the WANDERER

JAMES BUTLER HICKOK
and the AMERICAN WEST

CRAIG CREASE

Caxton Press

First Edition
ISBN # 978-087004-654-4
Library of Congress Control Number: 2024937838

CIP Information available at Loc.gov

Cover and book design by Jocelyn Robertson

Printed in the United States of America
CAXTON PRESS
Caldwell, Idaho
216352

TABLE *of* CONTENTS

INTRODUCTION

No one who met James Butler Hickok ever forgot him. He was at once unique, and yet also familiar. Many who expected to meet a stone-cold killer who was crude and coarse were stunned to find him a charming and cosmopolitan man, mannerly and well-educated, who rarely spoke of himself. Truly fearless and with a strong sense of fair play, time and again he walked away from men fired up with whiskey who wanted to test him. But should he see a terrified child or woman or man oppressed by someone formidable, he never hesitated to intervene, always to the detriment of the bully.

James Butler Hickok was a charismatic in the social sense, and probably in the clinical sense as well. Two things, among others, set him apart and projected his charisma: his personality and his unique physical presence. At a time when most men were 5'7" or 5'8", he was 6'2", with blue-gray eyes and long flowing blond hair; a very handsome man. Always clean and immaculately dressed, his body and strength were that of a frontier Adonis. Also, different and unexpected to many that met him, he was sophisticated, intelligent, and very well-spoken, unlike many of his peers. He was taciturn and quietly serious, yet not overly so; he had a good sense of humor, and there is evidence that he did not take himself or his legend all that seriously. It is these differences, some obvious and others subtle, that attracted people to Hickok. He was like no one they had ever met. These attractive differences, coupled with his penchant for selfless bravery, loyalty, and his well-documented defense of the weak, make his actual life story as compelling and relevant today as it was when his first biographer, George Ward Nichols, put pen to paper in 1865.

This is one book running along two themes. It is a conventional, straight-line, cradle-to-grave biography, supported by a factual basis. It is also a revelatory take-down of the many myths and legends that have clouded and obscured the real life of James Butler Hickok for nearly 150 years. After the myths and legends have been stripped away, the greatest

1

revelation remaining is the fact that the real life of James Butler Hickok is every bit as compelling and fascinating as any myth. James Butler Hickok, as Wild Bill Hickok, was the country's first real media star; he came of age just when the telegraph and railroad were first spreading across the nation. Suddenly, long-distance news by wire was instantaneous, and the railroad brought newspapers and magazines just as far by rail in only a few days. Every town along the westward-surging railroad had their own newspaper as well. Almost overnight, it seemed, the nation was connected, and coast-to-coast communication had arrived. The media influence of newspapers and magazines increased exponentially, the information served up almost instantly by the telegraph and railroads. This new, rapid and widespread media found its first national media star in February 1867: Wild Bill Hickok.

With very few notable exceptions, most of the men who gained fame in the post-Civil War American West, once stripped of the fanciful myths and falsehoods that made up their public persona, have little left to justify that fame and regard. James Butler Hickok was one of the notable exceptions. Hickok might be considered in today's parlance as an over-achiever. He excelled in almost everything he did, and his precocious proclivities were evident very early. He fell in love with a half-Indian girl, was a bodyguard for a U.S. senator, took part in two battles in the Border War skirmishes leading up to the Civil War, rode in the saddle day and night as a scout and spy in the Border War in Missouri and Kansas, and worked his first assignment as a frontier lawman...all before his twenty-first birthday. He was not even known yet as Wild Bill!

From 1866 to 1876, the decade that James Butler Hickok found national fame as Wild Bill Hickok and became a living legend, technology and a rapidly westward-expanding nation were hurtling forward, finding impetus in expending the pent-up energy gained by waiting out the five-year Civil War. Against that backdrop, James Butler Hickok's life played out for ten years. The scenes of much of his life were tied to the nation's settlement along the western railroads after the war.

In 1854, the Kansas-Nebraska Act created the Territory of Kansas, in anticipation of statehood which finally came in 1861. With that Act in 1854 came the abandonment of the previous ruling statute, the Missouri Compromise, which since the 1820s had stipulated that for every state scheduled to come into the Union as a free or abolitionist state, the next state admitted to the Union must come in as a pro-slavery state. The new law stipulated that states had free will to join the Union as

2

either abolitionist or pro-slavery. Kansas was slated to be the next state to join the Union. Pro-slavery factions wanted to ensure that Kansas would come in as a pro-slavery state. They began to move pro-slavery settlers into the Territory of Kansas in order to get control of the eventual vote for statehood. Out of this action came the Border War of Kansas and Missouri, a violent prelude to the Civil War from 1861 to 1865.

When the war ended in 1865, the railroad geared up to take the actions it had been waiting to accomplish after being forestalled by five years of war. The Union Pacific Eastern Division railroad started laying track west through Kansas as fast as it could go. Simultaneous with the railroad's westward movement, the war's end left many thousands of soldiers without a home to return to, and left many civilians homeless as well. This put the populace of many states east of Kansas on the move west, where they believed opportunity beckoned. The war-ravaged South in particular belched out many of its citizens to the west, especially Missouri, Arkansas, Tennessee and Kentucky.

As the railroad rushed onward laying track through Kansas, the Indians who had lived and hunted there for eons took exception to the planned railroad and unplanned hordes making their way into their homeland, and the frontier army found itself in an undeclared war with the tribes from 1866 to 1869. Life in Kansas at that time was subject to the constant threat of Indian attack, followed by reprisals from the frontier army, followed by more Indian attacks. In support of this Indian war in Kansas were Fort Larned (built in 1860), Fort Harker (1864), and Fort Hays, Fort Dodge and Fort Wallace (all 1865), as well as their two older counterparts, Fort Riley (1853) and Fort Leavenworth (1827). Wild Bill Hickok served duty at two of these forts and frequented all the others.

Starting in 1866, as the railroad moved west along the Kansas River valley, towns sprang up, and some city founders bet on the come and platted out their town even before the railroad arrived, hoping that their location would not be forsaken for another route. Some towns were already there. At the east end was Kansas City, Missouri, founded in the 1830s, whose twin sister across the Missouri River in Kansas held the railhead and railyard of the westward-building Union Pacific Eastern Division railroad. Upriver thirty miles was Leavenworth, established in 1854 in the Border War crucible, as was Lawrence, thirty miles west and on the Kansas River, also founded in 1854 by Massachusetts abolitionists determined to bring Kansas into the Union as a free state. A little further west on the Kansas River was Topeka, established in 1854, and Manhattan, founded 1855. Further west along the Kansas River valley were Junction City and Salina, both established in 1858. Notably, these Border War-era towns had time to build up some semblance of a civilized and organized town structure before the railroad and its work crews brought the onslaught of flotsam and jetsam from the last war to Kansas.

It is also notable that the four towns that owe their existence to the railroad, and who mark their founding as the day the westward-working Union Pacific track first reached their eastern environs, are Abilene, Ellsworth, Hays, and Sheridan. All four towns were the recipients of law enforcement actions of Wild Bill Hickok, either as a deputy United States Marshal, or as sheriff of that town.

Besides the railroad and the Plains Indian War, the other dynamic force that affected Kansas during this period from 1867 through 1871, and had national implications as well, was the Texas cattle trade. After the Civil War, Texas beef ranchers found they had a lot of beef on the hoof but no customers in cash-strapped Texas and the ravaged South. Illinois cattle broker Joseph McCoy recognized the problem held by the Texas beef ranchers. He sent agents into Texas to convince the ranchers they could drive their cattle north through Indian territory (Oklahoma) and into Kansas to waiting corrals and a railroad siding waiting to ship their cattle to the east and north to bring top dollar. From this, the town of Abilene was created from a site along Muddy Creek that had been a mail drop and a very occasional stagecoach stop. It was a brilliant plan, except that McCoy miscalculated the difficulty of dealing with the Texas cowboys who brought the cattle north. The Texas cowboys, after getting rid of their cattle, used Abilene as their own personal demented amusement park, complete with alcohol flowing freely twenty-four hours a day, illicit gambling, prostitutes, gunplay, and public drunkenness. Eventually the number of people who wanted a civilized and organized town outnumbered the cowboys. In 1871, McCoy tried to save his business by bringing a special man to Abilene to enforce the law, Wild Bill Hickok. In his most famous stint as a lawman, Hickok did his job well in Abilene, but the pending town contingent was not to be swayed, and after Sheriff Hickok's eight months in Abilene, and much to McCoy's chagrin, they voted to completely end Abilene's involvement in the Texas cattle business. The cattlemen moved operations first to Ellsworth, and eventually to Dodge City, Wichita, and Newton.

After Abilene in 1871, James Butler Hickok never again wore a sheriff's badge. For several years his wandering became more pronounced. In 1872, he traveled to Kansas City, to Georgetown, Colorado, and to Springfield, Missouri, followed by a trip in August to Niagara Falls for a one-day performance of his own wild west/buffalo hunt show. He then returned to his home in Kansas City, followed soon by a move back to Springfield, the scene of past glories. In September of 1873 he left Springfield and traveled the eastern United States for seven months as an actor playing himself with Buffalo Bill Cody and Texas Jack Omohundro in *Scouts of the Plains*. Hickok hated acting and soon returned to Kansas City. In the summer of 1874, Custer's expedition to the Black Hills found indications of gold, which set James Butler Hickok off on his last great adventure. He worked throughout 1875 trying to put together a Black Hills expedition to look for gold. In 1876, he traveled to Cheyenne, and in March of that year, to everyone's surprise, there married Agnes Lake, a circus owner and wealthy widow who Hickok had met in Abilene. She lived in the Cincinnati area, and they had corresponded by mail since Abilene.

Soon Hickok left for the Black Hills and a brand-new town rapidly expanding along Deadwood Creek, from which the town got its name. It seems that James Butler Hickok (aka Wild Bill Hickok) had been trying to find himself for the previous five years, and trying to decide whether to seek and repeat past glories, or to let go of his alter ego and walk away from it—what might be termed an identity crisis. At five years, it was a particularly long one. Perhaps he would find the answers at Deadwood that hot summer of 1876.

Think of the way that James Butler Hickok died: shot by the hand of an assassin while Hickok sat in a poker game. He was dead at just thirty-nine years of age, an instant death coming at the end of a nomadic life of adventure, danger and fame, death coming just months after he had married a wealthy widow, and surely just days before he would have turned his back on his old life forever and settled down into quiet anonymity. Shakespeare himself could not have plotted such a dramatic story and tragic ending, an ending guaranteed to perpetuate the wandering life of this remarkable man and his alter ego, Wild Bill Hickok.

There were thousands and thousands of men who lived out their lives in this unique post-war, ten-year period in the American West, 1866 to 1876. But just living anonymously in the midst of historical events does not necessarily put men in command of them. Further, these historical events in the frontier West are important to and illustrative of the general American belief that our collective character has been shaped by these men and events. It would take a special man of superlative ability and character to stand out in this crowded field and "make history." That man was James Butler Hickok.

Yet that is not to say that Hickok did not suffer from any faults or foibles. Like most men who swim against the river-current of history, his life and legend are complex, and Hickok's heroic legacy is sometimes colored by some very human errors and missteps. There are also misconceptions about him from which entrenched but false conclusions have been drawn. For instance, notwithstanding his awarded membership in the Poker Hall of Fame, and his gambling skills therefore considered akin to modern masters of the green felt like Amarillo Slim and Doyle Dixon, all indications are that Wild Bill Hickok was just an average gambler at the poker table or faro bank, if that. Hickok's friend John Malone said, "He would rather indulge in Poker than eat...On one occasion...played in his last earthly possession a black and tan terrier."[1] Charles Gross, who knew Hickok as well as anybody, said he would gamble the shirt off his back.[2] His passion for gambling, however, far exceeded his skill. "When he blew into Cheyenne on the big stampede to the 'Hills,' he was just a plain gambler and, I believe, not a very successful one, and with but little money." This observation by William Francis Hooker, who knew Hickok in Cheyenne.[3] John McClintock commented on Hickok's gambling in Deadwood: "I don't believe that... any other gambler in the town had any fear of Wild Bill, as he himself was a gambler. Though not a very successful one, it was his only occupation in Deadwood."[4]

Heavy gambling losses are implicated when Hickok was paid thousands of dollars for his seven-month stint acting as himself in the play *Scouts of the Plains,* yet just two years later and apparently broke, he was forced to ask a friend to stake him around twenty dollars, to be repaid when his "remit" came in from the East.

If it is not skill at gambling for which Hickok should be remembered, then it must be for being at the center of two poker games that are icons of gambling history and the American frontier West. The first one took place on July 20, 1865, in Springfield, Missouri. One Davis K. Tutt disputed the amount that Hickok owed him at the poker table. Hickok said he would check his records. Tutt grabbed Hickok's pocket watch off the green felt table, and stated he would keep it till the debt was paid. The feud simmered through that night and the next day, at six in the evening on July 21, 1865, they both stepped into the city square and simultaneously drew their pistols and fired. Tutt's bullet missed, but Hickok's bullet went through Tutt's heart, killing him almost instantly. They were seventy-five yards apart when they fired. This became the prototype for every walk-down shoot-out on a dusty frontier street that later appeared in books, films, and television.

The other took place in the #10 saloon in Deadwood, South Dakota on August 2, 1876. That afternoon Hickok joined Charlie Rich, Carl Mann, and William Massie at a poker table near the rear of the saloon. Hickok did not take his usual position with his back facing the wall. Later in the game a man walked in whom Hickok knew, because just the night before Hickok had beat him at poker, and he gave the man some money to buy breakfast with. The man walked towards the rear of the room, then suddenly turned towards the table, pulled his pistol, and shot Wild Bill Hickok in the back of the head, killing him instantly. James Butler Hickok was just thirty-nine years old. Along with the sheer dramatic impact of the killing itself, out of this event came the myth of Aces and Eights.

Something that writers have concluded, and allowed to become a part of the Hickok narrative, yet with no underlying evidence, is that Hickok was a heavy drinker. The presumption seems to be that since he was a heavy gambler, and gambling almost all took place in saloons, then Hickok must be a heavy drinker, with the implication and false conclusion that he was sometimes drunk. With the possible exception of one instance, there is no legitimate claim that Hickok was ever drunk or ever even drank to excess. That one exception took place on a train, in a train car filled with his friends. On the train was the editor of the Manhattan *Independent*. He reported on this rolling train party on October 26, 1867:

Wild Bill, the celebrated scout, with Jack Harvey and some dozen of their companions were upon the train having just come in from a scouting expedition under Gen. Sherman. All the party were more or less affected by frequent potations from their bottles, and Wild Bill himself was tipsy enough to be quite belligerent.[5]

Of course, this train party was a controlled environment, with Hickok surrounded by friends, where he must have for this rare moment not worried about being challenged or even ambushed by someone wanting to take out a legend. At just age thirty, he was already that—a legend. But in saloons and on dark streets Hickok could never relax like this. Because he was so concerned about this, he never drank to excess, or let himself become inebriated in public. It was self-preservation. After age thirty there were four assassination attempts on his life. The fourth attempt, tragically, was successful.

There have been twenty-one biographies of Wild Bill Hickok written from 1865 till 2022. This Hickok biography is the twenty-second. All of the previous biographies, with a few notable exceptions, have been mostly a rehash of what has been written before all the way back to his first two biographers, George Ward Nichols and James Buel, and characterized by repeating and building upon the most outlandish myths and falsehoods of those two writers. About fifty years after Buel, another biographer, William Connelley, added some new myths to the Hickok narrative that had no basis in reality, further clouding the real-life story of James Butler Hickok. Recent biographies that imply or claim directly to be the one true story of Wild Bill Hickok are not.

This is not a new phenomenon, however. In 1960, seventy-eight-year-old Howard L. Hickok, J. B. Hickok's nephew, wrote a scorching letter to the editor of *Newsweek* about his uncle. After a lifetime of trying to set the record straight concerning his uncle's life with authors, magazine editors and newspaper editors, his understandable frustration is reflected in this note to *Newsweek:*

Wild Bill Hickok was my father's brother. He was one of the best educated men in the West. He wrote legibly, was a good speller, and had almost a Harvard vocabulary. He was not an alcoholic nor a braggart. He never killed anyone that did not deserve killing. He was shy of women and a great friend of children. All America owes my uncle respect and homage. There are probably 5,000 relatives of Wild Bill in

America. Today they all hate you for saying bad things about him. I knew Buffalo Bill and Bat Masterson. They all loved my uncle.

Howard L. Hickok
Madison, Wis. [6]

In this book the writer has directly confronted and addressed the myths and legends that have clouded and obscured the actual life story of James Butler Hickok (aka Wild Bill Hickok). The majority of them have no basis in fact. They never happened. They are disputed and discarded in these pages with facts and evidence and logic, and relegated to the ash-heap of history. A few of these myths are overstated legends, where there is a factual event that occurred, but it has been so inflated and distorted that the story needs to be returned to its original basis by a reconsideration of all the evidence. It should not be a surprise that these few overstated legends are pivotal to the actual real-life story of Hickok. Finally, there is at least one legend that actually may deserve further consideration of the evidence, as will be shown.

After stripping away the myths and legends, the reader of this book will see that the real life of James Butler Hickok is every bit as exciting, unique and adventurous, dramatic and compelling, as any myth or legend. It's no wonder that his real life was such fertile ground for the mythmakers. His real life spoke of infinite possibilities, and the mythmakers wrote to those possibilities.

I am a pilgrim and a stranger and I am going to wonder*
till I am twenty-one and then I will tarry a while...

James Butler Hickok
Nineteen Years Old
Monticello, Kansas
November 24, 1856

* [wander]

JAMES BUTLER HICKOK

The child born James Butler Hickok who would one day become the man Wild Bill Hickok was born in the little village of Homer, Illinois on May 27, 1837. It is believed that the Hickok family is descended from the English family named Hiccox, that came from Stratford-Upon-Avon, Warwickshire, England, while another branch of the family hailed from London. The first members of the family to reach America settled in Connecticut in 1635. From there, other members of the Hickok family spread out over New England.

James' great-grandfather Aaron Hickok enlisted when the Revolutionary War started, serving as a private in Colonel Patterson's regiment of Minutemen. This outfit marched on April 22, 1775, in response to the alarm sounded by Paul Revere. Aaron is also believed to have been at the battle of Bunker Hill. Aaron Hickok was not only a fine soldier, but also a prolific father. Married twice, Aaron produced nineteen children between his two wives. One son, James' grandfather Oliver Hickok, fought in the war of 1812, and he died along with General Zebulon Pike at the battle of Sacketts Harbor in 1813. Oliver was just thirty-eight years old.

Oliver Hickok's son William Alonzo Hickok was born in 1801. William married Polly Butler in 1829. William and Polly moved around some in New England, living in Vermont and Maine while raising their first two sons: Oliver, born in 1830, and Lorenzo, born in 1832. In 1833 the family moved west to Illinois. Their third son, Horace, was born there in 1834. They lived in several Illinois towns before finally settling down in Homer in 1836. There in Homer their fourth son, James, was born in 1837.

James spent his entire childhood and teenage years in Homer, after which he left home to seek his own way. Homer eventually became the town of Troy Grove, that name adopted in the early 1860s after the discovery that there was another town named Homer in Illinois. James had a normal small-town, middle-class upbringing, and grew up in a close family.[1]

James' father William was an abolitionist, and as the anti-slavery movement gained momentum in the 1840s and 1850s, William became active in supporting the Underground Railroad. James' nephew Howard Hickok did not find out about the hidden cellar described below until 1906. Howard wrote:

> Grandfather [William] *built two cellars in his home, one a false hidden cellar which was lined with hay. This was used as a station of the Underground. I lived in this house...and was not aware of this hidden cellar. It was brought to my attention by my father [Horace], who had me remove some boards in the living room floor and under this floor was a dry earthen room, probably six foot square, and it was still lined with stems and traces of prairie hay.*
>
> *Running the Underground was a serious and dangerous undertaking: besides the Provost Marshals who were legally bound to reclaim the slaves, there were several men in the neighborhood who made the undertaking more difficult and dangerous. These were the kidnappers and bounty hunters. The kidnappers recaptured the slaves and resold them. The bounty hunters returned the slaves to their former owners for the bounty paid for them...Gould* [a friend and fellow abolitionist] *was lame and grandfather ill but both gave freely of their time and effort to help hundreds of slaves to their northern goal. Frequently they were fired upon by the bounty hunters. Dad told me that while riding one dark night they were fired at by a group of men, in an attempt to stop them.*
>
> *Grandfather pushed dad and uncle Jim from the wagon seat into the bed of the wagon with the negroes. The speed of the team and grandfather's knowledge of the country, enabled him to turn into a side road and return home while the disgruntled hunters went on towards Wedron.*[2]

Further corroboration of the abolitionist activities of young James and the rest of the Hickok family came years later in the town which would eventually play such an important role in James' destiny: Deadwood, South Dakota. In 1952, the Adams Museum in Deadwood received this revealing letter from one Milton D. Harper:

August 24, 1952
Hickok Museum
Deadwood, South Dakota
Gentlemen

    Upon our return from a recent trip to the west on which we stopped at your interesting museum, my mother refreshed my memory of the anecdote about Wild Bill, which may have some interest for you.
    My mother's family lived in Troy Grove, Illinois, having come west from Mass. in 1837 when her father Milton A. Dewey was seven years old. The Dewey and Hickok families were anti-slavery people and active in the underground railroad. The anecdote has it that from time to time the boys were entrusted with the job of driving the wagon at night to the next station, the presumption being that the posse would be less likely to suspect boys than men. Nevertheless on one occasion when Milton Dewey and Bill Hickok were driving a team made up of a Hickok horse and Dewey horse to be less easily recognized, the posse was heard following them and the boys drove off the road and into the field and spent a very nervous time rubbing the horse's noses to keep them from whinnying to the posse's horses, until the danger was passed when they proceeded to the station and made their delivery.
    Apparently Bill started out "agin" the law, although certainly on the right side morally.

                           Sincerely,
                           Milton D. Harper
                           2115 Sherman Avenue
                           Evanston, Illinois [3]

    Another incident so indicative of James' character is well told below by Howard Hickok:

    He [James] *and his brothers spent many hours swimming in the little river near their home. He was a fine swimmer. Few were the days in summer that did not find him in the water. The following was told to me by James Wylie in 1897. Another small creek, the Tomahawk Creek, ran through the Carr property. One day after a hard rain Jim and the boys of the neighborhood were swimming in the then swollen stream. One of the young men from the party was from Peru,*

Illinois. He was a good swimmer, and amused himself by bullying the younger boys, and ducking them under the water. Wylie, the son of a Scotch immigrant, could not swim, but amused himself by wading and splashing in the shallower water. The Peru joker shoved him into deeper water, and Wylie promptly went under. The bully frightened, left the water, and started dressing. Uncle Jim jumped in and rescued Wylie, brought him safely to shore. And then walked over to Mr. Bully picked him up clothes and all and threw him into the stream.[4]

Through the rest of his life, time and again, Hickok would turn the other cheek to insults hurled at him, usually by drunk men fired up with alcoholic courage, or by still-wet-behind-the-ears young men with lots of testosterone but no sense. But let James Butler Hickok witness the weak being taken advantage of by someone, and that would bring him into instant action. Edith Harmon, the Hickok family historian until her death in 2000, wrote in 1973 about James' early life in Homer:

He attended school in a log house near the Dewey property, and had, as his classmates, David Westgate, and the Deweys. Very early in his life, he had a teenage sweetheart, a girl next door. Josephine McLaughlin, who was later known as Josephine Ettinger, daughter of the proprietor of the Green Mountain Inn.

We were taught to be proud of Wild Bill Hickok. In no way, was his character questioned by his family, but in earlier days, grandfather and grandmother, did not extoll his virtues either. He was simply, Brother Jim, or Uncle Jim, and his exploits in the west, were not then considered to be greater than those, of his brother Oliver, or Lorenzo.

Contrary to many reports, Wild Bill did not run away from home, but went with the blessing of his family, and was aided by his brother, Lorenzo, who had been, before him, to the "west". He left Troy Grove in June, 1856, going directly to St. Louis on foot.

It is said that a party was held, on the night before Wild Bill left, in 1856, in hearsay, but by reliable people of their village, who have passed on.[5]

2

KANSAS TERRITORY

In June of 1856 nineteen-year-old James left his comfortable home in the little village of Homer, Illinois and struck out for the new Kansas Territory with his older brother Lorenzo. The Hickok brothers were seeking the rich new farmland they had heard about, just west of the Missouri River in this newly formed territory. James' nephew Howard Hickok recalled their trip as they neared St. Louis:

> The boys were amazed and bewildered. At the post office they found letters from home and the news that their mother was ailing. Lorenzo did not take kindly to the crowds and the bustle of the busy town. He worried about his mother and finally decided to return home. He was a quiet orderly man, dignified, much like his father. He was more of a realist than uncle Jim. So the brothers parted, Lorenzo went back to Homer after giving uncle Jim enough money to prove up on the homestead he was to take up for the family. Uncle Jim had a faculty for making friends and keeping them; and he was a popular member of any crowd he met. He engaged passage on the first steamboat bound up the Missouri River...
>
> He was much over six feet in height, strong and self-confident, still attuned to a code of gentle speech and manner: trained to a skill seldom attained in the use of firearms: skilled in woodcraft, taught to champion the weak, but encouraged never to let himself be "put upon." He was taught to believe in the freedom and equality of men.[1]

James booked passage from St. Louis to Leavenworth on the steamboat *Imperial*, contemporarily described as *"an immense, showy vessel, one of the first-class steamers, which completely dwarfs...others that we have come to look upon as leviathans.*[2] When he arrived at the crowded river landing at Leavenworth he found an angry crowd of pro-slavery men threatening the passengers, refusing to let some get off the boat, and intimidating others. James slipped quietly into the crowd and with his light baggage disappeared up the hill and into town.

James had just arrived at the flashpoint of pro-slavery and anti-slavery tension: Missouri's border with territorial Kansas. The Kansas—Nebraska Act of 1854 abolished "the Missouri Compromise" that had been in effect since 1820. The Missouri Compromise compelled parity among states; for each territory that came into statehood as a "free" state, another territory must come into statehood as a "slave" state. With that control gone after 1854, the new states were free to vote on whether they wanted to be abolitionist or pro-slavery. The very next territory to come into statehood after 1854 was Kansas. Missouri was a slave state, and had been since 1821. Much of the Missouri settlement of southerners who were pro-slavery were settled along the Missouri River, all across the middle of the state. Soon pro-slavery elements from the south began to pour into Missouri to try to affect whether Kansas would come into the Union as a free state or a slave state. Conversely, elements of free-state supporters began to pour into Kansas, hoping to put boots on the ground that would compel a free state when it came time for a vote. Lawrence, Kansas was born in that crucible.

That summer of 1856, James took up odd jobs around the Leavenworth area, hiring himself out as a plowman at one point. That summer he also became associated with the Free State movement and its charismatic leader, James Lane. Hickok family tradition, though unsubstantiated, tells of James winning his place with Lane's Free State militia in a shooting match, and winning thirty dollars. Contemporary evidence of a relationship with Lane, however, does come from the written observations of Bayless S. Campbell. He lived in Highland, Kansas and saw Lane giving a speech there in 1857. Campbell observed two men get off their horses and lie down in the grass near the foundation of a new hotel being built near where Lane was speaking. Campbell recognized the men. "These two men were General Lane's bodyguard, and one of them was Hickok."

The other man was John Owen. Campbell claimed to see Hickok with Lane another time at Grasshopper Falls, Kansas (modern Valley Falls), where Lane was delivering a rousing anti-slavery speech on a wagon that had been pulled up for that use. An unknown proponent of the pro-slavery faction took exception to Lane's remarks, and menacingly pulled out his pistol. Hickok drew his pistol and covered the miscreant, who quickly holstered his weapon and made his exit.[3]

By September 1856, young James was riding as a scout and spy for the Free State forces. On September 1, that put him with Lane's forces at the "battle that wasn't," the Battle of Bull Creek.

Throughout the summer of 1856 tensions between pro-slavery and anti-slavery factions were wound tighter than a drum. In May, Congressman Charles Sumner was beaten severely with a hickory cane on the floor of the House by South Carolina Congressman Preston Brooks, in retaliation for Sumner's anti-slavery speech, "*The Crime Against Kansas.*"

This single act lit a fire of indignant emotion across the nation. On May 21, the town of Lawrence, bastion of the Free-Staters, was attacked by pro-slavery raiders led by the sheriff of Douglas County, Samuel L. Jones. Sheriff Jones, not letting the fact that he was the sheriff for the people of Lawrence interfere with his pro-slavery views, ransacked both of the Kansas newspapers in Lawrence. He then turned his cannon on the Eldridge Hotel, and wreaked havoc up and down Massachusetts Street. Three days later, John Brown carried out the Pottawatomie Massacre in Franklin County, Kansas in retaliation for the Lawrence raid; five pro-slavery settlers were killed. Just days later, Brown and his men met pro-slavery men led by H. Clay Pate at Black Jack on the Santa Fe Trail in a pitched battle that has been termed by some historians as the first battle of the Civil War. On August 16, pro-slavery troops were routed at Fort Titus north of Lawrence, and at the end of August, pro-slavery militia almost captured John Brown himself at the battle of Osawatomie, a raid that resulted in the death of Brown's son, Frederick.

On August 25, acting governor of the Kansas Territory, Daniel Woodson, issued a proclamation that the territory was in open rebellion, and he asked for men to come forward to suppress the rebellion. Former Missouri senator David Atchison was already collecting pro-slavery militia across the border in Missouri, for the express purpose of hunting down James Lane and his followers. From Westport just a mile east of the Kansas border, Atchison led a column of men into Kansas. Missouri legislator John W. Reid led another column of men across the border into Kansas. A third pro-slavery force moved north from Fort Scott under the charge of George W. Clark, a former Indian agent. These three invading forces totaled about 1,600 men.

By August 29, Atchison's self-styled "Grand Army" was at New Santa Fe on the Missouri state line. Clark's column from the Fort Scott area was stillborn; it was routed by Free-State forces while moving north, and the column retreated. John W. Reid's forces, however, moved across the state line unimpeded and moved toward Osawatomie, looting and burning the town before turning north to meet up with Atchison's forces.

Now combined, this large pro-slavery force of more than 1,300 men camped on Bull Creek in today's southwest Johnson County, Kansas, and made their plans to find James Lane and the abolitionists. Lane was in Nebraska when he learned of Atchison's invasion into Kansas. The hunted became the hunter. Quickly Lane drew around him a fighting force of about 400 Free-State men, mostly from the Lawrence and Topeka area. Then he set about moving south to find Atchison. Nineteen-year-old Hickok rode with Lane's force, perhaps in his role as a scout and spy for Lane's forces, very likely.

Near dawn on September 1, Lane drew up his force on the north side of Bull Creek in a battle line. Recognizing that he was outnumbered by more than three to one, Lane and his forces devised and executed a bold ruse. While the surprised Missourians were scrambling to get into their own battle line, Lane sent one of his columns to the rear, out of sight of the pro-slavery troops, and then had them reappear outside of the opposite flank. Repeating this several times he created the illusion of a sizable or even a superior force, more than a match for Atchison's "Grand Army" on the other side of Bull Creek.

The heavy timber on the creek banks, along with the smoke of skirmishers' gunfire in the gray light of early dawn, served to cloud the vision of everyone on the battlefield. Soon Atchison's "Grand Army" was in a chaotic retreat, his untested and undisciplined militia convinced that a superior force was coming across the creek at them. No casualties were reported on either side. Lane and his troops left the battlefield victorious, and no blood was shed.

Just thirteen days later James found himself in the heat of a real battle. At Hickory Point, near present day Oskaloosa in Jefferson County, Kansas, Free-State forces under Colonel James A. Harvey clashed with pro-slavery forces. Though they won the battle, Free-State forces had nine wounded and one killed. At the end of the action, Free-State forces took the opposing troops prisoner. However, minutes after the battle ended, federal troops under the command of Philip St. George Cooke arrived and arrested Colonel Harvey and his remaining force and took them to Lecompton.

On September 28, James wrote to his mother Polly just a few weeks after the Hickory Point battle, taking care not to reveal any details of his new life in the saddle for the Free-State forces. He even went so far as to tell her that the "excitement is purty much over." Far from it.

(Punctuation added):

You say write often, how can I when it has been more then three months since I left home and only received to letters from home. You want to know what I am doing, you don't know what I came to Kansas for & you would not ask me that. I will tell you before long what I am doing and what I have been doing. the excitement is purty much over. I have seen sites here that would make the wickedest hearts sick. believe me mother for what I say is true. I can't come home til fall it would not look well. Tell the boys all to write.

This is from your son J.B. Hickok [4]

The same day, September 28, James wrote to his sister Lydia, indicating in this letter that the two letters he references above came from her and from his mother. He also makes a tongue-in-cheek statement about Colonel Harvey, his commander at Hickory Point (punctuation added):

Dear Sister, You requested me to write to you. I returned from the border yesterday and went strate to the post office expecting to get several letters from Illinois but I was disappointed only getting one when I expected several, but I was glad to receive one from you and mother...I will answer all letters wrote to me...[P]robably you have heard of [H]arvey, a Captin of a company of abolition trators. I have seen this tarable man.

Your brother J. B. Hickok [5]

Two months later, James wrote to his brother Horace, and revealed the wild and dangerous life he was leading in Kansas that he would not reveal to his mother, along with a bit of cynicism about the state of affairs in Kansas (punctuation added):

November 24, 1856

I received your letter Dated the 7 and was glad to hear from you and always be glad to get letters from home. But when you are ready to wright to me again, please leave it off an other week and mabe you

Can think of noncence a nough to fill a Letter withut writing Capital leters...

.....I opend your Letter when I was Coming home this evening to see who it was from and the first thing I read you wanted to no what was going on in Cansas. I looked a head of me to whare the roads Cross. I saw about 500 soldiers a going onn and I looked Down the river and saw some nice stemers and they ware all going onn and that is the way with all the people in Cansas, they are all going on. I guess they are going on to hell. [S]o you see I have told you what is going on in Cansas.

If I had [money] as mutch one month ago as I do now I would have had a Deed to 160 acres of land now but never mind thare is more Land to be sold in Cansas yet. thare is the finest Country in Cansas I ever saw, nice roling prary, nice timber on the crick.

[Y]ou mentioned something about my being in governor protection but I aint nor have not been but iff uncle sams troops had been at hickry point fifteen minits Sooner than they ware I might have had the honor of wriding with uncle sams troops, but captin Harvey had given orders that [S]couts should be sent towards Leavenworth city to see where abouts the companys of captin dun and miles Companys were camping. for you must no that they ware Camping all the while, only when provisions got scarce that they Could not help marching, and that is the way with all the proslavery Companys done.

Thare is 29 of our company in custody at Lacompton yet. I have been out to see them once. I had as good a horse and as good a gun as thare was in our Company. Thare was a man Living on Crooked Crick who furnished me with a horse and rifle and revolver. What I have told you is true. I have rode night after night without getting out of my saddle. Thare is no roads, no cricks, no trails, no groves, no Crossings, no springs, no partys of any kind between Leavenworth and Lorance or Lacompt...

...the Land sales commenced the first of November. thare is more speculators here than you can have any Idea of...I have been in masuria [Missouri] every day for a month and stopping in Kansas every night...

...I am a pilgrim and a stranger and I am going to wonder [wander] till I am twentyone and then I will tarry a little while.

From your brother James to H.D. Hickok [6]

Sometime in the fall of 1856, James met Englishman Robert H. Williams, who had come to Kansas seeking land in the Leavenworth area. Williams was a few years older than nineteen-year-old James, and an avid pro-slavery man; he was with Sheriff Jones in the May raid on Lawrence, and he was with the pro-slavery men defeated by John Brown at Black Jack in June. James, of course, was an avid Free-State man. Their relationship was a strange anomaly, yet it would not be the last time that James Butler Hickok would befriend someone of a different stripe than he.

Decades later, Williams wrote a book about his Border War-era adventures in America, *With the Border Ruffians.*[7] In it, he describes James as William Hitchcock, with no indication that he realized that his young William Hitchcock was none other than the legendary Wild Bill Hickok of later years.

In the spring of 1857, the lands of the Shawnee Indians south of the Kansas River came onto the market, as a result of their treaty that came out of the 1854 Kansas-Nebraska Act. James left the Leavenworth area and traveled with Robert H. Williams and a few others to seek out claims on this former Shawnee land in modern Johnson County, Kansas. Williams recalled their journey:

> ...*I made up my mind to leave Leavenworth and settle in Johnson County, across the Kansas River in the Shawnee country, intending to make my claim on Cedar Creek my headquarters. Forth I fared then, with my wagon and a pair of horses, my saddle-horse, provisions, whiskey, arms, and blankets, taking with me four of my claim-making party. These were named Shoemaker, Mike Mcnamara, William Hitchcock, and Wash Gobel, all who agreed to stand by me no matter what happened...I found that things were moving pretty fast in the reserve, and that joining the claim I had made on the Laramie and Kansas City road, a town had been laid out, which had been named Monticello, and that a tavern, groggery, and several shanties were in the course of erection.*[8]

Upon arrival in the new area, James did not immediately make his own land claim, but instead worked breaking ground for Robert Williams, who had already filed his claim along Cedar Creek that abutted the new town of Monticello. James spent some time with Williams, but that spring he also stayed with his friend and fellow bodyguard John Owen. S.T. Seaton, editor of the *Johnson County Democrat*, wrote to

William Connelley in 1924 with the recollections of Fred McIntyre during that spring of 1857:

> *My Distinguished Friend: I have your letter of Sept 26 asking for data on the life of the late William Hickok (Wild Bill) during his sojourn in Johnson County. I went out this morning to see my friend Fred McIntyre who knew Hickok, and is perhaps the only man now living who knew him when he lived in this county, unless it is Sol Coker who now lives in Desoto and is very aged...McIntyre was a boy about 11 years old when he knew Hickok. The McIntyres lived on the section cornering with the old town of Monticello on the N.W. He remembers that Hickok broke some prairie for R.H. Williams who owned the quarter adjoining the Monticello town site on the west. He used a lever plow and McIntyre used to get up and ride with him. He remembers that Hickok in those days was a good horseman and handy with a "gun".[9]*

Another recollection of nineteen-year-old Hickok that spring of 1857 in Johnson County:

> [He] *spent his time principally in having a good time with the boys, and astonishing them with his dexterity in hitting a target with a pistol. It was a common feat with him to take a stand at a distance of a hundred yards from an oyster can, and with a heavy dragoon revolver send every bullet through it with unerring precision. He had not then commenced his practice on human beings.[10]*

No letters from the pen of James Butler Hickok are extant from 1857. Perhaps they were lost or purloined. Maybe they were never written. That spring and summer passed, and by the fall of 1857 James had staked out his own claim to a160-acre quarter section a little over a mile southwest of Monticello, and three-quarters of a mile south of the California Road (Robert Williams "Laramie and Kansas City road" noted above). In 1857, this California Road was teeming with westbound emigrants trying to reach the Oregon-California Trail near Lawrence. Border War dangers had driven emigrant traffic off the Oregon-California Trail located further south in Johnson County to this comparatively safer northerly route from Westport to Lawrence. It also would have been the road that James followed for a short distance into Monticello and west to Lawrence and Lecompton. On this quarter section James built a cabin, and fished out of the cool waters of Clear Creek that bisected his claim. On February 10, 1858, James went to the Land Office at Lecompton to file a declaratory statement to further the process of gaining final ownership of his claim. Later that spring he wrote to his sister Celinda:

> *Monticello April 22nd 1858...you ought to see me fishing on my Clame. I can ketch any kind of fish that I want to. I have fed my fish till they are all tame. the girls Comes to my Clame a fishing some times and that I don't like, but I Can't help my self, this is a free country, every on dze as he* [pleases]...*from your effectionate Brother James Butler Hickok.*[11]

He wrote home to Illinois another day: *I have been mowing or reaping hay with the machine today and break it all to pieces...so I guess I shant have to wirk this afternoon. good luck at last.*[12]

Buffalo Bill Cody claimed in later years that he first met Hickok in October of 1857, as an eleven-year-old. The dubious tale as Cody tells it is that Hickok was with the ill-fated wagon train led by wagon master Lew Simpson that was burnt by Mormon militia in Wyoming. Supposedly eleven-year-old Cody was saved from a bully's thrashing by Hickok, and they became fast friends after that. The story is very unlikely—what is an eleven-year-old boy doing as an employee on a wagon train? Further, there is no record of Hickok being with that wagon train in 1857. But it is known that by the fall of 1859 Hickok was a friend of the Cody family, and must have known Lew Simpson by this time. The Cody family had moved into a large house in Leavenworth that fall, that they intended to use as a hotel. Cody's seventeen-year-old sister Julia listed one set of potential boarders in 1859: *James B. Hickok, Lew Simpson, John Willis, and George Ross.*[13]

Young James Butler Hickok (he had just turned twenty-one in May of 1858) had another distraction from farming well into 1858: the attention of a beautiful young woman named Mary Owen.

> *I would have finished this letter yesterday But was not at home. I was over at John Owen. I go there when I get hungry. Jest the same*

as I used to Come home to mothers to git some good things to eat. mary cut off a Lock of my hare yesterday and Sayed for me to Send it to my mother and Sisters. If she had not thought a great deal of you all She would not have cut it off for She thinks a grate deal of it. At least she is always Coming and Curling it, that is when I am hare.[14]

So wrote James about Mary Owen to his family in August of 1858. Born on April 24, 1841, to John Owen (Hickok's partner in guarding James Lane) and his Shawnee Indian bride Patinuxa, Mary was their only child. When she was a toddler, the family lived on the Shawnee reserve, until a flood in 1844 wiped out their little homestead near the Kansas River. At one time, Owen had worked for the Chouteau fur trade operation on the Shawnee reserve, and he sought employment again with them after the flood. Working for the Chouteau's, Owen and his family lived among the Kansa tribe until 1849, when they returned to the Shawnee reserve, where Owen found himself adopted into the tribe. Mary began her education in 1850 at the Shawnee Methodist Indian Mission school located in the Shawnee reserve in the northeast corner of modern Johnson County. The school was run by the county's namesake, Thomas Johnson. She lived in the dormitory at the mission during the school year. On her second year there, records show there were one hundred children attending, forty-seven of which were girls.

By 1856, at the age of fifteen, Mary completed her education at the mission and was back with her parents. When she first met James in the spring of 1857, she was a beautiful young woman barely sixteen years of age. She caught Robert H. Williams' eye also. Years later he recalled:

If there was plenty of hard work, there was also plenty of good fun too, and many a good dance we had that winter [the winter of 1857-1858] *We all of us girls as well as men, had to ride long distances to many of these, through the keen, frosty air, and the rides were almost as good fun as the dances. One of these, I particularly remember, was held at Olathy, the county seat of Johnson County, on New Years Eve. The occasion was the opening of a new hotel at this place, which was about ten miles from Monticello. I got together a party of five girls and seven or eight young fellows, all well mounted. It was a lovely starlit night, with an intense frost, and six inches of snow on the ground. All were in the wildest of spirits, and the gallop over the level trackless prairie was delightful.*

At the hotel we found quite a big gathering, and as soon as the ladies had divested themselves of their wraps we were all hard at work at the cotillions and polkas. Our host had provided an excellent supper, and of course liquid refreshments were in abundance.

...At many of the dances I have spoken of, I often met Shawnee half-breed girls, daughters, some of them, of well-to-do people and fairly well educated, others barely "tame". Amongst the first I remember the two Choteaus, and Mary Owens and Sally Blue Jacket. They all dressed like other Western belles, and were good dancers; but some of them were prone to take a little too much whiskey. Once, when dancing with Sally Blue Jacket, who was a remarkably handsome girl, she pulled a flask of whiskey out of her pocket and pressed me to join her in a drink. It would have been rude to refuse so delicate an attention, from so charming a partner, and I of course accepted the offer.[15]

Sally Bluejacket, the beautiful daughter of Charles Bluejacket, went on to marry Johnson County's first county attorney, Jonathan Gore. Mary Owen captivated James Hickok's heart, as evidenced by his letters home:

I went to see my gall yesterday, and eat 25 ears of Corn to fill up with. You ought to be here and eat some of her buiskits. She is the only one that I ever Saw that could beat mother making buiskits you no I aught to no for I can eat a Few you no. I [ate] ears of corn last Sunday. My gall washed them for me and a pack of dried corn and then was hungry.[16]

James' family back home in Illinois had serious misgivings about his romance with Mary, afraid that he might marry an Indian. They dispatched older brother Lorenzo to Kansas to try and break the couple up. James tried to relieve his family's anxiety in this letter to his sister Celinda:

Monticello April 22nd 1858

My dear sister...if I yoused you bad some times when I was angry you must forget it...you did not think that I was in earnest when I spoak of marrying did you. wy I was only joking. I could not get a wife if I was to try. Wy I am homlier than ever now days and you no that the wimen don't love homly men...[17]

27

Jule Hadley, interviewed in the June 6, 1901, *Olathe Mirror*, recalled the period, but with some misconceptions:

> *Hickok was one of the first constables of Monticello township and remained there a year after his term of office had expired in an effort to marry Mary Owen, a farmer's daughter and an eighth-blood Shawnee of great attraction. In 1858 I carried many notes to the lady for him as I made my home with the Owens. The public does not know it but his matrimonial failure and disappointment made him the "Wild Bill" and the most distinguished Son of the Border, the equal of General Funston, in his different and exacting line of duty.*

More than twenty years later, the editor of the August 31, 1922 Johnson County Democrat spread another misconception when he claimed that Hickok married Owens' daughter but they did not get along and separated, and the wife afterwards married a Dr. Harris. William Connelley, a Hickok biographer in the 1930s, believed for many years that James and Mary were married, until he was corrected by James' nephew Howard Hickok, who showed him letters of James that indicated they were not married. An indication of how strongly the Hickok family felt about this, even sixty-five years after the events took place, is evidenced by a letter written by Hickok's grand-niece, Susan Andrews, to Connelley in 1923:

> *Your letter dated May 2, should be ignored and would be only I feel some of your statements must not be published. Unless you send us records and proof of Jas. B. Hickok's marriage to a Shawnee Indian you will be persecuted...Your statements are ridiculous and show your immense ego.... Jas. Hickok has relatives living in Kansas a niece and nephew and until eight years ago a sister. I'm sorry he has no brothers or sisters to answer your impudent letter.[18]*

James did not marry Mary Owen. Lorenzo must have been persuasive, or perhaps James and Mary just drifted apart. Either way, by 1859 their relationship was over. Soon Mary was courted by a new suitor, Simeon H. Harris, a twenty-four-year-old doctor from North Carolina. On October 17, 1859, he married eighteen-year-old Mary Owen, in Monticello.

#3995

Twenty-one year old J.B. Hickok wrote from Kansas to his family in Illinois in August 1858 promising to get to Lawrence, Kansas and have his picture taken: *I will send you my likeness and you can see whether it looks like a whiskey face or not.* Several days later he wrote again, this time referring to his cousin Guy Butler:....*I think my mustache and goatee lays over hisen. Considerable the fact of it is hisen ain't no Whare.* This image is a tinted tintype. The original photograph is in an oval frame in a leather case. *Author's collection.*

29

Tragedy struck the young bride; after only fourteen months of marriage Dr. Harris died, shortly before Mary gave birth to their only child, a boy that Mary named Simeon. Two years later Mary was wed again, this time to Thomas Hagan. Again death cut short her marriage, but this time it was hers. Mary Owen died on February 11, 1864, at the age of twenty-two. Author and Hickok historian Gregory Hermon described her bittersweet legacy:

> *In her teenage years she knew the love of a man who would become one of the most famous and respected men in the annals of the Old West. Yet, she never knew the legendary "Wild Bill" Hickok. One of the tragedies of her life was that she died before the legend began.*[19]

Mary Owen is buried in the little Monticello country cemetery in Johnson County, not far from the land that James claimed as his own in 1858.

Monticello, Monday 16th, 1858 [August]

> *I will Write a few minutes While dinner is cooking. I have been and served three summonses this morning. There has been 25 horses stolen here Within the last ten days by to men by the names of Scroggins and Black Bob. They have narry one been taken yet, but I think they will ketch it soon. If they are caught about here they Will be run up awfull soon to the top of Some hill, I guess, where they won't steel any more horses.* [20]

Thus young Hickok described a day in the job he had undertaken in the spring of 1858—constable of Monticello; an inauspicious start in law enforcement for an unknown young man who would go on to be the most famous of the frontier peace-makers in the Old West. Hickok was appointed constable of Monticello on March 22, 1858. He was twenty years old. The election results that day included two names very familiar to James: Robert H. Williams as chairman of the Board of Supervisors, and John Owen as a member of the Board of Supervisors. These commissions were issued on April 21, 1858, by Governor James W. Denver of Kansas Territory. Surviving court records refer to James as both J. B. Hickok and William Hickok.

S.T. Seaton, editor of the *Johnson County Democrat*, recalled for William Connelley in 1924 James' days as a lawman in Monticello: *Hickok was a constable while he lived here, and the late J.L. Morgan of Desoto told me that he and Bill often rode together serving papers, and that Bill was handy with a gun.*[21] In an undated statement thought to be from early 1858, James described to his family back in Illinois the hardscrabble Kansas Territory and rough Monticello area that he was soon to be constable of:

> *It was the first time in my life that I ever saw a fight and did not go to see it out, and I am glad of it now. You don't know what a Country this is for drinking and fighting, but I hope it will be different some time and I no in reason that will when the Law is put in force. There is no Common Law here now hardly at all. A man Can do what he pleases without fear of the Law or anything els. Thare has been two awfull fights in town this week, you don't know anything about sutch fighting at home as I speak of. This is no place for women or children yet, all though they all say it is so quiet here...if a man fites in Kansas and gets whipped he never says anything A bout it, if he does he will get whipt for his trouble...*[22]

Monticello records indicate that James was one of the arresting officers of an accused murderer, in the first murder trial to ever take place in Johnson County.

As the year 1859 came around, James found himself facing several difficult issues. Not only had his relationship with Mary Owen ended, but he was faced with a startling revelation about his claim: the land that he had claimed and worked and farmed was not going to be his.

The quarter section that James had claimed was located on a so-called "floater." Even though it was on the Shawnee Indian reserve that had been opened to settlement by the 1854 Kansas-Nebraska Act, this particular land James had chosen was actually held by the Wyandot Indian tribe as a floater; by the terms of an 1842 treaty, the Wyandot tribe gained the right for certain tribal members to choose up to 640 acres on Indian land west of the Mississippi River. Of these thirty-five various square mile sections, James' land was located on Wyandot Float #18. Though James had filed his claim at Lecompton on February 10, 1858,

31

Wyandot member Samuel McCullough had exercised his floater option and filed his claim on it on April 1, 1857. The Lecompton office was either not aware of this floater claim when James filed, or failed to inform James at the time that there was already such a claim on the property.[23] Adding insult to injury, James' cabin burnt down. Speculation was the fire was set by pro-slavery men, or by someone who did not appreciate his law enforcement actions.

Faced with these issues, James returned to Illinois in the spring of 1859 and went to work on a wheat farm helping to bring in the spring harvest. It was his first visit back to Illinois since he had left home in June, 1856. Charles Gross, who knew Hickok well years later in Abilene, recalled in 1926:

> ...way back in 1859 my father was building a church in Buda., Ills. & our family spent the summer there. I was sent to a farm near Tiskilwa Ills. and put to work in the harvest field, the job being to carry water to the wheat binders. I was put to sleep with a young man named James B. Hickok, he lived near there somewhere...I was carrying bundles of grain into piles for me to shock, in the last I worked with Bill who was shocking. We both talked most of the time & slept together at night. I was then as now a very inquisitive boy, and just the age when I was much impressed by stories of any kind. Bill was a good worker, much older than I strong and athletic. At noon and after work he pitched horse shoes, ran races, jumped, Wrestled, and was the best at the game of others there.[24]

The Gibbs family of Princeton, Illinois was related to the Hickok family by marriage. Fred Gibbs recalled that his father had returned from Kansas with Hickok (which would be 1859) and they went to LaSalle, Illinois for haircuts and a shave before they had their picture taken. Fred Gibbs said both young men helped with the harvest. He said his father stayed in Illinois, but Hickok returned to Kansas.

Missing from the Hickok family records and letters is any mention or indication of James' return to Illinois in 1859. The letter below, written by Polly Hickok during the same period, laments that James has not returned home to Illinois. It seems that James did return to Illinois in 1859, yet did not go to his home or alert the family that he was in the general area. His reasons are unknown. Perhaps he felt he had failed to provide the homestead he had set out to build in Kansas and did not want to face his family. There may be other reasons as well.

James returned to Kansas after the spring harvest, probably early summer. It appears that very soon after his return to Kansas, James' brother Horace came to Kansas as well. Polly Hickok believed that Horace would be a good influence on James. But by August 16, and probably much earlier that summer, James signed on with a stage company running between Leavenworth and Denver, as a guard on the stagecoach. James' mother Polly wrote to his brother Horace in Kansas:

Homer August 16, 1859

I was sorry to hear that James had gone to Pikes Peak. I do not know what he means by doing as he has by not writing to us. We have had but one letter from him since you went away. If you hear from him I want you to let me know for I am very uneasy about him. Did he appear glad to see you or was he cold and distant [?] *Has he got anything or made anything or is he in det for his board* [?] *Do tell me about it. I was pleased when I heard that you had gone to Kansas instead of the Peak for I thought it would be much better for you and James both if you were together but it seems you did not stay together long.*[25]

Every mother knows their child like no one else does, even when that child is a grown man. Polly bares her soul in this letter and shows her concerns about her independent and unique youngest son, undoubtedly unlike any of his three older brothers.

On August 21, 1859, Horace wrote from Kansas to his brother Lorenzo:

Olathe Johnson County
August 21st, 1859

...James is getting Thirty Dollars a month for his pikes Peak trip...James took off [with] *my fine shirt and I think some of making one next Sunday.*[26]

No sooner had James left for the Colorado gold fields working for the stagecoach company as a guard, than a surprising development took place: he was being sued. More surprising, the plaintiff bringing the suit was his English friend Robert H. Williams. To add further intrigue, both of Mary Owen's future husbands were involved, Simeon H. Harris as a security for plaintiff Williams, and Thomas Hagan as a defendant; he was apparently dismissed from the case.

It appears from the case record filed on July 7, 1859 in Johnson County court that Robert H. Williams was seeking an injunction against Hickok and another defendant named Robert Catterson. Williams' complaint stated that he was trying to recover a debt from Catterson but was unable to because Hickok was holding a lien on Catterson; and so Catterson would not or could not pay anything to Williams. The complaint further asserted that there was a "connivance and conspiracy" between Hickok and Catterson, and charged that Hickok actually held no such lien. On September 12, 1859, the court ordered a summons to appear issued to both Hickok and Catterson, to be delivered by Johnson County sheriff Pat Cosgrove. Sheriff Cosgrove went out September 14, 1859, to deliver the summons. His handwritten notes on his copy of the summons read:

> *Executed by delivering a true copy to R. W. Catterson on the 14th day of September 1859.*
> *J.B. Hickok not found.*
> *Pat Cosgrove Sheriff* [27]

James was nowhere to be found in Johnson County, because he was riding shotgun on the Leavenworth-to-Denver stage.

Guy Butler was James' cousin on his mother's side. Guy had moved from Illinois to Kansas Territory to seek land, just like James. Guy purchased some land in eastern Douglas County at the now-defunct town of Black Jack, located on the Santa Fe Trail. By 1859, Guy lived in nearby Olathe. Hickok biographer Joseph Rosa surmised that in 1859, James left Monticello and moved in with cousin Guy in Olathe. Rosa cited no source for this statement. However, the rapid pace of events in the summer of 1859 leaves little time, if any, for James to live with Guy Butler. If James was in Illinois for the spring harvest and then, quickly upon his return to Kansas, went to work for the stagecoach company, the letter between Polly and Horace above indicates it was Horace whom James moved in with for a very short time, as indicated by Polly, not Guy Butler.

By the summer of 1859, James Butler Hickok's life had moved beyond Monticello and Johnson County. In three short years he had staked out a claim in the new Kansas Territory, fallen in love with a beautiful half-Indian girl, served as a bodyguard for a famous U.S. Senator, taken part in two battles in the Border War lead-up to the Civil War, ridden for days and nights as a scout and spy in those same actions, and got his first taste of being a frontier lawman...all before his twenty-first birthday. Though he was not yet known as the Wild Bill of fame and legend, certainly the exemplary upbringing and solid character of his that was forged in Illinois was further tempered to fine steel in hardscrabble Kansas Territory, and his time there as a young man contributed to the crucible that was about to receive the legend so well.

January 11, 1926

Mr. J.B. Edwards
Abilene, Kansas

My dear Mr Edwards:

I thank you for your favor of the 9th inst...The mother of the wife of Dr. Lindsay, an old physician here, knew Bill as a boy when he first came to Kansas, and I have secured a good statement from her. He worked for her father at Monticello, in Johnson County.
She says he was a good boy.[28]

3

RIDING SHOTGUN *on the* JONES & CARTWRIGHT STAGE

the MYTH THAT HICKOK RODE *the* STAGE FOR RUSSELL, MAJORS *and* WADDELL

the MYTH *of* J. B. HICKOK'S FIGHT *with a* BEAR

Numerous writers on Hickok, from James Buel in the 1880s to Richard O'Connor in the 1950s, and many in between, have asserted without evidence that Hickok, from the time he left Monticello in 1859 through his time at Rock Creek, Nebraska in 1861, was in the employ of frontier freighting monolith Russell, Majors and Waddell. Some writers then made a literary (and historical) leap of faith and stated that Hickok rode for the Pony Express. Hickok was never a Pony Express rider. Never.

Hickok had a slight and tenuous passing relationship with Russell, Majors and Waddell, but it was tangential at best. This will be seen in the following pages.

Putting this well-worn myth aside for now, there exists a compelling first-person remembrance of young James Butler Hickok that does tell much about him riding the stage at this period of his life in 1860. In 1931, Truman Blancett recalled for the *Denver Post:*

> *In 1860 my father, brothers and I were keeping the station at Ashpoint, Kan., between Seneca and Marysville, then the raw, western frontier. The town of Seneca was on the Nemaha River, eighty miles west of Fort Leavenworth. Marysville was situated on the Big Blue river, 125 miles west of the fort.*

37

The mail coach changed mules at our station, and was drawn by six or eight mules, depending on the load. Mexican mules, such as were used, are not very large, oftimes running with the coach like scared rabbits. They were mean and wild critters and two Mexicans were always at the station to make the change of teams. It was figured it took one Mexican to handle one mule.

Hickok was at our station once a week for about a half hour at a time while mules were being changed, and we would exchange stories of our experiences during the interim, a universal custom of the time. We were both young, he not being more then 20 years old, and I, 18. Both of us were trying to raise a mustache. "Wild Bill" was taciturn even at that age. He talked little of himself or about others. He was a man of action, not of words.

I never saw him with his feet off the cash box which was carried under the feet of the mail coach driver. This box was of metal construction, its carrying space equal to about a bushel. The box was the particular trust of the guard and he was under orders to watch it with his life.

Hickok handled a pistol with the speed of lightning. When he wished to emphasize something he had a way of throwing his right or left hand towards you with the trigger finger pointed straight at you. His hands moved with incredible swiftness and I believe he practiced this mannerism with such purpose that it became part of his nature, and probably resulted in making him the fastest two-gun man of his day.

Hickok was not a wanton killer and used his guns only in the line of duty. He had plenty of opportunities to kill oftener than he did, knowing he could start a graveyard at any time and the government would pay all funeral expenses.

We never knew him to be intoxicated and never knew him to kill but one man except in line of duty. The exception was a man named McCandless, who kept the Rock Creek station near the Little Blue river. The two got into a trivial dispute, no one knew just what, and Bill drew his gun first. My father and McCandless were friends and were both station keepers.

One day I returned to the Ashpoint station just as the coach pulled in. I was carrying a mighty good pistol, a Dragoon .45 caliber, and as I rode up to the coach I noticed Bill's eyes were directed toward my pistol. "That's a mighty dangerous looking gun for an innocent looking man," he said, asking to examine it.

After looking it over he remarked: "It's a mighty fine gun, but I don't see any notches on the handle."

I told him I hadn't got to that yet, and he said; "You will get to that before you cross the desert, that is if you don't get killed before you get into practice."

Anyone who wanted to make the acquaintance of Hickok and would mind their own business and not get too inquisitive would find him a perfect gentleman in every way. In those days he was he was not known as "Wild Bill."[1]

The Russell, Majors and Waddell story reined as common knowledge until the Hickok family provided Joseph Rosa two letters in the 1990s that cleared up the question of Hickok's employer for the two years from the summer of 1859 through the spring of 1861. These letters also knocked at least one more red herring out of the Hickok legacy.

Guy Butler, James' cousin, wrote to Horace Hickok on May 26, 1861, from his home in Black Jack, Kansas, with some shocking news (punctuation added):

I take this opportunity of writing to you not knowing when I may get another chance as I am about to enlist. I heard last week that James was dead. I do not know but that you have heard of it before. I got it from Mcintire of Monticello [George W. McIntyre, father of Fred McIntyre]. *he said he died with a disease called the newmonia a disease that has proven very fatal here in Kansas. I had not heard of his sickness before. if I had I should have gone up and taken care of him. He died at Salt Creek Valley four miles west of Levenworth. The circumstances surrounding his death I know nothing about. He was in the employ of Jones & Cartwright in whose employ he had been nearly two years. I suppose they must have been owing him considerable. when I left him last summer they were owing him about a hundred dollars. I will inquire into the matter more particular and let you know as soon as possible.[2]*

The family was stunned. Horace quickly wrote to Jones & Cartwright at Leavenworth, and they replied:

OFFICE OF
Pike's Peak Transportation Line
Under the Planters House
Leavenworth...June 6, 1861

Mr. Horace L. Hickok
Troy Grove, Ills
Dear Sir;

Yours of the 3rd is received. Mr. J.B. Hickok has not been in our employ since 20th April, at which time we settled with him and paid him what was due him. The Wagon Master under whom he worked, Geo. H. Ross, can probably tell his whereabouts, but he has now gone to Denver City and will not be back for two months. We will send your letter out to him when he can probably give you the information desired.

Yours respectfully,
Jones & Cartwright [3]

Guy Butler's letter to Horace above clearly shows that for the approximately two years from summer of 1859 through spring 1861, James was in the stagecoach and freighting business; he was not working for Russell, Majors, and Waddell, but instead was employed by Jones & Cartwright. This firm's principals were John S. Jones and Joseph Cartwright.

In the winter of 1858-1859 John S. Jones went to Washington, D.C. to bid directly against Russell, Majors and Waddell for a giant freighting contract that the government was about to grant in the wake of the Colorado gold rush. Jones & Cartwright already had a large wholesale store in fledgling Denver, and another one in Aurora. Jones was also at this same time a partner with William Russell in the Leavenworth & Pike's Peak Express, providing passenger and mail service between Leavenworth and Denver with a fleet of stagecoaches. Though Russell, Majors, and Waddell won the giant government contract, Jones & Cartwright did contract in 1859 to transport 150 wagon loads of military supplies to Utah. Earlier in 1859 they transported a trainload of merchandise to Denver.

Though a competitor of Russell, Majors and Waddell, Jones & Cartwright also functioned from time to time as a sub-contractor, filling in their stead when Russell, Majors and Waddell were struggling to fulfill a large contract, especially during those financially difficult years of 1860 and 1861, when bankruptcy was closing in on the freighting giant. That same sub-contractor status for Jones & Cartwright also applied to the Leavenworth & Pike's Peak Express, which was on shaky financial ground from the inception of the company until its demise in late 1859. It was Jones & Cartwright, sub-contracting under the banner of the Leavenworth & Pike's Peak Express, that young J.B. Hickok was working for when he pulled up on the stage at Ash Point each week and exchanged stories with Truman Blancett.[4]

Jones & Cartwright's letter above to Horace Hickok, dated June 6, 1861, also clearly indicates that Horace inquired not only about James' purported death to them, but also questioned if any past earnings were still due to James. In their response, Jones & Cartwright answered directly that they had settled in full with James. Guy Butler's statement that James had been working for Jones & Cartwright for nearly two years comports very closely with two benchmarks known to be true: James left Monticello in early summer of 1859, and he was at Rock Creek in Nebraska by late spring of 1861.

Finally, the mention of wagon master George Ross is germane to this issue. Buffalo Bill's sister Julia recalled both Hickok and Ross together in 1859 in a reminiscence. Now on the tail end of James' career at Jones & Cartwright, George Ross appears in their June 6, 1861, letter as Hickok's boss, and one most likely to know where James was at that time.

Almost forty years later, in 1900, James' sister Celinda Hickok wrote an unpublished manuscript about the life of her famous brother. Through the mist of a memory four decades old, and much muddled by memories of James written by others during those four decades, Celinda nevertheless provided further confirmation of those events of 1860 and 1861 in what she wrote (with editorial insertions added for clarity): "I very well remember the day we got word that he had been killed by the Notorious McKundlas band." (Celinda mis-remembers here. It was never written or stated that James was killed by McCandles. She has mixed up that memory with the letter from Guy Butler to the family that James had died of pneumonia.) "It was in '61 as near as I can recall the date...It was many weeks before we learned that he was still alive. I finally received a letter from a man by the name of Ross, in which he told me to write to the Wells Fargo Overland Company and they would tell us about him." (Here Celinda's memory "puts the cart before the horse." As shown in the Guy Butler letter above, the letter she received was from Jones & Cartwright, not Wells Fargo. The "man named Ross" is George Ross, Hickok's wagon master at Jones & Cartwright. Perhaps George Ross did write the family a letter about James, but more likely she is remembering the admonition from Jones & Cartwright that George Ross might know something about James, and they would forward the family's letter to Ross in Denver.) "I then wrote to this co, and received word to write to a Mrs. Cody, at Rock Creek and I would get the information so sadly wanted. I then received a letter from 'Julia Cody' a sister of William Cody, now known as Buffalo Bill. She told me that James was at their home...She said he would write as soon as he was able." (Of course "Mrs. Cody" was not at Rock Creek, she was at her home in the Salt Creek valley just north of Leavenworth, the same Salt Creek valley that Guy Butler claimed above that James died at. It is certainly plausible that Celinda would receive a letter from fifteen-year-old William Cody's older sister Julia telling Celinda and the Hickok family that James was alive and recuperating at their home.) "It was many months before he recovered, and when he came home to see us; After the Battle of Pea Ridge, in Missouri, He told us he had never been able to regain his usual weight, but he was seemingly as strong and active as ever." Glaring by its omission is any mention of Hickok's involvement in a bear fight, as alleged by Hickok biographer James Buel, which, if it had occurred, would have been seared into Celinda's memory even forty years later. [5]

It is curious that Celinda goes on in this unpublished manuscript of 1900 to remember James' notorious tangle with McCandles in 1861, almost verbatim with the sensational and completely false event as reported by George Ward Nichols in 1867. Yet her memory correctly finds no occurrence of a bear fight that never happened. However, this myth has been perpetuated in popular literature to the same level as Nichols' version of the McCandles fight, which takes us to the laying to rest of this myth.

In 1881, James Buel wrote the first widely-circulated biography of James Butler Hickok, devoting 221 of the lead-off pages to Hickok's life in the book *Heroes of the Plains -or- Life and Wonderful Adventures of Wild Bill, Buffalo Bill, Kit Carson, Capt. Payne,"White Beaver," Capt. Jack, Texas Jack, California Joe, and other Celebrated Indian Fighters, Scouts, Hunters and Guides.*

Buel's popular biography of Hickok was very influential on Hickok biographers who came after Buel. Many followed him verbatim. One of the legends started by Buel that has enjoyed a long and undeserved life concerned a bloody fight between Hickok and a bear. Buel wrote a long and gory and completely false passage about James' fight with this bear, mercifully edited below so the reader gets the general gist of the story:

> *While passing through the Socorro range with his team two miles ahead of Farley, Bill discovered a large cinnamon bear with her two cubs directly in the road in front of him. The bear, instead of manifesting any fear at Bill's approach, but moved entirely by her maternal instincts, boldly disputed his passage, and with further advance of the team she growled fiercely and showed her intention to attack him. Bill being provided with two excellent pistols and a large bowie knife gave himself no concern for the result of the encounter, thinking it an easy matter to kill the bear—a presumption in which he was most seriously mistaken.*
>
> *When the bear approached within twenty feet of him he fired one of his pistols, striking her squarely in the forehead, but the accurate aim instead of proving fatal had no other effect than to put the beast in a more desperate rage...the bear reared on her hind legs and grappled him. The struggle which now ensued was one of the most desperate ever known. Bill buried the knife rapidly in various parts of the bears body... but while doing this his shoulder was torn dreadfully, his left arm crushed from the elbow, his breast furrowed by the long poniard-like claws, and his left cheek was split open....The combat lasted nearly half an hour and at its close it was difficult to decide which presented the more horrifying spectacle, Bill or his dead antagonist...Bill was hauled to Santa Fe and placed under the charge of Dr. Sam Jones, an excellent frontier surgeon, who, by good attention, was able to so far restore his patient in two months' time as to permit Bill's return to Independence. But it was not until several months after his discharge from the surgeon's care that Bill was able to work again, and the scars from the wounds received in that encounter he bore to his grave. In the latter part of 1860 Bill left the employment of Majors & Russell to accept a position with the Overland Stage Co. as watchman and hostler at Rock Creek Station, a point on the Old Platte route fifty miles west of Topeka.*[6]

A fantastic and thrilling story, overly long and overwrought, written in the blood-and-thunder style of the popular culture of the time, and perpetuated by most Hickok biographers after Buel; but none of it was true. Buel thought he needed a manly and heroic reason that James had been banished to Rock Creek to work as a mere stable boy, and certainly pneumonia did not fit the bill. Further casting doubt on this dubious encounter with a bear is that the Hickok family had no knowledge of such a catastrophe, not at that time or later. The description of James' injuries does not hold up to scrutiny either; Hickok's later-in-life consistent skill and feats with a gun belie "a shoulder torn dreadfully" and his "left arm crushed from the elbow" at an earlier time. The many photographs of Hickok do not indicate that once "his left cheek was split open."

What actually happened, as is made abundantly clear by the two letters above and the Celinda Hickok manuscript, is that James caught pneumonia in the late winter of 1860 or spring of 1861. Guy Butler states that he died in the Salt Creek valley near Leavenworth. That is where the Cody family lived and ran a hotel. James was recovering there with the Cody family, when the word went out that he had died of "neumonia."

Anyone who has recovered from pneumonia knows its debilitating effect and the severe, months-long fatigue and weakness that the recovery entails. It also can cause unusual weight loss. Celinda recalled that James said he had "never been able to return to his usual weight." No wonder Hickok was tasked with menial jobs at Rock Creek to facilitate his recovery from pneumonia, not from the wounds of a bear fight.

Joseph Rosa believed that Buel got the idea for the bear fight from the files of one of the newspapers when Buel was a city editor there. Another "Wild Bill," from Fort Scott, in 1859 challenged some boxers in the editorial pages of the Westport *Border Star*. The paper described this "Wild Bill:"

[A] *Western ripsnorter who has proved himself a tight customer in a bear fight. He is a Cheyenne chief, well known for his power and spunk. He is a white man by birth, but in early life he joined the Indians and so well was he pleased with their manners, customs, and mode of life that he became a member of the Cheyenne tribe, and was finally chosen as their chief.* [7]

In addition to the fictional overtones of the editorial, James was not yet known as Wild Bill in 1859. This was probably the genesis of Buel's fantasy about James and a bear. This myth should be vigorously thrown into the ash bin of history. It never happened. Further evidence dismissing this myth of a bear fight appears in the next chapter.

These repudiations of Buel are not to say that there is nothing accurate or of value in his biography of Hickok. Buel has particular credentials not shared by any of Hickok's many other biographers. Other than George Ward Nichols, Buel is the only one who personally knew Hickok while he was alive.

Buel was a reporter for the *Kansas City Journal* in the 1870s; his office on 5th Street was just around the corner from where Hickok made his home on Main Street in the 1870s, at the St. Nicholas Hotel. By 1875 Buel had moved on as an editor for the *St. Louis Evening Dispatch*. Before James made his 1876 trip into the Black Hills, he stayed at Buel's St. Louis home. They were very familiar with each other. There will be more on Buel and his role in developing the Hickok legend in coming pages.

James left the employ of Jones & Cartwright on April 20, 1861, and working through his recovery from pneumonia, made his way to Rock Creek, Nebraska, arriving there in May, 1861. Circumstantial evidence indicates that he was employed by Horace Wellman, and it was Wellman who was employed by Russell, Majors and Waddell. It is known that Russell, Majors and Waddell, through one of their subsidiaries, had made an offer to purchase the east station at Rock Creek in April, 1861. It is also possible that James was not on anyone's payroll, since he had come to recover and recuperate and was assigned limited and menial tasks. Yet from these innocuous circumstances would come one of the most notorious gun fights of the frontier, and it would play a major role in propelling the story of James Butler Hickok into the legend of Wild Bill Hickok.

#4037

David McCanles. Leaving his wife and North Carolina home, McCanles made his way to Rock Creek in territorial Nebraska after discarding plans to seek gold in Colorado. In 1859 he bought the small relay station at Rock Creek that served stagecoaches and other travelers west on the Oregon-California trail. In 1861 on a hot July day at Rock Creek his plans for the future ended. *Author's collection.*

4

ROCK CREEK

With the possible exception of Wyatt Earp's shoot-out at the OK Corral in 1881, few frontier gun fights have generated as much controversy as the Hickok-McCanles affair that took place just a few miles north of the Kansas border in Nebraska at the Rock Creek station on July 12, 1861.

David McCanles came west from North Carolina in 1859, apparently because of debt troubles of some kind in the East. Though married, McCanles brought a different woman west with him: Sarah Shull, a beautiful young woman who was to figure in some of the mystery to unfold at Rock Creek. McCanles and Sarah came by steamboat to Leavenworth in spring of 1859, where they outfitted for an extended journey. It seems McCanles, like Hickok and many others, wanted to join the gold rush to Colorado and Pike's Peak. He and Sarah Shull set out on the Oregon-California Trail and encountered some disillusioned gold seekers. Further along the trail, McCanles came upon a small relay station at Rock Creek in Nebraska. This relay station was owned by a twenty-one-year-old named Newton Glenn.

This relay station served stagecoaches (the Leavenworth & Pike's Peak Express Company listed it as a regular stop), emigrants, gold-rushers, and other trail travelers. McCanles found that Glenn was willing to sell the property. McCanles saw economic promise in the station. He dropped his plans to chase gold in Colorado and bought the station in the spring of 1859.

That summer he made improvements; a new toll bridge over Rock Creek, and a new and larger ranch station on the east side of the creek. McCanles and Sarah moved into the original station building on the west side of Rock Creek. Inexplicably, McCanles sent for his wife back in North Carolina. She could not have been happy when she arrived to find McCanles' girlfriend there.

In April of 1861, the Central Overland California & Pike's Peak Express Company, commonly known as the Pony Express, though at that time deep in debt and hurtling towards imminent bankruptcy (as was their owner Russell, Majors and Waddell), approached McCanles about buying the east ranch station for use as a Pony Express station. It appears that they had already been renting the use of the east station for a period of time. Once they owned it, the Central Overland California & Pike's Peak Express Company would not only be able to take care of their own operation, but would now be the recipient of the receipts from other trail travelers that had previously gone to McCanles.

McCanles sold the new east side ranch station, that he had built, to the Central Overland California & Pike's Peak Express Company under these terms: one-third to be paid down and the remainder paid over the following three months. In May of 1861, at about the same time that James showed up at the station, Horace Wellman and his wife Jane arrived at the station. Horace Wellman was to be the station keeper at Rock Creek for the Central Overland California & Pike's Peak Express Company.[1]

There are only two eyewitness descriptions of the gun fight at Rock Creek: an expansive one by Monroe McCanles made in 1925, sixty-six years after the incident, and the few circumspect answers provided by Sarah Shull, also made in 1925 and a few years after.

The statement made by Monroe McCanles was made at the request of writer Frank Wilstach, who in1925 tracked down the now seventy-six-year-old man in Kansas City. Wilstach got some answers out of McCanles, but they reached an impasse when Monroe McCanles became angry that Wilstach was insisting that his father David had demanded taking the horses from the station on that fateful July day in 1861. Monroe finally relented and conceded to Wilstach that his father was going to take the horses.

Frank Wilstach was working on his Hickok biography at the time, as was William Connelley on his. They were communicating by letter regularly, sharing research and information about Hickok. At about the same period, George Hansen of Fairbury, Nebraska was putting together a study of the Rock Creek affair that would, in 1927, take up an entire issue of *Nebraska History Magazine*, the publication of the Nebraska State Historical Society.[2] The study was a not-so-subtle attempt to restore the reputation of McCanles, and besmirch the reputation of Hickok, all with little or no evidence either way.

October 30, 1926
Frank Wilstach to William Connelley

Oh, as to Hansen: He and the whole lot of 'em are getting on my nerves. They want to whitewash old Dave, and it can't be done right. If I am not mistaken, there was a fight at the cabin. Have some dope to that effect that looks good. In short, I do not believe Monroe's story. Do you?

Yours very truly,
Frank J. Wilstach [3]

December 16, 1926
Frank Wilstach to William Connelley

I am immensely obliged and pleased that you should try for the K.C. Journal "interview" with Monroe McCanles! I got one. That hain't no interview—as it is reported to be—by friend Sutton!!!
The truth of the matter is this: About a year ago I got (through a friend) McCanles to make a statement for me of what happened*; and that is what Fred S. has published as an interview—word for word. I didn't use McCanles' full story because* he withdrew it*, because I insisted that Wild Bill had put up the defense that his father demanded horses at the R.C. Station. McCanles finally admitted this, but became angry with me at the mere mention of horses! He finally admitted that—but you have seen it in my poor book. The McCanles statement, made at my request, (published as an interview by Sutton), was subsequently printed in a Fairbury newspaper. I have one—can loan it to you if you haven't seen it. A little more stuff in it than the Sutton "interview?" Fred S. shortened it, I think.*
What is Sutton's age, anyway? He was a cradle-side friend of Wild Bill. I fancy or the other way round.

Yours very truly,
F. J. Wilstach [4]

December 23, 1926
William Connelley to Frank Wilstach

> *I sent you a few days ago a copy of Sutton's alleged interview with Monroe McCanles. I see that this interview was a rehash of what you secured from McCanles. I am very glad indeed to have the information which you wrote to me on the 16th that McCanles admitted that his father had demanded horses from Wellman at Rock Creek. He made a demand for horses specially and also demanded that Wellman vacate the premises and turn the buildings over to him. Mr. McCanles was not the mild and injured party which his son makes him out.*
> *I have not seen yet or been able to ascertain the age of Mr. Sutton...*

> *Sincerely,*
> *William E. Connelley*[5]

Frank Wilstach's biography, *Wild Bill Hickok, Prince of Pistoleers,* was published in 1926. It was the first attempt to write a historically accurate story of James Butler Hickok's life, and Wilstach was able to dispose of a few, but only a few, of the myths. George Hansen's report appeared in the *Nebraska History Magazine* for April-June, 1927. William Connelley's biography, *Wild Bill and His Era,* came out in 1933, or at least a reduced version of it did. The book was published posthumously; Connelley died suddenly and unexpectedly on July 14, 1930. Fred Sutton, noted with some skepticism by Wilstatch and Connelley above, was a raconteur who managed to convince a gullible public that thirsted for tales of the American frontier that he was personal friends with a who's who of frontier icons: Hickok, Masterson, Earp, et al. More about Fred E. Sutton in Appendix Three of this book.

Monroe McCanles' long statement, that he pulled back from Wilstach in a fit of pique, appeared first in the Fairbury, Nebraska newspaper, then in the *Kansas City Journal*, and finally as part of George Hansen's report in the *Nebraska History Magazine* in spring of 1927. Notwithstanding the skepticism of Frank Wilstach, and taking into consideration that this, the only fully fleshed, blow-by-blow account of the gun fight at Rock Creek, is from an elderly man of seventy-six years recalling an event that took place when he was just twelve years old; and that he is considered a biased witness, as the deceased was his father.

These are the facts as stated by Monroe McCanles, sixty-six years after the incident. This is the only primary source available to determine what actually happened at Rock Creek on July 12, 1861:

> *My father, David C. McCanles, left North Carolina in March, 1859, his destination being Pike's Peak. This was during the gold excitement in Colorado. He came to Leavenworth, Kansas, and outfitted for a trip across the plains. He got as far as Rock Creek, Nebraska Territory, and having met several parties returning from Pike's Peak with such discouraging stories about the gold prospects there, he stopped at Rock Creek and bought of Newton Glenn the only ranch on the creek at that time. This was on the west side of the creek, and was the overland mail and stage station on the Oregon Trail at that time. During the summer of 1859 my father built a ranch house on the east side of the creek, dug a well and found plenty of water. There was no water to be had at the west ranch, excepting the creek water. Also, during this summer, he built a toll bridge across the creek, which was quite an undertaking, for it was the first bridge along the line and a great help to travelers on the Overland Trail. He built the house on the east side to house his brother, J.L. McCanles, who had concluded to come west, and in the latter part of August of that year, his brother and family with my father's family, his nephew James Woods, and Billie Hughes, an orphan boy, left North Carolina for Nebraska Territory. We came by railroad, steamboat, and ox teams, and landed at Rock Creek about the 20th of September, 1859.*
>
> *My uncle took up his abode in the east ranch house. Billie Hughes died with typhoid fever that fall. My uncle lived in this house until the spring of 1860 when he moved down to the ranch on the Little Blue river near the mouth of Rock Creek. Father then built a barn and a bunk house on the east side and rented that station to Russell, Majors and Waddell, who operated the Overland Stage and Pony Express to California, and they took charge and furnished their own station keeper and stock tenders.*
>
> *Early in the spring of 1861 father sold the west ranch to a couple of Germans, Hagenstein and Wolfe. The summer of 1860 was a very dry year and my uncle became somewhat dissatisfied with the conditions, so he picked up and moved down towards Nebraska City, and took up land in Johnson County, Nebraska. Now, after father sold the west ranch, he moved to the ranch on the Blue. We had a good lot of*

cattle and horses and a lot of work oxen. We had several hired men and were doing a regular ranch business. We furnished the hay for both of the ranches on Rock Creek. The Stage Company had at this time a man named H. Wellman and his wife as station keeper and Dock Brink as stock tender.

Early in the spring of 1861 the Stage Company sent James B. Hickok to the Rock Creek Station as assistant stock tender. Jim claimed to be a South Carolinian and father and he became quite cronies, both being from the south. The Wellmans and father were not quite so friendly. They were too slow with their payments. About the first days of July, 1861, Wellman and I went to Brownville, after a load of supplies for the station and some for father. We were gone about ten days, as it was 100 miles to Brownville on the Missouri river. We got home about four o'clock July 12th.

There was a little ranch upon the road southeast of the Station, kept by Jack Nye. When we got to the Station I saw some horses hitched up at Nye's and I thought I recognized them as some of ours, so I ran up to Nye's and found father, Woods, and Gordon there. Father seemed glad to see me, and wanted to know if Wellman had treated me right while we were gone and I told him that Wellman had treated me well. Then we all came back to the Station.

Father and I stopped at the house and Woods and Gordon went on down to the barn. Father went to the kitchen door and asked for Wellman. Mrs. Wellman came to the door and father asked her if Wellman was in the house and she said he was. Father said "tell him to come out" and she said "what do you want with him?" Father said "I want to settle with him." She said "He'll not come out." Father said "send him out or I'll come in and drag him out."

Now to make this more plain to the reader—while Wellman and I were gone to Brownville—father and Mrs. Wellman had some words, or a quarrel over the affairs at the ranch and Mrs. Wellman had told father when Mr. Wellman came home he would settle with father for his impudence and that is why father made the remark that he wanted to settle with him.

Now, when father made the threat that he "would come in and drag him out," Jim (or Bill) Hickok stepped to the door and stood by Mrs. Wellman. Father looked him in the face and said "Jim, haven't we been friends all the time?" Jim said "Yes". Father said "are we friends now?" and Jim said "Yes". Father said "Will you hand me a drink of water," and Jim turned around to the water bucket and brought a dipper of water and handed it to him. Father drank the water and handed the dipper back, and as he handed the dipper back he saw something take place inside that was threatening or dangerous. Anyway he stepped quickly from the kitchen door to the front door, about ten feet north of the kitchen door, and stepped up on the step and said "Now, Jim, if you have anything against me, come out and fight me fair." Just as he uttered these words the gun cracked and he fell flat on his back. He raised himself up to almost a sitting position and took one last look at me, then fell back dead.

Now Woods and Gordon heard the shout and came running up unarmed to the door, and just then Jim appeared at the door with a Colt's Navy revolver. He fired two shots at Woods, and Woods ran around the house to the north. Gordon broke and ran. Jim ran out the door and fired two shots at him and wounded him. Just as Jim ran out of the door Wellman came out with a hoe and ran after Woods who had run around the house, and hit Woods on the head with the hoe and finished him. Then Wellman came running around the house where I was standing and struck at me with the hoe and he yelled out "let's kill them all." I dodged the lick and ran. I outran him to a ravine shelter south of the house and stopped there. Mrs. Wellman stood in the door clapping her hands and yelling "kill him, kill him, kill him."

Father was shot from behind a calico curtain that divided the log house into two rooms, and was shot with a rifle that belonged to himself. He had loaned the gun to the Station keeper for their protection in case of trouble with the many hard characters that were traveling the trail. There were but four pieces of fire arms on the ground at this time, my small double barreled shot gun, small, or boys size, with one barrel loaded; fathers rifle that was kept in the house; a Colt's Navy six shooter that was in the house and a double-barreled shot gun that Dock Brink kept at the barn loaded with buckshot.

Now, to bear me out that Woods and Gordon were not armed when they ran up to the door: if either or both of them had been armed they surely would have had their revolvers in hand, and while Jim was shooting Woods don't you think one or the other of them would have done some shooting? Do you think that if Woods had been armed he would have let Wellman knock him in the head without trying to defend himself?

Now, for more evidence that Gordon was not armed: Gordon kept a blood hound that usually followed him where he went. This dog was with him at the barn when the fracas began. After Gordon had made his getaway, being wounded, the station outfit put this dog on his trail, and the dog trailed him down the creek and brought him to bay about 80 rods down the creek. When the bunch caught up, the dog was fighting Gordon, and Gordon was warding him off with a stick. Gordon was finished with a load of buckshot. Now, if Gordon had been armed don't you think he would have killed the dog?

All of the sensational writers have had those men loaded down with knives and firearms. When I made my escape from Wellman I ran three miles to the ranch and broke the news to my mother.

One of our hands hitched up a team and took mother and the other children up to the Station. I was so exhausted with my getaway that I remained at the ranch, or home place.

I went up to the Station the next morning. There was quite a crowd there that had gathered from twenty-five to thirty miles up and down the Oregon Trail. The first thing I saw when I got near the Station was a crowd of men burying Gordon. They had brought his remains from down the creek up near the station and had dug a grave on a little knoll and put him in, boots and all, wrapped in a blanket. They made a rude box for father and Woods and buried them in the same box in the hill south of the station, by the grave of Billie Hughes. Their bones lay there for twenty years. Then I moved them to Fairbury Cemetery about seven miles west of Rock Creek.

After the killing my uncle, J.L. McCanles, organized a crowd over in Johnson County and came over and arrested Hickok, Wellman and Dock Brink and took them before a Justice of the Peace at Beatrice, Nebraska, and they had a preliminary trial before old Pap Towle, an aged Justice and were acquitted. The county was not organized at that time and the trials were crude, merely sham trials.

My uncle then bundled us up and moved everything moveable over to Johnson County where he disposed of the stock and other property. Mother lived there until the spring of 1862, then moved back to the ranch on the Blue river. We surely went through some trying times. We had to run from the Indians several times. Went through all kinds of hardships, but mother kept her five children born in North Carolina, and one that was born in Nebraska, all together and they are all still alive, but she is dead. Died at the ripe old age of seventy-five years.

Her remains rest by fathers at Fairbury, Nebraska. My uncle moved to Colorado in 1863 and he became very wealthy and quite prominent. He was a representative and Senator in the state legislature. He laid out the town of Florence, Colorado. Oil was discovered on his land. He died at the age of 86 years.

I lost track of Jim, (or Bill) Hickok after this episode, and did not hear of him again until 1870. He was in Junction City, Kansas, that summer. Next he was in Abilene, Kansas then Dodge City, Kansas; Denver, Colorado; Cheyenne, Wyoming; and Deadwood, South Dakota. If Jim ever killed one man outright who had an equal chance for his life, I would like to have the evidence, and not fiction.

My father was no killer, horse thief, desperado, nor anything of the kind. We trace the family back to 1770 and there have never been any of our ancestors found hanging on a limb, so far.

This is written by
William Monroe McCanles,
3343 Bellefontaine Ave.
Kansas City, Mo.
October, 1925; at the age of 76 years.[6]

There are several points to consider about this statement of purported facts as written by eyewitness Monroe McCanles sixty-six years after the incident. First of all, his statements are not all eyewitness, and were probably told to him after the fact. He did not see Wellman kill Woods with a hoe, because Woods had run around to the north side of the building while Monroe McCanles was on the other side of the house with his deceased father. He did not see that the shot that killed his father rang out from behind the calico curtain, and he did not see that it was from the shotgun his father had provided for the station. He states that Hickok came through the door with a Navy Colt revolver. It is very unlikely that 12-year-old Monroe McCanles, anguished and suffering from extreme stress from seeing seconds before the death of his father, took time to note the type of gun Hickok was holding. Likely he read years later that the Navy Colt was Hickok's gun of choice, and applied it back to the incident. Young McCanles could not have seen what transpired with Gordon, as he had already made his escape from Wellman's hoe and was on the three-mile run to his home.

There is another glaring point about Monroe McCanles's statement: nowhere does he indict Hickok, or anyone else, as the killer of his father David, McCanles. He only states "The gun cracked and he" [his father] "fell flat on his back." He never considers who pulled the trigger of that gun.

Over the years many writers have speculated who killed David McCanles. Some incriminate Hickok, others indict Horace Wellman as the shooter. None of these speculations are built on any sort of material fact. Here is another suspect, not voiced until now, but not without logic and foundation: Jane Wellman. She had motive and opportunity. She hated David McCanles for the threats against her husband Horace, evidenced by Monroe's testimony above, and Jane Wellman's threat that Horace would "settle with him" [David McCanles] "for his impudence." There are also reports of David McCanles mistreating Jane's father, which certainly added to her animus. Lastly, at the scene she was gripped in the throes of a hysterical rage: "Kill him, kill him, kill him," she said, referring to 12-year-old Monroe McCanles, as she stood in the doorway clapping her hands excitedly. (Likely that Monroe actually heard her shouting "Kill 'em, kill 'em, kill 'em," referring to all of them.)

There are other statements that are very contradictory. Monroe claimed that Horace Wellman came after him with a hoe, yelling "Let's kill them all," but Monroe dodged it and made his escape. Yet Horace had just taken Monroe on a ten-day trip to Brownville, a trip on which, Monroe told his father,

Horace Wellman had treated him well. Yet moments after their arrival back at Rock Creek that July afternoon, Monroe claims that Horace Wellman was seeking to murder him with a hoe. Finally, if we can rely on Monroe McCanles' second-by-second account of events from the time he and his father approached the kitchen door of the east ranch station until David McCanles stepped upon the steps of the door ten feet to the north and was shot, then empirical evidence indicates that Hickok was not the person who shot McCanles. Monroe reports that his father asked Hickok for a drink of water, and his father drank the water and, "as he handed the dipper back" [to Hickok] "he saw something take place inside that was threatening or dangerous." David McCanles saw something "threatening or dangerous" by looking *over or around* Hickok, who was standing in the doorway accepting the dipper back from McCanles. So Hickok was not the object of McCanles' concern. "Anyway, he stepped quickly from the kitchen door to the front door, about ten feet north of the kitchen door," [one or two seconds elapsed for McCanles to move quickly ten feet] "and stepped up on the step and said 'Now, Jim, if you have anything against me, come out and fight me fair.'" It does not make sense that David McCanles would call out Hickok from the front door when he had seconds before, at the kitchen door, sensed a danger that was not engendered by Hickok, but someone else back in the room behind Hickok.

It is possible that sixty-six years after the incident Monroe mis-remembered the statement as being directed at Hickok. It is more likely that the statement he attributed to his father David McCanles was directed at the unseen danger in the house (Horace Wellman or Jane Wellman) that he had perceived looking over or around Hickok at the kitchen door, more like: "Now, if you have anything against me, come out and fight me fair." The next moment, Monroe claimed "the gun cracked and he fell flat on his back."

The shooting of Woods and Gordon raises many questions. Monroe McCanles' statement goes to great lengths to try to show that Woods and Gordon were unarmed. Yet shooting an unarmed man, especially in the back, does not square with everything known about the life of James Butler Hickok, both before Rock Creek and after. He was raised in a midwestern family with strong values in Illinois, and it is obvious they instilled in him a strong sense of right and wrong, and a sensitivity to the plights of others. After Rock Creek, notwithstanding Monroe McCanles' caustic sentence that appeared at the end of his statement that mis-characterized James' career after Rock Creek as that of a gutless cretin who preyed on others, James' career was exemplary. He shot a total of five men intentionally, all of whom threatened imminent harm. Three of those incidents took place when Hickok was an officer of the law, one of them took place when two soldiers tried to kill him, and one of them took place as a dueling shoot-out on a town square.

So it is very unlikely that Hickok shot at Woods or Gordon, unless they were armed and constituted an imminent threat. But, unless and until a new document is discovered, the facts concerning the deaths of McCanles, Woods, and Gordon remain undecided, supported only by the statement of Monroe McCanles.

George Hansen did discover the few trial documents that existed from 1861, and published them in the study he wrote in *Nebraska History Magazine* in 1927. Unfortunately, they really answered nothing about what actually happened. Many people were subpoenaed to testify, including Jane Wellman and Monroe McCanles. Young McCanles did not testify, and if Jane Wellman did, her testimony is lost, as is the testimony of the three defendants: James B. Hickok, Horace Wellman, and Dock Brink.

A warrant was issued on July 13, 1861, based on a written complaint made by the McCanles family. The three defendants were arrested on July 15 by Sheriff E. B. Hendee and taken in a wagon to Beatrice, Nebraska. Justice of the Peace T. M. Coulter held the hearing that took place July 15,16 and 18. Twelve-year-old Hugh. J. Dobbs attended the hearing, and recalled some intimate details years later:

> I remember that "Wild Bill" sat opposite to where I stood, and he was dressed in a gray suit; he was of light complexion, sandy bearded and with sandy hair; his eyes were quick and intense. There were times when he rose and paced the floor, and his tall, slim figure, well proportioned and quick in movement, made a deep impression on me..."Wild Bill" appeared nervous in the beginning of his trial, but this passed away as the trial progressed and he became calm and deliberate. I never heard in the whispers that went around the court room or in the yard outside, that "Wild Bill" had been attacked by a bear had been almost disembowled from this encounter, and that but a short time before he had been sent to Rock Creek Station to recuperate. He was to all appearances a strong, healthy man, in the prime of life, and had no appearance of an invalid or of one recovering from physical disability. If such had been the case, I believe there would have been talk of it among the onlookers and loiterers who came from miles around on the prairie—keen for talk of the happenings of prairie life; and as a prairie boy, almost twelve years of age, I would have remembered any bear story.[7]

The three defendants pled that they were defending company property, and Justice Coulter dismissed the murder charges against them, and so the trial ended. And what of Sarah Shull? In the same way that Frank Wilstach tracked down Monroe McCanles in Kansas City in 1925, he tracked down Sarah Shull that same year in North Carolina. She was ninety-one years old, and like Monroe McCanles, sixty-six years separated her from the Rock Creek incident. Wilstach wrote:

#4038

Sarah Shull came to Rock Creek in 1859 with David McCanles. Many years later she gave writer Frank Wilstach an interview about what happened at Rock Creek. *Author's collection.*

Having been located, she consented only with great reluctance to discuss the tragedy. Even after a lapse of more than half a century the incident is an exceedingly painful remembrance to her. Inducing her to talk was much like opening an oyster with a blade of grass.
It was a task of months to obtain anything significant from her.

Author Mark Dugan, who wrote an extensive study of Sarah Shull, believed that what little information she did divulge to Wilstach was given only in order to stop him from pestering her. Here follow the answers to such questions as Sarah Shull was willing to give:

Was money owed by Wellman the cause of the tragedy?
SS: No.
Were you at the cabin when McCanles was shot?
SS: No, I was at my home two miles away.
In your opinion, and from what you were told at the time, did Hickok kill McCanles in self-defense?
SS: Certainly-yes.
What makes you think this is true?
SS: Because on the morning of the tragedy I heard McCanles say he was going to clean up on the people at the Station.
You say McCanles stole horses?
SS: Yes, he stole horses.
Were those horses for the use of the Confederate cavalry?
SS: Yes. [8]

Yet seven years later in 1932, shortly before her death at the age of 98, Sarah purportedly told her close friend and confidante Jessie Williams that she had actually been at the east ranch cabin on July 12, 1861 when McCanles had been shot, and she added an unbelievable detail about hiding in the root cellar with Wood's blood dripping on to her head. To Jessie Williams, she said, "Hickok had steel-blue eyes that were beautiful and gentle but could change in a second and look dangerous. You had better watch his eyes; he wasn't one to run from a fight. I came close to having an affair with Hickok." [9]

Shortly after being acquitted, James left the Rock Creek area and made his way to Leavenworth, where a new destiny awaited him. The story of the incident at Rock Creek became well known on the plains of Nebraska and Kansas. The story would be exploited and exploded way beyond its factual details in a story by George Ward Nichols from an 1865 interview with Hickok in Springfield, Missouri. When it was finally published in *Harper's New Monthly Magazine* in February, 1867, it caused a sensation, and it propelled James Butler Hickok from midwestern notoriety to national fame.

5

J.B. HICKOK: UNION ARMY TEAMSTER, WAGON MASTER, SCOUT *and* SPY

James left Rock Creek in late July, 1861, and made his way to Fort Leavenworth to join the Union Army.

It has been stated before that he was brought in as a civilian scout, but he was actually brought into the army as a teamster. However, he participated in the Battle of Wilson's Creek that took place near Springfield, Missouri, not as a teamster but a sharpshooter. That battle that took place on August 10, 1861 was led by Union general Nathaniel Lyon. The Federal troops were defeated by the Confederates, and General Lyon himself was killed. In later years James' brother Horace recalled that before the battle started, James "was trying to locate a masked battery which opened fire the minute he discovered it. He never having been under artillery fire before said he was actually scared. The fire of that artillery brought on the battle of Wilson's Creek."[1]

By late October James was working as a wagon master for the Union Army. On October 28, 1861, he was hired by Captain James Swain at Sedalia, Missouri as wagon master from that date till November 30, 1861 at $100 a month, and from December 1 to December 31 at $60 a month.[2] Later Hickok was rehired by Captain James Swain at Otterville, Missouri as wagon master from January 1, 1862 till February 28, 1862 at $60 a month.[3] On February 10, 1862, Hickok was transferred to Capt. S.L. Brown, assistant quartermaster at Sedalia, apparently still as a wagon master.[4] No change in pay; and then we see that Hickok is named a chief wagon master at $100 a month on March 26.[5] On June 30, 1862 he is transferred to Rolla under Lieutenant S.C. Peck.[6]

George Hance, who served in Rolla throughout the war with James and his brother Lorenzo, and knew them both well, recalled that Hickok's wagon train was attacked by Confederates near Pleasant Hill,

Missouri in early 1862. Hance stated that the government purchased from Jones & Cartwright one hundred teams, each drawn by six yoke of oxen. Hickok was placed in charge of this train as wagon master. Hance related:

> *Early in the spring of 1862 he* [Hickok] *partially loaded at Fort Leavenworth, Kans., and started with the outfit to Sedalia, Mo., to finish loading for Springfield, Mo., for General Curtis's army, which was then in southwest Missouri, and northwest Arkansas. When he got down into Jackson county, Missouri, the rebels captured the train. Wild Bill made his escape and went to Independence, the county seat of Jackson county at that time, and got several companions and recaptured the outfit the next morning. The train then proceeded under heavy escort to Sedalia, finished loading, and went to Springfield. Mo. He then loaded for Batesville, Ark. From Batesville he went to Rolla.* [7]

There are only two extant letters known that James wrote during the war, though there surely must have been others. Both were written within a few weeks of each other, and written near the end of James' time as a wagon master and near the start of James time as a scout and spy for the Union Army in the fall of 1862.

On June 24, 1862, James wrote from Rolla to his friend William. The implication in the letter is that William lives in Homer (Troy Grove), and he is married to Jane. The letter also indicates that William is quite close to the Hickok family in Illinois. James' sense of humor comes through in the last part of this letter (punctuation added):

Rolla June 24 1862

> *William this is the first opportunity To write since I left home. The morning after I got Hear I Had to go to work and load 80 wagons with quartermaster goods for Batesville. when 30 miles from Rolla I received a Dispatch from Cheaf quartermaster Winslow to return to Rolla and Report to Capt. Peck quarter mstr Rolla Which I did yesterday evening. I am onloading Today and loading up for Springfield south west mosura With Commisary Stores. My escort to Batesville Consisted of 1200 men, 6 Peaces of artillery. It will take me 35 days to make the trip to Springfield and Back. Then I shall stay Hear one month. you can direct your letters to Springfield, all that you write in 20 days from this Date. I am in very good health. White river is open, and goods sent thare by water.*

I hope you are all well at home. give my respects to all and tell Liza when her Boy can say tater I will send him a hat. I would tell you to watch William Duey [Dewey] and see that he dont run of[f] With ma or ant Prissey. But I am afraid lid [Lydia] would tell him off it if I should. You can all write a grate deal easyer than I can, so you must all write. I want to find some letters when I get to Springfield. I shall write to you and Jane when I get to Springfield. direct your letters to Capt. J B Hickok Springfield Greene Co mo[8]

The only other known letter written during the war by James was written from Springfield to his sister Lydia on July 8, 1862, just two weeks after he wrote in the above letter about Springfield: "Then I shall stay Hear one month." In this below letter James noted the two letters from Lydia that he had received while unloading his ox train. He also told her he was glad to hear things were going well:

I expect to have Ruff times for some time On account of General Curtis Supplys Being cut off. I may be to Platesvill NBR as soon as I reach Rolla and I start from Rolla in the morning...

When next you write direct [it] to Rolla. Thare Was a farmer Just after me for Pay for 12.00 Rales my men Burnt of his fence yesterday and to day I told Him I Would make him some Rales next fall when it got Cool and feed His Corn for him to Boot. He walked off saying He was as good a Younion as I was. I told him he could afford to loose the Rales, then He went to cusin then and some of my men Put in the Variations. By Laughfing I guess he likes me Purty Well...When I get to Rolla I will write Again so Good By for the Presant From your Affectionate Brother.

Capt. J. B. Hickok [9]

The record shows that on September 26, 1862, Hickok was dropped from the wagon master rolls, yet no transfer or discharge is noted. The records are silent because James was being assigned to more dangerous work on behalf of the Union Army, work of subterfuge as a scout and spy that required a hidden identity. George Hance recalled that he was "personally & intimately acquainted with L.B. Hickok and his brother James B. Hickok, known in Rolla and Springfield as Wild Bill, where he served as a scout and guide from 1862 until the close of war."[10]

There is evidence that at some point from 1862 till 1865 Hickok was assigned to the 8th Missouri State Militia as a scout and a spy. Foster Keith, a resident of Dallas County, Missouri, who served with the 8th Missouri State Militia, recalled in later years riding on scouting missions with Wild Bill Hickok.[11] Hickok himself told journalist Henry M. Stanley in 1867 that he had served during the war with the 8th Missouri State Militia.

Part of the stated mission of the 8th Missouri State Militia was to use scouts and spies to get behind enemy Confederate lines. This regiment of militia was formed in 1861 and was active through 1865.

A protagonist and sometime leader of some of these covert expeditions was John Kelso, an eccentric man at best and a cruel fanatic at worst. He was described by contemporaries:

> ...fanatical in his Unionism, held all Confederates to be traitors, guilty of treason, and deserving of death...It is said that he always had a book of some sort in his saddle pockets, and frequently engaged in the study of mental philosophy and the subtleties of metaphysics while lying in the bush by the roadside waiting to "get the drop" on a rebel...But with all his whims and failings, Kelso had hosts of friends and admirers, especially among the soldiers.[12]

In his unpublished manuscript on Hickok, William Connelley reviewed the statements from an interview he did with John C. McKoin, who served with the 8th Missouri State Militia during the war:

> Springfield, Missouri was the home of John R. Kelso after the war. John C. McKoin, who served with Kelso and Hickok, always had much to say of them. He knew both men intimately and admired them. Most that he said of Hickok is recorded elsewhere. A Mr. Pearson also knew Kelso well and furnished some of the material for this account. He did not know Hickok except by sight and reputation...
> Once Hickok accosted Kelso in a bantering manner, unexpectedly he found a pistol cocked at his head, and Kelso glared at him with eyes that glittered with excitement and determination. Kelso would have killed him had not McKoin interfered the moment Kelso drew his revolver; it was all over in a few seconds. Bill apologized to Kelso and said he meant no offense and that the incident had not affected his friendship for Kelso. He took good care never to speak in a light vein to

Kelso. Kelso never refused to accompany Bill on any expedition which required they act together, even after this incident, but there was always jealousy between them, due largely to Kelso's attitude.[13]

McKoin recalled another wartime adventure with Kelso and Hickok. They were sent west with dispatches; McKoin supposed that they would return immediately to their headquarters. Yet Kelso and Hickok wanted to seize another opportunity; they located a rebel-guarded cattle herd some twenty miles distant from where they turned over the dispatches. McKoin found this plan very risky, but he relented and they undertook their plan that night; they fell upon the guard, killing several while the rest fled. They drove the herd to Springfield and surprised the quartermaster with the entire herd of 250 head of cattle.[14]

Hickok also served as a scout and spy with the 17th Illinois Volunteer Cavalry. This unit was formed in January 1864. Both it and the 8th Missouri State Militia were commanded at one time by General Sanborn. F.A. Carpenter, who served with the 17th and wrote the regimental history, described Hickok riding with the regiment's commander, Col. John L. Beveridge, pursuing enemy troops:"Wild Bill is with us, his horse running with a long easy stride, the front of his broad brimmed hat standing out of his line of vision." The Seventeenth was engaged in the fall of 1864 against the invasion of Missouri by Confederate militia and troops under Sterling Price. Lt. Philip McRae commanded Company C of the Seventeenth, and Carpenter described the admirable similarity of McRae and Hickok as "thrusting, daring, fearless men, both did good work for their country and took pride in doing so." At one point, Carpenter states that Wild Bill saved a number of soldiers of the regiment from capture by the troops of Price.[15]

Another soldier of the 17th Illinois Volunteer Cavalry, Albert Brock, recalled years later his recollection of Hickok during the Civil War. He knew Hickok was scouting for the regiment, but he saw him just once, apparently in disguise. Brock stated that a man "rode past on a mule. The man was dirty & unshaven, his clothing was dirty & needed repairs, so a young recruit made some disparaging remarks to the man about his appearance. The man made no answer but looked the young fellow over as tho he wanted to remember him. After the man was out of hearing, one of the cavalrymen said 'Young fellow, you're lucky to be alive. That man you just smarted off is Wild Bill Hickok, one of our scouts & he doesn't take that kind of talk from anybody.'" Brock remembered that the kid was terrified for weeks that Hickok would come back and find him, but Hickok did not return for him.[16]

True and verifiable records and recollections of Hickok, like McKoin's and Carpenter's above, are limited during his wartime spying years, because the very nature of what he was doing as a spy required secrecy, especially when the spy was working behind enemy lines, as Hickok often was. Yet another fine and concise recollection of Wild Bill Hickok during those years came from the pen of T. J. Estes. In 1864 and 1865, Yellville, Arkansas was occupied as a federal post. Located in Confederate Arkansas, yet just twenty miles south of the Missouri border, Yellville was an important crossroads point, and near the Union stronghold in Springfield, Missouri. Hickok worked out of Yellville for some period in 1864-1865. William Connelley writes that Hickok stayed at the Estes home in Yellville during that time, and that Mrs. Estes found Hickok to be "as nice a man at her home as she ever had about her house."[17] Years later, T. J. Estes recalled J. B. Hickok who stayed at his home in Yellville:

> Of course you have heard and read more or less, and also more or less falsehood, as well as truth, about "Wild Bill" (Bill Hickok) the Federal scout, and as he was at Yellville some and later at Springfield, Mo., where he killed little Dave Tutt, who was raised in Yellville, I will here introduce a sketch of his eventful life. I remember how he looked and about all the pictures I have seen of him were just like him. He was tall and straight, had long thin moustache and long, rather dark hair and he wore a broad brimmed hat. I believe what is said of him in the following sketch from the Springfield Democrat is pretty truthful...
>
> Everybody has read of Wild Bill and his wonderful exploits during and after the war, but everybody does not know that he lived in Springfield for a few years after the suppression of the rebellion.
>
> Many old citizens like J.M. Kirby, C.C. Avery, and D.M. Coleman, remember his career here having been acquainted with him...The real name of the former comrade of Buffalo Bill and the hero of Sundry Novels written by Ned Buntline, was J.B. Hickok. At the beginning of the war he left his home in Illinois and served as a scout in the wild and wooly west, in service of Uncle Sam. When peace was declared he located in Springfield. He was a magnificent specimen of manhood, six feet tall, weighed two-hundred pounds, and always wore a smile. He is described by D. M. Coleman as a good hearted fellow

who would give his last cent to anyone that needed it. He was genial and never sought a row, but always ready to take the side of the weaker party in any altercation. It is well known that he was an excellent shot and unflinching nerve, and that he killed a great many men during the war...

Albert Todd, colored, remembers an occurrence at Fayetteville, Arkansas illustrative of Wild Bill's character. It was during the war and in that country negroes were not allowed to drink at the bar with white people. There was a saloon kept by a strong secessionist, and Bill took six negroes, including Todd to the saloon to treat them. The negroes hung back timidly, but Bill said "I've got six good black republicans here and I am going to treat them at your bar." The saloon keeper, after some hesitation, set out the drinks.[18]

Probably the most important and dangerous foray behind enemy lines taken by Hickok as a spy was when he was able to fall in with the march of Sterling Price through Missouri in 1864. By the summer of 1864 the Confederacy was in serious military trouble. Supply lines to the South were now almost non-existent because they were in control of the Union, and the Mississippi River was considered uncrossable by large troops because of the preponderance of Union gunboats dominating the waterway. General Robert E. Lee was wedged deep in a battle of attrition near Richmond, and Union general William Tecumseh Sherman was advancing on Atlanta. Frantically they looked for one more bold plan to save the Confederacy. Sterling Price's invasion of Missouri was that bold, some would say outrageous, plan.

Fifty-five-year-old Major General Sterling Price was not only a military man, but a consummate politician as well. Before the war he had been a legislator, congressman, and governor of Missouri. As a politician he felt he knew and understood intimately the make-up and demographics of his former Missouri constituency. He was confident that southern culture and background existed all the way along both sides of the Missouri River across the state, from east to west. He counted on gaining many soldiers and militia from the Missouri River valley. He also projected that much of the west bank of the Mississippi held many recruits for him, from the Arkansas border up to St. Louis, which was a Union stronghold. Price's plan was to follow the west bank of the Mississippi north to St. Louis, and then make a hard left and a fast run west along the Missouri River to the area of Kansas City, where the Liberty Arsenal awaited the ammunition-starved Confederacy. Just thirty miles up the river from Kansas City was Fort Leavenworth, with the opportunity to completely shut off the Santa Fe Trail and take as war booty the treasures of a fully stocked fort. Price entered the state of Missouri on September 19, 1864 with 8,000 armed men and 4,000 unarmed. By the time he reached St. Louis and started quickly coming west along the Missouri River in early October, Union general Alfred Pleasonton had ordered General John B. Sanborn, commanding three brigades, to go after Sterling Price as an observation corps as well as to delay and harass Price's westward march as much as possible, until other Union forces could be brought to the fore. This Sanborn did well and expertly, and no doubt some of his success can be attributed to information from his man conducting a clandestine and dangerous spying mission inside Sterling Price's lines: James Butler Hickok.

Price eventually fought through Sanborn's delaying tactics and made his way west across the state to the Little Blue River just east of Independence, in the first battle of Price's effort to take the Kansas City area. Bloody actions were fought at the Little Blue River, then at Independence, then at Byram's Ford on the Big Blue River, and finally just south of Westport. There, the Confederates under Price capitulated and began the long retreat home to Arkansas, rushing south along the Fort Leavenworth Military Road from Little Santa Fe on the Kansas border onward. Indications are that Hickok was playing his dangerous surreptitious role almost to the end of Price's run for home.[19] Twenty years later Brigadier General John B. Sanborn confirmed in print Hickok's action with Price:

> My principal scout was William Hickok, "Wild Bill", the real hero of many exploits, and, according to the dime novels, the imaginary hero of many more. Bill was a fine scout and detective. He entered the rebel camps, was arrested as a spy, and even taken before General Price; but his inordinate nerve and great self-possession not only saved him, but made him an orderly on Price's staff. He eventually escaped and returned to me with valuable information during the battle of Newtonia.[20]

Hickok is recalled by a writer that rode with him during the war, and confirms in the February 1, 1867 *Leavenworth Daily Conservative* the events during the war that Sanborn notes above:

Since the publication of the paper in Harper's, setting forth the exploits of "Wild Bill", there has been a determined search in memory by those who participated in the closing scenes of the war in Northern Arkansas. Since the subject of the sketch in Harper has been prominently given to the country we have furbished our recollections, and the result is that we knew Bill Hitchcock in 1864 and recognize his portrait in the magazine for February. It is a fair representation for a wood cut.

"Wild Bill", as he is called, rode in company with the writer, and with the Adjutant Mackle and Lt. Col. Hoyt from Newtonia, subsequent to the battle in October, to the Arkansas River, we think, but perhaps he remained at Fayetteville...He came into Gen. Blunt's camp on the morning after the battle of Newtonia, having previously been with Price, and having spent several months in the camps in Arkansas, as stated in the article in question..."Wild Bill" has made his mark in the war for the Union, and we accord him full credit for his risks and reward for results attained.

There are more official and reliable glimpses of Hickok during the war that put him in place, time, and undertaking. Rolla, Missouri was his home base for much of the last three years of the war. Records show unclaimed letters at Rolla for J. B. Hichcock on November 29, 1862; J. W. Hitchcock on February 23, 1863; and J. B. Hicock on March 14, 1863.[21]

James' brother Lorenzo, a wagon master throughout the war and beyond, wrote to their brother Horace eight miles from St. Louis on July 16, 1863, and mentioned, "I left brother J.B.in Rolla if I should come Home I shall be there by the twentieth."[22] On March 4, 1864 he again wrote to Horace and gave this time news of substance about their brother James: "J. B. is in Batesville no Fayetteville at work for Capt. Squires who is Chief of the Detective Police, gets about $100. per month."[23]

The following month, on April 15, 1864, Lorenzo wrote from Rolla to James' sister Celinda and reports on the dangerous work James is involved in:

I have just returned from Springfield where I had been with a train Loaded with Forage and Ordnance. I saw James there. He left for Yellville Mo the day I left Springfield. he is Scouting for Genl. Sanborn and is getting Five dollars per day. The work he is doing is very dangerous Something that would not suit me. He told me that he could get me the same kind of a place if I wished. I most respectfully declined as I would have to work below Fort Smith...You will Excuse me for this short letter for I am in more of a hurry than Jonah was to get on dry land on a Certain occasion.[24]

On July 26, 1864, Lorenzo wrote again to his sister Celinda. President Lincoln's Emancipation Proclamation was issued on January 1, 1863, and Lorenzo found here in southwest Missouri a year and a half later former slaves now enjoying the benefits of that federal act. Certainly Lorenzo, scion of a strong abolitionist Illinois family, must have viewed the scene he describes with equanimity, even as he describes being brusquely escorted from the circus show by the Provost Marshal. Adding further tension to southwest Missouri while the state was still at war, the Union Provost Marshals were charged with enforcing these new rights of the former slaves; often having to enforce these rights against former slave owners. Also, many escaped slaves had made their way to Missouri from Kentucky, Tennessee, and Arkansas even before the proclamation. In almost the same breath Lorenzo describes the treacherous burning of a home by Bushwackers, "playing hell Generally" throughout the region. There is some mention of brother James towards the end of the letter. This is all in all a remarkable letter, describing the stressful introduction of a new social order in southwest Missouri, further aggravated by the slash-and-burn terror of the Bushwackers; this is the dangerous crucible that Lorenzo and James operated in during 1864 and 1865, and which continued even after the war's end for several years:

Rolla, Mo. July 26, 1864

Dear Sister
    Yours of recent date was received a few days ago...now I must tell you about the show. the Big Australian Circus of Mr. Melville's. Every Body went. I did not even leave the Babies or dogs at home but turned out En mass to give them a chance to take what little money they had left. I went with the balance...I disguised myself...and finally landed in the pit where were Congregated many, very many, of the Colored folks, who by their black looks were trying to frown me out of their Company, but I could not see it in that for I supposed that I was as good as they were if they had paid full fare and did not find out the difference until I was very politely kicked out by one of those Eighteen Inch Brogans. I then come to the conclusion that the Show was not that much and

#3991

September 10,1864 Lorenzo Hickok wrote to brother Horace about their brother James: *...he was going to have his photograph taken while he was here* [Rolla, Missouri] *but it was stormy all the time. Says he will send me some in a few days if he does I will send one home.* By this point in the war James was doing dangerous clandestine work as a spy behind enemy lines. He was twenty-seven years old. This small tintype was probably taken in Rolla in September or October of 1864 by photographer Albert Neuman, who worked in Rolla from 1860 to 1865. *Author's collection.*

went home a Sader if not wiser Boy having learned this lesson, that a Negroes rights are bound to be respected while some of Uncle Sams Provosts Marshals Reign in the Land of Many dissensions: so take the whole thing into Consideration. I think very little of the Show. Guess you would to if you had a Black Eye...

Wednesday...the Bushwackers are at work in this Vicinity. they Burned one House within three miles of Town Last night. Playing hell Generally. A scout went after this morning, what success they will have remains to be seen. I think of going to St. James to Morrow just for fun as well as see the races and to have a little recreation...I shall keep Oliver's letter a few days to see if James does not come down from Springfield. I have just learned that he was met by the Scout that went out this morning, if so I think he will give me a call before going back to Springfield. I hope so at least. I am really in hopes that the war will soon End so we can return to our regular pursuits...

Respectfully to all, Yours
L B Hickok [25]

Lorenzo's last letter to Horace that contains news of James is dated Rolla, September 10, 1864:

James has been here and made me a call of four days has now gone back where he will for the present. he says that if the War Ever stops he will go Home and stay for a month or two but as long as his services are needed here he will remain. he was going to have his Photograph taken while here but it was stormy all the time. Says he will Send me some in a few days if he does I will send one Home. [26]

By the time of Lorenzo's noting above of James' whereabouts in March, April and September 1864, it appeared that James had moved from spying to police work. Yet documents like those that follow, and the recollections of General Sanborn, indicate that James may have worked at these interchangeably during this period, at both spying and scouting as well as police work.

01-13-1864
Missouri Union Provost Marshal
Springfield, Greene County
Lieut. W. D. Hubbard

    Order that William Hickok, district policeman, is to go to Fayetteville, Arkansas and report on whether any soldiers are feeding more horses on public forage than allowed.[27]

The United States, to William Hickok Dr.
March 10, 1864

    For Services rendered as Special Police under the direction of Lt. N. H. Burns A Pro Mar Dist. S.W. Mo. at Springfield Mo from March 1, to March 10, 1864 inclusive being 10 days at $60.00 per month. $20.00
    I certify that the above account is correct and just, that the services were rendered as stated, and that they were necessary for the Public Service, as per my Report of "Persons and Articles", Abstract of Expenditures for March, 1864.

                    N. H. Burns
                    1 Lieut 1 Ark Inf. Actg. Pro. Mar.
                    Approved
                    John B. Sanborn
                    Brig. Genl. Comd.[28]

    The above payment voucher, as well as another one for forty dollars covering the period from March 11 till March 31, 1864, were both denied "for the reason that no authority was issued by the Pro Mar Genl of Dept of the Mo, for the employment of this man" [Hickok].[29]

    Yet Hickok was listed as a detective at the Springfield, Missouri District Headquarters, reporting to S. R. Squires, the chief of police. The police officers are listed as Wm. Hickok, J. W. McClellan, and Herman Chapman.[30]

03-21-1864
Missouri Union Provost Marshal
Springfield, Greene County
Thomas Andrews [Defendant]

Statement of James B. Hickok that he visited the saloon of Andrews and saw soldiers being served whiskey there.[31]

Head Qrs. Dist. South West Mo.
Springfield Mo. April 3rd, 1864
Special Orders
No. 89

J. B. Hickok, will be taken up on the Rolls of Capt. Owen, A.Q.M., as Scout, at these Head Quarters, from this date and will be furnished a horse, and equipments while on duty as a Scout. His compensation will be five dollars per day.

By Order of Brigadier General Sanborn
N. D. Curran
1st Lieut & Acting Asst Adjt General[32]

Now reporting directly to General Sanborn, Hickok is next heard of the following February in pursuit of scouting and spying for General Sanborn.

Cassville, Mo. February 10, 1865

Brigadier-General Sanborn:
I have been at Camp Walker and Spavinaw. There are not more than ten or twelve rebels in any squad in the southwest that I can hear of. If you want me to go to Neosho and West of there, notify me here. It was cold; I turned back.

J. B. Hickok[33]

#4024

Photographed in Rolla by Albert Neuman circa 1864-1865.
Here are the checkered pants, knee-length coat, and collarless
shirt favored by Hickok, though this time he has added a
flannel cape, indicating this picture was taken in fall or winter.
Author's collection.

The creator of the original photograph seen here, Albert
Neuman, was not accepted as such by Joseph Rosa because he could find
no evidence of Albert Neuman in Rolla city directories from 1863 to
1869. He speculated that Albert Neuman was an itinerant photographer
and that this photo might actually be a photograph that Neuman copied
from an original by Charles Scholten of Springfield.

Neuman was not an itinerant. He came to Rolla from nearby St. James, Missouri in 1860, known as a *Dagarrien Artist,* the first one in Rolla. He advertised in the Rolla newspaper as an *Artist and Dentist.* Records show he paid a $10 federal occupational tax in Rolla in August 1863. Neuman practiced a lucrative photograph business in Rolla through 1865. Then he gave up the photography business and opened an entertainment complex that included a bowling alley and wine garden. (See Paul L.Palmquist and Thomas R. Kalburn, *Pioneer Photographers from The Mississippi to the Continental Divide:1839-1865.* Stanford University Press, 2005, 460-461.)

General Sanborn replied back the next day:

Headquarters District of Southwest Missouri
Springfield, Mo., February 11, 1865
J.B. Hickok
Cassville, Mo.:

You may go to Yellville or the White River in the vicinity of Yellville and learn what Dobbin intends to do with his command now on Crowley's Ridge, and from there come to this place.

John B. Sanborn
Brigadier-General Commanding[34]

By 1865 James Butler Hickok was undoubtedly known throughout southwest Missouri and northwest Arkansas as Wild Bill, and this notoriety certainly made it increasingly difficult to remain unseen and unnamed as required of a clandestine spy and scout (punctuation added.):

Lawrence Co. Mo. February 15, 1865

Brigadier General J. B. Sanborn, Sir
I wish to know now of you wether or not that you have Wild Bill as he is called and one Mr. Jenkins, that was with you at Casvil last November. At this time on a Scout they were hear yesterday and acted very suspicious. Stating that they were on thur way to fort scot and had now business near hear and they started from hear north. and as soon

*as they were out of site of camp they turned South East in the direction
of Bredin's. They made particular inquiry what the nabors thought of
Bredin and Herrin being taken of. General as I told them everything
gos to prove that they were taken by their own party. This is the opinion
of all. I have heard excuses themselves. Pleas let me now wether they
were sent out hear by order or if not it was for som motive in connection
with the Bredin's.*

*S. A. Harshbarger Lt.
Co. A16 Mo Casvil* [35]

Near the end of the war in 1865, or perhaps just after the end,
Hickok still led his clandestine life, as evidenced by this undated arrest
order from the office of the Missouri provost marshal's office:

Tuesday Morning

Captain:
*I have ordered the arrest of a man known as "Wild Bill". With
the purpose of holding him till he can give a satisfactory account of
himself—he having told a variety of stories as to his belongings—&
these may lead me to believe he is not what he ought to be. Hinchman
made the arrest by my order & will leave him at the jail for safe keeping.*

Col. Tarbell [36]

---

*HeadQuarters Dist South West Mo.
Springfield, Mo June 9th, 1865
Div & Dept
Head Qrs
June 10th 1865 Special Orders
No. 142*

*1) Capt R.B. Owen A.Q.M. Dist Qr Mr. will settle up with
and drop from the roll of scouts the following named persons paying
them to include this date at the rates heretofore established*

*J.B. Hickok
Thos. G. Martin...* [37]

Finally the war ended on April 9, 1865 when Confederate general Lee surrendered his troops to Union general Grant at Appomattox Court House in Virginia. As noted in the report above, Hickok was mustered out in June, and soon found his way to Springfield, Missouri where dual destinies would manifest and propel him from regional notoriety to national fame.

6

SHOWDOWN *in* SPRINGFIELD

The field of war that Hickok had served in for three and a half years, mainly in southwest Missouri and northwest Arkansas, was the landscape of a civil war. Missourians fought against Missourians, neighbor against neighbor, sometimes even family against family. It was a particularly vicious and malicious war, made more so because the lines of loyalty and control remained fluid and unstable throughout the four years of war. Further fueling the progressive instability of the region, guerrilla bands and independent militia on both sides, Union and Confederate, roamed the Ozark hills, often dressing in Confederate or Union uniforms as subterfuge to gain safe access near enemy lines or to commit some atrocity, only to have it blamed on those who wore the uniform of the enemy. These guerrillas swept through the Ozarks with impunity, terrorizing and plundering and shooting citizens and soldiers alike. Prisoners were rarely taken.

The leaders of the conventional armies, especially Union officers, had a strong disdain for the guerrilla forces of the Confederates. "Let them swing," stated Lincoln's secretary of war Edwin Stanton. General J. G. Blunt exclaimed, "Give them no quarter." General J.A. Dix advised, "Shoot them on the spot."

"Execute them immediately," proclaimed General J. M. Schofield. General H.W. Halleck summed up the feeling of Union officers: "Let them be tried immediately by a drum head court, and punished with death." Halleck also admitted that Union guerrillas were treated by the Confederates as basically criminals; he stated, "which in many cases they were."[1]

As noted above, adding to the instability of the region, and even the entire state of Missouri, was the fact that the civilian populace, though leaning a bit more towards the Union, was about equally divided between Union and Confederate sympathies; between secessionist and anti-secessionist inclinations. The state remained politically divided

81

#4045

Is this James Butler Hickok? In about 2005 this photograph was discovered in Illinois. The image was considered at length by Hickok biographer Joseph Rosa, who determined it was not Hickok because the hair was not parted in the middle as indicated by other photographs. Setting aside the hair parting issue, all the subject's other features comport very well with known photos of Hickok from 1864 to 1865. (especially image 3991 and 4024) The hair is about the same length in these three photos. The prominent cheekbones are in evidence as well. The nose matches in all three photos. The known slightly pointed ears of Hickok are shown in this photo. Perhaps the strongest evidential feature is the eyes. The hair notwithstanding, it is this writer's opinion that this is a photo of James Butler Hickok, taken circa 1864-1865. But since this writer's opinion is not a primary source, a final determination awaits. In 2007 the original photograph sold at auction for $24,000. *Author's collection.*

throughout the Civil War. The disputed status of the state government was engendered by having two rival state governments; Missouri was claimed by both the Union and the Confederacy, and each sent representatives to the United States Congress and the Confederate Congress.

Although on November 28, 1861 the Confederates seceded Missouri from the Union and added it to the Confederate states, the Union government continued to recognize Missouri as a state, and by 1862 had established physical control of most of the state, yet the Confederate government ran a government in exile till the end of the war.

When the war ended in April, 1865, many of these battle-hardened guerrillas, as well as many Union and Confederate soldiers, were set adrift in the region. Many had no home to go to. The war had taken care of that. Hardened by the brutal violence of war, used to killing with firearms, and with no job or immediate means of support, they found themselves in kind of a lawless no-man's land. In the days following the end of the war, vendettas, retribution, and revenge killings were numerous, especially carried out by the victor, the Union, against the shattered losers, the Confederates. Before his interview with Hickok for *Harper's,* George Ward Nichols described the scene in July 1865:

> *In Southwest Missouri there were old scores to be settled up. During the three days occupied by General Smith- who commanded the Department and was on a tour of inspection- in crossing the country between Rolla and Springfield, a distance of 120 miles, five men were killed or wounded on the public road. Two were murdered a short distance from Rolla—by whom we could not ascertain. Another was instantly killed and two were wounded at a meeting of a band of "Regulators," who were in the service of the State, but were paid by the United States Government. It should be said that their method of "regulation" was slightly informal, their war-cry was "A swift bullet and a short rope for returned rebels!"*[2]

So afloat without a rudder, and no immediate prospects for the future, these battle-hardened soldiers and guerrillas gravitated to Springfield, Missouri, where a concerned populace watched as drinking, gambling, and general hell-raising came and overtook their town.

Founded in 1838 as the county seat of Greene County, in 1861 Springfield had a population of about 2,000. By 1865, its ranks expanded with the influx of war refugees and wandering soldiers and guerrillas,

Springfield probably had a population of about 3,000 people. Built around a public square that remains intact today, much of Springfield's early history happened at and around that public square. Its most famous piece of history, however, is the gunfight that took place the evening of July 21, 1865, between Davis K. Tutt and James Butler Hickok.

Davis Tutt was born in Yellville, Arkansas in 1839, making him just two years younger than Hickok. He joined the Confederate Army in June, 1862 at the age of twenty-two. Tutt served with the Confederates as a private with Company A of the 27th Arkansas Infantry. However, in February, 1863 he was assigned to the quartermaster's department as a brigade wagon master. By April 1863 he was listed in that capacity as being on "detached service," whereupon he promptly disappeared from Confederate Army records.

It has been speculated that perhaps he changed sides, yet much like Hickok's time in the war as a scout and spy, Tutt's ambiguous designation as "detached service" more likely indicates a clandestine position as a Confederate scout and/or spy. Circumstantial evidence supports that possibility, because by the time of his July gunfight with Hickok, Tutt had already lived in Springfield for a year, since July, 1864. He came at that time to Springfield with his half-brother Lewis, his widowed mother, and his sister. He may have even infiltrated the Union Army; there are vouchers extant that show the name of D. K. Tutt in a long list of individuals in the records of Richard B. Owen, the Union Chief Quartermaster of the District of Southwest Missouri. A final conclusion on Tutt's wartime activities during 1863-1865 awaits further study and material evidence.

Tutt and Hickok were friends. They frequently gambled together, and they had several mutual friends, including Thomas Green Martin, one of Hickok's erstwhile wartime scouting partners; another wartime scouting partner John Jenkins; and Larkin Russell, a policeman for the local provost marshal. James Orr and Eli Armstrong were also friends with both Hickok and Tutt. Orr and Armstrong would later become material witnesses in their trial.

Hickok and Tutt were friends until a fateful gambling game at the Lyon House hotel on South Street on the evening of July 20, 1865. The two of them were playing cards in Hickok's room at the hotel.

James Orr and W. S. Riggs were in the room also. At some point in the game, Tutt claimed that Hickok owed him $35 from past gambling debt. Hickok said he did not owe him $35, that he had recently paid Tutt $10 of the debt, and now he owed him only $25. Hickok told Tutt that they could go downstairs together and check his memorandum book where he kept records of his gambling debt. He thought he owed Tutt just $25, and after he had a chance to check his book, he could pay him that night. Hickok took his pocket watch off and laid it on the table; Tutt picked it up and told Hickok he would keep the watch until Hickok paid him after they went downstairs. Tutt then told Hickok the amount owed was $45, but he would take $35. Hickok told Tutt he still believed he only owed $25. Tutt left the hotel with Hickok's watch, stating again as he left that Hickok owed him $45. Later that night Hickok ran into their mutual friend, James Orr, and told him to "tell Tutt to bring his watch back in one Hour and he would receive the Twenty five dollars. If he did not return the watch something else would be done."[3]

The next afternoon Hickok and Tutt were sitting on the porch of the Lyon House with James Orr. Hickok still had not found his memorandum book, and Tutt still held his watch as collateral. About five p.m., another mutual friend, Eli Armstrong, joined them. Hickok and Tutt were continuing their dispute. They told Armstrong the amounts in dispute, and he told them if that was the only problem it could be fixed. Armstong took Tutt aside and asked if he would settle with Hickok for $35 to avoid further difficulty, and Tutt said he would. He took Hickok aside and told him the compromise Tutt had agreed to. Hickok refused to accept this settlement, insisting instead that he would find his memorandum book that would show what he owed. Tutt returned to the $45 demand, thinking that Hickok was unwilling to compromise, and he told Hickok again that he would keep the watch until he received payment. Hickok said, "You have accommodated me more than any man in town. I have borrowed money from you time and again and we have never had any dispute before in our settlement." Tutt said he knew that and he did not want difficulty, either.[4]

"Boys, that settles it then," stated Armstrong. "Let us all go and get a drink," said Hickok. Then Tutt, Hickok, Orr, and Armstrong went into the bar of the Lyon House and had drinks. Yet the stand-off still stood, and Tutt still retained Hickok's watch.[5]

After drinks, Tutt left the Lyon House and made his way north along South Street to the public square, making has way past the courthouse in the northwest corner of the square, and found a saloon near the livery stable. Hickok and Orr left the hotel and walked north on the east side of South Street to the public square. It was a few minutes before six p.m., Friday, July 21, 1865.

Orr told Hickok that he did not agree with him in his dispute with Tutt. Hickok responded that Orr must be Tutt's friend, and that he should leave. Orr said the street belonged to him as much as anybody, but he did not want to have a problem with Hickok, so he left. At that time John Tutt, Davis's brother, came to the corner and told Hickok he was sorry there was a difficulty between the two, and if he would come down Davis Tutt would settle it with him. Hickok walked away. At the corner Hickok told bystanders that he was waiting for Tutt, that he had taken Hickok's watch, and he had better not come across the square carrying his watch.

At about six p.m., Tutt left the saloon and walked to the south in front of the courthouse. Hickok left the corner of South Street and stepped out into the square. Tutt stepped out into the square in front of the courthouse. Hickok yelled across the square, "David you cannot come any further and pack my watch."[6]

Hickok and Tutt both stopped and drew their guns. Tutt turned to the side and raised his right arm to shoot. Hickok pulled his gun and fired. Both fired at almost the same time. Tutt missed Hickok with his shot, but Hickok shot Tutt in the right side of his chest. Tutt stumbled through one of the courthouse arches and then fell on his back into the square, dead.

The above detailed description of the day before and the day of the shootout is based on the testimony revealed in court documents discovered in the 1990s in the archives of the Greene County Court House. These fugitive documents included the coroner's inquest report, which include the testimony of eight witnesses to the events of July 21, 1865: Thomas D. Hudson, W. S. Riggs, John W. Orr, Lorenza F. Lee, Eli Armstrong, Oliver Scott, A. L. Budlong, and F. W. Scholten.

A mystery cleared up by these discovered documents is a Greene County court docket entry that reveals that on July 20, 1865, the very day before the shootout, Tutt was in court and charged with illegal gambling and resisting arrest from an event that had occurred the previous December. He was fined $100 and court costs. He was unable to pay and led to jail. Yet then Thomas Green Martin, Hickok's wartime scouting partner and friend of both Tutt and Hickok, came to his rescue and paid enough of his bail to get him temporarily released by the court. Much later after Tutt's death Martin was held to account for money owed by Tutt's estate to the court. These facts indicate that Tutt had compelling motivation to get money as soon as possible from Hickok, or any other source. But that still leaves a mystery; why didn't Tutt simply explain to his friend Hickok his situation and ask for help? Recall that Hickok had been indebted to him before.

On the square and witnessing the gunfight was Colonel Albert Barnitz, military commander of the Second Ohio Voluntary Cavalry at the Post of Springfield. Barnitz had Hickok arrested, who offered no resistance. Barnitz wrote his observations in his journal within a few hours of the shootout. He confirmed that there was a dispute over the watch, and he also wrote that Hickok and Tutt "fired simultaneously, as it appeared to me, at the distance of about 100 paces. Tut was shot directly through the chest."[7] Barnitz also made it clear that Tutt and Hickok were good friends when he wrote that they had been "intimate for years and had been gambling together to-day. The ill will seems to have originated at the gambling table."[8] But for unknown reasons, Barnitz was not called as a witness at the trial.

Hickok was originally charged with murder, but the charge was soon reduced to manslaughter. Barnitz wrote in his journal that after the gunfight, public opinion in Springfield was about equally divided between Tutt and Hickok.

On August 3 Hickok, through his attorney, entered a plea of not guilty and put his case "before the Country," meaning he would be tried by a jury. The trial opened on August 5, 1865 in the courthouse in front of which Tutt had died. The makeup of the jury favored Hickok. Just months after the official end of the war, anti-Confederate feeling still ran hot. The jury were each required to take the "Drake oath," a vow of loyalty to the Union. The jury contained no Confederate sympathizers or Confederates. Hickok was defended by one of the most respected lawyers in southwest Missouri, John Smith Phelps.

Not only an outstanding lawyer, Phelps was a popular politician who served in the U. S. House of Representatives from 1845 till 1863. When the war started in April 1861, the Union Home Guard of about 1,200 men was organized in May in Springfield, with John Smith Phelps as its commander. He was an unwavering Union supporter. Circuit Judge Sempronius Hamilton Boyd was the judge in the Hickok trial. Boyd was a strong Union supporter as well, and like Phelps, had served in the U. S. House of Representatives, from 1863 to 1865. The prosecuting attorney was Robert W. Fyan. He had served in the Union Army during the war as commander of the Forty-Sixth Missouri Voluntary Infantry.

The trial turned on Hickok's legal plea of self-defense. The law at that time stated, in essence, that if a defendant was an innocent party and was confronted by an assailant armed with a pistol threatening him with bodily harm, then he did not have to retreat. Any defensive action the defendant took then could be considered self-defense, However, if the defendant had played an active role in bringing on the assailant's belligerent action, a finding of self-defense could not be reached.

Though archivists do not have access to the missing trial transcript (it is doubtful there was one), the arguments of prosecuting attorney Fyan and defense attorney Phelps can be reconstructed from the proposed instructions to the jury that each attorney wrote for Judge Boyd, which are still extant.

Fyan would have presented evidence that Hickok played an active role in bringing on the shootout on July 21. He would have presented evidence that Hickok had been in an ongoing dispute with Tutt, that Hickok had not tried to avoid the conflict resulting from that dispute, and that Hickok turned away efforts made by his friends to resolve the issue. Fyan also would have shown evidence that Hickok came to the corner of South Street and the public square where he waited for Tutt, that Hickok told bystanders on that corner that there would be trouble if Tutt tried to cross the square, and that when Tutt showed himself at the square Hickok yelled out for Tutt not to cross the square with his watch. In other words, the defendant had made a public threat against the deceased just before the shootout. Attorney Fyan's argument centered around premeditation, which if found by the jury would defeat any plea of self-defense.

Defense attorney Phelps would have realized that Fyan's premeditation charge could be fatal to his defense of Hickok, so Phelps would have presented evidence about the shootout itself, as well as attempted to demean Tutt's character in a move to sway the jury away from considering premeditation.

Phelps tried to establish that Tutt was known as a dangerous man, one that threatened the defendant with bodily harm or death. Phelps would have argued that Tutt had threatened Hickok before, so that he had reason to expect the worst from Tutt. Phelps would argue that any reasonable person would defend themselves the same way Hickok had. Phelps made the unfounded contention that Tutt drew first.

Though that had no bearing on the law, the jury would have perceived this as an important point. In response, Fyan would have reiterated the material points he made during his argument; that if Hickok had helped bring on the conflict, and if he had yelled at Tutt threatening harm if he continued to walk across the public square with his watch, then his self-defense claim was null and he was guilty for the killing, regardless of who drew first.

As it still is in courtrooms today, what matters in a jury trial is convincing the jury. Knowing that he was facing an all-Union jury, Phelps made sure to bring out the fact that Tutt was a Confederate.

Among the list of twenty-two witnesses from the witness list (the names are known but their testimony is unknown) were numerous character witnesses including Hickok friends Thomas Green Martin and Richard B. Owen, as well as six former Union officers to testify on Hickok's wartime service for the Union: Colonel John B. Madill, Captain G. Maddison, Captain Small, Lieutenant John W. Goldston, Major Hart, and Captain Adams.

In the American legal system, in a jury trial both the defense lawyer and the prosecuting lawyer can (and almost always do) write proposed jury instructions for the judge to instruct the jury with. The judge can use the proposed defense instructions or the prosecution instructions, or the judge can ignore them both and write his or her own jury instructions. Obviously, each side's instructions are weighted toward vindication on the defense side and indictment on the prosecution side. The judge will use the lawyers' instructions that he or she believes best incorporate the facts and the law. In the Hickok trial, after hearing all the witnesses and evidence, Judge Boyd believed that Hickok was guilty, as evidenced by Judge Boyd's use of prosecutor Fyan's proposed instructions to charge the jury. Yet the jury deliberated a short time, and came back with a verdict of not guilty.

Looking back with the impartiality derived from a 159-year distance from the event, the physical and emotional wounds of the war that had just ended officially that April but continued in retribution in southwest Missouri that summer were still fresh and tender. Most Union people believed that the Confederates were traitors, a belief further confirmed, in their minds, by the secessionist war they had just waged on the republic. Phelps had played his judicial cards well, emphasizing again and again that Tutt was a Confederate and Hickok was a Union man. This one paradigm alone convinced the jury to ignore the law and the judge's instruction, and vindicate Hickok. Under the law, Hickok was guilty, and the judge believed him to be so. But he was a Union man, and Tutt was a Confederate, and that was that.

There are modern examples of juries going their own way on a

#4229

Davis K. Tutt met James Butler Hickok on the Springfield square on a warm July evening in 1865. A disputed gambling debt preceded this confrontation between these two apparent friends. When the smoke cleared, Tutt was dead. Hickok was arrested, and a trial soon took place in the very same courthouse where Tutt had died between its exterior columns after being shot. Legal documents show that the judge believed Hickok was guilty, yet the jury disregarded the judge's instructions and ruled Hickok not guilty. *Author's collection.*

verdict, but today there are a few rules adopted into the Rules of Civil Procedure that limit some of these sorts of actions by juries.

The Springfield *Missouri Weekly Patriot* on August 10 reported on the trial, expressing considerable dissatisfaction with the verdict by the Springfield citizenry, and to express further why the people were upset with the verdict, the paper printed the judge's instruction to the jury, the direct implication being that the jury had ignored those instructions when they found Hickok not guilty. As mentioned, in the 1990s more of the trial documents were discovered in the Greene County Archives, which included the proposed jury instructions written by defense lawyer Phelps that, back in 1865, had been rejected by Judge Boyd in favor of the proposed jury instructions written by prosecution lawyer Fyan.

Some modern writers have mistaken these rejected jury instructions proposed by defense attorney Phelps as some special document or supplementary instructions that were issued after the trial by the judge, implying that somehow these instructions were also given to the jury, and/or that these actually reflected the real conclusions of Judge Boyd. Neither of those conclusions are correct. Judge Boyd believed Hickok was guilty. Therefore, he provided the jury only with the jury instructions proposed by prosecuting attorney Fyan. Attorney Fyan's jury instructions are those published in the Springfield newspaper below. Unfortunately, additional studies of this trial have been undertaken in recent years using this faulty and incorrect interpretation as the basis of the writer's analysis.[9]

Following is the above-mentioned article from the August 10, 1865, issue of the *Springfield Missouri Weekly Patriot,* a damning editorial statement by the *Patriot* editor that also included the actual instructions from attorney Fyan that Judge Boyd charged the jury with:

> *The trial of Wm. Haycock for the killing of Davis Tutt, in the streets of this city week before last, was concluded on Saturday last, by a verdict of not guilty, rendered by the jury in about ten minutes after they retired to the jury room.*
>
> *The general dissatisfaction felt by the citizens of this place with the verdict attaches in no way to our able and efficient Circuit Attorney, nor to the Court. It is universally conceded that the prosecution was conducted in an able, efficient and vigorous manner, and that Col. Fyan is entitled to much credit for the ability, earnestness and candor exhibited by him during the whole trial. He appeared to be a full match*

for the very able counsel who conducted the defense. Neither can any fault be found with the Judge, who conducted himself impartially throughout the trial, and whose rulings, we believe, gave general satisfaction. As an evidence of the impartiality of his Honor, we copy the instructions given to the jury, as follows:

1st If they believe from the evidence that the defendant intentionally shot at the deceased, Davis Tutt, and the death of said Tutt was caused thereby, they will find the defendant guilty, unless they are satisfied from the evidence he acted in self-defense.

2nd That defendant is presumed to have intended the nature and probable consequence of his own acts.

3rd The defendant cannot set up justification that he acted in self-defense if he was willing to engage in a fight with deceased.

4th To be entitled to acquittal on the ground of self-defense, he must have been anxious to avoid a conflict, and must have used all reasonable means to avoid it.

5th If the deceased and defendant engaged in a fight or conflict willingly on the part of each, and the defendant killed the deceased, he is guilty of the offense charged, although the deceased may have fired the first shot.

6th If it appear that the conflict was in any way premeditated by the defendant, he is not justifiable.

7th The crime charged in the indictment is complete, whether there was malice or not.

8th If the Jury have any reasonable doubt as to the defendant's guilt, they will give him the benefit of such doubt, and acquit him.

9th But such doubt must be reasonable doubt, not mere possibility. It must be such a doubt as leaves the mind dissatisfied with a conclusion of guilt.

10th This rule, as to a reasonable doubt, does not apply as to matters set up in justification.

11th If the defendant claims to have acted in self-defense it is his duty to satisfy you that he so acted, and it is not sufficient to create a doubt in your minds whether he so acted or not.

12th The jury will disregard evidence as to the moral character of the deceased, and as to his character for loyalty, as the character of the deceased could afford no excuse for killing him.

13th Every murder includes in it the crime of man-slaughter, and if the jury believe that the defendant has committed the crime of murder in the first or second degree, they will find him guilty under this indictment of man-slaughter, the crime charged in this indictment.

14th The Court instructs the jury that they may disregard all that part of the evidence of Tutt's declaration to Lieut. Werner.

15th The Court instructs to disregard all Werner's testimony.

16th That the jury will disregard any threats made by Tutt against Haycock prior to the meeting at the Lyon House in Haycocke's room.

Those who so severely censure the jury for what they regard as a disregard of their obligations to the public interest, and a proper respect for their oaths, should remember that they are partly to blame themselves. The citizens of this city were shocked and terrified at the idea that a man could arm himself and take a position at the corner of the square, in the centre of the city, and await the approach of his victim for an hour or two, and then willingly engage in a conflict with him which resulted in his instant death; and this, too, with the knowledge of several persons who seem to have posted themselves in safe places where they could see the tragedy enacted. But they failed to express the horror and disgust they felt, not from indifference, but from fear and timidity.

Public opinion has much to do with the administration of justice, and when those whose sense of justice and respect for the law should prompt them to speak out and control public sentiment, fail to do so, whether from fear or from indifference, we think they should not complain of others. That the defendant engaged in the fight willingly it seems is not disputed, and lawyers say—and the Court instructed the jury to the same effect—that he was not entitled to an acquittal on the ground of self-defense unless he was anxious to avoid the fight, and used all reasonable means to do so; but the jury seems to have thought differently.

The jury deliberated for ten minutes, and returned a verdict: "We the Jury find the Deft not guilty in manner and form charged." Twenty-eight-year-old James Butler Hickok was a free man.

AFTERMATH

Hickok's shot on the public square was natural skill combined with catching lightning in a bottle. Witness Thomas D. Hudson testified that he saw Tutt go for his gun but Hudson turned his head away and heard a shot. He thought he only heard one shot.[10]

W. S. Riggs testified that he saw Tutt pull his gun but Hickok's back was to him so he did not see Hickok pull his. He saw smoke from Tutt's pistol, and he said he heard two shots. He stated that Hickok was about a hundred yards from Tutt when they fired.[11]

Lorenza F. Lee testified he saw Hickok talking to someone he saw on the corner of South Street. He then saw a man with a white linen coat appear that he did not recognize. He suddenly saw "the flash and smoke of two revolvers." He also "saw the flash & smoke from the revolver of Haycock which he held in his hand, but did not see the revolver in the other man's hand, but saw the smoke & flash did not know which fired first. Reports seemed to be simultaneous."[12]

Witness Eli Armstrong testified that he saw Tutt go to the livery stable and then return in front of the courthouse. He heard Hickok advise Tutt not to cross the square with his watch. "Tutt made no reply but placed his hand on the butt of his Revolver. Tutt fired & so did Haycock but witness could not tell which fired first. Tutt then turned round & placed his hand on his breast & said boys I am killed & ran into the Court House and fell at the door & rolled out on the ground at the door & died in about two minutes and perhaps not so long. Saw a bullet hole in his right side is satisfied both fired."[13]

A. L. Budlong testified that he did not get a clear view of the gunfight. But he was present when Dr. James came to Tutt and opened Tutt's vest and shirt and saw the wounds in Tutt's chest. Though he did not think Tutt fired, Budlong did notice an exploded cap on the nipple of Tutt's pistol.[14] Albert Barnitz, noted earlier as Hickok's arresting officer immediately after the gunfight, wrote that they "fired simultaneously, as it appeared to me, at a distance of about 100 paces."[15]

Various local historians and others have tried over the years to work out the actual distance of Hickok's shot, and the consensus is it was 75 yards, or 225 feet. It is believed that Hickok shot with an 1851 Navy Colt 36 Caliber cap and ball pistol. Ballistics experts put the top end of accuracy of the 1851 Navy Colt 36 Caliber at about a hundred yards, so the gun itself was capable of the kind of accuracy at seventy-five yards that Hickok exhibited that night. But he did so while simultaneously being fired on himself, that usually being a notorious modifier of shooting accuracy.

Logic indicates that Hickok must have fired a micro-second after Tutt stood sideways and raised his right arm to shoot, otherwise Hickok's shot would not have entered the right side of Tutt unimpeded by his right arm. Dr. Ebert, on the public square that evening, reached Tutt's body moments after the shootout, and upon removing Tutt's vest and shirt, "found that a bullet had entered on the right side between the 5th and 7th rib and passed out on the left side between the 5th and 7th rib...from his sudden death I am led to believe some of the large blood vessels were wounded."[16] Logic also indicates that the position of the wound, on the far-right side of Tutt's chest, shows that Tutt must have been standing sideways when he raised his right arm to shoot.

So it was his shot on that warm summer evening as the sun went down on the Springfield square that brought Hickok immediate regional notoriety, and soon national fame, as a gunslinger not to be tested.

That designation proved to not necessarily be a blessing. Hickok never again attempted such a difficult shot in a life-and-death situation.

Dexter Fellows, who was press agent for Pawnee Bill for two years, then with Buffalo Bill's Wild West Show for several years before spending the rest of his career as the business manager and publicity director for the Ringling Bros. Barnum & Bailey Circus, recalled conversations with James Kirby, the proprietor of a popular saloon on College Street just off of the Square. The last point that Fellow's makes below will be of interest to readers along the Kansas and Missouri border, especially those in the Springfield area:

> *Kirby, a friend of Hickok and saloon keeper in Springfield, Missouri, has told me of Wild Bill's duel with Dave Tutt. The two were in a poker game and Hickok was losing. Being short of cash he put up a watch, a present from his mother, with the understanding he could redeem it within a few days. The game ended with Tutt the possessor of the watch, which, as I recall the story, he refused to return when Wild Bill offered its equivalent in cash.*

Tutt was proud to have humiliated Bill and announced that he would wear the watch in public on the following day. Upon hearing of this boast Hickok sent word that he would kill Tutt if he carried out his plan. The intervention of friends was of no avail.

A duel was inevitable, and many were on hand in the public square to see the fireworks. Like boxers, Tutt started from one end of the square and Hickok came out of the other to meet him. They had taken only a few steps when both drew and fired. Tutt fell dead with a bullet through the temple as Hickok stooped over to recover his Stetson, which had been knocked from his head by a bullet from Tutt's six-shooter. Among the Hickok souvenirs that Kirby kept in his saloon is the very pistol with which Wild Bill killed Tutt. [!] [17]

Within months of the gunfight there began to be public thoughts that perhaps there had been more animus between Tutt and Hickok than just the fateful card game. Quartermaster Richard B. Owen, referring to the gunfight, told writer George Ward Nichols, "The fact is, thar was an undercurrent of a woman in that fight!" Whether this was just an artful device injected into the article by Nichols, or there was some truth to this statement, it started further speculation that there might have been a woman involved.

Hickok spent part of his time as a Union scout in Yellville, Arkansas in 1863. Tutt was born and raised in Yellville, and lived there till he and his family moved to Springfield in 1864. In 1923 the former Kansas secretary of state, John Thomas Botkin, wrote a remarkable letter to Willam Connelley. Botkin claimed that Hickok had an affair with Tutt's sister Letitia, and that from this affair a son was born to her. Botkin further claimed that Dave Tutt swore revenge. He told Connelley that he later saw the sister when she was a married woman of about fifty. Her husband was a physician in Marion County, Arkansas, of which Yellville is the county seat. Botkin stated that her son by Hickok was then a policeman in Oklahoma City. No further evidence has yet come to light regarding Botkin's remarkable statement.[18]

So ended the first and most famous face-to-face dueling gunfight on a public square in the American frontier West. There were few others, yet this iconic event has set the stage to be imitated and glorified in film, television, novel, and newsprint ever since. The Hickok-Tutt gunfight is the antecedent for every portrayal of a two-man shootout in a frontier town, from *High Noon* to *The Dirty Dozen,* from *Gunsmoke* to *Maverick,* from *Lonesome Dove* to *Shane.*

With the trial behind him, perhaps twenty-eight-year-old James thought about discarding his wild life and *nom de plume* of Wild Bill and returning to the farming that he sought to start when he first came to Kansas in 1856. But then, just weeks after the trial, George Ward Nichols and *Harpers New Monthly Magazine* came to Springfield.

7

HARPER'S SHOOTING STAR

the MYTH of BLACK NELL the HORSE

HARPER'S MYTH of ROCK CREEK and the MCCANLES FIGHT

Five weeks after the trial, J. B. Hickok ran for city marshal of Springfield. There were five men competing for the job. Hickok came in second with 63 votes. The winner, Charles Moss, won with 107 votes. Hickok's second-place finish indicated there were still those unhappy with the outcome of the trial, yet there were also many that supported him—just not enough, in this instance, to make him city marshal.

On almost the same day in September as the election, Hickok met writer George Ward Nichols. Born in 1831, Nichols was thirty-four when he met twenty-eight-year-old Hickok in Springfield in 1865. Nichols grew up in Boston. He was drawn to Kansas as a young journalist in the 1850s, reporting to newspapers back east about the simmering border war along the west boundary of slave-state Missouri and the east boundary of potentially abolitionist Kansas Territory. While in the area, it is reported that he lived for a time in 1855 and 1856 with the Shawnee, Delaware, and Wyandot Indians in future Kansas border counties Johnson and Wyandotte, thus in 1856 placing him serendipitously in the same general neighborhood as the subject on the streets of Springfield that Nichols would make famous nine years later. Nichols traveled to Paris after he left Kansas to study art and music. When he returned from

Paris, he became a reporter for the New York *Evening Post*. Nichols joined the Union Army in 1862, and soon became an aide under Maj. Gen. John C. Fremont. In 1864 he joined the staff of William Tecumseh Sherman, and wrote a journalistic report on Sherman's famous march to the sea. This was published as a book near the end of the war, titled *The Story of the Great March from the Diary of a Staff Officer*. The book sold sixty thousand copies and went through numerous printings.

Nichols' writing style glorified Sherman immensely, drawing on dubious accounts and sources and expanding anecdotes and interviews into grand and mythic stories. He wrote of Sherman that he was "terribly earnest in his method of conducting the war, but he is neither vindictive nor implacable.... Yet there is a depth of tenderness, akin to the love of a woman, behind that face which is furrowed with the lines of anxiety and care, and those eyes which dart keen and suspicious glances. Little children cling to the General's knees and nestle in his arms..." *The New York Times* complimented the book as a "spirit-stirring narrative." Nichols' book on the Sherman march foreshadowed the Sturm und Drang and legend-building that would characterize what he would later write about Hickok. Yet, Nichols' statements and assertions, in both his Sherman and Hickok works, would be based on some little fact, sometimes a tenuous circumstantial fact, but almost always stated with some kind of basis underlying. But there were also a few glaring exceptions having no factual underpinning. Nichols, talented, sophisticated and cosmopolitan journalist that he was, still wrote in the overwrought style that was prevalent in that era.

When Nichols arrived in Springfield he was finishing a novel, *The Sanctuary: A Story of the Civil War,* inspired by Sherman's march to the sea. It was published in 1866. He came to Springfield after having pitched the idea to his publisher, Harper and Brothers, for an article about a western hero to appear in their publication *Harper's New Monthly Magazine,* or he was simply free-lancing and speculated that *Harper's New Monthly Magazine* would jump at the chance to publish such a piece.

This article that was to cause a sensation back East was simply titled "Wild Bill." Nichols wrote a preamble describing hearing of Hickok's adventures from a multitude of persons throughout the area, even before Nichols had met Hickok. Inexplicably this preamble was placed on the second page of the article after Nichols had already described in glowing terms his first meeting with James. Here is that misplaced preamble:

Whenever I met an officer or soldier who had served in the Southwest I heard of Wild Bill and his exploits, until these stories became so frequent and of such an extraordinary character as quite to outstrip personal knowledge of adventure by camp and field; and the hero of these strange tales took shape in my mind as did Jack the Giant Killer or Sinbad the Sailor in childhood's days. As then, I now had the most implicit faith in the existence of the individual; but how one man could accomplish such prodigies of strength and feats of daring was a continued wonder.

Nichols began his article with this very disdainful description of Springfield, a description that would bring howls of recrimination from the local press when the article was published nationwide in February, 1867:

On a warm summer day I sat watching from the shadow of a broad awning the coming and going of the strange, half-civilized people who, from all the country round, make this a place for barter and trade. Men and women dressed in queer costumes; men with coats and trousers made of skin, but so thickly covered with dirt and grease as to have defied the identity of the animal when walking in the flesh. Others wore homespun gear, which oftentimes appeared to have seen lengthy service. Many of those people were mounted on horse-back or mule-back, while others urged forward the unwilling cattle attached to creaking, heavily-laden wagons, their drivers snapping their long whips with a report like that of a pistol shot.

In front of the shops which lined both sides of the main business street, and about the public square, were groups of men lolling against posts, lying upon the wooden sidewalks, or sitting in chairs.

These men were temporary or permanent denizens of the city, and were lazily occupied in doing nothing. The most marked characteristic of the inhabitants seemed to be an indisposition to move, and their highest ambition to let their hair and beards grow.

Here and there upon the street the appearance of the army blue betokened the presence of a returned Union soldier, and the jaunty, confident air with which they carried themselves was all the more striking in its contrast with the indolence that appeared to belong to the place. The only indication of action was the inevitable revolver which everybody, excepting, perhaps, the women, wore about their persons. When people moved in this city they did so slowly and without method.

No one seemed in haste. A huge hog wallowed in luxurious ease in a nice bed of mud on the other side of the way, giving vent to gentle grunts of satisfaction, On the platform at my feet lay a large wolf-dog, literally asleep with one eye open. He, too, seemed contented to let the world wag idly on.

After painting this picture of depraved squalor and malaise-like laziness on the public square and of the citizens of Springfield, Nichol's introduced his main protagonist, arriving like a Greek god riding a bolt of lightning.

The loose, lazy spirit of the occasion finally took possession of me, and I sat and gazed and smoked...when I and the drowsing city were roused into life by the clatter and crash of the hoofs of a horse which dashed furiously across the square and down the street. The rider sat perfectly erect, yet following with a grace of motion, seen only in the horsemen of the plains, the rise and fall of the galloping steed. There was only a moment to observe this, for they halted suddenly, while the rider springing to the ground approached the party which the noise had gathered near me.

"This here is Wild Bill, Colonel," said Captain Honesty, an army officer, addressing me.

He continued: "How are yer, Bill? This here is Colonel N——, who wants to know yer."

Let me at once describe the personal appearance of the famous Scout of the Plains, William Hitchcock, called "Wild Bill," who now advanced toward me, fixing his clear gray eyes on me in a quick, interrogative sort of way, as if to take "my measure."

The result seemed favorable, for he held forth a small, muscular hand in a frank, open manner. As I looked at him I thought his the handsomest physique I had ever seen. In its exquisite manly proportions it recalled the antique. It was a figure Ward would delight to model as companion to his "Indian."

Bill stood six feet and an inch in his bright yellow moccasins. A deer-skin shirt, or frock it might be called, hung jauntily over his shoulders, and revealed a chest whose breadth and depth were remarkable. These lungs had had growth in some twenty years of the free air of the Rocky Mountains.

His small, round waist was girthed by a belt two of Colt's navy revolvers. His legs sloped gradually from the compact thigh to the feet, which were small, and turned inward as he walked. There was a singular grace and dignity of carriage about that figure which would have called your attention meet it where you would. The head which crowned it was now covered in a large sombrero, underneath which there shone out a quiet, manly face; so gentle is its expression as he greets you as utterly to belie the history of its owner, yet it is not a face to be trifled with. The lips thin and sensitive, the jaw not too square, the cheek bones slightly prominent, a mass of fine dark hair falls below the neck to the shoulders. The eyes, now that you are in friendly intercourse, are as gentle as a woman's. In truth, the woman nature seems prominent throughout, and you would not believe you were looking into eyes that have pointed the way to death of hundreds of men. Yes, Wild Bill with his own hands has killed hundreds of men. Of that I have not a doubt. "He shoots to kill," as they say on the border.

In vain did I examine the scout's face for some evidence of murderous propensity. It was a gentle face, and singular only in the sharp angle of the eye, and without any physiognomical reason for the opinion, I have thought his wonderful accuracy was indicated by this peculiarity.

Nichols was awestruck at this first sight of Hickok, or at least he wanted the reader to believe he was. Regardless, the effect was the same. This would not be the last time over the next decade that someone, man or woman, would offer a fawning tribute to the physical presence and calm strength of the charismatic James Butler Hickok. There is an interesting point made above by Nichols as he adoringly describes Hickok; one that offers important circumstantial evidence of something. Nichols states that Hickok was standing before him "girthed by a belt which held two of Colt's navy revolvers." This, just seven weeks after the July 21 shootout on the public square, offers further circumstantial evidence that the pistol that Hickok used that day on the square was a Navy Colt.

Following this long and loving critique of Hickok as an Adonis, Nichols proceeds to give voice to Hickok, introducing the reader to Hickok as a country bumpkin:

"I allers shot well; but I come ter be perfeck in the mountains by shootin at a dime for a mark, at bets of half a dollar a shot. And then until the war I never drank liquor nor smoked," he continued, with a melancholy expression; "war is demoralizing, it is."

Why Nichols decided to use this linguistic literary effect to have Hickok using the language of an uneducated backwoodsman is unknown, especially since it is well established that Hickok had complete and intelligent command of the English language when he was speaking. Perhaps he thought that the use of that sort of language would naturally tie in with the uncouth citizens of Springfield that Nichols described. Nichols perhaps thought this backwoods language would better meet the preconceptions of his readers back East. Yet strangely, Hickok's syntax drifts back and forth between hillbilly and Oxfordian in Nichols' article. When the article appeared in February 1867, the outrage of those that knew Hickok and his command of the language was second only to those citizens of Springfield that took umbrage at Nichols' disdainful picture of their town and its people.

The first story Nichols tackled was the very recent Hickok-Tutt gunfight of July 21, 1865. He presented it through the words of Captain Honesty (Richard Bentley Owen): "The main features of the story of the duel was told to me by Captain Honesty, who was unprejudiced, if it is possible to find an unbiased mind in a town of 3000 people after a fight has taken place. I will give the story in his words."(Nichols has Captain Honesty speaking with the same fractured hillbilly syntax as that of Hickok) With some exceptions, Nichols did not let the gunfight story stray too far from the facts. He twisted up and embellished the gambling/watch story a bit (Hickok didn't want to gamble with Tutt because Tutt was a professional gambler; Hickok had killed Tutt's mate during the war; Hickok won $200 from Tutt but Tutt wanted $35 more.) Nichols changed the time of the gunfight from six p.m. to noon,forever predicating every future dusty street two-man shootout portrayed in novel or film to occur at high noon. Nichols set the distance between Hickok and Tutt at fifty yards. Nichols had Hickok immediately after firing at Tutt spinning around and pointing his gun at a group of Tutt's friends and threatening them. Captain Honesty said to Nichols: "The fact is, thar was an undercurrent of a woman in that fight." Other than these elaborations, Nichols' story generally followed the court testimony.

Next Nichols went into the story of Black Nell, Hickok's wonder-horse. This story had no underlying evidence like the gunfight did. Nichols structured it as being told to him by a lieutenant of cavalry who was standing nearby after Captain Honesty finished telling the story of the gunfight. Black Nell shoots forward like an arrow after Hickok waves his hand over her head. Escaping enemy lines in the war, Hickok whispers in her ear and she flees and leaps over a twenty-foot-wide ditch, Hickok turning and shooting two pursuers as Black Nell is still airborne over the ditch. They evade the enemy and reach their lines to rousing cheers. None of the tale is true.

Before continuing the adventures of Black Nell, Nichols digresses into a wonderful description of Hickok's hotel, where Nichols has gone to make their agreed afternoon meeting. That hotel, the Lyon House when Hickok stayed there in 1865, later the Southern Hotel and still later known as the St. James Hotel when Hickok returned to live again in Springfield in 1873, was located at today's modern address of 318 South Street. Today this historic location holds the Systematic Savings Bank. Nichols' first-hand description of the Lyon House and its saloon, which he indicates is the only hotel in Springfield at that time, deserves full treatment:

> *I went to the hotel during the afternoon to keep the scout's appointment. The large room of the hotel in Springfield is perhaps the central point of attraction in the city. It fronted on the street, and served in several capacities. It was a sort of exchange for those who had nothing better to do than to go there. It was reception-room, parlor, and office; but its distinguished and most fascinating characteristic was the bar, which occupied one entire end of the apartment. Technically the "bar" is the counter upon which the polite official places his viands. Practically, the bar is represented in the long rows of bottles, and cut-glass decanters, and the glasses and goblets of all shapes and sizes suited to the various liquors to be imbibed. What a charming and artistic display it was of elongated transparent vessels containing every known drinkable fluid, from native Bourbon to imported Lachryma Christi.[1]*
>
> *The room, in its way, was a temple of art. All sorts of pictures budded and blossomed and blushed from the walls. Sixpenny portraits of the Presidents encoffined in pine-wood frames; Mazeppa appeared in the four phases of his celebrated one-horse act; while a lithograph of "Mary Ann" smiled and simpered in spite of the stains of tobacco-juice*

which had been unsparingly bestowed upon her originally encarmined countenance. But the hanging committee of this undesigned academy seemed to have been prejudiced—as all hanging committees of good taste might well be—in favor of Harper's Weekly; for the walls of the room were well covered with wood-cuts from that journal. Portraits of noted generals and statesman, knaves and politicians, with bounteous illustrations of battles and skirmishes, from Bull Run number one to Dinwiddie Court House. And the simple-hearted comers and goers of Springfield looked upon, wondered and admired these pictorial descriptions fully as much as if they had been the masterpieces of a Yvon or Vernet.

A billiard-table, old and worn out of use, where caroms seem to have been made quite as often with lead as ivory balls, stood in the centre of the room. A dozen chairs filled up the complement of the furniture. The appearance of the party of men assembled there, who sat with their slovenly shod feet dangling over the arms of the chairs or hung about the porch outside, was in perfect harmony with the time and place. All of them religiously obeyed the two before-mentioned characteristics of the people of the city—their hair was long and tangled, and each man fulfilled the most exalted requirement of laziness.

Nichols was jolted out of his pleasant inspection by the arrival of Hickok and Black Nell. Now he claims he sees the amazing Black Nell in action himself:

I saw Wild Bill riding up the street at a swift gallop. Arrived opposite to the hotel, he swung his right arm around with a circular motion. Black Nell instantly stopped and dropped to the ground as if a cannon-ball had knocked life out of her. Bill left her there, stretched out on the ground, and joined the group of observers on the porch. "Black Nell hasn't forget her old tricks," said one of them. "No" answered the scout. "God bless her! She is wiser and truer than most men I know of. That mare will do any thing for me. Won't you Nelly?" The mare winked affirmatively the only eye we could see. "Wise!" continued her master; "why, she knows more than a judge. I'll bet the drinks for the party that she'll walk up these steps and into the room and climb up on the billiard-table and lie down." The bet was taken at once, not because any one doubted the capabilities of the mare, but there was excitement in the thing without exercise. Bill whistled in a low tone...

Nichols has Black Nell instantly rising and making her way up the steps and into the saloon of the Lyon House, climbing with perfect agility onto the billiard table, then letting several awestruck denizens of the bar climb onto her back, after which she gracefully got herself off the table, Then Hickok himself springs onto her saddle, they dash back through the high and wide doorway, and in one bound clear the steps and land in the middle of the street. As they walk towards Nichols' room at the Lyon House, Hickok tells of wartime adventures with Black Nell:

"Black Nell has carried me along through many a tight place," said the scout as we walked toward my quarters. *"She trains easier than any animal I ever saw. That trick of dropping quick which you saw has saved my life time and again...One day a gang of rebs who had been hunting for me, and thought they had my track, halted for half an hour within fifty yards of us. Nell laid as close as a rabbit, and didn't even whisk her tail to keep the flies off, until the rebs moved off. The mare will come at my whistle and foller me just like a dog. She won't mind anyone else..."*

Of all the Wild Bill legends started by the pen of George Ward Nichols, the story of Black Nell is one without any basis in fact, not even a circumstantial fact, no evidentiary record which can be considered, no eyewitness accounts, excepting that of Nichols, who made the whole thing up. When the article appeared seventeen months later the local and regional press were understandably skeptical about Black Nell, as well they should have been. Just two months after the article came out, Hickok, while being interviewed about the Nichols article at Fort Harker, Kansas by the correspondent of a Boston newspaper, denied the "horse story" ever happened,[2] confirming that Nichols made the whole thing up and Black Nell and her adventures were the work of Nichols' imagination. It is another one of many Hickok myths that must be thrown into the ash bin of history. You will read of the others here as well.

Nichols gave an accounting of Hickok's adventures with Sterling Price, stories set down, according to Nichols, "in the scouts own words." Were Hickok's words from an actual interview that Nichols had conducted with him? It seems unlikely. More probable that these were stories that army officers told Nichols about Hickok. Nichols stated as much. In turn, Nichols took what the officers had told him and interviewed Hickok by having him address these stories. Then Nichols mixed the stories with fantasies and falsehoods of Nichols' creation. The first few sentences below read like Hickok is responding to things he has been told by Nichols:

> *I hardly know where to begin. Pretty near all the stories are true. I was at it all the war. That affair of me swimming the river took place on the long scout of mine when I was with the rebels five months, when I was sent by General Curtis to Price's army. Things had come pretty close at that time, and it wasn't safe to go straight inter their lines, everybody was suspected who came from these parts. So I started off and went way up to Kansas City. I bought a horse and struck out onto the plains, and then went down through southern Kansas into Arkansas. I knew a rebel named Barnes, who was killed at Pea Ridge. He was from near Austin in Texas. So I called myself his brother and enlisted in a regiment of mounted rangers.*
>
> *General Price was just then getting ready for a raid into Missouri. It was some time before we got into the campaign, and it was mighty hard work for me. The men of our regiment were awful. They didn't mind killing a man no more than a hog. The officers had no command over them...I never let on that I was a good shot. I kept that back for big occasions; but ef you'd heard me swear and cuss the blue-bellies, you'd a-thought me one of the wickedest of the whole crew. So it went on until we came near Curtis's army. Bime-by they were on one side Sandy River and we were on t'other. All the time I had been getting information until I knew every regiment and its strength; how much cavalry there was, and how many guns the artillery had...*

Nichols has Hickok go on to describe in detail the "affair of me swimming the river" that James had cited above. In a nutshell, Hickok decided he must get this important information to General Curtis. So he baited a loudmouth show-off soldier to ride with him to see how close they could get to the enemy line. They approached the river with bullets flying all around from the Union soldiers on the opposite bank, until some soldier on the Union yelled out, "Bully for Wild Bill," whereupon the Confederate soldier riding next to Hickok drew his pistol to shoot, but Hickok beat him to the draw and he got blown out of the saddle. Hickok grabbed the reins of his horse and with the two horses plunged into the river and swam to the other side, while Confederate bullets splashed all around him.

Nichols self-corroborated this leap from the enemy lines to the Union lines with a similar tale, equally fanciful, of an escape from enemy lines. In this tale a Union officer told Nichols of Hickok's amazing escape with his partner over a wide expanse that confronted the two riders with a twenty-foot-wide, deep ditch, just as pursuing Confederates were closing in. They turned back for a hard run and leap at the ditch, but Hickok's partner was shot and went down. Black Nell makes the leap, and Hickok makes it to the Union side among the cheers of the soldiers witnessing the amazing jump. "Bill must have brought valuable information," continued the lieutenant, "for he was at once sent to the General, and in an hour we had changed position, and foiled a flank movement of the rebels."

Nichols saved his most grandiose fantasies for his report on the McCanles affair at Rock Creek, Nebraska. Here he really went off the rails and into parts unknown, much to the detriment of future writers, journalists, and historians, not to mention Hickok's legacy. Here is the complete passage in all its fierce and horrible and false glory:

> *I was especially desirous to hear him relate the history of a sanguinary fight which he had with a party of ruffians in the early part of the war, when, single-handed, he fought and killed ten men. I had heard the story as it came from an officer of the regular army who, an hour after the affair, saw Bill and the ten dead men—some killed with bullets, others hacked and slashed to death with a knife.*
>
> *As I write out the details of this terrible tale from notes which I took as the words fell from the scout's lips, I am conscious of its extreme improbability; but while I listened to him I remembered the story in the Bible, where we are told that Samson "with the jawbone of an ass slew a thousand men," and as I looked upon this magnificent example of human strength and daring, he appeared to me to realize the powers of a Samson and Hercules combined, and I should not have been inclined to place any limit on his achievements. Besides this, one who has lived for four years in the presence of such grand heroism and deeds of prowess as was seen during the war is in what might be called a "receptive" mood. Be the story true or not, in part, or in whole, I believed then every word Wild Bill uttered, and I believe it to-day.*
>
> *"I don't like to talk about that M'Kandlas affair," said Bill, in answer to my question. "It gives me a queer shiver whenever I think of it, and sometimes I dream about it, and wake up in a cold sweat."You*

see this M'Kandlas was the Captain of a gang of desperadoes, horse-thieves, murderers, regular cut-throats, who were the terror of everybody on the border, and who kept us in the mountains in hot water whenever they were around. I knew them all in the mountains, where they pretended to be trapping, but they were there hiding from the hangman. M'Kandlas was the biggest scoundrel and bully of them all, and he was allers a-braggin of what he could do. One day I beat him shootin at a mark, and then threw him at the back-holt. And I didn't drop him as soft as a baby, you may be sure. Well he got savage mad about it, and swore he would have his revenge on me some time."

"This was just before the war broke out, and we were already takin sides in the mountains either for the South or the Union. M'Kandlas and his gang were border-ruffians in the Kansas row, and of course they went with the rebs. Bime-by he clar'd out, and I shouldn't have thought of the feller agin ef he hadn't crossed my path. It 'pears he didn't forget me."

"It was in '61, when I guided a detachment of cavalry who were comin in from Camp Floyd. We had nearly reached the Kansas line, and were in South Nebraska, when one afternoon I went out of camp to go to the cabin of an old friend of mine, a Mrs. Waltman. I took only one of my revolvers with me, for although the war had broke out I didn't think it necessary to carry both my pistols, and, in all or'nary scrimmages, one is better than a dozen, ef you shoot straight..."

"Well, I rode up to Mrs. Waltman's, jumped off my horse, and went into the cabin, which is like most cabins on the prarer, with only one room, and that had two doors, one opening in front and t'other on a yard, like." "How are you, Mrs. Waltman?" I said, feeling as jolly as you please.

"The minute she saw me she turned as white as a sheet and screamed: 'Is that you, Bill? Oh, my God! they will kill you! Run! run! They will kill you!...It's Mkandlas and his gang. There's ten of them, and you've no chance. They've jes gone down the road to the corn-rack. They came up here only five minutes ago. M'Kandlas was draggin poor Parson Shipley on the ground with a lariat round his neck. The preacher was most dead with choking and the horses stamping on him. M'Kandlas knows yer bringin in that party of Yankee cavalry, and he swears he'll cut yer heart out. Run, Bill, Run!—But it's too late; they're comin up the lane!'

"While she was a-talkin I remembered I had but one revolver, and a load gone out of that. On the table there was a horn of powder

and some little bars of lead. I poured some powder into the empty chamber and rammed the lead after it by hammering the barrel on the table, and had just capped the pistol when I heard M'Kandlas shout: 'There's that d—d Yank Wild Bill's horse; he's here; and we'll skin him alive!' If I had thought of runnin before it war too late now, and the house was my best holt-a sort of fortress, like. I never thought I should leave that room alive."

The scout stopped in his story, rose from his seat, and strode back and forward in great excitement. "I tell you what it is, Kernal," he resumed, after awhile, "I don't mind a scrimmage with these fellers round here. Shoot one or two of them and the rest run away. But all of M'Kandlas's gang were reckless, blood-thirsty devils, who would fight as long as they had strength to pull a trigger. I have been in tight places, but that's one of the few times I said my prayers.

"'Surround the house and give him no quarter!' yelled M'Kandlas. When I heard that I felt as quiet and cool as if I was a-goin to church. I looked around the room and saw a Hawkins rifle hangin over the bed. 'Is that loaded?' said I to Mrs. Waltman. 'Yes,' the poor thing whispered. She was so frightened she couldn't speak out loud.

"'Are you sure?' said I, as I jumped to the bed and caught it from its hooks. Although my eye did not leave the door, I could see she nodded 'Yes' again. I put the revolver on the bed, and just then M'Kandlas poked his head inside the doorway, but jumped back when he saw me with the rifle in my hand. 'Come in here, you cowardly dog!' I shouted. 'Come in here, and fight me!' M'Kandlas was no coward, if he was a bully. He jumped inside the room with his gun leveled to shoot; but was not quick enough. My rifle-ball went through his heart. He fell back outside the house, where he was found afterward holding tight to his rifle, which had fallen over his head.

"His disappearance was followed by a yell from his gang, and then there was dead silence. I put down the rifle and took the revolver, and I said to myself: 'Only six shots and nine men to kill. Save your powder, Bill, for the death-hug's a-comin!' I don't know why it was Kernal," continued Bill, looking at me inquiringly, "but at that moment things seemed clear and sharp. I could think strong.

"There was a few seconds of that awful stillness, and then the ruffians came rushing in at both doors. How wild they looked with their red, drunken faces and inflamed eyes, shoutmg and cussing! But I never aimed so deliberately in my life. One—two—three—four; and four men fell dead.

111

"*That didn't stop the rest. Two of them fired their bird-guns at me. And then I felt a sting run all over me. The room was full of smoke. Two of them got in close to me, their eyes glaring out of the clouds. One I knocked down with my fist. 'You are out of the way for awhile' I thought. The second I shot dead. The other three clutched me and crowded me onto the bed. I fought hard. I broke with my hand one mans arm. He had his fingers round my throat. Before I could get to my feet I was struck across the breast with the stock of a rifle, and I felt the blood rushing out of my nose and mouth. Then I got ugly, and I remember that I got hold of a knife, and than it was all cloudy like, and I was wild, and I struck savage blows, following the devils up from one side to the other of the room and into the corners, striking and slashing until I knew that everyone was dead. All of the sudden it seemed as if my heart was on fire. I was bleeding everywhere. I rushed out to the well and drank from the bucket, and then tumbled down in a faint.*"

Breathless with the intense interest with which I had followed this strange story, all the more thrilling and weird when its hero, seeming to live over again the bloody events of that day, gave way to its terrible spirit with wild, savage gestures. I saw then—what my scrutiny of the morning had failed to discover—the tiger which lay concealed beneath that gentle exterior. "*You must have been hurt almost to death,*" *I said.*

"*There were eleven buck-shot in me. I carry some of them now. I was cut in thirteen places. All of them to have let out the life of a man. But that blessed old Dr. Mills pulled me safe through it, after a bed siege of many a long week.*"

Of all the legends Nichols put to print in his article, his exaggerated and outlandish version of the McCanles affair would be perpetuated the longest, and have the most adverse effect on the veracity of the historical record surrounding Wild Bill Hickok. Nichols' false version of what happened at Rock Creek deserves its own special and dishonorable place in the ash bin of history.

Nichol's wrapped up his article with one more story, a description of Nichols' in-person observation of Hickok's vaunted shooting skill with a pistol. This shooting exhibition took place from the street-side window of Nichols' second-story room in the Lyons House hotel:

"I would like to see you shoot."

"Would yer?" replied the scout, drawing his revolver; and approaching the window, he pointed to a letter O in a sign-board which was fixed to the stone-wall of a building on the other side of the way.

"That sign is more than fifty yards away. I will put these six balls into the inside of the circle, which isn't bigger than a man's heart."

In an off-hand way, and without sighting the pistol with his eye, he discharged the six shots of his revolver. I afterward saw that all the bullets had entered the circle. As Bill proceeded to reload his pistol, he said to me with a naivete of manner which was meant to be assuring:

"Whenever you get into a row be sure and not shoot too quick. Take time. I've known many a feller slip up for shootin' in a hurry."

Here Nichols describes an event not only possible, but plausible. Hickok is shooting at a target twenty-five yards closer than he undertook with Tutt. He is shooting from a second-story window, gaining whatever advantage that gives him. It would not be the last time he demonstrated his shooting ability for someone by blasting out the wooden center of the "O" on a sign. The next time he did would develop an iconic legend so compelling that frontier stalwarts Bat Masterson and Wyatt Earp claimed to have been a witness to the event. The facts surrounding it deserve reconsideration today, as will be shown later in this book.

Nichols made one final summary tribute to Hickok, followed by a short passage where Hickok purportedly pleads that Nichols must make his mother "know what'll make her proud," and Nichols closes with one more admonition to the reader that this story is true:

It would be easy to fill a volume with the adventures of that remarkable man. My object here has been to make a slight record of one of the best—perhaps the very best—example of a class who more than any other encountered perils and privations in defense of our nationality...

William Hitchcock—called Wild Bill, the Scout of the Plains—shall have his wish. I have told the story precisely as it was told to me, confirmed in all important points by many witnesses; and I have no doubt of its truth—G.W.N. [3]

When the story appeared seventeen months later, February 1867, in the popular and widely circulated *Harper's New Monthly Magazine,* it caused a sensation as well as generated much controversy. It made Hickok a media star, rising almost overnight from midwest regional notoriety to national fame. For the next ten years that fame would prove to be a mixed blessing.

The photograph #4023 on page 115 may have been requested by George Ward Nichols, as the body stance, Hickok's hand on his gun and his hat all appear on the woodcut that opened the article "Wild Bill" in *Harper's New Monthly Magazine.* Yet the woodcut also featured the collarless shirt, knee-length coat, and checkered trousers that Hickok favored at the time. Therefore the final woodcut may have been an amalgamation of two photographs, the one seen here and image 4024.

After the September Nichols interview, Hickok spent the rest of 1865 in Springfield. He was certainly still in Springfield in January of 1866, as borne out by two events that month. On January 13, a mysterious warrant was issued for Hickok's arrest, and a court hearing was set for January 18. Nothing in the warrant tells us what the charges are, or who the plaintiff is:

State of Missouri—County of Greene—As "By the Habeus Corpus act"

The State of Missouri to the Sheriff of Greene County said, under safe and secure Conduct together with the day and Cause of his being imprisoned and detained, by whatsoever name the said William Hickok may be known. You have before me, S H Boyd Judge of the Circuit Court for the 14 Judicial Circuit at Court House in the town of Springfield County of Greene state of Missouri on the 18th day of January 1866 to do and receive what shall then and there be considered concerning the said William Hickok so imprisoned and detained as aforesaid and hereof. Jail not at your peril.

Witness my signature this 13th day of January 1866 S H Boyd, Ct Court Jg [4]

#4023

Photograph by Charles Scholten circa September 1865. Scholten's granddaughter Mary Moore stated that this photo was taken in the Lyon Hotel, located on South Street just off of the square in Springfield, Missouri. The photograph was discovered in 1989 in Richard Bentley Owen's photo album in a military collectors store just off of the Springfield square. Owen was Hickok's good friend in Springfield and later at Fort Riley in Kansas. *Author's collection.*

Adding to the mystery of this warrant is the fact that later in January (or perhaps even in early February) Hickok testified under oath as a witness in court about a shooting that occurred on January 25, just seven days after Judge Boyd, in the warrant above, had demanded his appearance in court as a defendant.

On January 25, a man named James Coleman was shot and killed in Springfield by policeman John Orr. (Recall that Orr was a friend of Hickok. He was in the room when Hickok and Tutt had their famous poker game that resulted in Tutt absconding with Hickok's watch. Orr was on the square when Hickok and Tutt shot it out, and he testified at Hickok's trial.)

The circumstances leading up to the shooting were that James Coleman, his brother Samuel, and another man named Bingham came riding into Springfield that day, all very drunk. They rode down South Street and Bingham started whooping and hollering. Sheriff Charles Moss arrested him. Samuel Coleman apparently followed Moss and policeman John Orr as they were leading Bingham to jail, and tried to interfere with Bingham's arrest. James Coleman, who had stayed with the horses, came up to the group, and they all began to scuffle. In the scuffle, James Coleman was shot by Orr, and shortly after Samuel Coleman was shot by Orr. James Coleman died.

Hickok was an eyewitness to the event, which occurred in front of the Lyon House on South Street, where Hickok lived. His testimony under oath follows:

> *When I got where the fuss was, the police took a man off a horse. After they had got him off the horse, Chas. Moss came and took hold of him; he did not appear to want to come with the police; kept talking, and when they got opposite Jacob's store he commenced scrambling, and they threw him down the second time; then they took him along to where Ladd keeps grocery, and by that time one of his comrades came up; those they stopped; Samuel Coleman commenced talking, and the one that was killed had tied the horses at the blacksmith shop and came up and joined them at Ladd's, or near Ladd's grocery; the two Colemans wanted to stop the police and have a talk with the police; from that they got to jarring worse and worse until they commenced shooting; the first I saw of the shooting I saw John Orr jerk his pistol and put it up against the man and shot; did not see whether James Coleman had a pistol or not; his back was to me, and Samuel Coleman grabbed a stick*

and struck, but I do not know whether he struck John Orr or Charles Moss, and as soon as the first shooting was done Orr turned and shot Samuel Coleman; the crowd scattered around, and some person, or persons, grabbed the first man arrested and ran off down town this way; we pulled the man up on the platform and intended taking him into Ladd's, but he was locked up, and he was then carried to the drug store of N. P. Murphy & Co. The affray commenced first opposite the Lyons House and closed opposite Ladd's grocery, on South street, Springfield, Missouri.

J. B. Hickok[5]

8

1866

HICKOK RETURNS *to* KANSAS

GOVERNMENT DETECTIVE *at* FORT RILEY

the MYTH *of* HICKOK *the* BASEBALL UMPIRE

SCOUT *and* GUIDE *for* GENERALS SHERMAN *and* POPE

CODY *and* HICKOK

J. B. HICKOK: JUNCTION CITY SALOONKEEPER

On February 22, 1866, the Marble Hall Saloon opened in Kansas City in the 400 block of Main Street just off the city square. Described as "an elegant billiard parlor, the best lighted and ventilated in the city," the Marble Hall would come to figure large in Hickok's future time in Kansas City.[1]

Richard Bentley Owen became acting assistant quartermaster at Rolla, Missouri in July, 1862. It was in Rolla that he and Hickok first met. In April 1864 Owen became Hickok's boss when Brig. General John B. Sanborn issued "Special Order No. 89" stating that "J. B.

Hickok will be taken up on the Rolls of Capt Owen, A.Q.M., as Scout, at these Head Quarters, from this date and will be furnished a horse, and equipments while on duty as Scout." After the war Owen was made depot quartermaster at Springfield, Missouri in October 1865.

Richard Bentley Owen was Hickok's friend and supporter during part of the Civil War and on through Hickok's time in Springfield. Owen testified on behalf of Hickok at the Tutt trial. Owen was the "Captain Honesty" who introduced Hickok to George Ward Nichols, and who also gave information about Hickok to Nichols.

As the war closed, Owen was under orders to close the depot at Springfield, and in December 1865 he was assigned to Fort Riley in Kansas as assistant post quartermaster. Apparently when he took the position at Fort Riley in early 1866, he discovered numerous problems, not the least of which was the theft of government horses, mules and real property. He sent for Hickok, who came immediately; if not in February, certainly by March. James once again found himself living and working in Kansas. He left the Territory of Kansas in 1859; he returned now in 1866 to the five-year-old State of Kansas.

Danny Bohen, who served with Hickok through the Plains Indian Wars of the post-Civil War era, 1866 to 1869, recalled what drew Hickok to Fort Riley in 1866: "Bill Hickok came to Fort Reilly in 1866. The Railroad contractors and settlers were stealing mules from the Government and he was appointed Marshal." Bohen also stated, "In 1866, Hickok left Fort Morgan, Colo. with General Carr (he was a scout for him) to establish a stage line up the Smoky Hill route, by way of Bent's Fort. General Carr did not go any further than Fort Wallace. Fort Wallace was [then] called Pond Creek and Fort Hays [then] was called Fort Fletcher. The rebel soldiers were enlisted to fight Indians, not white men."[2] Bohen's rebel soldiers noted above references "galvanized yankees," Confederate prisoners who joined the Union army rather than face prison. These soldiers were stationed at Fort Morgan at that time. Though Bohen's statements about Hickok and Carr and the stage line in 1866 may be accurate, no corroborating evidence has surfaced.

George Hance, who knew both James and brother Lorenzo since 1862 when they were teamsters and wagon masters back in Rolla during the war, and who was now himself working at Fort Riley, described how Richard Owen and J. B. Hickok came to be at the fort:

In the winter of 1865-1866, the commissary and quartermaster's storehouse's at Fort Riley, Kansas, were burnt—it was common talk to balance some army officer's books. Captain Owen was ordered there and sent to Springfield, Mo., for Wild Bill to come to Fort Riley, and on the recommendation of General Easton, who was chief quartermaster at Fort Leavenworth, and Captain Owen at Fort Riley, Wild Bill was appointed a deputy United States marshal...On one trip over in the Council Grove and Little Arkansas River country, he brought in nine big mules and one big and two small men, army deserters. He did all this alone and was gone about three weeks. The largest man was riding on a mule by Wild Bill's side. I asked Wild Bill if he was not afraid to take such chances, as that big man could reach and draw one of the six-shooters, and then they would be on equal terms. He replied he could equally draw the other and shoot every one of them dead before they could fire a shot. I have seen him draw a pistol and hit a spot, not larger than a silver dollar, at 20 to 30 steps, before an ordinary man could fire a shot into the air or into the ground. [3]

Bohen and Hance above recall Hickok as a marshal, or a deputy United States marshal, upon coming to Fort Riley. The work Hickok undertook in early 1866 was all government-related tasks, synonymous with the duties of a deputy U. S. marshal: recovering stolen government mules and property, bringing in army deserters, transporting prisoners. Yet the records of Thomas Osborne, the United States marshal for Kansas that year of 1866, do not show Hickok as one of his deputies. This is not fully conclusive, however, because the records of the United States marshal, District of Kansas, for 1866 to 1871 are incomplete. Post reports from Fort Riley for 1866 do show Richard B. Owen on March 11, 1866 assigning J. B. Hickok, at $125 a month, to "hunt up public property." Yet Owen's reports also reflect that from April through September he is paid $75 a month, and Hickok is listed as a "guide" from May through September. Also, if Hickok was truly a deputy U. S. marshal in 1866, he would have reported to Thomas Osborne, not Richard B. Owen, and there would be no Fort Riley post returns mentioning his activities. So without further evidence, it must be concluded that James Butler Hickok was not a deputy United States marshal in 1866. Owen did, however, have two unnamed "detectives" on the payroll during the spring. It is possible there was no deputy U. S. marshal at that time to handle issues at Fort Riley, or if there was one, he was not available.

Hickok was probably one of those two unnamed government detectives. However, by April he was a guide and scout for the frontier army through Indian country. Fort Riley post returns also show that James' brother Lorenzo was employed at Fort Riley from October 1865 until December, 1866, receiving $75 a month as a wagon master. Surely James and Lorenzo had ample opportunity to see each other the ten or eleven months in 1866 they were both posted at Fort Riley. In January 1867, Lorenzo was posted at Fort Lyon in Colorado.

In 1865, General William Tecumseh Sherman was assigned as commander of the Military Division of the Mississippi, a vast western region that extended from the Mississippi to the crest of the Rockies, and from the southern border of Canada to Mexico. This vast area contained much of the westward movement along the ever-lengthening Union Pacific railroad and the great frontier overland trails, all coursing through the lands of increasingly hostile Plains Indians. Sherman, with offices in St. Louis, longed to get out into his designated territory on an inspection tour, and he finally did so in May of 1866.

It was then that Sherman came to Fort Riley, joined by one of his generals, John S. Pope. Richard B. Owen recommended Hickok as a guide and scout to Sherman, who agreed. The group left in May, 1866, initially traveling north to Fort Kearney in Nebraska. They went by Marysville, Kansas and crossed the Nebraska state line near the site of the Rock Creek station. One person there who recognized Hickok was Frank Helvey. Helvey, with his brother, had buried McCanles as well as Woods and Gordon in 1861. Frank Helvey later recalled:

> I did not see Wild Bill again until in 1866 or 1867, when he was with Gen. Sherman as a guide and escort, en route to the Indian troubles in Wyoming. Sherman had about 2000 men, and they encamped for the night on Little Sandy near our station. Before they had got fairly settled, Gen. Sherman, with Wild Bill accompanying him, rode up to the station, and warned us not to let the soldiers have any whisky. This we promised to do, and we kept it good, despite the entreaties of the men. Next morning, as the command rode by, Gen. Sherman and Bill stopped and thanked us for the favor. Wild Bill was a remarkable man in many ways, almost ideal of build, unexcelled as a shot, quiet of manner, hard to get acquainted with or talk with; was quick to take offense, and quicker to take action in retaliation. The only man that could equal Wild Bill as a shot was Bob Spotswood, who

was a division agent for the Stage Company out on the North Platte Divison. It was my good luck to see the famous contest of marksmanship between them, where the honors were exactly even.[4]

Sherman and his command continued northwest to Fort Kearney. At Fort Kearney, on June 11, 1866, Colonel James Meline recorded in the journal that would ultimately become his classic book, *Two Thousand Miles on Horseback,* his physical observations of Hickok, followed by his tongue-in-cheek assessment of James' leg-pulling stories:

By the way, I forgot to tell you about our guide—the most striking object in camp. Six feet, lithe, active, sinewy, daring rider, dead shot with pistol and rifle, long locks, fine features and mustache, buckskin leggins, red shirt, broad-brim hat, rifle in hand—he is a picture. Has lived since he was eleven on the prairies; when a boy, rode Pony Express on the California route, and during the war was scout and spy. He goes by the name of Wild Bill, and tells wonderful stories of horsemanship, fighting, and hair-breadth escapes. We do not, however, feel under any obligation to believe them all.[5]

At Fort Kearney, General Pope took leave of General Sherman, and seemingly under orders to do so, took his part of the troops and turned southwest for the very distant Santa Fe, New Mexico, apparently on an inspection visit of his own. Hickok continued on as scout and guide to Santa Fe for General Pope. Their route took them following the Platte River through Nebraska into Denver. From there, Pope's command followed along the front slope of the Rockies through Pueblo and Trinidad, picking up the Mountain Branch of the Santa Fe Trail over Raton Pass and on to Fort Union. They continued into New Mexico, through Mora, Las Vegas, Tecolote, and on into Santa Fe.

Reaching Santa Fe by late July, Pope's command spent almost three weeks in the area. Colonel Meline wrote of his extended visit in Santa Fe with Kit Carson. It appears he knew of Carson only by reputation, and had never met him before. Here are excerpts from the six pages that Meline wrote of his three days spent with Carson in Santa Fe:

The pleasantest episode of my visit here has been the society of Kit Carson, with whom I passed three days, I need hardly say delightfully. He is one of the few men I ever met who can talk long hours to you of what he has seen, and yet say very little about himself. He has to be drawn out. I had many questions to ask, and his answers were all marked by great distinctness of memory, simplicity, candor, and a desire to make someone else, rather than himself, the hero of the story.

In answer to questions concerning Indians, he frequently would reply—unlike so many I have met who knew <u>all</u> about them—"I don't know,"—"I can't say,"—"I never saw that."

...The conversation turning on grizzly bears...He laughed outright. "I have often and again seen grizzlies," said he, "of ten, eleven, and twelve hundred pounds. I distinctly remember killing one in the spring of 1846, that weighed 1200 pounds...Trappers have often told me of numbers rising to that weight, and I have no reason to doubt them."

General Carson (he is Colonel of the First Regiment New Mexican Cavalry, and Brevet Brigadier-General) usually resides at Taos, but is now in command at Fort Garland. He has been married many years to a Mexican lady (Senora Josepha Jaramilla) and has a family of three boys and three girls. I find that he is beloved and respected by all who know him, and his word looked upon as truth itself.[6]

Hickok and Pope's command were in Santa Fe for three weeks. Did Hickok seek out and meet legendary frontiersman Kit Carson during this time? Meline's three days with Carson indicate he was available and approachable. It is possible that they met, if only briefly, yet there is no evidence of Hickok and Carson meeting then in Santa Fe or any other time, notwithstanding William Connelley's completely fanciful story about Carson showing young Hickok through the "underworld" of Santa Fe. Another myth for the ash heap of history.[7]

On August 11, 1866, Pope's entire command left Santa Fe, guided by Hickok. They followed the Cimarron route of the Santa Trail northeast through New Mexico, the Oklahoma Panhandle, and into Kansas, crossing the Arkansas River at the Cimarron Crossing west of Fort Dodge. From there they followed the Santa Fe Trail on the north side of the Arkansas through Fort Larned and Fort Zarah, there leaving the Santa Fe Trail and continuing through Fort Ellsworth and finally home to Fort Riley in early September. Meline described their approach to the city that in the year of 1866 was Hickok's home, and their approach to the fort that was his employer:

Three miles west of Fort Riley we pass through Junction City, to which point the railroad is, nominally, completed, although not yet running [the Union Pacific]. City sounds, perhaps, a little premature, but with redundant stores, all the mechanical arts, handsome buildings of brick, and one of the finest architectural qualities of stone I have ever seen. I strongly suspect that Junction nurses secret dreams of metropolis.

Without reference to its military fitness, the site of Fort Riley is one of great beauty. Seen from its commanding position, the Republican and Smoky Hill Forks, here united, form the Kaw or Kansas River, one of the most picturesque streams in the country. A lovely valley, dotted with mills, hamlets, and villages, spreads out before you, and you might almost imagine yourself gazing down a long stretch of the Connecticut River.[8]

Hickok returned to Fort Riley in September, and resumed his job with Richard B. Owen as a government detective. Yet Owen released him once more to be a guide that fall. The post surgeon of the 5th U. S Voluntary Infantry was Dr. William Finlaw. James had gotten to know Dr. Finlaw and his family when the doctor was transferred to Fort McPherson in April, although his family came later in May with Sherman's troops. Now, in the fall of 1866, Dr. Finlaw and his family were being transferred back to Fort Riley. Hickok and ten soldiers went to Fort McPherson to escort the doctor and his family back to Fort Riley. A descendent of Dr. Finlaw's wife, Julia Snyder Rockwell, recalled that her mother, staying with a daughter who was the wife of the doctor "whose husband, Dr Finlaw, was an army surgeon at Ft. McPherson, Neb., arrived at Fort Riley under guard of Wild Bill Hickok, who with ten men had escorted her, her daughter and son, from Marysville, Kans., urging them not fear the Indians as he would sleep close to the ambulance."[9]

There is a cherished and much-published legend in Kansas City about J. B. Hickok and a baseball game in the year of 1866. This legend came from the pen of one of Hickok's three major myth makers, William Connelley (the other two being George Ward Nichols and James W. Buel). Here is Connelley's contribution to the history of frontier baseball in Kansas City. Connelley sets his tale in the summer of 1866:

About this time, baseball was beginning to develop into a real American institution. A Kansas City Club was organized and named the "Antelopes." The principal men of the city were its members: D.F.

Twitchell was president; William Warner, vice-president; and W.H. Winants, secretary. The field was in the vicinity of Fourteenth Street about Oak and McGee Streets. On the Saturday afternoons when games were played, there was a holiday by common consent. There was no enclosure and no fee for admission. Everybody was welcome. Chief Speers sometimes had trouble to keep the crowds off the "diamond" when the game became close and interesting, but they were good natured.

The Antelopes were invincible; everything went down before them—for a time. At Atchison, one Sunday afternoon, they were beaten, wallowed in the dust by the "Pomeroys." They took their defeat with true sporting spirit and invited the Pomeroys to Kansas City for another game. This time the Pomeroys were defeated, and a near-riot resulted. The umpire saved himself by flight, and the game ended with much bad feeling. The headline in the Times was "The Town Disgraced." The Pomeroys apologized and the Antelopes invited them back for another game, the following Saturday.

Wild Bill was an enthusiast for games of sport, and especially for baseball. He was an authority on the technique of the game as played in that day, so he was invited to be the umpire of the game. He consented, and when the Antelopes were ready, he was sent for. He was found at Jake Forcade's gambling rooms, at Fourth and Main Streets, playing poker with one of the founders of the city. He hurried out to the grounds and directed the game. Not a protest was made from any of his decisions. There was no dissatisfaction from any quarter. The Pomeroys were defeated by a score of 48 to 28. Wild Bill was asked to name the price of his services. "Send down to Frank Short's livery for an open hack and two white horses to carry me back to Jake's." The hack soon appeared with Short's crack team of white horses, and his compliments for "the distinguished guest of Kansas City for a day."

Imagine the stirring images this compelling report conjures up: Hickok behind the plate wearing a chest protector and two Navy Colts stuffed into the wide red sash beneath his brocade vest, long locks blowing in the breeze, a big-brimmed hat low on his brow as he crouches behind the catcher, awaiting the next pitch. "Strike three!" "You're out!" Not a word of protest from the batter or bench, nor a murmur from the crowd is raised.

It never happened.

There is some glimmer of fact in this story, which Connelley used as window dressing, but the payoff pitch is a myth. Consider Hickok's documented movements in 1866. Until February he was in Springfield, Missouri. From March until late in 1866 he was a government detective, living in Junction City and working out of Fort Riley. He was a guide for General Sherman in May and early June for a trip from Fort Riley to Fort Kearny in Nebraska. From June till September he was a guide for General Pope to Santa Fe, New Mexico and back to Fort Riley. Nothing in the record puts him in Kansas City during 1866. Though not yet nationally famous from the *Harpers* article that would appear in February, 1867, Hickok and his burgeoning reputation were already well-known in Missouri, Arkansas, Kansas, and Nebraska in 1866. Anything so novel as Hickok umpiring a popular baseball game in Kansas City that year would have been reported by the local press at the time of the event. There were no such contemporary reports in the press.

The Antelopes were indeed Kansas City's first team, formed in 1866. The players were civic leaders of the community. The records of the early press indicate that at that time the main competitor of the Kansas City Antelopes were the aptly named Frontier from Leavenworth, not the Atchison Pomeroys. There was a good reason for that: the Atchison Pomeroys team did not exist until 1885; almost ten years after the death of Hickok and almost twenty years after the purported year of this game in 1866.

These early baseball games were matches of gentlemanly congeniality played by prominent citizens. The game was usually followed by drinking and toasts, sometimes speeches. Rules were much different than today; the batter called for the pitcher to throw a high or low pitch, the pitch was thrown underhanded, and the fielders played with no gloves.

Connelley based his report almost verbatim on the recollections printed in an article called "First Team A 'Knockout'" in the *Kansas City Times* of April 28, 1927. Sixty-one years after the game came this reminiscence, run with this headline and more:

Old Timers Recall Antelopes' Debut Here In 1866
Return Game With Atchison Pomeroy's After A Rough Session The Week Before Was Kept Quiet With "Wild Bill" as Umpire

The article goes on to claim, based on the recollections of these "old timers," that there was a serious row between the Antelopes and Pomeroys "with much wrangling, disputing and coarse epithets. The umpire was pelted with sections of ripe watermelon and various vegetables. The game broke up in a row. Charley Whitehear, then city editor of the old *Times*, indignantly wrote a column story of it, headed 'The Town Disgraced.'" There is no record of such a fight ensuing in any game that the Antelopes engaged in. Further, the *Kansas City Times* was not in business until 1867. Note that Charley Whitehear above is actually Charles Whitehead, the editor and journalist for the *Times*, who in 1876 traveled to Deadwood to cover the gold rush there and ended up being jury foreman for the trial of Jack McCall. The article goes on:

> Just before the game "Wild Bill" who was at Jake Forcade's gambling saloon, Fourth and Main streets, playing poker with a highly respected citizen, had been sent for to act as umpire. "Bill" was a good player in his "army scout" days and knew the technique of the game pretty well.

Based on the fact that Hickok was not available to go to Kansas City in 1866 based on the documented record, considering that there is absolutely no contemporaneous press coverage of this novel baseball game, considering the fact that the purported opponents in this game, the Atchison Pomeroys, were not even in existence before 1885, and considering the numerous other contradictions in the *Times* article that were continued and perpetuated in Connelley's report, this charming and unique but completely false tale must be relegated to the ash bin of history.

It never happened.

Note that Joseph Rosa, after writing four biographies and histories of Hickok from 1965 until 2001, came to the same conclusion, that the story was probably false. He made that conclusion even without knowing the damning counter-evidence of the Pomeroys not existing till 1885, which is why he likely left it as "probably" false. His article on this subject, *Was Wild Bill Ever An Ump?* appeared in the June 2011 issue of *Wild West*.[10]

Showing up on Hickok's doorstep that fall of 1866 in Junction City was a tall, skinny twenty-year-old who James had not seen for five years. Will Cody was just a fifteen-year-old boy in 1861 when the Cody family nursed James back to health from a devastating bout of pneumonia at their little hotel in the Salt Creek valley north of Leavenworth. Young Cody, married earlier in 1866 to a wife that he left behind in St. Louis to seek out Hickok, was out of work and probably seeking the same sort of adventurous life of the man he idolized, James Butler Hickok.

Hickok was nine years older than Will Cody, and surely presented a father-figure to Cody when he was a boy. Having lost his father Isaac in 1857 when he was just ten, Cody was insecure, as any young boy would be from such a loss. Hickok entered his life when he was fifteen and Hickok was twenty-four. Hickok had already led an exciting couple of years on the frontier, as a young lawman in Monticello, as a scout and spy in the border war era, and as a guard riding shotgun on an overland stage. National fame was still in the future, but surely Hickok's life to that point must have thrilled and exhilarated fifteen-year-old Cody, and Hickok's image and personality would influence Cody deeply for the rest of his life, as will be seen in later chapters.

In Junction City that winter of 1866, Cody sought out Hickok, who helped his young friend out and got him a job as a scout. The work must have been intermittent, however, because it is reported that Cody spent some of that cold winter in a dugout with a man named Northrup.[11]

Junction City was founded in 1858, one city on the string of pearls built along the Kansas River in Kansas Territory prior to statehood, including Lawrence, Topeka, Manhattan, Abilene, and Salina. From 1866 through 1870, Hickok was in and out of Junction City quite a bit. It has been reported that Hickok boarded at the home of a family by the name of Dunston in the 300 block of West Sixth Street in the early time he lived here; i.e., 1866-1867.[12] That corresponds with the location of Hickok's saloon and gambling hall one street over on Seventh Street. On February 1, 1867, the *Leavenworth Conservative* mentioned the saloon obliquely, noting that Hickok "is now a gambler at Junction City, which statement we have no reason to doubt." Recalling Hickok's time residing in Junction City, the *Junction City Union* on August 19, 1876 stated that Hickok "formerly lived in this city and kept a saloon and gambling hell on Seventh street, about where Mrs. Kiehl's millinery store now stands." All of Hickok's saloon-keeping adventures in Junction City took place while he was a lawman of some sort and a scout for the frontier army. It would not be the last time he found himself in the saloon business.

9

1867

FORT RILEY *and* JUNCTION CITY

HARPER'S HITS *the* STREET

ANNA WILSON, *aka* INDIAN ANNIE

GOVERNMENT DETECTIVE *for* FORT RILEY

FORT HARKER *and* ELLSWORTH

SCOUT *for* CUSTER *and the* SEVENTH CAVALRY

DISPATCH COURIER THROUGH INDIAN TERRITORY

DEPUTY UNITED STATES MARSHAL

Fort Riley returns indicate that Hickok renewed his contract as a government detective with Richard B. Owen on January 1, 1867. On January 11, he and his partner Jack Harvey captured John Tobin and William Wilson, who had stolen mules from the fort. They confessed this to Hickok, who swore out a complaint the next day and delivered the pair for arrest to deputy U. S. Marshal Byron Farrell. By the time they came to trial in April, Hickok and Harvey were both out on the plains scouting for the army, yet the trial proceeded and the two mule thieves were convicted.[1]

In late January 1867, the February issue of *Harper's New Monthly Magazine* started filling mailboxes and store shelves throughout the country. Nichols' article on Wild Bill was the lead feature, with a full-length woodcut of James on the front cover, taken from a photograph made by Charles W. Scholten, made either in the lobby of the Lyon Hotel on South Street in Springfield, or in Scholten's studio located on the southwest corner of Springfield's public square. Thirteen pages long, with nine woodcut illustrations, it caused a sensation, especially in the East, but even in Europe, where *Harper's* had limited distribution. Yet it was immediately controversial as well, especially in southwest Missouri and Springfield itself, where James Butler Hickok was well-known and respected, even before the advent of *Harper's*.

On January 31, the *Springfield Patriot* responded on its editorial page. The editor must have had to buy extra printer's type to publish this editorial. Because it represents the response from Springfield, the home of Hickok and the location where much of Nichols' article took place, a location itself disparaged by Nichols' characterizations, it merits verbatim publication. Though the editor got a few facts wrong, for the most part the editorial is a razor-sharp, scorching indictment of Nichols and the lack of veracity in his article, "Wild Bill." Here it is in its long, unedited and compelling totality:

> *Springfield is excited. It has been so ever since the mail of the 25th brought Harper's Monthly to its numerous subscribers here.—The excitement, curiously enough, manifests itself in very opposite effects upon our citizens. Some are excessively indignant, but the great majority are in convulsions of laughter, which seems as interminable as yet. The cause of both abnormal moods, in our usually placid and quiet city, is the first article in Harpers for February, which all agree, if published at all, should have had its place in the "Editor's Drawer," with the other fabricated more or less funnyisms; and not where it is, in the leading "illustrated" place. But, upon reflection, as Harper has given the same prominence to "Heroic Deeds of Heroic Men" by Rev. J.T. Headley, which, generally, are of about the same character as its article "Wild Bill," we will not question the good taste of its "make up."*

We are importuned by the angry ones to review it. "For," say they, "it slanders our city and citizens so outrageously by its caricatures, that it will deter some from immigrating here, who believe its representations of our people."

"Are there any so ignorant?" we asked.

"Plenty of them in New England, and especially about the Hub, just as ready to swallow it all as Gospel truth, as a Johnny Chinaman or Japanese would be to believe that England, France and America are inhabited by cannibals."

"Don't touch it," cries the hilarious party, "don't spoil a richer morceaux than ever was printed in Gulliver's Travels, or Baron Munchausen! If it prevents any consummate fools from coming to Southwest Missouri, that's no loss."

So we compromise between the two demands, and give the article but brief and inadequate criticism. Indeed, we do not imagine that we could do it justice, if we made ever so serious and studied an attempt to do so.

A good many of our people—those especially who frequent the bar rooms and lager-beer saloons, will remember the author of the article, when we mention one "Colonel" G.W. Nichols, who was here for a few days in the summer of 1865, splurging around among our "strange, half-civilized people", seriously endangering the supply of lager and corn whiskey, and putting on more airs than a spotted stud-horse in the ring of a county fair. He's the author! And if the illustrious holder of one of the "Brevet" commissions which Fremont issued his wagonmasters, will come back to Springfield, two-thirds of all the people he meets will invite him to "pis'n hisself with suth'n" for the fun he unwittingly furnished them in his article—the remaining one third will kick him wherever met, for lying like a dog upon the city and people of Springfield.

James B. Hickok, (not "William Hitchcock" as the "Colonel" mis-names his hero) is a remarkable man, and is as well known here as Horace Greeley in New York or Henry Wilson in "the Hub." The portrait of him on the first page of Harper for February is a most faithful and striking likeness—features, shape, posture, and dress—in all it is a faithful reproduction of one of Charley Scholten's photographs of "Wild Bill", as he is generally called. No finer physique, no greater strength, no more personal courage, no steadier nerves, no superior skill with the pistol, no better horsemanship than his, could any man of the million

133

Federal soldiers of the war, boast of; and few did better or more loyal service as soldier throughout the war. But Nichols "cuts it very fat" when he describes Bill's feats in arms. We think his hero only claims to have sent a few dozen rebs to the farther side of Jordan; and we never, before reading the "Colonel's" article, suspected he had dispatched "several hundreds with his own hands." But it must be so, for the "Colonel" asserts it with a parenthesis of genuine flavorous Bostonian piety, to assure us of his incapacity to utter an untruth.

We dare say that Captain Kelso, our present member of Congress, did double the execution "with his own hands" on the Johnnies, during the war, that Bill did. This is no disparagement to Bill. Except his "mate" Tom Martin (who swore yesterday that Nichol's pathetic description of his untimely murder in 1863, in that article, was not true) Bill was the best scout, by far in the Southwest.

The equestrian scenes given are purely imaginary. The extraordinary black mare, Nell (which was in fact a black stallion, blind in the right eye, and "a goer"), wouldn't "fall as if struck by a cannonball" when Hickok "slowly waved his hand over her head with a circular motion," worth a cent. And none of our citizens ever saw her (or him) "wink affirmatively" to Bill's mention of her (or his) great sagacity. Nor did she (or he) ever jump upon the billiard table at the Lyon House at "William's low whistle;" and if Bill had (as the "Colonel" describes it on his own veracity) mounted her in Ike Hoff's saloon and "with one bound, lit in the middle of the street," he would have got a severe fall in the doorway of the bar room, sure, to make no mention of clearing at "one bound" a porch twelve feet wide, and five feet high, a pavement twelve feet, and half the width of the roadway (twenty-five feet by actual measurement) making a total of forty-nine feet, without computing any margin inside the room from which she (or he) "bounded."

We are sorry to say also that the graphic account of the terrible fight at Mrs. Waltman's, in which Bill killed, solitary and alone, "the guerrilla McKandlas and ten of his men"- the whole bilen of 'em- is not reliable. The fact upon which this account is founded, being, that before the war, and while yet out in the mountains, Wild Bill did fight and kill one McKandlas and two other men, who attacked him simultaneously. These little rivulets in the monthlies, weeklies and dailies, all run into and make up the great river of history afterwhile; and if many of them are as salty as this one, the main stream will be very brackish at least. We must, therefore tell the truth to "vindicate history."

Bill never was in the tight place narrated, and exhibited in the illustrating wood cut, where half down on the edge of Mrs. Waltman's bed, with his bowie-knife up to the hilt in one bushwhacker's heart, with half a dozen dead men upon the floor in picturesque attitudes; two of the three remaining desperadoes have their knives puncturing his waistcoat, and the final one of the ten is leveling terrific blows at his head with a clubbed musket. We congratulate Bill on the fact that that picture and narrative was rather not true. It would have been too risky, even for Bill, the "Scout of the Plains."

We have not time or space to follow the article further. We protest, however, that our people do not dress in "greasy skins", and bask in the sunshine prone upon our pavements. We will die in the belief that we have people as smart, and even as well dressed as "Colonel" G.W. Nichols. Mrs. E. M. Bowen advertises in our columns the latest styles of "postage stamp" bonnets, and Mde. Demorest's fashions, for our ladies; and we know that Shipley has not been in fault, if our gentlemen are not presentable in costume, even in the "salons" of the Hub.

We must add that so far as we are capable of judging, "Captain Honesty" (who can forget more than Nichols ever knew, and scarcely miss it) speaks very intelligible, good English. He was at least considered so capable and reliable an A.Q.M. as to be retained by the War Department for more than a year after the war had closed, and his regiment mustered out, to administer and settle the government affairs in one of the most important posts in the country.

In reading the romantic and pathetic parts of the article, "the undercurrent about a woman" in his quarrel and fatal fight with Dave Tutt; and his remarks with "quivering lips and tearful eyes" about his old mother in Illinois, we tried to fancy Bill's familiar face while listening to the passage being read. We could almost hear his certain remark, "Oh hell! What a d—n fool that Nichols is." We agree with "Wild Bill" on that point.

The die was cast. George Ward Nichols' *Harper's* piece would influence to a great degree the public's perception of James Butler Hickok's alter-ego Wild Bill for the rest of the nineteenth century and well into the twentieth century, especially after James Buel in the 1880s used Nichol's article as the main source shaping what he wrote about Hickok in the very popular and widely distributed *Heroes of the Plains*. It would be the 1920s before writer Frank Wilstach made an attempt

#4110

February 1867 photograph by Leavenworth photographer E.E. Henry. In February that year James visited Leavenworth with his common-law wife Anna Wilson. 1867 was quite a year for young Mr. Hickok, just 29 until his birthday in May. Harper's hit the street in late January, overnight catapulting him from regional notoriety to national fame with their lead story Wild Bill by George Ward Nichols. By April he was working as a scout and guide for George Armstrong Custer, both simultaneously receiving their initiation into Indian warfare that spring. By summer he was undertaking even more dangerous work at Custer's behest, as a courier delivering military dispatches by riding long distances by night on a swift and sure-fitted mule across the dark plains teeming with warring Indians. By early fall Hickok was undertaking his first work as a deputy United States Marshal. *Author's collection.*

to introduce some facts into the Hickok saga, yet that first attempt fell somewhat short. In 1964, a smart and motivated Englishman named Joseph Rosa wrote the first serious biography of Hickok, yet Rosa accepted some of Nichols', Buel's, and Connelley's myths in with his factual findings, and the edition suffered for it. But Rosa hit his stride in 1974 when he wrote the second edition of his 1964 biography of Hickok, *They Called Him Wild Bill*. By 1974, Rosa had gained command of all of the sources available at that time, along with the indispensable advantage of the Hickok family eager to provide him much information to set the record straight. The result was an almost completely new book from the first 1964 edition. This 1974 second edition of *They Called Him Wild Bill* was, for many years, the gold standard of Hickok biographies, and writers since 1974 attempting their own biography of Hickok walk through many fields plowed and seeded by the late Joseph Rosa.

Anna Wilson, a.k.a. Indian Annie, wife of James Butler Hickok, appeared on the scene in 1867. In its February 13, 1867 issue, the *Leavenworth Daily Bulletin* matter-of-factly reported the arrival of Hickok and his wife in Leavenworth: "...recently arrived from the Far West with trains loaded with furs, peltries, and buffalo robes. Wild Bill brings his wife along, and is resting at the Brevoort. The value of the furs and robes he brings with him is said to exceed $20,000."

The familiarity with which the newspaper mentions Hickok's common-law wife Anna Wilson (no marriage certificate has been found) indicates that it was already common knowledge in Leavenworth that he had a wife. It is generally accepted that the wife referred to was none other than Anna Wilson, as later events were to prove out.

Six days later, subtly noting Hickok's overnight fame engendered by the February *Harper's*, the *Leavenworth Daily Conservative* on February 19, 1867 reported: "'Wild Bill.' This somewhat noted individual was in the city yesterday, having recently arrived from Riley with a lot of furs and skins. He was the observed of a good many observers."

Two weeks later, James and Anna moved on to Atchison, where the editor of the *Atchison Weekly Free Press* took note in the March 2, 1867 issue:

PERSONAL.– Yesterday we had a call from Major James Butler Hickok, the "Wild Bill" of Harper's Magazine. The Major is in good health and fine spirits, and enjoys himself in the very best manner. He is stopping a few days in our place, on business entirely his own, and seems to be the observed of all observers. "Wild Bill" did good service during the war for the Union cause, although he is fierce as a lion when aroused on the side of right, he is ordinarily as gentle as a lamb. If we are the judge of human nature, "Wild Bill" has a heart as big as an ox, and would scorn to do a mean act.

Soon James and Anna returned to their home in Junction City, just south of Fort Riley. By April James was off again on a long trip, this time as a guide and scout with General Hancock's campaign to meet the Indians on the Pawnee Fork. Anna undoubtedly stayed home in Junction City.

Anna Wilson, aka Indian Annie, had parents who were born in North Carolina. Her father was a white man, and her mother was a Cherokee Indian. It is likely that her family came west on the Cherokee "Trail of Tears" in 1838. Anna was born in Arkansas, apparently in 1846 or 1847, which makes her about nineteen or twenty when she and James met. She claimed to have come to Kansas from the Indian Territory (modern Oklahoma).[2]

For almost five years Anna and James were together, from the winter of 1866 till the fall of 1871, spanning many of James Butler Hickok's legend- building adventures as Wild Bill: sheriff, deputy U. S. Marshal, government detective, guide and scout for the frontier army, Indian fighter, pistol shot extraordinaire, even saloon keeper. Through Junction City, Ellsworth, Hays City and finally Abilene they were together, yet only a few glimpses of Anna during that time are available.

In 1870 Anna was living in Hays City. The 1870 U. S. census, taken at Hays City on June 24 and 25, listed as living there "Annie Wilson, an Indian." James also lived in Hays City, presumably with Anna, yet he must have been away on those dates because he was not listed on the census. Yet he was certainly back in Hays by July 17, when he was in a legendary and deadly scuffle with two soldiers in Tommy Drum's saloon.

Anna and Hickok moved to Abilene in 1871, where Hickok, in his most famous law-enforcement role, became sheriff. J. B. Edwards of Abilene recalled, "One of his favorites in Abilene was supposed to have been an Indian girl whom he kept in a nice little cottage on the outskirts of town."[3]

We will revisit James and Anna later in this book, near the end of their relationship, for the rest of their story, and the previously little-known story of their child.

Fort Riley post returns show that in March and April Hickok was listed as a wagon master, yet by April he actually was a guide and scout for Hancock at pay of $100 per month. He served in this position from April through August for George Armstrong Custer and the newly formed 7th Cavalry.

Custer and wife Libbie had arrived at Fort Riley in about the middle of October, 1866. They came on the Union Pacific Railroad, Eastern Division (which would soon be known as the Kansas Pacific Railroad). They literally came to the end of the track: It extended about 110 miles from Kansas City to about 10 miles east of Fort Riley. Their small entourage and dogs came the rest of the way in three horse-drawn ambulances, the frontier equivalent of taxis.

On November 9, Custer reported to Washington to appear before an examining board that tested newly appointed officers. Custer took proficiency tests there to establish his suitability as an officer. He passed these tests easily, and returned to Fort Riley on December 16. Custer had come to Fort Riley to take command of the newly formed 7th Cavalry. By the end of 1866, the 7th Cavalry counted 963 men commanded by fifteen officers.[4]

On April 6, 1867, a soldier's letter from Fort Harker, Kansas was printed in the *Boston Transcript*. From it, Eastern readers read of the first days of the Hancock Indian campaign out West in this particularly insightful soldier's letter.

FORT HARKER, KANSAS

There are as yet no signs of Spring. March 13th our thermometer showed five degrees below zero at noon, and to-night as the north wind started anew on its wild journey and two of the neighboring tents blew down, we wondered if old Robert Thomas wasn't turning in his grave at such an upsetting of almanac predictions. The wind knows no rest; it rushes by with its hot breath in Summer, blasting and drying up all the garden vegetables. The dryness of the air is something wonderful. Meat never spoils. We tasted a beefsteak a month old, which was a little dry to be sure, but as sweet as ever.

We witnessed in February a curious specimen of mirage. One afternoon, as if to atone for non-appearance on preceding days, three distinct suns became visible in the heavens, and the same night the moon showed triple.

The great Indian expedition is at last on the war path. We quiet dwellers in mud huts and wall-tents were startled, April 1st, to see the soldierly form of Hancock enter garrison, followed by Generals Smith, Davidson, Custer and Mitchell. Five generals and thirteen hundred troops pouring in roused us from our squalor to something like excitement. They camped beside the Smoky River two days, and then departed for Fort Larned. The long, fair hair of Custer streaming in the wind, seemed most tempting to the scalp loving population. The expedition comprised six companies of the Seventh Cavalry, seven of the Thirty-seventh Infantry, a battery of the Fourth Artillery, and a pontoon train. "Wild Bill," whose incredible adventures you have all seen in Harper's Magazine for February, was with the party as courier, and a few Delaware Indians with their war paint on added to the interest of the procession. They hate their wilder brethren as only their revengeful race can hate, and their services will be correspondingly valuable to General Hancock...The greatest attraction in the whole procession to us was a Cheyenne boy six years of age, who is being carried back to his tribe. During the war a Colonel Chivington fell upon a camp of Cheyennes, and murdered men, women, and children, except two infants concealed and saved by some privates in the command. This boy is the sole survivor of the Chivington massacre. The other child died...

What is to be done by the expedition only the powers that be know. Perhaps following the example of the "King of France, with twenty thousand men," may be sufficient to awe the red man into decency; but General Hancock, followed by some of the men who fought under his banner on the Potomac, will not stop short of putting an end to all future trouble, at whatever risk. General Sherman has recommended that the Sioux be slaughtered without mercy, but such extreme measures may not be necessary with these southern tribes.

We are reduced to two companies of infantry here; one of these will be relieved next week by the 38th "Brunottes", as the U.S.C.I. are considerably termed. The expedition deprived us of our Post Commander, General Gibbs, whose genial presence is enough to make endurable a "lodge in a vast wilderness". He is one of the few left of the old Army, and a model soldier and gentleman for the younger officers of the new.

The many deserters from the Seventh Cavalry during the Winter are no doubt chuckling in their hiding places over their escape from Indian fighting, and rejoicing that they left stealthily the land where hair has an upward tendency. As six months imprisonment is the heaviest punishment which can be inflicted on a deserter, if he is caught, a man doesn't risk much in leaving Uncle Samuel's protection. Most hard cases would prefer six months in prison to a year in the service.

In July sutlers are abolished, and those officers who happen to be on duty in the Commissary Department will be the objects of pity, as the Government proposes to keep for sale to troops nearly all sutler's goods. As an officer expressed it, "If I am appointed Commissary after July 1st I shall resign; if I must keep a grocery store I prefer to do it in civil life, where it is rather more lucrative than on lieutenant's pay in the Army." Still, if the plan can be carried out successfully, troops can be supplied with all necessaries at the outposts much cheaper than sutlers can sell.

The Hancock Expedition left Fort Riley at 8:30 on the morning of March 27, 1867. The expansive column included 1,400 men: seven companies of the 37th Infantry, eight companies of the 7th Cavalry, Battery B of the 4th Artillery, many six-mule wagons, nine engineers, a canvas pontoon bridge, two Indian agents, fifteen Delaware Indians, interpreter Edmund Guerrier, and, among the scouts and guides, James Butler Hickok and James Harvey. Notwithstanding his sterling performance as a Union general during the Civil War, Custer had never before fought against Indians, He also had never before been on the plains of Kansas. This was the first formal Indian campaign for Hickok as well. Two journalists traveled with the column. Henry Morton Stanley of the *New York Herald* rode with the Hancock campaign, and Theodore Davis of *Harper's Weekly* joined Hancock at Fort Zarah. Stanley was instantly enamored of and thunderstruck by the charismatic Hickok. Theodore Davis, not so much.[5]

After their March 27 departure from Fort Harker, Henry Stanley (not yet having found Livingston in the wilds of Africa) wrote his first report on Hickok for the *New York Herald*. Writing after Hancock's column had reached Fort Zarah, and dated April 4, it appeared in print on April 16, just two months after the sensational and controversial Nichols article on Wild Bill Hickok in the February *Harper's New Monthly Magazine*. James was still somewhat uncomfortable with his newfound fame, and still somewhat embarrassed by the gross exaggerations that

Nichols put into print, especially Nichols' version of the McCanles story and his tales of Black Nell.

Sarcasm, irony and even satire sometimes do not translate well from the human voice and human facial cues onto the printed page. Read Stanley's report with that perspective; a very perceptive assessment by Stanley of Hickok's physical attributes and charismatic presence, followed by Hickok's sarcastic and tongue-in-cheek satirical report of a fanciful time in Leavenworth that thematically seems to be much like Nichols' exaggerated description of the McCanles battle:

James Butler Hickok, commonly called "Wild Bill", is one of the finest examples of that peculiar class known as Frontiersman, ranger, hunter, and Indian scout. He is now thirty-eight years old, and since he was thirteen the prairie has been his home. He stands six feet one inch in his moccasins, and is as handsome a specimen of a man as could be found. Harper's correspondent recently gave a sketch of the career of this remarkable man, which excepting a slight exaggeration, was correct. We were prepared, on hearing of "Wild Bill's" presence in the camp, to see a person who would prove a coarse, illiterate, quarrelsome, obtrusive, obstinate, bully; in fact, one of those ruffians to be found South and West, who delight in shedding blood. We confess to being agreeably disappointed when, on being introduced to him, we looked upon a person who was the very reverse of all we had imagined. He was dressed in a black-saque coat, brown pants, fancy shirt, leather leggings, and had on his head a beaver cap. Tall, straight, broad compact shoulders, herculean chest, narrow waist, and well-formed muscular limbs. A fine handsome face, free from any blemish, a light moustach, a thin pointed nose, bluish-grey eyes, with a calm, quiet, benignant look, yet seemingly possessing some mysterious latent power, a magnificent forehead, hair parted from the center of the forehead and hanging down behind the ears in long, wavy, silk curls. He is brave, there can be no doubt; that fact is impressed on you at once before he utters a syllable. He is neither as coarse and illiterate as Harper's Monthly portrays him...

The following verbatim dialogue took place between us: "I say, Bill, or Mr. Hickok, how many white men have you killed to your certain knowledge?" After a little deliberation, he replied, "I would be willing to take my oath on the Bible tomorrow that I have killed over a hundred, a long ways off." "What made you kill all these men; did you kill them without cause or provocation?" "No, by Heaven! I never killed one man without good cause." "How old were you when you killed the first white man, and for what cause?" "I was twenty eight years old when I killed the first white man, and if ever a man deserved killing he did. He was a gambler and counterfeiter, and I was in a hotel in Leavenworth City then, and seeing some loose characters around, I ordered a room, and as I had some money about me, I thought I would go to it. I had lain some thirty minutes on the bed, when I heard some men at my door. I pulled out my revolver and bowie-knife and held them ready, but half concealed, still pretending to be asleep. The door was opened, and five men entered the room. They whispered together 'let us kill the son of a b—h; I'll bet he has got money.' "Gentlemen," said he further, "that was a time—an awful time. I kept perfectly still until just as the knife touched my breast; I sprang aside and buried mine in his heart, and then used my revolvers on the others right and left. Only one was wounded, besides the one killed, and, then gentlemen, I dashed through the room and rushed to the fort, procured a lot of soldiers, came to the hotel and captured the whole gang of them, fifteen in all. We searched the cellar and found eleven bodies buried there- men who were murdered by those villains." Turning to us, he asked "Would you have not done the same? That was the first man I killed, and I never was sorry for that yet."

There are two versions of Stanley's report, and they are both credited as being published in the *St. Louis Weekly Missouri Democrat.* The version above is the more expansive of the two. The other version is heavily edited; some phrases are changed, and some passages are deleted completely. Most of what is edited out appears to be statements that might be offensive at that time to people of eastern and southern Missouri.

Theodore Davis, the other journalist riding on the Hancock expedition, found Hickok at Fort Zarah as well. Davis wrote his own report on Hickok, but he wrote it from memory almost thirty years later, probably supplemented with contemporary notes or a journal, indicated by the specificity of the report. Perhaps Davis wrote it to be published, yet for unknown reasons it never appeared until 1946. The enmity revealed in his recollection by both Davis and Hickok may have its roots in the fact that Theodore Davis was a journalist and illustrator for *Harper's Weekly.* For Hickok it gave him the opportunity to say to Davis what he really wanted to say to Nichols. For Davis it may have been jealousy that it was Nichols, and not Davis, that got to write the magnum opus "Wild Bill" for *Harper's*. That may have been exacerbated by the fact that Davis didn't like Henry Stanley, either; he once even accused him of being a forger. Libbie Custer, who knew Davis, referred to him as "an insufferable bore. His conceit confuses me."[6] Davis recalled, some three decades later, Hickok at Fort Zarah on April 4 or 5:

> *This was the situation, when toward dusk one afternoon I was seated on the ground wrapped in a blanket for warmth, and just by the opening of the tent to catch enough of the waning light to finish a drawing over which I was shivering—and my then special aversion, "Wild Bill" sauntered up. Seeing that he was not welcome, the Scouts stay was short and starting off remarked with some irony, "Ther's another dodgusted sardine of a newspaper cuss bunken in the sutlers shack what wants my mind."* [Shades of Nichols! Did everyone at Harper's apply a phony hillbilly syntax to every astute and educated frontiersman they interviewed and wrote about?] *I see you don't!" A fellow worker and sufferer in camp: This was news, and I was not long in starting, for the sod structure toward which the festive "Bill" who's right name was "Jim" had swaggered away in a miff.*
>
> *It was thus I found Stanley and promptly effected his rescue from the deluge of romance with which the voluble plains man was flooding him. The trip was Stanleys first experience of the Great American Desert—located by school geographers on their maps—It was not mine— And in characters novel to him Stanley was searching for the "Leather stocking" element of which as he said not even a shadow materialized. Both garments and character of honest old Natty Bumpo seemed a shocking misfit, for the self named "Wild Bills" and Texas Jacks.*

The next morning Stanley awoke and discovered that his saddle blanket and some personal equipment had been stolen, apparently by a group of deserters. Davis continued:

> *It is here worthwhile to describe "Wild Bill" whom we determined upon as the most available individual for chief operator, although our confidence in the critter was slim. This man was by nature a dandy, sufficiently vain of his personal appearance. phisique and constitution—gifts of nature which had thus far—proved armor for his mad gallop, amid regularities the end of which only: has connection with*

the word moral. Even his countenance was then unmarked by dissipation; In his usual array "Wild Bill" could have gained unquestioned admittance to the floor—of most fancy dress balls in metropolitan cities. When we ordinary mortals were hustling for a clean pair of socks, as prospective limit of change in wearing apparel, I have seen "Wild Bill" appear in an immaculate boiled shirt, with much collar and cuffs to match—a sleeveless Zouave jacket of startling scarlet, slashed with black velvet. The entire garment being over ornamented with buttons which if not silver seem to be. The trousers might be either black velvet or buck skin and like his jacket fitted with buttons quite beyond useful requirement. The French calf skin boots worn with this costume fitted admirably, and were polished as if the individual wearing them had recently vacated an Italians arm chair throne on a side street near Broadway. The long wavey hair that fell in masses from beneath a conventional sombrero was glossy from a recent anointment of some heavily perfumed mixture. As far as dress went only, "Wild Bill" was to border plainsmen what "Beau" Neil was to the Army of the Potomac—faultlessly clad under surprising circumstances. In fact I don't believe that it would have occasioned comment had the scout produced and deliberately fitted on, kid gloves matching perfectly his expansive necktie. Contrasted with this figure, the usual scout or guide, clad in such garments as his last opportunity for a ready-made outfit afforded, the gallus Wild Bill was a feature in the landscape to attract attention. Uncertainty was created as to Wild Bills legal name after it had been printed as Wm Hitchcock, Wm Hancock, and Wm Hickock, also Wm Haycock, and you were told that "Jim" Hicock was correct. This unique being, now the object of our quest, was with but little difficulty made favorably inclined to Stanleys proposition to go on a deserter hunt.

...when the Ranch was surrounded, "Wild Bill" upon his own suggestion stole noiselessly and alone to the door, gaining admittance after a short parley...An element of danger ample to interest every participant pervaded the movement and "Wild Bills" action dispelled something of a veil of doubt which in our minds clouded the title to genuineness of personal incidents narrated as fact by that gay party.[7]

Davis later conceded, however, that Hickok's "qualifications as an interpreter and scout are said, by those best qualified to judge, to be unsurpassed by any white man on the plains."[8]

March winds of the plains blew through March and into April; "a strong prairie wind blowing right in our faces, strong enough to blow us over," wrote one officer.[9] That night's first camp, Custer kept to himself in his Sibley tent. Within days he wrote to Libbie, "Contemplating these vast and apparently boundless prairies seems to give me new life."[10] As the column wound through the treeless prairie to Fort Larned, snow fell, piling up to two feet. Winter was not finished on the Kansas prairie, even in April. On April 1, the column reached Fort Harker, where two additional cavalry companies and an infantry company joined the entourage. On April 4 or 5, the column reached Fort Zarah, and soon continued on toward Fort Larned. The Hancock Expedition reached Fort Larned on April 7, and went into camp a mile east of the fort on the Pawnee Fork River. For five nights this large military force awaited contact with warriors from the Cheyenne and Sioux camp about thirty-three miles to the west.

The evening of April 12 found Custer and Hancock in front of a warming fire with fellow officers while fifteen men of the Cheyenne nation shook their hands. The Indian agent Edward W. Wynkoop introduced the leaders, Tall Bull and White Horse. Hancock spoke first, telling the Cheyenne that he had a great and powerful army, and that he had come to make war, because he had heard they wanted war. He demanded they return captives. He explained that great railroads were coming, and there was nothing the Cheyenne could do to stop it. For his part Tall Bull talked briefly to Hancock about a Cheyenne boy that Hancock had brought to return to his family with the Cheyenne. (See the notation in the article above mentioning that same Cheyenne child.) Tall Bull told Hancock, "The buffalo are diminishing fast. The antelope that were plenty a few years ago are now few. When they will all die away we shall be hungry. We shall want something to eat, and we shall be compelled to come into the fort. Your young men must not fire on us. Whenever they see us they fire, and we fire on them."[11]

At one point, Hancock interrupted Tall Bull and said that he was coming to their village with all his men. When Tall Bull finished speaking, Hancock rose and again addressed him: "We know that the buffalo are going away. We cannot help it. The white men are becoming a great nation. You must keep your men off the roads [the trails and railroads]. Don't stop the trains and travelers on the roads, and you will not be harmed." As he turned to return to his tent, Hancock said imperiously, "I have spoken." The meeting ended.[12]

Hancock thought the Indians had disrespected him at the meeting, and he set out to intimidate them. The very next morning the entire column was on the move west toward the Indian camp. The night of April 13, a few of the Indian leaders came into Hancock's camp to tell him that they would be bringing all of the Indian leaders in their camp to meet with Hancock. The next morning these few Indian leaders left for their camp. They never returned.[13]

Furious, Hancock broke camp at noon on April 14 and marched his troops toward the Indian camp.[14] They had traveled west just a few miles when, "reaching the summit of a little hill, we beheld in the valley, a mile distant, several hundred Indian warriors approaching us. They were in a line...everything now looked like war...," observed a Dr. Coates,[15] traveling with Hancock's column. Custer himself later wrote about the scene: "They were formed in a line, with intervals, extending about a mile. The sun was shining brightly, and as we arrived the scene was the most picturesque and novel I have ever witnessed. What rendered the scene so striking and so magnificent were the gaudy colors of the dress and trappings of the chiefs and warriors."[16]

Forestalling what seemed like an inevitable battle, several of the Cheyenne and Sioux chiefs persuaded Hancock that negotiations could continue when Hancock had moved further west and encamped near their village. These Cheyenne and Sioux chiefs returned to their line several yards away, and the entire line turned west and rapidly galloped away. Custer and his men pursued them at Hancock's order, yet, "Notwithstanding that the cavalry marched at its most rapid pace, there was not an Indian to be seen after marching five miles."[17] Custer returned to Hancock's column, and they moved to within a mile of the village the evening of April 14. Several Cheyenne men approached Hancock's encampment and said that the women and children had fled. One of the chiefs, Roman Nose, asked if Hancock had not heard of the Sand Creek Massacre. Later that evening Hancock's interpreter Guerrier reported that the men of the village were planning to leave shortly. Hancock ordered Custer to stop them.

Custer had the village surrounded by midnight. He led a small party into the village. From the moonlight he could tell the teepees still stood and fires were still burning. Going from lodge to lodge, they found that the village was completely abandoned. Albert Barnitz wrote about it the next day: "On entering the camp, I was astonished at its magnitude and magnificence. Each tent would contain twenty or thirty persons."[18] Hancock ordered an inventory: 272 teepees, 814 buffalo robes, 283 saddles, 243 whetstones, 165 frying pans, 49 coffee mills, and brass kettles, bridles, spades, ropes, hatchets, horn spoons, crowbars, tin cups and plates, and much more. Now Hancock and Custer realized that the impressive, mile-wide Indian line that looked for all the world like a hostile move was really a stalling technique. Outraged that the Indians had made their escape, in a fit of pique Hancock ordered the entire magnificent Indian village to be burnt to the ground. The order read:

Headquarters Department of the Missouri, in the field.
Camp No. 15, Pawnee Fork, Kansas April 18th, 1867
Special Field Orders No. 13

As a punishment for the bad faith practiced by the Cheyenne and Sioux who occupied the Indian Village at this place, and as a chastisement for murder and depredation committed since the arrival of the command at this point by the people of those tribes, the village recently occupied by them which is now in our hands will be entirely destroyed. All property within the village, such as tools, camp equipage etc., will be preserved and taken up as captured property by Captain G W Bradley, Chief Quartermaster of the Expedition. Brevet Major General J.W. Davidson, Major 2nd inf. Cavalry, Acting Inspector of this Department will take an accurate inventory of all species of property in the village, previous to the destruction. Brevet Major Genl A J Smith, Colonel 7th Cavalry, Commanding Dist of the Upper Arkansas, is charged with the execution of this order.

By Command of Major Genl Hancock
Signed W.G. Mitchell, Captn and A.A.A. General

The Indian agent of the Comanche and Kiowa, Jesse H. Leavenworth, later voiced his astonishment that Hancock "marched his column right up to the Indian village."[19] Hancock and Custer knew that these Cheyenne and Sioux feared another Sand Creek Massacre like the one Chivington carried out in 1864. Leavenworth added, "I am fearful that the result of all this will be a general war."[20] Leavenworth's fears came to pass. Hancock's missteps and bumbling resulted in a heightened and bloody Indian war across the Kansas plains. Instead of quashing the latent Indian uprising, Hancock set the Kansas plains on fire, figuratively and literally.

Scout Danny Bohen succinctly recalled these events years later for William Connelley: "In 1867 Hickok started with Generals Hancock and Custer. We moved up the Pawnee to the Arrapahoe Camp. The Indians agreed to come to terms, but deserted in the night. Hickok and myself took the dispatches to Fort Larned. General Hancock burned 185 tepees. Next morning General Custer followed the Indians, scattered them, and he turned back. We went overland to Fort Dodge. Hickok stayed with Custer, and I went to Fort Union with the 37th Infantry."[21]

Hancock ordered Custer and his men to pursue the fleeing Indians. Just before dawn on April 15, Custer led eight cavalry companies and numerous supply wagons northwest, along with interpreter Edmund Guerrier and six Delaware Indians, as well as J. B. Hickok and two other scouts. They headed northwest. At Downer's Station, Custer found two men who talked of a possible Indian attack at Lookout Station, thirty-five miles to the east. Later, riding up alone to Lookout Station, Custer recalled he "found the station house, stable, & haystack a pile of ashes, a few pieces of timber being still burning. The bodies of the three men were lying near the ruins. The hair was singed from their heads, the skin & flesh burned from their breasts and arms and their intestines torn out."[22]

The next day Custer and Hickok and the men reached Fort Hays. The horses were in dire need of forage, grain and hay that Custer expected to find at Fort Hays, yet there was virtually none at the fort. Custer asked Hickok to ride to Fort Harker to request forage to be sent to Fort Hays. Albert Barnitz recalled that Hickok was to ride the seventy miles overnight to Fort Harker on a fresh mule, and that Hickok "was armed with two revolvers (and a carbine I had loaned him for the trip), and thought that he was good for a dozen Indians at all events."[23] Scout Danny Bohen recalled: "Hickok and myself took the dispatches to Fort Larned [Fort Harker]."[24] Hickok made it through to Fort Harker, but there was very little forage they could spare. Thus ended Hancock's Indian campaign, and the first ever for Custer and Hickok.

By May 11, Hickok was back in Junction City. Jack Harvey was with him. The *Junction City Weekly Union* that same day reported: "Wild Bill came in from the west the other day. He reports all quiet at the front. Jack Harvey has also returned. Hancock will be in in a day or so. Custer will be the only notable left behind." Henry Stanley was in Junction City as well, awaiting the train that would return him east. On May 11 Stanley, still captivated by the ever-charming Hickok, filed another report for his paper, the *New York Herald*:

"Wild Bill", who is an inveterate hater of the Indians, was... chased by six Indians lately, and had quite a little adventure with them. It is his custom to be always armed with a brace of ivory-handled revolvers, with which weapons he is marvelously dexterous; but when bound on a long and lonely ride across the plains, he goes armed to the teeth. He was on one of those lonely missions, due to his profession as scout, when he was seen by a group of the red men, who immediately gave chase. They soon discovered they were pursuing one of the most famous men of the prairie, and commenced to retrace their steps, but two of them were shot, after which Wild Bill was left to ride on his way. The little adventure is verified by a scout named [Thomas] Kincaid, who, while bearing despetches for General Custer, was also obliged to use his weapons freely. The lives of these Indian scouts are made up of these little experiences.

Soon James was performing dangerous duty as a regular dispatch courier. Albert Barnitz on June 18 wrote from Stormy Hollow station, thirty miles west of Fort Hays: "Wild Bill is here—he has just come up, bearing dispatches to the posts further west."[25] Western Kansas was ablaze with rumors of Indian attack. Libbie Custer wrote to her husband a week after General Smith had removed her and other women from Fort Hays and moved them east to Fort Riley on June 16: "Rumors and true reports of Indians," she said, "came in so fast to General Smith that he knew he ought to be at Harker, and that we women ought to be in a safe place. We left in an amazing hurry...at dark a week ago Sunday."[26] Fanny Kelly had been a captive of the Sioux in Wyoming in 1864, gaining her national notoriety. She and husband Josiah came from Shawnee, Kansas, to the new upstart city of Ellsworth in 1867. She wrote: "I was the first woman located there. We lived in our wagon for a time, then built a hotel, and were prospering." She told of her fear of Indians that spring of 1867:

A terrible dread of again falling into their hands intensified my apprehensions for our safety. The scouts, Jack Harvey and 'Wild Bill', were constantly on the lookout, and eagerly would we look toward the hills for any one who could give us news and gather around them, when they came from the front, with anxious faces and listening ears...military companies were formed for protection. Thus we lived in a continual state of alarm, until at last one night the signal was given that the Indians

#4063

1867 photograph taken by the S. Weinsell Art Gallery in Junction City. Probably taken May 1867 in Junction City at the end of the Hancock Indian campaign, just a month before Hickok became a regular dispatch courier for Custer. *Author's collection.*

were approaching, when every man flew to his post and the woman and children fled to the places of refuge that had been prepared for them, an iron-clad house and a 'dug out', or place under ground. I fled to the latter place, where about fifty altogether had congregated...The Indians were repulsed, but they continued to harass us and threaten the town, so that it became necessary to apply for military protection.[27]

Charles H. Sternberg recalled an incident during this Indian panic taking place that summer of 1867 that involved J.B. Hickok. Seventeen-year-old Charles lived with his twin brother Edward on their homestead just over two miles from Fort Harker. He wrote:

In July, 1867, owing to the fear of an Indian outrage, General A. J. Smith gave us at the ranch a guard of ten colored soldiers under a colored sergeant, and all the settlers gathered in the stockade, a structure about twenty feet long and fourteen wide, built by settling a row of cottonwood logs in a trench and roofing them over with split logs, brush, and earth. During the height of the excitement, the women and children slept on one side of the building in a long bed on the floor, and the men on the other side.

The night of the third of July was so sultry that I concluded to sleep outside on the hay-covered shed. At the first streak of dawn I was awakened by the report of a Winchester, and springing up, heard the sergeant call to his men, who were scattered in rifle pits around the building, to fall in line.

As soon as he had them lined up, he ordered them to fire across the river in the direction of some cottonwoods, to which a band of Indians had retreated. The whites came forward with guns in their hands and offered to join the fight, but the sergeant commanded: "Let the citizens keep to the rear." This, indeed, they were very willing to do when the order was given. "Fire at will!" and the soldiers began sending leaden balls whizzing through the air in every conceivable arc, but never in a straight line, toward the enemy, who were supposed to be lying on the ground.

As soon as it was light my brother and I explored the river and found a place where seven braves, in their moccasined feet, had run across a wet sand bar in the direction of the cottonwoods, as the sergeant had said. Their pony trails could easily be seen in the high wet grass.

The party in the stockade were not reassured to hear the tramp of a large body of horsemen, especially as the soldiers had fired away all their ammunition; but the welcome clank of sabers and jingle of spurs laid their fears to rest, and soon a couple of troops of cavalry, with an officer in command, rode up through the gloom.

After the sergeant had been severely reprimanded for wasting the ammunition, the scout Wild Bill was ordered to explore the country for Indian signs. But although the tracks could not have been plainer, his report was so reassuring that the whole command returned to the Fort.

Some hours later I spied this famous scout at the sutler's store, his chair tilted back against the stone wall, his two ivory-mounted revolvers hanging at his belt, the target of all eyes among the garrison loafers. As I came up this gallant called out "Well Sternberg, your boys were pretty well frightened this morning by some buffalo that came down to water."

"Buffalo!" I said; "that trail was made by our old cows two weeks ago."

Later the general in command told me that they had prepared for a big hop at the Fort on the night of the fourth, and that Bill did not report the Indian tracks because he did not want to be sent off on a long scout just then.[28]

By July we find Hickok apparently moonlighting, in addition to his plains-wide courier duties, as a scout for Colonel Augustus Armes. Perhaps not really moonlighting; James was still on the payroll of the 7th Cavalry and would be till August. He would simply be carrying out whatever duties he was assigned by his senior officer; that is, Custer. This really indicates that James was in great demand for his wide-ranging and unique skills. Consider that top pay at that time for a scout or courier was considered to be $75 a month. Hickok never received less than $100 a month. Colonel Armes wrote in his journal:

Camp Near Bunker Hill, Kansas, July 9, 1867. Just as I sat down to breakfast this morning General Smith [of Fort Harker] *sent orders for me to take thirty men and scout up the Smoky Hill river to Wilson creek to capture and punish a war party of Indians reported to be depredating in that vicinity. Wild Bill, my guide, reports fresh signs of Indians this evening.*[29]

Later in July Hickok switched back to his prior assignment as dispatch courier. Theodore Davis, reporting while riding with Custer, wrote in the *Harper's Weekly* of July 29, 1867, a piece titled *General Custer's Scouts and Couriers*. He noted, "'Wild Bill' is at present one of General Hancock's couriers." In later years Hickok told his good friend, Captain Henry Lindsay of Topeka, that scouting for General Hancock (and for Custer), he passed through more danger every twenty-four hours than he had ever encountered in any week's service in the Civil War.[30]

Scout Danny Bohen left Hickok with Custer in early summer of 1867, and Bohen went to Fort Union. Returning in July, he recalled later: "I came back with the 5th Infantry 5th Company—Colonel Bankhead in command. I led him across the desert from Fort Lyon to Fort Wallace. I met "Buffalo Bill" or Cody, and Hickok at Fort Wallace when I arrived there. The cholera broke out at that time at Fort Wallace. Bill was still with General Custer. Custer moved down to Fort Harker and Hickok said he was going to quit when he got to Hays City."[31]

In July 1867 James was involved in an incident that showed he could settle disputes with his fists as well as his pistols. The incident was also a good illustration of his internal moral code, that did not tolerate any kind of abuse of the weak or those that could not stand up for themselves. As indicated by Barnitz, above, Hickok was then a dispatch courier. At that time there was no telegraph between Fort Hays and Fort Wallace. Hickok was carrying weekly dispatches between the two forts and posts in between. Hickok's regular overnight stopover was at Monument Station, located about ninety miles west of Fort Hays and forty-five miles east of Fort Wallace. He stayed here with William Comstock, then the post guide at Fort Wallace. Monument Station, in today's Gove County, still retains chalk formations at the site that gave the station its name.

The station was run by Oliver Wiggins, and he and his family lived there. The station was originally guarded by a company of 7th Cavalry soldiers, who were removed from the post earlier that year to fight elsewhere. They were replaced by a disreputable group of civilian guards, described as "former Denver jailbirds who had volunteered to guard the station." While Oliver Wiggins was away from the station, the leader of the disreputables, named Dolan, insulted Mrs. Wiggins. It is not known just what he said to her, but it infuriated Hickok. A fistfight ensued, and James beat him badly, at one point "jumping on his face with both feet." He told them that when Oliver Wiggins returned, Wiggins would kill them all for insulting his wife. It is presumed they made a rapid exit.[32]

That summer of 1867 found James one day at Salina, some thirty-three miles northeast of Fort Harker, where the Civil War's "angel of mercy," Mother Bickerdyke, was trying to establish a railroad hotel and inn near the Salina depot of the westward-building Union Pacific Railroad, Eastern Division. With James that day was his friend and employee of that railroad, C. J. Bascom. Bascom recalled the day for the *Kansas City Star* on June 8, 1913, in an article titled, "Wild Bill Days in Kansas:"

> *We at last reached Salina, where my headquarters were to be. This was a town of frame buildings of boarding houses, which lined the track. The food could not be recommended, as I remember it. Mother Bickerdike, the grand army nurse of Sherman's army, was trying to build a railroad hotel with very little money. Eastbound trains got breakfast here. Westbound trains stopped for supper. Mother had a little difference with Jim Hickok over breakfast. Jim had not been given the attention he felt was due him. Mother informed the gentlemen what kind of wood made shingles. Bill apologized, and Mother waited on him herself. They became good friends afterwards.*

In 1872 Custer wrote a series of articles for *Galaxy Magazine* that in 1874 were expanded into his book, *My Life On the Plains.* In the book appeared Custer's famous "pen sketch" of Hickok as he knew him in 1867, especially during the Hancock campaign and its aftermath. While parts of the book were panned by some critics, the Hickok piece was considered very well-written and insightful. *The Chicago Tribune* even chose to publish it as their excerpt from the book:

> *Among the white scouts were numbered some of the most noted in their class. The most prominent man among them was Wild Bill, whose highly varied career was made the subject of an illustrated sketch in one of the popular monthly periodicals a few years ago. Wild Bill was a strange character, just the one a novelist might gloat over. He was a Plainsman in every sense of the word, yet unlike any other of his class. In person he was about six feet one in height, straight as the straightest of the warriors who implacable foe he was; broad shoulders, well formed chest and limbs, and a face strikingly handsome; a sharp, clear,*

blue eye, which stared you straight in the face when in conversation; a finely-shaped nose, inclined to be aquiline; a well-turned mouth, with lips only partially concealed by a handsome moustache. His hair and complexion were those of the perfect blond. The former was worn in uncut ringlets falling carelessly over his powerfully formed shoulders. Add to this figure a costume blending the immaculate neatness of the dandy with the extravagant taste and style of the frontiersman, and you have Wild Bill, then as now the most famous scout on the Plains. Whether on foot or on horseback, he was one of the most perfect types of physical manhood I ever saw.

Of his courage there could be no question; it had been brought to the test on too many occasions to admit of a doubt. His skill in the use of the rifle and pistol was unerring; while his deportment was exactly the opposite of what might be expected from a man of his surroundings. It was entirely free from all bluster and bravado. He seldom spoke of himself unless requested to do so. His conversation, strange to say, never bordered on the vulgar or blasphemous. His influence among the frontiersmen was unbounded, his word was law; and many are the personal quarrels and disturbances which he has checked among his comrades by his simple announcement that "This has gone far enough," if need be followed by the ominous warning that when persisted in renewal the quarreler "must settle it with me."

Wild Bill is anything but a quarrelsome man; yet no one but himself can enumerate the many conflicts in which he has been engaged, and which almost invariably resulted in the death of his adversary. I have a personal knowledge of at least half-a-dozen men whom he has at various times killed, one of these being at the time a member of my command. Others have been severely wounded, yet he always escaped unhurt. On the plains everyone openly carries his belt with its invariable appendages, knife, and revolver, often two of the latter. Wild Bill always carried two handsome ivory-handled revolvers of the large size; he was never seen without them.[33]

By August, no longer employed by the 7th Cavalry as scout, guide, and courier, Hickok sought other employment. It was reported that he even drove a stage for a time. A local newspaper reported in the 1930s the recollections, "Charles Larkin, of Ellsworth, recalls hearing his father, the late Arthur Larkin, tell of seeing...Wild Bill...driving a stage between Fort Harker and Ellsworth, at intervals.[34] The article doesn't indicate why a stage was needed for the short three and a half miles from Fort Harker to Ellsworth.

On August 10, one-month-old Ellsworth County held a special election for county officers. James Butler Hickok announced his candidacy for sheriff but then withdrew from the race. When the vote was taken, E. W. Kingsbury, one of the first citizens of Ellsworth, won the office of Ellsworth County sheriff, and Chauncey Whitney won as undersheriff. In later years Kingsbury would become a major source of information on J. B. Hickok for James Buel, as the latter wrote *Heroes of the Plains.*

The *Leavenworth Daily Conservative* wrote of the problems facing the new sheriff, stating that in Ellsworth, "no fouler birds ever congregated around the putrid carcass of a departed ox than those which frequent and tenant the brimstone scented dens of this modern Sodom." The editor noted that four men in two days had been killed in Ellsworth.[35]

On August 13, the *Leavenworth Daily Times* published a letter written from a military camp on the Arkansas River on August 5, commenting on the ongoing Indian war and the fact that the Indians had relieved the army of "a few scalps and surplus ponies, and at the end of four months we return to our respective homes, covered all over with glory, each the hero of some hair-breadth escape—a second Lew Wetzel, Adam Poe, or Wild Bill, forsooth."

September brought Alexander Gardner, celebrated photographer of the Civil War and the American West, to Fort Harker and its suburb, Ellsworth. Gardner was on the payroll of the Union Pacific Railroad, Eastern Division, assigned to photograph the ongoing progress of that railroad from Kansas City west through Kansas in 1867. Gardner's significant photographs were put together as a book of mounted original prints titled *Across the Continent on the Kansas Pacific Railroad.* These are rare and much sought after today. Gardner also made a collection of enlargements of these photos, titled *Across the Continent on the Union Pacific Railway, E.D.* Rare also (there were only about fifty-two copies made), the size of these enlargements is about 13 x 18½ inches. It includes images from the *Kansas Pacific Railroad* group, as well as some unique images that only appear in this group of enlargements. In this group is the well-known group photograph taken at Fort Harker by Alexander Gardner that September, that includes thirty-year-old James Butler Hickok.

157

The photograph, made about September 27, 1867, is titled *Group at Quarter Master's Department, Fort Harker.* Hickok stands at the extreme left of the photo, towering almost a head above most of the roughly forty men in the group. Interestingly, Hickok and the three men immediately to his left are leaning to their left, almost appearing to be trying to make room for Hickok to get in the picture. Probably by the time this photograph was made Hickok was serving his first stint as a deputy United States marshal, reporting to then United States marshal for the District Of Kansas, Charles Whiting. The entire image is a fascinating and dynamic representation of the American West. The only known original print of this photograph is owned by the Getty Museum of Los Angeles.

On October 7, James took the train east from Fort Harker to Leavenworth to handle some unknown business or just to visit a friend. From Leavenworth he made his way back west to Topeka, arriving by October 15 to undertake his duties below.

The first official notice that confirms Hickok's position as deputy U. S. Marshal appeared in early October. At that time Hickok issued a subpoena for one James Quinlin to appear as a witness before the district judge in Topeka on October 15. The case was *United States vs. John Reynard.* Defendant Reynard was charged with counterfeiting United States currency. Another similar case was on the docket at that time as well, the *United States vs. John Hurst,* who was charged with passing counterfeit money. In this case in the Topeka courtroom J. B. Hickok was a witness for the prosecution, as was his boss, U. S. Marshal Charles Whiting, and fellow deputy U. S. Marshal B. Searcy. In court, Hurst was found not guilty.[36]

On October 26, the editor of the *Manhattan Independent* wrote of his encounter on the train with James Butler Hickok:

On Monday we took the cars of the U.P.R.W.E.D. for Leavenworth. We make no mention of this because there is any peculiar significance in our visiting the metropolis of Kansas. Like almost everybody in Kansas we do so occasionally. But upon this occasion it was our fortune to fall in with quite a number of persons of whom it might interest our readers to learn something.

Photo, right: September 1867 photograph by Alexander Gardner of group at Fort Harker, Kansas with Hickok at far right. *Author's collection.*

#4070

Wild Bill the celebrated scout, with Jack Harvey and some dozen of their companions were upon the train, having just come in from a scouting expedition under Gen. Sherman. All the party were more or less affected by frequent potations from their bottles, and Wild Bill himself was tipsy enough to be quite belligerent.

He is naturally a fine looking fellow, not much over 30 years of age, over 6 feet in height, muscular & athletic, possessing a fine figure, as lithe and agile as the Borneo Boys. His complexion is very clear, cheek bones high, and his fine auburn hair, which he parts in the middle, hangs in ringlets down upon his shoulders, giving him a girlish look in spite of his great stature. He wore a greatly embroydered sash with a pair of ivory hilted and silver mounted pistols stuck in it. Doubtless this man and his companions have killed more men than any other persons who took part in the late war. What a pity that young men so brave and daring should lack the discretion to sheath their daggers forever when the war terminated! But such is the demoralizing effect of war upon those who engage in it and certainly upon all who love the vocation.

We learn from a gentleman who has frequently met these wild and reckless young men, that they live in a constant state of excitement, one continual round of gambling drinking and swearing, interspersed at brief intervals with pistol practice upon each other.

At a word any of the gang draws his pistol and blazes away as freely as if all mankind were Arkansas Rebels, and had a bounty offered for their scalps. How long these Athletes will be able to stand such a mode of life; eating, drinking, sleeping (if they can be said to sleep) and playing cards with their pistols at half cock, remains to be seen. For ourself, we are willing to risk them in an Indian campaign for which their cruelty and utter recklessness of life particularly suit them.[37]

Of course, when the editor wrote this piece, Hickok was not a "scout" for "General Sherman." He was a deputy U. S. Marshal, returning from his above work in a Topeka courtroom to Fort Harker and Ellsworth. Like Hickok, Jack Harvey was probably a deputy U. S. Marshal at that time, and was also returning from his duties in that same Topeka courtroom. He was not just in from "a scouting expedition under General Sherman." Perhaps Hickok and Harvey ran into several old friends from the unnamed dozen there on the homeward-bound train and they celebrated the meeting.

On November 5, another election was held for sheriff of

#4071

October 1867 photograph by Charles T. Smith of Topeka taken of deputy United States Marshal J. B. Hickok. James was in Topeka that month to bring a defendant charged with counterfeiting to court, his first official act as a deputy U.S, Marshal. *Author's collection.*

Ellsworth county. The Ellsworth county commissioners' journal reflects that there were five candidates, of which "J. Hacock" was one. Of the top three contenders, Hickok prevailed in the city of Ellsworth, receiving 156 total votes—155 in the city and 1 rural county vote—while E. W. Kingsbury received 148 city votes, and M. R. Lane received 134. Yet when rural votes were included, M. R. Lane surpassed Hickok with 184 total votes, and E. W. Kingsbury won the election with 213 total votes (and thus retained the office of sheriff that he had been elected to in the special election in August).[38]

On November 9, the *Hays City Railway Advance* scolded a fellow newspaper in Illinois for an erroneous report that a captured bank robber named Henry O'Connor was actually James B. Hickok, when that paper wrote, "It may be interesting to the curious to know that O'Connor was a distinguished Union scout during the rebellion, and is no other than the Wild Bill of *Harper's Monthly*...," continuing: "We find the following in the *Democrat's* special from Springfield, Ill. The Wild Bill of *Harper's Monthly* was, at the time mentioned, in Ellsworth. He is Deputy U.S. Marshal and was a candidate for the office of that county, at the recent election, but was defeated. We set the *Democrat* right in justice to Mr. Haycock the original Wild Bill."

The *Hays City Conservative* published on December 14, 1867, an article from the *Hays City Advance*: "U.S. Marshal Whiting, Wild Bill, Jack Harvey, Surcy, and others called in at our quarters, Tuesday. They were all welcome. William is still around, probably engaged in preparing his LIFE for DeWitt."

E. F. Campbell came from Iowa to newly-minted Ellsworth in December 1867, intent on opening a city newspaper. The first issue of the *Ellsworth Tri-Weekly Advertiser* hit Ellsworth streets on Christmas day, 1867. Editor Campbell made this observation, certainly an affirmation of Christmas goodwill that belied Ellsworth's raucous image at that time:

> *Last Wednesday was a windy, disagreeable day, but we were determined, if there was pluck enough in Ellsworth, to get our press upstairs which was then lying in the street. Capt. Seavers and Wild Bill proved pluck doesn't go begging here. These two gentlemen doffed their 'good clothes', rolled up their sleeves and gathered hold of our Wells Power Press as if it were but a toy. To these two gentlemen we are under many obligations.*[39]

So as the Christmas spirit settled on Ellsworth, and the new year was so near, James Butler Hickok had accomplished the rarest of rare things in the year of 1867: he had transcended the fame brought by Nichols' legend-building article with the actions of his real life after the article had appeared the previous February. Government detective, Indian fighter, scout and dispatch courier for Custer and Hancock, deputy United States Marshal—all in one year, much of it accomplished while he was carrying dual duties. With this real-life resume James Butler Hickok splashed onto the history pages of 1868.

10

1868

FORT HAYS *and* HAYS CITY

DEPUTY UNITED STATES MARSHAL

J. B. HICKOK: HAYS CITY SALOONKEEPER

SCOUT *and* GUIDE *for* GENERAL PENROSE

Hickok's fellow scout Danny Bohen recalled that in 1867, after he left Hickok, who was still with Custer: "I did not see Wild Bill again until 1868. He was still Marshal at Hays City. He had no trouble at that time."[1]

Frank A. Root was at this time the editor of the *Atchison Free Press*. He wrote in the paper on January 6, 1868, after meeting Hickok just days before: "In Hays I made the acquaintance of Wm. Haycock, better known as "Wild Bill." He is a man about thirty years of age, over six feet high, straight as an arrow, with long black hair hanging over his shoulders. He is in the employ of Government as a detective, and is probably better acquainted with the plains than any other man living, of his age." What Root describes as a government detective misperceives Hickok's actual position at that time as a deputy U. S. Marshal.

On March 13, 1868, Hickok lost a good friend, fellow deputy U. S. Marshal Jack Harvey. He died of what was then called consumption (tuberculosis). Thirty-two-year-old Harvey had known Hickok during the Civil War, and they shared scouting duties together with the frontier military when Harvey went out West after the war. The Leavenworth press wrote of Harvey upon his death: "Brave. Cool in the hour of danger, and one of the best shots on the western border, Jack was always ready for a bold ride or a fight with the enemy. He was as generous and true-hearted as he was brave, and no man hereabouts had more friends." No wonder Hickok and Harvey were good friends. Birds of a feather.

Formerly a deputy U. S. Marshal in Ellsworth, James now based those official duties in Hays City. As deputy Marshal, he wrote on March 26, 1868 to the Commander of Fort Hays, Captain Samuel Ovenshine:

> *I have the honor to request that a guard of a Corpl and five men be detailed to assist me in conveying the prisoners of the U. S. Marshal now in the Post Guard House to Topeka Kans. I should respectfully call your attention to the number and character of these prisoners and the feeling in their behalf in this community which renders a guard of U. S. Soldiers absolutely necessary.*
>
> *I am Captain, very respectly*
> *Your obd't servt*
> *J.B. Hickok*
> *Dept. U. S. Marshal*[2]

Captain Ovenshine responded to deputy U. S. Marshal Hickok the same day, at the same time issuing an order for the six-man military escort requested by Hickok. The arrival of the escorted prisoners in Topeka was announced on April 2 by the *Topeka Weekly Leader*:

> *BAND OF ROAD MEN CAPTURED -*
> *W.F. Cody, government detective, and Wm. Haycock—Wild Bill—deputy U.S. Marshal, brought eleven prisoners and lodged them in our calaboose on Monday last [March 30]. These prisoners belonged to a band of robbers having their headquarters on the Soloman and near Trinidad, and were headed by one Major Smith, once connected with the Kansas 7th. They are charged with stealing and secreting government property, and desertion from the army. Seventeen men,*

belonging to this same band, were captured eleven miles from Trinidad, on the 13th of March, and sent to Denver, Colorado Territory, for trial.

The prisoners were housed in the jail underneath the Topeka courthouse. Eighteen men were under arrest for various violations of U. S. law. Early in April, "Major Smith," the leader of the gang, was also arrested. Smith's notoriety must have preceded him; his appearance in the Topeka courtroom on April 28 drew a large crowd. Hickok was there as a witness for the prosecution (perhaps another reason for the large courtroom crowd), as was U. S. Commissioner Lewis Haubeck. Smith was charged with stealing ten government mules on March 9, 1868. He would likely have been found guilty, except one of the witnesses for the prosecution admitted that he had committed perjury in testifying against Smith to shield himself in another case. A mistrial was declared and Smith walked out a free man, surely much to the chagrin of deputy U.S. Marshal James Butler Hickok.[3]

The five men in the photograph #4104 on page 168 have been identified left to right as J. B. Hickok, aka Wild Bill; James Hickey; Henry C. Lindsay; and, bottom row, Fry Giles and Cyrus Holliday. The informal postures, the fact that all five are smoking a cigar or pipe, and the large bottle that is held by Cyrus Holliday surely holding something stronger than lemonade all indicate a reunion party of old friends. Old friends indeed. All but Lindsay, the youngest of the group, were veterans of the Border War of 1856-1858. James Hickey had served alongside J. B. Hickok at the battle of Bull Creek. Fry Giles and Cyrus Holliday may have served alongside James in other battles of the Border War era. Hickey, Giles and Holliday were founding fathers of Topeka. When this photo was taken in April of 1868, Hickok was a deputy United States Marshal. Hickey was the deputy sheriff of Shawnee County, Giles was an officer of the first bank of Topeka, and Holliday was in the second of three terms he would serve as mayor of Topeka. Lindsay was a soldier in the 18th Kansas Regiment when he met Hickok during the Hancock Indian campaign. All four were close friends of James for the rest of his life.

Miguel Otero first met Hickok in Hays city in spring of 1868. Miguel's father, also named Miguel, was involved, as Miguel the younger described it:

#4104

April 1868 photograph by Topeka photographer Charles T. Smith. *Author's collection.*

The firm of Whiting & Otero was engaged in the multiform and very profitable activities of banking, outfitting, wholesaling, and retailing...Westport Landing on the Missouri River was the first location of the firm...On first going to Westport Landing we took rooms in the old Gillis House on the levee, facing the Missouri River, but during the summer of 1863 we moved to a small brick residence some distance from the river on the old wagon road leading to Lawrence, Kans. [aka the Westport to Lawrence Road, or the California Road.]

When James lived in Johnson County, Kansas in the 1850s his property was a half mile south from this road, and he often used it to travel west to Lawrence or east to Westport and Kansas City. From here Miguel and his family continued moving west, following the westward-moving end-of-the-track rail-heads of the Union Pacific, Eastern Division—to Ellsworth in 1867, and to Hays City in 1868. Otero recalled his impression of the town:

Hays City was, without doubt, a wild and wooly town from start to finish. Main street was almost a solid row of saloons, dance halls, barber shops and houses of prostitution kept by such characters as "Calamity Jane," "Lousy Liz," "Stink-foot Mag," and "Steamboat." Hundreds of freighting outfits had come to Hays City with the arrival of the railroad, and soon the surrounding country looked like a large tent city, except that covered wagons took the place of tents. It was an impressive sight to see a thousand or more covered wagons camped around Hays City at the same time, all waiting to be loaded with freight for Kansas, Colorado, New Mexico, Arizona and Mexico. At night the hundreds of blazing campfires made the scene look like a large illuminated city. Early in the evening, and frequently far into the night, we could hear the music of accordions, guitars, banjos and harmonicas, interspersed with songs—some sentimental, some boisterous. On the whole, it was a collection of humanity seemingly happy, even in the face of danger. Money was plentiful; it came easy and went easy. The saloons, dance halls and gambling rooms all did a thriving business. They never closed. It was a unique phase of life, this, of such terminal towns as Hays City, and its like will never be seen again.

Miguel describes his first meeting with Hickok:

It was in the year 1868 that I first met Wild Bill, and during my stay in Hays City I often came into contact with him. He dropped into the office of Otero and Sellar very frequently to talk to my father, who was a member of the Vigilance Committee. I took a great fancy to him and greatly enjoyed his company. At that time my brother Page and myself had a stable with several fine saddle horses...Wild Bill was very fond of good horses, and he was always welcome to any we had. Thus we became good friends. He often took my brother and myself on buffalo hunts.

Wild Bill was one of the most perfect specimens of manhood I have ever seen. He was tall—about six feet two—and his bearing was always erect and confident, though in no wise haughty or severe. His features were regular, clean-cut and expressive. His voice was low, yet firm, and carried with it a suggestion of indomitable will power. He was strong, vigorous, agile; yet he was as gentle as a child except when in a fight, and even then he was calm and bold. Without a sign of nervousness, he never became excited, always as cool and deliberate as a judge passing sentence.

Beyond a shadow of doubt he was the most fearless, and perhaps the most dangerous, man in an encounter on the frontier, but never in any instance is it recorded that he started a quarrel. There was only one Wild Bill. He was without a peer in the use of the rifle and the six-shooter. So quick was he on the draw and so perfect was his aim that almost every time he shot it meant certain death to his adversary.[4]

Sight of James is lost in the official record from May till August. Yet we find what must have occupied much of his time that summer of 1868 confirmed in the press. As he had been in Junction City, Hickok was a saloon owner in Hays. Writing on June 1 from the newspaper offices of the *Hays City Railway Advance,* which was located at that time at what was Eighth and Fort Streets, visiting Illinois journalist D. W. Barkley stated: "*Harper's* Wild Bill is an honored resident of the city. He keeps a saloon a few doors above, and is highly respected for his quick use of the pistol and general bravado." Barkley's full article on Hays City appeared in his hometown Illinois paper on June 11. From this we know that Hickok's saloon was located on the west side of Fort Street, between Eighth and Ninth. There are other written indications that Hickok may have entered the saloon business in Hays City early in 1868:

"Wild William- says the *Advance*, is building at Hays City," reported the *St. Louis Missouri Democrat* on January 6, 1868. The *Hays Sentinel* on February 2, 1877 recalled that Hickok "came to Hays in 1867 and engaged in the saloon business." The following year on January 18, the *Sentinel* recalled that "Wild Bill located on the south side of the track."[5]

Further confirmation of Hickok's second career as a saloonkeeper, and an intriguing attribution to Cody as a one-time bartender, come from the pen of William E. Webb, who was the founder of Hays City and president of the Big Creek Land Company. Webb was also the author of the book *Buffalo Land in 1872*, and the *Harper's* article "Air Towns and their Inhabitants" in 1875. From *Harper's* piece, Webb recalled:

> *Buffalo Bill and Wild Bill, whom I met often on the plains, much more fairly deserved their names. The former I knew first as teamster, then bar-tender, and finally scout. He certainly knew more about the plains than any one I ever met. Wild Bill, during the years that I was cognizant of his actions, filled at intervals the positions of scout, saloonkeeper, refugee* [from the shooting with the 7th Cavalry troopers] *and scout. The number of persons I knew him to kill was five, three at Hays and two at Abilene. It seems as if such men as Bill were designated by Providence to act as some sort of carnivore for keeping down the increase of their species.*[6]

Hickok owned saloons at Junction City and then at Hays City. In November 1866, a young Will Cody, down on his luck and having left his new bride in St. Louis to come west, sought out his mentor and father-figure James Butler Hickok in Junction City. Hickok found him work as a scout, though it was reported to be a spotty assignment, and Cody lived out most of the winter in a dug-out. To help Cody further, did Hickok have Cody tend bar at his saloon that winter? Webb's statement above makes that possibility more than just a fascinating rhetorical speculation. More historical detective work is needed here.

That spring or summer of 1868 James was confronted with another result of the *Harper's* article of the previous year: the adoring attention of females young and old. In this interesting recollection by someone writing as "C" in the August 25, 1876 issue of the *Chicago Tribune*, J. B. Hickok meets a young lady waiting for the train:

"Are you Wild Bill the Harpers Magazine tells us about?" The astonished scout bashfully replied "I believe I am." The mischievous eyes surveyed him complacently from head to foot, while their owner laughingly said, "Are you? Why, my papa told me to come out here and marry some great man like you?" The effect was wonderful, and for once in his life the man who had faced death almost times without number, and who could look into the muzzle of a "Colt's army" in the hands of a murderous assailant without a quiver, was thoroughly frightened, and, too, by the harmless weapons of a pretty woman. Pistols were of no use in such an engagement, and to steal away, and "blush unseen" was impossible. So, completely vanquished, he stood like the rural youth at his first "sparking," vainly trying to hide his feet and hands, until, tired of questioning a victim too overcome to answer, she bounded away to tell of her capture, and perhaps to find other "sons of the border" to conquer.

The summer of 1868 also found Hickok traveling away from Hays City, in June or July. On July 18, the *Leavenworth Daily Commercial* reported that "Numerous friends, of Hickok, the fiery, untamed William—familiarly styled by the vulgar—'Wild Bill', will be pleased to learn that this distinguished personage is now sojourning in this city." It was on this same trip east that Hickok traveled a few miles upriver from Leavenworth to Atchison, where unbeknownst to him, he started a starry-eyed boy on a career emulating his as a lawman. The boy's name was Bill Tilghman. Many years later, after his passing, his wife Zoe A. Tilghman wrote his recollections of the event that summer, working from her husband's notes. She provided this write-up to Joe Rosa in 1959:

It was on a blackberry excursion that young Bill Tilghman, 12 years old, unwittingly met with Destiny. With his sisters and Frank and some neighbor children, lunch and pails and baskets in the wagon, they set out for the [Missouri] river brakes where the long canes bent with their weight of juicy berries. Their way led for some distance along the main road West from Atchison and on it came another traveler who pulled up and greeted them. The children stared, round-eyed, and Bill especially noted every detail of the stranger's appearance.

He was mounted indeed upon no prancing charger, only a sturdy government mule. But he rode with the easy grace of a Plainsman. His buckskin jacket and broad hat were strange to their eyes, and savored of far regions. Two pistols hung from his belt. His boots were of fine tanned leather.

Tall, he was over six feet, splendidly built, and his face as handsome as his form, with strong, clear-cut features and keen dark blue eyes, long drooping mustache and hair curling upon his soldiers. Distinction sat upon him as a garment. He spoke in a slow, assured manner. "Good morning boys; and young ladies." The girls' eyes sparked as they strove to keep down embarrassed giggles. It was flattering to be called young ladies, especially by such a handsome stranger. "Did you happen to see a man driving a span of mules to a covered wagon?" he asked. Bill, from his position as driver, answered "Yes sir, we did. About two miles back."

"Uh. And does this road lead straight to Atchison? No turning off anywhere?"

[Tilghman answered] "Yes sir. It goes straight up to town."

"Thank you, good day." He swung off his hat gracefully and rode on.

"He certainly is handsome." "He must be somebody important." "That was a real deerskin shirt." Bill's remark was "I'd like to have a pair of pistols like his."

Mrs. Tilghman then provided a quote from the Atchison newspaper that her husband had written from memory in his notebook. She wrote out part of the Atchison article for Rosa: "Atchison had a distinguished visitor this week, Mr. William B. Hickok...known as 'Wild Bill', the most expert pistol shot in the West. He is now a Deputy U.S. Marshal and scout at Fort Hays, and came here following for four hundred miles a stolen team of mules and a wagon. The thief had just stolen them, but Wild Bill nabbed him before he left town, and took back the stolen property."

Mrs. Tilghman's report continues:

Wild Bill became the hero and pattern for adventure for young Bill Tilghman. He clipped the story from the paper, read and re-read it, and showed it to his boy companions. For weeks he talked of Wild Bill, even dreamed of him. He had a pair of cap-and-ball pistols, and now all the money he could get hold of, he spent for caps, powder and lead. He practised shooting pop-shots from the hip, with both hands in emulation of Wild Bill. Left-hand shooting was extremely hard at first; and the quick draw, and shooting as soon as the gun was leveled, aiming, in fact, in the very motion of drawing it, by judgment rather than actual sighting, was a refinement of skill that sometimes seemed impossible. But he kept determinedly at it, and the practice of a thousand shots told. The time came when he could hit a rabbit or a prairie chicken sitting in the grass thirty feet away, with a quick pop-shot.[7]

Based on the report in the Atchison newspaper quoted by Mrs. Tilghman above, we can see that James was still undertaking duties as deputy U. S. Marshal. After his meeting with young Bill Tilghman in Atchison, Hickok returned to Leavenworth to take the Union Pacific west back to Hays City. From Leavenworth, James stopped first in Topeka to visit his friend F. H. Chase, who recalled Hickok's summer of 1868 Topeka visit for William Connelley in 1913:

On the 28th of June, 1913, F.H. Chase, of Hoyt, Jackson County, Kansas, told me something about Wild Bill. Chase knew Bill well. In 1868 Chase lived at Topeka. That summer Bill came to Topeka. Chase was going north on Kansas Avenue, between Sixth and Fifth Streets, and on the west side of the avenue. Bill was going in the opposite direction on the other side of the avenue. When he saw Chase he stuck a potato, which he found in the gutter, on the end of his cane and threw it at Chase. The potato came with great force and struck the front of a jeweler's shop, jarring the little building. Then he came across to talk to Chase...He had just come to Topeka from Leavenworth...At Topeka he boarded at the Ashbaugh House, on West Sixth Street, just across the street south of where the Columbia Building now stands. He remained but a week or two.[8]

By August James was back in Hays City, making it in time to greet 200 "excursionists" that had come west to see the frontier, not through the pages of the newspaper, but with their own eyes.

The Topeka ticket agent for the Union Pacific, Eastern Division had organized a three-day trip to the end of the track, Hays City. On August 5, 1868, the following announcement appeared in the *Topeka Daily Kansas State Record:*

The Topeka Excursionists will leave the Depot on Thursday morning the 6th inst., at 6 o'clock SHARP, and run to the end of the track. Everybody is expected to take along their own eatables, and occupy as small a space as possible, as the baggage will not accommodate large boxes or trunks. Mr. Pape will furnish the refreshments, consisting of Ice Cream, Lemonade, Sherry Cobbler, Mint Julips, Wines, etc. A general good time is expected. All are expected to provide their own mode of conveyance to the Depot.

The excursionists numbered about 200 people, the implication made by no mention of a ticket price certainly an impetus for the big showing. The train, after making several stops for the passengers to take errant pot-shots at thundering herds of buffalo, made it into Hays City late in the evening. Excursionist John H. Putnam wrote of their arrival: "We got through to Fort Hays and Hays City lively as crickets, and met some acquaintances—among them 'Wild Bill' the great scout, a romantic but not o'er true history of whom you may find in *Harper's Monthly* of about a year ago. He said there were some hundreds of Cheyenne warriors camped a few miles out. Soon some of the braves came in. Clad mostly in red paint, feathers and bear-claw necklaces. Pleasant looking gentlemen these...pleasant images for dreams. The girls wondered if they would like some scalps of foreign hair."

While apparently the men slept that night on the train, the women were offered "a nice quiet residence" to pass the night in. At eleven o'clock that night the female entourage walked down the middle of the street to seek the house, accompanied by a few of the men to see them safely to their unknown destination. "We ask 'where does Mr. Joyce live?' Answer 'Just around the corner—Between the "Eldorado Club" rooms' and 'Pat. Murphy's saloon,' opposite the 'Prairie Flower Dance House.' A nice neighborhood surely. Find it with the help of 'Wild Bill.'...The 'nice clean beds' promised, three dirty blankets thrown on the floor." The ladies made their way quickly back to the train, and slept there that night.

The next day the excursionists continued on west to Monument Station. While the train returned to Topeka, Putnam described the populace of Hays City: "The people are worth seeing. There are men from every nation under heaven in their natural state, and then mixed with every style of American-Yankee, Westerner, Southerner, Negro, Mexican, and 'Injun,' with all imaginable crosses and mongrels of the same, presenting a conglomerate of human nature more curious than beautiful to see."[9]

#4114

GEORGE A. ARMES.
Major U. S. A.

J. B. Hickok was scout and guide for Major George A. Armes as his troops traveled from Fort Hays to Fort Lyon in Colorado in the fall of 1868, part of General Winfield Hancock's plan to attack Indians in their winter quarters instead of waiting till spring to do battle. *Author's collection.*

Later that August of 1868 Hickok returned to service with the frontier military. Fort Hays post returns show that on August 18, Hickok signed on as scout and guide for Captain G. W. Graham and Brevet Major George A. Armes of the 10th Cavalry, working on a reconnaissance expedition along the Republican River. When that mission ended thirteen days later on August 31, Hickok was paid $43.43 and released for service elsewhere, which came immediately. The very next day, September 1, he was signed on as a scout and guide with the 10th Cavalry, serving again, as he had in 1867, with Brevet Major George A. Armes. Hickok signed on at "Headquarters Detachment Tenth Cavalry near Skimmerhorn's Ranche." This assignment as scout and guide for Major Armes would take him to Fort Lyon in Colorado, and to a fateful encounter with the harsh and often unforgiving winter on the plains of Kansas and Colorado.[10]

Before the trip to Fort Lyon, Major Armes and Hickok struck out west to the Republican River. Major Armes entered in his journal:

Camp on Big Timber, August 21, 1868.

Major Kidd (who is still in command) failed to pay attention to the advice of Wild Bill, our scout and guide, in regard to the course we should take when we left camp yesterday, he appearing to know more about the country than those who have lived here for years. Under the circumstances, he has marched out of his course at least five or ten miles without prospect of finding any Indians.[11]

At the beginning of the trek from Fort Hays to Fort Lyon, Brevet Major Armes entered in his journal:

Camp above headwaters of Walnut Creek, September 2, 1868

We started out at seven o'clock this morning with Wild Bill as our scout, and while resting a few moments and allowing the horses to graze, he came rushing in with fifteen of his scouts to inform me that a fresh Indian trail had been discovered.[12]

The trek by the 10th Cavalry, led by Brevet Major Armes, and guided by James B. Hickok from Fort Hays to Fort Lyon in Colorado, was part of a plan by General Phillip Sheridan to undertake a new kind of warfare with the Plains Indians; he planned a winter campaign, when instead of burning homes, killing settlers and railroad workers, and in general committing atrocities, the Indians he had pursued relentlessly in futile runs all over Kansas were in their villages far away, repairing their moccasins, loving their wives and children, and anxiously awaiting springtime to renew their depredations. The village that Sheridan chose to strike was that of Black Kettle, a Cheyenne village on the Washita River in modern western Oklahoma. The 10th Cavalry, guided by Hickok, was ordered to make their way to Fort Lyon where they would be put under the command of General William Penrose. Under General Penrose, J. B. Hickok would be a guide, but not the general's chief of scouts. A Mexican, Charles Autobees, was assigned by Penrose as chief of scouts once the command left Fort Lyon and headed south for the Canadian. His son, Mariano Autobees, was also along with Penrose as a scout. There was a creeping tension between the American scouts and the Mexican scouts as soon as they left Fort Lyon. Sometime before James left Fort Lyon, he was at Fort Dodge for a short time in 1868. Danny Bohen recalled, "In the Fall I met him at Fort Dodge. He was there with General Sheridan. He told me he would go back to Hays City again. I went on to Fort Sill with Generals Sheridan and Custer."[13]

Penrose was to leave Fort Lyon with the 10th Cavalry three weeks ahead of General Carr, who would be following with the 5th Cavalry, both in support of Custer and the 7th Cavalry, who were working their way south to the Washita River in Oklahoma and to Black Kettle's camp. Penrose and Carr were to play defensive roles, forming a sort of blockade to keep the Cheyenne from coming north back into Kansas or Colorado if the attack on the village failed and all the Cheyenne warriors escaped.

Custer and the 7th Cavalry attacked the village at dawn the morning of November 27, the soldiers cheering, the band playing the 7th's regimental "Garry Owen." Custer killed over a hundred Indians, most trying to flee, including women, children and Black Kettle. In the battle at the village, Major Elliott and nineteen soldiers got cut off from the troops and were all killed. Captain Hamilton, the grandson of Alexander Hamilton, was also killed at Washita. Albert Barnitz was severely wounded, and though he lived, it ended his military career.[14]

Penrose and the 10th Cavalry took the brunt of the winter snowstorm head-on, and finally stopped at Palo Duro Creek, with no wagons, no tents, no supplies, no forage for the very few horses and mules that were still alive. With the snowstorm raging, they could not go forward, and they could not return. So they waited, and hoped that Carr could find them.

Carr went out to find Penrose, and almost got lost himself, but he had the horses and mules and wagons and supplies that Penrose did not. Finally Carr did find Penrose and the 10th Cavalry, and Hickok, on Palo Duro Creek.

These journal entries from Brevet Major Armes, written at Fort Lyon and beyond, describe the snowstorm that perilously stalled General Penrose with the 10th Cavalry and his guide, J. B. Hickok, and severely hampered Carr commanding the 5th Cavalry:

New Fort Lyon, C.T., October 20, 1868

> *We started out at 8 this A.M. Reaching this post at 1 P.M. I was introduced to Gen. William Penrose and Lieutenants Abel and Bonsall, who have just left my tent, inviting me to come and see them. General Penrose is to take command of our four companies of cavalry, and he notified us that we would have to start in five days, without wagons or forage, on a sixty day's expedition.*[15]

November 2nd, 1868

> *During the last few days we* [the 10th Cavalry] *have been practicing at target, preparing for a general campaign under which we expect to start at a moments notice, as General Sheridan has formed several expeditions to try to surround the Indians and destroy the village if possible. Gen. William Penrose, who commanded a division of the Sixth Corps during the war, has been placed in command of my battalion, consisting of four companies of cavalry and one of infantry, and as he was successful during the war, he has led General Sheridan to believe he will be a success now, but my impression is he will prove a failure if he undertakes to march without forage for the animals through the Indian Territory and New Mexico, where the grass is very scarce.*[16]

Armes traveled south with Penrose and Hickok until December 3. On that day Armes and two other officers, along with a small company of forty-four men, were sent back to Fort Lyon. Armes apparently was sent back because his entire command of 10th Cavalry was under the direct command of General Penrose, and perhaps he was also sent back

#4119

General William H. Penrose took command of Armes' battalion and others when Armes and Hickok reached Fort Lyon. Penrose failed to outfit his command properly to withstand the harsh winter, and his troops suffered greatly. *Author's collection.*

to enlist help for Penrose, who had lost most of their horses, leaving the cavalry on foot, and there were no wagons for cover from the pending snowstorm. Hickok stayed with the Penrose command.

As he and the small company moved back towards Fort Lyons, Armes wrote of the same sort of misery being suffered by Penrose and his command that included Hickok. Armes wrote on December 5, 1868: "Just before we reached camp it began to snow, and we are trying to make ourselves as comfortable as possible, considering that we have no shelter of any kind."[17]

And the entry for December 6th, 1868:

> *It has been snowing all night, and we are scarcely able to march today on account of the crust being just thick enough to break through, cutting the men's feet and the legs of the animals so as to leave a trail of blood, many of the men being barefoot. We are now in camp with scarcely anything to eat after marching thirty-five miles.*[18]

Armes and his group finally made it back to Fort Lyons on December 10.

> *December 22, 1868*
> *No news from General Penrose, who is in a terrible condition seventy-five or one hundred miles from this post.*[19]

> *December 24, 1868* [Christmas Eve]
> *No news from General Penrose.*[20]

> *December 28, 1868*
> *About 11 A.M. A small group could be discovered with our glasses out on the prairie, and upon a close investigation we soon found it to be a few men of the long-lost command of General Penrose, who was on the other side of the river coming into the post. They had been met by a party with rations, so they did not suffer from hunger, but the men were in a terrible condition, many of them barefooted, with scarcely any clothes of any description, and all the men on foot, the horses having starved to death or been killed during the expedition.*[21]

> *December 29, 1868*
> *...Lieutenant Abel and Lieutenant Bonsil started to look for General Carr's command, which had been sent out to look for General Penrose, but lost him, and now we are trying to find General Carr and his command.*[22]

11

1869

RESCUE *from* PALO DURO CREEK

COURIER *for* GENERAL CARR

WOUNDED *by a* CHEYENNE SPEAR

HOME *to* ILLINOIS

the MYTH *of* SENATOR HENRY WILSON *and* HICKOK

DEPUTY UNITED STATES MARSHAL

ELIZABETH CUSTER *and* J. B. HICKOK

SHERIFF *of* HAYS CITY *and* ELLIS COUNTY

the SHOOTING *of* BILL MULVEY

the SHOOTING *of* SAMUEL STRAWHUN

#4123

This is probably Hickok's best-known photograph. It was taken by photographer Wilbur Blakeslee of Mendota, Illinois in April 1869. *Author's collection.*

General Carr finally did find the lost and snowbound command of General Penrose in late December 1868 on the banks of Palo Duro Creek in northwest Texas. Will Cody, then the scout for Carr, led the advance search that found them. One of the first people he saw when he rode into Penrose's beleaguered camp was Hickok, who Cody saw was massaging his hands to keep them warm. By December 30 Carr had established a supply camp there, and soon the half-starved and frozen men could finally eat and warm themselves before a campfire. Sometime during the first week of January, 1869, Carr sent Hickok on a dispatch trip to Camp Supply. Hickok set off and made it through safely to Camp Supply. From there the dispatches were carried to Fort Dodge by Lieutenant C. Martin, along with a small guard of scouts and soldiers. Lieutenant Martin reached Fort Dodge late on January 10, 1869. He told the post commander that the previous Wednesday, "Wild Bill came into Camp Supply with Dispatches from Bvt. Brig. Gen. Penrose & Command for Major Genl. Sheridan."[1] The following report by Hiram Robbins described this particular trip.

Carr was searching for volunteers to ride from Palo Duro Creek to Camp Supply with a dispatch to request provisions. The scouts were lined up but no one stepped forward:

> *Finally Wild Bill, for whom Carr had no special regard, arose from his blankets, where he lay watching the proceedings, and said: "Well, General, it seems that you haven't any men in your crowd. I guess I'll have to make the trip." The offer was gratefully accepted, and Wild Bill, accompanied by an English teamster, started on the perilous journey. As Bill was well acquainted with the country, by taking a course along the base of a range of hills, he avoided a great many difficulties that would have opposed him had he taken the regular trail. Just as he arrived within sight of the fort, the Englishman fell from his horse. He was taken to camp, more dead than alive, and although he survived, one of his arms had to be amputated. Bill, after resting a short time, during which he was rubbed with whiskey, both inside and out,*

185

as he termed it, started on the return trip, passed the provision sleds and reached [Carr's camp on Palo Duro creek] *just ten days from the time of his departure.*[2]

Hiram Robbins was the manager and sometime scriptwriter for Will Cody's Combination during the year that Hickok spent on the stage with Cody. The report reads like an interview ["as he termed it"] and was probably told directly to Robbins by Hickok. Robbins' statements have to be used with care by writers, as he had a strong tendency to exaggerate. However, confidence in Robbins increases greatly when his story can be corroborated, as this one is. Brevet Major Armes wrote in his journal of the return of Penrose and the 10th Cavalry and Carr and the 5th Cavalry to Fort Lyon:

February 18, 1869

General Penrose, Lieutenants Beck and Hanna came in about one o'clock yesterday, leaving the command eighty miles off, which is slowly marching this way. Most all of the mules and horses gave out were shot to prevent their falling in the hands of Indians. General Carr, in command of the Fifth Cavalry, and Colonel Crittendon arrived this afternoon. They have gone into camp near the post.[3]

February 19, 1869
What is left of the Tenth Cavalry came straggling into the post this afternoon, forlorn-looking specimens of humanity. Mrs. Penrose, Mrs. Beck and I rode out to their camp this afternoon on horseback and witnessed the most pitiful sight we ever saw. The men were partly frozen; their pants had been burned and worn off, and many had not changed their clothing for weeks and months. Lieut. William Davis is in command of my company and has issued clothing for the men today.[4]

It is believed that Hickok returned to Fort Lyon on this day with the 10th Cavalry, if not the previous day with General Penrose. On one of the February days that remained an event happened that was to send James home to Illinois for the first time in years. Although details are sketchy, the end result is not. Hickok was outside of Fort Lyon, returning to Hays City, but still near to the fort. He was attacked by a small band of Cheyenne, and in the course of a running battle a Cheyenne warrior got close enough to thrust a long spear into Hickok's thigh. He shot his attackers or simply outran them, and made his way back to Fort Lyon. Cody was at Fort Lyon as well, and he was there when Hickok came in after the battle. He went out to the location of the fight. Hickok gave the spear that had wounded him to Cody, and William Connelley claimed that Cody still had it as of June 25, 1914. Joseph Rosa reported in 2001 that a Cheyenne lance once owned by Cody, that possibly is the one given to him by Hickok, resides today in the collection of the Buffalo Bill Museum in Cody, Wyoming.

On February 28, 1869, Hickok was discharged as a scout for the 10th Cavalry; it is likely that the official reason for his release was this spear wound. James made it back to Hays City, and wasted no time in working his way east on the railroad on a hastened trip back home to Illinois and medical care. On March 5,1869, the *Leavenworth Times and Conservative* reported, "J. B. Hickock, Wm. Cady [Cody], J. Estes, and Thomas Sherman" had arrived in Leavenworth and were staying at the Planter's House hotel. From Leavenworth, James made his way back to Illinois, arriving in mid-March at Mendota, just a few miles from the family home in Homer.

The photograph #4123 on page 184 was taken during James' visit home that March. He was of course visiting to see his mother and family, and to get medical attention for the spear wound he received near Fort Lyon. He stayed in Illinois for seven weeks, the last three weeks at the Passenger House hotel in Mendota, just a few miles from his home. Several writers have speculated that James was wearing a stage costume in this photograph. This was no stage costume. James did not appear on stage until 1873, when Cody coaxed him to act under the bright lights. Just eight months after Blakeslee took this photograph, Adolph Roenigk recalled Hickok on the plains of western Kansas in December of 1869 wearing this same buckskin outfit, or one very similar, as a deputy United States Marshal. Deputy Hickok was there to arrest men that were illegally cutting timber that belonged to the Kansas Pacific Railroad.

In 2003 a remarkable and previously unknown letter from James' mother Polly Hickok to James' older brother Lorenzo revealed much information about this heartfelt and joyful family reunion, and the letter confirmed many details about James' spear wound (punctuation added):

Homer May 10th 1869

My Dear Son
   It has been a long time since I have written to you...Celinda and Erastus wanted me to stay with them so I stayed there until James came home. We got a letter from James on Tuesday stating that he was at Fort Lyons also saying that he would be home on the 27 day of May which is his birthday and Wensday evening I received a Telegraph that he was in mendota and wanted me to meet him there on the 11 0 clock train so of cours Celinda and I came to Mendota and met the boy there. [Either Polly meant March 27 when she wrote that James planned to return on the "27 day of May," or James wanted to really surprise her when he showed up the Wednesday in March the day after she received his letter claiming it would be May 27 before he would come.] *He went down home with us and stayed three weeks. His leg was getting worse all the time, it was very painful but I could not keep him still. He would not let Houts dress his wound at all. He went to Mendota and Dr. Edwards tended to his leg three or four days. Then he got a Dispatch from Gen. Sheridan to meet him in Chicago so he went there and was gone a week and when he got back to Mendota his leg was much worse. He stayed at the Passenger House three weeks. The Lance went into bone in his thigh. The wound healed at the top but the bone was so affected that he had to have it lancet four or five times. I did not go to see him after he came back from Chicago. Horace and Hervy and Lydia went. Horace was there two or three times. He* [James] *came down last Sunday* [to tell Polly goodbye] *and on Monday Started for Leavenworth. From there he is going to Hays City. He does not expect to stay at Hays. He thinks that he will go some where on the Pacific Railroad. He says if you come home next winter he will surely come with you...Marshall* [James' sister Lydia's five-year-old son] *has been here for a week. He went home this morning. He talks a great deal about your coming home to fetch him a pistol. James bought him a Scotch Shephard dog. He gave five dollars for it. Marshall has been offered seventeen dollars in cash for his dog but he wont sell it... James say that I don't look any older than I did when he was home before. You had ought to have seen him take me up in his arms when I got off the Carrs to Mendota. When I stept down I turned round my back to the crowd on the platform to take my basket and the first* [I] *knew he had me in his arms, he says Mammy have y come? James fetcht me a nice large Fotograph in one of those large oval frames...From your ever affectionate Mother Polly Hickok.*[5]

Polly's letter reflects her great joy at seeing her youngest son after seven years of absence. (James had last made it back to Homer in 1862.) It also shows James' independent streak, refusing medical help until it was absolutely necessary. The letter shows a meeting with General Sheridan in Chicago (where Sheridan lived and maintained his headquarters, just months after both he and Hickok had returned to Kansas from the ill-fated winter campaign on the Washita.) That meeting has not yet been confirmed by historians, if any have even tried to confirm it.

Most of all this letter shows that the spear wound was very serious and was on its way to becoming septic when James finally had Dr. Edwards in Mendota work on him. Writing in the December 26, 1896 *Chicago Daily Record,* James' sister Lydia recalled the day she accompanied James to Dr. Edwards' office. Note that Lydia refers to him as Dr. Thomas, yet remember this is twenty-seven years after the event:

The longest time he ever remained [in Homer] *was three weeks, and that he was when he was wounded up in Minnesota by an Indian spear. It struck him in the hip, the point bending when it struck the bone so that he had to stop and get off his horse and pull it out. He paid little attention to the wound and rode to Fort Leavenworth, where there was a letter from me to him telling him that Mother was not well and asking him to come home. He came but said nothing of his wound for several days, although he had Dr. Thomas of Mendota Ill., to dress it and care for it. We learned of it only after he asked for some lint to put a fresh bandage on it. Later, it became necessary to lance the wound and scrape the bone...The doctor came one evening to perform the operation, but Bill would not take chloroform. The doctor made four cuts outward from the wound making a perfect cross with the lance. Then he drew the flesh back and began to scrape the bone. I was holding the lamp and felt myself getting faint. "Here, give it to me," said Bill. He took the lamp and held it while the doctor scraped away, never flinching once during the operation.*

There is something peculiar about this statement, and I don't mean the normal mistakes of memory exemplified above by "Minnesota" or "Dr. Thomas." What I find strange is that in all my years of studying Hickok and his life I have never, ever seen a Hickok family member refer to him as anything but James or Uncle Jim. I find it impossible that his own sister would refer to him as Bill. Lydia has been characterized as "a very outspoken lady who expressed great anger at some of the deliberate lies told about her brother." Yet here she refers to him as Bill twice. One likely answer is that the editor of the *Chicago Daily Record,* reading the statement before it went to press, substituted "Bill" for "James," believing that his readers would better understand that this was Wild Bill.

There are some other recollections of Hickok's visit to Homer in that spring of 1869. Paul McDonald lived as a young boy in Homer then, and he later told Howard A. Hickok (James' nephew) that during that time the boys of the village used to watch for Hickok to come uptown to visit the post office or store and would follow him around, "eager and anxious to hear him talk of the West. He witnessed the exhibition of shooting, told about by Mr. Wylie and was greatly impressed by what he witnessed."[6]

Howard Hickok recalled for Joseph Rosa in 1965 a wistful family memory from that 1869 visit home. Apparently James "brought with him many presents for his mother and the family. I believe somewhere in the family—probably in California—there is still one of the dresses he brought for my grandmother. There was never anything said, but it was felt that James should have given her money or something more practical, for although my dad and my mother took care of her, they felt he should have contributed something for her welfare. But I guess his presence at home was all she cared about."[7]

Polly Hickok's letter above shows that James spent seven weeks in Illinois: three weeks with her at the family home in Homer, one week in Chicago visiting General Sheridan at his request, and three weeks in Mendota at the Passenger House hotel. If James arrived in Homer by March 15 and then spent seven weeks in Illinois, he would have headed back to Kansas on about May 1 or 2. The *Leavenworth Times and Conservative* on May 7, 1869, announced his arrival there: "Hotel Arrivals at Planters House: J. B. Hickok of Hays City."

This brings us to a point in the timeline that we must dispel, hopefully for good, a myth that needs to die. Other historians have done their best to kill this hoary tale, and perhaps my attempt will finally push it off the proverbial ledge and into the ash bin of history. This fanciful tale was completely invented by James Buel, and then given substantiation when Hickok's next two biographers, Frank Wilstach and William Connelley, repeated it unquestioned in their widely-distributed books.

The story goes something like this. Towards the end of James' 1869 visit home, he received a letter from Henry Wilson, at that time a senator from Massachusetts. Wilson waxed eloquently in the letter about enlisting James to guide the senator and his party through the wilds of frontier Kansas.

James B. Hickok, Esq., Washington D.C.,

Dear Sir:
May 17th, 1869

> *A party consisting of several gentlemen, ladies and myself, desire to spend a few weeks in the far West during the warm season, and I hope it will be our fortune to secure your excellent services as our guide. I have heard much concerning your wonderful exploits in the West, and of such character, too, as commend you highly for efficiency in the scouting service of the government. If it be possible for you to accompany our party as guide some time during the following month, please write me at once at Willard's Hotel, Washington, indicating what compensation you will expect, and also what point in Kansas we had best start on the tour. I shall leave to you the selection of a pleasant route, as your general acquaintence [sic] with the places of interest between the Missouri river and the Rocky Mountains better qualifies you for deciding the trip that promises the most attractions. Hoping to hear from you at your earliest convenience.*

> *I am, yours truly,*
> *Henry Wilson* [8]

The story continues. Hickok is supposed to have set his fee at $500 and have arranged a trip beginning at Hays City in June. After the trip James was presented with a pair of Colt revolvers in appreciation of his services.

This trip never happened. Buel made the entire thing up, including the bogus letter from Senator Henry Wilson. The first piece of empirical evidence that it is fake is the date on the letter of May 17, 1869; the letter would never have made it to James in Homer. We have proof that no later than May 16, Hickok was already back in Hays City and undertaking once again his job as deputy U. S. Marshal. Furthermore, the press kept very close tabs on Hickok's activities during this period, and such an excursion with a standing United States senator would have drawn wide print coverage in the local press in Hays City and beyond. Yet the pages of these frontier papers are devoid of any mention of Hickok leading Henry Wilson and his party on an excursion west. Also, some opportunist, surely hoping to cash in on the story of the two presentation Colt revolvers, engraved "J. B. Hickock" right on the backstrap of a .36-caliber 1851 Colt Navy. The opportunist, obviously confident that he (or she) had chosen for this charade a Colt Navy, well-established as Hickok's favorite model, must have felt that offset the fact that James' last name was misspelled, a circumstance generally avoided on presentation trophies and awards. Joseph Rosa reported in 1987 that a photo of this gun was sent in the 1950s to the Colt company for comment, and the name of the current owner is unknown. We will meet the work of other creative opportunists in a later section of this book. Finally, no mention of Hickok was ever made in any of Henry Wilson's papers, personal and professional. Besides, Henry Wilson died in 1875, several years before Buel's biography, and could not have refuted Buel's statements. In summary, the Henry Wilson story was completely false. Never happened. Consider it officially dead. Throw it forcefully into history's ash bin.

James was back on his job of deputy U. S. Marshal almost immediately after arriving in Hays City. On May 8, U. S. Marshal Charles Whiting was notified by the post commander at Fort Wallace that he was holding two men (non-soldiers) that he had arrested for stealing government mules, and requested a deputy U.S. Marshal to come to Fort Wallace and get them. On May 16, the post commander advised the U. S. Marshal that he had "turned over to Mr. Hickox, Deputy U. S. Marshal... Baker and Carter, two citizen prisoners charged with stealing mules, also Edward Lane and James Dwyer witnesses in these cases have been sent to Topeka."[9] On May 18 the Fort Wallace post commander again wrote to U. S. Marshal Whiting, telling him that along with handing the prisoners over to Hickok, he had furnished government transportation, and as he would be charged for this, he wanted to be repaid by the U. S. Marshal's office.

Even before he went to Fort Wallace for the prisoners, James must have sensed that Marshal Whiting was in trouble. Though the problem did not actually involve Whiting, it did involve several of his deputies.

In March, 1869 (recall Hickok was home in Illinois and would be until mid-May), Pawnee Indians began showing up around Kansas. The citizens of Ellsworth and Hays City, along with those of the rural areas of Ellsworth and Ellis Counties, were very nervous and apprehensive about any Indians roaming about their communities. After almost two years of hit-and-run depredations against railroad workers, rural settlers, station managers, and even city folk that strayed too far from town, the inhabitants of the area were inclined to think every moving dust cloud on the horizon hid an incoming band of warriors. They were primed to overreact. Some of the Pawnee were arrested and told to go back to their reservation. Some Pawnee that showed up near Ellsworth were taken to Fort Harker for their own protection. There were unsubstantiated reports that these Pawnee were stealing property and frightening people.

Marshal Whiting was in Ellsworth on March 9, and sensing the citizens' concern, sent a telegram to Bvt. Lt. Col. E. H. Leib at Fort Harker, stating, "Twenty (20) Indians are in town send squad of soldiers." M. H. Henry also sent a telegram stating the Indians "are not arrested and are making themselves generally free."[10] By March 12, tension had almost reached critical mass, and when some of the Indians came to the outskirts of Ellsworth they were attacked by panicky citizens.

Some believed this attack on the Indians was unprovoked; letters were written to the governor and to Washington. On March 31, Major John W. Craig was ordered to Ellsworth to investigate. The situation then went from bad to worse. Major Craig reported that the Indians met on the main street of Ellsworth with deputy U. S. Marshal Chauncey Whitney (who at the time was also the sheriff of Ellsworth County) and deputy U. S. Marshal John Park. The deputy Marshals told the chief of the group he must be arrested until Fort Harker officials were made aware the Indians were in Ellsworth. The chief then made signs of using his bow and arrow, causing the other Indians to run away quickly. In the confusion, the chief was shot by several people, and another Indian was chased and killed outside of town by citizens.

Out of this fiasco a full federal investigation was opened on April 26. The attorney general in Washington was informed by the Department of the Interior that the "murder of friendly Pawnee Indians [was] alleged to have been committed by certain Deputy U.S. Marshals." Marshal Whiting responded in writing to the attorney general:

I am not at present advised of the facts, but have already taken the necessary steps to ascertain the entire history of the affair...The persons mentioned in your communication are well known to me. Parkes and Whitney are in my imploy as Deputies; the latter being also at the time of the murders, Sheriff of Ellsworth County, and has a very good reputation as an officer, Parkes has been a very active and efficient Deputy on the border of this State for some time, and up to the time of the receipt of your letter, I have never heard anything against his integrity as an officer. Circey is not in my employ. He is a man of bad character. One of the worst in fact to be found on the western border of Kansas.[11]

It is apparent that the attorney general had included Circey as one of the suspects in the shooting of the Indians on Ellsworth's main street. Though Whiting denied Circey was in his employ as a deputy U. S. Marshal, records indicate that before, during and after this incident, Circey was a deputy U. S. Marshal for Marshal Whiting. The reasons for Whiting's denial and fierce criticism of Circy (whose last name was actually Searcy) are unknown. While the feds deliberated on all this, the press began to pick up the story. Finally on May 20, just a week after Hickok had returned from Illinois to Hays City and resumed his job as deputy Marshal, Whiting was removed from office. Whiting continued to be active in local politics that year of 1869, yet in November he contacted an unknown illness, and he died on January 2, 1870.

The man who replaced Whiting on May 26, 1870 was Dana W. Houston. His first task was to interview all of Whiting's deputies and decide which were fit to remain. All the deputies were ordered to report to Marshal Houston in Leavenworth. The press took notice. The *Leavenworth Times and Conservative* reported on May 30: "They are all in now and counted. There are sixty-five (65) of them. Nobody had supposed that there were more than forty (40). We mean Whiting's Deputy Marshals. They all 'Interviewed' Col. Houston yesterday. They will do it again today. We think the Colonel will Mark sum of them off the list."[12] Hickok made the cut, and the first of June found him back in Hays City ready to resume his job as deputy United States Marshal.[13]

Writing about this summer of 1869, Elizabeth Custer wrote her well-known, candid, and even controversial comments about Hickok in Hays City and around Fort Hays:

Physically, he was a delight to look upon. Tall, lithe, and free in every motion, he rode and walked as if every muscle was perfection, and the careless swing of his body as he moved seemed perfectly in keeping with the man, the country, the time in which he lived.

I do not recall anything finer in the way of physical perfection than Wild Bill when he swung himself lightly from his saddle, and with graceful, swaying step, squarely set shoulders and well poised head, approachd our tent for orders. He was rather fantastically clad, of course, but all that seemed perfectly in keeping with the time and place. He did not make an armory of his waist, but carried two pistols. He wore top-boots, riding breeches, and dark-blue flannel shirt, with scarlet set in front. A loose neck-handerchief left his fine firm throat free. I do not at all remember his features, but the frank, manly expression of his fearless eyes and his courteous manner gave one a feeling of confidence in his word and in his undaunted courage.

The impression left upon my mind by the scouts of which Wild Bill was the chief was of their extreme grace. Their muscles were like steel, but they might have been velvet, so smooth and flexible seemed every movement. Wild Bill reminded me of a thorough-bred horse. Uncertain as was his origin, he looked as if he had descended from a race who valued the body as a choice possession, and therefore gave it every care. He not only looked like a thorough-bred, but like a racer, for he seemed, even in repose, to give evidence of great capabilities of endurance—of fine "staying powers," in his own vernacular. The days of the Greeks are slowly returning to us, when the human form will be so cared for that no development it is capable of will be neglected. Among the white aborigines of the plains, the frontiersmen and scouts, there have long existed fine specimens of physical development that one seldom encounters among people who live an in-door life.[14]

On July 31, 1869, the *Junction City Weekly Union* posted an article about a group of excursionists taking a trip on July 26 west to Sheridan, the "end of the track," and stopping in Hays City, where their friends George and Elizabeth Custer awaited them:

Excursion To Sheridan
On Monday last a party, consisting of Richard Bowne, Esq., a prominent member of the New York bar; Mrs. Bowne; Elizas and

Elizabeth Custer undoubtedly admired James Butler Hickok. But it was her husband General Custer that had her love and respect. After he died at the Little Big Horn in 1876 she spent the rest of her life telling his story. She died in 1933. *Author's collection.*

Annie Bowne; Mr. T.C. Bowne; Mr. E.W. Parsons, of New York City; Mr. Charles E. Alioth of Lausaune, Switzerland; and Mr. and Mrs. Boller of this place, started on a trip to Sheridan, the present terminus of the Kansas Pacific railway...

At Hays City, the excursionists had the pleasure of meeting "Wild Bill" of Harper's Magazine notoriety; and were besides greatly impressed with the air of respectability which characterized all the inhabitants of that wealthy and flourishing metropolis...

Elizabeth Custer wrote of this July meeting with that well-heeled group of friends noted above in Hays City that summer of 1869.

Occasionally we went to the train to meet excursionists who had telegraphed us to meet them. The officers were all of them more than strict in their injunctions to us to look neither to the right nor to the left in the town, and as they shut us in behind the closed curtains of the travelling-carriage they called out, laughingly, but nevertheless in earnest, "No peeking, now." The driver had his loaded carbine beside him, and listened attentively to some whispered instructions as he took up the reins. He was told, in addition, to draw up to the depot on the side farthest from the town, where our escort, having ridden beside the wagon, lifted us down and hurried us out of what seemed like a "Black Maria," it was so dismal in the carriage, and we were taken into the station, where the crowd was kept away by the dignity and authority of the officers' manner. One of the guests did "peek" through, and seeing the tables in the saloons with heaps of money, guarded by knives and revolvers, she was frightened into never looking again.

In one of these excursion parties were some of our Eastern acquaintances, and they begged to see Wild Bill. They sent the brakeman into the little street to ask him to come in, and they gave flowers to any bystander whom they saw, requesting that they be given to the renowned scout. But the more he was pursued with messages the more he retired from sight, hiding in the little back room of one of the drinking-saloons opposite. He was really a very modest man and very free from swagger or bravado. Finally, General Custer, persuaded by pretty girls, whom no one ever can resist, returned with the hero of the hour, for Wild Bill and General Custer were fast friends, having faced danger together many times.

Bill's face was confused at the words of praise with which General Custer introduced him, and his fearless eyes were cast down in chagrin at the torture of being gazed at by the crowd. He went through the enforced introduction for General Custer's sake, but it was a relief when the engine whistle sounded that released him.[15]

By the summer of 1869, Hays City was approaching two years of existence. The few main streets in town had, for the most part over those two years, upgraded from canvas tents and dugouts to frame buildings, even sporadic outbursts of rickety wooden sidewalks on Main Street and Front Street, divided from each other by the Kansas Pacific railroad track that ran down the middle. Back of Main Street was Second Street. Back of Front Street was Sproat Street. The north-south streets were Fort Street on the west and Chestnut Street on the east.

But if the streets were a little straighter and real buildings lined the main streets, little had changed to dispel the image of Hays City's early days when it was an end-of-the-track town; saloons, gambling dens, and dancehalls filled with the general flotsam of a westward-floating population following two steel rails from town to town; card sharps and con men, swindlers and grifters, pimps and prostitutes, gun men of all stripes, soldiers crazed in the last war, opportunists of all kinds seeking prey, all fueled by a regular supply of alcohol. Throw in frontier Fort Hays and its hundreds of soldiers less than a mile from the city, and all mixed in with an occasional preacher, a grocer, maybe a barber, maybe a teacher, all the latter mentioned trying to hold on until the circus moved on west, and hoping with that withdrawal would come structure and security, much of it through enforcement of the law. Yet it is that very enforcement of the law that fell short for a long time in Hays City, and compelled the birth of a vigilance committee to stand in the stead of formal law enforcement.

Matt Clarkson recalled when he and his brother arrived in the early days of Hays City, there were "twenty-two saloons, three dance halls, one little grocery, and one clothing store. We did not think anything of having one or two dead men on the streets nearly every morning. Some of them were soldiers from the fort. There was no law except the law of the six-shooter."[16] The *Junction City Weekly Union* posted this editorial in its May 8, 1869 issue:

There are probably eight or ten respectable men in Hays City, and why the eight or ten stay there God only knows. Gamblers, pimps, prostitutes, and dead beats run the town, and the most unblushing defiance of everything that is decent is the prevailing sentiment. One year ago, for the 'joke' of the thing, they elected a prostitute as one of the School Board, and another Street Commissioner. How it is to be expected that black or white soldiers will act any other way when they get a taste of the lightning poison vended there is a mystery to us. We hope the authorities of the State will incur no expense in protecting any such a class as runs Hays City.

The *Topeka Kansas State Record* had a correspondent in Hays City on June 11, 1869. He reported of Hays City, "No law in town – Thieves, robbers and pick-pockets, have undisputed sway."

Events had been building towards this out-of-control summer of 1869 in Hays City for quite a while. Ellis County's first sheriff was Thomas Gannon, elected into office on December 6, 1867. Gannon made his headquarters in Hays City. Records show that many times he had to request military back-up from Fort Hays in chasing and confronting outlaws. His time as sheriff was short, as by April of 1868 he had disappeared; many believed that he was ambushed and murdered to prevent his testimony in an upcoming criminal case.

During Gannon's short reign as sheriff of Ellis County, Hays City was incorporated on February 6, 1868. The new city trustees hired W. T. Butler, Isaac Thayer, and Peter Lanihan as the new city law enforcement officers. One Rufus Edwards later joined the group, but by August, two of the four had resigned for unknown reasons.

Gannon's successor as sheriff of Ellis County was J. V. Mcintosh, a druggist, with his pharmacy on Fort Street. He served as county sheriff from April 1868 until January 1869. After that, Isaac Thayer is shown as the sheriff of both Hays City and Ellis County. That same transition month of January, 1869, Governor Harvey of Kansas was shocked to hear that Hays City had been placed under martial law by Fort Hays military authorities. The governor demanded an immediate explanation and received this response from the fort commander, Lieutenant Colonel Anderson Nelson:

Fort Hays (about a mile from Hays City) has been the depot of supplies for Gen'l Sheridan's forces in the field and consequently it sometimes happens that three or four hundred, Wagonmasters, teamsters, &c are congregated here at one time. While here numbers of these men have been in the habit of visiting Hays City, after night-fall and what with the use of whiskey and their revolvers the town was rendered very uncomfortable for the better class of citizens.

It was on the representation of such citizens that I sent a patrol in a few nights since to stop the dangerous rowdyism then going on. Nearly fifty arrests were made and of that number there may have been five or six citizens, the balance were government employees. It can well be imagined that a few citizens might be arrested under such circumstances as much from accident as design, albeit they were in rather bad company as I am told nearly all the arrests were made in a bawdy dance house.

I feel assured, my Dear Sir, that you will justify me in any arrest I may deem it my duty to make in Hays City, for I will interfere with such a stretch of authority on the part of the military, only for the protection of life and property, and at such times when I am satisfied that the better class of citizens are unable to protect themselves.

I presume also that you have been informed that three colored soldiers were very recently taken out of the jail at Hays City at midnight and hung by the inhabitants of that town.

Martial law has never been declared in Hays City—should such a necessity arise I should certainly notify you immediately, believing that the circumstances which would call forth such an order would also in your estimation justify the declaration.[17]

Isaac Thayer's five-month reign as sheriff of Hays City and Ellis County was described by Hays City historian James Drees as "marred by shootings, lynchings, riots , and general disorder."[18]On May 5, 1869, Sheriff Thayer vanished from Hays City and never returned—yet he turned up several years later running a saloon in Newton, Kansas.

On July 7, 1869, the Ellis County commissioners, the probate judge, the county clerk, a deputy U. S. Marshal, and fifty-five citizens, including Alonzo Webster and Samuel Strawhun, petitioned Governor Harvey to appoint one R. A. Eccles as sheriff. But Harvey refused to appoint Thayer's successor; at the time, Kansas law made no provision for vacancies to be filled when there was no under-sheriff to take over. So Ellis County authorities would have to wait for the November election have a sheriff.

This was a serious conundrum that faced the Hays City Vigilance Committee, many of whom were also signees on the petition to the governor to appoint Eccles. To wait almost six months to place a new sheriff was unthinkable, especially considering the rapidly escalating violence and mayhem in Hays City. Where would they find such a man that could bring law and order to a town that had yet to know any? Surely they deliberated for a while, yet the decision was probably unanimous when they decided on their man.

While this political and practical crisis was playing out that summer, the more sedate citizens of Hays City persevered in trying to establish a safe and secure life in the chaos of this frontier town. In 1926, Annie Gilkeson recalled for William Connelley her struggle as a young mother in Hays City in the summer of 1869:

William Hickock – Gentleman.

Much has been written recently, of that picturesque figure commonly known as "Wild Bill". His historians seem to vary greatly in their estimates of his character and personality. In this connection I have been induced to relate an incident in my life, in which he played a prominent part. The very name "Wild Bill" conjures up a picture, vastly different from the one of him impressed upon my memory.

It was in the early part of the year 1868 [1869], when I arrived in Hays, with my oldest daughter Jessie, then just a babe of ten months. My husband had preceded me the year before, to establish his business as a druggist.

Saloons were so numerous, that they were in close proximity to every thing and place. My husband's store had one next door to it, and another directly across the street. The saloon next door was kept by a young man, who though engaged in the leading vocation of the place, never seemed to indulge in his own medicine. By such an exemplary young man, I was so favorably impressed that I did not hesitate when asked to loan him my baby. He liked to play with her in the mornings when his business was dull.

On one morning of a very hot day, he came for her as usual. The street was a mire of dust, at least six inches deep. When I thought it was time to bring her home, I went to my door to see why he was keeping her so long. I saw him sitting in his chair by the door. His eyes were closed, and his head hanging in a drunken stupor. But where was the baby? I looked again and there in the middle of the street in all that dirt, I saw her. She must have crawled there because she could not walk.

I flew to her rescue and in so doing roused my neighbor. Lurching to his feet he began suddenly to swear in a loud and angry voice. In horible oaths he called me all the vile names ever called women. I was at once amazed; terribly frightened and deeply humiliated. There I was in the street, with a drunken man labeling me a vile women, for all the town to hear. I felt utterly disgraced and unable to ever hold my head again. My husband was not at home. I was utterly alone and no one came near or offered to help me. To me it was terrible beyond belief. A strict Methodist, I had never heard profanity even in a mild form. Now it was being poured over me like a malignant rain. I can realize now that to Hays in its frontier period, a drunken man cursing a woman was a trivial affair. The town had its full quota of fallen women and their affairs and quarrels were frequent.

But my rescue was to come and from no less a personage then "Wild Bill." He happened to be sitting on the porch of a house near by. He alone—my gentlemen, seemed to sense the affair in its true aspect. Springing to his feet, I heard him call in a commanding tone "arrest that man." Instantly there was action and plenty of it, with "Wild Bill" taking a prominent part.

With my baby I fled to my house, where through a crack in the door I watched the conflict. The saloon keeper once aroused had a terrible temper and fought like a tiger. His face was soon streaming with blood. But my good friend, William Hickock—Gentleman, soon shut off that flow of profanity.

The next morning, a very contrite and much bandaged young man came to offer profuse apologies. These I accepted in the spirit in which they were offered. But never again did I loan him the baby. I did not have an opportunity to see or speak to "Wild Bill" and thank him for his kindness. I was much too frightened at the time to consider the amenities. However I have never forgotten the part he played in the incident. His chivalrous instincts made him quick to recognize the true facts in the case, and sent him promptly to the rescue; therefore I have written him down, William Hicock—Gentleman.

I never became acquainted with "Wild Bill", our paths seemed never to meet, but of course I saw him many times. In personal appearance William Hickock was certainly a picturesque figure. "Tall and well formed" as he has often been described I cannot describe his features exactly, as I was never near enough to know them. I know only his general form and appearance, which was most graceful and pleasing. His hair looked to me to be dark brown in color, but it may have been lighter as I have read it described. It was long and curiling however and reached to his shoulders. I know he wore the popular hat of the day—a soft felt with wide brim. His bloused shirts were of the dark, rich color known as magenta—not the bright vulgar red of today.

"Wild Bill" was not sheriff at the time of my incident but became so later. I know that he gained much notoriety because of his skill in shooting, "quick on the trigger" they said. I saw mute evidence of this one morning on the porch of the saloon opposite. A board upheld by two chairs, on which was stretched the body of a man fully dressed. A handkerchief over the face told the tale. I was told that Hickock had killed this man in the exercise of his duties as sheriff. I learned later that it was Straghan for whose death he gave up his own life.

It seems to me now, as I look back through the glamour of over fifty years in the retroscope, that he—"Wild Bill"- was like one of those knights of old. They rode forth seeking to dispense justice—each in his own way. With a specialty for rescuing females in distress. He needed but the graceful cape over his shoulders and a curling plume to complete the picture.

Annie Gilkeson
(Mrs) A.D. Gilkeson[19]

On July 23, Samuel Strawhun and Joe N. Weiss (a former deputy U. S. Marshal), both residents of Hays City, walked down Tenth Street mid-afternoon to the grocery store and post office of R.W. Evans to confront clerk Alonzo B. Webster. Webster, a member of the Vigilance Committee, had recently given both Weiss and Strawhan notices, on behalf of the committee, to leave town. The confrontation soon turned into a physical attack on Webster by the two. Then Weiss pulled a gun, but Webster was quicker with his pistol and shot Weiss in the gut, killing him. There is an unverified claim, made years later in a Dodge City newspaper, that Strawhun shot at Webster through a window as he was escaping, but the shot missed.

Evans was away from his business at the time. When he returned, Webster explained what had happened. Fearing that Strawhun would return with a cadre of men, they armed themselves and stood outside on the street corner awaiting their adversaries. Hickok was in town, and

#4125

Samuel Strawhun came west from Rolla, Missouri to Hays City, He was just 23 and Hickok was 32 when they had their fateful confrontation. *Author's collection.*

arrived shortly to support Webster and Evans. "Let them come," he was reported to say. "We are ready for them," he added, indicating he had his two Navy Colts. They never came.

Sometime before the middle of August the Vigilance Committee decided on their man for sheriff, James Butler Hickok. "The Vigilance Committee showed discretion and sound judgment in securing as town Marshal the famous 'Wild Bill' Hickok. He had his hands full in keeping order in the ranks of that motley and unruly horde of humanity, but he was equal to the task and proved himself one of the most efficient peace officers the West has ever known,"[20] Miguel Otero recalled, describing Hickok as sheriff in Hays City in 1869.

Indicating that Hickok had been installed by the Vigilance Committee as the sheriff of Hays City and Ellis County by August 18 was this entry in the *Leavenworth Times and Conservative* of August 22, printing their journalist's August 18 report on Hays City in general and Hickok specifically: "The greatest need of Sheridan is a magistrate. [The area in which Sheridan was located was attached to Ellis County for judicial purposes.] If Wild Bill arrests an offender in Sheridan there is a log jail to receive him, but no justice to try the case. Justices of the Peace have before been appointed but they resign so fast that the Governor has become disgusted and gone off to New York..."

In a later report in the *Hays City Sentinal*, Hays City's Martin Allen recalled that the date of Hickok's special election as sheriff took place on August 23, 1869. Yet the entry in the *Times and Conservative* indicates Hickok was clearly functioning as sheriff at least a week before that. On August 31, the *Times and Conservative* reported that in Hays City, "At the election held here a few days ago...J. B. Hickok, familiarly known as 'Wild Bill,' elected Sheriff of the County." What is most likely is that the Vigilance Committee probably had Hickok on the payroll from about August 1, and then ratified that decision on the back end with a special election held on August 23, making Hickok the elected sheriff of Hays City and Ellis County.

While the Vigilance Committee was finalizing the installation of Sheriff Hickok, he was still working steadily as deputy U. S. Marshal. Major George Gibson of Fort Hays wrote to his superior at Fort Leavenworth on August 26:

> *Sir: I have the honor to report that J. B. Hickok delivered at this post on the 21st a Mulatto and a negro whom he claims to be deserters from the 10th U S Cav. Troop "C". I have ascertained since the men have been confined at this Post, that they came from Sheridan, Ks., that they were deserters where they have been living for some time past, that they there acknowledged that they were deserters, and left precipitately, when Capt. Circy U. S. Marshal. attempted to arrest them. The name of the Mulatto is given as Ed Fry and of the Negro as George [Allen]...I have the honor, to request to be informed whether information of any such deserters has been received at Dept. Head'qrs, also what disposition be made of these prisoners.*[21]

James had only days before added sheriff of Hays City and Ellis County to his resume, when he was involved in his first shootout as a lawman. This press report dated August 23 in Hays City broke the story:

Last night Bill Hitchcock, better known as "Wild Bill", acting sheriff of the county, while attempting to preserve peace among a party of intoxicated roughs, or "wolves" shot a man named Bill Melvin through the neck and lungs. Melvin is still living, but the doctors say, with no hopes of recovery. He attempted to shoot several citizens, and was determined to quarrel with every one whom he met, using his revolver freely, but fortunately injuring no one.

The Leavenworth Times and Conservative ran these circumspect few lines on August 24: "J.B. Hickok (Wild Bill) shot one Mulrey at Hays Tuesday. Mulrey died yesterday morning. Bill has been elected sheriff of Ellis County."

Though this was Hickok's first shoot-out as a lawman, we know unfortunately very little about the man who died. Even his last name is in doubt; Mulvey, Melvin, Mulrey? On the federal census of 1870, Judge M. E. Joyce of Hays City recorded the deceased as John Murphy, twenty-five years old, a soldier born in New York. But we do have an eyewitness to the shooting: Miguel Otero, who recalled more than fifty years later the incident he witnessed in Hays City as a young boy, just one month short of his tenth birthday:

I was standing near Wild Bill on Main Street, when someone began "shooting up the town" at the eastern end of the street. It was Bill Mulvey, a notorious murderer from Missouri, known as a handy man with a gun. He had just enough liquor in him to be mean and he seemed to derive great amusement from shootng holes into the mirrors, as well as the bottles of liquor behind the bars, of the saloons in that section of the street. As was usually the case with such fellows, he was looking for trouble, and when someone told him that Wild Bill was the town marshal and therefore it behooved him to behave himself, Mulvey swore he would find Wild Bill and shoot him on sight. He further averred that the marshal was the very man he was looking for and that he had come to the "damn" town for the express purpose of killing him.

The tenor of these remarks was somehow made known to Wild Bill. But hardly had the news reached him than Mulvey appeared on the scene, tearing toward us on his iron grey horse, rifle in hand, full cocked. When Wild Bill saw Mulvey he walked out to meet him, apparently waving his hand to some fellows behind Mulvey and calling to them: "Don't shoot him in the back; he is drunk."

Mulvey stopped his horse and, wheeling the animal about, drew a bead on his rifle in the direction of the imaginary man he thought Wild Bill was addressing. But before he realized the ruse that had been played upon him, Wild Bill had aimed his six-shooter and fired—just once. Mulvey dropped from his horse—dead, the bullet having penetrated his temple and then passed through his head.

During this episode I had been standing about twenty-five feet from Wild Bill. My joy in the outcome was boundless, for I had been afraid that Mulvey, with his rifle trained directly on Wild Bill, would pull the trigger.[22]

The remains of the unknown Bill Mulvey were laid to rest in the Hays City Cemetery, as they have for more than 150 years. On September 1, Major George Gibson received an answer on the two deserters that Hickok brought in to Fort Hays on August 21:

In reply to your letter of the 26th Ult, referring to the cases of Ed Fry and George [Allen] who were delivered at your post by J. B. Hickok, as deserters from "C" Troop, 10th Cavalry;...you will send them to Fort Dodge under a suitable guard, from which point they will be forwarded to Camp Supply, I.T., with a view of their being sent from that Post to the company or companies to which they belong, at the first opportunity...[23]

There had been a reward posted for one of the two deserters, which Hickok received in December of 1869. The amount is unknown. Right on the heels of the Mulvey shooting came another one on September 27. Unlike Mulvey, much is known of Hickok's antagonist that day, Samuel Strawhun. One of four children, he was born on October 10, 1845, in Benton County, Missouri. Strawhun was twenty-three and Hickok was thirty-two when the Hays City shooting took place. Strawhun grew up in Rolla, Missouri, and there are still members of the Strawhun family living in Rolla today. Strawhun never married. As a young man he made his way west. Official records show that he was hired as a government teamster on November 1, 1868, and just six weeks later was promoted to be a courier between Fort Hays and Fort Dodge.

On February 8,1869, Judge John V. Macintosh of Hays City ordered Strawhun to serve papers on the commander of Fort Hays, requesting the commander to bring before the court a prisoner from the Fort Hays guardhouse. Yet on March 28, Strawhun himself was arrested by deputy U. S. Marshal John S. Park, based on a federal warrant. The charge on that warrant is unknown. As noted previously, Strawhun was one of the signees on the petition from citizens of Hays City to Governor Harvey, requesting the appointment of R. A. Eccles on July 7, just two weeks before he and Joe Weiss attacked Alonzo Webster in the Evans store.

Hickok had some history with Strawhun in Ellsworth before either of them had come to Hays City. It appears that in the winter of 1867, Strawhun and some friends were belligerently drunk and armed on the streets of Ellsworth. Sheriff E. W. Kingsbury and deputy sheriff Chauncey Whitney, with the help of J. B. Hickok, deputy U. S. Marshal, disarmed the drunk miscreants and tied them to posts to cool off, rather than taking them to jail. Strawhun probably remembered well those humiliating hours tied to that post.

The Hays City press broke the story on September 28:

Hays City, Sept. 27

A man named Sam'l Stranghan was shot and instantly killed by "Wild Bill," (J. B. Hickok) Sheriff, at one o'clock this morning It appears that Stranghan and a number of his companions being "wolfing" all night, wished to conclude by cleaning out a beer saloon and breaking things generally. "Wild Bill" was called upon to quiet them. In the melee that followed Stranghan was killed. The Coroner's verdict this morning was justifiable homicide. Stranghan was buried this afternoon.

The *Lawrence Kansas Daily Tribune* on September 30 ran the story from the *Leavenworth Commercial* that printed a dispatch from Hays City datelined September 27, that expanded details on the shootings at Hays City:

WILD BILL PRESERVES ORDER.—

About twelve o'clock last night a difficulty occurred in this place at the house [saloon] of John Bittles, between a party of roughs and the proprietor. Policeman Hickok and Ranahan [deputy Sheriff Pete Lanihan] interfered to keep order, when remarks were made against Hickok—Wild Bill. In his efforts to preserve order, Samuel Strangham was shot through the head by him, and instantly killed. Justice Joyce held an inquest on the body to-day, six well-known citizens being selected for the jurymen. The evidence in one or two instances was very contradictory. The jury returned a verdict to the effect that Samuel Strangham came to his death from a pistol wound at the hands of J. B. Hickok, and that the shooting of said Strangham was justifiable.

Finally, the Hays City press, probably the *Railway Advance*, ran this story by an eyewitness to the event, who may have been the editor of the *Railway Advance* himself:

PARTICULARS OF THE KILLING OF STRANHAN AT HAYS CITY
Hays City, September 30, 1869

Eds. Commercial:- Allow me, an eye witness, to relate to you the details of the shooting affair last Sunday night, during which a certain Sam Stranghan was killed.

It seems that there was on the part of this Stranhan and some of his associates bad feeling against certain citizens of this town, and members of the Vigilance committee. To satisfy their hatred, they mobbed together and went on Sunday night, about half past 11 o'clock to the saloon of Mr. John Bitter, with the intent to break up the establishment. The crowd, numbering about fourteen to eighteen persons, called for beer in a frantic manner. The glasses had to be filled up continually. Meantime the men were passing in and out of the saloon, and as it afterwards appeared carried the glasses to an adjoining vacant lot. Mr Bitter remarked that the number of glasses was diminishing, and saw that Stranhan had carried out some of them. The noise was fearful, all the men cryng at the top of their voices, beer! Beer! and using the most obscene language. This went on for a short time, when they began throwing the beer at each other. During all the noise one could hear threats as "I shall kill someone to-night just for luck," or "some one will have to go up to-night," etc.

Mr. Bitter finally called the policeman, Mr. Wm. Hickock, known as "Wild Bill," asking him to go out and fetch the missing glasses back. Wild Bill shortly returned with both hands full of glasses, when Stranhan remarked that he would shoot anyone that should try to interfere with his fun. Wild Bill set the glasses on the counter, Stranhan took hold of one and took it up in a threatening manner. He had no time to execute his design for a shot fired by Mr. Hickock killed him. He dropped down dead. The inquest was held next morning at 9 o'clock. The verdict of the jury was that deceased was shot by Mr. Hickock, and that the homicide was justifiable, the same being in self-defense. Too much credit cannot be given to Wild Bill for his endeavor to rid the town of such dangerous characters as this Stranhan was.

In 1876, years after the event, John Malone claimed that after bringing the glasses into John Bitter's saloon, Hickok said "Boys, you hadn't ought to treat a poor old man this way." Strawhun then said he would throw the glasses out again. Hickok replied, "Do, and they will carry you out."[24] Though unconfirmed and unlikely, local tradition has it that J. B. Hickok was master of ceremonies at the funerals of both Mulvey and Strawhun.

Recollections of incidents involving Hickok in Hays City are colorful and abundant. Buffalo hunter Joe W. Hutt recalled in 1925 seeing a demonstration of Hickok's amazing prowess with a six-shooter in 1868 or 1869: "I saw him draw his pistol in front of the old depot, throw it over his first finger, cocking it with his thumb as it came around and keep a tomato can jumping for a whole block down to Riley's saloon on the next corner and it also took a good horseman to do a trick like that. He was not a drunken, quarrelsome man-killer, but picturesque and a fine shot. It was not always the blustering bullies that were the bravest men in a western town."[25]

Harry Young, who in the future would gain notoriety as the bartender in the Number Ten saloon, on August 2, 1876, recalled how, at the age of nineteen, he first met Hickok in 1868 in Hays City:

Our first meeting is indelibly impressed upon my mind. I had been dancing all night in one of the numerous dance-halls of Hayes City, as was the almost universal custom in those days of strangers looking for pleasure and entertainment. Morning found me waiting outside for one of the dance-hall girls, for whom I had formed a boyish fancy. The night's entertainment had proved costly to me, my finances having dwindled from forty dollars to a dollar and a half. This extravagance on my part had been noted by Wild Bill, unknown to me. As I stood on the sidewalk, deliberating, someone touched me on the shoulder. I turned, and found myself face to face with the finest looking man I have ever seen or ever expect to see; a man who excited my greatest admiration. He was about six feet, two inches in height; perfectly formed and of strong physique, and at that time thirty-one years old. He had long auburn hair, and clear blue eyes; eyes that showed kindness and friendship to all, except the evil doer, to whom they meant the reverse. I was naturally drawn toward him, and instinctively felt that no matter how tough the town or its lawless characters, I had met a friend. He asked me where I hailed from and I replied: "From the Santa Fe Construction." He gave me some very wholesome advice regarding spending my money so foolishly and asked me what I was doing at Hayes City. I told him I was looking for work. After a long pause, during which he appeared to be sizing me up, he asked me if I could drive a six-mule team. I could not, and frankly told him so. He evidently thought I could learn quickly, for he took me into a near-by saloon and taught me how to tie a Government hame-string. The Government at that time used a leather strap with a knot on the end of it instead of the buckle and tongue of the present day.

The next morning he went with me to Fort Hayes, two and a half miles distant. There we met the corral boss, and Wild Bill asked him to put me to work, stating that he had taken a fatherly interest in me and wanted to see me get along in good shape. The corral boss asked if he could drive a six-mule team. To which Bill replied: "Yes." A mule collar was thrown on the ground, and I was told to tie the hames on, which I did. He then turned to Bill with a broad grin and remarked, "You have drilled him well." He then told me to remain at the post and he would put me to work. During the day I got acquainted with some of the mule drivers, who showed me how to harness a six-mule team. The term used for mule drivers in those days was "mule-skinners." The second morning Bill came out to see how I was getting along, and to his astonishment found me driving a six-mule team. He rode by my side for some distance, giving me pointers that afterward were very useful to me. I worked at this post for six months, during which I saw a great deal of Wild Bill, as I was in town nearly every night.[26]

211

C.J. Bascom, long-time employee on the Kansas Pacific Railroad, knew Hickok well and followed his activities in several towns along the Kansas Pacific. Writing in the *Kansas City Star* on June 15, 1913, Bascom recalled an incident in Hays City that, but for the quick and calm thinking of Hickok, could have easily brought his demise. Bascom stated that he was taking a walk around town with Jim Curry, the owner of a restaurant in Hays City. They came to Tommy Drum's saloon on North Main. Hickok was sitting there with his back to the door, but far enough in the rear not to expect any trouble. Bascom wrote:

> *Curry slipped up behind, and pressed his cocked revolver against his head, saying "Now, you son of a gun! I've got you!" Bill did not move a muscle. He showed no concern. He realized his danger but said in a casual way, "Jim, you would not murder a man without giving him a show!" Jim replied, "I'll give you the same you would give me, you long-haired tough!" Everyone present knew the peril in which Bill stood, and the suspense was awful. Tommy's oath was "By the boot." He was running about the saloon in great perturbation exclaiming "By the boot! By the boot!" Bill was the only cool, self-contained man in the room, and remarked "Jim, let us settle this feud. How would a bottle of champagne all around do?" The manner in which Bill had taken the whole incident, and the unconcern with which he made the remark relieved the tension, and all burst out laughing. Tommy Drum opened a pint bottle of champagne for everyone present. Curry and Bill shook hands and the feud between them was over.*

Incidents like the one above convinced Hickok to, where possible, always sit facing the door of whatever establishment he was in. As the sheriff of Hays City in particular, he realized that there might be attempts on his life by revenge-seekers or unpredictable and unstable characters like Jim Curry, above. Mrs. John Mueller related to her son, Henry, an incident where Hickok's life was in danger in Hays City. She told him how Hickok had evaded one of these rough types that was looking for him. At the time, Hickok was rooming with the Muellers. One afternoon she was opening the front door as Hickok was leaving. She quickly closed it and said, "Mr. Hickok, there's a man across the street and he has a gun. I saw him when you first came home and he's probably waiting for you to come out."[27] Hickok glanced out the window, then calmly borrowed an old hat and coat of Mr. Mueller's, stuffed his long hair up under the hat and put on the coat. Clothed accordingly and acting with a limp, he hobbled down the street, unnoticed by the gunman.

In early October, an event took place involving Hickok and his duties as a deputy U.S. Marshal while at the same time serving as the sheriff of Hays City and Ellis County. The event was precipitated by an incident that took place on September 15, when one Bob Connors murdered his employer near Pond City, a drover known by the name of Hammy. It seems Hammy awoke one morning to find Connors' hand under his pillow in preparation of smothering Hammy. In the morning he fired Conners. Hammy went to pay him off, and as he did, Conners shot and killed him. A few days later, while the search was on for him, Conners tried to blend in with the crowd at the train depot in Hays City before trying to get on the train and escape Ellis County. He was recognized and arrested by deputy U.S. Marshal Jack Bridges, and placed in the on-post jail at Fort Hays for safety's sake. He was concerned that a lynch mob might try to take him. Bridges believed he would be put on trial at Topeka or Sheridan.

However, on September 20, Fort Hays post commander Colonel Gibson wrote to Bridges, telling him that he had information from a Leavenworth merchant that if Connors were taken to Sheridan for trial, he would be lynched. Claiming he had no jurisdiction in this civil matter, he urged Bridges to get Connors safely to Topeka. Bridges could not, or did not, want to make this decision. Gibson then telegraphed Governor Harvey, who answered him with this curt response: "I know nothing of the case deliver Connors only to the proper legal authorities. Jas. M. Harvey."[28]

While the parties were denying responsibility, on September 28, there was a big jailbreak from the Fort Hays guardhouse, and Connors was one of the escapees. He was recaptured hours later, however. This is where things stood on October 3 when Hickok walked into Gibson's office with a warrant for Connors. Out of that meeting came this letter the same day to Governor Harvey. Much of the first part of the letter rehashed the details up to October 3, of which Harvey was already aware. Then Gibson got into the real reason for sending this letter to Harvey:

This morning about 10 o'clock Mr. J. B. Hickok (commonly known as Wild Bill) presented himself at my office accompanied by an Asst whom he called Pete, and made a formal demand for Connors, handing me what he claimed to be a Warrant for the arrest of said Connors signed by John Whitteford claiming to be a Justice of the Peace for the County of Wallace, Kansas. The document in question did not bear upon its face any seal.

Inasmuch as the Warrant directed Mr. Hickok as Sheriff of Ellis County to make the arrest I demanded to see his Commission which was not produced, he acknowledging that he had never been Commissioned by you. Under the circumstances I deemed it to be my duty to decline turning him over. Further I have no evidence that there was any regularly constituted Justice of the Peace for Wallace County.

Acting then purely agreeable to your instructions I have the honor to request that should any State Official endeavour to interfere with me in regard to my non Compliance in this case that you will at once interpose your strong arms in my behalf.[29]

Two days later, on October 5, Governor Harvey replied to Major Gibson. In part, it read:

Your refusal to deliver Conners on the demand of Mr. J. B. Hickok meets with my full approval. That person has no legal authority whatever to act as Sheriff of Ellis County, nor under the circumstances through which the vacancy occurred can any Sheriff be chosen until the regular election in November next...The execution of accused parties without trial must be stopped, and while I have no positive assurance that such is the design in this instance, I can see no hardship, no hindrance of justice, in safely retaining Conners until he can have a legal trial at the next term of the court of the Eighth Judicial District for Ellis County. Renewing my approval of your action in this matter, I beg to request that you will continue to retain Conners in your custody. I am obliged to leave the State to-morrow, to be absent some three weeks, and should any action be initiated hostile to your authority, I trust that its final determination may be withheld until my return.[30]

While Gibson and Harvey were in dual denial, deputy U.S. Marshal Jack Bridges decided he could wait no longer. On the morning of October 5, even before Gibson received Harvey's letter, Bridges sent deputy U.S. Marshal C. J. Cox to get Connors. Cox took Connors to Sheridan for trial, where inexplicably, and surely frustrating for Bridges and Hickok, he was acquitted.[31]

On November 2, the very elections took place that Governor Harvey had insisted were the only legal way for Hays City and Ellis County to install a sheriff. The candidates for sheriff were J. B. Hickok and his deputy, Pete Lanihan. The results were 89 votes for Hickok, and 114 votes for Lanihan. Hickok remained acting sheriff until December 31, when Lanihan took over.

After the election, James continued his work as a deputy United States Marshal, as well as his now-temporary assignment as sheriff of Hays City and Ellis County. In the *Leavenworth Times and Conservative* of November 21, a correspondent from Hays City described on November 16 the town and reported, "Wild Bill is sheriff and makes a good officer."

On November 17, Hickok visited Topeka and stayed at the Topeka House. The *Kansas Daily Commonwealth* noted him twice in their issue of November 18, the reporter taking a few poetic and literary liberties to make his point: "'Wild Bill,' whom they have attempted to kill, but who has the inexorable will to perambulate the earth still, and who is always ready for a 'mill,' save when he may chance to be ill, yesterday came up the Topeka hill to get a stomach fill." (Frontier haiku.) This was followed later that day by: "Sheriff Hickok, of Ellis County—yclept, in many a well-known story of border-life. 'Wild Bill,' is in town, registered at the Topeka House. Long may he be at Hays. 'Shake his ambrosial locks and give the nod, the stamp of fate, the sanction of a god!'" On December 8, the *Topeka Kansas State Record* made this report: "The papers are still electing Wild Bill, Sheriff of Ellis County. William himself, is content with being a private citizen of Topeka."

The next day, December 9, the *White Cloud Kansas Chief* stated firmly, "'Wild Bill' is going to spend the winter in Topeka." Yet the same day, the *Topeka Commonwealth* posted an article about an excursion party that had taken the Kansas Pacific all the way to Sheridan and back. The article mentioned, "Hays City under the guardian care of 'Wild Bill' is quiet and doing well."

Also on December 9, J. B. Hickok was in Hays City itself serving a notice on J. V. Macintosh. It seems that in the same election that James lost, the candidate who won the election for Ellis County representative, J. V. Macintosh, was accused by the losing candidate of election irregularities. As sheriff of Ellis County, Hickok served legal papers on the accused, at his residence. Hickok certified through his deputy the deliverance of these papers with the below statement:

Served the within notice at Hays City, Kansas, on the 9th day of December A.D. 1869, by delivering a certified copy of the same, at the usual place of residence of the within named J.V. Macintosh.

J.B. Hickok, Sheriff By Peter Lanihan.
Deputy Sheriff[32]

Kansas pioneer Adolph Roenigk recalled December of 1869, when he was a worker for the Kansas Pacific Railroad working at Fossil Creek Station (modern Russell, Kansas), and deputy U.S. Marshal Hickok came to the station:

There was quite a change at the station during my absence. A permanent telegraph office had been installed. A corporal's guard of seven or eight men from the 5th Infantry (General Nelson A. Miles' regiment) was stationed here, as was also every station along the line. Cook and his family had returned. The railroad was being extended to Denver, and this was a very busy place. A number of wood choppers' camps were located on Paradise Creek, north of Fossil Creek, where cordwood was cut, and ties were made, all of which was hauled to the station and shipped west to be used in extending the line.

While the work of making railroad ties was in progress at the woodcamps on Paradise Creek it had been reported that timber was being unlawfully cut on government land. Wild Bill (James B.) Hickok, who was then deputy U. S. Marshal at Hays City, came down to Fossil Creek Station to arrest the guilty parties. When he arrived on the train he wore a broad brimmed hat and a brand new buckskin suit with fringes on the elbow sleeves and trouser legs. A pair of six shooters strapped to his sides, he made the appearance of just such a picture as one could see on the cover of a dime novel. [This may be the same buckskin outfit that James wore just nine months earlier in April for the photographer Blakeslee of Mendota, Illinois, probably today Hickok's most widely recognized photographic image.]

While I was working at Fort Harker I had seen both Wild Bill and Buffalo Bill, who, with a number of others were carrying dispatches from one post to another. At the sight of them going and coming no more attention was paid than we do now to people in every day life. But on this occasion Wild Bill was dressed up for a purpose other than every day scout duty. He went to the wood camps on Paradise Creek and arrested five wood choppers for cutting wood on government land. With his five prisoners he took the train at Fossil Creek Station to Topeka where he turned them over to the United States court, who discharged them, no doubt, for want of evidence.[33]

Pertaining to these arrests, on November 26, 1869 Hickok appeared before U. S. Commissioner Haubeck and testified that "John Doe, Richard Roe, John Smith, Peter Jones all of whose Christian and surnames are to this affiant unknown...tenth day of November A.D. 1869 [did] unlawfully and feloniously...cut and cause to be removed certain timber...from the lands of the United States with the intent then and there to dispose and use the same other than for the use of the Navy of the United States...contrary to the Timber Act."[34]

Within a few days the names of the key offenders became known: Charles Hamilton, Charles Vernon, and John Hobbs. On December 14, Hickok went to Fossil Creek Station to arrest the offenders, as witnessed by Adolph Roenigk in the above entry. He took them before U. S. Commissioner Hill P. Wilson. Two witnesses appeared for the prosecution: Lieutenant L. W. Cooke and J. B. Hickok. Following is Hickok's testimony, including his answers while he was being deposed by one of the offenders, Charles Hamilton, who was apparently acting as his own defense attorney:

J.B. Hickok sworn:
My name is J.B. Hickok. I am a deputy United States Marshall. I went to the camp of the 3rd Inf. Det. about twenty four miles from the R W at Fossil Creek station perpendicular distance from the R road about twenty (20) miles on the 14th of Dec. A.D. 1869. Found prisoners cutting timber at a point (4 ½) four and one half miles to (5) five miles north from the camp of the 3rd. Inf., and about twenty four and one half (24½) miles to twenty five and one half (25½) miles from the line of KPRW. I saw Charles Hamilton cutting wood at this place, was cutting the wood into a R Rd tie. Saw Charles Vernon hauling ties from the creek to a place for loading. Saw John Hobbs trimming up timber and assisting in the general work of making ties. This is while they were in the Employ of Mr. Harris tie contractor.
Question by Chas. Hamilton to Witness: You say it is twenty miles from the 3rd. Infy to the R Rd.?

217

Answer: I do.
Question: How do you know it is that dist?
Answer: From having traveled it a great many times, as often perhaps as twenty times.
Question:From the Camp of the 3d Inf to where we were arrested is how far?
Answer: About four and one half (4 ½) miles.
Question: In what direction?
Answer: The camp of the 3rd Inf is from (¼ to ½) one fourth to one half of a mile east of a line running from the place of your arrest perpendicular to the R/Rd. Witness states further: The ties were cut along the line of the creek for a distance of one mile and one half (1 ½). Mr. Harris informed me that the ties hereinafter described were cut for him.

(Signed) J.B.Hickok U. S. Dept. Marshall [35]

Commissioner Hill P. Wilson found that the accused produced no exculpatory evidence, and that the defense of Charles Hamilton, that he was cutting timber on his own land that he soon intended to settle on under the Homestead Law, was pretextual and false. Wilson set bail at $1,000 each, and on December 19, Deputy Marshal J. B. Hickok was supposed to set out to deliver the prisoners to the prison in Topeka. It appears, however, that Hickok and the prisoners did not actually leave till two days later. The *Topeka Commonwealth* issue of December 21 reported that "Jas. B. Hickok, alias Wild Bill sent a whole buffalo to McMeekin yesterday, from Hays City. Mac serves up buffalo roasts and steak to-day with the usual etceteras." McMeekin was the proprietor of Topeka House, James' hotel of choice when in Topeka. The Topeka Record of December 22 stated that Hickok and his prisoners had arrived in Topeka on December 21. There is no official record of the ultimate determination of this case; however, some believed at the time that this indicated that the charges were dismissed.[36]

Late in December, Private William Gleason of Company I, 3rd Infantry, was sitting in the Fort Hays guardhouse charged with murder. Colonel Gibson requested that the proper civil authorities remove him for trial. No one appeared, so Gibson wrote his superiors: "I have held him until Hicock Deputy U.S. Marshal should arrive."[37] Hickok did not come, and Gibson arranged a military escort to Topeka. James had already left to spend the rest of the winter in Topeka.

12

1870

the WANDERER WANDERS

DEPUTY UNITED STATES MARSHAL

ONE FINAL DATE *with* DESTINY *in* HAYS CITY

In Topeka, J. B. Hickok sought out an old friend, Colonel H.C. Lindsay. Hickok knew Lindsay from back in Border-War era of the late 1850s, and they probably met up again on the western Kansas plains during the Indian campaigns of Hancock and Sheridan, when Lindsay served in the 18th Kansas Battalion. At one point in his visit with Lindsay, Hickok accompanied him on a trip to Kansas City when Lindsay was taking a drove of horses and mules there. Lindsay later recalled for William Connelley that James pointed out landmarks from the Border War located on or near the old California Road they were following. James used this same road back then for moving between Lawrence and Kansas City. East of Lawrence, they passed through old Franklin, now almost abandoned, and James remarked that he saw a thousand Border Ruffians camped here during the summer of 1856.[1]

Junction City, Ellsworth, Hays City, and Sheridan all had their share of people who, for whatever reason, wanted to challenge the famous James Butler Hickok. Topeka was no exception. On about February 6, near the corner of Sixth and Topeka, a man walked right up to Hickok and started to insult him. Provoked, James knocked him to the ground.

The *Topeka Commonwealth* of February 8 reported the incident: "Wild Bill was up before Judge Holmes yesterday, and fined five dollars for striking straight out from the shoulder and consequently hitting a man."

James' well-published intention to stay in Topeka for the winter ran up against his natural restlessness. Later in February he traveled by train to Warrensburg, Missouri, as a guest of another old friend, Joseph W. McClellen. The *Warrensburg Standard* on February 24,1870, reported, "J.B. Hickok is in town visiting his old friend J.W. McClellen." James and Joseph had served together as police detectives in Springfield, Missouri during 1863 and 1864, both reporting to the Provost Marshal's office. McClellen's German wife ran a restaurant in Warrensburg, and he had two children when Hickok visited, eight-year-old Maggie and eleven-year-old Benjamin. While with the McClellens, Hickok had his photograph done with Joseph's daughter, Maggie. The photographer was D. E. Sedgwick of Warrensburg. On March 3, in tribute to James and his visit to their town, the *Warrensburg Standard* ran the entire *Harpers* article of February 1867 in their March 3, 1870 issue.

In mid-March, James left his friend Joseph McClellen and rode the train ninety miles east to the state capital of Missouri, Jefferson City. He had come here by invitation from an unknown legislator. James caused a sensation visiting the floor of the Missouri House of Representatives. Among its numerous members were past friends of his as well. The *Topeka State Record* reported on March 22, 1870:

> *"Wild Bill," alias Sheriff Wm. Hickok, has recently been "lionising" at Jefferson City. Here is what the* St. Louis Democrat *correspondent has to say about it: Quite a sensation was created on the floor of the House by a visit from Wm. Hicock, Sheriff of Ellis county, Kansas, better known as "Wild Bill of the Prairies," a cognomen secured by his hair-breadth escapes, his personal encounters, and his services as a scout in the Union army. He has had great experience among the Indians, and as a trapper and hunter, and meets many old friends among the members.*

Come April, Hickok had returned to Topeka. "'Wild Bill'" is in the city again," reported the *Topeka Daily Commonwealth* on April 29. He may have arrived in Topeka a week or so earlier. By May he had moved on west sixty miles to Junction City, returning to his first home in Kansas after the war, when he came back to Kansas and Fort Riley at the request of Richard Owen in the spring of 1866.

#4127

March 1870 photograph taken in Warrensburg. Missouri by photographer D.E. Sedgewick. Eight-year-old Maggie McClellen and Wild Bill Hickok. *Author's collection.*

In 1923, J. C. Prine recalled for William Connelley Hickok in Junction City in Spring, 1870:

> *Your letter of the 12th is before me. I have delayed hoping I could see some of the old crowd that associated more intimately with W.B. then I ever did and knew him better. Of course I saw him often. The first time I saw him was the first time he appeared on the streets of Junction City. He was dressed to make a show and strutted like a turkey gobler. I should judge he was the proudest man in town. John A. Anderson said to me what do you think of him. I said to Anderson he wants to show off.*
>
> *About this time Anderson was building the Presbyterian Church. Somehow Anderson interested Wild Bill. All sorts of schemes were adopted to raise money, such as voting for the most popular lady [?] and Wild Bill helped to swell the vote. Gamblers were plenty in those days Wild Bill took a part...*
>
> *I will try to look up some of the old fellows and if I can gather any facts that will interest will send these forward. Old Mr. Pauteu knew Wild Bill in Ill. where he was a boy. He told me W.B. was his neighbor and a nice boy. Wild Bill lived in an era of Carnage and Slaughter. Finally it came his turn and he went the same route he had sent others. I will soon write further in regard to Wild Bill.*
>
> *Truly Yours, J C Prine*
>
> *PS I am sure Wild Bill was Marshall for a time or Assistant Marshall. I will learn more & write you.*[2]

There is anecdotal information in Junction City that Hickok was a lawman there at one time, but nothing in the official record to substantiate it. Prine recalls Anderson's building of the Presbyterian Church correctly. On March 8, 1868, John A. Anderson became pastor of the newly established Presbyterian Church in Junction City. Initially, services were performed in a building known as the "Corn Crib." By September of 1868, the congregation moved to Brown's Hall. Finally, plans were made to build a church, and construction began in June, 1870, to be built partially with funds generated by Hickok and the Junction City gamblers that spring. The church was completed and first used on Christmas Eve, 1870. In 1873, Reverend John A. Anderson was elected as the first president of Kansas State Agricultural School, today's Kansas State University in Manhattan. He served as president of the college until 1879. The 1870 Presbyterian Church in Junction City lasted for fifty years, until 1920, when a larger facility was required.

A very recent (2020) recollection of Hickok in Junction City has surfaced. Titled *Bertha Church Went To Town With Wild Bill Hickock*, it provides an interesting, and up to this time unknown, anecdote of Hickok in Junction City in spring, 1870:

> *Bertha Church lived at what was then 120 East Second Street and was probably the only person in Junction City who could boast that the location of the Municipal Building marked the site of her birthplace. Bertha was born in a frame building when Wild Bill Hickok was making regular visits to Junction City.*
>
> *She was the daughter of Mr. and Mrs. E. Church and was born on June 13, 1868. She lived in Junction City all her life. Her birthplace was a rooming and boarding house run by her parents. The old house had been added onto and came to be known as the Central Hotel. There were eight rooms in the hotel.*
>
> *Wild Bill Hickok was a frequent visitor at the Central Hotel when he came to town from Abilene. When Bertha was a baby, occasionally Bill would push her around town in her baby buggy. Bertha stated that she was "too small to remember much about it, but he used to take her downtown. Every other place in town was a saloon in those days and sometimes he would take me into a saloon with him." Bertha also said that some of her mother's friends, used to tell her mother that she shouldn't let Bill take her with him because of that, "but mother wasn't afraid for me. He was a gambler, but he was a good man and a gentleman."* [3]

Bertha would have been about two years old in the spring of 1870 when Hickok was there. Perhaps Annie Wilson was with James on these buggy strolls to downtown Junction City, further alleviating Bertha's mother's concern.

Born and raised in Junction City, L. S. Sargent recalled seeing Hickok often at his father's drugstore. The Sargent family at one time had a photograph of what they believed was Hickok and young L. S. Sargent together, purportedly made about 1870. The photograph appears on page 127 of Joseph Rosa's book, *The West of Wild Bill Hickok*.

Rosa found it "obviously not Hickok," but proposed it might be Thomas James Smith, the Marshal of Abilene in 1870, until he was violently murdered on November 2 of that year, soon to be replaced as Marshal of Abilene by none other than James Butler Hickok.

There were other sightings of Hickok that spring in Junction City. Henry Theile recalled watching in the city park as silver dollars were shot out of the cleft of a stick by Hickok, who was a substantial distance away from the target.[4]

At some point that spring or summer, James decided it was time to move on from Junction City. He made his next stop a return to his home of the last several years, Hays City. His name does not appear in the 1870 census, which was taken by temporarily-assigned deputy U. S. Marshal Marcellus S. Jones in Hays City, on about June 24 and 25. So, he returned to Hays City sometime after those dates. It is unknown why he returned to Hays City. Perhaps he wanted to return to Anna Wilson; she is shown as a citizen of Hays City in the 1870 census: "Annie Wilson, an Indian." Perhaps he wanted to re-start his career as a lawman in Hays City. The one thing that is known for certain about his return to Hays City is he was there by July 17, 1870.

On the evening of that day a legendary battle took place in Tommy Drum's saloon in Hays City. James Butler Hickok was attacked by two 7th Cavalry troopers who attempted to murder him. The murder weapon mis-fired, however, and in defense, Hickok shot one trooper, who died the next day, and shot the other trooper in the knee. Hickok fled the saloon by throwing himself through the back window and made his escape, expecting retaliation from other 7th Cavalry troopers.

Those are the raw facts of what transpired that evening. The frontier press covered the incident. The Topeka *Kansas Daily Commonwealth* on July 22 reported: "On Monday last 'Wild Bill' killed a soldier and seriously wounded another, at Hays City. Five soldiers attacked Bill, and two got used up, as mentioned above. The sentiment of the community is with 'Bill', as it is claimed he but acted in self-defense."

The *Junction City Union* stated on July 23:

> "Two soldiers of the Seventh cavalry were shot at Hays City last Tuesday night by Wild Bill. The names of the men were Langan and Kelly. The greatest excitement prevails in the town owing to the outrage. After the shooting was over Wild Bill made for the prairie and has not been heard of since. The citizens were out en masse looking for

Bill, so that he might be summarily dealt with. The parties were all under the influence of liquor at the time."

The *Clyde Republican Valley Empire* on August 2 reported: "Wild Bill, of Harper and plains notoriety, got into a friendly scuffle with a soldier at Hays City on the 20th, which ended in a row. Bill shot and mortally wounded another soldier who had a hand in the muss and left for parts unknown."

Though all three newspapers got the date wrong, they were not too far off the mark in telling what happened. The actual date was Sunday, July 17, 1870. That night Privates Jeremiah Lonergan and John Kile were admitted to the Fort Hays post hospital for treatment of gunshot wounds. Kile died on July 18, and Lonergan was released for duty on August 25.

When Buel got ahold of the story in 1881, it expanded to fifteen troopers that Hickok battled that night. Wilstach's version in 1926 had Hickok killing three, maybe four soldiers after they attacked him for beating up their sergeant. Then General Sheridan ordered the arrest of Hickok dead or alive. In 1933, Connelley made the attackers out to be a group of ruffian soldiers led by Tom Custer out to kill Hickok.

Yet, setting aside these wild-eyed accounts of over-the-top biographers, there are compelling secondhand accounts; these entries below are all recollections by people who were in Hays City at the time, and could have received reports from an eyewitness, or someone near to an eyewitness. Following these entries is the one compelling true eyewitness to the event.

In the summer of 1870, attorney Allen D. Gilkeson was living in Hays City at the Commercial Hotel. Gilkeson reports that Hickok was then living at the Commercial Hotel as well. Gilkeson had come several years before to Hays City, and he lived his entire life there (he died in 1928), becoming a respected judge. Some years after this incident in Tommy Drum's saloon, Gilkeson recalled that Hickok shot three soldiers, and General Custer held a court of inquiry which exonerated Hickok.[5]

That summer of 1870 Annie Roberts, the niece of Colonel George Gibson of Fort Hays, was staying with her uncle. Annie wrote in her diary on July 18, 1870: "In the middle of the night, [July 17] we were aroused by a man wanting the priest, Fr. Swembergh to go over to the town with him—for 'God's sake'—that two men were shot. He went over—'Wild Bill,' a celebrated Desperado shot them. One died

225

this morning—there were shots fired backward and forward across the bridge. We thought the good father was in danger. Wild Bill is reported shot. The two men were cavalry soldiers & their comrades threatened to burn down the town." The next day Annie wrote in her diary: "The soldier was buried this evening with the honors of war."[6]

Matthew Clarkson was a buffalo hunter who had settled early on in the Hays City area. He and his two brothers were well known in the area by 1870. Clarkson recalled the event this way:

> *Wild Bill got into trouble with some soldiers at Tommy Drum's saloon & drew two six-shooters & started firing & backing towards the door. when he got outside two more soldiers began shooting at him so he kept the fellows in front covered with his left hand & threw his right hand up over his right shoulder shot backward & killed a soldier. he realized what he had done & thought he had better leave. his horse was tied up behind the saloon & he jumped on him & started north. In 30 minutes there was a bunch of soldiers started in pursuit. when Bill got to North Fork he started down the creek & the soldiers thought he had gone North towards Stockton. Bill went down North Fork to Big Creek & on down to a wood choppers camp. there he had his wounds bound up and & staid in camp about a week & the next thing that was heard of Wild Bill he was Marshall of Ellsworth.* [7]

C. J. Bascom was a long-term employee of the Kansas Pacific Railroad and well known in Hays City, Ellsworth, Ellis, and Abilene. He recalled the event that summer of 1870 in the *Kansas City Star* of September 13, 1913:

> *I was at North Fork, this place was just a section house and water tank...Wild Bill came there and wanted to know if there had been any strangers that day. I told him "no". he said he was looking for two horse thieves. I asked him if he had had any dinner, if not to come into the Section house and I would get him a lunch. he said, "no," he did not care to do that and requested I should bring him a hand out. I went in and brought him out some Corn Beef and Cabbage, bread and butter and Coffee. After eating what he wanted, he gave me a dollar to give the Missie, and said he would go up the Creek a ways. Inside of an hour an ambulance from Fort Hays drove up with a Lieutenant and four Soldiers, this Snob I had seen his kind in the Civil war, got out*

*and come blustering up to me saying, "who are you?" I replied none of
your damn Business. He wanted to know did I live there, I replied, "no,
I live at Ellsworth" and was an officer of the road. "Do you know Wild
Bill?" "No I don't know Wild Bill." He got in his wagon and told his
men "that man knows more than he cares to tell." and they drove down
the Creek in the Direction of Old Fort Fletcher.*

John McDaniel was a respected engineer on the Kansas
Pacific Railroad, as well as later the founder of Bonner Springs, Kansas.
McDaniel piloted the very first Kansas Pacific passenger train out
of Kansas City to Topeka on January 1, 1866. On July 2, 1933, the
Kansas City Star ran this recollection: "...John McDaniel founder of
Bonner Springs, who was a pioneer locomotive engineer on the Kansas
Pacific railroad and was in Hays that night. He was a friend of Wild
Bill and persuaded him to leave Hays until the matter quieted down.
McDaniel argued that Bill could not fight the whole 7th regiment,
and that he would have to do it if he remained in Hays. So Bill rode out
of Hays that very night on McDaniel's engine and went to Topeka."
William Connelley, who lived in Bonner Springs for many years himself,
interviewed McDaniel directly sometime before 1915 (McDaniel
died that year.): "John W. McDaniel, founder of Bonner Springs,
was the pioneer locomotive engineer of the Kansas Pacific. He was in
Hays that night. He was Bill's friend, having carried him back and forth
over the road since 1866. He went to Bill to make a last appeal. It was
just before he had to pull out with a freight train for Kansas City. He
finally prevailed on Bill to go with him. They went down to the train,
and McDaniel pulled out. He has often told the author that he made
passenger time with that freight for a few miles, for as they boarded the
engine a body of men could be seen riding in from the fort."[8]

Elizabeth Custer was at Fort Hays when the incident occurred.
She surely heard the details from General Custer, who certainly received
a detailed report on what happened. It is plausible that report came from
Sergeant Ryan of the 7th Cavalry, which in the final entry below reveals
himself as an eyewitness to what happened in Tommy Drum's saloon on
July 17, 1870. Elizabeth Custer, in her inimitable writing style that was
blunt and informative, but always gracious, tells her version of events:

*When not in camp, Wild Bill was off duty, and consequently
ruling his realm, the tuerbulent town. Some of our men having received,*

as they considered, a deadly insult to their company, determined to right their wrongs, and assassinate the renowned scout. In these feuds there was very little margin for the right on either side. In our ranks were just as lawless men as were found in Hays City, but the strict discipline of military life soon subdues the most violent spirits. In the town however, with restraints removed, the bluff and the bully showed forth in his true colors. A little of the very bad liquor sold there turned the obedient soldier into a wrangling boor. Three desperate characters, planning to kill Wild Bill, decided that no one of them stood any chance if the scout was left the use of his arms; not only was his every shot sure, but he was so lithe and quick, and so constantly on the alert for attack, that it was next to impossible to do him injury. It was planned that one soldier should leap upon his back, and hold down his head and chest, while another should pinion his arms. It is impossible in the crowded little dens, imperfectly lighted, and with air dense with smoke, to always face a foe. Wild Bill was attacked from behind, as had been planned. His broad back was borne down by a powerful soldier, and his arms seized, but only one was held in the clinching grasp of the assailant. With the free hand the scout drew his pistol from the belt, fired backwards without seeing, and his shot, even under these circumstances, was a fatal one. The soldier dropped dead, the citizens rallied round Wild Bill, the troopers were driven out of town, but not without loud threats of vengeance. There was no question among the citizens but that every threat would be carried out, and it was decided that if Wild Bill hoped for life at all he must flee. It was impossible for General Custer to interfere in such a contest. His jurisdiction did not extend to the brawls of the town; the soldiers off duty were not punished, unless the citizens found something so flagrant, and proof of the dereliction so positive, that the offence must be investigated by a court-martial.

So Wild Bill, the most daring and valuable scout in the West, had to leave. I have heard General Custer say that he did not believe the scout ever shot a man except in self-defence; but no one who mingled in such mel'ees, where infuriated mobs of men followed every savage impulse of their nature, could possibly hope for justice.[9]

Sergeant John Ryan of the 7th Cavalry appears to be the only eyewitness that reported what he saw the night of July 17, 1870. The specificity and sharp detail that only an eyewitness could know are very apparent in Ryan's report. He makes a somewhat nuanced statement that leaves the impression that he possibly came in just after the fight was done, but his detailed report belies that. It is this author's opinion that Ryan may have felt he might be criticized for not coming to the aid of the two privates, since they were in Company M along with Ryan, and he was their sergeant.

Ryan first reported this event in 1909, writing in the Newton, Massachusetts *Circuit* of September 3. In 2000, Ryan's original manuscript journal that was the basis of the *Circuit* article was discovered, and in 2001 it was published in a book, *Ten Years With Custer.* It is the expanded version from the journal that is printed below, along with some interesting comments Ryan made about Hickok from the same journal, as well as some comments about the man killed in Tommy Drum's saloon, John Kile, who Ryan calls John Kelley in his journal:

#4128

Gamblers, gunfighters, and thirsty 7th Cavalry soldiers from Fort Hays could easily find Tommy Drum's saloon from the distinctive three-window second story false front. Here on a hot July evening in 1870 two soldiers tried to take Wild Bill Hickok's life. *Author's collection.*

I was present at Hays City, Kansas, when Wild Bill held full sway there...I will give here a general description of Bill Hickok, better known as Wild Bill, and my impressions of him. Bill was a noted scout and scouted a great deal with Custer's command. He was a very fine looking man, being large and broad shouldered and was very neat in his dress. He wore long jet black hair, a black moustache, and a black imperial. He generally wore a black broad rimmed sombrero hat. He wore on some occasions a blue flannel shirt with a sailor's collar, on other occasions he wore what we called out there, a boiled shirt, which was the same as one of our white laundered shirts here. He generally wore a pair of black broadcloth pants and high topped black patent leather boots with Mexican spurs on them. A Mexican spur differs a great deal from the spurs we have in this section of the country. They have rolls in them with very long teeth with bells attached to them so that a person walking along with a pair of these spurs on makes a regular jingle. He also wore a waist belt with a pair of open pistol holsters strapped around his waist. These holsters contained a pair of very handsome ivory handled Colts pistols, forty-four caliber. I have seen him on different occasions sitting in front of Tom Drum's saloon reading a newspaper, his eye evidently cast on that paper. All the time he took in every detail of the people who passed him and had his eye open all the time. He was the only man according to my estimation who was able to hold his own among the tough element in that city. Although he was known as an all around bad man, he had his good points.

There was a saloon keeper in Hays by the name of John Bitters, a German; Bitters had in front of his saloon one of those old-fashioned bucket windlasses used for drawing water from a well. I have seen Wild Bill while sitting on the railroad track draw his pistol, take aim, shoot and cut the rope that the bucket hung from and drop the bucket into the well, then turn around and pay John Bitters to get the bucket out.

...On another occasion Wild Bill had a dispute in the temporary post office with another man named Strawhorn [Strawhun], *and when Wild Bill had played his hand there was another murder added to his list.* [Ryan conflates the post office incident with the separate shooting of Strawhun on September 27, 1869.] *I have often sat down and talked with Wild Bill with regard to scouting and other matters, and have always found him to be quite a sociable kind of man. Nevertheless he had a reputation as an all around bad man with whom it was best to have nothing to do.*

230

It will be remembered that I have mentioned that a great many men deserted while on the expedition of 1867 and among those from my company was a corporal by the name of Kelley and a trumpeter by the name of Augustus Anthony. While lying in camp here on Big Creek, we got some recruits assigned to the different companies in the regiment. Co. I's tents were being pitched on the right of my company line, the recruits that were assigned to that company were obliged to march by my company from headquarters to get to Co. I. There was a 1st sergeant by the name of Varden in Co. I. And a sergeant in my company that were pretty chummy. As those recruits were going to Co. I., this sergeant from my company spotted this former Corporal Kelly and reported it to Sergeant Varden. This sergeant of my company and Varden were making up money to go on furlough. They already apprehended one deserter and were laying for some more. It was hinted that Kelley was among the recruits Kelley was a good man while serving in the company and whatever possessed him to desert on this occasion, I do not know. I thought it was too bad to have him arrested, so I immediately proceeded to Co. I to where the recruits were and spoke to Kelley. I said "Now Kelley, you have one thing or the other to do. You will be apprehended as a deserter in a few moments and the best thing you can do is to go over and surrender to General Custer and I will go with you." He told me he didn't know what to do. He said he was not feeling well, so I told him to come down to my company tent. I walked him down to my tent, got him towels and one thing or another so as to clean himself up. I then tied up the front of the tent. I immediately strapped on my belts with my pistol and holster. I no sooner had done that when down came Sergeant Varden from Co. I. to my tent.

He pulled the tent open and he said "Kelley, I want you." I was sitting on the outside. I jumped up and shook my hand at Varden and said "Sergeant, the jig is up. That man has surrendered to me as a deserter and I am going with him right over to General Custer's quarters." Varden went back to his company. Kelley started with me to Custer's tent and in crossing the parade grounds, we had to pass by the squadron commander's tent, he being the captain of Co. I., Captain Keogh. I was a little afraid that Varden would report the circumstances to his company commander and that the captain would call me before I got across the parade grounds, but as it was everything passed off all right and I got by the captain's quarters without being spoken to. I approached General Custer, saluted him, and said to him, "General, I have brought a man to you by the name of Kelley. He has surrendered to me as a deserter." The general asked me what company he deserted from and I told him Co. M. He asked me where from and I told him in the Department of the Platte on the expedition of 1867. He also asked me what kind of man he was and I told him that he was a very good soldier and a corporal in my company but what possessed him to desert I could not say. During the time that Kelley had been away from the 7th Cavalry, he enlisted in the 5th U.S. Cavalry and served under General Carr over in the Department of the Platte and had some meritorious papers from that general....

General Custer said, "well Sergeant Ryan, you take him back and report him to the 1st sergeant of his company for duty." I was somewhat perplexed to know which company to take him to at the time. I asked the General which company I would take him to. I told General Custer that Kelly deserted from Co. M, my company, and he was now assigned to Co. I. The general told me to take him back to the 1st sergeant of Co. M. and turn him over for duty, which I did. I did as I was directed, so there was no apprehension money paid for this man to anybody...

After Kelley had reported for duty, he told me, and in fact I could see that he was not feeling well, and he was put on the sick list of the company, and remained sick for several days, and, of course, was excused from duty. Before Kelley deserted from my company he was a neat, tidy, good-looking soldier, and was considered so by the men in the company. At this time we had a private in the company by the name of Lonergan. He and Kelley got to be quite chummy and were in each other's company quite often.

One beautiful moonlight night after tattoo roll call, about half past eight, they both left camp to visit Hays City, which was about two miles west from our camp. I think they left without permission. As I have mentioned before, there was a man in Hays City who kept a regular bar-room, for which Hays City was noted, by the name of Thomas Drum. This saloon was frequented by the men of this camp, and these two men visited this saloon. When they got into this saloon, Wild Bill, whom I have spoken of before, was standing up at the bar having a sociable talk with the bartender, Mr. Drum. Lonergan was a big powerful man and considered one of the pugilists of M troop. He had not been in the company a great while before this occurrence.

Lonergan walked up behind Wild Bill without being discovered, and as quick as a flash he threw both arms around Wild Bill's neck from the rear and pulled him over backwards on to the floor. He got a straddle on Wild Bill on the floor and held his two arms out at arm's length. It appears that Lonergan and Wild Bill had some trouble once before which caused this action. In the meantime, Wild Bill got one of his hands loose and slipped one of his pistols out of his holster. Some of the men in leaving camp were in the habit of carrying their pistols stuck down inside the waist band of their pants, with the hilt of the pistol protruding and covered up by their blouse, and a man could whip one of those out in an instant.

It appears that this was the position that Kelley had his pistol in when this affair took place. Kelley immediately whipped out his pistol and put the muzzle of his pistol into Wild Bill's ear and snapped it. It missed fire, or it probably would have ended his career right there. Lonergan was holding Wild Bill's right wrist, but Wild Bill turned his hand far enough to one side, and the first shot he fired shot Kelley through the right wrist. He fired a second time, and the bullet entered Kelley's side and went plumb through his body and could be felt on the other side. Of course, that put an end to Kelley then and there in a few moments. Wild Bill tried to kill Lonergan who was holding him down but Lonergan was holding his wrist in such a position that it was impossible for him to get a shot at his body. He finally fired again and he shot Lonergan through the knee cap. That caused Lonergan to release his hold on Wild Bill, who jumped up from the floor and made tracks for the back of the saloon and jumped through a window, taking glass and sash with him and made his escape. I was in this saloon just about the time that Kelley breathed his last and a doctor was sent for. The doctor asked me if I knew Kelley and I told him that I did and that both men were members of my company. He examined him very thoroughly and took off a gold ring that was on his finger and asked me if I was a friend of Kelley's. I told him that I was and so he gave me the ring. I kept the ring for some years afterwards and I never could find any of Kelley's relations, which I tried very diligently to do, and I think he was under an assumed name. I was informed later that his right name was Kyle, and that he belonged either in Chicago Ill., or Cincinatti, O. Finally,

I gave this ring to a friend of mine by the name of John Murphy, who was a trumpeter in my company and was wounded in the Battle of the Washita.

The news of this affair got to camp very soon and a number of men seized their guns and immediately proceeded to Hays City in search of Wild Bill. Here I joined this party and we visited all the saloons and dives in the place, but we could not find Wild Bill. If we had found him, we will leave it to the reader to imagine what would have happened to him.

In the meantime, Kelley's body was taken to our camp and Lonergan was brought to the post hospital at Fort Hays. Wild Bill immediately left the city and that was the last of his career as far as I know in Hays City.

I saw him about a year later about thirty miles from Fort Harker on the Kansas Pacific Railroad, either at the little town of Abilene or Salina, I have forgotten which [most likely Salina, which is thirty-four miles from Fort Harker. Abilene is about sixty miles from Fort Harker], *going south in May 1871. Some of the officers and myself and a number of the men had a long talk with him. He told us that after leaving Drum's saloon, he immediately proceeded to the room that he occupied in that city* [Hickok went to the Commercial Hotel on Main Street in Hays City, a few doors south of Tommy Drum's saloon, maybe 150 feet away down the alley between Main Street and Second Street] *and there he got his "needle gun"* [Winchester rifle] *and one hundred rounds of ammunition and proceeded to the cemetery, a little west of town* [about a half mile], *which I will describe a little later in my story. There he laid until the next morning, as he expected that the soldiers would round him up and put an end to him.*

However, he made the statement that he never intended to be taken alive while in that cemetery and would make many of those soldiers bite the dust before he would be taken. After daylight, he left there and proceeded to Big Creek Station, on the line of the Kansas Pacific Railroad, about eight miles east of Hays City, and boarded a train. I had a long talk with him the last time I saw him in regard to this affair. I understood some years afterwards that a brother of one of the men that he shot in Hays City followed him into the Black Hills and assassinated him. [This is the false story that Jack McCall made up to justify his killing of Hickok; that supposedly McCall had a brother in Hays City that Hickok had shot and killed.] *Wild Bill told me on one occasion that he never ran up against a man that he was afraid of in a square fight but he said, "I do expect sometime or another some desperado will come up and shoot me from behind," and I think likely it was the case with him.*

It happened to be my pleasure about a year ago to visit a man that owned several hundred relics from the different wars and the Indian frontiers. Among them, I saw a pistol engraved on the handle "Wild Bill." The pistol which I saw in that collection was similar to one which I had seen Wild Bill carry but whether it was his or not, I cannot say.

A couple of days after the affair at Drum's saloon, Kelley was buried from our camp and I had charge of the funeral ceremonies. We marched with the body and it was entered in the Fort Hays Cemetery. Lonergan recovered from his wounds and joined the company again, from which he deserted sometime afterwards and I understood he was killed by a man named Kelley belonging to an infantry regiment a little later on in Kansas.[10]

William E. Webb, the founder and developer of Hays City, had been gone from the city for several days when the fight in Tommy Drum's saloon took place on July 17, 1870. Webb's comments, written and published in 1872, indicate that he had talked to an eyewitness to the fight, perhaps even to Ryan himself, as Ryan's first published comments did not appear until 1909. Referring to Hickok, Webb stated:

"Only a short time after we left Hays two soldiers attempted his life. Attacked unexpectedly, Bill was knocked down and the muzzle of a musket placed against his forehead, but before it could be discharged the ready pistol was drawn and the two soldiers fell down, one dead, the other badly wounded. Their companions clamored for revenge, and Bill changed his base." Note that Webb's statement about the mis-firing pistol is the only mention of it other than Ryan's mention.[11]

Ryan's report is literally a blow-by-blow rendition of what happened that night inside Tommy Drum's saloon. Hickok's escape has led to some diverse speculations about what he did and where he went after he jumped through that back window of the saloon. But the truth of his flight can be reconstructed from a quick analysis of the entries above and where they corroborate each other.

The evidence shows, from Hickok's own testimony, and from the other entries above, that he went to his nearby room at the Commercial Hotel, grabbed his rifle and loads of ammunition, and made his way to the Hays City cemetery about a half mile from town. He hid out there all that night, and sometime early the next morning made his way some eight miles east to Big Creek Station, near where he boarded the eastbound Kansas Pacific train, whose engineer was Hickok's friend John McDanield. From there he traveled on the train to Ellsworth.

When James got to Ellsworth, he probably made it to the home of his friend Harry Pestana, an attorney. Historian James Drees believed that Hickok likely had received a gunshot wound to the leg in the fight. Matthew Clarkson above mentions Hickok's wounds. Annie Roberts wrote in her diary that same night, "Wild Bill is reported shot." If he was shot in the leg, it must have been a surface wound, because reports show Hickok active again within weeks. Hickok sought out the protection of the Pestana home in Ellsworth, and he probably realized he would need a lawyer if a warrant was issued for his arrest. One was never issued.

Anna Wilson either fled with James to Ellsworth, or made it from Hays City to Ellsworth at a later time. Recall that she was listed in Hays City on the census taken on June 24 and 25. James was not listed because he had not yet returned for his date with destiny.

Recent important research by historian Jeff Broome informs much that was previously unknown about the 7th Cavalry brawl, and especially about Lonergan and Kile. Jeremiah Lonergan was born in Cork, Ireland. At age twenty-two, he enlisted in the U. S. Army. Six months after the fight in Tommy Drum's saloon, he threatened a sergeant and, in a drunk stupor, defecated on the barracks floor. He was court-martialed and sentenced to almost three years in Leavenworth prison, and then was dishonorably discharged. After his release, he vanished from the record. Ryan reported erroneous information when he said Lonergan was shot after the fight. Kile was a Medal of Honor recipient, based on his bravery in an important Indian battle on July 8, 1869, in Colorado. He was described at the time as having good character. Yet one year later, he was shot in Tommy Drum's saloon and died the next day.[12]

Though working now out of Ellsworth, Hickok was still a deputy U. S. Marshal. On August 15, 1870, John McAllister passed a counterfeit twenty-dollar bill at Abilene, and it was traced back to him. On September 15, 1870, a warrant was issued on Hickok's complaint. At the hearing, Hickok stated that he had arrested McCallister "*3 or 4 weeks* *ago, at Abilene for counterfeiting money. Defendant said he obtained the money from some Col._____. Money was a $20 bill; Defendant said he got it of another man and* [he] *would not take it back. Did not search him. Defendant gave it to another to bet and..."* The rest of the transcription of Hickok's testimony is missing.

James King testified at the hearing that he had taken the money to the Junction City bank and was told it was bad. He said it was E. W. Kingsbury that made the bet. King gave Kingsbury $30 and Kingsbury brought him a $20 bill and a $10 bill in "good money." King testified that he refused to take the $20 bill, and offered Kingsbury a $10 bill in exchange. McCallister was bound for trial at Topeka in October 1870, yet he did not come to trial until October 1871; by this time, Hickok was sheriff of Abilene. He was subpoenaed, however, as a witness, and when he arrived in Topeka on October 19 for the trial, the press noted that he was in town and looking good and natural as ever. On October 21, the judge rendered a verdict of not guilty for McCallister. This brought to an end J. B. Hickok's five-year career as a deputy United States Marshal. [13]

From October until December, 1870, we lose sight of James Butler Hickok. We can only presume that after recovering at Harry Pestana's home in Ellsworth, he and Indian Annie remained in the Ellsworth area for the rest of the year. Perhaps Hickok was concerned that soldiers from Fort Hays might pursue him after the shooting of Kile and Lonergan in Tommy Drum's saloon in July. If so, he could be confident that his numerous friends at Fort Harker, just a few miles from Ellsworth, would forestall any such action by the soldiers from Fort Hays.

We regain sight of Hickok for a fleeting moment in December, 1870, while he is in Junction City, likely visiting one of his friends from that town or Fort Riley nearby.

Englishman Percy Abbutt of London, while visiting Junction City and other points west, took note of Hickok in Junction City. "Wild Bill was a fine looking fellow, with long curly hair hanging down his back, and was dressed in rather a dandified fashion. He was said to have twenty-seven nicks cut on the handle of his revolver, each signifying a man whose life had been taken by him. And yet he walked the streets as free as any man."[14]

13

1871

ELLSWORTH

SHERIFF *of* ABILENE

the MYTH *of* JOHN WESLEY HARDIN *and* HICKOK

AGNES LAKE

the SHOOTING *of* PHIL COE

ANNA WILSON *aka* INDIAN ANNIE

After the Civil War, Texas cattle ranchers found that many of their southern shipping points had been decimated by the war, and the economic downturn engendered in the South by that war also reduced the local demand for beef. There was a strong market for beef in the East and the North, but Texans had no way to get their cattle to these markets.

Joseph McCoy was an Illinois livestock dealer that accumulated some wealth before and during the Civil War. He understood the plight of the Texas cattle ranchers, and he recognized an opportunity. He set out to find a single shipping point on the tracks of the westward-building Union Pacific Railroad in Kansas. McCoy went to two well-established towns in Kansas, Junction City and Salina, to pitch his idea for huge shipping pens and more. He was rebuffed by both towns. Finally in 1867, he found the little whistle-stop of Abilene, then barely a cabin or

239

two and a few sod dugouts next to the railroad tracks. Soon he made a deal with the railroad to pay him five dollars for every carload of cattle shipped from Abilene east to Kansas City. The deal was finalized on July 1, 1867, too late in the season to see many cattle from Texas. But the rest of that year much effort was expended at Abilene, as McCoy brought in workmen and laborers to build the huge holding pens to handle the anticipated throngs of cattle, as well as the building of a new and magnificent hotel, the Drovers Cottage, to handle all the cattle buyers and others from the East. Meanwhile, McCoy sent publicists into Texas to bang the drum for Abilene and entice the cattlemen north to McCoy's new shipping yards.

The Texans were receptive to McCoy's plan, and the season of 1868 was a huge financial success for McCoy as well as for the Texas cattlemen. What McCoy had not counted on were the considerable problems that came with the cowboys that drove those cattle: widespread violence and gunplay, liquor-fueled mania, illicit and crooked gambling, and rampant prostitution. While the cowboys and their herds were all situated south of the railroad tracks, McCoy did not foresee in 1867 that north of the railroad tracks, a town would form in just a few years, and the citizens of the town would eventually bring unrelenting pressure to terminate McCoy's Texas cattle-shipping business. Theophilus Little recalled the heyday of Abilene as a cattle town:

> In the early spring great herds of Texas Cattle began to arrive for shipment to eastern markets, thousands upon thousands. With them came cowboys, cattle owners, cattle buyers, gamblers, thieves, thugs, murderers, the painted women, the rich, the poor. Money poured like the waters. Thousands upon thousands of people came. It was said that there were 7,000 people by June 1st...My lumber yard was on the corner of Walnut and First Street, right in the red hot center of Hell. We called first street Texas street. It had no other name. It was Texas close down to the Gulf of Mexico. It wasn't Kansas. It was full—jam full—of saloons, gambling dens, dens of infamy of all kinds of character, cutthroats, robbers, murderers. I am not exaggerating. I have not half told it. It was indescribable and I was there on Texas street selling lumber.
> All the cattle were herded west of town. Every cowboy that came into town had to pass my office door. There were hundreds of them every day and every "son of a gun" had two guns and I thought every gun was as long as an Ohio fence rail. These boys came to town and did

not leave Texas street, would drink and gamble, get rip-roaring crazy drunk and towards evening would jump on their Texas ponies and then begin to shoot hundreds of shots, yelling like a million Indians, ponies on the dead run. Every boy passed my office and by the time they got there the air was lurid as they shot upwards. At first I would run to the door to see the show, but I soon learned to crawl into a hole and pull the hole in after me or pull a pile of lumber over on to me. Then down into the creek and up the west bank and disappear over on the unlimited prairie and then back the next day and repeat.[1]

The best authority any historian can rely on are eyewitness recollections by perceptive and intelligent observers. These are rare. Yet the frontier history of Abilene gives the historian an abundance of riches: three sharp-eyed eyewitnesses with a penchant for detail named Charles Gross, J. B. Edwards, and Theophilus Little. Charles Gross in 1922 recalled the early days of frontier Abilene:

I have always taken an interest in Abilene because in a way I feel responsible for its being started as a cattle town. And then being there for so long as one of the first on the ground with the McCoys. I saw from a post with a number where the mail Bag was hung on a Hook with a board shelter above to Keep out rain, to a good sized town. When I came there to stay via Stage from Junction City. I spent my first night with Tim Hersey. My 2nd in a tent. Going east from Mud Creek just south of what is now the RR came a dug out & a queer party whose name I cannot recall who had a Prairie Dog Village which he guard with Care...

When the McCoys sold all their landed interests to Augustine & Lebold, they being general Boomers, Made the town & county too, grow rapidly. Up to their advent no one thought of anything but Texas Cattle, selling goods & liquor to Cow men, & gambling and prostitutes. With the advent of swarms of actual settlers & their familys things began to hum about the town & County with the real Home seekers who have made Abilene what it is today. The cattle trade left the town when McCoy was elected Mayor.[2]

Abilene was incorporated in 1869, and for the next two years it was under the management of a board of trustees. For a time Joseph McCoy was the chairman of that board; for the remainder of its existence,

T. C. Henry was the chairman. The Board of Trustees from the very beginning knew they had a challenge in front of them attempting to control the Texas cowboys and prostitutes. They hired the first sheriff of Abilene in May 1870—Thomas James Smith.

Smith came to Abilene with an obscure background. T. C. Henry, who probably hired Smith, claimed that he was born in New York in 1849, which makes Smith about twenty-one years old when he became Abilene's first Marshal. Yet the census for 1870 listed Smith as forty years old. Henry also claimed that Thomas Smith had been Marshal of Kit Carson, Colorado, before his Abilene assignment.

Stocky and muscular, Smith proved to be an anomaly among law officers of the time; he preferred using his fists over his guns to enforce the law. He found himself trying to enforce law on the lawless: cowboys, gamblers, prostitutes, grifters, and more, all clustered around the saloons emanating from the intersection of Texas Street and Cedar Street. Smith hired a deputy, James H. McDonald, and went to work.

For the first time firearms were banned in Abilene. Smith made his rounds up and down Texas Street on his horse, always a moving target. When he found something wrong that needed his attention, he dismounted and approached the miscreant. Though he carried two six-shooters, it was well known among the cowboys and their ilk that fists or a rap on the head with the butt of his gun were Smith's go-to weapons, if needed after confronting the wrongdoer. Smith's "gun-as-a-last-resort" policy was very popular with the citizens of Abilene, so much so that in August, the Board of Trustees raised his monthly salary from $150 to $225.

For the seven months that Smith was the Marshal of Abilene there was extremely little press coverage of his doings. The *Abilene Chronicle* only mentioned Sheriff Smith twice in those seven months from May to November, and one of those times was to report his death in November. It has been suggested that the paucity of press coverage might have been because he did little that was press-worthy; that his "guns-as-a-last-resort" policy was really a live-and-let-live policy towards the Texas cowboys and their cohorts.

In July, Smith tracked down and captured a horse thief who had stolen horses at Abilene. The August 2 *Republican Valley Empire* of Clyde, Kansas, reported on the incident: "Under sheriff Smith, of Dickinson county, called on us on Monday. He had just returned from Brownsville, Nebraska, whither he had been in pursuit of Buckskin Bill, who stole horses at Abilene not long ago, an account of which we published. Bill had sold some of the stock at Pawnee City, and they attempted to prevent the sheriff from getting the property by telling him he had better get out. Or he would soon have nothing to go out on. The sheriff captured nearly all the stock..." On September 5, Sheriff Smith ordered the red-light district of Abilene closed, as reported by the Abilene Chronicle on September 8:

> *Cleaned Out.—For some time past a set of prostitutes has occupied several shanties, about a mile north-west of town. On last Monday or Tuesday Deputy Sheriff Smith served a notice on the vile characters, ordering them to close their dens, or suffer the consequences. They were convinced beyond all question that an outraged community would no longer tolerate their vile business, and on yesterday, Wednesday morning, the crew took the cars for Baxter Springs and Wichita. We are told that there is not a house of ill fame in Abilene or vicinity- a fact, we are informed, which can hardly be said in favor of any other town on the Kansas Pacific Railway. The respectable citizens of Abilene may well feel proud of the order and quietness now prevailing in the town. Let the dens of infamy be kept out, the laws enforced and violators punished, and no good citizen will ask more. Chief of Police, T. J. Smith and his assistants, and C.C. Kuney, Esq., deserve the thanks of the people for the faithful and prompt manner in which they have discharged their official duties. A grateful community will not forget the services of such efficient officers.*

The editor's optimism that prostitution had been driven out of Abilene through the closing of two little shanties was severely misplaced. Prostitution in Abilene continued thriving and almost unabated through Marshal Smith's tenure in 1870, and Marshal Hickok's in 1871.

On November 2, Sheriff Thomas James Smith, in the process of serving a warrant, was brutally murdered. *The Chronicle* reported on November 3:

> *On Wednesday of this week officers T.J. Smith, and McDonald, went out to McConnell's dugout to arrest him [for murder]. Upon reaching the dugout they found McConnell and Miles. Officer Smith informed McConnell of his official character, and that he had a warrant for his arrest, whereupon McConnell shot Smith through the right lung; Smith also fired, wounding McConnell; the two being close*

together grappled; Smith, although mortally wounded, was getting the better of McConnell, when Miles struck him on the head with a gun, felling him senseless to the ground, and seizing an ax chopped Smith's head nearly from his body. At this stage of the tragedy officer McDonald returned to this place for assistance. A posse was raised, and repaired to the scene of the murder, but McConnell and Miles had fled, and up to this morning had not been arrested. They were both wounded, and it is reported that they were in Junction City last evening. It is hoped that they will be speedily arrested. We give the above named particulars as we gather them from reports current in town.

The body of Mr Smith was brought to this place last evening, and will be buried at 10:00 to-morrow. The sad event has cast a gloom over our town. Our citizens had learned to respect Mr. Smith as an officer who never shrank from the performance of his duty. He was a stranger to fear, and yet in the private walks of life a most diffident man. He came to this place last spring, when lawlessness was controlling the town. He was at once employed as chief of police, and soon order and quiet took the place of the wild shouts and pistol shots of ruffians who for two years kept orderly citizens in dread for their lives. Abilene owes a debt of gratitude to the memory of Thomas James Smith, which can never be paid. Although our people will never again permit the lawlessness which existed prior to his coming to the town, yet it will be a long time before his equal will be found in all the essentials required to make a model police officer...

McConnell and Miles were captured three days after the crime. Their trial came up the following March. McConnell received twelve years in the penitentiary, and ax-wielding Miles got sixteen years.

The first city election was held in Abilene on April 3, 1871, and Joseph McCoy was elected as Abilene's first mayor. In the same election the first city council was elected as well. Neither McCoy nor the new council wasted any time in implementing plans to control the Texas cowboys and prostitutes.

McCoy realized, after the murder the previous November of popular Abilene sheriff Thomas Smith, that it was going to take a special man to bring law enforcement to Abilene. McCoy believed that it was only by subduing the Texas cowboys who terrorized the town, and the multitude of prostitutes who walked the streets of Abilene, that he could broker a co-existence between the cattlemen and the citizens of Abilene. Others in the town, including some of the members of the council, felt like the cattle trade in Abilene needed to be eliminated completely. Charles Gross, McCoy's assistant manager at the Drovers Cottage, recommended James Butler Hickok. Gross knew Hickok back in Illinois in the 1850s, and they became re-acquainted at Fort Harker and Ellsworth in 1868 and 1869. Gross knew of Hickok's fearless ability and charisma, and he knew Hickok was the special man McCoy was looking for. McCoy sent Gross west to find Hickok. Gross caught up with him in the Fort Harker/Ellsworth area and convinced him to come to Abilene. Mayor McCoy and the new city council looked at Hickok as their agent of change.

The new mayor and city council were up and functioning right out of the gate on April 3, and anxious to get someone into the position of sheriff before the Texas herds and their trouble-making cowboys would arrive. On April 15, they made it official that their enforcer had arrived. The minutes read: "J. B. Hicocks appointed by the Mayor as Marshall. Unanimously confirmed."[3] At the next council meeting four days later they unanimously approved an ordinance that set Hickok's monthly salary at $150, plus twenty-five percent of fines against violators he personally arrested. On August 21, the council wrote an ordinance detailing the new Marshal's duties:

> *The Marshal shall be industrious & vigilant, not only in preventing any infraction of the ordinances of said city, and bring offenders against them to justice, but also in causing the prosecution or punishment of offences against the penal laws of the State of Kansas committed within said City, and in suppressing disturbances, affrays, riots, and other breaches of the peace therein. He shall keep an account of all moneys received by him for the use of the City, and pay the same to the treasurer thereof on the first Saturday of every month and take his reciept therefor, and do & perform all such other duties as are now or hereafter may be required of him by said Council.*[4]

By April 24, if not sooner, Hickok was at work on the streets of Abilene. After a request by the council to purchase balls and chains for prisoners he did so, presenting the council with the bill of $42.96 to reimburse him.

That same spring, to deal with the multitudes of prostitutes that plied their wares every day on every street in Abilene, McCoy decided to move them into a special and restricted area where they could carry on their business, far away from the schools, homes, and churches of Abilene's citizens. He located this special place about a mile south of Texas Street, and a little southeast of the town. He had large frame barrack-like buildings built for the prostitutes to live and work in, and McCoy had the entire area fenced. The prostitutes were all moved there with the firm admonition that they could carry on their business, but they could only do it in what came to be known as McCoy's Addition. If they wished to come north into town, it was only to carry out important errands having nothing to do with prostitution. Charles Gross was a witness to Mayor McCoy's action, and years later recalled it:

> The lawless Element was ruling the town, & the genuine good citizen together with wife, rose in open rebellion & demanded the town be made safe for their wives and daughters to go to the stores, post office, or else where in the town without being insulted & outraged by the prostitutes, often drunk, were everywhere. Gamblers were plentiful. McCoy was hard pushed. He felt the Cow men were on the Search for the gambling, & the prostitute, & the Liquor. Joe was a conscientious man himself & after long thought he started what was called McCoy's Addition & made all the Prostitutes go there. This did not fully satisfy good People & some always Howled but it helped some & matters got quieter.[5]

Ironically, some eighty plus years later in the 1950s, the location of McCoy's Addition was covered by Old Abilene Town, the faux frontier land amusement park that thrilled baby-boom children and others of all ages.

On May 8, the city council met, and it was at this meeting that the notorious "missing councilman" incident took place. It seems that in the face of an important vote that required a quorum, Councilman S. A. Burroughs left the council suddenly and without permission. On the motion of Councilman Brinkman, Marshal Hickok was instructed to compel the vanishing councilman's attendance. Burroughs was brought back to the room, but made his exit once again. Hickok went again to get Burroughs, and this time brought him back thrown over his shoulder, and surely placed him in his chair with a firmness that indicated he should not attempt another escape. This normally would have ended the affair, with the result leaving Councilman Burroughs with a bruised ego that few

#4131

J. B. Hickok, Sheriff of Abilene. McCoy wanted a marshal who could corral the wild cowboys that came north to Abilene with their cattle every year. He sent Charles Gross to find his friend Mr. Hickok. The rest is history. This photograph is credited to W. Ames of Topeka and was probably taken in the first quarter of 1871. *Author's collection.*

#4136

McCoy added his word balloons to Henry Worrall's newspaper cartoon of the "councilman incident", then had them printed up for distribution around the country. *Author's collection.*

in Abilene would even have known about. However, Mayor McCoy, who had little love for some of the members of the Abilene city council, was at the meeting or found out about the meeting and leaked the story to the Topeka press, who promptly had their illustrator draw up a cartoon to run in the newspaper. Not just any illustrator; it was produced by the noted nineteenth-century Kansas artist Henry Worrall. To make sure the council got the message, McCoy had a blurb added to the illustration that said "Who's Mayor Now?" McCoy also arranged to have a Topeka photographer provide multiple photographs of the Worrall image, to be sold across the country. Worrall either knew Hickok well enough to draw him accurately from memory, or he had a current photograph of Hickok available, or Worrall was in the council room when Hickok returned with Burroughs on his shoulder (doubtful). This cartoon by Worrall is one of the very few images showing Hickok with a goatee. Worrall's image matches perfectly with the photo of Hickok #4123 on page 247 .

The editor of the *Abilene Chronicle*, V. P. Wilson, who had his own vendetta against McCoy, found another opportunity to criticize the new mayor when he heard of the council room incident. He editorialized in the *Chronicle* on May 18, 1871:

The Picture Man- A short time since our Mayor, J.G. McCoy, ordered the Marshal to arrest and bring into the meeting of the council, only two members being present, one of the members who did not wish to be present. The councilman was arrested and carried into the room by the Marshal. There was not the least shadow of law for such a proceeding, there being no ordinance to compel the attendance of councilmen. Of course the Marshal simply obeyed orders—whether legal or not—and is not to blame. But our silly mayor goes down to Topeka, publishes his exploit in the papers, gets up a picture that pretends to represent the transaction, carves upon it in big letters, "Who's Mayor now," and sends them all over the country to be hawked about and laughed at as a standing disgrace to his own town. If boyish silliness can beat such a small trick we'll acknowledge that Abilene is blessed with a mayor of prudent sense. If you wish to see such nonsense continued vote McCoy's ticket for councilmen on next Tuesday 21st; but if you prefer a council that will oppose the eccentricities and extravagances of our picture mayor, be sure to vote for Boudinot and Carpenter. They are men of good sense, and will do what they think is right.

As still happens today, back then Wild Bill Hickok and Buffalo Bill Cody were sometimes confused with each other, though more times people mistook Buffalo Bill for Wild Bill than Wild Bill for Buffalo Bill. A passenger on the Kansas Pacific Railroad confused the identities even more by implying they are both names for the same person, as the train pulled in to the Abilene depot in May 1871, very near the day of the "missing councilman" incident:

Passing Abilene we saw Buffalo Bill at the Depot; he is tall, slender, black hair hanging to his shoulders. From a belt around his waist, hung two navy revolvers and a large bowie knife; being Marshal of the town, he moved around with an air of authority; a terror to all evil doers. The council of Abilene were to decide some very important measure, at an appointed time, the majority of whom, wishing to shirk their duty in regard to the question, did not put in an appearance, consequently there was not a quorum present. Wild Bill being equal to any emergency, went out into the Gambling houses and saloons, and carried members of the council on his back, until he had got a quorum, when they proceed to business.[6]

With May came the approach to the end of the school year in Abilene. Theophilus Little recalled the day of the end-of-school play, or "closing exercises":

Sometime during the cattle season a large barn like structure was erected on the ground now occupied by the Steam Laundry on the south side. It was intended for public entertainment. In fact it was the "Grand Seelye Theater: of the day. I do not recollect if it was built by the citizens of the "400" of the Texas element, but I do remember that some of the high toned plays put on the boards were somewhat on the high kicking and "whoopdee-doo-dee-noo" order. Anyhow when the public schools were about to be closed probably in May, the south side "Seelye Theater" was secured for the closing exercises in the evening. Of course the citizens were "permitted" to go.

The cowboys exercised their inalienable rights of the Texas American citizen to go where they damned please on the south side, were there and filled the edifice to the roof with words to that effect, but hundreds were there, citizens, cattlemen, cowboys, gamblers, the elite from the addition on Fisher's farm—in fact—a cosmopolitan gathering. The cowboy element was in the ascendancy being most numerous.

The exercises were very satisfactory and of great interest to the parents and patrons. The cowboys held themselves steady just as long as human endurance could endure, but finally got tired and grew restless and noisy and more noisy and very noisy, interrupted the proceedings. Mrs. Little and I and the two little boys, Eddie and Willie were seated together in chairs, immediately in front of us were two big Texans. Each one big enough to swallow me whole. They became very noisy and offensive and I remonstrated with them quietly, pled with them to keep quiet. They turned and laughed at me, asking what in hell I was going to do about it. I quit talking and began to get mad, madder yet. I was young then, if not handsome. I began to think I could just whip 20 wild cats right with a lot of Texans thrown in. They standing up right in front of me, swearing and laughing, having the biggest time in town. I lost sight and sense of everything but mad and fight.

I jumped up and caught one of them by the throat and jammed him into his chair and choked him till he gurgled, in a flash I had the other huck by the throat. You too I yelled and choked him until his Texas tongue ran out of his mouth, jammed him into his chair and hissed into their ears, another word out of you tonight and I'll smash every bone in you bodies.

It's a wonder I was not shot to pieces, but I thought then that I could smash every cowboy in that big shanty. I think they thought so too for I tell you silence reigned profound the balance of that evening. They were so utterly astonished at the audacity and foolhardiness of the act that they were cowed and helpless.

Just as the exercises closed, Wild Bill strode swiftly toward us with his silk hat in his left hand, his right thrown across the left breast and with a low and courtly bow to Mrs. Little, in most gracious tones he said "Mr. Little if you will allow me. I will walk home with you and your family this evening." I thanked him saying, "We would deem it an honor but not a necessity." Said he "I think I understand this case better than you do, Mr. Little," and he went to our home with us.[7]

It was June of 1871 in Abilene when a legend/myth purportedly took place that needs to be clarified and then discarded into the ash bin of history. As it is told, eighteen-year-old John Wesley Hardin came up the Chisholm Trail that spring, working with one of the many north-bound cattle herds destined for Abilene. Hardin was a homicidal killer that murdered over twenty men in his lifetime. When he arrived in Abilene, he was eighteen and Hickok was thirty-four. In the 1890s, long after Hickok was dead and unable to dispute it, Hardin wrote in his autobiography that back in 1871 in Abilene, Hickok drew his six-shooter and told Hardin he was under arrest. Hardin claimed that he presented his two pistols butt-forward to Hickok and then Hardin rolled them over his hands and cocked them at the same time and stuck them in Hickok's face. Hickok purportedly said, "You are the gamest and quickest boy I ever saw." Hardin writes that the two men put away their guns and went and ordered some drinks and became friends.

Hardin was notorious for writing exaggerations and fabrications. There are no legitimate witnesses nor any legitimate corroborations of this event between Hardin and Hickok anywhere. Hardin's own biographer, Dr. Richard C. Mahron, found no evidence that it ever took place and he believed Hardin made it up to assuage his ego late in life. Mahron notes that Hardin wrote to his wife from prison and referred to Hickok as a brave man, suggesting that Hardin saw Hickok in a heroic light.[8] Hardin was an insecure man, and he would likely have been jealous of the esteem in which Hickok was held. It is doubtful that Hardin ever even met Hickok in Abilene. Throw this myth into the ash bin of history.

It is widely reported that when Hickok was not at the Abilene jail working, he was at the Alamo Saloon working. The Alamo was located just south of the railroad tracks, at the intersection of Cedar Street and Texas Street. Positioning himself at the Alamo gave Marshal Hickok a chance to be right in the thick of the troublesome Texas cowboys, and to forestall problems before things got out of hand. The impressive Alamo was described by George Cushman in the 1940s:

The Alamo was the most elaborate of the saloons, and a description of it will give an idea of the plan of them all. It was housed in a long room with a forty-foot frontage on Cedar street, facing the west. There was an entrance at either end. At the west entrance were three double glass doors. Inside and along the front of the south side was the bar with its array of carefully polished brass fixtures and rails. From the back of the bar arose a large mirror, which reflected the brightly sealed bottles of liquor. At various places over the walls were huge paintings in cheaply done imitations of the nude masterpieces of the venetian Renaissance painters. Covering the entire floor space were gaming tables, at which practically any game of chance could be indulged. The Alamo boasted an orchestra, which played forenoons, afternoons, and nights. In the height of the season the saloons were the scene of constant activity. At night the noises that were emitted from them were a combination of badly rendered popular music, coarse voices, ribald laughter and Texan "whoops," punctuated at times by gun shots.[9]

A Junction City reporter visiting Abilene had this eyewitness report describing the Alamo Saloon printed in the *Junction City Union* on August 19, 1871: "...[at the Alamo] Crowds within and about its doors. At night it is brilliantly illuminated. There are tables covered with 'the green cloth.' On them are piled the checks of ivory, the gold, and silver. About the bar costly mirrors, pyramids of sparkling glasses, and vases of the choicest flowers give the place an air of elegance. The harmonious strains of piano and violin temper the intense excitement of the games with a sort of weird enchantment."

In the middle of June, the Abilene city council ordered Hickok to have printed and posted new liquor license regulations and a new ordinance covering brothels. The brothel ordinance stipulated, "It shall be the duty of the City Marshall to make such detail of assistant

Marshals or police as may be provided him so as to rigidly enforce this ordinance."[10] Three deputies were brought on under Hickok: James Gainsford, Tom Carson, and J. H. McDonald. Gainsford was already serving as a deputy U. S. Marshal at the time. Tom Carson was a relative of Kit Carson. J. H. McDonald had notoriety of the unwanted kind: many in Abilene still thought that even though he was a deputy to Tom Smith, he had abandoned Smith at the time of his murder. For the first time in his life in law enforcement, Hickok had three deputies.

The Abilene city council momentum continued. On June 24, a new Miscellaneous Ordinance was added to Hickok's plate. It prohibited the carrying and/or discharge of firearms in the city limits, as well as carrying dirks or bowie knives.[11] The council also made Hickok street commissioner, but with no increase in pay. His new duties included investigating about street obstructions, to use prison labor or hired labor to clear these obstructions, and in general see that all laws and contracts issued by the council were enforced concerning sidewalks, streets, alleys, gutters, and bridges. Seems the council was trying to maximize its investment in the one man that could get people's attention and compliance.

However, the *Abilene Chronicle* noted two weeks earlier, on June 8, that Marshal Hickok "has posted up printed notices, informing all persons that the ordinance against carrying fire arms or other weapons in Abilene, will be strictly enforced. Thats right. There's no bravery in carrying revolvers in a civilized community. Such a practice is well enough and perhaps necessary when among Indians or other barbarians, but among white people it ought to be discountenanced." So either Hickok was giving the miscreants advance notice of what was coming, or the city council implemented its policy even before they wrote the ordinance that supported it.

On June 28, the city council was called into special session to investigate an altercation that same day between deputies Carson and Gainsford. No details are provided, but the deputies were reprimanded. On July 2, a new ordinance was written up that stated that if Sheriff Hickok found hogs running in the streets at large and with impunity they would be "taken up and impounded by the Marshal and shall by the Marshal be advertised for the period of three days, and if not called by the owners, before or at the expiration of said three days, the Marshall shall proceed to sell the same at public auction."[12]

On July 15, a more serious matter was considered and a plan was implemented. As sheriff of Abilene, Hickok was ordered to "stop dance houses and the [unlicensed] vending of Whiskeys, Brandies, &c in McCoy's Addition."[13] That was the fenced brothel district southeast of Abilene. Further tightening the vise on the prostitutes and Texas cowboys, a week later, on July 22, the council told Hickok to "close up all dead & Brace Gambling Games and to arrest all Cappers for the aforesaid Games."[14] In other words, to shut down crooked gambling. All of the new laws and rules infuriated many of the Texans. They understood that all of these draconian regulations were directed at them (and the prostitutes). The cowboys focused their anger on the most visible perpetrator of their agony, Marshal Hickok. Yet their fear of him and his prowess with his two Navy Colts kept them at bay. Hickok knew that paradigm might not hold the line forever. In his mind in Abilene also had to be remembrance of two recent assassination attempts on him in Hays City: one from maniacal and unpredictable restaurant owner Jim Curry, the other from two drunk 7th Cavalry privates, John Kile and Josh Lonergan.

Charles Gross recalled years later several summer days in Abilene in 1871 when he witnessed Hickok's ability with a pistol:

> *Bill got up leasurely and as he sat side ways on the Bed I saw he had his 6 shooter in his right hand and on the Bed spread lay a sawed off Gun (Double Barreled) with a strap on it so he could swing it over his shoulder and Carry it under his Coat out of sight. I dont think the Barrel was More than a 1-1/2 feet long.—to my surprise as soon as Bill was dressed, all but Coat & Hat—he went carefully to the door, looked all around for several mts & then Emptied one 6 shooter. He had the one in Each hand, returned to the room, cleaned & reloaded it, then went to the door & Emptied the Other one & reloaded it the same way. Bill used powder & Ball—We had pistols then with Metal Cartridges but Bill would not use them, he used powder & Ball, moulded his own bullets & primed Each tube using a pin to push the powder in so he was sure of powder Contact and before putting on the Cap he looked at the interior of Each Cap. Now this all strange to me & new too, for I had roomed and slept with Bill all the time he was at the [Drovers] Cottage (2 months or more) & he never did it there, so I said did you get your Guns damp yesterday Bill? He said "no, but I aint ready to go yet & I am not taking any chances, when I draw and pull I must be sure. You are the Only person in Abilene I will go to sleep with in the same room that I do not make things as sure as I Know how when I awake."*

I went fishing with Bill once at Hoffmans Dam & when we got in the Buggie Bill threw on two extra pistols and on our way home we stopped at a clear spot by some Cottonwoods & he & [I] put up a piece of paper on a tree as near the size of a mans body as we could guess & about the hight of Navel—(a 6 foot man). The paper was about 6 in long [wide] with a spot in the Center halfway. We stepped off 20 feet & he asked me to "wait a few moments," he Kind of slouched and did not appear to be looking at anything. he said "Keep talking & then suddenly without any hesitation in your talk, say Draw (Kinder quick)".

He shot six times so quick it startled me, for his six was in his Holster when I said "Draw". I was looking directly at him and only saw a Motion & he was firing. No use to ask how he drew. I don't Know. I only saw his arm was not straight and stiff. There was a perceptible Curve to his arm, but very slight—Every shot was in the paper and two in the spot, but all of them within one inch of an up & down line like this. We put up another paper and Bill tried his left hand with the result that all were in the paper but none in the spot but all of them [on] the up and down line, Each almost over the other or in the same hole. I said Not quite so good Bill—He said "I never shot a man with my left hand Except the time when some drunken Soldiers had me down on the floor & were trampling me & then I used both hands." [Kile and Lonergan, Hays City, the previous summer]

I do not recall that I ever heard Bill say "Killed." He always said "shot." I have wandered away from Your question & I will now return to it only pausing to say, Bill said "Charlie I hope you never have to shoot any man, but if you do, shoot him in the Guts near the Navel. you may not make a fatal shot, but he will get a shock that will paralize his brain and arm so much that the fight is all over."[15]

James Butler Hickok was good with his fists when needed, and strong in a fist fight. Dexter Fellows, for many years the business manager and press agent for the Ringling, Barnum, & Bailey Circus, recalled this rather humorous anecdote of J. B. Hickok in Abilene that showed he did not always resort to his pistols, or even his fists, to resolve a conflict:

Hickok would stand for all kinds of abuse from men whose courage was fired by drink, but let a chap strike town preceded by an announcement that he was coming to get Bill, and Hickok would live up to his reputation of always being the first on the draw. Many persons are of the belief that Wild Bill was helpless without a six-shooter, but Victor Murdock of the Wichita Eagle *has told me a story of one of Bill's fights while he was Marshal in Abilene, Kansas that disproves this. Bill, it seems was standing at the bar of a saloon when a strapping young man lurched up to him and said:*

"I know I'm not a match for you, Bill, with guns, but if you'll throw them aside I'll whale the lights out of you."

Hickok calmly put his pistols on the bar, seized a smoked buffalo tongue from on the free-lunch counter, and gave the boastful wight an unmerciful beating.[16]

In Abilene, James had ties to the two most important women in his life, aside from his mother and his sisters. Agnes Lake entered his life in Abilene, and Anna Wilson left his life in Abilene.

Agnes Lake's husband, William Lake, was murdered by a disgruntled circus patron at a performance of *Lake's Hippo-Olympiad and Mammoth Circus* in Granby, Missouri on August 21, 1869. Agnes was suddenly thrown into total responsibility for the management of their large circus. Her son-in-law Gil Robinson wrote that she gathered the circus employees together and told them of her plans: "Although Mr. Lake is dead, I intend to carry on his circus just as though he were here with us. If any of you think I am incapable, all I ask is that you will give me two weeks' notice and I will endeavor to fill your places. I am determined to keep the show on the road and I shall succeed."[17] Another account stated that all of the employees vowed to stay, and Agnes broke down when she heard of their loyalty.

Her determination paid off. After her husband's death in August, Agnes led her circus in 1869 through the rest of the fall and winter season, covering almost a hundred appearances, without missing a date. Performances were at one and seven p.m. Admission was one dollar for most attendees, fifty cents for children under ten.

That first season under her management was a strong financial success, proving that Agnes had natural business sense as well as the performing abilities of a circus star. Gil Robinson claimed in his memoir that "Mrs. Lake's success as a circus owner and manager was remarkable and the show became a gold mine under her direction."[18] The *Missouri Republican* of January 21, 1870, remarked that her circus had "made the tour of Arkansas, Mississippi, and part of Tennessee, clearing over $20,000" in the last half of 1869 alone.

Two years later, in 1871, the business now called *Madame Lake's Hippo-Olympiad and Mammoth Circus* came to Abilene. Like all the cities on their tours, they performed there just one day, yet two performances, at one and seven p.m., on July 31, 1871. They had come from a previous performance in Salina on July 29, apparently giving their roustabouts July 30 to set up on the west side of Abilene near the Drovers Cottage. The circus left Abilene either late in the evening of July 31, or very early in the morning of August 1; they had a show in Topeka scheduled on August 1. So they were in Abilene for a very short time; July 30, that night, and July 31. Two days and one night. Not much time for romance. *The Abilene Chronicle* reported on the July 31 performance: "The attendance was large at each performance."

Agnes surely knew of James Butler Hickok, aka Wild Bill Hickok, nationally famous at that point in his life. He probably knew of her as well. She had been a well-known circus performer for many years. When they met in Abilene, Agnes was forty-four, James was thirty-four. At some point, probably on July 30, Hickok, in his job as Marshal of Abilene, went to meet her where the circus was being set up. He may have needed to collect a licensing fee, or perhaps to discuss security matters for the next day's performance. There must have been an immediate mutual attraction, because Hickok's referral to what various historians have delicately termed "something essentially feminine" about her indicate they slept together before she left Abilene. That leaves the conclusion that their tryst took place the evening of July 30.

Hickok's above mentioned comment comes from the pen of Charles Gross, who knew Hickok back in Illinois in the 1850s, knew him again in the 1860s, and was Hickok's close friend in Abilene in 1871. In fact, it was Charles Gross who Joseph McCoy sent west to find Hickok and bring him back in the spring of 1871 to be the sheriff of Abilene. Years later, in the 1920s, Gross wrote numerous letters to J. B. Edwards in Abilene, recalling his remarkable and intimate knowledge of James Butler Hickok, Agnes Lake, Anna Wilson, and much more. One of these letters (this one, eleven handwritten pages long), mentioned Agnes Lake:

When Mrs. Lake the Widow of "Old Lake" of Circus fame Came to Abilene she set up her tent just West of the D Cottage on the vacant ground. Bill was on hand to keep order. Bill was a Handsome man as you Know & she fell for him hard, fell all the way <u>Clear to the Basement</u>, tried her best to get him to marry her & run the circus. Bill *told me all about it. I said why dont you do it—He said "I Know she has a good show, but when she is done in the West, she will go East & I dont want any Horse Collar any way—No it wont do—Now that one remark of Bills indicates to me that <u>there was no Legal reason</u> for his refusal to Marry Mrs. Lake. I know she was Keene for it (wonder if her name was Agnes?) she wrote to him after leaving Abilene, I know for the letters came to me under seal to the Cottage* [the Drovers Cottage].[19]

It is likely that Gross is not only describing the feelings developed between James and Agnes during the very few days or single night they spent together in Abilene, but he is describing as well the feelings developed in the letters that Agnes wrote to James after she left Abilene, which Gross delivered to James. He probably responded to at least some of her letters as well. Though they may have existed, none of these letters have ever surfaced.

Almost five years later James Butler Hickok married Agnes Lake.

On August 2, the Abilene city council took under consideration a motion to cut the four-man police force in half, but no action was taken. The same meeting considered "the looseing of twenty Dollars in controversy Wm Hickok and J.H. McDonald."[20] No further details are provided. On August 16, the council voted on whether to reduce the police force by half. The vote ended in a tie. On September 2, Hickok was instructed by the city council "to suppress all Dance Houses and to arrest the Proprietors if they resist after the Notification."[21] That same day, the city council discharged from the police force J. H. McDonald and James Gainsford, thus reducing the force by half. On September 6, Hickok was directed by the city council to "inform the proprietor of the Abilene House to expell the prostitute from his premises, under the pain and penalties of prosecution."[22]

After the long hot summer and the continual little regulations war the Abilene city council waged that summer against the Texas cowboys, and with the saloon owners and the prostitutes being collateral damage in that action, no one was surprised when the keg exploded on the evening of October 5, 1871. Theophilous Little recalled the dangerous build-up that evening, and the resulting incident at the Alamo saloon:

I remember the evening so well. About dusk I left my office to go to the Gulf House on my way home. I saw this band of crazy men. They went up and down the street with a wild swish and rush and roar, totally oblivious to anything in their path. It was a drunken mob. I hurried home and got my family into the house, locked the doors, and told my folks not to step outside, that the town was liable to be burned down and the people killed before morning. There were two men killed before 9 o'clock that night. As I have said the Marshall had been apprised of this plot and was on the ground fully prepared. The howling mob gathered around but Wild Bill had singled out Phil Coe, who had his gun out, but the Marshall had his two deadly guns leveled on Coe and pulled a trigger of each gun and just at that instant a policeman rushed around the corner of the building right between the guns and Coe and he received both bullets and fell dead. The Marshall instantly pulled two triggers again and two lead balls entered Coe's abdomen. Whirling on the mob his two 44 six shooters drawn on them, he calmly said, "If any of you want the balance of these pills, come and get them." Not a word was uttered, they were sobered and paralyzed. "Now every one of you mount his pony and ride for his camp and do it damn quick." In less than five minutes every man of them was on the west side of Mud Creek. Coe did not die that night, and this son of a Presbyterian Elder, Wild Bill, got a preacher out of bed and had him go to the dying gambler, Phil Coe, and pray with and for him. He died the next day.

The police man whom the Marshall killed was the son of a widow of Kansas City, Missouri. He sent money to the mother to come to Abilene, procured a fine burial casket, had a large funeral and shipped the body to Kansas City for burial, paying all expenses.[23]

Charles Gross was at the Alamo Saloon that evening:

I was in the saloon when Wild Bill shot his partner by mistake & then shot Dan [Phil] Cole the Texas gambler who had come to Abilene by request of his old cronys who were in the Conf army with him to get Bill. But Bill was too quick for him.[24]

Because the incident took place the evening of October 5, 1871, and the *Abilene Chronicle* was published each Thursday, their report on the shoot-out between Hickok and Coe did not appear in their pages until the following Thursday, October 12. The first press report of the incident came in the Junction City Union of October 7, 1871:

Two men were shot at Abilene, Thursday evening. The circumstances were about as follows, so our informant says: Early in the evening a party of men began a spree, going from one bar to another, forcing their acquaintances to treat, and making things howl generally. About 8 o'clock, shots were heard in the "Alamo," a gambling hell; whereupon the City Marshal, Haycock, better known as "Wild Bill," made his appearance. It is said that the leader of party had threatened to kill Bill, "before frost." As a reply to the Marshal's demand that order should be preserved, some of the party fired upon him, when, drawing his pistols "he fired with marvelous rapidity and characteristic accuracy," as our informant expressed it, shooting a Texan, named Coe, the keeper of the saloon, we believe, through the abdomen, and grazing one or two more. In the midst of the firing, a policeman rushed in to assist Bill, but unfortunately got into his line of fire. It being dark, Bill did not recognize him, and supposed him to be one of the party. He was instantly killed. Bill greatly regrets the shooting of his friend. Coe will die. The verdict of the citizens seemed to be unanimously in support of the Marshal, who bravely did his duty.

The *Abilene Chronicle* reported an expansive review of the incident on the following Thursday:

SHOOTING AFFRAY
Two Men Killed.

On last Thursday evening a number of men got on a "spree." and compelled several citizens and others to "stand treat," catching them on the street and carrying them upon their shoulders and into the saloon. The crowd served the Marshal, commonly called "Wild Bill," in this manner. He treated, but told them that they must keep within the bounds of order, or he would stop them. They kept on, until finally one of the crowd, named Phil. Coe, fired a revolver. The Marshal heard the report and knew at once the leading spirits in the crowd, numbering probably fifty men, intended to get up a "fight." He immediately started to quell the affair and when he reached the Alamo saloon, in front of which the crowd had gathered, he was confronted by Coe, who said that he had fired the shot at a dog. Coe had his revolver in his hand, as had also other parties in the crowd.

As quick as thought the Marshal drew two revolvers and both men fired almost simultaneously. Several shots were fired, during which Mike Williams, a policeman, came around the corner for the purpose of assisting the Marshal, and rushing between him and Coe, received two of the shots intended for Coe. The whole of the affair was the work of an instant. The Marshal, surrounded by the crowd, and standing in the light, did not recognize Williams whose death he deeply regrets. Coe was shot through the stomach, the ball coming out of his back; he lived in great agony until Sunday evening; he was a gambler, but a man of natural good impulses in his better moments. It is said that he had a spite at Wild Bill and had threatened to kill him—which Bill believed he would do if he gave him the opportunity. One of Coe's shots went through Bill's coat and another passed between his legs striking the floor behind him. The fact is Wild Bill's escape was truly marvelous. The two men were not more than eight feet apart, and both of them large, stout men. One or two others in the crowd were hit, but none seriously.

We had hoped the season would pass without any row. The Marshal has, with his assistants, maintained quietness and good order—and this in face of the fact that at one time during the season there was a larger number of cut-throats and desperadoes in Abilene than in any other town of its size on the continent. Most of them were from Kansas City, St. Louis, New Orleans, Chicago, and from the Mountains.

We hope no further disturbances will take place. There is no use in trying to override Wild Bill, the Marshal. His arrangements for policing the city are complete, and attempts to kill police officers or in any way create disturbance, must result in loss of life on the part of violators of the law. We hope that all, strangers as well as citizens, will aid by word and deed in maintaining peace and quietness.

The Texas press saw Hickok and Coe and the shooting in a different light. The *Austin Daily Democratic Statesman* reported on October 12: "A telegram from Abilene, Kansas, to Mr. Bowles of this city, announces the death of Phil Coe, a citizen of Austin. He was killed by 'Wild Bill the terror of the West,' a notorious gambler and desperado, at one time sheriff of Ellsworth in that State. The remains of the deceased will be sent to the city." The Brenham, Texas *Banner* of October 16, 1871, reported: "The remains of Phil Coe, who was murdered at Abilene by a notorious character known as 'Wild Bill,' arrived on Monday evening

#4237

This photograph of Phil Coe was probably taken in 1871. Texan Coe took over the Bull's Head Tavern after his friend and fellow Texan Ben Thompson left Abilene. Born in 1839, he was two years younger than Hickok. *Author's collection.*

last, and was interred at our city Cemetery on Tuesday morning, by his relatives and friends, with whom we deeply sympathasize." The *Saline County Journal* reported on October 12 that Coe "had resided in Salina a short time during this past summer, and was regarded by those who knew him as a quiet and unoffensive man."

It is reported that Hickok was devastated by the accidental shooting of his friend Mike Williams. There are claims made, though no proof, that Hickok paid to have his body shipped to Kansas City, and paid for the funeral as well. Williams had left his home and wife in Kansas City and gone to Abilene about four months prior to the fatal shooting, seeking a position as a policeman. In Kansas City he had been keeping a saloon at Twelfth and Walnut Streets, and later was a bartender at another saloon on Fourth Street. In 1871 Williams was twenty-nine years old and his wife was nineteen. That fatal night in Abilene, Mike Williams was working as a private policeman hired by the Novelty Theater to keep the Texans in line and away from the chorus girls.[25]

On November 4, the Abilene city council approved Hickok to bring on another deputy in addition to Tom Carson: J. W. "Brocky Jack" Norton. Carson and Norton's monthly pay was set by the council at $50 per month. That day the council reported that "the City Clerk was instructed to draw an order on the Treasurer, Payable to J. B. Hickok, for the purpose of sending R. E. McCoy, wife & child who were paupers, to Kansas City."[26]

The council met again on November 27; they directed Hickok to discharge deputies Tom Carson and short-timer Brocky Jack Norton from the force.[27] November 30, the *Abilene Chronicle* ran this stunning report:

ATTEMPT TO KILL MARSHAL HICKOK
—

He Circumvents The Parties
    Previous to the inauguration of the present municipal authorities of Abilene, every principle of right and justice was at a discount. No man's life or property was safe from the murderous intent and lawless invasions of Texans. The state of affairs was very similar to that of Newton during the last season. The law-abiding citizens decided upon a change, and it was thought best to fight the devil with his own weapons. Accordingly Marshal Hickok, popularly known as Wild Bill,

was elected Marshal. He appointed his men, tried and true, as his assistants. Without tracing the history of the great cattle market, it will suffice to say that during the past cattle season there has been order in Abilene. The Texans have kept remarkably quiet, and, as we learn from several citizens of the place, simply from fear of Marshal Hickok and his posse. *The Texans, however, viewed him with a jealous eye. Several attempts have been made to kill him, but all in vain.*

He has from time to time during the last summer received letters from Austin, Texas, warning him of a combination of rangers who had sworn to kill him. Lately, a letter came saying that a purse of $11,000 had been made up and five men were on their way to Abilene to take his life. They arrived in Abilene, but for five days kept hid, and the Marshal, although knowing their presence, was unable to find them. At last wearied with watching and sleepless nights and having some business in Topeka, he concluded to come here and get some rest. As he stood on the platform of the depot at Abilene he noticed four desperate looking fellows headed by a desperado about six feet, four inches high. They made no special demonstrations, but when the Marshal was about to get on the train, a friend who was with him overheard the big Texan say, "Wild Bill is going on the train." He was informed of this remark and kept a watch upon the party. They got on the same train and took seats immediately behind the Marshal. In a short time, he got up and took his seat behind them. One of the party glanced around and saw the situation, whereupon they left the car and went into the forward car. The Marshal and his friend, then, to be sure that they were after him, went to the rear end of the rear car.

The Marshal being very tired, sought rest in sleep, while his friend kept watch. Soon the Texans came into the car, and while four of them stood in the aisle, the leader took a position behind the Marshal, and a lady who was sitting near, and knew the Marshal, saw the Texan grasping a revolver between his overcoat and dress coat. The Marshal's friend, who had been a close observer of the party, went to him and told him not to go to sleep. This occurred about ten miles west of Topeka. When the train arrived at Topeka, the Marshal saw his friend safely on the bus and reentered the car. The party of Texans were just coming out of the door, when the Marshal asked them where they were going. They replied, "We propose to stop in Topeka." The Marshal then said, "I am satisfied that you are hounding me, and as I intend to stop in Topeka, you can't stop here." They began to object to his restrictions, but a pair of 'em convinced the murderous Texans that they had better go on, which they did.

While we cannot condone lawlessness or recklessness of any kind, yet we think the Marshal wholly justifiable in his conduct toward such a party. Furthermore, we think he is entitled to the thanks of law-abiding citizens throughout the State for the safety of life and property at Abilene, which has been secured, more through his daring, than any other agency.

The Texas cattle season had ended, so the city of Abilene no longer had need of their agent of change and enforcer, J. B. Hickok. It was to be the last season that Texas cattle drives would come to Abilene. Whereas Mayor Joseph McCoy was seeking a way for the city to co-exist with the Texas cowboys by attempting to control the cowboys and prostitutes through enforced laws and regulations, most Abilene citizens had endured them long enough after five years, and their voices eventually won out. At a special session of the Abilene city council on December 12, 1871, this motion was made, put to a vote, and unanimously agreed upon: "Be it resolved by Mayor & Council of City of Abilene That J B Hickok be discharged from his official position as City Marshal for the reason that the City is no longer in need of his services and that the date of his discharge take place from and after this 13th day of December A D 1871. Also that all of his Deputies be stopped from doing duty."[28]

February, 1872, most of the citizens of Abilene signed the below petition. It spelled out the final doom of the Texas cattle trade in Abilene, effectively turning off the lights on the cattlemen coming to that town. That season the lights were turned back on for the cattle trade in Ellsworth, sixty-four miles west of Abilene:

"We, the undersigned, members of the Farmers' Protective Association, and officers and citizens of Dickinson county, Kansas, most respectfully request all who have contemplated driving Texas cattle to Abilene the coming Season to seek some other point for shipment, as the inhabitants of Dickinson will no longer submit to the evils of the trade."

Years after his Abilene endeavors, Joseph G. McCoy wrote:

"For my preserver of the Peace, I had 'Wild Bill' Hickok, and he was the squarest man I ever saw. He broke up all unfair gambling,

made professional gamblers move their tables into the light, and when they became drunk, stopped the game."[29]

Some forty-five years after McCoy made that statement in 1908, President Dwight Eisenhower generated some attention with this quote from a speech given in 1953 in Washington DC:

> *I was raised in a little town of which most of you have never heard. But in the West it is a famous place. It is called Abilene, Kansas. We had as our Marshal for a long time a man named Wild Bill Hickok. If you don't know anything about him, read your Westerns more. Now that town had a code, and I was raised as a boy to prize that code. It was: meet anyone face to face with whom you disagree. You could not sneak up on him from behind, or do any damage to him, without suffering the penalty of an outraged citizenry. If you met him face to face and took the same risks he did, you could get away with almost anything, as long as the bullet was in front.*

In the same way that the Tutt and Hickok walkdown shootout on the town square of Springfield became the real-life prototype for every Western featuring a man-to-man shootout on the town square, James Butler Hickok's eight months at Abilene became the real-life prototype, in fact the only known real-life prototype, for the eternal Western theme of a strong, chisel-faced but taciturn sheriff brought into town to save the frightened citizenry from a variety of bad guys and evil-doers, all leading up to the inevitable shootout on the town square.

J. B. Hickok did everything in Abilene that McCoy and the Abilene city council demanded of him. He did his job well, he did it fearlessly, and then he left town with dignity. A better prototype could not be found.

It is not known just when James B. Hickok and Anna Wilson left Abilene and parted ways, but it probably occurred when James was discharged in December of 1871 as Marshal of Abilene. It is known where they went: James B. Hickok went east to Kansas City, and Anna Wilson west back to Ellsworth.

J. B. Edwards recalled Hickok and Indian Annie in 1871: "One of his favorites in Abilene was supposed to have been an Indian girl whom he kept in a nice little cottage on the outskirts of town. He was rarely seen with her."[30] What Edwards did not realize was that before Abilene, Anna Wilson (aka Indian Annie) had been with James from Junction City to Ellsworth to Hays City, and back to Ellsworth, and finally to Abilene. Five years. Perhaps off and on they were together, living the ups and downs, ins and outs of a serious relationship. Whatever their commitment to each other may have been, their relationship was considered a common-law marriage on the Kansas plains, especially in the Ellsworth area, where they and their long relationship both were well known.

Anna Wilson's parents were born in North Carolina. Her father was a white man, her mother was a Cherokee Indian. It is plausible that her family came west on the Cherokee "Trail of Tears" in 1838. Anna was born in Arkansas, in 1846 or 1847, which makes her about nineteen or twenty when they met; James was twenty-nine or thirty. Anna claimed to have come to Kansas from the Indian Territory (modern Oklahoma).[31]

Anna Wilson and James B. Hickok had a son together. His name was William Wilson. Based on some deductive research into the 1875 Kansas state census by historian James Drees, son William was born in 1870, sometime after the federal census for that year was taken in Hays City on June 24 and 25. Yet, Anna Wilson was somewhat careless with her own age when responding to the census taker (she reported that she was thirty-two years old on the 1870 census; in 1875 she reported that she was thirty-one years old' and finally settling down in the 1880 census and the 1885 census, she reported ages of thirty-three and thirty-eight respectively, making her actually born in 1846 or 1847). So it is possible that she reported her son's age off by a year, most likely reporting his age as five when he was actually only four. This would make his year of birth 1871, not 1870.[32]

Edwards referred to the "nice little cottage" where James and Anna lived in Abilene. Charles Gross recalled this same cottage and the woman who lived there with Hickok; all indications point to that woman being Anna Wilson. Gross wrote to J. B. Edwards in 1925. In the same eleven-page manuscript letter so full of information, Gross gave his recollection, among many other things, of Hickok and Indian Annie:

You have asked me a question that I can only answer by giving an opinion. The many talks I had with Bill I do not now recall any remark, or refference to any Woman other than those he made to the

One he lived with in the Small house & he did not Ever show bifore me any Especial affection for her—What he called her I do not recall but I do Know he was on Guard Even against her.

I was there alone with the two Many times but I was Very carefull never to go unless I knew Bill was Home & always there was good reason for my going. Having to go Early one morning Bill was still in bed & when I went to the door and the woman came to let me in she saw through the window who I was.—she was only just up & was still in night dress. Bill said "let him in; you dont give a Dam for Gross seeing you"; but she did and showed it in looks. she went into the next room & Bill got up leasurely...[33]

It is worth noting that Gross, who clearly indicates that he knew both of them well, and visited their cottage often, never mentions a child. If James' son William had been born in 1870, he would have been there at their Abilene home in 1871. This is another indication that William may have born in 1871, probably late in the winter, when Gross may not have been to their cottage before Hickok was discharged as sheriff of Abilene in December. That would make William actually four years old in 1875, in spite of Anna reporting him five years old in the 1875 state census.

There is another point to be clarified in Charles Gross' long letter noted above. Later in the letter to J. B. Edwards, Gross writes: "He [Hickok] always had a mistress. I Knew two or three of them. One, a former mistress of his was an inmate of a cottage in McCoy's addition. Bill asked me to go with him to see her to be a witness in an interview. I believe she was a Red Head but I am not sure. She came to Abilene to try & make up with Bill. He gave her $25.00 and made her move on. There was no Row but Bill told her he was through with her. She moved On."

Several writers on Wild Bill Hickok have taken this passage to be about Indian Annie, apparently reasoning that since Anna Wilson and Hickok broke up in Abilene, this passage must also be about her. An understanding of the context shows that it is not about her, but another woman. McCoy's Addition was a derisive term the citizens of 1871 applied to the fenced property southeast of town that McCoy had built to house the prostitutes. Indian Annie was not a prostitute, as Gross describes the woman above. Gross thought the woman had red hair. Indian Annie had straight black hair (see her daughter's letter on page 275). Gross describes this woman as a former mistress who had a

JAMES BUTLER HICKOK AND THE AMERICAN WEST

falling-out with Hickok in another town and came to Abilene to patch things up with him. That woman is not Indian Annie.

Unknown are the reasons that James and Anna ended their five-year relationship in Abilene. But evidence indicates they parted ways for good, and their son William went with Anna. Charles Lyon, the author of the 1879 *Compendious History of Ellsworth County, Kansas,* claimed that he got the information on Hickok directly from Anna Wilson. He wrote: "From Abilene he [Hickok] went to Cheyenne, thence to Deadwood, while Mrs. 'Wild Bill' came to Ellsworth, where she now resides. The latter is a half-breed, her father being a white man and her mother a Cheyenne Indian." James may have told Anna he was going to Cheyenne, but all available records show that he went directly to Kansas City that December of 1871, after leaving Abilene.[34]

In 1875 Anna Wilson and her son were still living in Ellsworth. The state census shows them as citizens of Ellsworth, showing her as Annie Wilson, age thirty-one, an Indian born in Arkansas, came to Kansas from the Indian Territory. The census showed her son as Willie Wilson, age five, a white male born in Kansas who had attended school within the census year.

Ellsworth resident Charles Larkin, the son of Arthur Larkin, the hotel owner that was Anna Wilson's employer, claimed that in early August, 1876, he went through the front door of his father's hotel, the Grand Central, and saw "Indian Annie" on her knees scrubbing the floor of the hotel lobby. He said, "Annie, father has just heard over the telegraph that Wild Bill was shot in Deadwood." Looking up into his face, Anna Wilson gently said, "I'm damned glad of it." Then she turned back and continued scrubbing.[35]

Anna and her and James' son continued to live their quiet life in Ellsworth, though occasionally approached by visitors and journalists interested in their ties to the legendary James B. Hickok. One visiting journalist made this report in the *Leavenworth Daily Times* of October 21, 1877:

ELLSWORTH October 20

    WILD BILL'S WIDOW, or one of them at least, who goes under the name of Mrs. Wilson, lives here, and supports herself by taking in sewing. Young Wild Bill, now a lad of nine or ten years of age, is exactly like his father, built upon the same architectural plan, and is possessed of the same spirit. It takes a tough lad to get away with him, and he 'runs the ranch' usually wherever he goes. One marked feature of the lad is his eyes, which are bright and piercing, and in that particular, if in no other regard to his physical make-up, he resembles his father. Mrs. Wilson, or Mrs. Wild Bill, or Mrs. Hickock, or whatever-name-you-choose-to-call-her, is an Indian, of low stature, not bad looking.

Anna Wilson met another man in Ellsworth, also with the last name of Wilson. With him she had her second child on April 17, 1878, a daughter that she named Birdie Daisy. Like her brother and mother, Birdie was of mixed heritage. One census reported her as Indian, while another census entry said she was white.

On September 26, 1878, the *Ellsworth Reporter* described a sad event:

> *As we look out of our office window Monday afternoon we saw pass a wagon, containing two men, a veiled woman, seated in a chair, and a coffin. This is all we know of the funeral of Willie Wilson. He was being carried to his grave, without a mourner, save his mother, without prayer, unless unuttered prayer, nor any ceremony.*
> *It was a sight sad enough to move any heart to pity.*
> *A sort of waif in the world, Willie had grown to the age of eight years in Ellsworth a smart, active child, eager in his sports and plays, being a sort of leader among the boys of his age, and was becoming quite useful to his mother by doing numerous errands for her. He was taken with diphtheria last week and died after an illness of a few days. We shall miss him on the street, and the little boys he used to play with, will feel sorry that they can never play with Willie any more—he is laid away out of sight forever. His mother, familiarly known as "the little Indian woman" has our pity and sympathy and we hope some faith in the Great Spirit may comfort her.*

So the young son of Anna Wilson and James Butler Hickok passed away.

It has been reported that for most of her time in Ellsworth, Anna Wilson and her family lived in a small two-room house near the old county jail. On May 1, 1879, the Ellsworth *Reporter* reported that on "Wednesday morning one of the hardest rains poured down on this community, that we ever saw. The streets were overflowed and in fact the whole town on the low ground was covered with water. The house which the widow of 'Wild Bill' occupies, was afloat, and the lady had to be carried out on horseback. The colored family that lives across from the jail were almost drowned out..." In the 1950s, eighty-six-year-old Bessie Beatty set down in writing her recollections of Anna Wilson in 1879 and 1880:

> *In 1879, when a child eight years of age, I came with my parents, brothers, and sisters from the state of Iowa to the new little town of Ellsworth, Kansas. This was a newly settled country, windswept, treeless prairie, wild and desolate, compared to the wooded country with abundant fruit and beautiful flowers of the home I had lived in. Some years previous to this I was told the settlers had been in danger from the attacks of Indian tribes.*
>
> *While attending school, a young classmate asked me to go with her to the cabin where Mrs. Wild Bill Hickok lived, to watch her tell fortunes with cards. My young friend told me that she was an Indian woman called Indian Annie. I said, "No, I can't go with you, I'm afraid of Indians." She assured me that there were no other Indians there so I went to the little cabin where Indian Annie lived with her little daughter and stood in the doorway watching her tell fortunes.*[36]

After this meeting with Indian Annie, Bessie Beatty stated that Indian Annie and her daughter Birdie Daisy entered the County Home for destitute people. Annie had contracted tuberculosis. On November 10, 1885, at the age of thirty-eight, Anna Wilson (aka Indian Annie) died of tuberculosis. On November 12, 1885, The Ellsworth *Reporter* published her obituary:

> *AT REST*
> *WILSON—*
>
> *At the county poor farm, Tuesday November 10, 1885, Mrs. Anna Wilson, of this city. The deceased had been a resident of Ellsworth for a number of years, coming here as the wife of Wild Bill, who shortly after their arrival, deserted and left her to struggle through life alone, as best as she could. She was an industrious and kind hearted woman and leaves one child and many friends to mourn her untimely death.*

Rest you; no more shall ill befall,
Nor pain, nor anguish hard to bear,
Nor mortal grief, nor earthly care,
For death has overcome them all.

Anna Wilson was buried near her son Willie Wilson, in the area designated as the Potters Field on the grounds of the County Home where she lived the last few years of her life. The location of the Potters Field today is on the grounds of a modern golf course. The location by modern directions is the northeast corner of the intersection of U. S. 156 Highway with the tracks of the Union Pacific Railroad. There is a limestone marker denoting the Butterfield Overland Despatch that passed this spot in 1865 and 1866. At the base of the hill on the northeast corner is a small, flat stone marker with a metal plaque that reads:

INDIAN ANNIE
LIES ON THE KNOLL ABOVE
COMPANION OF
WILD BILL HICKOK
IN ELLSWORTH KANSAS
DIED 1885

Another Ellsworth newspaper, the *Ellsworth Democrat*, also reported Anna's passing, and mentioned Anna's little girl Birdie Daisy: "Mrs. Wilson, well known to our citizens as the 'little Indian woman' died last Tuesday morning at 5 o'clock. She leaves a little girl about seven years of age, who will be provided for by Mr. Thompson, of Mulberry Creek."

The Search for Birdie Daisy

In the 1920s, William Connelley was gathering material for his forthcoming biography of Hickok. He found indications that Hickok had been associated with an Indian woman in Ellsworth. Connelley wrote to Ira E. Lloyd in Ellsworth, an attorney who settled in Ellsworth in 1873, and asked him questions about this Indian woman. Lloyd wrote back to Connelley, confirmed that he knew Indian Annie, and provided information to Connelley of what Lloyd thought he knew. Lloyd told Connelley that she lived in a house near the old courthouse. She took in

#3999

Anna Wilson, aka Indian Annie with her daughter Birdie Daisy, about ten years after she and James had parted ways. Taken about 1881, Birdie Daisy is three years old here. *Courtesy of Ellsworth County Historical Society, Ellsworth, Kansas.*

washing and sewing to make extra money. She had a little girl; Lloyd said no one in Ellsworth believed the little girl was Hickok's daughter. The girl later went to Oklahoma. Lloyd knew of the girl's father but he did not reveal his name. Obviously, Birdie Daisy was that little girl.

Somehow Connelley found the name and address of the woman he believed was Indian Annie's daughter, but in Texas, not Oklahoma. On January 21, 1926, he wrote to her:

> *Mrs. Ed Berry*
> *Palacios, Texas*
>
> *Dear Madam:*
> *I am writing a biography of James Butler Hickok, better known in Kansas as "Wild Bill." In securing the recollections of those now living, I find that he had an Indian wife who used to live in Ellsworth, Kansas, in a little house where the old courthouse stood, and that she had two children, a boy and a girl. When she was unable to longer work and support her children she gave them homes with farmers near the Elk Horn. A man named Reuben Sparks furnished a home for the boy. My information is that he died at the age of fourteen. I have not been able to find the name of the person who furnished a home for the girl. I think you must be the girl, and I wish you would write me fully concerning your mother and her marriage to Wild Bill.*
> *I should like to know when this marriage was, the tribe of Indians to which your mother belonged, her age and general appearance at the time she met Bill if you can give it. Also write me any recollections you may have of your mother. Tell me when she was born and when she died. If you know of any incidents in the life of Wild Bill, or adventures, please give me an account of those. He was a wonderful scout and did a great deal to secure information from the rebel lines in southwest Missouri and northeast Arkansas in the Civil War. All the generals pay him a high tribute for his services as a scout. I do not want to write a sensational book and do not intend to. I want a statement of plain facts. The information I have concerning the daughter is that she married in Lincoln county, Kansas, but of course this may not be correct.*
> *If you can do this for me it will be a great favor and I will return it if opportunity occurs.*
>
> *Sincerely yours,*
> *William Connelley*[37]

Connelley wrote to Ira E. Lloyd on January 26, 1926, and thanked him for the report on Indian Annie that "contain[ed] information which I had not been able to secure before." Connelley finishes his letter to Lloyd with an update on his search for Birdie Daisy: "I have traced the girl, the daughter of Indian Anna, to a town in Texas, and have written her to give me what information she has about Wild Bill and her mother. I am not sure she will do it, but she may do it. She married a man named Berry."[38]

On February 8, 1926, Birdie Daisy Berry, the daughter of Indian Annie, responded in writing to Connelley:

Palacios, Texas
Mr. Wm. E. Connelley
Topeka, Kans

> *Dear Sir: In reply to your letter of Jan. 21st. It is impossible for me to give you much information in regard to my mother life. I was only seven when she died and remember very little about her. After her death I was taken by J.P. Thompson who then live in Ellsworth Co. near the Yordy School house which is near the east line of the county. I had a brother six years my senior. He died when I was three year old. My mother lived in Ellsworth until her death.*
>
> *I have no knowledge of her being with Wild Bill. But have been told she was his wife. I think when she lived with him she was at Wamego, Kans or somewhere there about. My Brothers name was William.*
>
> *Some twenty-four or five years ago a lawyer Brown of Topeka Kans tried to help me find some information concerning my mother. We corresponded quite extensively but failed to find out much about her. We were unable to find what tribe certainly she belonged to. This lawyer Brown is dead now. But I think his son Chauncey is practicing law and he might have some of the information we secured.*
>
> *Some thought my mother was a Choctaw. But we could [not] establish the fact enough that I could get a claim from the government. I do not know my mother age when she died. But I expect somewhere [near] 35 yr. She was very dark very black straight hair and small stature.*
>
> *I would appreciate should you find out any thing about my Mother if you let me know. Many think I am entitled to a claim on the government if I could find out what tribe she belong too. Any other question you wish to ask I will be glad to answer if I can.*

My brother lived with my mother and myself until he died. I lived with my mother until her death.

Sincerely,
Mrs. Ed Berry

P.S. I was married at Beverly Kans Jan 1, 1906.[39]

There are several errors of memory pertaining to her brother in Birdie Wilson/Mrs. Ed Berry's response to Connelley. The empirical evidence of Willie Wilson's September, 1878, obituary in the Ellsworth *Reporter* shows beyond any doubt that her brother died then at eight years of age, when she was barely five months old (she was born April 17, 1878). Mrs. Berry's letter also shows that most of what Connelley thought he knew about Indian Annie was wrong before he communicated with Mrs. Berry. She also does confirm that when her mother died, she went to live with a Mr. Thompson. Tellingly, she says nothing about anyone else furnishing her a home. Connelley responded back to Mrs. Ed Berry on February 13, 1926:

Mrs. Ed Berry
Palacios, Texas

Dear Madam:-
I was pleased to have your favor of the 8th inst. but regret you are unable to tell me the tribe in which your mother belonged...

Connelley then described Hickok's relationship to Mary Owen back in Monticello in the late 1850s, who was also the child of a white father and an Indian mother, ending the passage with "This may be of importance to you or it may not be." Then he continues with a tantalizing clue and more:

There is an account of his having married another Indian woman. He told Mrs. Smith, who lives in this city [Topeka] *and who knew him at Monticello, that he was married to an Indian woman. But this was during the Civil War or after the war, and may have been another Indian woman* [i.e., a different Indian woman than Mary Owen]. *Mrs. Smith does not know anything more than that he said he was married to this Indian woman.* [Indian Annie and Hickok are first noted together in 1866, one year after the Civil War.]

Your account of yourself and your brother confirms closely to what Mr. Lloyd of Ellsworth, told me. The man Brown you mention is not now in Topeka and I think it would be useless to look for him. He may be dead. Do you remember your mother's Christian name, that is her given name. Was it Mary, Jennie, Lucy, or what was it.

I shall be glad to hear from you at any time.

Sincerely yours,
William Connelley[40]

Birdie Daisy, aka Birdie Wilson, aka Mrs. Ed Berry, lived a long life and died in 1957 at the age of seventy-nine or eighty, unlike her brother who died of diphtheria at age eight, and her mother who died of tuberculosis at just thirty-eight.

James Butler Hickok, man about town in Kansas City.... J. B. Hickok came east to Kansas City in 1872 looking for some relief from the stress of law enforcement in the rough and tumble towns along the Kansas Pacific railroad. He moved into the St. Nicholas hotel at 4th and Main, just up the street from the Marble Hall Saloon at 520 Main Street. Here he made his headquarters for an extended Kansas City vacation, one that lasted most of the year. The original 1872 photograph is credited to Andrew White, whose studio was a few blocks further south at 712 Main. The original photograph was given by James to his Kansas City friend Dan Pixley. On the back of the photograph is inscribed James B. Hickok Wild Bill, written in Hickok's own hand. *Author's collection.*

14

1872

KANSAS CITY

an IMPOSTER *in* BOSTON

JAMES BUEL

DR. JOSHUA THORNE *and* E. W. KINGSBURY

BUFFALO HUNT *at* NIAGARA FALLS

TROUBLE *with* TEXANS... AGAIN

SPRINGFIELD REDUX

James B. Hickok came directly east to Kansas City from Abilene in late December, 1871. On the Kansas Pacific Railroad en route to his new home, he surely mulled the previous two years: the tragic accidental shooting just three months past of his dear friend Mike Williams, three assassination attempts on his own life, and the final breakup, after five years, with Anna Wilson. Never again would he wear the badge of a lawman. He had been paid quite well in Abilene and Hays City as sheriff of those towns, enough to have saved a good sum back. The national fame and recognition that he had garnered for the last five years, though he did not seek it, had

279

#4136

St. Nicholas Hotel,

(NEWLY FURNISHED AND RE-FITTED.)

CORNER FOURTH AND MAIN STREETS, OPP. OLD COURT HOUSE;

KANSAS CITY, MISSOURI.

JOE. SIGEMUNT, Proprietor.

S. S. BAKER AND H. B. MIDLAM IN THE OFFICE.

J. B. Hickok's home in Kansas City, the St. Nicholas Hotel. *Author's collection. From the 1872 City Directory of Kansas City, Missouri.*

brought him some pleasure but also some pain, and some danger. Over those five years he had been a scout and guide for the frontier military in two Indian campaigns, he had served as a deputy U. S. Marshal for most of those five years, he owned two saloons, one in Junction City, and one in Hays City, and he had served as sheriff of Hays City and Marshal of Abilene. As a lawman he had shot and killed three men in the line of duty. He had been wounded by an Indian spear, and may have been shot in the leg in the brawl with two 7th Cavalry privates. In Kansas City he would seek some peace and quiet. He was thirty-four years old.

For the next four years, off and on, sometimes for long periods, other times for short periods, Kansas City, Missouri and the St. Nicholas Hotel would be his home. The St. Nicholas Hotel, owned and run by Joe Sigemund, was a large, four-story hotel on the southwest corner of Fourth and Main Streets. Directly across Main Street, on the southeast corner, was the Kansas City police station. South on Main from Fifth Street to Missouri Avenue was known as Battle Row, mostly occupied by saloons and gambling halls, the most popular and lavish being the Marble Hall at 520 Main Street. Across the street from the Marble Hall and slightly north was Coates and Bullene Dry Goods, located in a four-story brick building, at 529 Main Street. The top floor of the building was the meeting room of the International Order of Odd Fellows, with its own entrance on Missouri Avenue. In the neighborhood a few blocks west at Third and Wyandotte was the elaborate home of notorious madam Annie Chambers and her house of ill repute. And, probably most important to the legacy of James Butler Hickok, the offices of the *Kansas City Journal* were at 6 West Fifth Street, just around the corner from the St. Nicholas

#4148

This 1872 photograph of J.B. Hickok wearing the buffalo overcoat of his friend Dan Pixley, was probably also taken by photographer Andrew J. White. Both Pixley photos passed down through the Pixley family of Pawhuska, Oklahoma until 1996 when the Pixley family donated them. *Author's collection.*

#4148

This 1872 photograph came to light in Kansas City in 1993 when its undisclosed owner asked Joseph Rosa to verify it as Hickok. In 2008 it came up for auction, yet any action on it was undetermined. It carries the inscription of photographer Andrew J. White. Hickok wears the same hat as in Image 4001. *Author's collection.*

Hotel. In the offices of the *Journal* was the desk of their ace reporter, twenty-two-year-old James W. Buel.

James Buel was born October 22, 1849, in Golconda, Illinois. At the age of eight he went to work in his father's tannery. As a child, Buel was an avid reader, and he developed wide interests and knowledge. In 1863, at the age of fourteen, he and a friend ran away from home and tried to join the Union Army. They were sent home.

In 1868, Buel enrolled in the Illinois Industrial University (today's Illinois University). While at college, his roommate was poet Eugene Field, then unknown. Buel started off studying law. It is unclear if he ever graduated. By 1870 he had moved west to Kansas, landing at the small town of Spring Hill in Johnson County, near the Missouri border and about thirty miles southwest of Kansas City.

Enlisting a partner, Buel started a small weekly newspaper in December of 1870 called the Spring Hill *Enterprise*. During this time, Buel was admitted to the Kansas bar. In January, Buel bought out his partner and shortly after, he partnered with a Dr. Parker; they continued to publish the *Enterprise* through 1871. In August of that year, Buel married Eliza Brawner of Illinois and brought her to Spring Hill.

A view of Main street in Kansas City in 1872 looking north from Sixth street. On the west side at 520 Main is the Marble Hall Saloon, Hickok's gambling headquarters. On the east side and just out of the picture at 529 Main is the three or four story building holding Bullene's Clothing Story on the bottom floor and the International Order of Odd Fellows Hall on the upper floors. North on Main on the west side at Fourth and Main was the St. Nicholas Hotel, Hickok's Kansas City home. Across the street was police headquarters. *Courtesy Missouri Valley Special Collections, Kansas City Public Library, Kansas City, Missouri.*

In early 1872, W. H. McGowan bought the newspaper from Buel and Parker. Buel and his bride moved to Kansas City and Buel took a job as reporter for the Kansas City *Journal.* He held that job for four years, until 1875. During that time, he got to know James Butler Hickok quite well, and they became friends. In 1875, he took an editorial position with a St. Louis newspaper, and he and Eliza moved to St. Louis. In 1876, Hickok came to St. Louis to put together a group to visit the Black Hills in South Dakota, and he stayed at Buel's St. Louis home.

After Hickok's stunning and untimely death in August of 1876, Buel went from journalist to biographer. He started working on writing up the life of Hickok. Titled *The Life and Marvelous Adventures of Wild Bill, the Scout—Being A True and Exact History of all the Sanguinary Combats and Hairbreadth Escapes of the Most Famous Scout and Spy America Ever Produced,* this ninety-two-page booklet in wrappers was published in 1880. It has been reissued many times over the last 141 years, and under a wide variety of titles. A good copy of the scarce first edition of the title above can bring as much as $3K on the rare book market.

Buel followed this up one year later with a greatly expanded version of his Hickok biography, encompassing the first 221 pages of Buel's *Heroes of the Plains.* That book had wide distribution and cemented Hickok's fame and celebrity for future generations. Buel was the most influential Hickok biographer for eighty-plus years, until Joseph Rosa came along in the 1960s. Buel claimed to have received Hickok's diary from his widow, Agnes Lake. No trace of it has ever been found, if it even existed in the first place, which is doubtful. Buel's papers and notes have not been found either, despite searches by several historians, including Joseph Rosa.

Heroes of the Plains sold very well across the country, and Buel was encouraged to write more. In 1882, he went to Russia to observe the turbulent political conditions there. That trip resulted in Buel's book, *Exile Life in Russia,* published in 1883. That same year, he struck up a partnership with W. S. Bryan and founded a publishing house known as The Historical Publishing Company. They eventually had offices in St. Louis, Chicago, and Philadelphia.

Buel wrote prolifically, both on his own and in collaboration with others. The publishing company was successful. The books were sold by subscription; door-to-door salesmen carrying sample copies and taking orders. The books published by Historical Publishing were profusely illustrated, bound with gilt and embossed leather or fabric, and printed with quality in mind.

More popular titles followed, including *The Border Outlaws: An Authentic and Thrilling History of the Most Noted Bandits of Ancient and Modern Times; The Younger Brothers, Jesse and Frank James and their Comrades in Crime; Heroes of The Dark Continent, America's Wonderlands,* and *Buel's Manual of Self Help.*

In 1907, Buel issued his final work, a fifteen-volume set entitled *The Anglo-Saxon Classics.* He retired from writing and publishing, and moved to San Diego, where he purchased a wholesale laundry company. He took a partner, Ruben Town. The business was known as the Buel-Town Company, and today the building that housed their business is known as the Buel-Town building. James W. Buel died on November 16, 1920, at the age of 71.[1]

Along with all the information he had gleaned from Hickok during their years together in Kansas City, and what he had read in the newspapers, Buel relied on two primary informants for information on Hickok: Dr. Joshua Thorne and Ezra W. Kingsbury, both of Kansas City.

During the time that Hickok called Kansas City home, Dr. Joshua Thorne had his office on the northeast corner of Third Street and Walnut, in close proximity to Hickok's place at the St Nicholas Hotel and Buel's office at the Kansas City *Journal,* just across the city market grounds. Dr. Thorne was born in England in 1832. After his family moved to the United States in 1845, Dr. Thorne studied medicine at St. Louis and Charleston. He opened his medical practice in Charleston in 1853, and in 1855 he took a post-graduate course in homeopathic medicine. He married in 1857 and came to Kansas City in 1859, where he lived the rest of his life.

During the Civil War he opened a general hospital in Kansas City at the request of the U. S. surgeon general. During the Price Raid, he was in charge of the wounded and supervised all the hospitals in the area. After the war ended, he was appointed by the federal government as assessor of internal revenue in the region, a position he held until 1873. He also served as secretary of the Board of Pension Surgeons until 1885. Dr. Thorne also served as president of the Missouri Institute of Homeopathy.[2]

Dr. Joshua Thorne has been described as "a man of strong character and much originality—an influential citizen, conspicuous in professional circles, an interesting public speaker of more than local reputation, and a forcible, convincing writer..."[3]

It is very hard to believe, with these sterling credentials noted above, that Joshua Thorne would ever lie, or even exaggerate to James

Buel. Yet Buel claimed, among other things, that "Dr. Thorne informed the writer that he had removed eleven bullets from the body of Wild Bill, nearly all of which were shot into him at the Rock Creek fight..." On a more believable note, Buel wrote, "Returning to Kansas City, he [J. B. Hickok] remained for some time inactive due to an attack of opthalmia superinduced no doubt by the exposure he underwent while in the Black Hills. Dr. Thorne treated him for several months with such success that his eyesight, which for a time was entirely destroyed, was partly restored, but he never again regained his perfect vision."[4]

Buel may have felt that his readers would believe that Dr. Thorne's word was beyond reproach, and that he could handle any complaints Thorne himself might have about Buel's exaggerations, even as outrageous as they might have been.

Ezra Wolcott Kingsbury (commonly known as E. W. Kingsbury) knew Hickok even before Dr. Thorne did. They may have met during the Civil War in southwest Missouri, but they definitely knew each other by 1867, when both were in the Ellsworth area. Kingsbury was one of the first residents of Ellsworth; in fact, he built the first structure there in May, 1867. It housed a store and a hotel. In August that year Hickok and Kingsbury were both candidates for sheriff of Ellsworth County. Kingsbury won the election. That winter Hickok and Kingsbury and undersheriff Chauncey Whitney teamed up to arrest several men that were very drunk and raising hell in Ellsworth. They tied them to posts to have them cool off. Ironically, a few years later, J. B. Hickok had another confrontation with one of the men, Samuel Strawhun.[5]

By 1872, Kingsbury had moved to Kansas City, and renewed his acquaintance with Hickok there, and met Buel for the first time in Kansas City. Buel claimed that Kingsbury was on the scene in the immediate aftermath of the McCanles affair: "The particulars as here recorded [concerning the McCanles incident] are unquestionably correct, for they were obtained from Capt. Kingsbury, who heard Bill's first recital of the facts right on the battleground..."[6] To state the obvious, Kingsbury was never there. Again, as with Thorne, Buel may have thought that Kingsbury, who was a former frontier sheriff, would be readily believed by people.

Buel took an uncharacteristic posture when describing Hickok's actions in Kansas City; he was very straightforward and apparently stuck with the facts, which may be because he was an actual witness to those events in Kansas City, unlike Hickok's other adventures elsewhere; thus

Buel could be the one taken to task on the veracity of events in Kansas City that he described. Buel did not let that stop him from assigning some exaggerated statements, however, to Dr. Joshua Thorne and Ezra W. Kingsbury. In *Heroes of the Plains,* Buel described Hickok's coming to Kansas City in 1872:

> *Becoming tired of the life which Hays City afforded, Bill resigned his position as U.S. Marshal, and in the spring of 1872 went to Kansas City, where he found a place bristling with sports and entertainments well suited to his disposition. About the same time the writer, who had been occupying an editorial position on the Fort Scott Daily Monitor, accepted an offer made him by the proprietors of the Kansas City Journal and took up residence in the Bluff City [Kansas City], where he became intimately acquainted with the heroic scout and learned much concerning his marvellous career.*

Buel knew that Hickok came to Kansas City after being Marshal of Abilene, not Hays City. This was just a slip of Buel's writing pen. And it is known today that Hickok came to Kansas City in December of 1871, not the spring of '72. Buel continues:

> *Kansas City was a brisk town in 1872. It contained a population of nearly 30,000, and was the parent block off which was chipped all the gambling towns along the Kansas Pacific railroad. Games of chance, cards, keno, faro, dice, cock-mains, dog fighting, and kindred means for hazarding money ran day and night. On the west side of Main, between Fourth street and Missouri avenue, there was nothing in the upper stories of the buildings except gamblers and gaming outfits. But this district was peculiar only in presenting an unbroken chain, as it were, of gambling dens. Fifth street, between Walnut and Main, was equally bad, even worse, because the rooms were less inviting and patronized by a more disreputable class. The lower end of main street and the levee were given over to brothel houses, about which a first-class item could nearly always be found. The writer now recalls to mind one evening when he was detailed to report three murders and one suspicious death.*
> *But today the infamies and demoralizing characters which once filled the streets of Kansas City exist only in the history of her progress, and the hum of her commerce has long since displaced the*

sonorous voice of the keno caller and the death-crack of the revolver. Not withstanding the lawless, turbulent elements that once gave character to Kansas City during the period of Wild Bill's presence in the place, he kept himself aloof from them, in his quiet, dignified, reserved way, and thus never had occasion to unloose the tiger that slumbered beneath his calm exterior.[7]

The *Kansas City Times* on January 19, 1872, reported: "Wild Bill distinguished himself in the parquette of the Opera House last night."

The *St. Joseph Daily Gazette* reported on January 31, 1872, that Charles Whitehead, the editor of the *Kansas City Times,* was feuding with another editor, Frank Grice. Later a very drunk Charles Whitehead searched for the whereabouts of Grice. "He went to the Walnut Street Theatre, where he had some words with Wild Bill," stated the paper. Whitehead continued on his search, and upon finding Grice a scuffle ensued, ending when editor Grice shot editor Whitehead with a derringer in the left thigh. Though just a flesh wound, it ended the scuffle. Charles Whitehead's name would appear once more in the Hickok narrative, when he became the jury foreman in the trial of Jack McCall in 1876.

A Hickok imposter showed up in Boston in January of 1872. *The Saline County Journal* reported on it in their issue of January 18, 1872. The writer indicates his disgust with this faker (although he does not know it is a fake Wild Bill) by calling him a criminal and castigating him as a "libertine and a rowdy." Of course, the real Hickok was none of these:

> It is said that Hacock, the scout, known in this country as "Wild Bill", is exhibiting himself to the inhabitants of Boston. Ever since his achievements were narrated in Harper's New Monthly Magazine, three or four years ago, Wild Bill's star has been ascending, and now the credulous New Englanders have an opportunity to interview in person the man who has shot down men in cold blood by the scores and is big a criminal as walks the earth. If it is pleasure for those down-easters to welcome a gambler, a libertine and a rowdy, we can furnish those of the same ilk, just as deserving, by the hundreds, from our "wicked plains." Bill is making money showing himself, so they say. "A prophet is not without honor save in his own country."

This was the first known Hickok imposter, and it would not be the last. Various unscrupulous people tried to cash in on Hickok's fame and following, during his life as well as after it. A few more of these fakers will be met in later pages of this book.

In March 1872, James left his Kansas City home at the St. Nicholas Hotel and traveled to Georgetown, Colorado to visit his friend Charley Utter. Hickok and Utter probably met more than a decade before, in 1860 or 1861, when James was riding shotgun on a Jones & Cartwright stage between Leavenworth and Denver. In 1872, no stagecoach was needed. Hickok would have purchased his ticket to Denver at the Kansas Pacific ticket office just a block away from his hotel, and made his way to the depot. On the train trip west he surely would have considered the vagaries of the national fame he had garnered since he had gone to Kansas in 1866, because the tracks of the Kansas Pacific took him right through the very towns and near the frontier forts where his life, over those years, had played out: Junction City and Fort Riley, Abilene, Ellsworth and Fort Harker, Hays City and Fort Hays, and on to Denver.

Charley Utter owned a boarding house in 1872 in Georgetown, and many of his tenants were miners at the nearby O. K. Mine. One of them, A. D. McCanless (Ironically, a relative of David McCanles) wrote this recollection: "When I went to Georgetown, Colorado in March 1872, and began working at the O.K. Mine I boarded, when not at the mine, at Charley Utter's (known as Colorado Charley) and Wild Bill was there for six or eight weeks after I got there. He was out of work and put in most of his time playing poker. He was very pleasant and agreeable, and never had any trouble while there." [8] By June, James was back in Kansas City.

In July of 1872, Sidney Barnett, from Niagara Falls, New York, tracked down Hickok in Kansas City. Barnett desperately needed something or someone to rescue his vision of a Niagara Falls buffalo hunt, a vision that he had been pursuing since 1869. Barnett needed a celebrity frontiersman that would fill the Niagara Falls bleachers on his name alone. He found that person in James Butler Hickok. It is not known how much money Barnett paid Hickok for his services, but it must have been substantial to lure Hickok from his comfortable Kansas City home at the St. Nicholas Hotel and travel to Niagara Falls.

Sidney Barnett was the son of Thomas Barnett, and they owned the Niagara Falls Museum. Thomas Barnett started his museum in 1827. He and Sidney traveled the world seeking exotic relics that would bring in tourists to their museum, located on the Canadian side of Niagara Falls.

In spring of 1872, Sidney Barnett set in motion plans to carry out their long-considered buffalo hunt. He and others came to the Midwest to engage cowboys and Indians for the show. In June, Barnett reached Fort McPherson, Nebraska, seeking to engage Texas Jack Omohundro to lead the show. The *Omaha Weekly Herald* of June 12, 1872, ran this report from June 3:

> *A novel undertaking is on foot here, and is of gigantic proportions. Colonel Sidney Barnett, of Niagara Falls, is getting up a grand Buffalo hunt at Niagara Falls, from the 1st to the 4th of July. He is now here for the purpose of completing arrangements and superintending the starting of the enterprise, and shipping the buffaloes East.*
>
> *He has secured the services of the celebrated scout and hunter, Mr. J.B. Omohundro, better known as "Texas Jack," the hero of the Loup Fork. "Texas Jack" is a partner of "Buffalo Bill," and nothing that skill and foresight can accomplish will be spared to make this hunt a perfect success.*
>
> *Through the kindness of Major North, the commander of the Pawnee scouts, arrangements are being made for a party of Pawnee Indians- the deadly and bitter enemies of the Sioux—to go to Niagara with their fleet ponies and lodges, and full war and hunting equipment. The buffaloes will pass through Omaha the latter part of this, or early part of next month.*
>
> *We here think this is a grand affair, and believe there can be no question of success from the reputation of the parties engaged in it. The spectacle that will present itself to the scores of thousands who will be spectators at Niagara will be the most novel and thrilling ever seen east of the great plains, and it will give our eastern friends an idea of what buffalo hunting is in Nebraska.*

For Barnett and the buffalo hunt, things started going from bad to worse very quickly. Texas Jack wrote to Jacob Troth, the agent for the Pawnee Indians, asking for permission to take the Pawnee to Niagara Falls. Troth refused, telling Texas Jack on June 13 that such a trip was forbidden by the Agency. Barnett was getting anxious. He telegraphed the commissioner of Indian Affairs in Washington, asking to have agent Troth's decision overturned. With no immediate answer from the commissioner, Barnett telegraphed him again the next day, frantically: "I have incurred expenditure of five thousand dollars. This disappointment will utterly ruin me. Can refer you as to my character to Col. Parker ex Comm. to Mr. Chilton ex Consult at Clifton or any person at Niagara will give any amount of security. Please reconsider."[9] The commissioner of Indian Affairs replied bluntly: "Matter cannot be reconsidered."[10]

Though frustrated and disappointed, Barnett had too much invested to turn back now. To make things worse, after the Pawnee Indians could not come for the show, Texas Jack backed out. Barnett was then notified that most of the buffaloes had died in captivity. Barnett still decided to persevere. He went to Indian Territory, and he was able to engage some Sac and Fox Indians and Mexican cowboys, as well as a new little group of buffalo for the show. He went to Kansas City in July, having already passed the show's proposed date of the Fourth of July weekend. In Kansas City he found his replacement for Texas Jack: the famous Wild Bill Hickok. Barnett set the new dates for the buffalo hunt to be August 28 and 30, and set about getting his show business entourage to Niagara Falls. It is not known how much publicity was generated for the buffalo hunt before the show, but this advertisement appeared in the *Niagara Falls Gazette* on August 28, the very day of the first performance:

> GRAND BUFFALO HUNT
> AT NIAGARA FALLS
> *28 & 30 August, 1872*
>
> *This novel and most exciting affair will positively take place on the days mentioned and will be under the management of "Wild Bill" (Mr. William Hickok), the most celebrated Scout and Hunter of the Plains. No expense has been spared to make it the most interesting, the most exciting, and the most thrilling spectacle ever witnessed east of the Missouri River.*

The actual performance was reviewed by the Gazette on September 4, 1872:

> *The great Buffalo Hunt over the river came off last week according to the programme. The managers of the enterprise used every endeavor to make the exhibition one of interest and amusement to the spectators, and to meet the expectations of all concerned. No doubt some were disappointed in not seeing a herd of wild buffaloes instead of 3.*

#4184

Sidney Barnett's printed advertisement for the buffalo hunt at Niagara Falls. *Author's collection.*

Some 3,000 people were present the first day and a large number on Friday. "Wild Bill" was on hand with several Indians and Mexicans accustomed to the western plains, and exhibited what they knew about lassooing wild cattle and buffaloes.

The large race course gave ample room for an exciting chase and the whole field was traversed. The skill of these men in riding and lassooing is remarkable. A large number of Cayuga and Tuscarora Indians played a game of "La Crosse" which was novel to good many and quite exciting. In fact, the whole show was such as every person would like to see.

Other reviews were not as enthusiastic. *The Toronto Globe* wrote this blistering report on August 28:

THE BUFFALO HUNT
THE WHOLE THING A FARCE.

(By Telegraph from our own Correspondent)
Clifton, Aug. 28

The buffalo hunt to-day was a failure. The buffalo had been caged up for some years past, and did not appear to manifest any disposition to run. "Wild Bill," mounted on a low-sized mustang, careened about after a small-sized ox, and, finally, by the aid of some of his satellites, managed to secure a cow, which required to be goaded to desperation before it would run at all. The throwing of the lasso, or lariat, was a mere sham, inasmuch as many of the Indian chiefs had defacto to take the bull by the horns to make him run. The chase after the Texan cattle was also a farce, as the Indians, disguised in the traditional war paint, wandered about on ponies after a cow that had evidently been roaming about for the last two years in the pastures of some peaceful agriculturist in the neighborhood of the Falls. The whole affair is to be repeated on Friday next, and if no better fun is to be offered to those who patronize the entertainment, the exhibition will be but poorly attended. The proceeding was somewhat enlivened by the band of the 44th Battalion.

Another Niagara Falls area newspaper stated: "The first game struck was a Texas ox, but he was not taking a lively interest in the affair and was soon turned out to grass." The buffalo failed to create the expected "thrilling spectacle" and she "loafed around and then laid down."[11]

Yet probably the real thrill for most was the chance to see Wild Bill Hickok in person. A writer years later made that point: "The Buffalo hunt and rodeo may not have been a happy event in the lives of the Barnett family but it gave local lads his first glimpse of a real wild West show and a chance to see that hero of the old West, Wild Bill Hickock. Clifton and Drummondville [towns around Niagara Falls] had witnessed something that was to be the talk of the town for many days to come, the like of which is still yet to be seen by today's generation."[12]

The show was indeed a financial disaster for the Barnetts. Even before he had hired Hickok, Barnett stated that he had already expended five thousand dollars on the project. The heavy expenses of transporting animals and men from the West to Niagara Falls, as well as Hickok's unknown fee and numerous other expenses such as building the fence for the eighty-acre field, all far exceeded what was brought in in the two days of the show. Even at 2,000 or 3,000 people attending per show (the given estimates), at fifty cents a person entry fee, that was only $1,500 income per show, at the most. Barnett blamed the two delays that ended up putting the show at the end of the tourist season in late August and greatly reduced the number of people who attended. It was apparently too much of a financial hit for the Barnetts to absorb, and five years later they were forced to sell the museum.[13] The first week of September, Hickok boarded the westbound train in New York City and made his way home to Kansas City and the St. Nicholas Hotel.

In *Heroes of the Plains,* Buel told of an incident later that September between Hickok and a young trouble-maker, told with such specificity as to date and place that it must have originally been a report of his in the Kansas City *Journal,* or at the very least Buel was an eye-witness to the event. Buel wrote:

> The peaceable tenor of Bill's way was disturbed on but one occasion while he remained in the Bluff City, and this circumstance developed into a ludicrous rather than a sanguinary scene. Joe Siegmund, now proprietor of a railroad eating-house in Malvern, Arkansas, was at that time owner and keeper of the St. Nicholas Hotel, on the west side of the public square. Attached to the hotel was a bar and billiard room, which gathered an excellent patronage from the gambling gentry, and was nearly always full of excited young bloods taking their initiatory

lessons in broils and drinking. On the occasion referred to, September 17, 1872, Bill walked into the saloon with an acquaintance and took a seat near the billiard tables, to watch a game then in progress. He had been in the saloon only a few minutes when four "larks," two-thirds full of Western cussedness, and the other third full of whiskey, straggled around the room and stopped in front of Bill. One of the quartette, desirous of establishing a reputation for belligerency, having heard much about Wild Bill, and knowing him by sight, in a most insulting manner halloed out to his companions: "Here, boys, is the great wild man of the prairies; the mighty untamable giaftycutus that eats three men every night before retiring and rises so hungry that he sometimes chews up a whole town for breakfast. Look out, I tell you, its just about his meal time now."

This harangue very naturally excited Bill's anger, but with apparent indifference to the insult, he only replied: "See here, young man, I'll lift you with the toe of my boot if you don't get away from here in five seconds."

The young fellow was spoiling for a row, and showing the butt of his pistol he abused Bill in a manner absolutely unbearable, calling him every vile name that a wicked native was capable of uttering. Persuading efforts only serving to increase the belicose fellow's propensities, Bill at length got up, and catching hold of his shoulder, administered a stunning blow on the young man's head which brought him to a realizing sense of his assailant's true nature. Then holding him by one ear, Bill boxed the impudent fellow's face until howls for mercy preserved him from a more severe beating. The lesson thus imparted was productive of excellent results, for the abashed "larker," with tears in his eyes, slunk away, followed by his amazed companions.

After the crowd had departed Bill expressed many regrets for having to use the young man so roughly, but every one present pronounced the whipping a most deserving act. As it would probably serve to make the fellow more respectful and considerate in his future conduct.[14]

On September 28, 1872, the Topeka *Kansas Daily Commonwealth* reported on an incident that took place at the Kansas City fairgrounds at Fourteenth and Broadway. With the sheer force of his personality and charisma he backed down fifty gun-pointing Texans who took offense when Hickok stopped the band from playing their anthem of past glory, *Dixie*.

TELEGRAPHIC
DOMESTIC
*The Kansas City Fair...Wild Bill and the Texans...Pluck Superior
to Pistols Special Dispatch to the Commonwealth*

*There were 30,000 people on the fair grounds yesterday, and
to-day the crowd was not lessened. Wild Bill made a big point at the
fairgrounds. A number of Texans prevailed upon the band to play
Dixie, and then the Texans made demonstrations with the flourishing
of pistols. Wild Bill stepped forward and stopped the music, and more
than fifty pistols were aimed at William's head, but he came away
unscathed.*

In *Heroes of the Plains*, Buel provides an undated example of
Hickok's outstanding marksmanship in Kansas City, or anywhere, as
provided to him by Dr. Joshua Thorne. Buel follows that with several
other examples of Hickok's prowess with a pistol, some to be believed,
some not to be believed without corroboration:

*On one occasion, during his residence in Kansas City, he gave
Dr. Thorne examples of his wonderful shooting. It was a sultry Sabbath
afternoon, when the two were sitting out in the side yard connected
with the Doctor's residence engaged in desultory conversation. A flock
of chickens were strolling about the place, among the number being a
large rooster whose propensity was for chasing every other gallinaceous
male off the place. Dr. Thorne having informed Bill of the troublesome
qualities of the fowl, expressed a wish that, as it was too old to eat, some
one would kill it out of compassion for the other male chanticleers.
Thereupon Bill remarked:*
*"I'll bet you five dollars, Doctor, that I can cut the rooster's
throat with my derringer, at thirty paces, without breaking his neck or
touching the head or body."*
"You can't do it," responded the Doctor, "and I'll take the bet."
*The chicken was chased to the required distance, and while it
was still walking Bill raised his pistol and fired, without even bringing
the weapon to his eye. The rooster ran a short distance and then dropped
and fluttered about until it died. Upon examination it was found that
the chicken's throat and windpipe had been cut with the same cleverness
as if a knife had been used, while its neck was evidently not touched.*

This shot, surely as perfect as could be made, so astonished the Doctor that he claimed it was an accident. Bill then, to convince him that it was not, fired several times from the two cartridge derringers he carried, first at small objects and then at sparrows in the trees; each shot went directly to the mark, not a single miss being made. The Doctor was satisfied.

Among the great number of fancy shots Bill was accustomed to make in amusing his friends, was one driving the cork through the neck of a bottle and knocking the bottom out without breaking the neck. This shot was also performed at a distance of thirty paces.

For a lucrative pastime, at which he won no inconsiderable amount of money, Bill would get up a shooting match, and then take bets off from one to ten dollars that he could shoot a hole through a silver dime at a distance of fifty paces. This seemed so utterly impossible that there was but little difficulty in getting a number of such bets, until he demonstrated his ability to perform the act nine times out of ten. Of course, at such a distance, it is almost impossible to see so small an object as a silver dime, but this difficulty was readily overcome by placing the money in such a position as to that the sun's rays would be gathered on its surface, thus presenting a brilliant spot for a target.

In rifle shooting Bill was also an adept, but at short spaces he was much dextrous with the pistol. In using the former weapon he took deliberate aim, while with the latter he fired at seeming random, the bullet, apparently, going straight to the mark of its own volition.[15]

After nine months in Kansas City, drinking and gambling at the Marble Hall Saloon and Old Faro Bank Number Three, performing shooting demonstrations for friends and tourists, and hanging out with Buel and other associates, James' restless nature began to assert itself, and the Wanderer wandered again, this time back to Springfield, Missouri; the very place his national legend began.

15

1873

SPRINGFIELD...REDUX

the NEWS *of* MY DEATH *has* BEEN GREATLY EXAGGERATED

A SPRING FLING *or* SUMMER ROMANCE?

SCOUTS *of the* PLAINS—ACTS ONE *and* TWO

In October of 1872, Hickok made his way to Springfield, Missouri and took out boarding at the St. James Hotel, located on the east side of South Street between the Square and Walnut; in other words, the same hotel that formerly was the Lyon House Hotel back in 1865, the same hotel that was Hickok's home then, and the same hotel from which he had walked north to the square on a warm July evening to meet his destiny with Dave Tutt. Now the hotel had a different name, and a different live-in proprietor as well, J. C. Ackley. But structurally it was the same building. The comfort of familiar places.[1]

Springfield had changed substantially in the seven years since James was there in 1865. In 1865 the city was still wracked by the war that had just ended. By 1872, those wounds created structurally, physically, and emotionally by having two major battles fought near and in the midst of the city, and the years of lawless, post-war retribution that followed, were finally healed. Yet Springfield in many ways was still a frontier town.

The town square remained the center of city business. The Scholtens had moved from their photography business in the southwest corner of the square; it was here, or at the Lyon House Hotel, that Charles Scholten had shot the famous photograph of Hickok that was the basis for the cover of the notorious issue of *Harper's New Monthly Magazine* in February, 1867. Now in 1873, the Scholtens were in the entertainment business; Charles and E.T. Scholten ran a saloon featuring bowling, billiards, and cards in the South Street alley. Their advertisement promised "One of the most private saloons in the city... The bar is supplied with the best of Liquors, not surpassed by any in the city. Remember a GRAND LUNCH every Saturday."[2]

In the early part of 1873, a flurry of reports started appearing across midwestern newspapers concerning the demise of J. B. Hickok. It is unknown what caused this outburst of misinformation. Perhaps Hickok had told very few people that he was leaving Kansas City and going to Springfield; editors sensed the absence of any reports on Hickok, said reports always being newsworthy. So glaring by their omission, editors speculated that Hickok was no more.

It started in Abilene. On February 20, 1873, the *Dickinson County Chronicle* reported:

> WILD BILL—*It is stated that Wild Bill was murdered in Galveston, Texas, about two weeks ago, by some of Phil Cole's friends, who it will be remembered by our citizens, Bill shot in a fracas, while he was Marshal of Abilene. Cole's friends vowed vengeance and finally accomplished it. So they go.*

From there more rumors sprung up. On March 1, the *Kansas Daily Commonwealth* reprinted this article from the *Kansas City News*:

> WILD BILL
> *Lionizing in New York*
> *Visiting Friends in Springfield, Mo.*
> *Killing Indians in the West*
> *Killed in Galveston*
> *And Riddled With Bullets at Fort Dodge*
> *From the* Kansas City News.

A few days ago we published a short item stating, on the authority of an Abilene paper, that Wild Bill, or William Hickox, who gained so much notoriety as scout during the war, was a famous frontiersman afterwards, and subsequently Marshal of Abilene, and who made this city his headquarters this past year and a half, until within the past few months, had been killed recently in Galveston, Texas by a brother of the man Cole, who was shot by him while acting as Marshal of Abilene. The report started many others in regard to the whereabouts of Hickox.

Mr. Dan Pixley [see note below] *a few days ago, saw a letter of recent date, stating that he was visiting relatives or friends near Springfield, Mo., others produce letters and papers to prove that within three weeks he has been in New York airing his long hair and exciting the wonder of the timid by perambulating the streets of that city; others again declare upon the authority of Omaha papers that he is far out on the Union Pacific railroad, where, the other morning, in a fit of pleasantry, and because they objected to drinking cold coffee with him, insisting that it should be hot, he shot and killed three Indians—these same parties stating, also, that they read a letter from him received only a few days ago, by McDaniels* [J.H. McDonald], *his former deputy at Abilene, and which was dated at some point on the Union Pacific.*

Last evening, however, a man arrived from Fort Dodge with an entirely different report. He says Wild Bill is dead, that he was murdered in a saloon in Fort Dodge last Saturday night week, and that he, the informant, was present when the affair occurred. He says Bill had been there for some time, but was very careful of his person, and guarded himself as well as possible, from danger, knowing he had enemies. Finally, two men whom he had thought were friends, proved treacherous, and murdered him in the following manner.

The three were going about the small town on the night of the murder, and the assassins being very friendly, and finally they entered a saloon where at a signal the lights were all extinguished. Simultaneous with the going out of the lights, firing commenced, with the first report, the tall form of the man who had proven such a terror on the plains fell at the feet of his enemies, vanquished by death, a bullet having pierced his brain, entering his skull in the center of his forehead. The firing was kept up in the dark by the assassins, one shot entering Bill's heel another his shoulder, and four others perforating his body in different places. Then all ran out, and when the lights were again turned on all that was left of Wild Bill was a dead and bleeding body, fulfilling the prophecy in connection with him and all his class that he would "die with his boots on." It is almost certain that the two false friends at least were concerned in the murder, although others may have joined in the firing. It was dark; no one could see another do the deed, and in that country they consider that they have no evidence sufficient to warrant the arrest of any one for the crime.

The informant says he is positive the man killed was Wild Bill, ex-Marshal of Abilene, as he knew him well at that place. Notwithstanding this last report, many of the friends of Bill in this city refuse to believe that he is dead, or that he was in the section where his murder is reported to have been committed.

The above named Daniel Pixley was a good friend of Hickok in Kansas City in the early 1870s. Pixley was a contractor, and in 1873 he lived at 1217 Cherry Street, the southernmost "suburbs" of Kansas City at that time.[3] Of the almost forty photographic images known today of James Butler Hickok, two of them come from descendants in the Pixley family. Both photographs are the original; there are no known copies, as there are with many of the other Hickok images. Several weeks later the *Kansas Daily Commonwealth* on March 14 reprinted an article from the *Kansas City Journal of Commerce* (probably written by James W. Buel), refuting the lengthy report of the *Kansas City News* report above:

"WILD BILL"
The Fiery, Untamed Individual Still Survives

From the Kansas City Journal.

If anybody in the city has shed tears or rejoiced because of the late announcements of the death of Mr. William Hickox, better known as Wild Bill, these presents will inform them that they have had their trouble for nothing. William isn't dead; the public placed some reliance in the report of his demise, when the scene thereof was located in Galveston; it was the first report; but when it came to killing him in Ft. Dodge also. The thing began to look fishy; nobody believed he had been killed twice. Now, here comes a communication from Springfield, to say that he has not been killed at all. Those papers that have been wringing their hearts for a suitable obituary of Wild William, had better adopt the plan of a certain Kansas paper in reference to another individual whom it had killed and buried several times, and wait with their obituaries until he notifies them of its necessity.

Springfield, Mo., March 6, 1873
Journal of Commerce:

The paraded accounts of Wild Bill, or Wm. Hickox's death, are simply farces. I have seen the gentleman "in flesh and blood" in this city to-day, and from his appearance should judge that he was not accustomed to "laying in his gore" in saloons at Fort Dodge.

His friends in Kansas City may be pleased to hear an authentic report concerning him.

Yours, C.

On March 15, the *St. Louis Daily Missouri Democrat,* by way of a retraction, reprinted and disavowed an article it had run on March 13 proclaiming J. B. Hickok dead. Following the reprinted article was a letter from J. B. Hickok himself, proclaiming to that paper and any other interested party that he was very much alive:

NOT "CORRALLED" YET

In last Wednesday's Democrat the following item of news appeared, and though the source of our information was supposed to be reliable, the following letter received yesterday, proves that it is not:
"It begins to look as if "Wild Bill" was really dead. The latest report is that the Texan who corralled the untamed William did so because he lost a brother to Bill's quickness on the trigger. When the Texan shot Wild Bill, he asked the crowd in the bar-room if any gentleman had any desire to 'mix in;' if so, he would wait until he was 'heeled', and take great pleasure in killing him. No gentlemen expressing a desire to be killed, the Texan got on his horse, and remarking that he had business in Texas, slowly started for the Lone Star State."
Springfield, Mo., March 13, '73
TO THE EDITOR OF THE DEMOCRAT:

Wishing to correct an error in your paper of the 12th, I will state that no Texan has, nor ever will *"corral William."* I wish you to correct your statement, on account of my people. Yours as ever.

J.B. Hickok

P.S. I have bought your paper in preference to all others, since 1857. J.B. Hickok or "Wild Bill"

We take much pleasure in laying Mr. Hickok's statement before the readers of the Democrat, most of whom will be glad to learn from his own pen that he is still "on deck." But, in case you should go off suddenly, William, by writing us the particulars we will give you just as fine an obituary notice as we can get up, though we trust that sad pleasure may be deferred for many years.

"Wild Bill", or any other man killed by mistake in our columns, will be promptly resuscitated upon application by mail. It is not necessary for the deceased to call in person. He will receive just as much—in fact, more—attention by simply writing.

On the same day this editorial also appeared, possibly in the St. Louis Republican:

The Dead Returned To Life
Autograph Letter From Wild Bill
The Noted Indian Scout

A few weeks ago we published an account of the shooting of Wild Bill by some Texans who decoyed him into a saloon under pretense and shot him from behind. We have seen no denial of the statement and never doubted its correctness until the reciept of the following letter minus the faintest smell of brimstone and bearing the well known imprint of Uncle Sam. We don't like to take anything back nor insist that a man is a ghost who handles shooting irons so familiarly and carelessly, but circumstances over which we have no control have modified our opinions and Wild Bill, (William we meant to have said) is undoubtedly "korrect."

Here following is J. B. Hickok's last public comments on the matter, apparently appearing also in the St. Louis Republican that March:

Springfield, Mo. March 26th, 1873

I wish to call your attention to an article published in your paper on the 19th in regard to my having been killed by Texans. You say when I was murdered it was fufilling a prophecy that all men of my kind should die with their boots on. Now I would like to know the man that prophecies how men shall die, or classes of men, so that the public may know who is right and who is wrong. I never have insulted man or woman in my life but if you knew what a wholesome regard I have for damn liars and rascals they would be liable to keep out of my way.

J. B. Hickok, or Wild Bill
from LaSalle County, Ill.

N.B. Ned Buntline of the New York Weekly has been trying to murder me with his pen for years; having failed he is now, so I am told, trying to have it done by some Texans, but he has signally failed so far.

J.B.H.

On May 21, 1873, the New York *Herald* reported that the Atlantic and Pacific Railroad in May had brought a trainload of New York businessmen west to Springfield, Missouri. A reception was held there with state and civic dignitaries and prominent citizens, James Butler Hickok among them. The *Herald* reporter wrote that Hickok was "a splendid specimen of a man. He is tall, sinewy, lithe, graceful in his every movement; has a keen gray eye and steady hand...Bill is a true son of the West, a fearless fellow and one who is ever ready to help a friend with the same characteristic energy as he would 'get square' on an enemy."

James may have had a spring fling or a summer romance in Springfield in 1873. Or did he have a secret admirer with a poetic touch? Could he be the poet himself?

Do I love thee go ask
The flowers if they
Love sweet refreshing
Showers.
Sadia

#4167

Here is the informal 1873 photograph that accompanied the slip of paper upon which "Sadia " wrote poetic lines of love for J. B. Hickok. *Author's collection.*

In 1985 a San Antonio art dealer came into knowledge of a small tintype photograph and a small slip of paper with writing on it that was inside the leather case that held the image. The tintype was speculated to be of J. B. Hickok, as was the writing, several short lines of poetry as written above and more. The art dealer, of course, contacted the expert on Hickok, Joseph Rosa, and asked him to verify the image and the writing. Rosa identified the image as Hickok without much hesitation, and upon first review thought the writing might be Hickok's as well, although later he was doubtful.

The tintype image of Hickok is surely one of the most informal of the known Hickok images. The tintype is small; 3½" high and 2 ¹/₈" wide. In it he wears the checkered pants he seemed to favor, as the checkered style shows in several of his known images. He also wears a matching checkered vest, over a collarless, long-sleeved dark-colored shirt. It appears to have been taken in a studio with a pictorial backdrop behind him; though it is difficult to make anything out on the backdrop because of damage to the tintype, there is a perceptible image of a small house with a chimney just off of Hickok's right hip. On the reverse of the tintype are scratched-in the number 42 in the upper left corner and 3480 in the lower left corner. Hickok's initials, J. B. H., are written on the inside of the case. Something else is written on the inside of the case as well, but it is too indistinct to make it out.

The most interesting part of the grouping, outside of the image of Hickok, is the slip of paper that came with it. On it is written several lines of poetry, as shown above. Below the poetry are five hand-drawn flowers, all the same. Under the flowers is the full name, James Butler Hickok, written in cursive, above a dashed line. On the next line is written Springfield; below that is the abbreviation for Missouri, Mo., over a dashed line.

There is another interesting attribute to this image. There is a tintype of Hickok that was known even before this image showed up in 1985. When the two are compared together they appeared to have been made at the same time and in the same Springfield studio. In this other image Hickok has removed the checkered vest and is wearing the long-sleeved, collarless dark shirt and the checkered pants. There are traces of similarity in the two backdrops. And this image reflects the same sort of informality that the other one does.

Rosa studied the few lines of poetry. He consulted an associate, Robin May, about whether it might have its roots in something written

#4168

This is the other informal 1873 photograph taken at the same time and place in Springfield as Image 4167. Hickok has donned a hat and removed his vest for this shot. *Author's collection.*

by William Shakespeare. May told him it was not tied to Shakespeare, but something about it reminded him of something written by John Godfrey Saxe. Later in 1985, Rosa visited the Kansas Historical Society at Topeka, and there discovered that Saxe had written a poem titled "Do I Love Thee." It went like this:

Do I love thee? Ask the flower
If she loves the vernal shower,
Or the kisses of the sun,
Or the dew when day is done.
As she answers, Yes or No,
Darling! Take my answer so.

Rosa came to the Kansas Historical Society with the notion that Hickok wrote the lines of poetry. Now he knew the lines were not original; they were crafted off of the John Godfrey Saxe poem. Rosa told the ladies at the Society of his belief that Hickok wrote the lines, even if the words were not his. The ladies, Rosa said, shook their heads and told him: "That was written by a woman, for it is obviously a feminine hand and the flowery drawings are a definate feminine touch."[4] Rosa accepted their analysis, which sent him off on another search; who was Sadia or Sadie?

Rosa searched the 1870 federal census for Springfield, and could find no matches for Sadie or Sadia. The closest he found in the 1870 census was a Salina Stubbs, twenty-one years old, who was shown as an employee at the hotel of a Mr. James Vaughn. The hotel was located near the St. James Hotel, where Hickok was staying in 1873.

From these tenuous ties Rosa concluded that this Salina Stubbs was the closest thing he had to a suspect. Yet he was unsatisfied with this conclusion, and stated himself, "...I suspect that the answer to the riddle of Sadia may yet lie in Texas."[5] A logical conclusion, since the image and poem first surfaced in Texas.

Joseph Rosa wrote all this up in an excellent article for *True West* magazine in the September 2001 issue, entitled, "A Pistoleer Poet?" Rosa was delighted to find proof that Hickok was living in Springfield in 1873, listed in the 1873 city directory as J. B. Hickoh, boarding at the St. James Hotel. Yet, inexplicably, he continued to seek "Sadia" and the derivatives of that name in the 1870 census, and apparently did not conduct that same search in the 1873 city directory. Had he done so he would have seen that there were two single woman listed in 1873 Springfield named Sallie, and thirteen named Sarah. He would have also found that Salina Stubbs was not listed in the 1873 city directory, apparently no longer living in Springfield. Interestingly, one of the two Sallie's is listed as a widow, and twelve of the thirteen Sarah's are listed as a widow. A further review of the other single women listed in the 1873 city directory reflects that a vast majority are shown as widows, far more than statistically would normally appear in such a document, even in post-war Springfield. Did Springfield actually have a disproportionately large number of widows living there in 1873, or was there some custom to report all single women as widows regardless of whether they simply had never been married, or were divorced, or were actually widowed by the death of their spouse?[6]

There were three photographers in Springfield in 1873.[7] Of the three, W. H. Morehiser is the most likely candidate, because of proximity to the St. James Hotel. Morehiser's studio was located in 1873 on the east side of South Street between the Square and Walnut Street. That is the same location description of the St. James Hotel in the 1873 city directory; Morehiser was either adjacent to the St. James Hotel or very near it on the same side of the street. Because the Hickok photograph is very informal, and certainly not posed, Hickok may well have acted impulsively when he had the tintype made, supporting the theory he made it for a certain woman; the unknown Sadia.

On April 24, 1986, the tintype, leather case, and poem came on the auction block at Swann Galleries in New York City and sold for an undisclosed sum. Twenty-eight years later, in 2014, the same grouping came up for sale at Heritage Auctions in Dallas, the consignor believed to be the original purchaser at Swann in 1986. For whatever reason, it did not sell. On July 10, 2016, the three items came up for auction at Cowan's Auctions, and went for $9K, including the buyer's premium.[8]

It was none other than Ned Buntline who persuaded Buffalo Bill Cody to take to the stage as an actor. Ned Buntline was born Edward Zane Carroll Judson in 1821. His father was a lawyer, and young Judson did not want to be an attorney. They argued about it, and at thirteen he ran away from home and became a sailor. At seventeen, Judson received some national attention; at great risk to himself and exhibiting much bravery, he saved a group of men from drowning because the Fulton Street ferry had capsized their small boat in the East River. President Van Buren heard of this brave act, and appointed Judson as an acting midshipman in 1838. This was followed by a career at sea. In fact, the pseudonym he chose for his last name, Buntline, comes from the word for the rope at the bottom of a square sail: the "buntline." He always seemed to attract some sort of trouble, and as an alcoholic made a living from time to time delivering temperance speeches about the evils of liquor. As a writer, he was beyond prolific; it is estimated that he wrote in his life more than two hundred novels.[9] In 1869, Buntline decided to go west to find material for his dime-novel writing. It is believed that he was looking for Wild Bill Hickok specifically. Hiram Robbins, who was the manager of Buffalo Bill's combination show that included Hickok, recalled:

> *He would have been Buntline's hero, but for his disregard, I may say, dislike of notoriety. When Buntline came out in search of a real life hero, he saw Wild Bill in a saloon one night. Bill was dressed in regular scout fashion, with pistol belt and buckskin leggins. When he entered a saloon where Buntline had, according to his habit, stationed himself, he immediately awakened enthusiasm in the breast of the romancer. "There's my man," he exclaimed, and rushing forward he approached Bill; and exclaimed: "I want you." Now in that country, it was not altogether polite for a man to rush up and say "I want you." There was something about it at that time which the rough and tumble man from the states did not fancy.*
>
> *"What do you mean," exclaimed Bill, while his hand suggestively sought his pistol.*
>
> *"I mean that I want you; that you are my man."*
>
> *"Well, if you can take me, all right." Bill replied, drawing his pistol. Buntline drew back, and realizing his rudeness, said: "I am representing Street and Smith, of the New York Weekly, and am in search of a real life Indian fighting hero. Seeing you, while my thoughts were on the subject, I recognized you as my ideal of such a character."*
>
> *"That's all right," Bill replied, "That is a pretty good talk, but let me tell you, my friend, I'll just give you twenty-four hours to leave this community. I don't care what your business is, but I don't like your looks no how."*
>
> *Buntline, after inquiring around, learned that Bill was a man of his word, and left. Afterwards, meeting Buffalo Bill in Texas Jack's saloon, Buntline was presented to him. Buffalo Bill was a ward of Wild Bill, for when Cody was a boy, Wild Bill, concieving a fancy for him, took him under his wing of protection. Buntline agreed that if Texas Jack would furnish the whiskey, a necessary incentive to Cody's*

free narrative of Wild Bill's exploits, he would make both of them heroes. Jack, who had read Buntline's stories, readily agreed, and under a pretence of playing billiards, Buntline received from Cody many of Wild Bill's exploits, of which he made hurried notes, substituting Buffalo Bill for Wild Bill. True to his promise, Buntline made heroes of both Buffalo Bill and Texas Jack.[10]

If this actually happened, and it took place in 1869, then it probably occurred in Hays City, where J. B. Hickok was the acting sheriff at that time.

Aside from Robbin's invented dialogue between Buntline and Hickok (Robbins was not there to know what was said), there is much truth in what he says above about Cody and Hickok. Young Will Cody, having lost his father Isaac when he was just eleven years old, idolized Hickok in his youth. J. B. Hickok, ten years older than Will, had already at the age of twenty-one had a life that would enchant any young boy on the American frontier: stagecoach guard, lawman of Monticello, scout and spy in the Border War era. When Cody reached adulthood, it is no wonder he adopted the tenor and demeanor of his mentor Hickok, and as he undertook his own career on the Kansas frontier, he carefully guided it to mirror the life and exploits of his hero. When Cody ultimately went into show business as Buffalo Bill, the persona of Cody was so like Hickok that then, as well as now, 150 years later, some people think that Buffalo Bill and Wild Bill are two different names for the same person, or that they can be flexibly intermixed, such as Wild Bill Cody or Buffalo Bill Hickok.

The idea that Hickok was upset with Cody for appropriating his exploits as his own has some merit. One press report in 1876 stated bluntly: "Wild Bill accuses Buffalo Bill of having given Ned Buntline incidents of his (Wild Bill's) life, and claiming them as his (Buffalo Bill's) own adventure."[11]

Scouts of the Plains—Act One

Buntline met Cody at Fort McPherson in Nebraska in the summer of 1869, and found him to be a viable substitute for the apparently unapproachable J. B. Hickok. Buntline went to work on the idea of getting Cody on the stage to play himself. He began a letter-writing campaign, peppering Cody with letters encouraging just that. Soon Cody was brought to New York City by persons he had been a hunting guide for out west. While in New York City, Buntline got Cody to go and see a play by actor and playwright Frederick Maeder that had dramatized one of Buntline's dime-novels: *Buffalo Bill: King of the Border Men.* As Buntline had hoped, Cody was "curious to see how I would look when represented by someone else." [12] The play, like Buntline's dime-novel, actually was a reworking of J. B. Hickok's exploits in the Civil War, yet as carried out by the actor playing Cody. At the play the audience caught sight of Cody and wanted him to go up on stage. Many years later Cody recalled the moment: "I felt very much embarrassed—never more so in my life—and I knew not what to say. I made a desperate effort, and a few words escaped me, but what they were I could not tell, nor could any one else in the house."[13] The theater manager saw the audience reaction to seeing the real live Buffalo Bill, and he offered him on the spot $500 a week to play in this production. Buntline must have been pleased.

Cody went back west, and Buntline continued to press him by mail and telegraph. His fellow scout, Texas Jack, said he would go with Cody on stage if he went. Ultimately it was the money that drew him to the stage. Here was a western scout and guide, used to being paid $100 to $150 per month, being offered $500 a week, $2k a month to go on stage and just be himself.

Buntline met Buffalo Bill and Texas Jack at the Chicago train depot on December 12, 1872. They would start their theatrical career in Chicago. Buntline sat down soon after and wrote their first script in four hours. He hired three or four dozen men to act as Indians, providing them tan frocks and black flannel wigs. Buntline hired for his heroine popular Italian actress Giuseppina Morlacchi to act as the love interest as well as the obligatory Indian maiden.

The scouts and other actors undertook long rehearsal hours, until all felt they were ready. The day before the opening night of *Scouts of the Prairie, and Red Deviltry As It Is,* the *Chicago Times* wrote that the play was the "red-hot type" and it had been written by "the prince of sensation-mongers." Four days after their arrival in Chicago, Buffalo Bill and Texas Jack peeked out from behind the stage curtain to see an eager audience filling every chair in the theater. Battle-hardened veteran scouts though they were, the sight must have terrified them.[14]

The play opened with a western scene, with Buntline playing trapper "Cale Durg." (Perhaps this is the right moment to state something unique about Buntline: the numerous photographs taken of him around this time show that he was a dead ringer for Bert Lahr as the cowardly lion in *The Wizard of Oz*, right down to his slouching demeanor.) The play closes in the third act with the annihilation of all the Indians, in retaliation for the Indians killing their friend trapper, Cale Durg. The scouts must fight or die! Cody's line here is, "Give it to 'em, boys." The Indians start a prairie fire, but the scouts win in the end. Dead Indians are everywhere on the stage, yet the scouts find time for a tender, romantic moment with a woman. The final standing tableau, as the curtain comes down, is described in the press as "wild and weird in the extreme and worth the price of admission."[15]

It was reported that General Sheridan was in the audience that night. The opening night brought in $2,800, validating Buntline's confidence in the star power of the scouts. So it went for the rest of the season, a blockbuster success wherever it played. Yet Buffalo Bill and Texas Jack made no claim that they could act. One critic for the *New York Clipper* remarked in the April 12, 1873 issue that criticizing them as legitimate actors would be "unjust as well as absurd." But Cody and Texas Jack had learned much and gained substantial confidence from their theatrical first season, so much so that they believed they could manage their own show. With that, they dismissed Ned Buntline. He carried on and opened his own show two months later. Yet the presence of Cody was what drew the crowds, and Buntline's show soon folded.

Cody knew he would have to bring in somebody to replace Buntline on stage, and he now understood enough about show business that he knew it had to be a drawing power, as he and Texas Jack were. He did not look very far.

Cody recalled thinking, "Wild Bill would be quite an acquisition to the troupe, we wrote to him at Springfield, Missouri, offering him a large salary if he would play with us that winter [of 1873]. He was doing nothing at the time, and we thought he would like to take a trip through the States, as he had never been East."[16] Cody of course at that time was not aware of Hickok's buffalo hunt at Niagara Falls in August, 1872.

Scouts of the Plains—Act Two

The photograph by Rockwood could have been made during any one of four trips Hickok made to New York City. He was there in September of 1872, perhaps for a day or two, catching the train back to his home in Kansas City after the disastrous buffalo hunt at Niagara

#4180

This photograph of J. B. Hickok was taken in New York City by prominent photographer George Rockwood, who maintained a prestigious studio on Broadway over fifty years from 1859 till 1911. This is one of three shots that Rockwood took that day. *Author's collection.*

Falls. His second visit was when he went to New York City, when he first joined Cody and Texas Jack on stage for a week-long theater run, from September 1 to September 6, 1873. Another visit to the city came when the stage company returned for a three-day encore to New York City from September 11 to the 13. James may have made one final trip to New York City for a rendezvous with Agnes Lake a few days after he left Cody and Texas Jack in March, 1873.

Hickok joined Cody and Texas Jack in New York City in early September, 1873. Cody had written specific instructions to Hickok: "I am staying at the Brevoort Hotel, and you will land in New York at the 42nd Street Depot. To avoid getting lost in the big city, take a cab at the depot and you will be driven to the hotel in a few minutes. Pay the cabman two dollars. These New York cabmen are regular hold-up men, and your driver may want to charge you more, but do not pay more than two dollars under any circumstances."[17] Hickok followed the instructions, and when the cab pulled up in front of the Brevoort Hotel, he handed two dollars to the driver. The driver said his charge was five dollars, and he climbed down from his cab and prepared for a fight. Hickok punched him into the gutter, from which he was dragged and replaced in his cab by the jeering little crowd of spectators that had gathered. Hickok entered the Brevoort, apparently met in the lobby by John Burke, at the time an advance agent for Cody's Combination Show. Burke recalled that evening: "Wild Bill arrived in New York dressed in a cutaway coat, flowered vest, ruffled white shirt, pepper-and-salt trousers, string tie, high-heel boots, and a broad-brimmed hat."[18]

Hickok made his stage debut a brief one, appearing that first night in a New York City theater alongside Cody in the play *Buffalo Bill, King of the Border Men* on Thursday, September 4, 1873. Cody described that night:

> We had two or three rehearsals together before Bill made his appearance, and even then he was only required to say only a few words. The first scene in which he was cast represented a campfire around which Wild Bill, Texas Jack, and myself were sitting telling stories. In order to carry out the scene so that it would be a faithful counterfeit of the reality, we had a whiskey bottle filled with cold tea which we passed from one to the other at the conclusion of each story. When it came to Bill's turn to relate an adventure I passed him the bottle, and taking it in the way with which he was so familiar, he commenced draining

the contents. I say commenced because he stopped very suddenly and spurted the tea right out on the stage, at the same time saying in a voice loud enough for the audience to hear him: "You must think I'm the worst fool east of the Rockies that I can't tell whiskey from cold tea. This doesn't count, and I can't tell a story under the temptation unless I get real whiskey." I tried to remonstrate with him, while the audience shook down the galleries with their cheers. At first I was mortified, but it did not take long to convince me that Wild Bill had unconsciously made a big hit. I therefore sent out for some whiskey, which Bill drank, and then told his story with excellent effect.[19]

When Buntline left the group, Cody knew that he would need a new writer as well as a new actor to fill Buntline's dual roles. He had his actor in Hickok, and late in September he found his new writer, Hiram Robbins. Robbins wasted no time in creating a new play, and November of 1873 found the group performing Robbin's new production, *Scouts of the Plains*, all across Pennsylvania, packing theaters all the way, while critics alternated praising and panning this play and others before it. Remarking on the latter, one press report found no plot, only "a succession of raids by the Indians, in which the young ladies are carried off and afterwards rescued in an impossible manner by their lovers... However the very absurdity of the scenes lends an interest which would probably be lacking if they approached nearer a true representation of border life."[20]

M. B. Leavitt was at one time the manager of Cody's Combination. He recalled Hickok and *Scouts of the Plains* in 1925 for writer Frank Wilstach, some fifty years after he first saw the play:

The play that I saw Wild Bill act in was Buffalo Bill's "Scouts of the Plains," written by Ned Buntline. Wild Bill played one of the scouts and had only a few lines. But all of the action that he did was very creditable. The play was sort of Wild West affair, with all the trimmings thrown in: plenty of red fire and Indian fighting. The principals, outside of Cody, were Wild Bill and Texas Jack. Cody was the only real Thespian. The play was well written, a real thriller, and a fine success.[21]

Cody's Combination played Terre Haute, Indiana, October 9 through 11. The *Terre Haute Daily Express* reported that the three scouts

#4182

This photograph was taken during the seven months that Hickok appeared on stage with Buffalo Bill Cody's *Scouts of the Plains*. Hickok, Cody, and Texas Jack Omohundro appear in the middle. On the far left is Elijah Greene, on the far right is Eugene Overton. Greene and Overton were friends of Cody and Omohundro after they all except Hickok went on a summer hunting trip together in 1873. *Author's collection.*

were their own best promoters. When Cody, Hickok, and Texas Jack walked the streets before a show, "their long, ambrosial locks streaming in the wind,"[22] they never failed to draw attention.

The photograph #4182 shows all five men in stage costumes. Elisha Greene married Ella Remington, whose father, grandfather, and brothers ran the noted gun and rifle manufacturer E. Remington & Sons. When Cody and company played Utica, New York in February of 1873, Elijah Greene presented Cody and Texas Jack with special, gold-mounted Remington rifles. The following month, Cody and Texas Jack mentioned the Remingtons in glowing terms on stage in New York City. That summer the hunting trip was undertaken, and it included Eugene Overton, a friend of Cody and Texas Jack.

Gordon Lillie, who one day, as Pawnee Bill, would mount a Wild West spectacle to rival Buffalo Bill's, saw the *Scouts of the Plains* in Bloomington, Indiana as a teenager:

One day after school, I went on an errand in downtown Bloomington. As I passed along Main street looking west, I saw a large crowd in front of the St. Nicholas Hotel, which was then the best and most popular hotel in town. Thinking it was a fight, boylike, I hurried to the spot as fast as I could run. But the thrill I got was the greatest I ever had in my life, for there in the center of this immense crowd sat three frontiersmen, clad in big sombreros, with long hair falling to their shoulders and wearing buffalo robe coats. They were relating their experiences of the plains to each other. These men were Buffalo Bill, Wild Bill, and Texas Jack Omohundro. They appeared that night at Schroeder's Opera House in a play called "The Scouts of the Plains." [23]

Gordon Lillie attended the show that night at the opera house. He claimed that very night he decided to forego a life of working at the mill in a small Indiana town, and decided instead to go West. Dexter Fellows recalled when he was a young child seeing the scouts on the street:

I had seen Cody several years before as he, "Wild Bill" Hickok, and "Texas Jack" Omohundro led a group of Sioux Indians through the streets as a ballyhoo for the Prairie Waif, in which they were playing at our combined theater and city hall.

No finer looking men ever appeared in public life than these three. You may have your Johnny Weismullers and Clark Gables, and if they truly represent present-day ideals of masculine comeliness, I'll stick by the frontier Apollos. Buffalo Bill, Wild Bill, and Texas Jack were Lochinvars from out of the Wild West. They were not promoted as men possessing irresistable charms to women. They represented a masculine ideal. Men's chests swelled to the bursting point if there were only a hint that they faintly resembled any one of those hairy Olympians. Women, old and young, had crushes on them, and many a perfumed pillow has a photograph of one of these IT men.

Of the three, Wild Bill cared the least for his public. This great scout, gambler, and Marshal joined up with Cody much against his will, and the one time I saw him riding in parade with his two stage colleagues he impressed me as being bored to death by the music, the cheers, and the ballyhoo. [24]

The photograph #4176 on page 327 is a well known formal portrait taken in Syracuse, New York on March 6 or 7, 1874, of the three scouts together, dressed in their best suits and boots, Hickok and Cody sitting in chairs with Texas Jack standing between. Even a quick glance at the photo shows Hickok with the same "Why am I here?" expression on his face described above by Fellows. Cody and Texas Jack loved the stage, but it was misery for Hickok. As time went on in the theatrical season of 1873-74, his misery seemed to increase and be reflected in various ways that could not have pleased Cody and Texas Jack.

On the plains, J. B. Hickok was gracious and polite, taciturn and self-effacing, unless faced with belligerent opposition. On the stage, contrary to his normal demeanor, he was compelled to speak such banal lines as "Fear not, fair maid! By heavens, you are safe with Wild Bill, who is ever ready to risk his life and die, if need be, in defense of weak and defenseless womanhood."[25] Surely part of his discomfort on the stage was found in these insipid lines that were a standard of the day's melodramas.

Intermission —

Hickok was on stage with Cody and Texas Jack from September 1873 through the middle of March, 1874. Presuming that the hard winter months of November, December, January, and February would have precluded an outdoor shooting demonstration, it is very likely that the amazing shooting demonstration described below by Robert A. Kane took place sometime during the first two months of Hickok's short stage career, September or October.

Robert Kane was no wide-eyed kid. He was a big game hunter, a gun expert, and the editor of *Outers Book,* a popular early-day sportsman's magazine. Kane recalls this event took place in Milwaukee, Wisconsin, which was probably Kane's hometown, because Milwaukee is where Kane edited and published *Outers Book* years later. Yet if Hickok, Cody, and Texas Jack did play in Milwaukee during the six months that Hickok was with the troupe, the event is unrecorded. Or perhaps Kane, writing some thirty-five years later, misremembered the city where it happened. Either way, the shooting demonstration by Hickok took place, as evidenced by Kane's compelling report in *Outdoor Life* magazine in 1906:

Along in the 70's W.F. Cody (Buffalo Bill), Wm. A. Hickok (Wild Bill), and Texas Jack, as members of Buffalo Bill's "Prairie Waif"

Company, played a three-nights' engagement in Milwaukee, Wisconsin. Several of the local marksmen, including myself, called on the celebrities at their hotel, where in a little social session shooting and shooting methods were discussed. Mr. Hickok treated us with great courtesy, showed us his weapons, and offered to do a little shooting for us if it could be arranged for outside the city limits. Accordingly the early hours of the afternoon found us on our way to the outskirts of the city. Mr. Hickok's weapons were a pair of beautifully silver plated S.A. 44 Colt revolvers. Both had pearl handles and were tastefully engraved. He also had a pair of Remington revolvers of the same caliber. The more showy pair of Colts were used in his stage performance. On reaching the place suitable for our purpose, Mr. Hickok proceeded to entertain us with some of the best pistol work which it has ever been my good fortune to witness.

Standing in a railroad track, in a deep cut, his pistols cracking with the regularity and cadence of the ticking of an old house clock, he struck and dislodged the bleaching pebbles sticking in the face of the bank, at a distance of about 15 yards.

Standing about 30 feet from the shooter, one of our party tossed a quart can in the air to a height of about 30 feet. This was perforated three times before it reached the ground, twice with the right and once with the left hand.

Standing midway between the fences of a country road, which is four rods wide, Mr. Hickok's instinct of location was so accurate that he placed a bullet in each of the fence posts on opposite sides. Both shots were fired simultaneously.

Located midway between the two telegraph poles he placed a bullet in one of them then wheeled and with the same weapon planted another in the second. Telegraph poles in this country run about thirty to the mile, or 176 feet distant from each other.

Two common bricks were placed on the top board of a fence, about two feet apart and about 15 yards from the shooter. These were broken with two shots fired from the pistol in either hand, the reports so nearly together that they seemed but one.

His last feat was to me the most remarkable of all: A quart can was thrown by Mr. Hickok himself, which dropped about 10 or 12 yards distant. Quickly whipping out his weapons, he fired alternatively with right and left. Advancing a step with each shot, his bullets striking the earth just under the can, he kept it in continuous motion until his pistols were empty.[26]

Six years later, Kane recalled again Hickok's amazing shooting ability in the November, 1912 issue of *Outdoor Recreation* magazine*:*

> *On the single occasion which the writer was privleged to witness the methods of Mr. Hickok in handling his six shooters, I was deeply impressed with his almost exasperating deliberation. No matter how elusive the target, even when shooting at objects tossed in the air, he never seemed hurried. This trait was, of course, natural, and in part due to his superb physique and superior mentality, which, combined with and supplemented by his methods of practice and free, wild life in the open, developed in him that perfect coordination of hand and eye which was essential to perfect mastery of the one-hand gun.*
>
> *The writer has himself seen Mr. Hickok shoot, using a Colt single action revolver in either hand, firing simultaneously or alternately, and I am prepared to believe any story of his skill or prowess that does not conflict with the laws of gravitation or physics.*
>
> *I have seen Wild Bill fire two shots simultaneously, using both hands, at stationary targets, and alternate shots with either hand at moving objects, for a limited number of shots, and score with each shot. It was while giving an exhibition of his skill with a six-shooter that I* [first] *saw him hit a quart tomato can while in the air, with two Colt six-shooters. He did not seem to be hurried and I feel sure he could have fired another shot with his left hand.*[27]

Kane's expert observation of Hickok's "almost exasperating deliberation" reflects the same conclusion reached by even less gun-knowledgeable observers. The extra split second taken by Hickok to insure accuracy surely saved his life more than once in face-to-face shootouts.

— Intermission Over

On November 6, 1873, the troupe played in Titusville, Pennsylvania at the Parshall Opera House. Cody recalled the day:

> *One day at Titusville, Pennsylvania, while Burke, the business agent was registering our names and making arrangements for our accommodation, several of us started for the billiard room, but were met by the landlord, who stopped me and said that there was a party*

of eight roughs from the lower oil regions who were spreeing, and had boasted that they were staying in town to meet the Buffalo Bill gang and clean them out. The landlord begged of me not to allow the members of the troupe to enter the billiard room as he did not wish any fight in the house. To please the landlord, and at his suggestion, I called the boys up into the parlor and explained to them the situation. Wild Bill wanted to go at once and fight the whole mob, but I persuaded him to keep away from them during the day.

In order to entirely avoid the roughs the members of the company entered the theater through a private door from the hotel, as the two buildings joined each other. While I was standing at the door of the theater taking tickets, the landlord came rushing up and said that Wild Bill was having a fight with the roughs in the bar-room. It seemed that Bill had not been able to resist the temptation of going to see what kind of a mob it was that wanted to test the pluck of Buffalo Bill's party; and just as he stepped into the room, one of the bruisers put his hand on Bill's shoulder and said "Hello, Buffalo Bill; we have been looking for you all day."

"My name is not Buffalo Bill; you are mistaken in the name," was the reply.

"You're a liar!" said the bruiser.

Bill instantly knocked him down, and then seizing a chair, laid out four or five of the crowd on the floor. This was all done in a minute or two, and by the time I got downstairs, Bill was coming out of the bar-room whistling a lively tune.

"Well!" said he. "I have been interviewing that party that wanted to clean us out."

"I thought you promised to come into the Opera House by the private entrance?"

"I did try to follow that trail, but I got lost among the canyons, and then I ran in among the hostiles," said he. "But it's all right now; they won't bother us any more."

We heard no more of them after that.[28]

On November 13, the troupe played Buffalo, New York, and it was here on that day that they introduced to their audience for the first time the play that Hiram Robbins had been working on since early October, *Scouts of the Plains*.

Scouts of the Plains played the rest of 1873 to sold out houses. When they played Williamsport, Pennsylvania on November 26 and 27, the local press reported twelve hundred people in attendance each night, "an unparalleled success."[29] On December 15, the show came to Easton, Pennsylvania, and were greeted with a poem by the *Easton Daily Express:*

> *Hark; Hark; the dogs do bark,*
> *The Indians are in town -*
> *Buffalo Bill and Texas Jack,*
> *William the Wild, the peerless Morlac*
> *Chi, as the maiden brown.*[30]

16

1874

SCOUTS *of the* PLAINS —ACT THREE

a MEETING *with* AGNES LAKE *in* NEW YORK CITY

KANSAS CITY...AGAIN

HUNTING GUIDE *with* TEXAS JACK

CHEYENNE

Scouts of the Plains—Act Three

For Hickok and the troupe, 1874 certainly started off with a bang, literally. Cody's troupe played Philadelphia on January first to the third. The show included a rented calcium spotlight. It was also termed a limelight; when the lime was heated, it created brilliant, focused illumination. Hiram Robbins claimed that sometime during the three-day run in Philadelphia, Hickok shot out this calcium light up in the rafters during a performance. Robbins assigned Hickok's motivation for this act to be his desire to have the light focused more on him, and less on Cody and Texas Jack. That is absurd. Throughout the six months with the Cody troupe, Hickok was trying to avoid publicity, not seek it. What's more, Robbins falsely claimed several times that Hickok was recklessly

325

belligerent with his pistols. In one false recollection of Robbins', he has Hickok as a scout drawing down with his Colts on General Carr to get an order rescinded.

If the shooting of the light occurred, it was probably as described by Cody in this offhand manner:

> *When the curtain fell at the close of the first act he and I and Wild Bill were supposed to stand out near the front of the stage clasping rescued maidens to our breast in the white glare of the calcium. But Wild Bill was never out there where he belonged. He invariably hung back in the shadows at the rear or remained half-hidden behind a painted rock or tree. He was a poor hand to pose or show off and hated to have a lot of people staring at him. One night when the spot light found him leaning against a gnarled oak in the background, it made him mad, and he took a shot at the spot light machine in the central aisle of the balcony, shattered the bull's eye and broke the machine. The show had to go on to the end without the usual calcium effects. If Wild Bill was not a star on the stage, he was a sensation off it.*
>
> *Crowds followed him about everywhere. I didn't wonder at it, for aside from his picturesque Western garb he was the one of the handsomest men I ever knew.*[1]

At the end of January, *Scouts of the Plains* played Portland, Maine for two nights. On one of those nights at the hotel, Hickok was having trouble sleeping due to loud noise in the room next door; raucous laughter and clinking glasses, punctuated by an occasional shout. Getting dressed, he went next door.

He found a group of businessmen playing poker. They looked at sleepy-eyed James, and invited him to join the game. Hickok asked them to tell him a bit about the game they were playing, as he was not entirely familiar with it. He made a few "blunders" to set them up, and then proceeded to gain a few hundred dollars from the businessmen. Bidding them goodnight, he advised them: "Adios, my friends, better think twice after this before waking a man up and inviting him to play poker."[2]

By the end of January, 1874, J. B. Hickok had finally concluded that the theatrical stage was not where his future was. Acting out his frustration, he was tormenting the "Indian" members of the cast by shooting at their legs instead of over their heads in the battle scenes. Though his pistol was underloaded with just a few grains of black powder,

#4176

Cody's manager John Burke recalled that this photograph was taken at Syracuse, New York during the latter part of Hickok's tenure on stage with Cody and Texas Jack. Latter indeed. Cody and company played Syracuse on March 6th and 7th, 1874. Their very next play date was Rochester on the 10th and 11th, where Hickok parted ways with Cody and Texas Jack. Hickok's indifferent slump and subtly scowling visage in this photograph reflect the apex of his frustration and disdain for stage acting. After this photo was taken in Syracuse, just three or four days later Hickok walked out. It has been proposed that this photograph was taken by George Rockwood or Gurney and Sons, both photographers with New York City studios. That is not likely; Syracuse is over 250 miles from New York City, and neither Rockwood nor Gurney traveled in their business. The photographer is unknown. Note that Hickok's black fur hat sits on the table. *Author's collection.*

a shot could still sting. Instead of falling and dying on stage, they would dance and jump. The extras complained to Cody, and threatened not to go on stage, so Cody went to Hickok and pleaded for him to stop these antics. Hickok promised Cody he would cease.[3]

Actor Harry Irving had joined the troupe a few months earlier. In a newspaper interview many years later, he recalled an event in early February, 1874, when *Scouts of the Plains* was playing at another cold city in Maine: "Arriving on a very cold day at one of the Maine venues the troupe registered into a hotel. Wild Bill requested a fire lit in his room. In the middle of the night loud cries of 'Fire' awakened the guests. The hotel clerk and several guests ran into the street and looked up to see Bill in nightshirt with head out of window yelling 'Fire.' The clerk shouted 'where's the fire?' Bill yelled back, 'that's what I want to know, I ordered one four hours ago and it hasn't been built yet.'"[4]

Increasingly, James became frustrated with the show and his partners. He felt they were being laughed at and made to look foolish. Increasingly he talked of leaving. Robbins reminded Hickok how much money he was making in hopes that would persuade him to stay. It did not. The tension reached critical mass on March 11 in Rochester, New York. Once again, Hickok resorted to trying to singe the extras' legs. Offstage, Cody was furious over it and told Hickok so. Hickok stormed off to the dressing room, stripped off his buckskins and threw on streetwear, and exited onto the street through a back door. Cody was told after he finished the next scene by a stagehand: "That long-haired gentleman, who passed here a few minutes ago, requested me to tell you that you could go to thunder with your old show."[5]

When the show ended, Cody found Hickok at the hotel: "By this time he had recovered from his mad fit and was in good humor as ever. He had made up his mind to leave for the West the next day. I endeavored to persuade him to remain with me till spring, and then we would go together; but it was of no use. I then paid him the money due him, and Jack and myself made him a present of $1,000 besides."[6]

Robbins made up a preposterous story claiming he then tried to get Hickok an acting job with another acting troupe for $50 a week, whereupon Hickok took the job for one night, then quit, but came back later another night and beat up the actor hired to play his part. None of this is to be believed. Hickok wanted off the stage in the worst way, and yearned to be back out west. Besides this, Hickok made thousands of dollars during his time on stage with Cody and Texas Jack, and being

#4178

This photograph was taken at the same session in Syracuse, New York and by the same photographer as Image 4176 on March 6th or 7th, 1874 just days before the breakup. Hickok wore the black fur hat for this photograph, and he has added skin-tight leather gloves for this shoot. As with Image 4176 he sports a white silk tie and wears dress pants with a subtle plaid pattern. He also holds something in his hands, maybe a rolled-up magazine or a fan. This is one of Hickok's most formal portraits. The photographer is unknown. *Author's collection.*

THE WANDERER

flush with cash when he left, he would never have accepted an acting job for $50 a week.[7]

Major John Burke, Cody's business manager and press agent for thirty-five years, from the early days of *Scouts of the Plains* through and into the twentieth century, probably characterized Hickok's time on the stage with Cody and Texas Jack best, when he told early Hickok biographer Frank Wilstach:

> "The trouble with Bill as an actor was that he had a sense of humour and the public uproar over him he could not take seriously. It annoyed him. It made him tired. He couldn't endure it. The business to him seemed preposterous. He was sighing all the while for the freedom of the plains. With his good looks, striking figure, and excellent speaking voice, he would have made a fine actor; but the fact is he hated the business with a deep abomination."[8]

The day after Hickok walked off the Rochester stage, a reporter for the Rochester Democrat and Chronicle glimpsed him walking down State Street in Rochester, and knowing that the troupe had left for performances in Lockport, caught up with him and gained a remarkable interview that ran in that paper March 13, 1874:

> *WILD BILL*
> *He Leaves Troupe For The Western Frontier—The Way His Friends Treated Him*

> *Having seen the stalwart form of Wild Bill (J.B. Hickok) passing down State street yesterday afternoon, and knowing that the troupe of scouts, with which he has been appearing upon the stage for sometime past had departed for Lockport where they performed last night, we ventured to approach the hero and enquire the reason why he tarried behind his fellows. Our hand was grasped with considerable warmth in his which appeared to be an iron vice from which we were glad to be released. After devoting a few words not all complimentary, to the blustering March winds that were swirling the snow through the streets, he began to relate why he was not with the troupe, and we should have had the whole matter explained then and there, had not an impudent youngster crying "Union" or "Express" come down the street with the loud cry of, "Oh! stag his nibs wid the long hair!" Now it is*

well known that Bill wears his hair in the flowing style prevalent on the frontier; and this, together with the tall form and manly deportment of the man, attracted the attention of the newsboy, and caused him to give vent to several exclamations of no particular importance to the student of polite literature, but very well calculated to draw the attention of everyone within the sound of his voice to us.

Bill was not at all affected by this strange proceeding. He remarked that he had witnessed it in hundreds of towns, so often, in fact, that it was an old thing to him. We suggested, however, that we should move along, to which he willingly consented. The few staring open-mouthed children of the pave who had gathered were soon left behind, and as we passed into Exchange place, there was but one left, and he took to his heels because Wild Bill stopped and looked at him. We were then informed that Bill had received a call to the frontier. Recognized as one of the best scouts and Indian fighters that have appeared upon the great western frontier, his services are highly valued and eagerly sought for when there is danger of war with the Red man. Just now there is considerable commotion at Fort Laramie and some of the Indian agencies, especially Red Cloud and Spotted Tail agencies. The Sioux has been seen in his war paint and General Sheridan thinks he may begin his attempt to seek the paleface in a few weeks.

At this time and amid such scenes as these, the services of Wild Bill will be invaluable to the United States troops. It is this, together with a longing desire to return to the free, wild life he loves so well that has called our hero away. He will first proceed to New York where he has some business to transact, remain there a few days and then go direct to the frontier. Buffalo Bill, Texas Jack, and the other scouts did not like to have him leave, but when he said he must go, the noble-hearted fellows presented him with $500 apiece, and each gave him a splendid revolver, bidding him to make use of it among the "Reds." He had nothing but kind words to speak of the boys, as he familiarly termed the other scouts. He wished them all manner of good fortune and was sure they would receive it. Wild Bill is a noble fellow, a true-hearted child of nature, one of those men which one occasionally come in contact with and ever after retains a place in his memory. We shook hands with the hero, bade him good-bye, and wished him a pleasant journey to his far western home. He left at 12:15 this morning for New York.

There was no call to the frontier by General Sheridan. Probably leaving Hickok with mixed feelings, and being embarrassed to admit to a reporter that he was leaving his job for something less than a heroic reason, Hickok invented for the reporter a more palatable and seemingly likely reason; duty calls me at the request of General Sheridan. The other time, like this one, has no supporting evidence of any request for James to come to General Sheridan; in 1869 when he was home in Troy Grove convalescing from an Indian spear wound, he told his mother that he must leave for a week to meet with the general in Chicago. There is no indication that this meeting ever took place.

The trip to New York, though, mentioned above, bears consideration. There has been uncorroborated speculation that Hickok went to New York to drink and gamble. More likely is that he went to meet with Agnes Lake and her daughter, Emma. Though not mentioning Hickok, the New York *Clipper* reported on February 28 and March 7, 1874, on Agnes and Emma's trip to New York City that March. On February 28, the *Clipper* reported succinctly on Agnes' pending arrival from Cincinnati: "Mme. Agnes Lake will arrive in New York on March 1." On March 7, the *Clipper* announced some specifics: "Mme. Agnes Lake has seceded from the Great Eastern Circus, and, with her daughter, Miss Emma Lake, will be at the St. Nicholas Hotel, New York, during the present week." Nowhere in the report did the *Clipper* give a reason for Agnes' sojourn in New York. Perhaps it was just a coincidence that James and Agnes were both in New York at the same time in March, 1874. Yet this circumstantial evidence indicates they may have planned to meet in New York.

Whatever the reason for Hickok's trip to New York, soon he left there on the train heading west, this time for Kansas City. When he returned to Kansas City and the St. Nicholas Hotel, it is unknown what his future plans were. He had plenty of money from his time on the stage with *Scouts of the Plains.* Perhaps he simply wanted to enjoy springtime in Kansas City at the poker tables of Marble Hall on Main Street or around the corner at the Faro bank of Old Number Three on Sixth Street.

By July, however, J. B. Hickok was on the move again. At Kansas City on July 18, Hickok joined a "party of about twelve English lords and noblemen. The party are bound about 200 miles west on a general hunting excursion. Wild Bill was picked at this place and taken along as scout."[9] On July 21, 1874, the *Topeka Daily Commonwealth* reported on Hickok's plans, and made the first public mention of possible eye problems for James: "Wild Bill passed through North Topeka on Saturday, on his way to Cheyenne, where he is expected to join Buffalo Bill and Texas Jack, and proceed with a party of English tourists to the Yellowstone country. Wild Bill is suffering with an affection of the eyes, caused by colored fire used during his theatrical tour."

By July 22, Hickok was in Cheyenne. "Mr. William Haycock, more familiarly 'Wild Bill' is in town," announced the *Cheyenne Leader* that day. From there he moved on to Denver. He left Denver on July 27, with the group of English hunters. In Denver, the *Rocky Mountain News* of July 31, 1874, wrote: "Those English millionaire hunters, with 'Buffalo Bill' and 'Wild Bill' for guides, who came out here to out-do the sporting achievements of the Grand Duke Alexis, took to the saddle last Monday, and by this time, have fairly commenced the extermination of all the wild game in the Platte valley. Major Moore, with a company of cavalry, has gone out with the party, merely to keep the Englishmen from destroying the redskins, while exterminating the buffaloes."

Buffalo Bill was actually not yet with Hickok and the English hunters noted above, but even more glaring by its omission was any mention of Texas Jack. Preliminary newspaper reports had indicated that Texas Jack and Hickok together would be leading a party of English gentry on a hunting expedition through Colorado, Wyoming, Utah and Montana. The *Denver Daily Times* ran this report on August 8, 1874, unequivocally confirming that Texas Jack and J. B. Hickok would be leading the party of English lords together:

HUNTING IS HIGH LIFE

Mr. J. B. Omahundro, better known throughout the west as Texas Jack, gave the Times a call today, having just arrived from Boston to take charge of a hunting party to accompany the Earl of Dunraven on a three-months trip. Jack has been with the Earl before, and together they have done some pretty tall hunting. They will outfit here, go over the mountains to Salt Lake, thence to the headwaters of Yellowstone, thence south into the Big Horn mountains—a route which is a couple of thousands of miles in length, and which will take them through the roaming haunts of warlike Indians. Texas Jack's party will consist of several very prominent plainsmen, including J. B. Hickok, otherwise known as Wild Bill.

Scooped by the *Denver Daily Times* above, the next day, on August 9, the *Denver Rocky Mountain News* reported that " 'Texas Jack,' a noted plainsman, is in town. He is to guide the Earl of Dunraven and party on a hunting expedition." Dunraven later recalled the details of that hunting trip in his book *The Great Divide,* and made no mention of Hickok whatsoever. Texas Jack had led the Earl of Dunraven in 1872; this 1874 trip was their second together. Texas Jack did not mention Hickok on this trip in his later writings. Did Hickok leave Denver with the English hunters on July 27 and then keep them in camp until Texas Jack arrived? Did Hickok leave for Kansas City as soon as Texas Jack showed up? Did Hickok and Texas Jack have a falling-out in Denver, causing them to part ways? These questions remain unanswered until new evidence turns up indicating what happened and why Hickok disappeared from the records of this excursion.

There are statements recorded that show that by some time in August, 1874, Hickok had returned to Kansas City. Ed Moore, a soldier in the Indian Wars, and later a frontier newspaperman, provided written information in the 1920s to William Connelley of his pertinent recollections of Hickok. Moore stated that in 1874 while traveling with Cody and Texas Jack in *Scouts of the Plains,* one night a footlight exploded and hurt Hickok's eyes, enough to send him to a hospital. Moore claimed that Hickok was in the hospital for some time and after he left he wore thick-lensed [darkened?] glasses, until whatever was afflicting his eyes would heal.[10]

Moore further stated that while in Kansas City that August of 1874, Hickok, Moore, and several friends attended the horse races at the Kansas City fairgrounds at Fourteenth and McGee Streets. Hickok's eyes were not yet fully recovered. Moore perceived that Hickok's right eye was the most injured. At the races Hickok donned the glasses, and it was immediately noticed that the right lens was missing. There were laughs all around, and they adjourned to the bar as Hickok promised to pay for the first round.[11]

That same August the Custer expedition to the Black Hills discovered indications of gold. Though Custer's official report stressed that the expedition had not stayed at any camp long enough to make a satisfactory check on deposits of valuable minerals that indicated the possibility of gold, the public was not deterred. The public recalled the 1849 gold rush to California, and the 1859 discovery of gold in Colorado. They knew fortunes had been made by some, and some were pushed out of there by the multitudes who mined nothing. Fueling the urgency was the fact that the country was struggling financially; some banks had closed, and work was hard to find. Negative reports on gold in the Black Hills were disregarded. Optimistic reports spread quickly.

Another over-arching impediment to prospecting in the Black Hills: It was Sioux country. Not yet even a territory, let alone a state, the Dakotas were off limits to white prospectors or settlers. General Philip Sheridan, commander of the Division of the Missouri, issued orders to leaders of all frontier posts to be prepared to halt the expected gold rush. Sheridan instructed Brigadier General A. H. Terry to burn wagons and arrest all people trying to enter the Black Hills, home of the Sioux.

All this pent-up gold fever started to gather at Cheyenne. Located right on the Union Pacific railroad and outside the western demarcation of the Black Hills, set on a high vast open plain, Cheyenne was a natural jumping-off point for when and if the Black Hills might open. About midway between Denver to the south and Fort Laramie to the north, and with a population of about five thousand, Cheyenne expected that influx of hopefuls. Hickok returned to Cheyenne that September of 1874.

James came to Cheyenne that September for the same reason as all did at that time: Black Hills gold. His old friend Charley Utter came to Cheyenne that month as well. In addition to gold, Charley had come to see if the burgeoning population of Cheyenne would support a supply and express outfit.

On July 22, the *Cheyenne Leader* reported that J. B. Hickok was in town, just prior to leaving for Denver with the English lords on the hunting trip that never came about for Hickok, noted earlier in these pages: "Mr. William Haycock, more familiarly 'Wild Bill' is in town." Yet when he returned to Cheyenne in September, the press made no mention of it. When he came to Cheyenne he rented a room above Dave Miller's jewelry store. Next door to Dave Miller's jewelry store was Luke Murrin's liquor store and bar. For other entertainment, Hickok made the Gold Room his headquarters. The Gold Room was a popular Cheyenne saloon, dance hall, and sometime theater. It was located at 310 W. Sixteenth Street, next door to the popular Rollins Hotel.[12]

James' first trip to Cheyenne lasted just five days in late July, until he moved on to Denver to lead the Earl of Dunraven and his party on an excursion that, for whatever reason, he never participated in. Now he had returned to Cheyenne for an extended period that would last through the fall of 1874 and into 1875. It would be during this period in Cheyenne that a storied event would purportedly take place involving J. B. Hickok, his cane, an unscrupulous Faro dealer, and the Gold Room.

The first to report this story was Buffalo Bill Cody, in his autobiography published in 1879. Cody here sets the events in 1874, soon after James had left his employ in *Scouts of the Plains:*

> *This was the last time that Wild Bill appeared on the stage. He shortly afterwards returned to the West, and on arriving at Cheyenne, he visited Boulder's gambling room and sat down at a faro table.* [As will be explained, Cody probably got this story directly from Hickok himself, sometime before he died in 1876. Cody's memory of what Hickok told him may be slightly off but still logical; for instance, Boulder did not own the Gold Room, he was a faro dealer himself.] *No one in the room recognized him, as he had not been in Cheyenne for several years.* [Actually, James had first been in Cheyenne back in late July, never before that.] *After losing two or three bets he threw down a fifty dollar bill and lost that also. Boulder quietly raked in the money. Bill put a second fifty dollar note on another card, when Boulder informed him that the limit was twenty-five dollars. "You have just taken in a fifty dollar bill which I lost," said Bill. "Well you needn't make any more such bets, as I will not go above my limit," replied Boulder. "I'll just play that fifty dollar bill as it lays. If it loses, it's yours: if it wins, you'll pay me fifty dollars, or I will know the reason why." "I am running this game, and I want no more talk from you, sir," said Boulder.*
>
> *One word led to another, until Boulder threatened to have Bill put out of the house. Bill was carrying the butt end of a billiard cue for a cane* [much more likely that Hickok was carrying his grandfather's cane; more about this cane later], *and bending over the table, he said: "You'd rob a blind man." Then he suddenly tapped Boulder on the head with the cane, with such force as to knock him over. With another sweep of the cane he tumbled the "lookout" from his chair, and then reaching over into the money drawer, he grabbed a handful of greenbacks and stuck them in his pocket.*
>
> *At this stage of the game four or five men—who were employed as "bouncers" for the establishment to throw out the noisy persons— rushed up to capture Bill, but he knocked them down right and left with his cane, and seeing the whole crowd was now closing in on him, he jumped into a corner, and with each hand drew a revolver and faced*

the enemy. At this moment the barkeeper recognized him, and sang out in a loud voice: "Look out boys—that's Wild Bill you've run against."

That settled the matter; for when they heard the name of Wild Bill they turned and beat a hasty retreat out of the doors and windows, and in less time than it takes to tell it, Wild Bill was the only man in the room. He coolly walked over to Dyer's hotel, and retired for the night. Boulder claimed that he had taken $500, but he really only got $200. Boulder, upon learning that it was Wild Bill who had cleaned him out, said nothing about the money. The next day the two men met over a bottle of wine, and settled their differences in an amicable manner.[13]

Though James W. Buel did not include the story in his first biography of Hickok, a small pamphlet published in 1880, he did capture it in *Heroes of the Plains*, published in 1881. Buel virtually mirrored what Cody had said:

Leaving the East, Bill went directly to Kansas City, and from there to Cheyenne, a place he had not visited for several years. Here he drifted into a faro bank which was run by a gambler named Boulder. Bill had only two hundred dollars with him and he commenced the game by staking small amounts. Losing all these, he played up for an average by doubling. Staking fifty dollars he also lost that, but immediately put down a another fifty dollar bill. Boulder, who was banking, told Bill, who was a stranger to him, that the limit was twenty-five dollars and that he couldn't play above that sum.

"Why," enquired Bill, "didn't you just take fifty dollars of my money?" "Well," answered Boulder, "I won't let you play that amount any more." "You won't," replied Bill, "then I'll see why; that fifty dollar bill lays on the tray, and if my card don't turn, the money is yours, but if it does come out, then I'll have fifty dollars of your money or there'll be fun here, that's all."

From this a war of words followed, until Bill struck Boulder on the head with a heavy walking cane, which rolled him off a substantial seat. Several bouncers for the establishment rushed upon Bill, but he knocked them down in a most artistic manner, until finding the fighting too progressive he jumped into a corner and jerked out two pistols. At this juncture the bar-keeper, attending the saloon downstairs, hearing the noise, ran up and discovering the situation, cried out: "Look out, boys, that's Wild Bill!" This information acted like magic; the tempest was becalmed, and a moment later Bill was alone. On the following day Boulder, although still nursing a badly damaged head, called on Bill and producing champagne and cigars, the two settled their differences amicably.[14]

This story never really caught fire with the general public and become embedded in the popular culture like the *Legend of the O* (see Appendix One), written by Alfred H. Lewis. Lewis wrote the Gold Room into his version of what Cody and Buel had written that Lewis titled, "How Mr. Hickok Came to Cheyenne."[15] The story as told by Lewis was like Cody and Buel on steroids, culminating in Lewis's usual over-wrought and over-the-top prose and high satire. In it, Lewis exercised his penchant for satirizing people's names, substituting Bowlby for Boulder. After Lewis wrote "How Mr. Hickok Came to Cheyenne" in 1904 for the *Saturday Evening Post,* Frank Wilstach in 1926 and William Connelley in 1933 both followed the story as written originally by Cody, yet both showed the strong influence of Alfred H. Lewis' version, right down to the change from Boulder to Bowlby.

Well-known and notorious riverboat gambler George Devol, in his book *Forty Years A Gambler on the Mississippi,* published in 1887, claimed to have been dealing Faro in the Gold Room when the Hickok-Boulder impasse took place. He had obviously read Cody and/or Buel and caught all their salient points in what he wrote, but placing himself falsely at the scene in the Gold Room.

In addition to his considerable talent as a historian, Hickok biographer Joseph Rosa was a careful and meticulous researcher. Yet he overlooked Cody as the actual genesis of the story in 1879 and believed that Buel's was the first publication of it in 1881. Rosa believed that after Buel in 1881 came Lewis with the story in 1904, and Rosa believed the first publication of the story by Cody did not appear until 1911.[16] The October 15, 1911 issue of the *Chicago Inter-Ocean* featured an article by Walter Noble Burns that included some of Cody's memories of Hickok. In this version, Cody (or Walter Noble Burns) recalled that Hickok "could stand flat footed and jump sixteen feet." As far as the Gold Room event, Cody stated that it was $800 that Hickok took from the till, not the $200 stated in Cody's 1879 autobiography. After reading this 1911 article by Walter Noble Burns, Joseph Rosa believed that Cody, or Walter Noble Burns, had used Buel and Lewis as their source. Yet unknown to Rosa, what actually happened was that Cody or Burns in

1911 were simply updating the story as originally published in Cody's autobiography in 1879. Rosa also speculated that the Gold Room story was based on the passage on page 341 about Doc Howard that begins "Later that fall of 1874 Doc Howard joined the Cheyenne police." [17] That is not likely. The only ties that Doc Howard's event described below have with Cody's original 1879 story are that Howard mentions Charley Boulder and Hickok, and it takes place in the Gold Room. That's it. The event described by Howard has nothing to do with the Cody story. It is completely different.

What is most plausible is that J. B. Hickok told this story himself directly to Cody sometime before 1876. Cody used it in his 1879 autobiography, adding some of his own embellishments, as Cody was prone to do. Which leaves this final question to be resolved: Was Cody's Gold Room story true? Even at a mere glance, the story is possible. There is no physical or logical impediment that would keep this story from actually occurring. It is also plausible. It is known that Hickok brought his grandfather's cane to Cheyenne. John Hunton recovered Hickok's cane near the time of his death in 1876. (See Chapter Eighteen.) Dave Miller, the owner of the Cheyenne jewelry store over which Hickok's apartment was, told John Hunton when showed the cane that he recognized it as one which Wild Bill had owned. Boulder did not own the Gold Room, but he did run a Faro bank there. Hickok, just like anybody, did not like to be cheated or treated unfairly. But was it probable? The Gold Room story is easily one of the most believable of the Hickok legends. It is really nothing more than a story about the emotions that compel certain actions between a cheater and his victim, making it probable. The only thing the Gold Room story lacks is proof. Empirical evidence. A verifiable and legitimate witness to the event and their written report—a letter from Doc Howard addressing the specific Gold Room event; Charley Boulder's deathbed confession. Any of these, or similar, will mandate a permanent waiver from the ash bin of history for this tale.

Faro was a deceptively simple gambling game. It was one of the few games where the cheating more often then not was done by the dealer, commonly called the banker, rather than the player. Faro had been played in the United States since the late 1700s, coming to this country from France. Though in popular culture poker is portrayed as the game that reigned at the tables of riverboat gamblers and saloon gamblers of the Old West, it was Faro that actually dominated gaming tables at least through the 1870s.

On the Faro table was a green felt top with thirteen cards painted on it, ace to king. Often the painted suits were all spades, but the suit was irrelevant, only the face value was used in the game. The dealer dealt twice from a fifty-two-card deck; each deal was two cards. The object of the game was for the players to predict what cards would be turned up. Players could bet a win for the bank or the player on the turn of each card. The player placed his bet by placing poker-style chips, called checks in Faro, on any painted card on the felt. Hexagonal tokens called coppers marked the players' bets backing the banker's card. Players could also bet whether the card drawn would be odd or even, or the higher denomination of the two cards dealt. An abacus, called a casekeeper or cue box, kept track of what cards had been dealt. Many Faro banks provided paper sheets printed with the various cards, called tabs, with which players could keep also keep track of the cards dealt. From this came the common modern phrase of "keeping tabs." Though poker surpassed Faro in gambling popularity in the late 1800s, the last Faro bank in existence closed down in Nevada in 1955. Upton Lorentz recalled Hickok and Utter in Cheyenne in September:

> *The writer first saw both Wild Bill and Utter in September, 1874 at a resort known as the "Gold Room," a combination theater, dance hall, gambling place and saloon, paralleling the Union Pacific Ry. Line at Cheyenne, Wyoming. This resort was the noted meeting place for cattlemen and other early Western characters, and nightly Wild Bill stood at the east end of a long bar, opposite the the entrance from the south or railway side of the building, while the western end of the room was occupied by a raised platform for dancing. Between the bar and the platform were tables for games of various kinds, and also private gaming rooms at the side.*
>
> *Never far from him, generally in front of the bar, could be seen Colorado Charley, a slight, well -dressed man, with long fair curls to shoulder also, and perhaps but five feet six inches tall. It was said at that time that the position maintained at the bar by Hickok at the east end and Utter fronting him a short distance away, was a precaution against attack from enemies known to be looking for a chance to get the drop on Bill...*[18]

Lorentz recalled, ten years later in Socorro, New Mexico: *I mentioned to Utter of having observed Hickok at the "Gold Room" in Cheyenne some ten years before. He said he was only a friend to Hickok and never acted as a bodyguard.*[19]

In Cheyenne that September, James met an old friend from his scouting days in the Indian Wars, J. W. "Doc" Howard. When James was a scout for General Penrose in 1868, he met Howard, who was a sergeant in the 5th U. S. Cavalry. After settling in Cheyenne, Howard went to work at Luke Murrin's liquor store and bar, and later he was with the Cheyenne police force. Howard recalled a humorous anecdote with Hickok in Cheyenne that September:

> *Wild Bill came from the east to Cheyenne. He was with Buffalo Bill on the stage, but the lights affected his eyes, so he had to give it up. He made his headquarter's at Murrin's. We often talked over old times on the plains.*
>
> *He roomed next door to Murrin's, over Dave Miller's Jewelry Store. One night he was in the saloon and said, "I don't feel very good; guess I'll go up and go to bed." I didn't think much about it, but when he didn't come down in the morning at the usual time, I got uneasy, took a good drink, went up to his room, turned the knob and walked in. The curtains were down and it was dark. I stopped and looked, and there was Bill dying (so I thought). He was lying across the foot of the bed. I said "What is the matter, Bill?" He raised up and said "What is the matter?" I said, "I thought you were stretched out dead at the foot of the bed." But he informed me that he always slept that way. "You see if I have an argument with anybody and they come upon me unexpectedly, I can pull my pants and boots on all together.*[20]

On October 7, the *Cheyenne Daily News* reported, "Wild Bill is among the number that will shortly go out to the Laramie Peak country exploring for gold." Today, as well as in Hickok's time, Laramie Peak dominates the Laramie Mountains, at 10,275 feet. None of the other mountains in the range exceed 10,000 feet. Laramie Peak is a little over 100 miles north of Cheyenne.

Later that fall of 1874, Doc Howard joined the Cheyenne police. He was new on the force and recalled the following:

> *One of my first experiences came while I was passing Jim Allen's Variety Show* [aka The Gold Room]. *I heard loud talking and shifted my gun from the pocket holster into my right pocket and kept my hand on my gun. I entered the main hall. I noticed Wild Bill leaning up against the door jamb. I passed by him to see what the quarreling was about. I saw Charley Rich grab the table to turn it over. The men around the table held it down, so that he could not. He had been loser and he wanted to put an end to the game. There was quite a lot of money on the table when I entered. I said, "What's the matter? Stop that!" With that, Charley swirled around, grabbed me by my slipknot necktie and tried to choke me. Then Wild Bill jumped in and grabbed me around the arms, so that I could not use my gun. Charley Boulder, a noted gambler, stuck his gun right into my stomach. I grabbed his gun and stuck it into my left coat pocket. I said, "Bill, let loose of me," and he said, "Doc, if Boulder had got you I'd have got him." I took Boulder out and turned him over to Fallon, another cop, who was peeping in the window, afraid to come in.*[21]

Doc Howard was persuaded not to arrest Charley Rich or Boulder. Rich would later achieve notoriety as he sat at the poker table with Hickok on August 2, 1876, in Deadwood. Boulder later murdered two men and was sentenced to ten years in prison.

On December 3, 1874, the *Cheyenne Daily News* took notice of Hickok once again: "Wild Bill is still in the city. He is a noble specimen of Western manhood."

17

1875

WILD BILL'S GOLD EXPEDITION

CHEYENNE

J. B. HICKOK, VAGRANT?

ANNIE TALLENT

RETURN *to* KANSAS CITY

DR. THORNE *and*
J. B. HICKOK'S OPTHALMIA

Hickok's fellow scout and guide from the Indian Wars of the 1860s, Danny Bohen, caught up with him in Cheyenne years later: "In the winter of 1875 I had charge of a ranch 15 miles from Cheyenne. I met Hickok in Cheyenne and brought him out to camp. He hardly knew me at first, his eyes were so bad. He stayed a week with me...Bill was always afraid of someone shooting him in the back...I never knew Bill to start a quarrel. He drank, but never to excess. Every bad man that came to Texas wanted to get rid of Bill Hickok.[1]

During the fall of 1874, James undoubtedly began to make his own plans for the Black Hills, as soon as the federal government opened up the Dakotas. He envisioned a large, well-financed and supplied expedition to enter the Black Hills, and it is apparent that he believed that a large draw for getting people to join his group would be his fame as Wild Bill Hickok. On March 26, 1875, the *Cheyenne Daily News* ran this letter in support of Hickok's plan:

> *How is this?*
>
> *The following is an abstract from a letter to Mr. Wm. Hickok, familiarly and friendly known as "Wild Bill." It is from a gentleman of highest standing in Portsmouth, Ohio and reflects as greatly as it expresses.*
> *"Great excitement prevails here. People by the hundreds are getting ready to go to the Black Hills. I was recently in Chicago and St. Louis and know that there are thousands waiting at each place for the chance to go. Throughout our section of the country the general belief is that the government will succeed in obtaining an abrogation of the Sioux treaty, and that the excitement will be intense for the coming season. The excitement to the California or Pike's Peak rush will be remembered as tame affairs compared with the Black Hills rush."*
> *The author, Mr. Hiram Robbins, has indicated quite broadly in another part of his letter, that six only lead them to the Hills from the city of Cheyenne.*

The "gentleman of the highest standing," Hiram Robbins, is of course James' former manager in *Scouts of the Plains,* who obviously sent this advocacy letter at James' request. Though an obvious attempt to drive demand to Hickok's door, the letter does reflect accurately the pent-up desire for all sorts of people to pursue the mountains of gold they believed awaited them in the Black Hills.

By 1875, Cheyenne had been in existence for eight years, and it was steadily moving from a dusty little town that fronted each side of the Union Pacific railroad track with thrown-up frame structures that held saloons and gambling halls and whorehouses, to a real city with structure and laws and families and promise of a future. Gamblers and saloon-keepers and prostitutes were not part of Cheyenne's long-term ambitions, and so just as happened when the city fathers of Abilene wanted to become a viable city, Cheyenne decided to give their law enforcement officers laws and regulations to use to restrict, reduce, and eventually remove what they perceived to be undesirables. But law enforcement cast a wide net with these regulations, and it caught many in its net. One prepared regulation applied arbitrarily in Cheyenne was the one governing vagrancy.

Vagrancy was not of the homeless, sleeping on the sidewalk in a cardboard box sort of infraction as perceived today, but rather a catch-all that included regular gamblers, of which Hickok was one. The fact that he was a living legend and nationally famous didn't help James skirt the vagrancy regulation; in fact, it probably annoyed the sheriff of Cheyenne, Jeff Carr, immensely.

Doc Howard, who worked for Jeff Carr, called him a "hard boiled stiff." Howard saw Jeff Carr spot Hickok across the street one day and Carr hollered out to Hickok "Bill, I guess I'll have to run you out of town." Hickok was unflappable. He looked over at Carr and nonchalantly said, "Jeff Carr, when I go, you'll go with me." Then Hickok walked on down the street.[2]

A story that has long been around is that sometime in the spring or summer of 1875, a notice was posted in Cheyenne listing people who were considered vagrants, and Hickok's name was on it. The listing gave those included on it twenty-four hours to leave town, or risk being forcibly ejected. Hickok drew his knife and slashed the notice to shreds, stating that he would leave town when he wanted to. Whether this story is accurate or apocryphal, it is a fact that on June 17, 1875, J. B. Hickok as a gambler was charged with vagrancy, and an arrest warrant was issued the same day. Yet no arrest was carried out, and by November when the trial was set, a continuance was granted because he could not be found. The warrant was never processed.

Three weeks after the vagrancy charge, J. B. Hickok faced another challenge. On the Fourth of July, a fire started on Eddy Street, most likely in the McDaniel Theater. The fire spread quickly, and soon it reached Murrin's liquor store and bar (Doc Howard's former employer), and spread next door to David Miller's jewelry store, where Hickok had a room on the second floor. Finally the Cheyenne fire companies, with outside help from nearby Fort Russell and Camp Carlin, were able to put out the fire. Yet Hickok's apartment was destroyed. It has been reported that for a period of time in Cheyenne, 1874 and 1875, James lived at a house located at 421 West Twenty-Seventh Street. Perhaps it was to this address that James moved in the summer of 1875, after the fire that destroyed his rented room above the jewelry store.[3]

Annie Tallent came across Hickok on a Cheyenne street that summer of 1875 and wrote about him later:

One day during the summer of 1875, while walking along one of the principal streets of Cheyenne with a friend, there appeared sauntering leisurely towards us from the opposite direction a tall, straight, and rather heavily built individual in ordinary citizen's clothes, sans revolver and knives; sans buckskin leggings and spurs, and sans everything that would betoken the real character of the man, save that he wore a broad-brimmed sombrero hat, and a profusion of light brown hair hanging down over his broad shoulders. A nearer view betrayed the fact that he also wore a carefully cultivated mustache of a still lighter shade, which curled up saucily at each corner of his somewhat sinister looking mouth, while on his chin grew a small hirsute tuft of the same shade, and, barring the latter two appendages, he might easily have been taken for a Quaker minister. When within a few feet of us, he hesitated for a moment as if undecided, then, stepping to one side, suddenly stopped, at the same time doffing his sombrero and addressed me in good respectable Anglo-Saxon vernacular substantially as follows:—

"Madam, I hope you will pardon my seeming boldness, but knowing that you have recently returned from the Black Hills, I take the liberty of asking a few questions in regard to the country, as I expect to go there myself soon. My name is Hickok." I bowed low in acknowledgement of the supposed honor, but I must confess, that his next announcement somewhat startled me.

"I am called Wild Bill," he continued, "and you have, no doubt, heard of me,—although," he added, "I suppose you have heard nothing good of me."

"Yes," I candidly answered, "I have often heard of Wild Bill, and his reputation at least is not at all creditable to him. But," I hastened to add, "perhaps he is not as black as he is painted."

"Well, as to that," he replied, "I suppose I am called a red-handed murderer, which I deny. That I have killed men I admit, but never unless in absolute self-defense, or in the performance of an official duty. I never, in my life, took any mean advantage of an enemy. Yet, understand," he added, with a dangerous gleam in his eye, "I never allowed a man to get a drop on me. But perhaps I may yet die with my boots on," he said, his face softening a little. Ah, was this a premonition of the tragic fate that awaited him?

346

After making a few queries relative to the Black Hills, which were politely answered, Wild Bill made a gracious bow, that would have done credit to a Chesterfield, passed on down the street out of sight, and I neither saw nor heard more of him until one day early in August, 1876, when the excited cry of "Wild Bill is shot," was carried along the main street of Deadwood.

During our brief conversation he incidently remarked that he thought I possessed a good deal of "sand" to undertake so long and dangerous a journey into the Black Hills. Now while Wild Bill, no doubt, intended that as a great compliment—it being his ideal of "pluck,"—would you believe I did not at first quite like the imputation. You see I was not as well versed in Western phraseology then, as I have since become.

It was a rather startling circumstance to be "held up" in the main thoroughfare of a large, busy town in broad daylight, by a noted desperado, yet Wild Bill performed that daring exploit with a single wave of his swift unerring right hand. No reflection is meant on his memory when it is hinted that perhaps he was not well up in street etiquette. Be that as it may, I have been strongly impressed ever since with the thought that Wild Bill was by no means all bad. It is hard to tell what environments may have conspired to mould his life into the desperate character he is said to have been.

Before coming to Black Hills in 1876, Wild Bill was at one time sheriff somewhere in the State of Kansas—in which capacity he is reputed to have been a holy terror to law-breakers. He was also for many years the notable as a government scout, having acted in that capacity during the Civil War. The greater part of his life had been spent on the plains, among the lawless element of the Western border, where, as an officer of the law, he was brought in frequent conflict with all such desperate characters, as usually infest the frontier settlements; murderers, horse-thieves, road-agents, and other criminals, who seem to believe that the world owes them a living which they are bound to have at any cost. Wild Bill was in consequence mixed up in many a desperate encounter, in which the first to press the trigger came off victor, and he was usually the first.

Perhaps the most remarkable peculiarity in the make-up of Wild Bill, was his wonderful nerve, and marvelous swiftness as a shot—his aim being steady, and his shot like a flash of light, it is easy to believe that he never allowed a man to get the drop on him.

347

Whether he possessed any redeeming traits is a disputed question; that he had numerous ardent admirers is an admitted fact.

This bold dashing frontiersman, who met his fate in the Black Hills, upon a time met a daring and accomplished equestrienne of the circus ring, called Madame Agnes Lake, and mutually admiring each other's dashing characteristics, they finally loved and were married in Cheyenne, Wyoming, in 1874. The widow survives her murdered husband and now lives somewhere in the State of Kansas.[4]

Annie Tallent (1827-1901) in South Dakota history is a legendary figure herself. When gold was discovered in South Dakota she, her husband, and their nine-year-old son joined twenty-five other men and left New York for the gold fields of South Dakota. The government had not yet opened the area to settlement; in fact to do so, which the government finally did in 1876, the treaty with the Sioux nation would be abrogated. The Gordon Party, as Annie's group was known, moved into the area and erected a stockade fort for protection against inclement weather as well as against the Sioux Indians. Annie became the first white woman to enter the Black Hills. Four months after they arrived, in April, 1875, the government found and removed the entire party. Annie and her family moved to Cheyenne for a year, and that is the period she met Hickok on a Cheyenne street. In April, 1876, Annie and her family returned to the Black Hills. Here she helped open several schools, and in 1895 was president of the Rapid City school board. She wrote and published in 1899 her classic treatise on the area, *The Black Hills: or, The Last Hunting Ground of the Dakotahs,* in which her perceptive assessments of Hickok printed above first appeared. In 1978, Annie Tallent was inducted into the South Dakota Hall of Fame. [5]

William Francis Hooker also knew Hickok in Cheyenne, and he recalled his perceptions of the legendary gunfighter, lawman, and gambler in his book, *The Prairie Schooner:*

Wild Bill Hickok was perhaps the best-known character in Cheyenne in the 70's He was a ministerial-looking person, but was not a confidence operator. He was just a plain gambler, but he managed to escape the "halter" every time he put a notch in his gun. Bill killed no one in Cheyenne; in fact, his days there were quiet and prosy. His killings were all done at the time the K. P. was being built from the Missouri River to Denver. When he was in Cheyenne, he was on his last legs- had begun, as they say nowadays, to slow down. Nevertheless, he was feared by a great many, although among certain classes it was understood that he had lost his nerve..."Bill" was more than six feet tall, straight and thin. He carried two big revolvers in his belt and they protruded sometimes from the side of his long broadcloth coat. He also carried a bowie knife.[6]

In *Adventure Magazine* in 1920, Hooker recalled Hickok again:

If my estimate of Wild Bill Hickok is worth anything, I am willing, in the interest of history and to help straighten out the record, to give it. It is this: He was a man of nerve, and had, as city Marshal of Abilene, kept the town in fairly good order for those times; and in doing it he was obliged to scatter a bit of lead among the garroters, then the pest of every camp along the K. P.

Of course he killed a number of men, and when he blew into Cheyenne on the big stampede to the "Hills," he was just a plain gambler and, I believe, not a very successful one, and with but little money. I doubt if he owned a horse, something nearly every one had in those days (and blankets), although I have a faint recollection of seeing him emerge from Tracey's corral a-straddle a fine looking sorrel and gallop off toward Fort A. D. Russel. Tracey's corral and barn were located on the outskirts of Cheyenne on the Loraine Trail, and our camp was on Crow Creek, not far away, in plain sight of Fort Russell and Camp Carlin. For all I know Bill was headed for Custer.[7]

J. B. Hickok's movements, if any, for the last half of 1875, are hard to confirm as to time and place with total certainty. It is confirmed that by spring of 1875, he had undertaken plans to lead a gold expedition into the Black Hills. Buel indicates that James left Cheyenne and returned to Kansas City sometime in the fall of 1875: "Bill therefore returned to Kansas City. His five months stay in the Hills [Buel errs; James was in Cheyenne from September 1874 until at least July 1875, eleven months], however, convinced him of the rich deposits of gold which that section contained, and he decided to organize an expedition from the States, with the view of leading a force into the auriferous region of such strength as would provide security against molestation from the Indians."[8] Buel also indicates that later in the fall, probably in October, 1875, James visited several cities to enlist expedition participants. Those cities visited were most likely the river towns of Kansas City, Omaha, and St. Louis. Buel continues in the matter-of-fact and seemingly truthful style that characterizes everything, uniquely, that he wrote about Hickok and Kansas City. Many of Buel's statements about Hickok and Kansas City are corroborated by other people's statements:

> In furtherance of his scheme Bill visited several cities, but the season was now so far advanced that those whom he found willing to join such an expedition, prevailed upon him to wait until the following spring, 1876, when the trip could be made more advantageously.[9]
>
> Returning to Kansas City [probably in November, 1875] he remained for some time inactive owing to an attack of opthalmia superinduced no doubt from the exposure he underwent while in the Black Hills. Dr. Thorne treated him for several months with such success that his eyesight, which was for a time entirely destroyed, was partly restored, but he never again regained his proper vision.[10]

What were the facts underlying the reports of eyesight problems that had been surfacing after Hickok left *Scouts of the Plains* in March, 1874?

The first contemporary report addressing this eyesight issue, as the reader has already seen, was the public report in the *Topeka Daily Commonwealth* of July 21, 1874, just four months after Hickok's departure from *Scouts of the Plains*: "Wild Bill is suffering with an affection of the eyes, caused by the colored fire used during his theatrical tour."

The next month, August 1874, brought Ed Moore's statement about seeing James in Kansas City after a footlight had exploded and damaged Hickok's eyes while touring with Cody and Texas Jack. Moore also observes that in Kansas City, Hickok is wearing thick-lensed or darkened glasses until whatever is ailing his eyes might heal.

The following month, September, 1874, Doc Howard met Hickok in Cheyenne, where he stated, "He was with Buffalo Bill on the stage, but the lights affected his eyes, so he had to give it up."

In November or December, 1875, Hickok sought treatment for his eye affliction with Dr. Joshua Thorne in Kansas City.

In addition to being a fine historian and narrative writer, Joseph Rosa was an indefatigable researcher. Rosa applied his investigative skills seeking to find out if J. B. Hickok really had suffered an eye problem, and if so what was the affliction and what was the cause. Rosa found that writer Mari Sandoz had noted Hickok's eye problem in her book, *The Buffalo Hunters*. Sandoz wrote:

> *When he* [J. B. Hickok] *had trouble seeing the spoor of the otter and mink up in the Yellowstone country, he slipped secretly to the army surgeon at Camp Carlin near Cheyenne. The doctor had looked very grave. It was advanced glaucoma, incurable, and in a few months he would be in total darkness.*
>
> *Sworn to secrecy— "There's a hundred as would brace me on any street, if it gets out how little I can see"—the doctor promised to do what he could, but it would be little.*[11]

In 1956, Rosa wrote to the Adjutant General's office and the Armed Forces Medical Library in Washington to track down this fugitive Camp Carlin medical report noted by Sandoz. Neither facility had any records pertaining to a Camp Carlin medical report on an examination of Hickok. Other prospective sources were a dead-end as well. So he wrote directly to Mari Sandoz for more information.[12] She responded back with a rather condescending note to Englishman Rosa:

> *Here in America the progressive blindness of Wild Bill is no longer questioned by even the cursory investigator. Hickok made repeated trips to Topeka to a doctor about his eyes in the Kansas period, and the final evidence was in the medical records of Camp Carlin in the days when the material was in storage over at Virginia Avenue, Washington D.C., in 1937-38. I've never checked on what became of these documents since the material has been moved into the National Archives building.*[13]

Rosa contacted the National Archives, who explained that several people besides himself had come looking for these records at one time or another, and that the searches for the Camp Carlin material had been fruitless.

Rosa also experienced frustration with Mari Sandoz when he read other things she had written in *The Buffalo Hunters*, particularly the fictional aspects she applied to the actual murder of an Indian, Chief Whistler, and to her conclusion that Wild Bill Hickok was the murderer. Rosa's investigation into this story proved that it was not Wild Bill Hickok who killed Chief Whistler, but another notorious character,

Wild Bill Kress, sometimes referred to as Wild Bill of the Blue.[14]

All of this frustration with Mari Sandoz led Joseph Rosa to write: "It is unfortunate that for reasons best known to herself, Miss Sandoz was not averse to causing confusion by producing references to historical characters that eventually turned out to be fictional, frequently involving others in months of fruitless research."[15]

Considering different possibilities, Rosa speculated that Hickok's eye problem might have been caused by gonorrhea, caused by "brief affairs with the Cyprian sisterhood."[16] Others have suggested trachoma may have been the culprit, an infection of the eye caused by lack of cleanliness and bad hygiene. A speculative conclusion of gonorrhea is unconvincing; Hickok was a very handsome man by any standard, and a nationally famous figure for the last ten years of his life, and many women were obviously attracted to him, some famous in their own right. As far as trachoma, that also does not jive with the man we know Hickok was; fastidiously clean, dressed like a fashion plate, and from his dozens of photographs, vigorously proud of his long, clean, curly locks.

Until a contemporary medical report turns up, it must remain an open question. Yet the experts that Rosa queried, optometrists and ophthalmologists, all believed that something must have been bothering Hickok's eyes late in his life, even if there is still no definitive diagnosis to rely on.

18

1876

RETURN *to* CHEYENNE *in* FEBRUARY

JAMES BUTLER HICKOK MARRIES ALICE LAKE *in* MARCH

APRIL *and* MAY *in* ST. LOUIS *and* CHEYENNE PLANNING BLACK HILLS GOLD EXPEDITION

CHEYENNE *to* DEADWOOD— HICKOK'S LAST TRAIL

the MYTH *of* CALAMITY JANE *and* WILD BILL HICKOK

DEADWOOD

#10 SALOON, AUGUST 2, 1876

JAMES BUTLER HICKOK'S DESTINY ENDS *and* WILD BILL HICKOK'S DESTINY BEGINS ANEW

JACK MCCALL

a CONSPIRACY *at the* #10 SALOON?

the MYTH *of* ACES *and* EIGHTS

1877: DEADWOOD AFTERMATH

After being treated for his eye ailment by Dr. Thorne in Kansas City that winter, by February of 1876 James had taken the train back to Cheyenne. Soon what seemed to be a serendipitous event occurred. Journalists, and even historians, have considered this sudden crossing of each other's path by J. B. Hickok and Agnes Lake, each unaware that the other was in Cheyenne, and the marriage that resulted, a perfect event upon which to ascribe all sorts of motivations to James and Agnes.

Remember that before 1876, the relationship of James and Agnes consisted of one night together in Abilene, Kansas in July of 1871, several possible days together in New York City in March of 1874, and purported letters written to each other in the interim between 1871 and 1875. (None of the purported letters written by James or Agnes prior to their marriage have ever turned up; the existence of these letters is based on Charles Gross' statement in Abilene that "she wrote to him after leaving Abilene, I know for the letters came to my care under seal to the Cottage"[1] [the Drovers Cottage]. That they exchanged letters before they were married is corroborated by Agnes' letter of June 30, 1876, to Celinda Hickok, published later in this chapter.

Several events occurred that worked toward placing Agnes Lake in Cheyenne in February, 1876. On November 16, 1875, Agnes Lake's daughter, Emma, married Gil Robinson, scion of the wealthiest and most influential circus family in America at the time. This freed up Agnes from her self-stated responsibility for her daughter. Agnes left the circus company in January of 1876 so Emma could become used to being an equestrienne circus performer who was married and no longer relying on her mother.

Leaving from Chicago, Agnes made her way to San Francisco. A number of her former circus friends had put together year-round shows in sunny California, playing in large theaters and dance halls, and Agnes went to visit them. Several weeks after her visit, probably in February, she returned east, but only as far as Cheyenne, where she stopped to visit an old friend, Minnie Wells.[2]

Minnie Wells had a circus career as a female lion tamer. She worked for several circuses, including Haight's Empire City Circus. By 1876, she had left the circus life and was living with Sylvester L. "Wes" Moyer, whom she would marry in June of 1877. Their home was at the corner of Eighteenth and Central in Cheyenne. It seems evident that Agnes' visit to Cheyenne was to see her friend Minnie, and she anticipated nothing else happening during that visit.[3]

Yet somehow J. B. Hickok found out that Agnes Lake was in Cheyenne. Despite all of the highly speculative reasons for their meeting given by many historians and biographers, all without a shred of evidence, it is unknown how they found out the other was in Cheyenne. They met, and with virtually no courtship, and the almost non-existent, in-person intimacy over a five-year period as described above, they decided to get married.

On March 5, 1876, they were married in the home of Minnie Wells and Sylvester Moyer, by the Reverend W. F. Warren. Minnie and Sylvester served as witnesses; it is unknown if anyone else was in attendance. A formal photograph was taken on that wedding day of a sitting J. B. Hickok and Sylvester Moyer standing behind. Agnes was just a few months shy of turning fifty. James was thirty-eight. It is one of two photographs that have been proposed as Hickok's last known photograph ever taken. Surely the photographer took a wedding picture of Agnes and James. It has never turned up.

Reverend Warren wrote in his church register: "Don't think the[y] meant it."[4] It has to be asked, why would he say that? Did they say as much to him by their words and actions? Did they not seem to take the ceremony seriously? These five words written in the margin of the church register have perplexed biographers and historians for decades, including this writer. Yet the letters that Agnes wrote to the Hickok family after she and James were married, and the two known letters that James wrote to Agnes after they were married, all indicate abiding and mutual love for each other.

On March 7th, 1876 the Cheyenne *Daily Leader* published their wedding announcement.

Married—By the Rev. W. F. Warren, March 5th, 1876, at the residence of S. L. Moyer, Cheyenne, Wyomimg Territory, Mrs. Agnes Lake Thatcher, of Cincinnati, Ohio, to James Butler Hickok, Wild Bill, of this city.

#4194

Thirty-eight-year-old James Butler Hickok married forty-nine-year-old Agnes Lake Thatcher at the home of Sylvester and Minnie Wells in Cheyenne on March 5th, 1876. This is a picture taken on his wedding day of James and his best man Sylvester Moyer. There were surely photographs taken of James and Alice that day, yet they have never turned up. *Author's collection.*

On March 8, the Cheyenne *Daily Sun* weighed in:

"Wild Bill," of Western fame, has conquered numerous Indians, outlaws, bears and buffaloes, but a charming widow has stolen the magic wand. The scepter has departed, and he is as meek and gentle as a lamb. In other words, he has off the coils of bachelorhood.

On March 31, the Omaha *Daily Bee* had a different perspective:

Mrs. Lake came to Cheyenne ostensibly for recreation, but really to take advantage of the privileges which leap year gives the ladies. Hickok has always been considered as wild and woolly and hard to curry, but the proprietress of the best circus on the continent wanted a husband of renown, and she laid siege to the not over susceptible heart of a man who had killed his dozens of both whites and Indians. The contest was "short, sharp and decisive," and "Wild Bill" went down in the struggle clasping his opponent with his brawny arms, and now sweet little cupids hover over their pathway and sugar, cream and honey for a delicious paste through which to honeymoon. Success and happiness attend them, and while on the road of life they may have every joy vouchsafed to mortals, and we feel confident that Mr. Hickok will see to it that they are never lacking for small Bills.

The above reference to leap year references a tradition that held sway at that time, that February 29 was the day it was socially appropriate for a lady to propose marriage to man.

Shortly after the wedding, the newlyweds took the train to St. Louis, where Agnes and James visited her brother, Joseph Mersman.[5] It is probable that James, and perhaps Agnes as well, visited James Buel in St Louis. Buel was now editor of the influential *St. Louis Evening Dispatch*, and a strong supporter of James' plans for a Black Hills expedition.

After a few days James and Agnes continued by train to her home in Cincinnati at 10 W. Ninth Street. Gil Robinson, Agnes' new son-in-law of four months, answered the door. Robinson later recalled the moment: "When he came to my home in Cincinnati and I first laid eyes on the worlds greatest pistol fighter, with his long frock coat and high hat, I thought he was a preacher!"[6] In 1928, towards the end of his life, Robinson gave an interview to the *Cincinnati Commercial Tribune* about all the famous people he had met in his long circus career. The reporter wrote:

#4195

This image of Agnes Hickok has been consistently misdated. It is actually the photograph that Agnes had taken and sent to Polly Hickok and the Hickok family in 1876 after she had married James. She was fifty years old in this photograph. This is all confirmed by the letter she wrote to the Hickok family telling them she was having this photograph done and was going to send it to them. *Author's collection.*

#4196

It has been proposed that this photograph may have been taken in either Denver or Cheyenne. Yet there is evidence that it was produced in Cheyenne. The back of the original photograph has a hand written census of nine people in the image from left to right; #1 unknown, #2 Doc Middleton [a notorious horse thief], #3 unknown, #4 Doc Howard, #5 Wild Bill, #6 unknown, #7 California Jack, #8 unknown, #9 Bloody Dick [Seymour] If these identifications are right, as they appear to be, they effectively date this photograph as taken in Cheyenne in the spring of 1876. *Author's collection.*

"He shook hands with Abraham Lincoln when that dignitary was in Cincinnati in 1861, bound for Washington. Since then he has known Gen. Ulysses S. Grant, Gen. Robert E. Lee, Buffalo Bill, Wild Bill Hickox, the King of Siam, and Edward, Prince of Wales, among other celebrities.

Indicating that he was proudest of his relation to Hickok, Robinson commented:

'Do you remember hearing of Wild Bill Hickok? He was an in-law of mine. Coolidge doesn't need to think he's the only celebrity that spends time in the Black Hills. Look here!' And Robinson showed a letter from Wild Bill dated July 17, 1876, in the Black Hills, South Dakota."[7]

More about Gil Robinson and the letter he brandished above, later in this book.

After two weeks together in Cincinnati, in about the middle of March, the newlyweds parted at the train station. James planned to go on to St. Louis to work on putting together his Black Hills expedition, while Agnes would stay in Cincinnati to help take care of daughter Emma's newborn child, Agnes' infant granddaughter. From St. Louis, James would go on to the Black Hills to seek his fortune, and Agnes would await him in Cincinnati.

It appears that Polly Hickok and Celinda Hickok wrote on March 28 to their new daughter-in-law and sister-in-law. Polly and Celinda's letter has not been found. Below is Agnes' response.

Cincinnati April 26 [1876]

Dear Mother and Sister
  Your kind letter of April 28 [Agnes means March 28] *has this Moment been received and with joy and pleasure. I have arrived Home all right, in fact I have been Home for a week to day: have not heard from James as yet. I expect a letter to day: he is very busy in St. Louis where he will remain until the middle of May and then he will go West again: and I expect to join him sometime in the Fall. He is going to take a party to the Black Hills and I expect to remain in this place until he sends for me: it is hard to part so soon after being Married but it is unavoidable and so I am content: such is life at any rate: My Daughter does not travel this Summer as she will be confined sometime in August. She was Married last November to a Mr. Robinson a Circus Proprieter and well off, hence my Marriage. I would never have Married as long as my Daughter remained single as it was my Duty to remain with her and take care of her: but now I am superceaded and she has a protector ahead of me: although I loved James for three years before I Married him I would not get married before my Daughter did. I wanted to see her settled in the World first as I considered myself a minor consideration.*
  Loving James as I do and being a Woman of tender fealings I don't see why we will not git along together: I shall doo all in my power to git along: I will send you my Picture as soon as I git it taken: I have a very bad cold just now. I don't sleep at nights at all: I have such fearful night[s] and my eyes are so swollen that just as soon as I git so I can have them takin I will doo so. Dear Mother I want you to give me James exact age as I want to put our Berths on our Marriage Certificate. He plays and larkes with me so mutch that I wont put it down until I git

it from you: the Day of the Month and year: my Daughter Emma was Born the 22nd of February, Washingtons Birth Day: only not the same year. She was born 1856. I was Born the 2nd of August, 1832. I have one Sister and one brother in St. Louis. My sister is heer.

My Kind Love to all and belive me to be your
Loving Daughter Agnes Hickok

PS you spoke in your letter of being [poor?] *people. That is what I am.*[8]

As Agnes relates in her letter above, James expected to be in St. Louis in April and planned to be there till the middle of May. James Buel writes here with fact-based clarity and corroborates her statement about Hickok's plans:

> *Wild Bill remained with his wife in Cincinnati nearly two weeks, and then giving her an affectionate goodby, went directly to St. Louis for the purpose of getting his proposed expedition organized. Excitement over the Black Hills discoveries was now at fever heat, and a lively business was being done at Bismarck and Cheyenne in fitting out parties who were rushing into the gold region with reckless haste. A great number of those intent on reaching the Hills went by boat from St. Louis to Bismarck and then overland. But Bill considered the route from Cheyenne as the most expeditious and practible; and his company was organized that way, where outfits could be had much cheaper than at Bismarck.*
>
> *It required several days to make up the desired number of men, as Bill had fixed upon not less than one hundred and fifty, and during this period of organization he daily visited the writer, who was then city editor of the* Evening Dispatch, *and reported the progress of his scheme.*[9]

Notwithstanding Agnes' stated belief that James went directly from Cincinnati to St. Louis, and James Buel's mistaken claim that James did the same, it appeared that Hickok had a change of plans, perhaps necessitated by an increased urgency to get to Cheyenne to firm things up there for his expedition, because he did not go directly to St. Louis; he went directly to Cheyenne. A reporter for the *St. Louis Republican* in Cheyenne sent this report to his paper that appeared on March 23:

362

"Wild Bill is in Cheyenne at the 'Miners Home' where he makes his headquarters. He is a trifle pale now because of a recent illness...I had a conversation with him and he spoke of the prospects in the new El Dorado as soon as the weather opens."

The photograph #4196 on page 360 was taken in Cheyenne. There is no record of Doc Howard in Denver, yet he held various bartending jobs in Cheyenne in 1875 and 1876. Bloody Dick Seymour did not arrive in Cheyenne until April 1876, and was soon recruited as a partner in Charley Utter's express service to run between Deadwood and Fort Laramie. Seymour was also with the party of Utter and Hickok that made their way to Deadwood in July, 1876. Lastly, there is a photograph of a similarly-named billiard hall in Denver, but the building is substantially different than the one in this photograph; much smaller sign on the front, different windows, and an awning, whereas the building in this photo has none. The Metropolitan Billiard Hall in this photograph must be in Cheyenne. One final identification to speculate upon: If this image was taken in the spring of 1876 in Cheyenne, and all indications are that it was, and Bloody Dick Seymour is correctly identified in the group, could this actually be J. B. Hickok's good friend Charley Utter next to Hickok? Utter was reported to be about 5'6", Hickok reported to be about 6'2". Also, in this photograph Hickok appears to be holding his grandfather's walking cane, which he would go on to lose on the way from Cheyenne to Deadwood in July, 1876.

On April 14, the *Cheyenne Leader* not only placed Hickok still in Cheyenne, but also managed to chastise him as well: "Wild Bill still lingers with us and the same may be said of winter. He is in his element nowadays and makes a business of stuffing newcomers and tenderfeet of all descriptions with tales of his prowess, his wonderful discoveries of diamond caves, etc. which he describes as located 'up north.'"

Shortly after this April 14 report, James must have rushed to St. Louis to wrap up affairs on the east end of his planned expedition enterprise. On April 30, 1876, the Cheyenne *Daily Sun* made this report:

Black Hills and Big Horn Expedition

Wild Bill (J. B. Hickok) sends us from St. Louis, circulars and posters announcing that he is raising a company for the Black Hills and Big Horn country, which will leave St. Louis, Jefferson City, Sedalia, and Kansas City on Wednesday, May 17th. He adds that for reasons which will be fully explained to all who make application to become members of the expedition, we deem it not prudent to start earlier than the above named time. He wants parties joining his command to be outfitted as follows: One good rifle each, and 200 rounds of ammunition; one tent for two, four or seven men; camp supplies; one rubber blanket, two woolen blankets, and four to six months' provisions. Bill is not sure whether he will take the Cheyenne route or Sidney route, but intends to purchase the supplies at one of the two places.

He says: We hope to secure a large body of men for this expedition, not only for better self-protection on the route, but also to enable us to get cheaper rates of transportation, and lower figures on our supplies, and make a formidable settlement in the famous gold region.

Not to be outdone by the *Daily Sun*, the *Cheyenne Leader*, Hickok's chief critic in Cheyenne, ran this report on May 3:

> *Black Hills Breezes*
> *Wild Bill Organizing an Expedition in Saint Louis*
> *Wild Bill's Expedition*
>
> *We have received circulars from St. Louis announcing that Wild Bill (J. B. Hickock) is organizing an expedition for the Hills, which will leave St. Louis, May 16, coming to Cheyenne by special train, coming here via Kansas City, Lincoln and Omaha. The expedition will go from here to Custer City, where it will stop about ten days and then probably proceed to the Big Horn country. The fare from St. Louis to Cheyenne will be $25; and from St Louis to Custer City $33.65.*
> *Contracts have been made with our outfitting houses as to prices of outfits, and with forwarding houses as to freight rates etc. The circulars give details as to the outfits required, and state that Wild Bill proposes to lead the expedition to points where plenty of gold can be found.*

On May 13, another report surfaced from St. Louis and was printed in that day's Cheyenne Weekly Leader:

> *Wild Bill's Expedition*
>
> *J.B. Hickock (Wild Bill) writes from St. Louis to a friend in this city that he is working night and day completing the organization*

of his Black Hills and Big Horn expedition. He says he has to "buck" against the Yankton route, for which active agents are working in St. Louis, but that he is steadily convincing people of the advantages of the Cheyenne route and will bring his expedition here to outfit. He reports that he has everything working smoothly and will soon be on the road.

In a letter to the Hickok family just a few years after James' death, James Buel made it clear that they were good friends in both Kansas City and St. Louis, and that James stayed at Buel's St. Louis home for the six weeks before his last trip to the Black Hills: "I was well acquainted with James during his residence at Kansas City, during which time I was city editor of the *Journal*. I came to St. Louis in 1873, and during the time James was organizing his last expedition to the Black Hills he made his headquarters with me. I entertained a warm friendship for him and I assure you that in writing his life I have dealt chiefly on the good qualities of heart which distinguished him."[10]

James Buel's St. Louis home was at 3214 S. Eighth Street. Certainly staying with Buel would have facilitated the "daily progress" reports James provided to Buel, then the city editor of the *Evening Dispatch*.

By June 2, Hickok was indeed back on the road, and headed west on the train to Cheyenne. On that day, from the Metropolitan Hotel in Omaha, Nebraska, he wrote to his wife Agnes for the first time since they parted in Cincinnati back in March (punctuation added):

June 2nd, 1876

Doll one word from Omaha I was very sick last night but am feeling very well and happy now. god Bless and Protect my Agnes is my prair. would I not like to Put my big hands on your Shoulders and kiss you right now. Love to Emma One Thousand Kises to my wife Agnes.

From you ever loving Husband
JB Hickok
Wild Bill
By By [11]

#4191

This image has been credited to photographer D.D. Dare of Cheyenne and is estimated to have been taken in 1875 or 1876. Because of the serious and weary countenance of James and the apparent wrinkles around his eyes due to eye strain, some writers have proposed that this might be Hickok's last photograph. Image 4194 has also been considered as a possible last photograph of James Butler Hickok. *Author's collection.*

On June 8, the *Cheyenne Leader* succinctly noted Hickok's return to Cheyenne: "Wild Bill is with us again." No fanfare, no mention of a Black Hills expedition, nothing. What happened? Buel noted in *Heroes of the Plains* that "In the latter part of March about one hundred persons had joined the expedition at St. Louis, and nearly as many more had enlisted under Carpenter at Kansas City, so that the two companies were consolidated and started for the Black Hills via Cheyenne on the 12th of April."[12] The St. Louis press had indicated that one C. C. Carpenter was organizing an expedition scheduled to leave St. Louis on April 3. Did Carpenter take over Hickok's expedition? If so, why? Whatever the reason, it is plain that J. B. Hickok had dropped his plans to lead a formal expedition to the Black Hills, and he had returned to Cheyenne to strike out for the Black Hills on his own or with like-minded friends he might meet there. George Stokes of Denver was in Cheyenne during this same period. He reported that Hickok stayed at Wagner's Hotel in Cheyenne, ate sparingly and did not drink at all, but he did play some poker.[13] James did find at least two like-minded friends when he reached Cheyenne: Charley Utter and White Eye Anderson.

Charley Utter had long been friends with J. B. Hickok, even earlier than the one time we know they were together in Georgetown in 1872. Charley Utter came back to Cheyenne in early June with his brother, Steve. Charley Utter and Hickok had been in Cheyenne together in March, and probably discussed their respective plans: James' plan to bring a one-hundred-man gold expedition in the Black Hills from points east, and Charley's plan to organize a Black Hills transportation business, as well as a Pony Express-style mail line between Deadwood and Fort Laramie. Yet they both left soon; Hickok for St. Louis to implement his expedition plans, and Utter back to his home in Georgetown, Colorado, where he was promoting his own plans for the Black Hills. Now it was early June, and Charley Utter had returned to Cheyenne with his brother, Steve. J. B. Hickok himself was also back in Cheyenne by early June, and undoubtedly very happy to see his close friend, Charley. He would have confided in Charley then what had happened to kill his well-laid plans for a gold expedition.[14]

In that early June period, James and Charley went to the Elephant Corral in Cheyenne to purchase horses and wagons for a trip into the Black Hills. The Elephant Corral advertised:

#4190

This photograph of Joseph "White Eye" Anderson was taken in Leadville, Colorado by photographer J. T. Needles in 1879. *Author's collection.*

#4218

This 1877 photograph was taken in Deadwood and is credited to photographer F. Jay Haynes. Though the two figures on the right are unidentified, the two standing figures on the left are believed to be Steve Utter and his brother Charley Utter, J.B. Hickok's best friend. The Utter brothers were still in Deadwood through most of 1877, and their unique wear set them apart from everyone else in Deadwood. Known are two illustrations of Charley Utter in similar or the very same clothing. *Author's collection.*

> *Elephant Corral, formerly the Old Union is now opened. Finest Lot of Mules and Horses in Wyoming Territory for sale at prices to suit buyers. Parties Outfitting for the Black Hills Could not do better than to visit the Elephant Corral before buying elsewhere.*

The Elephant Corral was located at the corner of Eighteenth and Eddy in Cheyenne.[15] It was at the Elephant Corral that James and Charley met White-Eye Anderson. White-Eye recalled the meeting:

> *Charlie* [this Charlie was White-Eye's brother] *and I took the railroad to Cheyenne, Wyoming, which was the starting place for the Black Hills. We went over to the Elephant Feed Corral to try and find*

a conveyance to take us to Deadwood. While we were looking up an outfit we ran across some old friends and acquaintances who were doing likewise, Wild Bill and Charley Utter. It had been several years since I had seen Wild Bill, but he recognized me and the first thing he said was "Touch Flesh, my boy," which was an old time saying we used when we shook hands. Then he told Charley Utter how we got acquainted several years before. Steve Utter, Charley's brother, was there too and had just finished serving five years with the Texas Rangers. When Bill introduced me to friends I did not know he would say "This is my boy, the white-eyed kid." Now you can bet that I surely was stuck on myself to know that I had such a friend as Wild Bill Hickok. It was through my friendship with Wild Bill that "Colorado Charley" Utter told my brother and I that we could travel with them if we wanted to.

Wild Bill and his partner, a man named "Pie" [historians have yet to discover the identity of the mysterious Mr. "Pie"], *bought a light, two-horse wagon and horses. We took passage with the Utter boys as they had just bought a wagon and four-horse team and had plenty of room to stow away our plunder. Charlie and I had already bought two saddle horses. The six of us had our grub together.*[16]

White-Eye Anderson believed he had first met J. B. Hickok at Fort McPherson in western Nebraska in 1873 when Hickok came to the fort to meet Will Cody and Texas Jack to discuss going on stage with them. That is doubtful. Furthermore, Cody never recalled this meeting. Cody wrote that he and Texas Jack had contacted Hickok in Springfield in 1873 and made him their offer to join them onstage. He accepted and came directly to New York to meet them.[17]

But by the way White-Eye describes James' obvious fondness for him indicates that they must have met someplace before, and met long enough to develop a friendship. A slight error, considering White-Eye was making these recollections some fifty years after the events.

Joseph "White-Eye" Anderson was born September 2, 1853, in Ohio. He left home at age sixteen and made his way out west. He landed at Fort McPherson and got a job herding the milk cows that went with the fort. He cleared $40 a month. At one point, when he was eighteen, while at Fort McPherson he was out on the Nebraska plains and being chased by a group of Indians. They could not catch Anderson or his partner, so they set fire to the tall, dry grass. The wind was blowing hard, pushing the fire towards the boys. Anderson and his partner made for a large buffalo wallow that was filled with water about a foot deep. They let their horses go and never saw them again. They lay down in the water hoping the fire would pass over them. All was covered by water except their face. A cinder came down and caught Anderson right on the eyebrow. It hurt so bad he thought he had lost an eye, but when things calmed down and his eyebrow grew back, it was snow white. In 1871, Anderson was in Saskatchewan, Canada and spent time beaver trapping with the notorious Liver-Eating Johnson. After Hickok's death in 1876, Anderson spent three more years in the Black Hills. In 1879, he was in Leadville, Colorado, panning for gold, where he claims he met Frank and Jesse James. He spent time in Arizona mining in the 1880s, and in 1886 he left the frontier and moved to San Diego and, in his own words, "From that time on I never set foot in a saloon and had nothing to do with cards or any other games of chance." He was thirty-three years old.[18]

In the 1970s, writer William Secrest became interested in a series of articles written by Raymond Thorp in 1940, based on the life of Joseph "White-Eye" Anderson. Earlier, Joseph Rosa had also been interested in Thorp's articles, and he included some of the material in his biography, *They Called Him Wild Bill*, when it came out in 1964, and also in the expanded and improved second edition that was published in 1974. In 1970, White-Eye's eighty-one-year-old daughter found that Rosa mentioned her father in his book, and she wrote to him in England. Joseph Rosa knew of Secrest's interest in the Thorp material and was surprised to find out that Secrest had obtained a large file of the late Raymond Thorp's material and notes, including Thorp's correspondence with White-Eye. Rosa put White-Eye's daughter in touch with William Secrest; they found that she and Secrest lived just a few miles from each other in Fresno, California. When they met, she told Secrest it was her cherished desire to have her father's full manuscript published. With her support William Secrest undertook the task, and the wonderful result was *I Buried Hickok: The Memoirs of White Eye Anderson*, published in 1980. Incorporated into the book is a twelve-page manuscript about Hickok that White-Eye had prepared for Captain Jack Crawford in 1900. Anderson was a particularly adept observer of people and events, and the memoirs fairly crackle with electric immediacy. White-Eye Anderson died in 1944 at the age of ninety-one.[19]

On June 19, Agnes wrote again to her new mother-in-law:

Cincinnati June 19th [1876]
Polly Hickok
My Dear Mother

> *I wrote in answer to Celinda's letter and sent you my picture.*
> *[D]id you git them? [N]ot gitting any answer I thought that perhaps*
> *you did not git my letter. [I]f such is the case I will send you others: and*
> *if you answered my letter I did not git it. James has gone West: and I*
> *am going to remain heer until sometime in the fall as I can not leave*
> *until after my Daughter's confinement: for she thinks that iff her Ma*
> *Ma is only with her all is sure to go right and I am glad she has so mutch*
> *confidence in her Mother: well my Mother how are you gitting along is*
> *your health any better: if I can possible git of some time this Summer*
> *I am coming to see you: I feel very lonely away from my husband and*
> *long for the time to come when we will meet again: Emma sends Love*
> *to all: I will write long letter next time when I see iff this reaches its*
> *destinasion so I will close by sending you all my Love from your Loveing*
> *Daughter*
>
> *Agnes Hickok* [20]

Agnes' statement that "James has gone west" in her letter indicates
she had received James' very short letter of June 2 from Omaha. She also
states that she answered Celinda's letter and sent a picture of herself as
well, yet she had not yet received an answer, which must have concerned
her. The picture Agnes sent is now in the Hickok Family Collection at
the Kansas Historical Society. It is photograph #4195 on page 359.

The Hickok/Utter party left Cheyenne in late June, the same
week that Custer met his fate at the Little Big Horn in Montana on
June 25. The day before they left Cheyenne for the Black Hills, James
approached Doc Howard, who recalled later:

> *One day, as I was walking on Sixteenth Street, Wild Bill came*
> *over to me and said "Doc, Charley Utter and a few of the boys are going*
> *up to Deadwood and I'd like to go with them, but my remittance hasn't*
> *come from the East." I said "Bill, how much do you want?"*

With that we went over to Unfug Brothers grocery store in the old Rollins House, where I staked him to $22.30. He was very grateful and said he would pay it back as soon as he could. I remember saying, "Bill, if you ever get flush, pay it back; if not, forget about it." I thought a great deal of Bill. He was as good a friend as a man could have. He deserved much more credit than he ever got for bravery and loyalty to all. After I staked him we said goodbye and he left with the gang in the morning. Shortly after that, I heard he had been shot. He was in a poker game with Charlie Rich, the same fellow who I had a fuss with in Jim Allen's Variety Show, and two other fellows.[21]

It is unknown where James' "remittance" was coming from. Perhaps Agnes, yet she made no indication of it. Perhaps Polly Hickok, or brother Lorenzo? Or maybe there was no pending remittance. To a bigger question, where was James' money? He had earned thousands of dollars less than two years before on the stage with *Scouts of the Plains*. Had he spent it all on preparations for his apparently forestalled Black Hills expedition? Had he gambled it all away in Kansas City and Cheyenne?

The Hickok/Utter party left Cheyenne on about June 27 for the Black Hills and the new, ramshackle settlement of Deadwood, only up and running since April. On June 30, they arrived at John Hunton's ranch, south of Fort Laramie, and camped for the night. Years later, John Hunton recalled their visit:

I will now refer to...'Wild Bill', whom I knew fairly well in 1874 and late in the year 1875, when he was making his home in Cheyenne. During that time I do not think he knew 'Calamity Jane'.

On June 30, 1876, Bill" and a party of men who were on their way to the Black Hills mines, traveling with a four-horse team and wagon, camped about two miles south of my ranch. The next morning they passed my place and 'Bill' stopped long enough to say 'How'. He then said, 'So long, Jack' and went away. A few hours afterward, Waddie Bascom, one of my men, came in and said 'Mr. Hunton, I met a man down the road who said he was 'Wild Bill' and wanted you to go to the place he camped last night and get his cane, which he stuck in the ground at his head where he made his bed last night in the edge of a patch of bushes, and send it to him at Deadwood by someone you trust to deliver it to him. Be sure not to send it except by some mutual friend

#0002, #0004

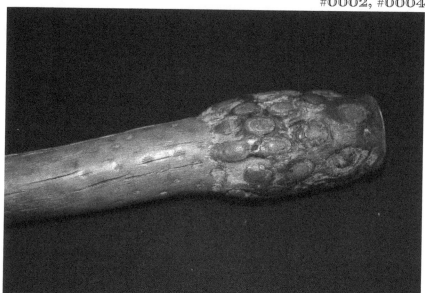

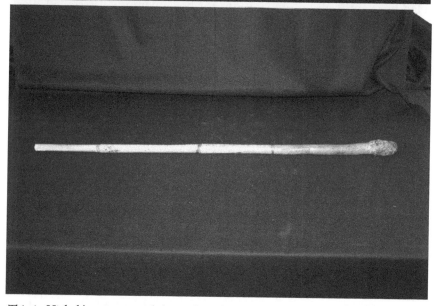

This is Hickok's cane, passed down from his grandfather, that John Hunton saved and eventually turned in to the Wyoming State Museum. This is the cane that Hickok held in the group photograph taken in front of the Metropolitan Billiard Hall in in Cheyenne in the spring of 1876. If the story about the Gold Room brawl in Cheyenne is true, this is the cane with which Hickok cleared the room. This cane, perhaps over two hundred years old now, has a carved pine cone handle, a wooden cane decoration popular even today. *Courtesy of Wyoming State Museum, Cheyenne, Wyoming.*

*whom you both know, as he did not want to take any chance of losing it.'
I sent the man for the cane, and he brought it to me.*

*In less than a month, I heard of Bill's death...I kept the
cane until 1921 and then gave it to Miss Eunice G. Anderson, State
Historian, to be deposited in the museum of the Wyoming Historical
Society, where it is now deposited and can be seen.*[22]

Left are photographs of the Hickok cane, still located today
in the Wyoming State Museum. This is very likely the same cane that
Hickok used in Topeka to stab a potato in the gutter and hurl it across
the street at a friend, shaking mightily the glass of a jewelry store instead.
(See Chapter Ten.) It is the same cane shown in Hickok's hand in the
group photograph taken in front of the Metropolitan Billiard Hall in
Cheyenne. As noted in Chapter Sixteen, this cane was recognized by
David Miller of Cheyenne as owned by Hickok, after being shown the
cane by John Hunton. Miller would have had occasion to see Hickok
almost every day in Cheyenne; Hickok's apartment was right on top of
Miller's jewelry store.

Also on June 30, Agnes wrote her third letter to the Hickok family in
Illinois, this time to James' sister Celinda.

Cincinnati June 30 [1876]

Dear Sister Celinda
*Your ever so kind and welcome letter I received some days ago
but have not been able to answer on account of having run an ice pick
clear through my fore finger but it is dooing very well but badly swollen
but it don't amount to any thing only an inconvenience: I am happy to
see that Mother is gitting along as well as can be expected. [M]ay [G]
od bless her is the preyr of her unseen Daughter.*
*[Here part of the letter is missing, either torn out or fallen
out.]...put of[f] the trip until the first of June. I will remit you his letter
from Omaha. I have not herd from him since: and I feal so bad about
it that I can not sleep at night: but the only consolasion that I have is
that he is where he can not communicate: iff I was sure it was that I
would not feal so bad but I am afraid he is sick: and iff so he will not
write nor alow eny one els to doo so: before we ever got married I did*

not get a letter from him for five weeks: and the first...time he told my... [missing]*some Day before long iff all goes well* [in margin at top of letter, upside down].

> *Your loveing Sister*
> *Agnes Hickok*
> *Emma sends love to all.*[23]

This letter confirms that Agnes did receive letters from James before they were married. None of these letters have ever turned up.

White-Eye's recollection of the trip to Deadwood continues:

> *We traveled from Cheyenne to Fort Laramie, a distance of about seventy-five miles. There were lots of soldiers there and the officer of the day told us we would have to wait until there would be a party of over one hundred to travel together. This was to protect ourselves from the Indians who had been killing all the small outfits that had traveled alone. We had to wait only a day or two until we had more than a hundred in our party.*
>
> *We were also told to go to the Government Farm, which was sixteen miles further up the road to the Black Hills, and there to organize our wagon train. We were to elect a captain and a wagon boss so that the wagons could be properly corraled in case of Indian trouble. They wanted to elect Wild Bill captain, but he was not very well and did not want to be bothered with it so Colorado Charley was elected captain and my brother was selected as wagon boss.*
>
> *While we were at Fort Laramie, the officer-of-the-day asked us if we would take a young woman with us. It was just after payday and she had been on a big drunk with the soldiers and had been having a hell of a time of it. When they put her in the post guard house she was very drunk and near naked. Her name was Calamity Jane.*[24]

Some historians doubt that Calamity Jane rode with the Hickok/Utter party from Fort Laramie to Deadwood. They believe that research has not turned up real evidence that she was on this trip, and point to the fact that she was on trial in Cheyenne on June 9 for grand larceny, but was acquitted and released, whereupon the next day she got very drunk and rented a buggy and, intending to go to close-by Fort Russell, instead ended at Fort Laramie, some seventy-five miles away. She was reported from there at Fort Reno and Fort Fetterman. However, the Deadwood paper reported on July 15 that "Calamity Jane has arrived" in Deadwood. The Hickok/Utter party arrived by July 12, "or a few days later," as White-Eye remembered it. There is corroborating evidence supporting White-Eye's contention that Calamity Jane traveled with his wagon train from Fort Laramie to Deadwood. John Gray heading into the Black Hills to mine for gold, claimed to have joined the Hickok/Utter party at the Government Farm. Gray was interviewed by writer Doane Robinson in 1904, who wrote this about John Gray: "In June following he started for the Black Hills with what was known as the Colorado Charlie and Wild Bill train, the first being captain of the expedition, while Wild Bill and the husband of Madam Mustachio were his two lieutenants, the three being well-known characters on the frontier." Gray further recalled for Robinson in this 1904 interview that, "Among the women in the party were Calamity Jane (whose death occurred about a year ago), Madam Mustachio and Dirty Em, each of whom will be remembered by the old timers."[25]

An article in the *Cheyenne Daily Leader* confirms to some extent that Calamity Jane was at Fort Laramie at about the time the Hickok/Utter party was there. The paper stated that she had driven out of Cheyenne on June 10 in a rented buggy. She started drinking, and she eventually found herself at Fort Laramie, some ninety miles away. *The Leader* reported that "She turned her horse out to grass, ran the buggy into a corral and began enjoying life in camp after her usual fashion." *The Leader* article implies strongly that Calamity Jane was at Fort Laramie near the end of June when the Hickok/Utter party was there. Finally, consider that White-Eye puts their arrival in Deadwood on July 12 "or a few days later." July 15 certainly comports with "a few days later," when the *Black Hills Pioneer* stated bluntly, "Calamity Jane has arrived." White-Eye's description of the trip from Cheyenne to Deadwood continues as he addresses what Hickok thought of Calamity Jane:

> *Calamity Jane had a wonderful command of profanity; that is, she could cuss to beat the band. She was also a good shot with a six-shooter and could skin mules for further order. I believe it was the first time that Wild Bill had met her and he surely did not have any use for her. She looked to be about twenty-five years of age and was as tough*

as they came. She laid up with Steve Utter and ate her meals with us during the trip.[26]

J. B. Hickok wanted nothing to do with Calamity Jane. The final argument proposed by those who want to believe they had a tryst ask, why then are they buried together, in eternal love? The late James McLaird, history professor at Dakota Wesleyan University, who produced learned studies of both Wild Bill Hickok and Calamity Jane, answered this very well:

> *Shortly before Calamity Jane's death on 1 August 1903, amateur photographer John Mayo coaxed her to pose in front of James Butler Hickok's grave. His picture of her there added to growing impressions that these two famous characters were intimately related. This notion was a relatively recent one. During the interval between Hickok's death in 1876 and Calamity Jane's in 1903, biographers relating Wild Bill's adventures did not even mention Calamity Jane...The burial of Calamity Jane next to Wild Bill, only ten days after Mayo took his photograph, was the most important early event associating these two individuals. Although it is alleged that this occurred at Calamity's request, Deadwood promoters likely had a hand in the decision. The Hickok family protested the proximity of the graves, and several of Hickok's friends, including Captain Jack Crawford, denounced implications that Wild Bill and Calamity Jane were ever intimate. Local officials made the decision to place the graves near each other, for they could have disregarded Calamity's purported dying wish to be buried close to her old friend and thus have avoided the controversy. The Belle Fourche Bee may have spotted the real reason for their decision when it suggested that Deadwood would now have two attractions.*[27]

There was no love nor affair between Calamity Jane and Hickok. Toss this myth into the ash bin of history.

White-Eye continues:

> *Our wagon train consisted mostly of westerners: prospectors, gamblers, saloon men, bartenders and wholesale liquor men. There were thirteen or fourteen ladies of easy virtue in the train; Calamity Jane and Madam Moustache, the noted twenty-one dealer, were two*

of the famous ones. Madame and Bill Erbb, Nutchell Bill and Soapy Smith were other noted characters in our group...There were about thirty wagons in our train and some one hundred and thirty people... There was not much of a wagon road in those days, Teams were always getting stuck in the mud and having to cross streams of water. At times, Calamity Jane, with a black snake whip and lots of cussing, would have to help the teams over the rough, bad places...

When we started from Cheyenne, Wild Bill bought a five-gallon keg of whiskey from a wholesale liquor dealer. He said he wanted enough for himself and his friends on the trip, and thought it would be good to have in case of snake bites, cramps or colic. Every time we would go into camp, the first thing in the morning there would be a crowd of fellows around Bill's wagon to sample some of his liquor. Bill was a good-hearted and whole-souled fellow. I often think of how he would say to me when the cup was passed around and emptied, "Fill her up my boy and pass her around again."

We were not much more than halfway to Deadwood when Bill's whiskey barrel ran dry. He went to a man named Shingle who had a six-mule load of whiskey along, and got his barrel filled again. This time he told the boys his liquor was private stock and he wanted it to last till we got through. No one was to have any outside of our own party except in the case of sickness or snake-bite.[28]

The "man named Shingle" was George Shingle, on his way to Deadwood to open a saloon, hence his "six-mule load of whiskey." George Shingle also would find himself in the #10 saloon on August 2, 1876. Considering that Doc Howard loaned Hickok the specific and unusual amount of exactly $22.30 in Cheyenne the day before they left for Deadwood, it bears wondering if $22.30 was the exact price of a barrel of whiskey in 1876?

Bill Hickok never talked much, but what he said was right to the point. He was over six feet tall, very broad in the shoulders and narrow in the waist. I think the reason he was so slim was that he always had a belt with two six-shooters and this didn't give his belly a chance to grow. If I remember right his hair was dark brown and not very thick. His eyes were a kind of bluish, steel-gray and when he looked at you it seemed he was staring right through you. I think the reason he was such a good poker player was that he could tell what you were thinking just by looking at you. He never had much to say, was very good to his friends and polite to strangers.

We were over two weeks on the road from Cheyenne to Deadwood and at night there would be a bunch of us around the campfires telling stories. We had a lot of fun and some lively times. Bill Hickok never had much to say, but you can bet there was something doing when Calamity Jane was around. I think she told some of the roughest stories I ever heard and there would always be a big crowd come over to the campfire to hear her talk. I done most of the cooking and got very well acquainted with Jane. She was a big-hearted woman and she and I became good friends.

....Going down through Cedar Bluffs the road was very steep and we all had to help each wagon to the bottom of the hill. When we reached Hat Creek we found General Crook and his command on their way to Sitting Bull and his red devils...Buffalo Bill was chief of scouts and he had along several other old-timers whom we knew. Cody and Wild Bill had some words over a manuscript they were interested in together, but it was settled peacefully.

There was more to this argument between Cody and Hickok than White-Eye let on, or recalled. It may have been simmering for quite a while. Hiram Robbins, Cody's stage manager for a period, said that Cody provided Ned Buntline many stories of Hickok's exploits from which Buntline wrote plays and dime novels, only substituting Buffalo Bill Cody's name for Hickok's. In 1875 and 1876, Cody appeared on stage in the play *Wild Bill, or Life on the Border*, by Buntline. With that, Cody moved from appropriating Hickok's exploits as his own to also promoting himself on stage as Hickok. That was certainly the main subject of contention between the two of them at the meeting at Hat Creek. Other observers noted that the meeting between Cody and Hickok was "boisterous."

Referring to this incident at Hat Creek, or to the longer-running issue, the *Jefferson City People's Tribune* on August 23, 1876, reported: "Wild Bill raised Cody to manhood's estate, after which the two separated over some personal difficulty, and have never been on good terms since. Wild Bill accuses Buffalo Bill of having given Ned Buntline incidents of his (Wild Bill's) life, and claiming them as his (Buffalo Bill's) own adventures."

White-Eye Anderson continues:

Wild Bill had his old buffalo rifle with him. It was what we called a big 50. It was .56 caliber with a long barrel and we called it the Springfield single shot needle rifle. When he shot a buffalo with it, it would make a hole big enough for a calf to jump through.

Bill had discarded the Colts navy cap-and-ball pistols and had two of the latest Colts .36 caliber cartridge six-shooters. He generally filed the trigger off and the hammer smooth so they would pull very easy. He had lots of cartridges and we would do a little practicing about every day. Sometimes I would throw up my old broadbrimmed hat high up in the air and he could put six shots in it before it would hit the ground. Bill had worn buckskin when I first met him at Fort McPherson, but on our trip into the Black Hills he wore just plain western clothes.

Bill was always ready for duty. I remember one night when we were camped at Alum Springs and it was Bill's turn to herd the stock at night. It was one of the worst spots on the road for Indians and we could see dozens of signal fires in the hills. Bill and five others were supposed to be on guard duty until midnight and it was my brother Charlie's job to detail the guard. When he told Bill to go on guard, Bill said, "To hell with your guard." Charlie told him he would either have to serve or else get a substitute and then he walked away. Bill suddenly called back, "Captain, come back here and kick me. Of course, I'll go on guard, especially on a night like this." He picked up his rifle and went right to his post and stayed until morning, although he was only required to stay til midnight. We traveled on until we came to the South Fork of the Cheyenne River and crossed it, traveling up through Red Canyon where the land stands on edge. The road was very bad...We camped that night at Lost Springs, at the head of Red Canyon. Charley Utter and myself located the Springs, and we afterward started a road and stage station there.

...The next day we arrived at Custer City and some of the people on our trail stayed there...We arrived in Deadwood about the twelfth of July, or it might have been a few days later, but I know it was not before that. My brother and I had bought two good saddle horses in Cheyenne and a few miles before we got to town we let Wild Bill and Charley Utter have them to ride ahead of the train into Deadwood. They were to pick out a good camping place.

We pitched our camp on Whitewood Creek, about one hundred and fifty yards above its mouth. The timber and brush were so thick we had to cut a road out and had to clear up the brush on the ground we camped on. It was a nice flat in a grove of spruce and pine trees and made a beautiful summer camp. Wild Bill, the Utter Boys, Pie, my brother Charlie, and myself camped there, and sometimes Calamity Jane came to camp when she got hungry.[28]

Dakota Territory was established in 1861. It originally covered the future states of Wyoming, Montana, North Dakota and South Dakota. By 1876, the territories of Wyoming and Montana were established as independent territories on their way to eventual statehood; Dakota Territory now covered just North and South Dakota.

The Fort Laramie Treaty of 1868 had stipulated that the Black Hills of South Dakota were a part of the Sioux Indian Reservation, and would be for perpetuity. The treaty mandated that no non-Indian could come into the Black Hills except for members of the federal government or the military. No one else could enter the reservation for any reason. The treaty was signed by Sioux chief Red Cloud and other Sioux chiefs, as well as by General William T. Sherman and General William S. Harney. It was ratified by Congress and signed into law by President Andrew Johnson.

Seven years later, in February of 1876, the United States broke this treaty with the Sioux for a one-word reason: Gold.

Custer led a military expedition into the Black Hills in 1874, its purpose being to explore and map the area for a good site for a military post. As part of this military expedition, which included geologists as well as geographers, they searched the area for mineral deposits. They found traces of valuable mineral deposits, including trace indicators of gold. In the winter of 1874, news of this discovery began to filter out to the public. Though the geologists wrote that these were just indicators of possible gold and not a discovery yet of the actual precious metal, the public only heard the word "gold," and very soon there were attempts to trespass onto the Sioux reservation in the Black Hills.

The military was at that time under specific orders to enforce the treaty and keep non-Indians out. Probably the first group of trespassers to avoid the military was the Gordon group. Around Christmas day of 1874, the group, which included Annie Tallent, made their way onto the reservation and found their way to the same area where Custer's

#4204

This image is dated Main Street, Deadwood D.T., June 15, 1876. Tents, lean-to's, a few frame buildings, and a meandering dusty street. *Courtesy Deadwood History, Inc., Adams Museum Collection, Deadwood, SD.*

expedition had located the trace indicators of gold. They managed to elude the military for several months, and even found time to erect a stockade fort, until the military caught up with them in the spring of 1875, and they were all removed from the reservation.

News of the Gordon party's audacious move to find gold on the Sioux reservation spread across the nation, and generated much excitement. Soon other individuals and small parties were chasing gold illegally on the Sioux reservation. In May of 1875, the government sent out from Fort Laramie the Jenny Expedition, to try to evaluate Custer's findings from the previous year.

By the summer of 1875, new groups were filtering illegally into the Black Hills, many following the route of the Jenny Expedition. All the while this was going on, negotiators were working behind the scenes trying to get the Sioux to abandon their treaty and the Black Hills. General Crook, in charge at this time, and under considerable political pressure to satisfy both the trespassing miners and the Sioux, allowed the miners to form a town on French Creek. This became Custer City, the first town in the Black Hills. Also that summer, two small parties ventured onto the reservation and discovered gold samples on what would become known as Deadwood Creek and Whitewood Creek.

This move by Crook infuriated the Sioux, and negotiations broke down completely, the Sioux finally realizing that the U. S. government was going to take their land and the Black Hills, whether the tribe agreed to it or not. Naturally, that put the Sioux on the warpath, and by the spring of 1876, it had become very dangerous for small parties to enter the Black Hills.

Soon the real gold rush was on, and by March of 1876, the flood of people pouring into the Black Hills was unstoppable. Some of the best areas for mining appeared in Deadwood Gulch, which in the summer of 1876 held three mining camps: Elizabeth City, Crook City, and Deadwood. Located at the head of the gulch, against a canyon wall, Deadwood was the most desirable location for panning for gold, as it sat right on Deadwood and Whitewood Creeks. Laid out on April 28, 1876, within days, Deadwood was teeming with an estimated 15,000 to 25,000 people.

Yet for all the people that flooded into Deadwood that summer of 1876 seeking gold, there was a multitude of opportunistic entrepreneurs who sought riches by selling essentials and non-essentials, services and entertainment: hardware stores, bakeries, grocery stores, lumber yards, butcher shops, gun stores, and more. Added to this was a subset of gamblers, grifters, con men, prostitutes, whorehouses, liquor stores, saloons, gambling hells, and mining-camp entertainment.

Amazingly, the denizens of Deadwood threw up cheap, wood-frame false-front buildings all along the sometimes muddy, always dusty rut that passed for Main Street in less than two months, May and June of 1876. During May, Deadwood was mostly a tent city; the building explosion really took off in mid-June. The first frame structure was built in June by C. V. Gardner, who in this building brought Deadwood its first real grocery store. Two other grocery stores were up and running before the end of June as well. Apparently in May, Judge W. L. Kuykendall had provided a sort of curbside grocery for freighters and miners to pick up essentials, sort of like a modern-day convenience store. The first drugstore was built on the east side of Main, below Lee Street. The Custer House hotel was built that June on the corner of Main and Lee Streets. This was a two-story, wood-frame building. The Custer House opened for business in July. The Grand Central hotel was also built in June, but was initially used as just a restaurant. Later, a second story was added to the building and it was then run as a hotel. The first hardware store in Deadwood was owned by a partnership, Boughton and Berry, and built on the ground afterwards occupied by Sol Star and Seth Bullock's hardware store. As early as May, J. Shoudy's meat market was opened. The first regular restaurant in Deadwood, the IXL, was opened early that summer of 1876.[29]

The Senate Saloon, Al Swearingin's Gem Saloon and Dance Hall, the Deadwood Theatre, George Shingle's Saloon, and the #10 Saloon (located next to the Bella Union Variety Theatre being built for a September opening), and many more, were all up and running by the middle of July when J. B. Hickok and Charley Utter first entered Deadwood. Houses of prostitution abounded, from one-room hovels to private boxes on the interior of saloons like the Gem, to upstairs bedrooms above the gambling and drinking below. Gambling was available almost everywhere, and liquor flowed twenty-four hours a day.[30]

To James, Deadwood at first glance must have looked much like the end-of-the-track railroad towns in Kansas, in their early, wide-open lawless heyday, where much of his national fame had been generated; Junction City, Ellsworth, Hays, Abilene. Yet Deadwood that summer of 1876 was an extreme version of those towns, hurtling toward an unknown future, bursting with the promise of untold riches, unhampered by any laws or restrictions or boundaries other than human emotion, and all thrown together frenetically in less than two months to satisfy every need or whim of the tens of thousands of people crowding Deadwood Gulch. James must have felt right at home.

James Butler Hickok arrived in Deadwood sometime between July 12 and July 15. His life ended on August 2, 1876, when he was shot by Jack McCall in the #10 Saloon. At the outside he spent just one day short of three weeks in Deadwood. So much has been written about these last three weeks of his life, some fact, some fiction, that it would seem that he had spent three years in Deadwood, not three weeks. There are, however, two individuals who spent much time with Hickok in Deadwood, and were eyewitness to the events in his life those last three weeks: White-Eye Anderson and Leander P. Richardson. They were not only there at the time; they each wrote about what they knew and had seen. White-Eye Anderson's bona fides have already been introduced, and need no further explanation.

#4202

One month later, the middle of July, Hickok and Utter's party arrive in Deadwood. Now both sides of Main Street are covered with new buildings and businesses: The IXL restaurant, the Custer hotel, the Senate saloon, the Number 10 saloon and much more. The summer of 1876 the businesses served thousands of miners, and the businesses made more that summer than most of the miners panning Deadwood Creek for gold. *Courtesy Deadwood History, Inc., Adams Museum Collection, Deadwood, SD.*

Leander P. Richardson was already an accomplished journalist at age twenty when he made the trip to Deadwood , arriving July 30, 1876. By age sixteen, Richardson was a correspondent for the Chicago *Inter-Ocean*. His trip to Deadwood was funded by a Massachusetts newspaper, the *Springfield Republican*. His journalistic plan was to write about the Black Hills gold rush by sending regular dispatches to the Republican. Those contemporary dispatches, sent by telegraph, as well as an article he wrote for *Scribner's Monthly Magazine* in 1877 based on those same experiences in the Black Hills, all led to a considerable amount of publicity and recognition for Richardson. For the next twenty years, Richardson continued to write about his time in the Black Hills, and although there were some occasional discrepancies, for the most part the reports were consistent. Like any good journalist, Richardson had made extensive written notes when he was in Deadwood. Even though he was there for just five days, they were five critical days that included the killing of Hickok and the ensuing murder trial of Jack McCall. Richardson also interacted close-up and first-hand with Hickok for several days. En route from Cheyenne to Deadwood, he traveled with one John Marsh, a Deadwood resident. In Deadwood, Richardson came across Charley Utter's brother, Steve, who provided him with a letter of introduction to Charley.[31]

When the driver hired by Richardson dropped him and John Marsh off in Deadwood and returned to Cheyenne, he reported to the local paper that Richardson, Marsh and Wild Bill Hickok were drinking together when he left them. Soon Richardson made his way to Hickok and Utter's camp and introduced himself to Charley and gave him Steve's letter, whereupon Charley Utter insisted he stay in their camp, which he did the entire time he was in Deadwood.[32]

White-Eye Anderson wrote of his first impressions of Deadwood:

> *Deadwood was a mighty lively camp in those days. Gold dust was the currency, $18 and $20 per ounce. Some of the miners were making as high as $7000 per day to the claim. Board was $18 per week, meals $1, drinks and smokes, 25 cents, potatoes 50 cents per pound and onions 50 cents apiece, when you could get them...Sunday was a big day in Deadwood that summer. Nobody worked and everyone came to town. All the saloons, damce halls and gambling dens ran full blast and many of the gambling games moved out on the sidewalks. Lots of horses were sold at auction on the streets.*

> *The Gem Theater* [take note, all fans of HBO's cult classic TV series, Deadwood] *was a beer hall with a platform stage and*

*curtains. It was a variety show with all kinds of tough performances.
There were lots of small tables and chairs with benches lined up along
the walls. Also along the walls were private boxes six to eight feet square
where the ladies of secret virtue would get the drunken miners to spend
their dust and treat them to champagne. Sometimes they would keep
the bottle corks flying pretty lively. There were lots of beer jerkers, girls
and women to keep the crowd well-supplied with drinks and smokes.*

*Right across the street was the Bella Union Theater. It was
about the same as the Gem, only worse. They had a big cancan dance
at midnight about three times a week. Billy Nuckel [Bill Nuttall] ran
that show and he was a tough nut. Before he came to Deadwood he ran
a tough joint in Salt Lake City. He got so bad that the authorities gave
him just twenty-four hours to leave town. He said it would not take
him fifteen minutes if his mule didn't buck.*

*Mr. Languish brought a theatrical troupe to Deadwood from
Montana that summer. It was a pretty good outfit and they played in
the McDaniels Theater in Deadwood and also in Lead City, Central,
and Gayville.*[33]

Leander P. Richardson wrote of his first impressions of Deadwood:

*Down the side of a steep hill the road wound its way into the
lower end of Deadwood Gulch. The gulch is about ten miles long, and
very winding in its course. Through its bottom stretches a long line
of shanties and tents forming in all, four towns. At the lower end is
Montana City, then come Elizabethtown, Deadwood City, and
Gayeville (or Gaye City). Our train finally halted in Deadwood City,
and we were immediately surrounded by a a crowd of miners, gamblers,
and other citizens, all anxious to hear from the outer world. It was
Sunday afternoon, and all the miners in the surrounding neighborhoods
were spending the day in town. The long street was crowded with men
in every concievable garb. Taken as a whole, I never in my life saw so
many hardened and brutal-looking men together, although of course
there were a few better faces among them. Every alternate house was
a gambling saloon, and each of them was carrying on a brisk business.
In the middle of the street a little knot of men had gathered, and
were holding a prayer-meeting, which showed in sharp contrast to the
bustling activity of wickedness surrounding it.*[34]

White-Eye Anderson:

A day or so after we arrived in Deadwood, Calamity Jane came to my brother and me and said, "Boy's, I wish you would loan me twenty dollars. I can't do business in these old buckskins. I ain't got the show the other girls have." We gave her a twenty and then didn't see her for several days. When she did come back to camp she was all togged out in a good outfit of female clothes. She pulled up her dress, rolled down her stocking and took out a roll of greenbacks and gave us the twenty she had borrowed. She said she was doing a good business, but didn't express it in just that way...Calamity was a great friend in time of trouble. If anyone got sick or hurt, she nursed them until they got well. She knew how to be rough, but could also be kind and good.

...We had many callers at our camp; old friends, parties who had come into the hills with us, and others who stopped by just out of idle curiosity. California Joe came to our camp to see Wild Bill. His hair was long and a regular mat of cockleburs and he told us he was going to get him a squaw to comb his hair and get the burrs out.

The first thing Bill would do in the morning was empty his pistols in target practice at an old cottonwood tree that grew on the bank of the creek. Then he would take a stiff drink of whiskey and he would be ready for breakfast. We cut pieces of white paper about one inch square, stuck a tack in the center of the paper and then drove it into a board. We leaned the board against the tree and then stood off about twenty-five steps. Sometimes all our party would try it, but we would seldom make a center shot. When Wild Bill would shoot, the paper would almost always drop to the ground for the bullet would drive the tack into the board and there would be nothing to hold it up anymore. Sometimes Bill gave me lessons on how to make a quick draw-and-shoot.[35]

Leander P. Richardson:

I had been in town just a few moments when I met Charley Utter, better known in the West as "Colorado Charley," to whom I had a letter of introduction, and who at once invited me to share his camp while I remained in the region. On our way to his tent, we met J. B. Hickock, "Wild Bill," the hero of a hundred battles. Bill was Utter's "pardner," and I was introduced at once. Of course I had heard of him, the greatest scout in the West, but I was not prepared to find such a man as he proved to be. Most of the western scouts do not amount to much.

389

They do a great deal in the personal reminiscence way, but otherwise they are generally of the class described as "frauds." In "Wild Bill" I found a man who talked little and had done a great deal.

He was about six-feet two inches in height, and very powerfully built; his face was intelligent, his hair blonde, falling in long ringlets upon his broad shoulders; his eyes, blue and pleasant, looked one straight in the face when he talked; and his lips, thin and compressed, were only partly hidden by a straw colored moustache. His costume was a curiously blended union of the habiliments of the borderman and the drapery of the fashionable dandy. Beneath the skirts of his elaborately embroidered buckskin coat gleamed the handles of two silver-mounted revolvers, which were his constant companions. His voice was low and musical, but through its hesitation I could catch a ring of self-reliance and consciousness of strength. Yet he was most courteous man I had met on the plains.[36]

On July 17, 1876, James wrote the last letter he would ever send to his wife Agnes. Optimistic, upbeat, and looking to their future, yet in this letter James lies to her about his prospecting activities. There is not a shred of evidence that James ever dipped a gold pan in the waters of Whitewood Creek or Deadwood Creek or any other creek. Whatever fortune, if any, that James hoped to bring back from Deadwood to Agnes would be from the poker table or Faro bank. Understand also that James knew he was marrying a wealthy woman in her own right, and whose daughter Emma had recently married into the richest circus family in America. As a practical matter, Alice did not need James to make her fortune. She already had one.

[Punctuation added.]

Dead Wood Black hills, Dakota July 17th 1876

My own darling wife Agnes. I have but a few moments left before this letter Starts. I never was as well in my life but you would laugh to see me now. Just got in from Prospecting, will go a way again to morrow. will write In the morning but god nowse when It will start. my friend will take this to Cheyenne if he lives. I don't expect to hear from you but it's all the same. I no my Agnes and only live to love hur. never mind Pet, we will have a home yet, then we will be so happy. I am all most shure I will do well hear. the man is huring me. Good by Dear wife. Love to Emma.

JB Hickok
Wild Bill

More on the story of this remarkable letter and its last known whereabouts later in this book.

White-Eye Anderson:

Bill put in a good deal of his time playing poker and generally was very lucky. Usually he would go up to a saloon on on the corner of Main and Lee streets which was not very far from our camp. He told me not to get stuck on faro or poker as I was not smart enough to beat the game. Bill was generous and I know lots of times he would give fellows who were not in the game money "to eat on." One time Bill made a big winning at poker and he invited all of us—Charley Utter, Steve, my brother Charlie and myself—to a good Sunday dinner at Joe Gandolpho's Palace Restaurant, the best place in Deadwood to eat.

Seth Bullick, the hardware man, got in some nice sheet iron cook stoves and Bill bought one for our camp. I did most of the cooking and it was a dandy. After another big poker winning, he bought a whole wagonload of grub from a Nebraska rancher who had just come into town. He had a two-horse outfit loaded with bacon, hams, beans, dried fruit, corn meal, butter and eggs. I was in our camp at the time and Bill got up from his poker game and walked up Main street to where it intersects Lee. He shouted for me to come over and pilot the rancher to our camp and help him unload the grub. Then Bill went back to his poker game.

One evening after supper, Seth Bullick, Mr. Clark, a Mormon who had a big secondhand store, and several other prominent men of the camp came to see Wild Bill. They wanted him to be Marshal of the town and said if he would agree they would call a miner's meeting and get some kind of law and order established. Bill did not make them any promise and said he would let them know later in a week or so. Bill, Charley Utter and my brother had a big talk about it, but I did not know what conclusion they came to. It was not long after that Seth Bullick was appointed sheriff of Laurence County and Captain Willard was made U.S. deputy Marshal.[37]

William Secrest, the editor of *I Buried Hickok*, from which the above comments are drawn, correctly points out that Seth Bullock arrived in Deadwood on August 2, 1876, the day Hickok was shot and killed.

Perhaps Hickok bought the stove off of their incoming supply wagon of hardware that morning of August 2. More likely is that Anderson simply mis-remembered it and it was someone else from whom Hickok bought the stove.

Along the same line, and also corrected by editor Secrest, is the fact that Bullock, having arrived on August 2, could not have been one of the prominent men of the camp who asked Hickok to be Marshal. Secrest acknowledges that Anderson spent three years in the Black Hills, and recalling fifty years back some minor errors would be expected.

It is worth noting that some of the citizens of Deadwood were looking at that early date for some kind of law and order, and they thought they had found the answer in J. B. Hickok. Surely word of this meeting was spread in Deadwood, and must have increased the miner's anxiety that they might be facing Hickok sometime soon, especially the criminal element which abounded at that time on the streets of Deadwood.

Leander P. Richardson:

> On the following day I asked to see him use a pistol and he assented. At his request I tossed a tomato can about 15 feet into the air, both his pistols being in his belt when it left my hand. He drew one of them, and fired two bullets through the tin can before it struck the ground. Then he followed it along, firing as he went, until both weapons were empty. You have heard the expression "quick as lightning?" Well, that will describe "Wild Bill." He was noted all over the country for rapidity of motion, courage, and certainty of aim. Wherever he went he controlled the people around him, and many a quarrel has been ended by his simple announcement "This has gone far enough."
>
> Every morning, just before breakfast, he used to crawl out, clad in his shirt, trousers, and boots, tie his hair in a knot at the back of his head, shove his big revolver inside the waistband of his trousers, and run like a sprinter down the gulch to the nearest saloon. In a few minutes he would come strolling back, with a cocktail or two stowed away where it would do the most good, and would complete his toilet.[37B]

White-Eye was eye-witness to the Monday, August 1 poker game between McCall and Hickok that may have created the animosity that McCall carried over into Tuesday, August 2. Though White-Eye recalls the Monday late-evening poker game happening at George Shingle's saloon, Carl Mann testified that the Monday night poker game between Hickok and McCall took place at his saloon, the Number 10. White-Eye said:

> *The night before he was killed, Bill in was in a poker game at Shingle's saloon on the corner of Lee and Main streets. Shingle was a friend of Bill's who had come in on our train from Cheyenne. There were three men in the game besides Bill. One was named Jack McCall, but the other two I did not know. When McCall started to play he gave the bartender his sack of dust, saying there was an ounce in it and to give him chips in that amount. The bartender gave him $18 worth of chips and he sat down.*
>
> *I went down to the saloon about 11 o'clock to bring Bill back to camp. There was something the matter with his eyes and he could not see good in the dark. Some said he was moon-blind and he always had one of us come and lead him back to camp at bedtime. I waited almost an hour before the poker game broke up. Bill had won all of McCall's chips, but when he went to cash them there was only $11 worth of dust in the sack.*
>
> *"The next time you play with me," Bill told McCall, "you better not call for more than your sack or there will be trouble." McCall replied that he thought there was an ounce in the sack.*
>
> *"I'll keep the sack and call it even," replied Bill. "The sack is worth about four-bits and I need a sack to keep my dust in."*
>
> *"No," replied McCall, "I want my sack back and if you won't let me have it tonight, I'll get it tomorrow."*
>
> *Bill wouldn't give him his sack, but he asked if he was broke. When McCall replied that he was, Bill handed him a dollar saying "This is to get your breakfast with." We then went to camp, got a lunch, and went to bed.*[37C]

As noted above, Carl Mann remembered the Monday night game was played at his place, the #10 Saloon. Mann said:

> *...saw McCall only twice before this happened, and in this house. Bill was there and McCall weighed out some gold dust to get some poker chips to play with Bill and the others. McCall won $23 or $24. Am not certain of the amount. He then went out and came back and played again. After playing a short time he took a purse from his pocket and bet five or six dollars and Bill bet twenty or twenty-five more. McCall shoved his purse further onto the board and says "I call you." Bill won and they came to the bar and asked me to weigh out $20*

or $25. The purse was $16.50 short. Bill said "You owe me $16.50." McCall said "Yes" and went out. He came back shortly after and Bill said "Did I break you?" McCall said "Yes." Bill gave him all the change he had, 75 cents, to buy his supper with and told him if he quit winner in the game he was playing he would give him more. McCall would not take the money and went out in fifteen to twenty minutes.[38]

Though the versions of Carl Mann and White-Eye Anderson differ as to the location, they both follow the general theme that McCall bet more than he had money to back it up, then when J. B. Hickok found out he was broke, he offered McCall money (White-Eye said one dollar, Carl Mann said seventy-five cents). Carl Mann's statement is from the Yankton trial several months after the event. White-Eye's statement was probably made about twenty-four years after the event, so White-Eye perhaps mis-remembered the location, but not the details of the event.

August 2, 1876

On Tuesday, August 2, 1876, J. B. Hickok probably followed the routine he had maintained for the almost three weeks he had been in the Black Hills and Deadwood. He would have practiced his shooting a bit that morning on the big old cottonwood tree near Whitewood Creek and their camp. That morning he might have taken a bath and washed his hair. In a town and a time when a man's bath might be closer to a monthly routine or weekly routine than a daily one, Hickok's penchant for cleanliness was an anomaly. Then around noon or a bit after, he might shuffle down to George Shingle's saloon at the corner of Main and Lee Streets, one of his favorites, or perhaps to the Senate saloon, or another favorite, the Number 10 Saloon, owned by his friend Carl Mann. On this Tuesday he decided on the Number 10, and as he entered it he found Carl Mann, Charley Rich, and Captain Massie already seated and ready for an afternoon of poker. Harry Young was working the bar and keeping the gamblers in poker chips. Next door the under-construction and unfinished Bella Union Theatre was connected with the Number 10 Saloon by an open, arched doorway. In the Bella Union was eighteen-year-old Peter LaFlemme, a laborer doing some kind of work in the new building.

Carl Mann, the co-owner of the Number 10 Saloon along with Bill Nuttall, knew Hickok back in his Hays and Abilene days. Charley Rich was the youngest at the table. It has been reported that he was

#4221

This photograph was taken in the spring of 1877. The frame building with four windows next to the Bella Union was occupied through most of 1876 by the Number 10 saloon, where James was murdered that August. The building holds an auction house in this photo. Delmonico's restaurant has taken over the building that held the IXL restaurant in 1876, Deadwood's first restaurant. *Author's collection.*

twenty in 1876. Yet his gravestone in Ohio shows he was born July 28, 1859. If that is correct he was seventeen (barely) when he sat at the table with Mann, Massie, and Hickok on August 2. Recall that he tried to flip over a poker table at the Gold Room in Cheyenne when he was losing, and Doc Howard was there then to stop him. He would have been fifteen then. So either the birth date on his gravestone is wrong, and he was actually born in 1856, or he must have been big for his age. Charley Rich was a twin, the other twin dying at birth. He was the oldest of thirteen children. His daughter recalled that he told his children that Wild Bill was a fine man. He told them about Charley Utter as well. She stated, "My father never owned a gun in his life. I don't even know if he knew how to shoot." Modern descendants of Charley Rich have genealogical proof that the Rich family is collaterally related to J. B. Hickok, through James' great-grandfather, Aaron Hickok.[39]

Captain William Massie was about forty-seven years old in 1876. He was born near Franklin, Missouri in 1829. From his earliest years he wanted to be a riverboat captain, and that is what he spent his entire life doing. In 1861, Massie was captain of the steamboat that brought the first letters to St. Joseph to be transported to California on the Pony Express. Massie found himself in Deadwood that summer of 1876 to pan for gold and play poker. Like Hickok, he probably played more poker than anything else he did in the Black Hills.

Unknown to these three men as they started their afternoon game of poker, they were about to be participants in one of the most iconic moments in American frontier history.

As Hickok entered the saloon he noted that Charley Rich was sitting in the one chair that placed his back against the wall. He asked Rich to give him that seat, which Charley Rich refused to do. Hickok sat down, but a few minutes later he asked for that chair again, and again was refused by Rich. Hickok was good-naturedly chided by the other two players that he had nothing to worry about. He then let it go and found himself for the rest of the day sitting with Charley Rich against the wall on his right, Carl Mann on his left, and Captain Massie straight in front of him. This gave Hickok a clear view of the front door over Massie's shoulder, but the rear door was not in his view.

The afternoon poker game progressed for several hours. Later in the day George Shingle entered the saloon to weigh his gold dust, probably in anticipation of joining the game in progress. At about three p.m., Jack McCall opened the front door of the Number 10 Saloon and stepped in. Hickok undoubtedly recognized him from the previous night's poker game, but he did not perceive him as a threat. Charlie Rich had just dealt the table their hands, and Hickok was studying his cards. George Shingle was weighing his gold dust on the scales at the end of the bar. Harry Young had just returned, or was about to return, behind the bar after handing Hickok $50 in chips. Laborer Joseph Mitchell was at the rear of the Number 10 Saloon, installing wainscoting.

After entering the saloon, Jack McCall walked to the end of the bar as if he was going to weigh gold dust on the scale. As he approached the rear of the saloon, he apparently hesitated for a moment. At the same time, Captain Massie laid his cards on the table, which drew Hickok's full attention. At this precise moment, McCall left the scale and moved towards the rear door, out of Hickok's vision. Hickok tossed his cards on the table and said good-naturedly, "The old duffer, he broke me on that hand." It was the last thing James Butler Hickok ever said. Suddenly McCall moved within two or three feet behind Hickok, pulled his pistol from his loose-fitting jacket, and shouting, "Damn you, take that!", he shot Hickok in the back of the head at point-blank range. The projectile killed J. B. Hickok instantly, and after exiting, it lodged in the wrist of Captain Massie. Hickok was perfectly still for a moment after being shot, and then slumped dead to the floor from his stool.

Immediately after shooting Hickok, McCall began backing towards the rear door of the saloon, at one point shouting, "Come on, you sons of bitches." He pointed his pistol to the rear of the room and pulled the trigger. The pistol didn't fire. He pointed his gun at George Shingle, who had moved to where Hickok was on the floor, and shot at him, but the gun misfired again. At this point Charley Rich, Captain Massie, Harry Young, and George Shingle went out the front door of the saloon. Carl Mann remained. For a third time, McCall tried to fire his gun, this time at Mann. Again it misfired. Mann moved to find his weapon behind the bar, but by this time McCall had left the saloon through the rear door and was attempting to make his escape.

McCall tried to mount his horse, but the loose saddle slipped to the side when he stepped into the stirrup, and he fell to the ground. At this point he decided to forego righting the saddle and instead try to make his getaway on foot. Peter LaFlemme, the laborer next door in the Bella Union, recalled years later for reporter Joe Koller:

> *Saloon No. 10 was next to the dance hall. An arched doorway connected the two places. LaFlemme heard voices and knew there was a card game in progress. Suddenly came the shot. It had been fired in the saloon. The lumber walls trembled with concussion. Peter LaFlemme, age 18, got behind a post. He realized in a few seconds that there would be no exchange of shots so he moved toward the archway to see what had happened. All his life he was to remember the details of the Wild Bill death scene.*

Card players were on their feet. There was shock and hate in their eyes and strained attitude. McCall backing towards the street had his gun on them, mouthing threats, and they stood with their hands up, their glances darting from the killer to the victim of the assassin. The drama of the occasion held Peter LaFlemme in its grasp. To watch Wild Bill's body slump as tension relaxed, and see his arm and hand slide limply down and hang there, was uncanny to behold. The hand that held no equal in draw or trigger speed was stilled forever.

There was defiant action then. Men jumped to steady Bill's figure in the chair. McCall's gun had failed to explode three times in succession. Bartender and players chased after McCall as he raced to escape.[40]

White-Eye, working close by the Number 10 Saloon that day, recalled, "I heard the shot and someone at the door of the saloon 'Wild Bill is killed!'"[41]

In Deadwood time stood still for a few seconds, then pandemonium broke out. James Butler Hickok, the legendary Wild Bill Hickok, was dead. White-Eye saw Jack McCall running fast up the street with a pistol in his hand. White-Eye tried to get a shot at him, but the street was filled with people running every which direction, many with a pistol in their own hand, looking for their own open shot at McCall. Because there were so many people crowding the street, no one would take a shot at McCall for fear of hitting an innocent party.

While on the run, McCall tried to shoot several people but his caps were bad and the shots would not go off. Finally, the crowd cornered him at or near Shoudy's Meat Market and he was captured. Someone shouted "Bring a rope!" While the crowd prepared to string McCall up, an odd thing happened, an event that probably saved McCall's life, if only temporarily. Almost at the same time that a rope was being thrown over a tall, strong tree branch, a rider came flying down Main Street, causing a commotion. The Mexican rider held the decapitated head of a dead Indian by the hair, telling the crowd on Main Street that the hills around Deadwood were alive with Indians. He said they had already captured Crook City and were intent on wiping out Deadwood Gulch.

The hanging was postponed as the town prepared to grapple with an imminent Indian attack, that luckily never came to be. The Indian head was later purchased by an ambitious entrepreneur who placed it in a room at the Wide West Saloon and charged ten cents for people to view it.

At the #10 Saloon, steps were being taken to take care of the body of J. B. Hickok. Ellis T. "Doc" Peirce, a local barber working at Flaherty's barbershop across the street from the Number 10 Saloon was one of the first on the scene. Peirce had received some limited medical training before the Civil War, then served as a surgeon's assistant during that war. Though there were several practicing physicians in Deadwood at the time, Peirce became the de facto doctor and coroner for the crime scene, probably just because he showed up right away. Peirce later described the crime scene:

> *Now, in regard to the position of Bill's body, when they unlocked the door for me to get his body, he was lying on his side, with his knees drawn up, just as he slid off his stool. We had no chairs in those days—and his fingers were still crimped from holding his poker hand. Charlie Rich, who sat beside him, said he never saw a muscle move...When Bill was shot through the head he bled out quickly, and when he was laid out he looked like a wax figure. I have seen many dead men on the field of battle and in civil life, but Wild Bill was the prettiest corpse I have ever seen. His long moustache was attractive, even in death, and his long tapering fingers looked like marble.*[42]

White-Eye Anderson recalled what happened next:

> *I went to where Bill was killed and helped to take the body to camp. They had locked the doors of the Number Ten saloon and sent word to Charley Utter who was with my brother at our camp on Whitewood Creek. They got a man—I don't remember his name, but they called him "Doc" and he was a barber—to go with them. A Mr. Rutherford, who had a one-horse express wagon, brought the body to our camp in his wagon and Doc and the two Charley's took his boots off and fixed the body in good shape...Back at camp we had a carpenter make Bill a coffin out of rough pine lumber. He was a large man, over six feet tall and broad shouldered. The coffin was covered with black cloth on the outside and white cloth on the inside and it looked pretty good for a homemade coffin. We put Bill's old buffalo rifle in the coffin and Charley Utter put in a few other trinkets.*[43]

In the meantime, the frenzied residents of Deadwood had confirmed that there was no Indian attack imminent. At least some of them must have realized that hanging McCall might be problematic in an unorganized territory with no law or government of its own. Therefore they decided to put together an impromptu and improvised court of their own. Judge William Kuykendall wrote of what happened next:

> *That night [August 2] one hundred and five business men met behind closed doors in Langrishes Theater. To observe the proper formalities, I was to act as chairman. After stating the object of the meeting to be the organization of a second miner's court to try the case the next day, I stated that if any man present were not in harmony with the movement then was the time for him to leave. All remained. It was decided the jury should be selected by making out a list of the twenty names of miners from each of the three mining districts, the name of each to be written on a separate slip of paper and well shaken in a hat, the twelve drawn from there to be the jury, lists to be made by a committee to be selected by the meeting when court convened next morning. On motion I was elected Judge, Issac Brown, sheriff; John Swift, clerk; Colonel May, Prosecuting Attorney, and Judge Miller, attorney for the prisoner. Both were able lawyers at the time, although without clients, for there was no law in force then or for months afterward.*
>
> *While willing to assume the responsibility, I refused to serve unless all those present agreed to be present with their revolvers when the court convened to see that a proper jury committee was selected and to remain through the trial and see the proceedings through to the end. I told them that if any of them would not do this, to retire immediately. Again all remained and by a rising unanimous vote pledged themselves.*
>
> *When the court convened the committee and jury were selected and sworn according to program. Officers and everybody except the prisoner were armed, and the theater was packed with men. The prisoner was brought in and entered a plea of not guilty...the trial proceeding under all the forms of law. Evidence of the killing by the prisoner developed an absolutely cold-blooded, cowardly assassination without any warning or extenuating circumstances whatever. Wild Bill had met his death while playing cards, the muzzle of the pistol being within six inches of the back of his head, the bullet coming out near his nose and wounding the man he was playing with in the arm.*
>
> *Evidence showed no provocation whatever and no motive save a love for notoriety, coupled with a full glass of whiskey taken in a saloon opposite, from which he could see the two players and the bartender, who were the only persons in the place. At noon the sheriff informed me that*

he had carefully listed those present who were in the meeting the night before and besides the officers only five had been present at the trial. For a moment I lost my faith in humanity. He said there could only be a verdict—"guilty," to which I replied that I would do the sentencing in short order and expected him to be as expeditious with the immediate hanging. He assured me he would.

The prisoner, by way of bravado, made a statement that he killed Wild Bill because the latter killed his brother. This I knew was false. After arguments of counsel I charged the jury about sundown, and as the theater could not be used that night, the saloon where the killing had occurred was selected as the place to receive the verdict, the prisoner being confined in a cabin immediately in its rear, in front of which stood a large pine tree having a limb just right for the hanging. Conferring with the sheriff, we agreed that he should select fifteen of his and my nerviest friends, arm them, draw a chalk line across the floor, leaving a few feet in rear for the court proceedings, place three of the men at the alley nearby, to halt and, if necessary, shoot anybody attempting to pass through, it being the only place accessible to the hanging from the street.

Then we would bring in the prisoner and the other twelve men, seat him between me and the clerk, have the men line up with a revolver in each hand back of the chalk mark (as that eighty foot room would pack full of men) and then bring in the jury. When the prisoner was seated, his feet beat a tattoo on the floor, and his teeth were chattering. He was a pitiable object of abject fear. The outside space in the room filled with men even up to the chalk line and a pin could have been heard to drop.

When the jury was in place I asked the foreman if they had agreed on a verdict. He answered yes. "Mr. Foreman," I said "you will pass the verdict to the clerk, who will read it." The verdict was "We, the jury, find the defendant not guilty."

McCall hurried out through the back door and was soon on a swift horse, fleeing the country in the darkness with California Joe and Texas Jack, friends of Wild Bill in hot pursuit. He escaped, was arrested a few days afterward in Laramie City, Wyoming, taken to Yankton by the United States Marshal, indicted by the United States Grand Jury, and hanged for the crime. While I was a member of the Legislature of Dakota, I was shown the four posts where the hanging occurred.[44]

On August 17, 1876, the Cheyenne *Weekly Leader* summed up the general feeling in the Dakotas:

Wild Bill's Murderer Acquitted

Bill Sutherland [McCall's alias], *who shot Wild Bill Hickok down in cold blood on the 8th inst., was tried by jury and acquitted. The trial was in regular form, but our correspondent characterizes it as a regular farce.*

August 3, James Butler Hickok was buried. The previous evening Charley Utter had gone to the offices of the *Black Hills Pioneer* and arranged to have a funeral notice printed inside a black border:

Funeral Notice

Died, in Deadwood, Black Hills, August 2, 1876, from the effects of a pistol shot, J. B. Hickok (Wild Bill), formerly of Cheyenne, Wyoming. Funeral Services will be held at Charles Utter's Camp, on Thursday afternoon, August 3, 1876, at 3 o'clock P.M. All are respectfully invited to attend.

White-Eye recalled the funeral and burial:

Mr. Rutherford brought his body to the grave in his little express wagon. There were no pallbearers that I could see. A man I didn't know read the Episcopal funeral service. There were six or seven women in the procession, including Calamity Jane. I remember Jane gathered some little blue flowers that grew beside the road and threw them into the grave before they filled it with sod. Some of the girls that were there were named Big Dollie, Tid Bit, Dirty Em, Smooth Bore, and Sizzling Kate. A large pine tree grew at the head of the grave. I think Bill was the second or third person buried in Deadwood cemetery.[45]

Leander P. Richardson, another attendant and eyewitness at Hickok's funeral, wrote his observations:

The next day, "Colorado Charley" took charge of the remains of the great scout, and announced that the funeral would occur at his camp. The body was clothed in a full suit of broad cloth, the hair brushed back from the pallid cheek. Beside the dead hero lay his rifle, which was buried with him. The funeral ceremony was brief and touching, hundreds of rough miners standing around the bier with bowed heads and tear-dimmed eye,—for with the better class "Wild Bill" had been a great favorite. At the close of the ceremony the coffin was lowered into a new made grave on the hill-side—the first in Deadwood. And so ended the life of "Wild Bill," a man whose supreme physical courage had endeared him to nearly all with whom he came in contact..."[46]

White Eye Anderson described above the graveside funeral service, and Leander Richardson described the funeral that took place at their camp.

Writer O. W. Coursey, writing some fifty years after the event, stated that there were pallbearers at Hickok's funeral. He listed them as Bill Hillman, John Oyster, Charley Rich, Jerry Lewis, Charles Young, and Tom Dosier. Coursey does not state his source for this information.[47]

Hickok's first grave marker, a tree stump at the head of his grave, was inscribed: *A brave man, the victim of an assassin / J.B. Hickok (Wild Bill), age 39 years / Murdered by Jack McCall, Aug.2, 1876*

On August 7, 1876, Agnes sent another letter to Polly and Celinda Hickok. Ironically, she received his letter dated July 17, 1876, from Deadwood at the very moment that she was writing to Polly and Celinda. Though she stated she would forward to Polly and Celinda this latest letter, she did not. Agnes kept it after she found that it was the last letter she would ever receive from her husband, or perhaps there was something in James' letter itself that caused Agnes to hold onto it. However, as of this August 7 date, none of the three knew James was dead.

[Punctuation added]
Cincinnati August 7th 1876
Dear Mother and Sister

Your kind and welcome letter has this morning been handed to me by the letter carrier, and while I was reading it he handed me another one from my Husband witch I will send with this so you can see where he is and what he is doing. Emma so far is well: but I am afraid that I will not be able to come and see you all this Summer as by the time that Emma gits through with her confinement and is able to be around again, James will send for me to come out West. You ask what sort of an Actor James is: it would be hard to tel as he does not like it: but His wife is a good Actress as I plaid in the German Language in Berlin Prussia before the King about two Dozen of times and can git five thousand Dollars a year and all expenses paid but my Husband says he did not Marrie me to work. He only wants me to please him and not the Public: and that is what I am trying to doo; and iff duty and Love can doo it I will succeed and Dear Mother I hope that you will live to see me in a good Home and happy, me and my Daughter.

Love to all. Answer soon. Look for pictures from me.[48]

The first newspaper to report the murder of Wild Bill Hickok was the *Black Hills Pioneer* on August 5, 1876:

ASSASSINATION OF WILD BILL

He is Shot Through The Head by John McCall while Unconscious of Danger—Arrest, Trial, and Discharge of the Assassin, who Claims to Have Avenged a Brother's Death in Killing Wild Bill.

On Wednesday about three o'clock the report was started that J. B. Hickok (Wild Bill) was killed. On repairing to the hall of Nuttall & Mann it was ascertained that the report was too true. We found the remains of Wild Bill lying on the floor. The murderer, Jack McCall, was captured after a lively chase by many of our citizens, and taken to a building at the lower end of the city and a guard placed over him. As soon as this was accomplished a coroner's jury was summoned, with C. H. Sheldon foreman who after hearing all the evidence, which was to the effect that while Wild Bill and others were seated at a table playing cards, Jack McCall walked in and around directly back of his victim and when within three feet of him raised his revolver, and exclaiming, "Damn you, take that" fired, the ball entering the back of the head and coming out at the center of the right cheek, causing instant death, rendered a verdict in accordance with the above facts. Preparations for a trial were then made by calling a meeting of citizens at the theatre building...

At two o'clock the trial was commenced, and lasted till six. The evidence in the case was the same as that before the coroner's jury, so far as the prosecution was concerned. The defense was that the deceased, at some place in Kansas, killed the prisoner's brother, for which he killed the deceased. The Jury after being out an hour and thirty minutes, returned the following verdict: We the jury find Mr. John McCall NOT GUILTY.

Charles Whitehead, Foreman

J.J. Bump, J.H.Thompson, J.F. Cooper, K.E.Towle, L.A.Judd, John Mann, L.D. Bokaw, S.S. Hopkins, Alex Travis, J.E. Thompson, Ed Burke, Jurors.

Thus ended the scenes of the day that settled a matter of life and death with one living, whose life was in the hands of twelve fellow men whose duty it was to decide upon the guilt or innocence of the accused, charged with the murder of Wild Bill, who while it was in progress, was being laid in the cold, cold ground: in the valley of Whitewood, by kind hands that were ever ready to administer to his sufferings while living, and ready to perform the painful duty of laying him in his last resting place.

The Cheyenne *Leader* had the story of Wild Bill's demise front page by August 12. By August 15, the whole nation was reading the news. What a summer it was for the country. On June 25, the unthinkable happened, as Custer and the 7th Cavalry went down in ignominious death and defeat at the Little Big Horn. On July 4, the nation celebrated its Centennial, a 100-year-celebration that was sweeter still because it had never been a foregone conclusion that the country would make it that far, and then on August 2, a shock wave rolls across the country: James Butler Hickok, aka Wild Bill, probably the nation's first living legend since George Washington, and well-known across the country, was shot dead by an assassin in the Number 10 Saloon, killed before he even reached forty.

The Kansas City *Times* wrote a proper obituary for J. B. Hickok, one that reflected the respect and affection the people of Kansas City had for him:

It appears that Bill died in just the way and manner he did not wish to die—that is, with his boots on. His life during the past five or six years has been one of constant watchfulness and expectation, as more than one reckless frontiersman had coolly contracted to take his life. But Bill was never off guard, and woe unto the wretched devil who failed to "get the drop" on the long haired William. More than one fool has had a bullet crushing through his brains from the ever ready pistol of this cool silent desperado...

William Hickok was a quiet, courteous gentleman when sober, and seldom allowed himself to drink to excess. He dressed well, carried a small, fancy cane in his hand, and rather avoided than sought company. While he was a frontiersman in every sense of the word, he was not an Indian scout. He was well known in nearly every frontier town, and seldom went out on the trail. Gen. Custer speaks well of him...He has many warm friends in this city, as well as all over the West, who will regret to hear of his tragic end, the end he has so long been expecting.

The Ellis County *Star*, weighing in for Hays City on August 17, filed a report that surely reflected the feelings of other one-time, end-of-the-track railroad towns like Junction City, Abilene, and Ellsworth:

We learn from recent dispatches that Mr. J. B. Hickok, (Wild Bill), well known to the older citizens of Hays City, was shot in the head and instantly killed, by a man named Bill Sutherland, while playing cards in a saloon in Deadwood Gulch, Wyoming. From the report it seems that Bill had killed a brother of Sutherland's in this city, several years ago, and in revenge the latter shot Bill, taking him unawares.

This is the long-looked for ending of the career of one who deserved a better fate. For nearly his whole life time Bill was on the frontier, a portion of the time acting as scout, and then as an officer of the law in some frontier town. He was elected Sheriff of this county in 1868, and did good service in keeping order. While here he killed several men; but all their acquaintances agreed that he was justified in so doing. He never provoked a quarrel, and was a generous, gentlemanly fellow. In person he was over six feet tall, broad-shouldered, and a specimen of perfect manhood throughout. He was a dead shot, wonderfully quick in drawing and shooting, the latter faculty filling his enemies with a very wholesome respect, when in his presence. Living as he did in constant fear of his life, he always kept his revolvers with him, and had the fellow that shot him given him a fair fight, and not taken the cowardly advantage that he did, Wild Bill would not have been killed.

The nation mourned J. B. Hickok's passing, yet for his family, a proud family who always supported James, but worried about him, his death was particularly painful, because the Hickok family, neither his mother nor any of his three brothers and two sisters, had seen or had direct communication with James in almost seven years. They read about him in the papers, and they knew some aspects of his life from the news.

On August 17, 1876, James' sister Lydia wrote to one of her two brothers—Horace or Lorenzo—that still lived in Troy Grove, and pleaded for confirmation of what she was reading about her brother, James. At this time, Lydia was married and lived in Kansas. Inexplicably, she called the brother she is writing to "Bill." (punctuation added):

Thursday
Dear Brother

Barnes has been in town to day and seen in the tri-weekly Inter Ocean an account of James B. Hickoks death. Is it true? It seems awful hard as to be true but I want you to write and tell all you have heard or all that you do or hear about it. Oh Bill I do wish I could be there with Mother. Now if this is true it will nearly kill her. Oh dear I feel so bad down here alone. I would much rather he had been killed with Custer. Tell me what his wife writes about it, and give me her address. I have felt so hard towards her because I thought Jim loved her better than he did us and now it is all over with the Poor boy. I cant feel any rest till I hear from you dear brother and how Mother is. I wish I was up there. I feel so awful Bill but it may not be so after all, tho Barnes said the paper gave names, date and all particulars but he could not get the paper to bring home to me. I am so anxious as I have been most down sick ever since Barnes got better. He is not well yet. Baby is well. Brother if Ma gets sick you must let me know right off. My head is bursting. Good night.

Dear Mother, there is few women love their brothers as I do even if I do not always show it. I feel most crazy about Jim.

Write soon
Your sister
Lydia [49]

407

Twenty years later, in 1896, Lydia, in a printed article, recalled the day her mother Polly found out that her son James had been killed. As per her above letter, Lydia was married and living in Kansas in 1876, so what she is probably remembering is what her sister Celinda told her about what happened that day in Troy Grove. Note that the editor changed her deceased brothers name to "Bill," rather than James, apparently thinking that this would keep his readers from becoming confused as to why the family called him James:

> *I remember the day the paper came with the news of Bill's murder. Mother had been a sufferer of inflammatory rheumatism for two years before that and had not taken a step for eighteen months. My sister [Celinda] was standing at the gate when a neighbor came by and brought the Chicago paper, giving an account of Bill's death. He handed it to my sister. She took it and saw the headlines, but did not read all of it. She folded it up and hurried into the house, hiding the paper in the kitchen behind the mirror on the shelf. Then composing herself she went in where Mother was sitting. "Mother" she said, "I am going over to the store a minute and will be right back." She put on her bonnet and ran to the little store about two hundred yards away to tell one of my brothers. All came back to the house together. When they entered the sitting room, there sat Mother, the newspaper lying at her side, while the blood from a hemorrhage of the lungs dyed the front part of her dress. "I saw you get the paper, Lydia [actually Celinda] she said, "and when you did not bring it in, I went and got it." She never fully recovered from the blow, and she died two years later, still mourning Bill's terrible death.*[50]

Was there a conspiracy to murder J. B. Hickok at the Number 10 Saloon on August 2, 1876? On August 3, 1876, the jury in the trial of Jack McCall in Deadwood declared him "not guilty" of murdering James Butler Hickok. The outcry was immediate. Judge Kuykendall was flabbergasted. He was so sure of a guilty verdict, he had told the sheriff to make the hanging quick. Prosecuting Attorney George May was outraged. He was sure the jury was made up mostly of people that wanted Hickok dead, and may have paid McCall to carry it out. To May, nothing else could explain the verdict, and the fact that the jury had simply ignored all of the empirical evidence indicting McCall. It appears that McCall stayed in the

Deadwood area for a few days, until California Joe found him and made it clear in no uncertain terms that he must leave Deadwood, or else.

McCall left Deadwood and went to Cheyenne, and from there to Laramie City, Wyoming. Attorney George May followed McCall to Laramie City. McCall's new-found notoriety must have made him brag about killing Hickok, especially after heavy drinking. George May brought deputy United States Marshal Balcome one evening to a saloon that May knew McCall was frequenting in Laramie City. After overhearing McCall all but admit killing Hickok, the officer arrested McCall on August 29, 1876. Without George May's tenacity, McCall probably would not have been caught. When McCall was caught, May wrote to Agnes Hickok and asked for funds to prosecute the murderer of her husband and seek justice for James, and for her as his wife. Agnes did not respond. Tragically, May was never able to prosecute McCall in court, as he died of a sudden and unknown disease on November 21, at the Merchant's Hotel in Yankton where he was staying. The local bar association paid off his debts and set up his funeral.[51]

In Laramie City, McCall was examined by Judge Blair. He confessed to the judge that he had committed the murder. On September 1, the Cheyenne *Daily Leader* ran a report stating authorities believed that McCall might have killed someone else after he shot Hickok: "The reason for this belief is that when McCall was tried in Deadwood he had but forty three dollars on his person, while on the very next day he was sporting a costly gold watch and chain, and had also a large sum of money. An investigation is now being made, and startling developments may be expected."

In Yankton on October 18, McCall was indicted for murder. On November 9, McCall and his cellmate tried to break out of jail. They attacked the jailer, and were close to gaining their freedom, when the sheriff and an assistant arrived with pistols drawn, thwarting their plan.

The next day, McCall decided to turn state's evidence. He alleged that John Varnes had paid him money to kill Hickok. The broad implication to be drawn was that Varnes had instructed McCall to claim that Hickok had killed his brother back in Kansas. If so, that ruse got McCall acquitted at the Deadwood trial, but would not play in Yankton.[52]

The Cheyenne *Weekly Leader* of November 23, quoting the Black Hills *Pioneer* of November 11, reported action taken on McCall's indictment of John Varnes:

> *Wild Bill—A Strange Sequel to the Tragedy. The Black Hills Pioneer of November 11th says: From Mr. Sheldon was learned the following facts regarding the Wild Bill tragedy: A deputy United States Marshal with a posse of five men have started in pursuit of John Varnes, now out on the "new stampede," who is charged with having procured the death of Wild Bill by paying a sum of money to Jack McCall alias Sutherland, for the committing of the deed. It appears that some time ago Wild Bill and Varnes had a difficulty in Denver, and the animosity between the two was augmented by a dispute over a game of poker at the "Senate" saloon in this city, a short time previous to the death of Wild Bill at which time Bill interfered in a dispute with Varnes and another man. Bill covered him with his pistol and arrogated to himself the position of umpire, after which friends interfered and ended the difficulty. It is not necessary to speak of the arrest and trial of the murderer McCall; suffice it to say that he was arrested by the United States authorities at Cheyenne and taken to Yankton for trial. It appears that he now desires to turn state's evidence, and charges Varnes with having paid him money to murder Wild Bill.*

In the next issue of the Cheyenne *Weekly Leader*, November 30, the story was updated:

> *Wild Bill's Murderer. The trial of McCall, for the murder of Wild Bill, was set for Nov. 27th , at Yankton, D. T., but owing to the length of time which will be consumed in getting witnesses from the Hills, the trial will probably not begin until Dec. 1st. As previously stated, a party of men were sent to Deadwood to arrest one Varnes, who is said to be an old enemy of Hickok's, and to have bribed McCall to kill him. This witness is undoubtedly on his way to Yankton.*

Curiously, in the very same issue of the *Weekly Leader*, November 30, the paper printed this retraction:

> *A Hoax—This is the way the* Black Hills Pioneer *ventilates the yarn, published in our last issue, in which the name of John Varnes was connected, turns out to be a falsification. The only foundation which the story appears to have had was that the murderer made some such statements upon his trial, with some hope of excusing his own great crime; but as he before had made so many varying and different*

statements, even his own attorney refused to take cognizance of this latter subterfuge. Where our own informant received his information we do not know, but we do regret sincerely if the name of an innocent man has been coupled with McCall's atrocious deed.

This above retraction by the *Daily Leader* was in response to the below report in the Black Hills Pioneer of November 18, that included the very unusual written denial of a deputy United States Marshal that any warrant had been issued for John Varnes:

> *Wild Bill: The sensation story about Wild Bill's murder, published in our last issue, in which the name of John Varnes was connected, turns out to be falsification. The only foundation which the story seems to have had was that the murderer made some such statements upon his trial, with some hope of excusing his own great crime, but as he before had made so many varying and different statements, his own attorney refused to take cognizance of this last subterfuge. Where our informant received his information we do not know, but we do regret, sincerely, if the name of an innocent man has been coupled with the McCall's atrocious deed. The following will explain itself:*

> *Deadwood, Nov. 12th, 1876*
> *I, the undersigned, do declare that the statement published in the* Pioneer *of the 11th inst., is a fabrication cut from whole cloth as no warrant has been issued for John Varnes.*

> *H.C. Ash,*
> *Dep'y U.S. Marshal for Dakota.*

It may be that Deputy U. S. Marshal Ash responded so quickly and so publicly denying the reports that a posse of which he was in charge was seeking John Varnes, because his targeted audience was as much the governor of Dakota Territory, John Pennington, as it was the people of Deadwood. Pennington had made clear that he believed that people who lived in the Dakotas who were charged and then acquitted by a jury should not be subjected to "double jeopardy" by being charged for the same crime again, notwithstanding the empirical fact that no controlling law or judicial system existed in Deadwood at that time. Though his opinion did not carry the weight of law, it did influence cases such as McCall's. When McCall's lawyers sought clemency for McCall by appealing to President Grant, Pennington's signature was among those on the petition. On January 22, 1877, the Black Hills Pioneer ran a story by their correspondent in Yankton that laid out Governor Pennington's beliefs, and strongly implicated that the deputy U. S. Marshal was compliant to those beliefs and therefore was not pursuing Varnes because of them, which further implies that Marshal Ash published a false statement, above, claiming that no warrant had been sworn out for John Varnes:

> *By the way, the Deputy U.S. Marshal arrived the other day, and I was surprised to find that he brought no prisoners, but the reason, I have no doubt, was that he understood the views of Governor Pennington with regard to such matters. In a conversation yesterday the governor said that he was opposed to the re-arrest of persons tried and acquitted in the Hills, and thought as we were trespassers, we should abide by the laws made unto our selves, and persons tried under these laws should not have their lives the second time put in jeopardy for the same offence.*

There were many people in Deadwood in the summer of 1876 who thought the jury in the August 3 trial was tainted at best, and conspiratorial partners in murder at the worst. Many voiced evidence that the better citizens of Deadwood recognized that Deadwood could not continue down the path of having the most important and influential people in town be gunfighters, gamblers, saloonkeepers, and prostitutes, and a populace whose primary driving forces were greed, lust, and alcohol. In many ways, the Deadwood of 1876 recalled Hays City of 1869 or Abilene of 1871: doomed unless someone could restore order. As in Hays and Abilene, that someone the citizens of Deadwood sought was J. B. Hickok.

The most reliable observer of Hickok and his activities during the almost three weeks he spent in Deadwood before his untimely death at age thirty-nine is White-Eye Anderson. Not only do his statements about Hickok and the events surrounding his time in Deadwood ring true, most of his statements can be corroborated by others. Adding to Anderson's veracity is the fact that much of what appears about J. B. Hickok in *I Buried Hickok*, edited by William Secrest and published in 1980, was actually part of what White-Eye Anderson wrote about Hickok in 1900, just twenty-four years after the events in Deadwood.

White-Eye recalled that Deadwood citizens called on Hickok to consider becoming sheriff of Deadwood:

> *One evening after supper, Seth Bullick, Mr. Clark, a Mormon who had a big second-hand store, and several prominent men of the camp came to see Wild Bill. They wanted him to be Marshal of the town and said that if he would agree they would call a miner's meeting and get some kind of law and order established. Bill did not make them any promise and said he would let them know later in a week or so. Bill, Charley Utter, and my brother had a big talk about it, but I do not know what conclusion they came to.*[53]

White-Eye may have mis-remembered Seth Bullock at this meeting. If Bullock came to Deadwood on August 2, as is generally accepted, then he could not have been at this meeting. Though there is a minority opinion that Bullock came to Deadwood a few days before Hickok died, then it would be technically possible that he was there at the meeting, but it is doubtful he had developed any influence as one of the "prominent men" in just two days in camp. It is known, however, that Bullock did eventually become very influential in Deadwood, and one of its prominent men. White-Eye must have remembered this aspect of Seth Bullock and his memory placed Bullock in Deadwood earlier than he actually was. The "Mormon who had a big second-hand store" was either Craven Lee or Ike Brown, one of whom, or both, were Mormons. Their "big second-hand store" was the Zion's Cooperative Mercantile Institution.

Leander P. Richardson, being an observant journalist even in the short five days that he was in Deadwood, believed there was a conspiracy to kill J. B. Hickok:

> *There were a dozen or so men in Deadwood who wanted to kill Wild Bill because he would not 'stand-in' with them on any 'dead-beat' games, but not one man among them all dared to pick a quarrel with him. They were all waiting to get a chance to shoot him in the back. It was this "clique" that put McCall up to the killing and ensured that he was not convicted afterwards.*

Later in 1877, when Richardson learned McCall had been arrested in Wyoming and sentenced to death by hanging in Yankton, he wrote: "At the trial it was proved that the murderer was hired to do his work by gamblers who feared the time when better citizens should appoint Bill the champion of law and order—a post he formerly sustained in Kansas border life, with credit to his manhood and his courage."[54]

White-Eye Anderson remarked on the Deadwood jury and the purported conspiracy:

> *"They picked out three hundred men from the three mining districts, but they could not get a jury out of that bunch. Finally they did get a jury, but they were mostly rough Irishmen and proved to be friends of McCall's, and they cleared him...The next we heard he was in Laramie City making his brag that he got one thousand dollars for killing Wild Bill and got away with it too.*[55]

Seth Bullock, who became the sheriff of Deadwood when he became sheriff of Lawrence County in March, 1877, which put him in the best position as an officer of the law to find information about Hickok's murder, wrote about the jury in the Deadwood trial and the McCall verdict, and the conspiracy to murder Hickok:

> *This verdict was not a surprise to those cognizant of the way the jury had been chosen. While there were a few members of the jury who were supposed to be square men, a number of them were associates of the gang suspected of hiring McCall to murder Wild Bill. One of them about a year later, was killed by a sheriff's posse while attempting to hold up a stagecoach enroute to Cheyenne. Immediately after the rendition of the verdict, McCall left Deadwood on a good saddle horse, provided by the men who employed him to commit the murder and went south, followed in a couple of hours by California Joe and Colorado Charlie who expected to overtake him and avenge the death of a fellow scout...*[56]

If John Varnes was indeed guilty of conspiring with Jack McCall to murder Hickok, he was surely elated with the jury's "not guilty" verdict in the Deadwood trial of McCall. Varnes would have no reason to leave Deadwood in August, now that McCall was free and on his way to Wyoming. As will be shown, Varnes was not just another unknown drifter in Deadwood.

Gayville, founded by namesake William Gay in April 1876, was located on Deadwood Creek about two miles upstream from Deadwood. Here John Varnes owned a small eating place with the unusual name of X-10-U-8.[57]

Within a week of Hickok's death, Deadwood was faced with another crisis. There were many horses in Deadwood, and feeding costs for the horses was becoming prohibitive. Four men came up with the idea of keeping many of the horses in a herd outside of town on what was known as the Centennial Prairie, where they could graze. The men charged a small fee for each horse, and it was thought to be an ideal situation for both the horse owners and the four businessmen. It was known as the Montana herd. The herd was about two hundred horses.[58]

But one Sunday in August tragedy occurred. The four men were killed by a band of Sioux Indians, and the Montana herd was driven off by the Indians. Harry Young, the bartender from the Number 10 Saloon, wrote what happened next: "This occurrence left very few horses in Deadwood. Those there were used primarily for teaming purposes. However, we formed a party, consisting of Carl Mann, Tom Dozier, Seth Bullock, Ed Milligan, Pat Kelly, John Varnes, Charley Storms, and a man named Brown, who had high aspirations to be appointed to be our first sheriff. These men, with about twenty others, including myself, started on the Indian chase, who had gone north."[59]

This group, that included John Varnes, did not find the band of Sioux Indians that had stolen the horses, but they did meet up with one Indian who managed to shoot and kill two men, one of whom was Ike Brown, the Mormon co-owner of the Zion Cooperative Mercantile Institute mentioned above. Young said "We secured the two bodies and returned to Deadwood, a tired and disgusted lot."[60]

On August 18, John Varnes and Charley Storms, apparently both blind drunk, had a shoot-out on Gold Street in Deadwood. The August 19 Black Hills *Pioneer* reported:

Two sporting men, named Storms and Barnes [sic; Varnes]*, who had some difficulty, agreed to settle the dispute by setting themselves up as targets for each others aim. They met in Gold Street yesterday about six o'clock, and as the lively notes of the revolver fell upon the air, the balls whistled thick and fast, some of them crossing Main Street and entering the windows of the store of Wertheimer & Co., and one unfortunate man, named Joe Ludwig, was hit in the thigh. The wound is not thought* *to be of a serious nature. Mr. Neuman, partner of Mr. Wertheimer, who was standing a few feet from the window on the east side of the building, received a shot so close to his head that the glass from one of the panes through which a ball penetrated lodged in his hair...*

In the last week of August, 1876, John Varnes was noted again by Harry Young, this time as a member of a small group seeking a new gold strike: "In the latter part of August, a report was circulated that a great strike had been made at the base of what was called Sun Mountain, situated about a hundred miles northwest of Deadwood. Myself and four others taking our horses and a pack mule, started on our stampede. Those with me were Pat Kelly, Ed Milligan, Tom Dozier, and Johnnie Varnes..."[61] Three days after leaving Deadwood they ran into a band of Sioux Indians, about twenty-five of them. Young and the group built some breastworks out of dirt, and awaited the inevitable attack. When it came, the Indians mounted attack after attack, yet Young and his small band killed one Indian and wounded another. The Indians finally withdrew, and the group ventured out to inspect the one dead Indian. Young continued: "I had a scalp. Kelly took his war bonnet, Milligan his breech-clout, Varnes his moccasins and Dozier his gun. We then started for Deadwood. We had had enough of the stampeding business to last awhile. We shared in the venture and trophies of war, but arrived in Deadwood with no gold."[62]

McCall was arrested on August 29, 1876, in Laramie City, Wyoming. After the three events described above involving John Varnes during August of 1876, he was never seen in Deadwood again. Young does say that after the drunken shoot-out on August 18 in Deadwood, Charley Storms and John Varnes became "great friends." In 1881, Charley Storms was shot and killed by gunfighter and gambler Luke Short outside the Oriental Saloon in Tombstone, Arizona. With just a touch of animosity, Harry Young states that Varnes died in Denver, Colorado, "an opium fiend."[63] Varnes did die in Denver in March, 1881. His body was discovered outside an opium den. He was thirty-one years old.

There is at least one minority opinion, from a respected source, that does not believe the McCall/Varnes conspiracy. John S. McClintock came to Deadwood in April, 1876, living there the rest of his life until he died in 1942. His 1939 book *Pioneer Days in the Black Hills* is a respected source of information on Deadwood, especially the gold-rush era of 1876-1880. McClintock had a keen memory and a penchant for only telling about things and events he had personally seen or been involved in; occasionally he would inform on a subject based on information he had received from persons he deemed a reliable source. He was prejudiced on some subjects: for instance, he was particularly disdainful of Wild Bill Hickok, and it shows in McClintock's writing about him. That disdain may have played a part in McClintock's complete dismissal of the McCall/Varnes conspiracy.

McClintock wrote:

> I have described these conditions to show that, from my point of view as an everyday observer in those memorable days of '76, while there was no question but what the city of Deadwood was at that time in need of better local government, it was not in need of a notorious man-killer as peace officer [referring to Hickok]. There may have been talk by his friends that he was to receive the appointment as Marshal, it was not generally known, as I never heard of it. [Here is seen an example of McClintock's tendency to presume that if he did not know about it, it did not happen.] As regards the stories about Johnnie Varnes, a professional gambler whom I knew very well, and Tim Brady, a man I never heard of, conspiring to have Wild Bill killed, it is my opinion that it is without foundation, and has been related by hero worshipers for the purpose of leading readers into belief that their hero was greatly feared by the tough element in Deadwood. One writer states that "Cold Deck Johnnie" gave Jack McCall seven hundred dollars to kill Wild Bill. Another says that he gave him a few drinks of whiskey to do the job. I don't believe that Varnes or any other gambler in the town had any fear of Wild Bill, as he himself was a gambler. Though not a very successful one, it was his only occupation in Deadwood.[64]

Hickok biographer O. W. Coursey believed in the conspiracy when he wrote in 1924:

> Deadwood was growing tougher every day. So many gunmen had been attracted there by the lure of gold that decent folk scarcely dared to appear on the street—particularly after dark. It was becoming rumored—and no doubt with considerable authority, that Deadwood, within a week or two, was to be organized into a municipality, with a full set of officials, and that Wild Bill was to be appointed City Marshal. The toughs of the city feared him. If robed with police authority, he would be still more dangerous. Something had to be done to get rid

of him. Accordingly, two of these characters, Tim Brady and Johnny Varnes, took a desperate character, John McCall, filled him up on liquor, and then suggested that he kill Wild Bill.[65]

Writer Frank Wilstach reported on the conspiracy in 1926, indicating that he received the information from Ellis T. Peirce:

> *The citizens sought to preserve order without resorting to lynch law, and after the Hinch murder trial, which took place upon a pile of logs in the middle of the street, the question of selecting a Marshal was considered. As Wild Bill had arrived in June and his official acts at Abilene and Hays City were known and appreciated, a suggestion was made to offer him a large salary and have him duplicate his Kansas record. Tim Brady and Johnny Varnes, two of the undesirables, got Jack McCall drunk and then told him that Bill was to be Marshal of the town and that all gunplay would stop. It was said at the time, and never denied, that they told Jack that the boys could not afford to have Wild Bill Hickok created Marshal and that they would give him two hundred dollars if he would slip across the street and shoot Bill. They gave him twenty-five dollars in dust on account and promised to pay him the remaining one hundred and seventy-five dollars when the bloody work had been performed.*[66]

William Connelley reported on the conspiracy in 1933, mirroring some of the same information from the Wilstach entry above. That is not unusual; Frank Wilstach and William Connelley were researching for their respective Hickok books at about the same time, and they shared much information with each other (note that Connelley's book was issued posthumously in 1933; he died suddenly on July 14, 1930):

> *Jack McCall was the drunken, degenerate tool of more clever men. These lawless ones, knowing that it was now or never, used Jack McCall as the instrument placed in their hands by an evil Providence... As to his actual and immediate preparation for the affair, that consisted of a conversation with Tim Brady and Johnny Varnes, two leaders of the bad men. They stressed the fact that if Wild Bill was appointed Marshal their days were numbered. They urged on Jack McCall the glory he might claim as the slayer of the most famous of gunmen. They*

promised him absolute immunity from punishment and quick release if captured. They gave him twenty-five dollars in gold dust and were to add to that one hundred and seventy-five more, after the deed was done. And as a last assurance, they filled him up on raw whisky, the kind that make even a coward crazy and reckless. So fortified, he set forth to commit the crime.[67]

This almost 150-year-old cold case cries out to be re-opened by some talented historical detective. The game is afoot, Watson.

On November 12, 1876, Agnes Hickok wrote her last letter to the Hickok family (punctuation added):

Dear Mother and Sister
I suppose you think with the death of my beloved and lamented Husband you think that our friendship has ceased, but not so. I have had more trouble than I could live up to and tired, nature gave way at last and I have not been able to write, but in future will do if God spares my life; my daughter has had a hard time of it, and the Baby is so cross that there is no rest for her night or day, and she has gone to Housekeeping and just got fixed nicely; and I am having the first leasure moment to Day Sunday that I have had in about 3 months.
Dear Friends I am longing to pay you all a visit this Spring before going West to remain next to the scenes that my beloved Husband loved so well, and try and end my days out West. I am going to the Black Hills and remain near his grave; I have been bothered to death with lawyers wanting a job on the case. I suppose you know that Jack McCall has been arrested and taken to Yankton to be tried for Murder, and friends of James told me not to get any lawyer because as they was out there and would attend to all that needed attending to so you see my husband had Friends out there that loved him as well as I do, God bless him. It is impossible for a human being to Love any better than what I did him. I can see him Day and night before me. The longer he is Dead the worse I feel. I am not quite so busy now that my daughter has got well. Now I have more time for Retrospection. I grieve all the time. My intention if nothing happens to take an overland route to the far West to ride Horse back all the way: I suppose you think it a funny notion so it is, but I am able to the task and not afraid to do it. How is

our Dear Mother, has she recovered from the sudden news yet or not? I am anxious to see the mother of so noble a son as James was. Excuse bad writing as I have the Dropsy so bad that my hand is quite numb all the time. Out West it dont bother me at all. Give my love and a kiss to Mother and tell her that God willing I will see her in the spring.

> *Answer soon and believe me to be your Loving Sister.*
> *Agnes Hickok* [68]

Despite her written intention, there is no record of Agnes ever visiting the Hickok family in Illinois.

To end this important year of 1876, we come to the most long-lived, tenacious, widespread legend to ever be associated with *Wild Bill* Hickok. It is so deeply embedded in American culture that no amount of empirical evidence will probably dislodge people's belief in it. It has been celebrated in song, poems, books, on beer labels, t-shirts, and television. It is ubiquitous. Like stop signs, it is everywhere. It is Aces and Eights—the Dead Man's Hand.

Understand that the legend of Aces and Eights is based on a single mid-sentence phrase written about fifty years after the purported incident, by a person about whom it is generally agreed never let the truth get in the way of a good story: Ellis T. "Doc" Peirce.

In preparation for his book on Wild Bill Hickok, in 1925 Frank Wilstach tracked down in South Dakota the still-living, eighty-something Doc Peirce, seeking information on Hickok's last days in Deadwood. Peirce responded to Wilstach, and it appeared in Wilstach's 1926 book this way:

> *In his letter to the writer Mr. Peirce gives several details that have not heretofore been revealed. Doc Peirce was the impromptu undertaker who took charge of the remains and looked after details of the burial:* "Now, in regard to the position of Bill's body," *writes Mr. Peirce,* "when they unlocked the door for me to get his body, he was lying on his side, with his knees drawn up just as he slid off his stool. We had no chairs in those days—and his fingers were still crimped from holding his poker hand. Charlie Rich, who sat beside him, said he never saw a muscle move. Bill's hand read 'aces and eights'—two pair, and since*

that day aces and eights have been known as 'the dead man's hand' in the Western country.[69]

There is no question that Peirce, a barber with some rudimentary medical knowledge, working in a barber shop across the street from the Number 10 Saloon on August 2, 1876, was one of the people to examine Hickok's body in the saloon after the shooting. He then followed the wagon, driven by a Mr. Rutherford and carrying Hickok's body, to the camp on Whitewood Creek maintained by Charley Utter, White-Eye Anderson, and the late J. B. Hickok. White-Eye recalled:

> *I went to where Bill was killed and helped to take the body to camp. They had locked the doors of the Number Ten saloon and sent word to Charley Utter who was with my brother at our camp on Whitewood Creek. They got a man—I don't remember the name, but they called him "Doc" and he was a barber—to go with them. A Mr. Rutherford, who had a one-horse express wagon, brought the body to our camp in his wagon and Doc and the two Charleys took his boots off and fixed up the body in good shape.*[70]

Just the fact that Doc Peirce was there means nothing. No one at the fateful table in the Number 10 Saloon on August 2, 1876, said anything about "aces and eights," or any other cards that Hickok might have held when the shot was fired, though they all testified in detail about that afternoon at McCall's trial—not Carl Mann, not Charley Rich, and not William Massie. George Shingle, in the saloon weighing gold dust when McCall entered and fired the shot, said nothing about "aces and eights" or any cards in his expansive testimony. None of these men recalled it in later years, either. White-Eye Anderson said nothing about "aces and eights" as well. Peter LaFlemme, watching through the open archway in the Bella Union next door that day, reported nothing about aces and eights. Laborer Joseph Mitchell, putting up wainscoting at the rear of the Number 10 that day, testified about what he saw and said nothing about "aces and eights." Number 10 bartender Harry Young said nothing about "aces and eights," but he did have a recollection of a hand that Massie beat Hickok on that afternoon. Young recalled, "They had been playing not to exceed twenty minutes, when Massie beat a king full for Bill with four sevens, breaking Bill on the hand. They were playing table stakes. Bill then asked me to bring him fifty dollars worth of checks, which I did...I placed the checks on the table in front of Bill, standing as I did between him and Carl Mann. Bill looked up at me and remarked: 'The old duffer (meaning Massie) broke me on the hand.' These were the last words he ever uttered."[71]

Young's comments on the hand are ambiguous. They could be read to mean that the next hand dealt after Massie beat Hickok was not dealt yet, thus the hand Hickok was holding when he was shot was the "king full" described by Young. It could also be read to mean that hand had been discarded and the next hand, whatever it was, had already been dealt and was in their hands when the shot was made by McCall. The second scenario would seem more likely, because for Young to know what the hands were he would have had to probably (but not absolutely) see them *after* they were discarded. Still, there is no mention of "aces and eights."

Joe Rosa received many cards to look at over the many decades that he studied Hickok, all coming with a claim that they were in Hickok's hand when he was shot. Some even came with blood-stains on the cards. All were bogus: some on cards that were not printed until after 1876, some with paper that was not right, some with fake blood stains. All failed even a cursory examination.

In 2008, writer and historian Des Wilson wrote an acclaimed poker history, *Ghosts At The Table*. In it, Wilson attempted to get to the bottom of the Aces and Eights legend. He went right to the place where the legend started, Deadwood. Here he believed he might find the truth. He read several statements from respected Hickok historians that basically stated that the cards in Hickok's hand when he was shot are simply not known. Much to his surprise, he arrived in Deadwood to find that the Adams Museum told him they had the actual cards. [72]

He was told "A few years ago, a family called Stephens claimed that one Richard Stephens had been making a delivery in Number 10 Saloon on August 2nd and was actually there when Wild Bill was shot. In the midst of the uproar he scooped up the cards and took them home, and they were on the family mantelpiece for years. Then they were donated to the museum."[73]

Taken aback, Wilson found the cards in a glass case in the corner of the museum. The five cards are the ace of diamonds, ace of clubs, eight of hearts, eight of spades, and queen of hearts. He asked for and was given contact information for the great-granddaughter of delivery man Richard Stephens. Wilson promptly sent the lady an email with questions about the family story of these cards. He received back a quick reply. Richard Stephens was a dairy farmer, and that day he was delivering buttermilk to the Number 10 Saloon, she said. No one saw him pick up the cards because there was a shooting going on, she told Wilson. His picking up the cards was not a conscious act: "Apparently he didn't even realize he had them until he got home the following day...He just picked up Hickok's hand as the cards slipped from his fingers...My dad, Dick Stephens, donated the cards to the Adams Museum in the 1970's."[74]

The curator at the Adams Museum wrote to Des Wilson concerning the Stephens cards as well. Their policy about the cards seems reasonable and prudent:

> At this time, our official policy, is to display the cards, report the details we received from the family, refer to the displayed cards as the "purported dead man's hand," and leave the rest to our visitors. After all, in Deadwood, Wild Bill Hickok has attained almost a mystical status. We've more or less decided to let the cards be as mysterious as the man... So, in the end, the Adams Museum's position is that we believe we have the cards held by Wild Bill, but nobody can say for sure whether we do or we don't.[75]

As Des Wilson points out, it somewhat undercuts the validity of Aces and Eights when we know that the very first mention of Aces and Eights is about fifty years after it allegedly happened. Add to that the only carrier of that message, Doc Peirce, is remembered in South Dakota as a notorious jokester who delighted dropping shocking and often nonsensical statements into his writing, statements sometimes surprising enough to draw a double-take from the reader.

Wilson finishes his study of Aces and Eights in Deadwood with the conclusion that "there is no satisfactory evidence that Wild Bill ever held aces or eights...but no one in town is going to admit it."[76]

That should be the conclusion of all students of the subject of Aces and Eights...there is no satisfactory evidence. Plant your flag on that hill. Do I think this will stop the continued perpetuation of this legend? Do I think that Aces and Eights will go kicking and screaming into the ash heap of history? Don't bet on it.

On a hillside overlooking Deadwood, South Dakota, James Butler Hickok rests for eternity. Yet Wild Bill Hickok continues to wander through American popular culture and our minds, reminding us of this unique and charismatic man, so different yet so recognizable, as he wanders through time. James' brother Lorenzo once remarked ruefully that if James had not died in 1876, "his restless spirit and adventurous streak would doubtless have kept him roaming the West."[77]

Wild Bill is with us, his horse running with a long easy stride, the front of his broad brimmed hat standing out of his line of vision.

F. A. Carpenter, ca. 1864

1877

DEADWOOD AFTERMATH *and* BEYOND

A s 1877 came around, Jack McCall had been convicted of the murder of J. B. Hickok in December. On January 3, 1877, he was sentenced to death by hanging. On January 23, McCall's lawyers advised the Yankton court that they were filing a clemency plea with the president of the United States.1 On February 19, they received a telegram that stated that the attorney general of the United States "declines to interfere with the sentence pronounced by the Court."[1]

On February 25, McCall's sister wrote from Louisville, Kentucky to the Marshal of Yankton:

> *Dear Sir:*
>
> *I saw in the morning papers a piece about the sentence of the murderer of Wild Bill, Jack McCall. There was a young man of the name John McCall left here about six years ago, who has not been heard from for the last three years. He has a father, mother, and three sisters living here in Louisville, who are very uneasy about him since they heard about the murder of Wild Bill. If you can send us any information about him, we would be very thankful to you.*
>
> *This John McCall is about twenty-five years old, has light hair, inclined to curl, and one eye crossed. I cannot say about his height, as he was not grown when he left here. Please write as soon as convenient, as we are very anxious to hear from you.*
>
> *Very Respectfully,*
> *Mary A. McCall.*[2]

On March 1, 1877, at 10:15 in the morning, Jack McCall was hung for the murder of James Butler Hickok.

Agnes Hickok returned to Cheyenne in the spring of 1877, reportedly to train horses for the circus. The Cheyenne papers reported in July that she was in town. From Cheyenne, she traveled to Deadwood in the late summer, following the same route her husband had used to come to Deadwood the year before.

The Black Hills *Daily Times* reported her arrival on September 4:

> *Madame Lake Hickok, the widow of the late Wild Bill, accompanied by Charles Dalton, (Buckskin Charley) and wife, and George Carson arrived in the city late on Friday evening. On Saturday the widow visited Bill's grave, and proposes as soon as it is definitely settled that the graveyard will not be deserted, to erect a fenced monument in his memory, in which kind action Buffalo Bill, Texas Jack and Buckskin Charley, will assist her. Madame Hickok, when she leaves here, will proceed to Havana, Cuba, via Cincinnati and New York, in company with her daughter, whither they will take two young horses the Madame has trained this summer, at Cheyenne, for the circus ring.*

The Cheyenne *Daily Sun* reported on September 14:

> *Mrs. Hickok paid several visits to her husband's grave during her sojourn in the Hills, and is very enthusiastic in her praises of Charley Utter, who treated her so kindly while here. He proved himself a true friend of "Wild Bill," her husband, for which she feels truly grateful.*

Agnes came to Deadwood to remove James' body back to Cincinnati or Cheyenne for re-burial. She brought an open wagon to Deadwood for that purpose. O. W. Coursey wrote that Agnes had initially planned to come to Deadwood to take James' body back to Cheyenne for burial:

> *In 1877, she hired Charley [George] Carson, a noted hunter, to take her to the Black Hills, so she could get Wild Bill's remains and take them back to Cheyenne for burial. At Custer she met "Doc"*

Peirce who had prepared her husbands remains for burial. To him she disclosed her errand. He told her when she saw how well her husband's body had been disposed of in Deadwood, and considering the fact that he was lying in historic ground, she would perhaps be content just to let him remain there. After arriving in Deadwood, and after looking over the grave and its location, she, too, decided that this was the best thing to do; and so she and Mr. Carson drove back to Cheyenne where they were immediately married.[3]

Near the end of September, Agnes Hickok returned to Cheyenne. On September 27, she and George Carson took out a marriage license, and on that same evening they were married. The *Cheyenne Daily Sun* reported the next day:

Married: Hickok-Carson. At the residence of the bride, in Cheyenne, on Thursday evening, September 27th, 1877, by Probate Judge C.F. Miller,—Mrs. Agnes Lake Hickok to Mr. George Carson. The bride was the widow of the late J.B. Hickok ("Wild Bill"), who was murdered at Deadwood by Jack McCall about a year ago.

Records show that at this marriage between Agnes Hickok and George Carson, the witnesses for the marriage were the same as when Agnes married James: her friends Wes and Minnie Moyer. Since this wedding took place "at the residence of the bride," as reported above, it took place at the home of Wes and Minnie Moyer, the same place Agnes had wed James. Alice had no residence of her own in Cheyenne. She always stayed with the Moyers at their home at Eighteenth and Central in Cheyenne.

On October 2, the Black Hills *Daily Times* reported the news that must have confounded and perplexed the citizens of Deadwood as much as it has later historians and biographers of Hickok: "Madam Lake, the widow of Wild Bill is married again. She was married to Geo. Carson, of Cheyenne, on the 27th of last month." The bride was fifty-one. The groom was twenty-nine. After the wedding he disappeared from the historical record. He literally was never heard from again.

Agnes returned to Cincinnati and continued to be involved with the circus, both in managing her daughter's career and making occasional appearances in the circus ring itself. She also bought a farm in Kentucky and trained horses for the circus. Agnes died in 1907, and is buried in the family plot in Cincinnati.

AFTERWORD

the WANDERER KEEPS WANDERING

From that moment on a warm August afternoon in the Number 10 Saloon, James Butler Hickok's destiny ended, and Wild Bill Hickok's destiny began anew. Even before his death in Deadwood, the Hickok narrative was first controlled by the dime novels. Just five months after the publication of Nichols' article in the February 1867 issue of *Harpers New Monthly Magazine,* the July issue of DeWitt's *Ten Cent Romances* published "Wild Bill the Indian Slayer." Several issues later came "Wild Bill's First Trail." After a two-year hiatus, J. B. Hickok appeared again in a dime novel; this time in a supporting role to Buffalo Bill in Ned Buntline's *Buffalo Bill, The King of the Border Men.* This was serialized in *The New York Weekly and other publications.* Buntline killed off Wild Bill Hickok in this story; Dave Tutt's girlfriend stabbed Hickok in the heart. It is worth considering that all the attention garnered for Hickok by these dime novels was happening while Hickok was alive and his "real life" was playing out.

After Hickok's death, author Prentiss Ingraham took a different approach than Buntline in writing dime novels. Ingraham's writing technique, much like James W. Buels, was to mix fact and fiction, making it more believable to a less-than-discerning public. Beadle's Pocket Library in 1891 published Ingraham's *Wild Bill, The Pistol Prince,* said title probably the inspiration for Frank Wilstach's titling his 1926 biography *Wild Bill, Prince of Pistoleers.* Beadles published eight more Hickok dime novels, with titles like *Wild Bill's Gold Trail, Wild Bill's Sable Pard, Wild Bill's Trump Card, Wild Bill's Weird Foes,* and *Wild Bill, the Wild West Duelist.* Soon Hickok's dime-novel adventures began appearing in Britain. In the early twentieth century, the *Original Buffalo Bill Library* came out in England, in which Wild Bill Hickok often appeared. These dime novels were published in England into the 1940s.

Many dime-novel authors eventually graduated to conventional new journalism, yet many worked in both fields simultaneously. The era of the dime novels ran roughly fifty years, from about 1860 to 1910. Running on a parallel track from 1883 until 1909 was William F. Cody's traveling real-life dime-novel show, *Buffalo Bill's Wild West,* that literally imprinted on the American and European psyche the lasting image of the western American frontier for audiences in the East and Europe, who had never set foot in the West. Traveling throughout the United States and abroad, doing two-a-day shows drawing 30,000 people to each show, Buffalo Bill brought a frontier to live shows that strongly implicated much of Wild Bill Hickok's life and legend. Many of the play acts and vignettes in the live show were actually based on real incidents in Hickok's life. Cody's presence and persona was and always had been a carefully crafted homage to his mentor and father figure, James Butler Hickok. It is no wonder that even today, people confuse Cody with Hickok, and vice-versa.

Soon after the dime novels faded in about 1919, a new media came along. Silent moving pictures first, and then the talkies came not long after. The motion picture industry was born. The first silent movie depicting Wild Bill Hickok was probably *The Pioneer Peacemaker,* a two-reel film that came out in 1913. In 1915 the next silent movie about Hickok was released: *In the Days of '75 and '76, or The Thrilling Lives of Wild Bill Hickok and Calamity Jane.* This movie was filmed in Nebraska and South Dakota. Ironically, some of the actors were descendants of the McCanles family. By 1923, the first Hickok movie featuring a well-known actor came to the screen. William S. Hart played the lead in Wild Bill Hickok. Hart was almost sixty when he portrayed Hickok. The movie's premise is that Hickok wants to retire and play cards in Dodge City, but Custer convinces him to holster his guns and work with other lawmen to restore law and order. After Hart's 1923 portrayal, Wild Bill Hickok shows up again in *The Iron Horse (1924), The Last Frontier (1926), The World Changes (1933), Aces and Eights (1936),* and *Custer's Last Stand (1936).*

Probably the most influential Hickok movie ever made was *The Plainsman* in 1936. A Cecil B. DeMille epic of a Western, some of it was based on Frank Wilstach's 1926 biography, *Wild Bill, Prince of Pistoleers.* *The Plainsman* was influential if for no other reason than it put young Joseph Rosa on a path that would, thirty-eight years later, produce the groundbreaking book, *They Called Him Wild Bill,* that would be the first-ever factual biography of Hickok, with much input and information from the Hickok family themselves. The movie was also influential because it had legendary Cecil B. DeMille as director, and popular, Academy Award-winning actor Gary Cooper playing Hickok. *The Plainsman* packed movie houses across the country. It was sweeping and dramatic; an epic with a big national story that included the Civil War, manifest destiny, Abraham Lincoln, and more. Yet it had little to do with J. B. Hickok's actual life. In *The Plainsman,* Hickok musters out of the army at Leavenworth. He heads for Hays City. Mention is made that he is the killer of the whole McDaniels gang. The Sioux and Cheyenne are on the warpath. Hickok and Cody are guarding an ammunition train with about fifty men. Custer has been slain at Little Big Horn. Hickok handles the gun runners at Deadwood. Just as the cavalry arrives, Jack McCall shoots Hickok. Fade to black. Gary Cooper portrayed Hickok as masculine, and solidly moral, strong and quiet. Cooper's portrayal of Hickok's personality may have been the closest the film got to reality.

The forties brought several more Hickok films to the screen, all playing fast and loose with the facts. There was *Young Bill Hickok,* which took the McCanles and Rock Creek story as it appeared in William Connelley's 1933 *Wild Bill and His Era,* and conflated it with several other Hickok legends to make another Hickok film untethered from the facts. In 1941, the film *Wild Bill Hickok Rides* put Hickok in Montana helping homesteaders against a Chicago swindler. In 1953 *I Shot Jack McCall* came out, a bizarre tale where Hickok is a dangerous desperado and Jack McCall is the hero. In 1956, the equally forgettable *I Killed Wild Bill Hickok* hit the screens.

Television really came into its own in the 1950s, and the increasingly limited amount of Westerns on the silver screen was inversely proportionate to the flood of Westerns appearing on television. It would be 1967 before another full-length movie about Wild Bill Hickok would again appear, *The White Buffalo,* starring Charles Bronson. In his first appearance in the movie, Bronson appears to be wearing a pair of Ray-Bans. Kim Novak was co-star Poker Jenny. The ghostly white buffalo was a full-size puppet on a rail track. The movie was roundly panned by critics.

In 1995 came a much-anticipated Hickok movie, to be simply titled *Wild Bill.* It was much anticipated because of the stellar cast, including Jeff Bridges as Hickok and Ellen Barkin as Calamity Jane; and legendary director and screenwriter of many Westerns, Walter Hill, was to write and direct the movie. Strangely enough, Hill used two works of fiction as his sources to develop the script: Pete Dexter's *Deadwood* and Thomas Babe's strange and macabre play, *Fathers and Sons.* One critic and reviewer thought that Hill could not decide "whether to celebrate the past or send it up." In the movie, Hickok and Calamity Jane make love in an empty saloon to a background tune of the *Battle Hymn of the Republic.* Hickok sits in a chair to have a shoot-out with a man across the street in a wheelchair, to make it a fair fight. Hickok is an opium addict. The movie, so anticipated as one that might actually tell a factual story of Hickok's life, failed in that effort completely. 1995's *Wild Bill* was a commercial disappointment, losing almost twenty-eight million dollars, and a critical failure as well.

A factual motion picture about Wild Bill Hickok still awaits the silver screen. If Hollywood would only learn that the actual life of James Butler Hickok is just as compelling and dramatic as any of the myths and legends, then that long awaited bio-pic of Wild Bill Hickok could be made.

If any media has addressed the Hickok narrative and brought it to masses of Americans, it is television. Baby Boomer children, and many of their parents, were thrilled from 1951 through 1958 through 113 episodes of *The Adventures of Wild Bill Hickok.* From 1951 till 1956, the Mutual Radio Network broadcast *The Adventures of Wild Bill Hickok* on radio as well. On the television show, Guy Madison played Hickok and Andy Devine played Jingle P. Jones, his deputy Marshal and sidekick. The show was sponsored by Kellogg's Corn Pops, later called Sugar Pops. At Kelloggs' insistence, whenever possible, Hickok was supposed to outwit the outlaws rather than shoot and kill them, and he was to stay away from saloons. Many times the Kellogg's cereal boxes were adorned with cutout cardboard badges, or instructions for sending in a number of box tops for a plastic gun. The show first appeared on CBS, then later was switched to ABC. Guy was a former lifeguard and telephone lineman who had appeared in a few forgettable films for RKO. Andy Devine was better known, and he had been offered the sidekick role after Burl Ives had turned it down. Wild Bill and Jingles galloped around the country on their horses Buckshot and Joker in each twenty-five-minute episode, chasing down outlaws in all kinds of situations. In 1954, the show landed the much-sought-after six o'clock slot on ABC, going up against the respected CBS Evening News. Out of this one show came a merchandising bonanza: Wild Bill Hickok shirts, belts, jackets, action figures, board games, puzzles, bubble gum cards and much more. Because of The Adventures of Wild Bill Hickok, the television iconic image of 1950s Westerns is Wild Bill Hickok, and the show's influence on the Hickok narrative is immeasurable.

In 2004, David Milch brought out the *Deadwood* series on HBO. Not that it added anything to the Hickok story: Hickok was killed off in the fourth episode by Jack McCall. But what it adds to the Hickok legacy is a screen version that shows a spot-on take of what the end-of-the-track and end-of-the-line lawless towns like Deadwood, Abilene, Hays City, Ellsworth, and Sheridan looked like, smelled like, and felt like. Wild Bill Hickok knew them all.

The print version of what was being watched on television in the 1950s came out in comic books. Avon Periodicals published twenty-eight issues of *Wild Bill Hickok* from 1949 till 1956. Charlton Comics, after the end of the television show *The Adventures of Wild Bill Hickok* in 1958, published seven issues of *Wild Bill Hickok and Jingles* in 1958 and 1959.

It is not just popular media that has contributed to the Hickok narrative. Interest and recognition of him run far afield. In 1923, when the decisions were being made on who to carve into Mount Rushmore, Doane Robinson, then the state historian for South Dakota, proposed that Wild Bill Hickok and Buffalo Bill Cody be carved into the mountain. Robinson's view did not prevail. In 1943, the United States Navy christened one of their ships the James B. Hickok. It served with distinction in the war. In the flower world, there is a beautiful, tall, bearded iris called Wild Bill Hickok.

So the Wanderer wanders...forever.

APPENDIX ONE

the LEGEND *of the* "O"

or

a STUDY *in the* GROWTH *and* PERPETUATION *of a* LEGEND

There is a fascinating, long-running legend that has its most well-known incarnation taking place in Kansas City in either the summer of 1872 or the spring of 1874. This legend has two reality-based prerequisites; it is both possible and plausible. It is a story of James Butler Hickok's well-established shooting ability with two Navy Colts in his hands. This is a wide-ranging tale. Its actors include *Harper's* George Ward Nichols, satirical humorist Alfred Henry Lewis, gunfighters Bat Masterson and Wyatt Earp, novelist Emerson Hough, Kansas City's first police chief Thomas Speers, novelist Thomas Berger, and, of course, James Butler Hickok. In addition to being a long-lived and long-loved story, it is a tale so compelling that notable people have tried to establish a case for their presence at the event, or at least create a narrative supporting direct, first-hand knowledge of the event, thereby increasing their own fame or notoriety just by the purported association.

Few stories resonate in the vast shooting-skill legacy of James Butler Hickok like this one that took place at or near the city market around Fifth and Main in Kansas City. The second and third members of what the general public considers the gunfighter's triumvirate, Wyatt Earp and Bat Masterson, both claimed at different times to have witnessed the event and/or its aftermath in Kansas City. Nineteenth-century humorist

Alfred Henry Lewis (think Mark Twain with more snark), a close and influential friend of Bat Masterson, gave the story wide circulation when he published his version of the story in the *Saturday Evening Post* in 1904. Novelist Thomas Berger used it as a literary device in *The Return of Little Big Man* in 1999. It is the longest-tenured Hickok legend, dating back to 1865, when George Ward Nichols got the ball rolling, at least thematically, when *Harper's New Monthly Magazine* published in February 1867 what Nichols claims he saw that summer of 1865:

> *"I would like to see yer shoot."*
>
> *"Would yer?" replied the scout, drawing his revolver, and approaching the window, he pointed to a letter O in a sign-board which was fixed to the stone-wall on the other side of the way.*
>
> *"That sign is more than fifty yards away. I will put these six balls into the inside of the circle, which isn't bigger than a man's heart."*
>
> *In an off-hand way, and without sighting the pistol to his eye, he discharged the six shots of his revolver. I afterwards saw that all of the bullets had entered the circle. As Bill proceeded to reload his pistol, he said to me with a naivete of manner that was meant to be assuring, "Whenever you get in a row with someone be sure and don't shoot too quick. Take time. I've known many a feller slip up for shootin' in a hurry."*
>
> *It would be easy to fill a volume with the adventures of this remarkable man. My object here has been to make a slight record of one who is one of the best- perhaps the very best- example of a class who more than any other encountered perils and privations in defense of our nationality.*

Next up was James W. Buel, who missed this story completely in his 1881 *Heroes of the Plains*. If it happened in Kansas City in 1872, perhaps Buel was out of town. If it happened in 1874, perhaps Buel was out of town, or maybe Buel had already left Kansas City to take an editorial position with a St. Louis paper that year. However, the fact that Buel does not mention it cuts against this legend's potential veracity. Buel wrote about almost everything in Hickok's life. But he missed or ignored Aces and Eights as well.

Before he published his more famous piece in the *Saturday Evening Post*, Alfred Henry Lewis wrote his version of the Kansas City shooting event in the August 3, 1895 Kansas City *Evening Star*, entitled "Wild Bill Hickox." The piece was syndicated to several other newspapers around the country:

"Wild Bill Hickox was for a long time chief of scouts in my command." It was a retired army officer that was talking. He leaned back in his chair at the Army and Navy Club and became reminiscent. *"Hickox got his nom de guerre of Wild Bill at Independence, Mo., when he was about nineteen years old. This was sometime in the late fifties, when Independence was the busy end of the Santa Fe Trail."*

"He was a natural born pistol shot and could shoot in the dark by ear. In fact he could hit any object once he had located it, and he aimed a pistol by nervous instinct rather than by sight. He could hit a dime tossed in the air and shot with his left hand as well as his right. He stood on Market Square on one occasion in Kansas City, just after the war, and with a pistol in each hand put twelve bullets in one of the O's in an I.O.O.F sign which was tacked to the third story of the building in the center of what was called Battle Row. He fired both pistols together and the twelve shots sounded like six."[1]

Lewis's use of the "retired army officer" may be a literary device, but if the interview was real, and if it took place within weeks or months of publication, then the officer being interviewed was probably John B. Sanborn, who was J. B. Hickok's commanding officer in southwest Missouri near the end of the Civil War. Of the other officers associated with Hickok, General Hancock died in 1886, General Sheridan in 1888, General Sherman in 1891, and General Pope in 1892. General Penrose lived until 1903, yet probably did not command Hickok long enough to make these statements. Which leaves Sanborn, who is further implicated by earlier statements he wrote praising Hickok and his role as a spy and scout under Sanborn's command.

Nine years later, Alfred Henry Lewis wrote his famous and widely-read piece on Hickok that appeared in the March 12, 1904 issue of the *Saturday Evening Post*. Entitled "How Mr. Hickok Came To Cheyenne," as the title implies, the general thrust of the story is about Hickok coming to Cheyenne, (which he actually did for the first time in 1874), but the prelude of the story is once again about Hickok shooting full of holes one of the O's in an I.O.O.F. sign in Kansas City. This time the story is much expanded. The pertinent excerpts are:

Mr. Hickok, then of Kansas City, might have been seen walking in that portion of Main Street known as Battle Row. For one of his optimism Mr. Hickok's mood showed blue and dull. One might tell it by a brooding eye and the droop which invested his moustache with a gravity not properly its own. Moreover, there was further evidence to prove the low spirits of Mr. Hickok. His hair, long as the hair of a woman, and which in lighter moments fell in a blond cataract about his yard-wide shoulders, was lifted away beneath his hat...

What should it be to prey upon the sensibilities of Mr. Hickok? Kansas City was a town of mud and dust and hill and hollow that quenched all happiness and drove the inhabitants to drink. Was it that to bear him down? No; if it were mere environment Mr. Hickok would have made his escape to regions where the sun was shining.

Not to run the trail too far, Mr. Hickok was ruminating the loss of his final dollar, which had fled across a faro layout in the Marble Hall saloon. As he strolled dejectedly in Battle Row he couldn't have told where his next week's board was coming from, not counting his next week's drinks. It was the dismal present, promising a dismal future, which exhaled those mists to take the curl from Mr. Hickok's moustache and teach his hair to hide beneath his hat. A short-haired man may be penniless and still command respect: a long-haired man without a dollar is a creature to be laughed at.

Having nothing to engage him but his gloom, Mr. Hickok glanced upward and across the street where, over the fourth story windows, an Odd Fellows sign was bolted. The sign was painted black upon white. The "O" that stood as initial of "Odd" showed wood-color inside of the black.

It was years before when, to please a bevy of tourists and by permission of Mr. Speers, then chief of police, Mr. Hickok emptied his six-shooters into the center of that "O." It was a finished piece of shooting; the tourists told of it about their clubs when safe in the East again. The "O", where the original white paint had been splintered into wood-color by these dozen bullets it had stopped, showed plain as print.

Mr. Hickok sighed as he admired his handiwork.

Mr. Hickok did not sigh because of any former accuracy with pistols: but he recalled how on that fine occasion—in contrast to present bankruptcy—he harbored 1400 dol. in his clothes. He had beaten the bank at Old Number Three, and was rich and gay in consequence.

"I think I shoot better when I've got a roll."

Thus murmured Mr. Hickok as he meditated on that miracle of the guns, done seven years before, Mr. Hickok might have extended his surmise: a man does all things better when he has a roll...Mr. Hickok, *having sufficiently surveyed his bullet work of another day as set forth by the Odd Fellows emblem, was about to resume his walk, when telegraph boy rushed up. His rush was over. The urchin gazed upon Mr. Hickok with the utmost satisfaction for the space of thirty seconds.*

"Be you Mr. Hickok?" he asked.

"Yes my boy," replied Mr. Hickok blandly. Mr. Hickok was tolerant of youth.

"Mr. Wild Bill Hickok?" [2]

The next year, in June of 1905, Alfred Henry Lewis wrote a fictionalized biography of his friend Bat Masterson. Lewis and Masterson probably met in the 1880s or 90s in Kansas City, where Lewis was then a newspaperman and attorney, and Masterson often visited the city. Lewis's 1905 biography of Masterson was entitled *The Sunset Trail*,[3] and in the book Lewis included, almost verbatim, his piece, "How Mr. Hickok Came To Cheyenne," that had run the previous year in the *Saturday Evening Post*. The broad implication by including it in *The Sunset Trail* was that Lewis wanted the reader to believe that Bat Masterson was the source for the story and somehow involved in it.

Following his cue from Lewis, five years later, in 1910, Bat Masterson, his six-shooters put away and now a resident of New York City, wrote in the July 17 issue of the *Denver Republican* an article entitled "A Few Scraps," reviewing Bat's alleged heyday on the gunfighter frontier. The story was syndicated in numerous papers across the country. In it he gave his version of the legend of the "O":

I remember one of Wild Bill's more humorous stunts used to be shooting the center out of the O's of an I.O.O.F. sign in Kansas City, across from Police Headquarters. Imagine a man amusing himself with that kind of target shooting today! I dropped in for a talk with the chief of that town one day while Bill was in his prime, and, chancing to see the sign, asked what had happened to it.

The chief swore roundly and said it was the work of that blasted madcap Wild Bill. It appears that Bill used to spend his winters in Kansas City, and much against his will was required by the chief of police and the law to give up his shooting irons while he was in town. Bill hated the idea, for it naturally made him feel like a fish out of water. So he invariably used to relieve his feelings by emptying his guns at that hapless sign. He would repeat the operation in the spring when the guns

were returned to him, saying it was to keep them from getting rusty...
Wild Bill was a close personal friend of mine and he'd have fitted into
the pages of a novel.[4]

Western novelist Emerson Hough introduced the legend of the "O" into
popular culture when he included it in his popular 1923 novel *North of*
36:

> *Hickok rose lazily, leaving the liquor in his glass. "Let's take a*
> *walk out of doors," he said. They stepped to the front of the saloon and*
> *stood looking up and down the street. Some forty yards away a sign*
> *hung out over the walk: "Dance Hall and Saloon."*
> *"I'll take the right-hand O," said Hickok quietly.*
> *With the ease of great practice and native genius—and all the*
> *Army men rated Hickok as the best shot with rifle or revolver that the*
> *West ever saw—he raised one of his weapons to a high level and fired the*
> *six shots of the single-action piece with unspeakable rapidity. He carefully*
> *returned the gun to its place. He did not look at the sign. He knew!* [5]

In 1926, the first limited attempt at a factual Hickok biography
was written by Frank Wilstach, entitled *Wild Bill Hickok: The Prince of*
Pistoleers. Wilstach did not cover the legend of the "O," though he was
surely aware of it, because he does cover Hickok's trip to Cheyenne as
written by Alfred Henry Lewis, just not the prelude that takes place in
Kansas City.

Not to be out-gunned by Bat Masterson, so to speak, the third
member of the gunfighter triumvirate, Wyatt Earp, inserted himself into
the legend of the "O," though not until twenty years after his old Dodge
City partner, Bat Masterson, had weighed in. Perhaps it was his biographer
Stuart Lake, and not Earp who placed him in the story, for it was published
almost two years after Earp's death, and his widow Josephine Earp
notoriously pushed hard on Stuart Lake to wildly expand the length and
breadth of Earp's frontier career. It is now known that Lake capitulated to
many of her demands, leaving Earp's first biography, *Wyatt Earp, Frontier*
Marshal,[6] largely a work of fiction. Before the book was published in 1931,
an excerpt was published in the *Saturday Evening Post* in the November
30, 1930 issue, titled "Guns and Gunfighters." Here Stuart Lake hitched
Earp's star to the legend of the "O" in Kansas City:

But let me go back to Bill Hickok's marksmanship. That summer in Kansas City he performed a feat of pistol shooting which often has been cited as one of the most remarkable on record. It was all that, but the accounts which have been so widely circulated have invariably given the impression that Wild Bill did his shooting from the hip. What really happened may be of some interest.

Hickok was on Tom Speer's bench showing a pair of ivory-handled six-guns which Senator Wilson had given him in appreciation of his services as guide on a tour of the West. Tom knew, as we all did, Bill's two favorite exhibitions of marksmanship—one, driving a cork through the neck of a bottle with a bullet; the other, splitting a bullet against the edge of a dime; both at about twenty feet, the sign across Market Square in K. C., a hundred yards away.

Wild Bill continues his distant smile. "The Odd Fellows sign," says he. "I couldn't do that at no paces." So when Tom asked Bill what he could do with the new guns, he added that he did not mean at close range, but at a distance that would be a real test.

Diagonally across the square, possibly 100 yards away, was a saloon, and on the side wall toward the police station a sign that carried a capital letter, O. The sign ran off at an angle from Hickok's line of sight; yet before anyone guessed what his target was, Wild Bill had fired five shots from the gun in his right hand, shifted weapons and fired five more shots. The he told Tom to send someone over to look at the O. All ten of Bill's slugs were found inside the ring of the letter.

That was shooting. There were twenty or more witnesses to the feat, yet in every account of it that I have read in recent years, it has been stated that Hickok fired those ten shots from his hip. I am not detracting from Wild Bill's reputation or ability when I bear witness that while he was shooting at the O, he held the gun as every man skilled in such matters preferred to hold one when on action—with a half-bent elbow that brought the gun slightly in front of the body at about, or slightly above, the level of the waist.[7]

In 1933, William Connelley's *Wild Bill and His Era* was published, and Connelley completely missed the legend of the "O." Or perhaps he did not actually miss the story, as *Wild Bill and His Era* was published posthumously by his daughter after Connelley had died suddenly in 1930. Connelley's daughter cut out two-thirds of his manuscript before it was published, and she decided what would ultimately be in the book. Perhaps Connelley's version of the legend of the "O" ended up on the cutting room floor.

By 1999, the legend of the "O" had become a fixture in popular culture, as evidenced by this exchange in Thomas Berger's novel, *The Return of Little Big Man*. This was Berger's follow-up to his 1964 novel *Little Big Man,* which was made into the award-winning 1970 movie of the same title, starring Dustin Hoffman (as 112-year-old Jack Crabbe) and Faye Dunaway. Here Jack Crabbe talks to Hickok about the Odd Fellow's sign in Kansas City:

> *Wild Bill's eyes was squeezed into sightless slits, and its funny that what I thought was how helpless he would be if someone was to shoot him at that instant.*
>
> *He take me by the elbow of my shirt and bends down and in a subdued voice he says "Hoss, I seem to recall being in your company once in a certain kind of establishment, or am I wrong?"*
>
> *"That's right, Bill, you and me went to a whorehouse."*
>
> *He flinches and says, "Keep your voice down, willya?"*
>
> *I had not been shouting, but I did as asked, and went on. "That was right after you shot Strawhan's brother, which was the damndest thing I ever witnessed. Not only did he have the drop on you, he was able to shoot you in the back. You seen him in the mirror. My god, you was fast."*
>
> *He showed me a thin smile, lifting his head and opening his eyes away from the sun. "I'm not that good anymore, hoss. I don't say I'm bad, but I don't see as well as I used to. They still get me to shoot coins on edge, but nowadays it's dollars, not the dimes of old days."*
>
> *I reflected that one of the dollars he give me had a nick in it. "I saw you put ten loads into that O in the sign across Market Square in K. C., a hundred yards away."*
>
> *Wild Bill continues his distant smile. "The Odd Fellows sign", says he. "I couldn't do that nowadays. I'm taking something for my eyes. It makes me pale, and maybe it is doing something to my well-being..."* [8]

Consider the written evidence. Nichols in 1867. Lewis in 1895, 1904 and 1905. Masterson in 1910. Hough in 1923. Earp in 1930. Berger in 1999. Eight different entries. There may be more. One hundred and thirty-two years of covering the legend of the "O."

Though Nichol's version rings true, it happened in Springfield, not Kansas City. Hough's is a fictional reconstruction of the legend of the "O" that was taken from Lewis and/or Masterson. Berger's version is a fictional amalgamation of what had been written before. Which leaves consideration of Lewis, Masterson, and Earp.

Consider the Earp version. The late Joseph Rosa, Hickok scholar and biographer, took a strong look at the Earp version in the first edition of Rosa's 1964 biography, *They Called Him Wild Bill*. Rosa made the effort to field test Earp's comments before he wrote about them. Rosa wrote from England to fellow Westerner James Anderson of Kansas City, who was also at that time the president of the influential historical advocacy organization, the Native Sons of Kansas City. Among other details, Rosa requested from Anderson the dimensions of the Market Square. Anderson wrote back in August 1956:

> *I have consulted two old atlases of Kansas City. Market Square is the same now as when dedicated by the town company, between Main, Walnut, Fourth and Fifth Streets. It is 300 feet on each side. Because of the Police Headquarters being on the north-west corner* [in the 1870s] *and the Market House being on the north-east corner of the square* [in the 1870s] *a shot from the former would have to be somewhat diagonal, measuring the distance as a minimum of 325 feet and a maximum of 350 feet, according to the atlas, and assuming that the sign was on the corner of the east building line of Walnut Street, somewhat more than a hundred yards.*[9]

Today the dimensions of the Market Square extend north from Fifth to Third Street for 530 feet, and from Main east to Grand for 660 feet. Rosa went on to have the distance tested by a modern marksman using similar weapons, including a pair of 1851 .36 Colt Navy revolvers, known to be Hickok's pistol of choice. The marksman concluded, "Ten successive shots in a two-foot circle at a hundred yards, offhand, is possible with Hickok's weapons but very, very unlikely. With modern weapons it is difficult but not spectacular."[10]

Ten years after the issue of Rosa's first edition of *They Called Him Wild Bill* in 1964, and after frustratingly finding out that much of what Stuart Lake had written about Earp was false and unsupportable, Rosa took a different tone with Earp's purported witnessing of Hickok's Kansas City shooting feat. In his second edition, published in 1974,

Rosa, ever the English gentleman, wrote his understated assessment of Lake's falsehood: "In 1931 in a fictional biography of Wyatt Earp, the author [Stuart Lake] alleged that his hero had witnessed such shooting in Kansas City...no contemporary reference has been found."[11]

Rosa lost faith in the veracity of what Lake wrote. There were also indications in Lake's writing itself that indicated this was a false report. The story about Senator Henry Wilson giving Hickok ivory-handled six-guns has already been thrown into the ash bin of history in earlier pages of this book. Tom Speers became town Marshal in 1870, and would not become chief of police until 1874. The so-called Flood manuscript, a biography written of Wyatt Earp written by engineer John H. Flood Jr., and purportedly based directly on statements made by Earp to Flood, does not mention Hickok, Kansas City, or the shooting of the "O." The groundbreaking and expansive biography of Wyatt Earp by Casey Tefertiller published in 1997 does not mention the incident. Stuart Lake made it up, or more likely adapted it from what he had read of Masterson and Lewis to include a witness who was never actually there: Wyatt Earp. The Stuart Lake/Wyatt Earp version of this event can be thrown into the ash bin of history.

Which leave the versions of Bat Masterson and Alfred Henry Lewis to consider.

Bat Masterson and Alfred Henry Lewis were very good friends, having probably met for the first time in Kansas City. Bat frequented Kansas City often; he even lived there for six months in the last half of 1880. That year of 1880 was the last year of legalized gambling in Kansas City, Missouri. Considering Masterson's occasional manipulation of the truth, Masterson's biographer Robert K. De Arment once wrote that "after a long career during violent times, in violent places and in associations with violent men, there is no hard evidence that Bat Masterson ever killed anyone." [12]

Somewhat like his friend Wyatt Earp (who definitely did kill some people in the American West), Masterson's actual life was almost eclipsed by his legend, and both he and Earp tried in later years to backfill and promote colorful stories and events commensurate with their legend and public image. They both had many years after the gunfighter frontier was gone to accomplish that. Masterson died in 1921, Earp in 1929. Alfred Henry Lewis was a skilled narrative writer and a social gadfly who had friends in high places who became Masterson's friends as well. Those well-heeled friends included President Teddy Roosevelt. Lewis had no compunction about writing stories about his friend Masterson's purported gunfighter career that had little relationship to what actually happened. So Masterson's reports can be considered a secondary version of what Lewis wrote that Masterson wrote as his own experience.

Masterson himself sometimes stretched the truth to the breaking point. In the article "A Few Scraps," Masterson states a falsehood: "Wild Bill was a close personal friend of mine..." There is no record that Masterson ever met Hickok, or that Hickok was even aware of his existence. (Masterson was just twenty-three when Hickok died in 1876.) This is just one example of Masterson's attempt to backfill and promote colorful stories and events into his legend and public image. Where Hickok had his James Buel, and Earp his Stuart Lake, Masterson had his Alfred Henry Lewis. In the 1880s, Bat Masterson could often be found at the Marble Hall Saloon on Fifth Street, then managed by Joe and Charley Bassett, formerly of Dodge City and good friends of Bat. This is the same Marble Hall Saloon favored by Hickok in 1872 when the legend of the "O" took place, if at all. Bat had visited Kansas City as early as September 1878, and visits of his to the town are known in 1880, 1883, and 1884. There surely were others.

Bat Masterson was an unknown nineteen-year-old in 1872. If Hickok's shooting display did take place in that year, Masterson was not there to witness it firsthand. On the other hand, he had numerous opportunities in later years, as noted above, to visit Kansas City and speak to Tom Speers, who became Marshal in 1870 and was chief of police from 1874 to 1895. Furthermore, Speers' police station sat on the southeast corner of Fourth and Main, just two blocks north of the Marble Hall Saloon at 520 Main. So Masterson's favorite saloon and gambling hangout was in close proximity to the police station and the Market Square.

In 1872, across the street from the Marble Hall Saloon, on the east side and slightly south of it at 529 Main, was the I.O.O.F. building. There had been an Odd Fellows building at this exact location since 1859. Early Kansas Citian Theodore Case described the immediate area in 1859: "Beyond the 6th Street no streets were cut through crossing Main and the only houses were on the west side...Speer's Woman's Shop, a frame building, opposite the present [1859] Odd Fellows Hall."[13]

Masterson wrote that Hickok's "more humorous stunts used to be shooting the center out of the O's of an I.O.O.F. sign in Kansas City, across from Police Headquarters." If he meant that the I.O.O.F. sign was across the street from police headquarters, that would be wrong, for the only I.O.O.F. sign available to shoot was one on the same side of the street as police headquarters, and quite a distance away at 529 Main. (This important location will be discussed shortly.) The straight distance between police headquarters at Fourth and Main and the I.O.O.F. sign hung off the side of the building at 529 Main is about 660 feet, or 220 yards. If Masterson meant shooting at the sign from the point across the street from police headquarters at the hanging I.O.O.F., the distance might be slightly more. If we don't take Masterson's statement literally, it can be interpreted that Hickok's shot was probably made from the west side of Main across from police headquarters and substantially south on Main, likely shooting from the northwest corner of Fifth and Main. From that corner to the I.O.O.F. sign on the other side of the street and further south is about 325 feet, or about 108 yards, well within the capacity of an 1851 Navy Colt and certainly within the skill level of a gunman with the nerve and control and natural ability of J. B. Hickok.

The search for the truth behind the legend of the "O" ends with Alfred Henry Lewis, and may have begun with him as well. Lewis grounded in his story factual details of the landscape. The streets are correctly named, the Marble Hall salon is accurately located, and most importantly the exact location of the Odd Fellows building with its purported bullet-riddled sign can be determined with accuracy.

By the time Alfred Henry Lewis first wrote about the building and the I.O.O.F. sign in 1895 (then Lewis referred to James as Wild Bill Hickox), the three-story building of 1872 that had four windows on the stories facing Main had been replaced (in about 1884) by a four-story building, with three windows on the stories facing Main. That building continued to house the Odd Fellows on the upper floors well into the twentieth century, and the building still exists today, virtually unchanged on the exterior; even the original, stone-arched entrance to the Odd Fellows rooms remains today on the Missouri Avenue side. Standing on the west side of Main today, about where the Marble Hall stood at 520, it is easy to look across at 529 and imagine in your mind's eye a hanging Odd Fellows sign. Did Masterson actually talk to Tom Speers one day when they both gazed up at the blackened "O" on an I.O.O.F. sign?

By 1872, the Sixth Street that Case notes above was designated as Missouri Avenue (as it continues to be in modern times). Frank Wornall, the son of well-known early Kansas Citian John Wornall, recalled the location as it was in 1872:

Another photograph, taken a year or so previously, shows that this was the dry goods establishment of L. Bullene and Brother—their first in Kansas City—four storerooms facing on Main street...The building, a brick structure, was owned by my father, John B. Wornall. The covered walk seen in front and fronting most other stores in the block was a typical feature of the period. It obviated snow-shoveling in the wiuter, kept shoppers dry on rainy days. There were two more storerooms in a part of the same building The more eastern of these was occupied by Kansas City's first volunteer fire department. By an arrangement with my father, the Independent Order of Odd Fellows owned the second and third floors of the building on Main, father holding a majority stock. Above the stores on the Missouri avenue frontage was a printer named George Gaugh.[14]

Lewis knew of where he spoke and the lay of the land because he lived much of the 1880's and 1890s in Kansas City. But was what he wrote about the legend of the "O" the truth, or one of Lewis's renowned fables that he later became well-known for? The legend perhaps has been perpetuated so easily over a hundred and fifty years because the story is possible and plausible. Possible because this shooting feat in Kansas City was well within J. B. Hickok's ability to accomplish; plausible because it is well-established that Hickok frequently gave demonstrations of his shooting prowess to his friends. The story needs just a little more empirical evidence to move it into the probable ranking. So the legend of the "O" sits teetering on the edge of the ash bin of history, not quite ready to be discarded, not quite ready to be believed. We will see what the next hundred and twenty-nine years brings.

APPENDIX TWO

WILL ICONS *be* BYGONES?

Ellis T. "Doc" Peirce recalled in 1924 the burial of Hickok: *"We buried him in a rough coffin with his big Sharps rifle by his side. (His pistol, Utter, his partner, wished to keep.) His left arm was laid crosswise, beneath his back, just as he carried it in life. His right arm was extended downward by his side, with his hand on his rifle.*[1]

In 1925 someone alleged that an undertaker had stripped Hickok's body and found that it was covered "with knife and bullet wounds." Doc Peirce wrote and denied this:

> *The fact is I never undressed Bill. What was the use? He had no other clothes to put on. He was clean, except for clotted blood in his hair. I washed that out nice and clean; plugged up the hole where the bullet entered the back of his head; closed the perfect cross which the bullet made where it came out under his right cheek bone; fixed up and dressed his long fine moustache; cut a lock of hair from the back of his head which measured (if memory serves me right) about 14 inches in length; placed his right hand on his right hip where Bill always carried it, next to the stock of his Smith and Wesson gun; placed his left arm across his breast, then put his fine Sharps rifle in the box on the right hand side; I was thru.*[2]

Note that there are some contradictions in the two statements above by Peirce, especially the mention of the Smith and Wesson in one statement but not the other, and the peculiar and nonsensical description of the placement of Hickok's left arm in the first statement. The lock of Hickok's hair, though, is accurate, although Peirce when questioned about it could not remember what happened to it. The lock of hair went to Charley Utter, who gave half of it to Leander P. Richardson. In the *Denver Rocky Mountain News* issue of November 1, 1876, Richardson wrote: "Charley Utter...gave me a lock of the famous scout's hair. It is more than a foot long, and as fine and glossy as a women's locks." In the *New York Sun* he wrote, years later (channeling his inner dime novel inclinations), that "a lock of the dead man's hair was cut off after his body had been prepared for burial. Utter took half of the long brown strand and I have the other half to this day. It is glossy as spun glass and as soft as down. Near the roots there is just a touch of roughness, where the life-blood of a brave great-hearted American gushed out as the assassins bullet burst through his brain."[3]

Richardson kept the lock of Hickok's hair for many years, until one day in 1907 he met up in New York City with Gil Robinson, Agnes Lake's son-in-law. Robinson wrote of their meeting in his book *Old Wagon Show Days*:

> *Several years ago, while conversing with Leander Richardson, Bat Masterson, and other well-known characters in New York City, the subject of the early days in Deadwood was broached, and Richardson remarked that he was a friend of "Wild Bill" Hickok and was in Deadwood the day he was killed. "Why," I said, "that is curious. 'Wild Bill' was the second husband of my wife's mother." Richardson then related that "Wild Bill" who was rooming with him, remarked that he was going to the cafe to play poker. "He had been gone only a few minutes when I heard a shot, and running out across the street to the saloon, I discovered "Wild Bill" with his head resting on the table, dead. I took out my knife and cut off a lock of the dead man's hair with thought of sending it to his widow."*
>
> *When I reminded him that I was the son-in-law of Mrs. Hickok, he said: "Come over to my office to-morrow and I'll give you the lock of hair that I've carried around for over thirty years expecting some day to meet Mrs. Hickok."*
>
> *The next day I met him and he gave me a small package wrapped in a piece of the* New York Herald. *The paper was yellow and faded and the date showed it was thirty years old. On opening it I found the lock of hair. It was over twenty inches long, of a light-brown hue, and as soft and silken as a childs tresses.*
>
> *When Mrs. Hickok learned of her husband's death she went to Deadwood and had a shaft erected to his memory. Among his effects*

which she secured was the hat he wore when he was shot. It had been perforated by a bullet. The hat was retained as a souvenir, and I intended to give it to Richardson, but found it had been thrown away by Mrs. Hickok after the moths of a quarter century had nearly destroyed it.[4]

In his writing, Doc Peirce was a master at dropping mid-sentence *bon mots* that answered questions that weren't even asked, apparently seeking a double-take on the part of his reader. One example is when he wrote about how he found Wild Bill Hickok after he was shot by McCall. Peirce wrote, "Now, in regard to the position of Bill's body, when they unlocked the door for me to get to his body, he was lying on his side, with his knees drawn up just as he slid off the stool. We had no chairs in those days — and his fingers were still crimped from holding his poker hand."[5]

Of course there were chairs in Deadwood in those days. Perhaps the table Hickok was shot at had only stools, but the city of Deadwood had plenty of chairs in 1876. There is an even more influential "mid-sentence *bon mot*" from Peirce, one that started a legend that is now part of American culture and refuses to die. Aces & Eights.

Here is another example from Peirce, even more head-turning: Doc Peirce wrote a report that appeared in the Deadwood *Daily Pioneer Times* on September 14, 1919 telling the story, in his own style, of the drunken shoot-out in Deadwood between Charley Storms and John Varnes.

Old Time Trails—The following story is from the pen of E. T. Peirce of Hot Springs, and is taken from a late issue of the Hot Springs Star, *for which newspaper Mr. Peirce has been writing a series of old time stories. Mr. Peirce is well known in Deadwood and his stories nearly always tell something of the early life in Deadwood. This one is no exception.*

A gun play that was intended to end in tragedy but switched to the comedy column was pulled off on Main Street in Deadwood in the early days. The actors were John Varnes and Charley Storms, a Hebrew gunman. It seems that they had been playing cards in a saloon when a dispute arose and Storms invited Varnes to pull his gun. "My gun is over at my shack," replied Varnes. "Go get it and I will wait for you," said Storms, "but when you return come a shooting or I'll not wait for you." "All right, Storms, I'll not keep you waiting long." Storms followed Varnes out of the saloon and to the corner of the street leading back to the Montana Corral. There he stopped and waited for Varnes.

When Varnes came out of his cabin he saw his mark and the meeting was opened in due form. Storms was the better shot, so Varnes took refuge behind a lumber wagon in the street and Storms proceeded to shoot the spokes out of a hind wheel. When his pistol was emptied he threw it on the ground and took a fresh one.

His guns were of large calibre and shot bullets that belonged to the croquet family...Storms had purchased Wild Bill's old cap and ball pistol just a few days before Bill was assassinated, and it is a wonder that he did not use it in this fight [emphasis added]. Perhaps the reason was Bill never used triggers on his short guns, as he was what they call a pulse shot, and threw his gun forward with his thumb on the hammer and the weight of the barrel would raise the hammer, and as the top of the hammer was filed smooth it would slip from under his thumb, and believe me, it was some rapid shooting. It would make an amateur go and hide his gun.

...I can agree with the old timers and globe trotters—there never was but one Deadwood. Varnes died soon after in Denver. Storms was killed by Luke Short, one of the noted gunmen of the southwest.

This shoot-out took place on August 18, 1876. J. B. Hickok died on August 2, 1876. If Peirce is truthful and accurate in this statement, Storms must have purchased Hickok's cap-and-ball pistol between July 29 and July 31, 1876. Corroboration of Peirce's statement above that Charley Storms owned one of Hickok's cap-and-ball pistols is this eyewitness statement in Deadwood by the reliable White-Eye Anderson: "Bill had discarded the Colts cap-and-ball pistols and had two of the latest Colt's .36 caliber cartridge six-shooters."

Though there has been much speculation over the years about which guns J. B. Hickok actually had in Deadwood, to date there has not been a conclusive determination. John McClintock rather matter-of-factly wrote of his knowledge of the subject in 1939:

Wild Bill had several revolvers, one of which was a finely carved, ivory-handled Colts forty-four caliber, model of 1850. This

452

gun, he said, was a present from Kit Carson. The gun had been used until it was completely worn out, and when it was fired every chamber would be discharged simultaneously. This fine, though useless revolver, was turned in by Wild Bill to Captain Dotson in part payment of a board bill. Subsequently it came into possession of Laverne Wolfe of Deadwood. He owned two other forty-fours and a small pistol. The whereabouts of these is not definitely known by this writer.[6]

John S. McClintock is the only Deadwood-based writer that claims Hickok carried a single 1850 Colts 44 caliber pistol in Deadwood. Consider, however, that although he wrote extensively about Hickok in his book *Pioneer Days in the Black Hills,* and lived in Deadwood when Hickok was there, missing in the book is any indication that McClintock ever actually met Hickok during the several weeks Hickok lived in Deadwood.

What of the bullet that killed Hickok and planted itself in Captain William Massie's wrist? Richard Hughes was in Deadwood that summer of 1876 at the age of twenty, seeking gold like almost everyone else. In 1957, his journal of that time was published. In it Hughes wrote of McCall and the bullet that killed Hickok; McCall "stepped behind Hickok, and with a revolver of large caliber shot him through the head, killing him instantly. The bullet passed entirely through his head and lodged in the wrist of Captain Massie the player sitting opposite...It was extracted by Dr. A. M. Overman—then a physician in Deadwood."[7] Hughes goes on to write that Dr. Overman opened a drugstore in Deadwood in May, 1876, and that he was a physician—surgeon. There is no corroborating evidence currently known that supports Hughes' statement that Dr. Overman extracted the bullet from Massie's wrist.

Hickok biographer O. W. Coursey wrote in 1924, "The bullet passed through Wild Bill's head, came out under his right cheek bone, struck Captain Massey in the wrist—knocking him from his stool—and then passed up between the bones in his forearm and lodged in his elbow joint. A frontier doctor, named McGowan, extracted the bullet, and Massey promptly departed for his home at Bismarck, D. T., thankful to be alive.[8] Coursey provides no source for this claim.

Writer Raymond W. Thorp knew Captain William Massie well in the early twentieth century. Thorp wrote of Massie and the bullet:

Seated directly across the table from Wild Bill when the fatal shot was fired was another famous man—whose fame and adventures antedated those of the dead man—Captain William Rodney Massie. The shooting occurred August 2, 1876, and on the following Dec. 6, this man testified at the trial of Jack McCall: "My left arm was resting on the table when the pistol was fired. I felt a shock and numbness in my left wrist...The ball was not found on examining my arm. It is there yet, I suppose."

It stayed there. This bullet, possibly the most controversial in American history, because no person living knows its caliber or the make and model of the gun from which it was fired, stayed with the greatest and most famous steamboat pilot who ever navigated the Missouri river. Since it was in his left forearm, and he was left-handed, it might be surmised that it caused him trouble at times, but if so, no one ever heard him complain. He had a much worse wound in his hip, caused by the presence of half a stone arrowhead. I knew Captain Massie, and after a steamboat career of my own, determined to follow him and the famous leaden ball.

..."Doctor" Hill, one of the horse-doctors at Deadwood, told him that he could extract the bullet, but since it was lodged in the muscles, it would be a difficult job with the tools at hand. Massie said: "It doesn't bother me at all. I'll just leave it there."

...Traveling with Massie in 1885, the famous leaden ball was heralded by the Democratic Leader *of Cheyenne on July 30, as copied from the* Bismarck Tribune:

The Ball That Killed Wild Bill

The ball that killed Wild Bill arrived in the city yesterday. It is in the wrist of Bill Massey, an oldtime steamboat pilot, who arrived from below yesterday...He was playing cards with Bill in Deadwood when the latter was shot; the ball passed through Wild Bill's head, lodging in Massey's arm, where it now remains.

*In all the bars along the rivers...the great Captain threw his gold to the winds and roared the friendly greeting to the hangars-on: "Shake the hand that holds the ball that killed Wild Bill!"*⁹

Captain William Massie died in St. Louis on January 29, 1910, at the age of eighty-one. He is buried in Bellefontaine Cemetery in downtown St. Louis, where many of the movers and shakers of the American frontier are buried. Tradition has it that he was buried with the ball in his wrist. Yet Captain Massie's family tell a different story. William Secrest notes their story in *I Buried Hickok:*

> *It has always been presumed that Massie took the Wild Bill bullet to his grave, but perhaps this was not the case. According to William Keith, a Massie nephew, the bullet was removed in later years and made into a watch fob. Still later the bullet was made into a lavalier which Ada Massie, the captain's daughter, wore for some years. Keith remembered seeing Miss Massie wear the pendant many times, but didn't know what happened to the bullet upon her death. If it would be located perhaps the pendant could at last identify the weapon that killed Wild Bill Hickok.* [10]

The search for iconic items owned or associated with James Butler Hickok and his alter-ego Wild Bill has been well underway since 1876, with the pace of discovery quickening some in the last twenty-five years, perhaps due to the advent of the Internet and sites such as eBay and Amazon. Whether it's his guns, original photographs, letters, documents, artwork, autographs or more, there is continued strong interest in items associated with Hickok and his legacy.

The greatest auction of Hickok material since 1876 came to market in 2003. This auction of Hickok items came to market with unimpeachable provenance. The items had one owner only during their existence, and that owner was the Hickok family; Celinda Hickok, to be exact, James Butler Hickok's sister. The auction house to handle this was Greg Martin Auctions, a new auction house founded in 2002 by three respected auction executives formerly with well-known auction house, Bonham's. The Celinda Hickok auction was eagerly anticipated, and it received a big media buildup. Its accolades were well deserved. Included in this offering was an 1858 letter from James to his sister Celinda, sent back to Troy Grove from Monticello, Kansas when he was just twenty years old; a wonderful Civil War letter written to a friend back in Illinois signed *Capt J B Hickok;* a compelling and very informative letter from James' mother, Polly Hickok, in 1869, telling his brother Lorenzo all about James' first visit in many years home to Troy Grove; and much, much more. Included in the auction was what was probably the original print of the hauntingly beautiful and evocative formal portrait of thirty-one-year-old J. B. Hickok that graces the cover of this book, and has been copied many times by others. But the prize of the twenty-two Hickok lots offered was undoubtedly lot number fifteen, the second to the last letter to his wife Agnes that he would ever write, a few lines followed by his sign-off: *From your ever loving husband J B Hickok Wild Bill ByBy*. That letter, written on the stationery of the Metropolitan Hotel in Omaha, sold for $190,400. The 1858 letter to Celinda from Monticello brought $64,400. James' Civil War letter came in at $47,040. Polly Hickok's 1869 letter brought $7,840. Hickok's original formal portrait was purchased for $24,640. In all, the Hickok auction on June 16, 2003, at Greg Martin Auctions, brought in almost half a million dollars in just twenty-two lots. Provenance is everything.[11]

In 2007, at the Coeur d' Alene Art Auction in Reno, Nevada, N. C. Wyeth's 1916 oil painting, *Hickok at Cards*, brought a winning bid of $2,000,000. This was the most ever paid for an N. C. Wyeth oil painting up to that time. Experts said what drove the bidding was not just the artist, but the subject matter as well.[12]

A search has long been on to find J. B. Hickok's 1851 Navy Colts, and any other pistols that he may have owned or been associated with. Today there are respected museums that hold what they claim to be one of Hickok's revolvers, yet they all have weak or no provenance: the sort of empirical evidence engendered in such things as serial numbers, contemporary photographs, official documents and more. Most of what passes for provenance on Hickok's pistols is uncorroborated family tradition held by the previous owners. In 2013, a family came forward with a particularly strong and convincing family tradition, concerning a particular Smith & Wesson #2 revolver they claimed was not only one of Wild Bill Hickok's guns, but it was also the very gun he had on him in the Number 10 Saloon when Jack McCall shot him. They took their gun and its story to Bonham's Auctions, who agreed to put it up for auction and promote that auction.

Working back in time to 1876, the chain of possession went like this. In 2013, the current owner of the gun was Eric Hoppe and his family. Mr. Hoppe's grandfather was Leo Zymetzke, who was the head electrician at the Chicago Merchandise Mart for thirty-five years. While working there, Mr. Zymetzke became close friends with a lady named JoAnn Willoth. She was from Deadwood, was an only child, and had never married. She had in her possession this Smith & Wesson #2 revolver that she said at one time was Wild Bill Hickok's. Because she had no remaining family, in 1972 she gave the gun to her close friend Leo Zymetzke. Mr. Zymetzke turned around that same year and gave the gun to Eric Hoppe's mother and father. His parents, realizing the importance and value of the gun, put it into a safety deposit box in 1973, where it remained until a few days before it was taken to Bonham's in 2013. Apparently for the fifteen years prior to taking it to Bonham's, Eric Hoppe had worked to develop information on who and how the gun came to be in the possession of JoAnn Willoth.[13]

He discovered that her parents, Emil Willoth Jr. and Hazel Willoth, were also from Deadwood, and that Hazel Willoth's maiden name was Fishel. He found corroborating statements in the book *Fast and Fancy Revolver Shooting*, by shooting expert Ed McGivern, that describe that writer's trip to Deadwood in 1932 in search of Wild Bill's guns. McGivern wrote, "One of his guns, a Smith & Wesson, is in possession of Mrs. Hazel Willoth, nee Fishel...The gun was given to Mrs. Willoth by Seth Bullock. The Willoth gun is quite generally established as being one of Wild Bill's guns, and all reports seem to support such claim quite convincingly."[14]

On Bonham's promotional piece, and apparently appearing nowhere else, was this following statement at the bottom of the page, in very small type, and almost looking like a disclaimer: "Germane to the question of the gun's provenance is a conversation that JoAnn Willoth had with the Zymetzke family when she decided to give them the gun, in which she recalled that Adolph Fishel, Emil Willoth's father-in-law, had founded a stationary, tobacco, and sundries store with his brother Max, later known as Fishel's Bazaar, in Deadwood in 1876. According to family history, Wild Bill had run up a tab at the store before he was killed and the Smith & Wesson was given to the family by Seth Bullock as reimbursement for the tab."[15]

Eric Hoppe produced numerous signed statements and affidavits establishing and supporting this line of ownership. The McGivern statement from 1932 certainly looked like some good evidence that the gun started off in the possession of the Willoth family of Deadwood. Much excitement was generated in the auction community, as it appeared at last that one of Wild Bill's actual guns with supporting evidence was coming onto the market. Bonham's set the pre-sale estimate at $300,000 to $500,000. The auction was set for November 13, 2013.

The days after the auction the papers carried an unexpected headline: "'Wild Bill' Hickok's revolver fails to sell as bids stall at

$220,000."[16] Bonham's had started the bidding at $150,000, but the prospective buyers only bid it up to $220,000, less than the reserve (a privately held minimum number that the item can sell for, usually established by the auction house in concert with the item's owner). So what went wrong? It appears that prospective buyers of this gun, surely many of them experts in the field, were concerned about the lack of hard evidence of the first two transactions; i.e., Bullock obtains Hickok's gun, then Bullock gives the gun to the Willoths. They may have hesitated because even if Bullock gave this gun to the Willoths, there is no evidence that it was actually Hickok's. Finally, they may have paused if and when they read the biographical material on Adolph and Max Fishel that appeared in John McClintock's 1939 book *Pioneer Days in the Black Hills*. McClintock states that Max Fishel came to Deadwood in 1876 and engaged in the stationery and notions business, while his brother Adolph Fishel did not come to Deadwood till 1879, and was employed for some time by a clothing merchant. McClintock does confirm that Adolph Fishel is the father of Hazel Fishel, who married Emil Willoth.[17]

Though it did not sell at Bonham's auction in 2013, this Smith & Wesson #2 entered that auction with a stronger provenance than all the other purported Hickok guns known today, except for one. Read about that one shortly.

2022 update: Nine years after its 2013 failure to sell at Bonham's, this same Smith & Wesson #2, with the same provenance, came on the auction block at Rock Island Auction House in Illinois. The gavel came down on August 27, 2022, at $235,000, as the Smith & Wesson #2 finally sold.

On May 22, 2022, another purported Hickok gun came on the auction block at Rock Island Auction. As the story goes, this 1851 Colt Navy was purported to be part of a matching pair, the other matching gun having been for many years at the Cody Museum in Wyoming. They are considered to be a matching pair, perhaps wishfully, because their engraving is similar and the serial numbers are just thirteen numbers apart. (The gun in the Cody Museum is Serial #204672 and its "match" is Serial #204685.) They were both manufactured in 1868 at the Colt factory.

These pistols were purported to have been sold at an auction in Deadwood after Hickok's death. This event itself is suspect. There is no reliable record of an auction of Hickok's belongings taking place in

Deadwood after his death. It seems evident that Charley Utter, perhaps with the help of White-Eye Anderson, would have paid for Hickok's funeral. As the story goes, the pistols were separated after the so-called auction, one of them ending up in the hands of one William Burroughs. The pistol (serial #204672) stayed in his family and was eventually gifted to the Cody Museum by Burroughs' descendants, Florence Jenkins and Donald Becker. The other 1851 Colt Navy (Serial #204685) provenance is a bit more convoluted.

In about 1982, H. Sterling Fenn bought a rifle and pistol from a junk dealer/antique dealer in Bloomington, Minnesota. The dealer told Mr. Fenn that about a year earlier an old man came into the shop and claimed that he got them from another old man who owned them for many years in South Dakota. Both the rifle and the revolver were dirty and in poor condition. The old man sold the rifle and pistol to the dealer, and in turn the dealer a year later sold them to Mr. Fenn for not very much. Joseph Rosa analyzed both of the pistols in the 1980s, and he concluded, "the provenance of both pistols is more hearsay than fact."

The pre-sale auction estimate for the 1851 Navy Colt (serial #204685) projected $140,000 to $225,000. On May 22, 2022, notwithstanding the shaky provenance, the winning gavel came down at $616,875.

In 2013, an auction came about in Harrisburg, Pennsylvania, full of association items of the Old West, including an expansive selection of Hickok items. The auction was controversial in several different ways. A contemporary report that summer of 2013 summed up the situation and its controversies:

> The insolvent city of Harrisburg, which attempted to declare bankruptcy in 2011, closed a chapter in the shameful tenure of Mayor Stephen R. Reed last week by auctioning off 8,000 Old West artifacts for an estimated $3.85 million. After paying commission fees, the city will walk away with $2.7 million. According to Penn Live, once you add in earlier sales, the Harrisburg take comes to $4.4 million, or a little more than half of the $8.3 million the city spent acquiring the items. What, might you ask, was Pennsylvania's capitol city (pop. 50,000) doing in possession of a document signed by Wyatt and Mattie Earp (which fetched $55,000), a coat belonging to Annie Oakley ($6,000), Wild Bill Hickok's knife in a box ($14,000) (emphasis added) and Doc Holliday's dental chair ($40,000)?

During a disastrous 28 years in office that earned him the title "mayor for life," Reed mortgaged the city's future to finance a wide array of misconceived schemes and projects. While crime soared, the middle class fled, and schools deteriorated, Reed focused his attention on buying a hotel, building a baseball stadium, buying a baseball team, erecting many failed commercial developments, and throwing good money after bad in an attempt to repair a garbage incinerator that was never necessary in the first place.

A history enthusiast, Reed treated himself to taxpayer-funded junkets in which he traveled the country buying Old West artifacts of questionable authenticity. He paid for these goodies out of a slush fund carved into the budget of the Harrisburg Authority, an agency charged primarily with maintaining the city's water supply. Reed's vision was to create a Wild West museum—one of five cultural institutions that would help turn Harrisburg into an international tourist destination.[18]

That Mayor Stephen Reed spent $8.3 million of the city's money to buy Old West items, some of dubious authenticity, some legitimate, was just a guess. Reed kept no receipts or invoices, only various notes in a logbook. Because the city had declared bankruptcy, to the tune of a bit over $600 million, and the Old West items of Reeds had been used as collateral on one of the loans subject to the bankruptcy, the court ordered the sale of all the items. Thus the 2013 auction.

The Hickok items in the auction all fell into the dubious category, and if there had been such a ranking, the extremely dubious category. A silver-plated pocket watch with a decorative beaded fob, and the words *J. B. Hickok* scratched into the inside rear of the watch cover in block letters, went to someone who must have believed that its complete lack of provenance was outweighed by their hope it was Hickok's watch that Tutt had grabbed. They paid $8,500 for it. Another offering was an old-appearing enamelware spittoon that conveniently had "Saloon Number 10" printed on the top edge. It is not known what it went for.

But the truly deceptive pieces were the Hickok knives. Note that there is absolutely no record nor evidence of J. B. Hickok ever paying off a gambling debt with a knife of his, yet in this auction there were three of them. The one mentioned above that went for $14,000 carried its own written "provenance."

Typed on paper on the inside lid of the knife box:

James Butler Hickok, alias Wild Bill Hickok, who was aware of his own fame, would collateralize many of his gambling debts with knives that bore his name. This is one such knife, won in a card game by Jacob Nash of Lawrence, Kansas. He was very proud of this knife and the fact that he beat Hickok in a game of poker. This is all I know.

> *Samuel Osborn, Topeka*
> *Brethern in Christ Church, Topeka Kansas.*

The second knife, mounted on a board with the name James Hickok on the handle, had a small plaque underneath it describing "lore" about how Hickok's knives were used in gambling and that this one had been won in Kansas City by a John Buel. It went for $11,000.

The third knife had a particularly interesting "provenance." It had been won by no other than Captain William R. Massie, the riverboat captain that sat in on the infamous game in the Number 10 Saloon on August 2,1876. The knife came in a glass box with an ornate metal frame indicative of old age. The knife had "engraved" on the blade, *Wild Bill Hickok 1874*. Inside was a printed plaque that read:

Won July 23rd 1876

Wild Bill Hickok's Boot Knife Won In A Card Game By Capt. Bill Massie, in Deadwood, DK Ter. Hickok Was Killed August 2nd Holding Aces And Eights.

The inside of the lid held this writing that must have sealed the deal:

May 17, 1929

My Grandpa, William R. Massie, won this personalized boot knife from James Hickok in Deadwood on July 23, 1876. My Grandpa carried the fatal bullet of Hickok's Death in his arm till he died.

> *S. Richard Massie*

At the auction, for this item, the gavel came down at $32,000.

Somewhere there is a little old man with a cobbler's bench, a knife lathe, and a few old books on Wild Bill Hickok. There the little old man works away at that bench, supplementing his retirement with the fruits of his creative mind, secure in the knowledge that sometimes people will throw caution to the wind and spend whatever it takes to hold in their hands what they believe is an iconic piece of history.

James Butler Hickok died on August 2, 1876, and was buried the next afternoon, Thursday, August 3, 1876. White-Eye Anderson was there:

> *"Back at camp we had a carpenter make Bill a coffin out of rough pine lumber. He was a large man, over six feet tall and broad shouldered. The coffin was covered with black cloth on the outside and white cloth on the inside and it looked pretty good for a homemade coffin. We put Bill's old buffalo rifle in the coffin with him and Charley Utter put in a few other trinkets."[19]*

Doc Peirce was there, and helped prepare the body for burial: "We buried him in a rough coffin with his big Sharps rifle by his side, with his hand resting on his rifle."[20]

Frank Wilstach wrote what Doc Peirce had probably told him: "Colorado Charley had placed beside him in the coffin the Sharps rifle that Bill had carried for many years."[21]

Three years later, there was a decision to move Hickok's body up the hillside to Deadwood's Mount Moriah cemetery, and on August 3, 1879, Charley Utter, John McClintock, Lewis Schoenfield, and the cemetery caretaker undertook that task. John McClintock wrote about that day:

> *On the first day of September, 1879, Colorado Charlie returned to Deadwood and on the third of September* [McClintock mis-remembered here, it was August, not September], *he, with the writer, and Lewis Shoenfield, the writer's cabin mate, went with a team and spring wagon to the grave of Wild Bill, which had been opened by the cemetery care-taker William Austin, a large man, an old soldier*

who died many years ago at Hot Springs, South Dakota.

Mr. Austin had, after preparing a new grave on Mt. Moriah, opened the first grave of Wild Bill. The four of us took up the body and transferred it to the new grave. Here the box was opened and the lid of the casket was removed. The body down to the hips was exposed. To our great astonishment it appeared to be in a perfect state of preservation. Being perfectly white, it seemed to have a coat of lime finish...

The writer took a stick the size of a cane and tapped many places on the body, face, and head, discovering no soft places anywhere. While the body appeared to be solid, petrified, the sound from the tapping was much the same as would result from the tapping of a wall, and not of solid stone. Some of the party were inclined to believe that the body was in process of petrification. Mr. Austin estimated the weight of the casket at five hundred pounds. While it was an extremely heavy load for four able-bodied men to carry up the hill, the writer would not place the weight above four hundred pounds, nor did I concur in the belief that it was a case of petrification, though there may have been such cases in existence. It was my belief that it was the result of a natural embalming by percolation of water containing embalming substances, depositing these in the tissues of the body.

...It has been stated by the acting undertaker [Doc Peirce?], who was in charge of the original funeral, that Wild Bill's big Sharps rifle was buried by his side. This statement the writer knows to be incorrect, as he saw the gun in the coffin when it was opened on reinterment. It was not a Sharps rifle, but a carbine, or a short cavalry, fitted into an old-fashioned Kentucky rifle breech, with the name J. B. Hickok engraved in the wood. After his death his personal effects were disposed of, and John Bradley of Spearfish, South Dakota, purchased the Sharps rifle. Subsequently it came into the possession of Allen Toomey, of Spearfish, now deceased.[22]

Note that McClintock above avoids mentioning that the rifle was removed from the coffin in 1879, thus his confusing statement, "After his death his personal effects were disposed of, and John Bradley, of Spearfish, South Dakota, purchased the Sharps rifle." This is not correct. John Bradley bought it in 1879 after it was removed from the coffin, and McClintock calls it a Sharps rifle and then says it is not a Sharps rifle. Even writing many decades after the event, McClintock was still obviously concerned about being accused of grave-robbing, the very thing his "cabin mate" Lewis Schoenfield was accused of on a different date and in a different circumstance.

The Black Hills *Weekly Times* of August 9, 1879 reported: "As previously announced in these columns, Wild Bill's remains were exhumed and reinterred in Mount Moriah cemetery on Sunday last... Everything in the coffin was found just as it had been placed there, and the rumor that the grave had been rifled is all bosh. The only article buried with the body was a carbine, and that was in as good a state of preservation as ever. There was no knife and revolvers buried with him as reported, and those who should know say that he never owned a pistol in the Hills."

From John Bradley the rifle made its way to the Toomey family of Spearfish. It appears the Toomeys put it on loan at the Adams Museum of Deadwood in the 1950s, and they eventually requested the rifle back from the Adams Museum, perhaps to sell it to well-known collector of the Old West James H. Earle. It remained with Earle until September of 2021. On September 27, 2021, the collection of Jim and Teresa Earle came on the auction block at Bonham's. The rifle was described by Bonham's as "Wild Bill Hickok's Springfield Trapdoor Rifle Buried By His Side At Deadwood South Dakota On August 3, 1876." The pre-sale estimate was $150,000 to $250,000. The rifle sold for $475,312. Provenance, provenance, provenance.

Of all the iconic items that came out of Deadwood associated with Wild Bill Hickok, his long-sought last letter, dated July 17, 1876, that he sent to his new wife Agnes from Deadwood, is the ultimate object of virtue...and it is lost. Yet this letter has a long and winding provenance that may indicate where it can be found.

First to discard a myth that only muddies the provenance of the above letter: The last letter Hickok wrote is not the spurious few maudlin lines written by Captain Jack Crawford and then back-dated by others to August 1, 1876, to be sure that it might be accepted as Hickok's absolute last letter; the following day he was dead. This phony letter reads: "Agnes Darling, if such should be we never meet again, while firing my last shot, I will gently breathe the name of my wife—Agnes— and with wishes even for my enemies I will make the plunge and try to swim to the distant shore."[23]

Anyone familiar with the style and syntax of J. B. Hickok's writing recognizes this just doesn't sound like something Hickok would write. No written manuscript letter from Hickok written August 1, 1876, has ever shown up, only published versions. There is no record of Agnes Hickok ever receiving this letter. In Frank Wilstach's 1926 biography of Hickok, he wrote, "There are two letters written by Wild Bill at the time to his wife." Wilstach goes on to print the true final Hickok letter written July 17, 1876, though Wilstach incorrectly dates it July 19. Although Wilstach may have been referring to the spurious letter written on August 1, 1876 by Captain Jack Crawford as the second letter, it is not. The final two letters written by J. B. Hickok are the June 2, 1876 letter to Agnes from the Metropolitan Hotel in Omaha, and the July 17, 1876 letter to Agnes that she received in Cincinnati on August 7, 1876, five days after he died.

The spurious letter dated August 1 and written by Captain Jack Crawford actually appeared first as a stanza in a much longer poem written by Crawford, called *Wild Bill's Grave,* published in the Virginia Evening Chronicle, August 4, 1877. The lines that became the purported letter are preceded by these lines:

> *And now let me show you the good that was in him-*
> *The letters he wrote to his Agnes—his wife.*
> *Why, a look or a smile, one kind word could win him,*
> *Hear part of this letter—the last of this life.*

Note that there was no place or date of August 1, 1876 appended to this poem or letter, and when James Buel re-published the entire poem again in *Heroes of the Plains* several years later, there was no August 1 date attached either, and Buel made no claim that he had the manuscript letter. That is because the letter never actually existed.

Incredibly, adding insult to injury, respected historians and biographers have facilitated this charade by adding "Dead Wood Black Hills, Dakota August 1, 1876," to the heading, and "J. B. Hickok, Wild Bill" to the salutation, said heading and salutation taken directly from the actual Hickok letter of July 17, 1876. The August 1 letter does not actually exist. It was invented by Captain Jack Crawford. Another one for the ash bin of history.

Yet the true final letter did exist and probably still does. J. B.

Hickok wrote to Agnes on July 17, 1876 (punctuation added):

My Own Darling Wife Agnes.

I have but a few moments before this letter starts. I never was as well in my life, but you would laugh to see me now—just got in from prospecting. Will go away again tomorrow. Will write again in the morning, but God knows when the letter will start. My friend will take this to Cheyenne if he lives. I don't expect to hear from you but it is all the same, I know my Agnes and only live to love her. Never mind, pet, we will have a home yet, then we will be so happy. I am almost sure I will do well here. The man is hurrying me. Good-bye, dear wife, love to Emma.[24]

Where did this letter go? It left Deadwood July 17. Agnes received it in Cincinnati on August 7, 1876, not knowing that James has been killed five days earlier in Deadwood. She received this letter just as she was writing a letter of her own to Polly and Celinda Hickok in Illinois. Agnes described receiving this July 17 letter from James: "Your kind and welcome letter has this morning been handed to me by the letter carrier, and while I was reading it he handed me another one from my Husband witch I will send with this so you can see where he is and what he is doing." Apparently without even looking at the letter from James, she promised Polly and Celinda that she would forward it to them after she had read it. Probably by August 15 she found out that James had been murdered. This letter being the last communication she ever received from James, she decided to keep it.

After finding out James has been killed, Agnes could not bring herself to contact the Hickok family until November. The letter she sent in November, despite assurances that she still considered them her family, is the last known communication they have.

After Agnes had retired from the circus, and before she married Wild Bill Hickok, she made some business investments in a business up and coming at the time in Cincinnati, lithography. She invested in a firm that used the lithographic printing process to manufacture playing cards and large, full-color posters and billboards advertising circuses, magicians, and the theater. Out of the early days of the company came two companies: the United States Playing Card Company and Strobridge Lithographing Company. Today, the United States Playing Card Company is the largest playing card manufacturer in the world, and Strobridge Lithographing Company, though no longer in business, is highly respected for the beauty and quality of its posters, many of which sell today to collectors for thousands of dollars each.[25]

One of the founding members of the board of directors of the United States Playing Card Company was Gil Robinson, Agnes Lake Hickok's son-in-law. Agnes died on August 21, 1907, three days before her eightieth birthday. At the time of her passing, she was living with her daughter Emma and Emma's husband Gil Robinson. Ownership of the July 17, 1876 letter went to Emma, along with the lock of James' hair given to Gil Robinson to give to Agnes Hickok by Leander P. Richardson earlier that same year of 1907.

Agnes' daughter Emma died on May 11, 1911 at the age of fifty-six, reportedly of the long-term effects of a fall from a horse she was riding in the circus ring three years before. Ownership of the letter moved to her husband Gil Robinson.[26]

In 1900, the United States Playing Card Company opened a small company museum at their offices in the Cincinnati suburb of Norwood. It started out as a museum holding a small collection of playing cards, many dating back to the 1400s, to be used as a way to promote the company's business. The core of the collection at that time was the purchase the company made of a collection from England. In addition to old and rare playing cards, the collection included a large assortment of books on gambling and playing cards and related subjects. The book collection eventually grew to almost 1,000 volumes.[27]

Enter Frank Wilstach, theater agent and author, who sought out Gil Robinson in the early 1920s to find out more about Agnes and James for the book on Wild Bill Hickok he had planned. At the same time, Wilstach had taken up communication with William Connelley, who was writing his own book on Wild Bill Hickok.

On September 23, 1925, Wilstach wrote to Connelley, both seeking information and sharing information with Connelley about their mutual writing interest, Wild Bill Hickok. Wilstach had been in touch with Gil Robinson, who was eighty years old at this point. Wilstach writes: "I am after the last letter he wrote his wife. Know where it is, and have demanded it back for Gil Robinson [emphasis added]. I HAVE A LOCK OF HIS HAIR. Got it from Gil Robinson. Will send you a couple of the long hairs if you like."[28]

Two weeks later, on October 5, 1925, Wilstach wrote again to Connelley. This time he mentioned nothing about the letter, but

Wilstach does say, "Don't you want a thread of Bill's hair? You say nothing on this score."[29]

On February 23, 1926, five months later, Wilstach writes again to Connelley and he makes it clear that he has obtained the letter in the interim since his October 5, 1925 communication. He and Connelley are looking for confirmation of the marriage of James and Agnes. He writes some interesting things about their marriage certificate:

> *I have yours asking for a tracing of Wild Bill's signature. I am enclosing the same. Hope it will serve your purpose. I haven't the data at hand as to the marriage. One of the Robinsons was in a couple of weeks ago, having with him the original marriage license. I was out. Sorry,— for I would have had a photostat of it made. And now the party has carried it off with him, and the last I heard of him was from Frisco, on his way to the far East. He wont be back for six months or so. Too bad.*
>
> *I am at a sketch of the life of Bill, as you know; but, I would like to help you in any way possible.*
>
> *Bill was married to Mrs. Lake. No doubt about it. And Mrs. Lake did not marry again, as reported by writers in the Deadwood papers. They were married in Cheyenne. I missed getting my hands on the marriage license. Missed it by an hour.*
>
> [second page]
>
> *The signatures below are from Wild Bill's letter to his wife dated July 17th, 1876—from Deadwood. The top one was done with a stub pencil; the one below with a sharp one. The lines, except where the shading is indicated, is a little sharper in the original. It was written with a sharp pointed pen, evidently.*
>
> *F.J. Wilstach*[30]

Below Wilstach's signature are three tracings of J. B. Hickok's original signature on the letter of July 17, 1876.

On December 16, 1926, Wilstach wrote again to Connelley. Wilstach still has the original letter of July 17, 1876. In this letter he itemizes the things he has that he will make copies of for Connelley. Wilstach writes:

Yours of the 13th. As to pictures, I have the positives of or rather negatives of:
1) Wild Bill's mother.
2) Mrs. Lake.
3) Texas Jack & B.B & N.B.
4) Dr. Pierce
But no prints. Brought them down and shall have prints made today.
5) Wild Bill's letter to his wife. I have the original but no print at hand I think the negative is at the P.L. [public library] *Shall have one made with the other.*[31]

Frank Wilstach's book, *Wild Bill Hickok, The Prince of Pistoleers* was published later in 1926, and in it he stated when introducing the July 17, 1876 letter: "Here follows the letter, *now in the possession of Gil Robinson* [emphasis added], whose wife was Wild Bill's daughter-in-law, Emma, who is mentioned in the letter..."[32]

Wilstach makes clear in his letters and book excerpt above that he knew where the missing July 17, 1876 letter was and he intended to get it for Robinson. Although the location is unknown from which Wilstach got the letter returned to Robinson, a reasonable conclusion is that it was located in Cincinnati at the playing card museum of the United States Playing Card Company (USPCC), having been placed there by former USPCC board member Robinson himself at some point. At eighty years of age, Robinson may have been reticent himself about asking for the letter back.

On January 29, 1928 eighty-three-year-old Gil Robinson was interviewed by the Cincinnati *Commercial Tribune* about people he had met during his long life with the circus. The reporter wrote: "He shook hands with Abraham Lincoln when that dignitary was in Cincinnati in 1861, bound for Washington. Since then he has known Gen. Ulysses S. Grant, Gen. Robert E. Lee, Buffalo Bill, Wild Bill Hickox, the King of Siam and Edward, Prince of Wales, among other celebrities." Robinson commented during the interview, 'Do you remember hearing of Wild Bill Hickok? He was an in-law of mine. Coolidge doesn't need to think he's the only celebrity that spends time in the Black Hills. Look here!' *And Robinson showed a letter from Wild Bill, dated July 17, 1876, in the Black Hills, South Dakota*" [emphasis added].[33]

Eight months later, on August 17, 1928, Gil Robinson died. But apparently before he passed away, he placed the Hickok letter back in the museum of the United States Playing Card Company, or perhaps his estate placed it there after he passed away, as evidenced by the following newspaper report one year after his death. It appears that Robinson also turned over to the museum the original marriage certificate of James and Agnes as well. On August 29, 1929, this newspaper article appeared:

They say that 'gold is where you find it.' It might be remarked that the same thing is true of documents which tell of the historic past. For such papers have a queer habit of bobbing up in the most unusual places, and to the historian there is no thrill quite like that of unexpectedly coming across some such memento of the past.

The museum of the United States Playing Card company in Cincinnati, Ohio, where one can see the history of playing cards for the last five hundred years graphically portrayed, is probably the last place on earth to which you would go, seeking relics of Wild Bill Hickok, famous gunman of the Old West. Least of all would you expect to find there evidence of the more tender side of this grim-faced cold-eyed killer, before whose blazing six-shooters more than a score of men went down to their deaths. Yet, in a glass case at one end of the big room which houses the unique collection there, you will find these things, an elaborately ornamented marriage certificate...close beside it is a single sheet of letter paper somewhat yellowed with age but the writing upon it is still decipherable and it reads as follows:

"Dead Wood Black Hill Dacota, July 17th, 1876

My own darling wife Agnes I have but a few moments left before this letter starts I never was so well in my life but you would laughf to see me now Just got in from Prospecting will go away again tomorrow but God nowse when it will start my friend will take this to Cheyenne if he lives I don't expect to hear from you but it is all the same I no my Agnes and only live to love hur never mind Pet we will have a home yet then we will be so happy I am all most shure I will do well hear the man is huring me Good by Dear wife Love to Emma

J.B. Hickok
Wild Bill"[34]

470

187_

Deadwood Black hills. Dacota July 17th

My own darling wife Agnes I have but a few moments left before this letter starts I never was so well in my life but you would laugh to see me now Just got in from Prospecting will go a way again to morrow will will In the morning but you nouse when it will start my friend will take this to Cheyenne if he lives I dont expect to hear from you but it is all the same I know my Agnes and only live to love her never mind Pet we will have a home yet then we will be so happy I am all most shure I will do well hear the man is hurrying me Good by Dear wife Love to Emma

J B Hickok

Wild Bill

This image is a photograph of James Butler Hickok's last letter, written to his wife from Deadwood on July 17th, 1876. The location of this important and historic letter is unknown today. Maybe it is in a forgotten backroom box at the Cincinnati Art Museum. Perhaps it is folded into the leaves of a book in a Tennessee college library, or tucked away and forgotten in an untended storage room in Erlander, Kentucky or maybe it somehow made its way back to the Robinson family and rests unknown in the attic of a descendant. The search continues. *Author's collection.*

Thus the original letter of July 17, 1876 was, as of August 1929, in the possession of the United States Playing Card Company at their museum. Yet the USPCC's own company statements as well as other supporting statements indicate that although the playing card museum collection began in 1900, the entire collection was given to the Cincinnati Art Museum in 1929 on "permanent loan." Therefore the book and playing card collection, as well as the July 17, 1876 letter and the marriage certificate of James and Agnes, must have been shut down and transferred to the Cincinnati Art Museum sometime in the remaining four months of 1929. But the "permanent loan" was not permanent. In 1983, the collection was returned to the USPCC offices by the Cincinnati Art Museum, and the USPCC reopened their playing card museum.

Since the 1940s and perhaps earlier, the Adams Museum in Deadwood has had a photocopy of the July 17, 1876 letter. That photocopy may very well have come from Frank Wilstach, who indicated in his letter above that he was going to make a photocopy of the letter while it was in his position. Wilstach died in 1933.

Uncorroborated claims were reported in 2015 that the USPCC ended public access to their museum collection suddenly on October 30, 2001, and that by 2007 a small number of items from the collection were on display at the USPCC gift shop, while an unknown part of the collection had been sold, and the rest remained boxed up in storage. Yet there are reports in 2009 that state (after the company announced plans to move to Kentucky) that "USPCC will continue to have operations in Cincinnati, including a display of the company's museum of historical playing cards dating back to the fourteenth century."[35] Fifteen years later, however, as of 2024, USPCC has still not reopened the playing card museum. In 2017, USPCC sold the collection of almost 1,000 books on gambling and playing cards held by the former playing card museum, many of them rare, to Vanderbilt University in Nashville.

If this long-lost letter of July 17, 1876 still exists, the last letter James Butler Hickok ever wrote, where might it be? Overlooked in a backroom box at the Cincinnati Art Museum? Buried and forgotten in a storeroom in one of the boxes at the United States Playing Card Company, with all the carefully boxed playing cards still awaiting rebirth in a museum? Tucked in the pages of a gambling treatise at Vanderbilt University? Maybe even forgotten in the attic of a Robinson family descendant? This treasure awaits a seeker.

APPENDIX THREE

SHYSTERS, SHADY CHARACTERS, IMPOSTERS *and* MORE

All frontier icons, including Wild Bill Hickok, Wyatt Earp, and Bat Masterson, have a variety of suspicious characters with suspicious motives that seem to pop up out of nowhere, often wanting to establish their place in history by a purported relationship to one of these frontier icons. Some have even darker motives. As with all iconic media stars, there are always people seeking the physical items associated with those icons, creating a market for less than reputable people to fill that desire to hold one of those items. Here are the stories of some of those people associated with the Hickok legacy.

For the two years after his death Deadwood continued to grow, much of that growth near Ingleside where James was buried. Deadwood citizens made plans to move the bodies at Ingleside to a new and permanent cemetery at Mount Moriah. In June of 1879, Charley Utter made plans to return to Deadwood to have James Butler Hickok exhumed and moved to this new cemetery. Wild rumors took hold in the west, rumors about Hickok's grave already being opened and robbed. None of this was true, of course, and the rumors subsided as quickly as they came on.

On August 3, 1879, Charley Utter, John McClintock, cemetery caretaker William Austin and one Lewis B. Schoenfield moved the body of J. B. Hickok to Mount Moriah. The Black Hills *Times* on August 5 reported:

As announced in these columns, Wild Bill's remains were exhumed and reinterred in Mount Moriah Cemetery on Sunday last. For the information we have derived of the removal, we are indebted to Mr. Lewis Schoenfield, an old time acquaintance of Bill's, and in whose memory Bill's many endearing qualities are still bright and green. Colorado Charley, a partner of Bill's at the time of his death, has purchased a lot in the new cemetery, and at his own expense procured a fitting monument of Italian marble, that is now daily expected, which will be raised over his new resting place as soon as it arrives. At 4 o'clock Sunday morning the body was uncovered and at 9 o'clock it was taken out of the grave. The body at internment weighed 180 pounds, but upon its removal it weighed not less than 300. There was no odor and no perceptible petrification had taken place, as it was hard as wood, and returned the same sound as when struck with a stick.

Everything in the coffin was found to be just as it was placed there. And the rumor that it had been rifled is all bosh. The only article buried with the body was a carbine, and that was in as good a state of preservation as ever. There were no knives ot revolvers buried with him as reported...His hair was as glossy and silky as when in life, and a lock of it is now in the possession of Wm. Learned, musical director of the Gem Theatre. His moustache was hard, and seemed like his body to have been petrified and thus endeth the third and last chapter in the life of this truly remarkable man, whose true friends, and he seems to have many of them, still cherish his memory although three years have rolled past into eternity since they laid him in the tomb.

Lewis B. Schoenfield was no friend of Hickok's, which it did not take Charley Utter very long to find out. Among others he wrote to Dick and Brant Street, true friends of Hickok and Utter, having been with them in Deadwood that summer of 1876. To them, Charley Utter made his disgust with Schoenfield known when he wrote to them on January 20, 1880 (punctuation added):

Dear Dick and Brant

Yours of January 4/1880 came to hand the day before I left Deadwood and Dick I was glad to hear from you. Well Dick I will explain all about that man Scholfield you spoke about. In the first place he is a dead beet and a bilk and I can prove it, he is a tenderfoot and wants to come into noteriety, he never seen Bill in his whole life nor was he in the Hills when Bill got killed. Well he made my acquantanship on the strength of Odd Fellowship. he claimed to be an Odd Fellow and was introduced to me as such and when the City of Deadwood layed out the new burriel ground he took several contracts to move the boddies of parties corpses from the old ground to the new one and he came to me and wanted the contract to move Bill that was about six months before I took Bills boddy up. I told him when the proper time came that I would have him moved, and I did not want anyone to meddle with the grave and if they did that I would kill any one that I found tampering with the grave at all. Well on the 1st of August I went to the City Clerk and bought a burriel lot and on the 3rd I hired two men to dig him up. I bought a new outside box for the grave and paid the expressman for hawling the boddy and Paid for digging the new grave. well the night before on the 2nd this man Schoolfield came to me and sayed he would go up and help the men dig Bill up. I told him all right he went to a Saloon and got some whiskey and took it up to help him along and I paid for the whiskey to. They went up early in the morning to dig, and I told them just as soon as they got to the coffin to come and get me for I would not allow any one to raise the boddy until I was there. well they did so and I went up with some friends and we raised him and opened the coffin and found him just as I described to you before so now you have the whole truth about the man Schoolfield and he is a liar. Well good by old friend.

From Charlie H. Utter Colorado Charlie[1]

On September 6, 1879, Lewis B. Schoenfield wrote to Lorenzo Hickok that "your brother was a good friend of mine." He told Lorenzo that he had bought a plot in the new Mount Moriah cemetery because he was sure Wild Bill would have done the same for Schoenfield. He also told Lorenzo that he had "invited" Charley Utter to the exhumation and removal to Mount Moriah. He also claimed he had a deed to the lot where Hickok was buried.[2]

The very next day, Schoenfield sent Lorenzo another letter, claiming he forgot "Some particulars So will fill up with them." He claims he had been overwhelmed with requests from the press for stories about J. B. Hickok, that he had been so bothered by them he told them all, "go to the devil." Working hard to ingratiate himself with Lorenzo, he says he felt duty-bound to help him in any way, "Even if you want him

Shipped home at Some future time I will See to it for you." He offers to get a lock of James' hair from someone else who has it, and send it to Lorenzo.[3]

On April 19, 1880, Schoenfield contacted Lorenzo again by letter, and pressed his scam. He told Lorenzo that some Easterners had arrived with the intention to dig Hickok up and steal the body. He begged Lorenzo to move the body from Mount Moriah to protect it. Schoenfield said he would do it, but he was short of cash. He then claimed that he had paid for almost all the work to move Hickok's body, and that Lorenzo should pay for all expenses.[4]

Five years later, on April 12, 1885, Schoenfield popped up again with a letter to Lorenzo, asking for a letter of introduction to Buffalo Bill. Lorenzo sent him a letter but the meeting never took place.[5]

A month later, on May 19, 1885, Schoenfield was back with another annoying request, a copy of Buel's book. Apparently Lorenzo ignored this request.[6]

Finally, in 1893, the Hickok family was informed by Henry Robinson, a Deadwood undertaker and one-time sexton who had cared for James' grave, that Schoenfield had been charged with grave robbing and forced to leave the country, and not to believe anything he said nor have anything to do with him. With that, Lewis B. Schoenfield faded into obscurity.[7]

In the summer of 1881, Western papers were reporting news of a son of Wild Bill Hickok and his stepmother Agnes Lake. An example of this preposterous story is below, printed in the Black Hills *Daily Times* on July 6 , 1881:

> *A son of Wild Bill, the well known frontier character, who was killed by Jack McCall at Deadwood, is in the city, on his way to join an uncle in the Black Hill's. His mother was accidently killed at Denver not long since by a shot fired by a drunken man at someone else. The young man is lame from a bullet lodged in his leg by a younger brother of his father's murderer, with whom he had an altercation. His step-mother, Madame Lake, lives in Cheyenne. She took charge of her husband's circus after his death, and while traveling with it was married to Wild Bill. It will be seen that a pay streak of tragedy runs through the whole family.*

At about the same time, the following version of "Hickok's son" was making its way through the fifth estate in the West. This came from the Black Hills *Daily Times* of July 23, 1881:

> *According to the Pierre Journal, Jos. B. Hickok, the only son of the late "Wild Bill", who was murdered in Deadwood by Jack McCall, is en route to this city. The lad is only fifteen years old, according to the information of our Missouri river contemporary, and is a deaf mute. That paper also says that the young boy's mother resides here. This is a mistake. She died in Cuba some time ago, and what is more there was no issue from the marriage of Wild Bill and Madame Lake. The youth is evidently an imposter, a victim of ten cent literature.*

The most far-reaching impostor to frustrate and anger the Hickok family is Jean McCormick. Miss McCormick burst upon the scene on Mother's Day, May 6, 1941, when she appeared on the popular and influential radio show *We the People* and announced to a nationwide audience that she was the daughter of Wild Bill Hickok and Calamity Jane. In June, the Billings, Montana *Gazette* published a story about this lady from Billings calling herself Jean Hickok McCormick. McCormick produced an old photograph album which she claimed had been used as a diary by her mother, Calamity Jane. It was letters written to her daughter, in diary form. In these letters, Calamity Jane stated she had been married twice; once to James Butler Hickok, a cousin of Wild Bill Hickok. The second marriage was to Clinton Burke, in 1891. Jane claimed that Wild Bill's cousin, James Butler Hickok, was the father of her daughter. September of 1941, McCormick even attended a Hickok family reunion in La Crosse, Wisconsin. But once Jean McCormick started receiving increasing publicity that year, things began to change.

Now she claimed to be the daughter of the real Wild Bill Hickok, not his cousin. McCormick also produced a page torn out of a bible that she claimed was the marriage certificate of Wild Bill and Calamity Jane. She said that her parents fell in love and were on their way to Abilene, Kansas when they met Reverend W. F. Warren and Reverend W. K. Sipes. Reverend Warren, Jane claims, married them on the spot, proclaiming on the page torn from a bible: 'I, W. F. Warren, Pastor not having available a proper marriage Certificate find it necessary to use as a substitute this Page from the Holy Bible and unite in Holy Matrimony—Jane Cannery, age 18. J. B. Hickok—31 Witnesses—Carl Cosgrove Abilene Kansas

Rev. W. K. Sipes Sarasville Ohio Tom P. Connel Hays City Kansas."

Historian Clarence Paine reported a different "marriage certificate of a page torn from a bible" for Calamity Jane, dated 1873. Also, curiously, the Reverend Warren appears to be the same pastor that married Agnes Lake and J. B. Hickok in 1876. The handwriting from the marriage certificate of James and Agnes has been compared with the bible certificate of Calamity Jane, and has been shown to be two different people, not the Reverend Warren's writing on both.

McCormick claimed she was born on September 25, 1873 in Wyoming. She said she was raised by an English sea captain named James O'Neil, who had befriended Calamity Jane right after she had given birth to McCormick. Calamity Jane and the baby traveled to Omaha, then by train to Richmond, Virginia, where Captain O'Neil and his wife adopted the baby and took her to England. When Calamity Jane died in 1903, her papers went to Captain O'Neil, and when he died in 1912, the papers went to McCormick, she said.

She claimed she kept the papers secret, even from her first husband. Then, she claims, during World War I she fell in love with an airman named Ed McCormick. They met in a wartime hospital where she was a nurse and he was recovering from war wounds. She further claimed that they were married on Armistice Day, 1918, but he died a few hours before the "cease fire" was sounded.

McCormick pressed on with her scam. She applied to the United States government for an old-age pension. She provided the government with Calamity Jane's diary as evidence. Throughout the 1940s she was a minor celebrity, appearing in rodeos and at fairs. She rode several times in the *Wild Bill Day* parade in Abilene.

During the 1940s, Martha Dewey, a niece of J. B. Hickok, went to the Billings *Gazette* and other papers and proclaimed that Jean McCormick was an impostor. It doesn't appear that it did much to slow Jean McCormick down. However, it has been reported that before she died, Jean McCormick admitted she was not born until 1880, four years after the death of Wild Bill Hickok. Jean McCormick died February 21, 1951.[8]

Along with the sort of all-encompassing impostors exemplified by Jean McCormick, there were also the "I was there" impostor, the person claiming relationship with all sorts of famous people; and/or the person claiming to have made an unrecorded appearance at a historic and iconic event. A good example of the "I was there" type is Fred E. Sutton.

Fred E. Sutton was born in Michigan on July 9, 1860. Mark that birth date. It is germane to this story. Sutton's family moved from Michigan to Kansas in 1869. As a child, Sutton was plagued by health issues that apparently kept him from regular attendance at school, so "in place of schooling had the rugged training of the plains school, on the cattle range and in the rough and tumble existence of the wild west... It was in 1878 that he went to Kansas and became a cow puncher, with headquarters at Fort Dodge," claimed one short biography of Sutton, and probably written by him.[9]

As an adult Sutton became a successful businessman in the oil business in Oklahoma and Kansas. He also carried his childhood passion for the Old West into adulthood, continuing as an adult a deep and abiding interest in its stories and history, especially its gunslingers, lawmen and outlaws. He obviously studied what books and articles were available then about his favorite Western heroes. He was particularly interested, however, in three of them: Wild Bill Hickok, Bat Masterson, and Wyatt Earp. At some point, he began to imagine himself involved with these men, and he began to build a paradigm of history that included himself as well as his heroes. It is not known if Sutton really believed what he said, or if it simply got away from him as more and more people seemed to believe what he said.

As a young adult, Sutton lived in Guthrie, Oklahoma, yet it appears he moved to Kansas City at about age forty, and that was his primary home the rest of his life. In Kansas City, Sutton met and became friends with a like-minded lover of the Old West, A. B. MacDonald. MacDonald was a Pulitzer Prize-winning investigative reporter for the Kansas City *Star*. It is unknown how long they knew each other before they collaborated, but collaborate they did, and in a big way; on April 10, 1926, they published an article in the respected, and at that time widely-read, *Saturday Evening Post*. It was entitled "Fill Your Hand," by Fred Sutton, as told to A. B. MacDonald. It was the country's first look at Sutton's Wild West. It featured two of Sutton's favorites, Wild Bill Hickok and Bat Masterson: "Wild Bill Hickok, the deadliest shot of them all, was a close friend of Bat Masterson, and that made Hickok my friend, too. I was with him often in Dodge City and Hays City, Kansas."[10]

Hickok was the law in Hays City in 1869. Sutton was nine years old in 1869, and a sickly child according to his biography. Hickok spent little or no time in Dodge City. Masterson and Hickok never met. "My father, a contractor who helped build the Santa Fe railroad across

Kansas, took me with him to the sutler's store at Fort Leavenworth, and there I saw General George A. Custer and his two scouts, Wild Bill and Buffalo Bill, buying goods."[11]

There is no record of J. B. Hickok ever being at Fort Leavenworth with Buffalo Bill. Hickok was a scout for Custer in the summer of 1867. Sutton was a sickly seven-year-old in 1867. Buffalo Bill was never a scout for Custer.

> *When he was Marshal of Hays City I was walking up the plank sidewalk there and I saw Bill coming down the middle of the street, walking slowly, a sawed-off shotgun in the crook of his left elbow. He came over to shake hands and I asked him, "Why the middle of the street, Mr. Hickok? Isn't the sidewalk good enough for you?"* [12]

As above, it is 1869. Sutton was nine years old, and a sickly child. This meeting between Hickok and Sutton never happened. And again:

> *A drunken soldier rode his horse into a saloon in Hays City one day and tried to make it mount a pool table. Wild Bill interfered, the soldier reached for his gun, and Bill killed him. The next day a troop of the Seventh Cavalry, stationed at Fort Hays, turned out to slay Bill. Seven of them set upon him. He killed three and then fled. He came over to Dodge City, ninety miles across the prairie, to visit with Bat Masterson, who was sheriff then. I heard him telling the story to Bat.* [13]

Here Sutton has taken George Ward Nichols' false claim from 1865 that Hickok would ride his horse Black Nell onto the pool table in Springfield saloons, and made it the illegal action of a Fort Hays soldier. This phony story is a poor substitute for the real story of Hickok and two soldiers in Tommy Drum's saloon one fateful night. Once more, with emphasis: *Hickok and Masterson never met*, and certainly not with child Sutton standing by.

Two weeks later, Sutton and MacDonald collaborated again on a piece in the *Saturday Evening Post*. This time the article was titled "Hands Up!", and again is full of Sutton's fantasies of his life with the famous movers and shakers of the West.[14]

The following year, building on their two appearances in the *Saturday Evening Post* in 1926, Sutton and MacDonald teamed up again, this time on a book: *Hands Up! Stories of the Six-Gun Fighters of the Old*

Wild West. Historian Ramon F. Adams, a highly respected bibliographer of the American West, had this to say about the book *Hands Up!*:

> *The author makes many questionable statements. According to his narrative he appears to have been personally acquainted with all the outlaws of the West. But in view of his age at his death in 1927, such acquaintances would have been impossible. He claims that he saved the life of Billy the Kid in Dodge City, but he would have been only three years old at the time, and I can find no record that the Kid was in Dodge City. The author claims to have been present at many exciting events in the lives of outlaws; for example, he claims to have seen the body of Jesse James immediately after he was killed by Bob Ford. He also, he says, happened to be in Dodge when Wagner and Walker killed Ed Masterson and says he held Ed Masterson's head on his knee while the gunman was dying...The author's accounts of Billy the Kid, Wild Bill Hickok, and all the rest have many errors, too many to list here. On the whole, it is a most unreliable book.[15]*

Adams states Sutton's death is in 1927, but that is surely a typo; he died in 1937, and was still writing up to that year. (See below.) Adams continues. He points out that most of the quotations from Wilbert E. Eisele's 1931 book, *The Real Wild Bill Hickok*, are from unreliable sources, "among them Sutton's *Hands Up!*, a most untrustworthy book."[16]

Fred Sutton wrote an article, "The Killing of Billy the Kid." Ramon Adams flatly stated, "The whole account is absurd."[17]

Referring to Paul I. Wellman's 1961 book, *A Dynasty of Western Outlaws*, Adams states, "He [Paul I. Wellman] defends the book *Hands Up*, Sutton's dictation to A .B. MacDonald, and states that MacDonald was a reliable reporter, a winner of a Pulitzer Prize. That may be true, but McDonald certainly swallowed Fred Sutton's tall tales without investigating their truthfulness."[18]

Adams's last point is well taken. Why would highly respected and Pulitzer Prize-winning investigative journalist A. B. MacDonald have accepted Sutton's statements at face value? Investigative reporting was what he did for a living, and he was nationally known as one of the best in the country. Even a person with no specific knowledge of the frontier west should have been skeptical of Sutton's continued claims to be at the scenes of history and with its famous proponents again and again. MacDonald's archives recently came on the manuscript market (he died in 1942), and the holding includes a description indicating his interest in outlaws of the frontier west: "MacDonald was fascinated also with the outlaws and lawmen of the Old West, seeking out those who were still alive and interviewing their descendants. Among the clippings and correspondence here are photographs of the mother and children of Jesse James, letters from Emmet Dalton and Henry Starr, and original photographs of Cole Younger and Al Jennings. Conversations with one witness to the old days, Fred E. Sutton, led to MacDonald's book, *Hands Up! Stories of the Six-Gun Fighters of the Old Wild West*."[19] It appears that Sutton found the perfect scribe in MacDonald, who must have thought he had found the perfect subject in Sutton.

In 1931, the Western movie *Cimarron* came out, starring Richard Dix and Irene Dunn. It was a big-budget, major motion picture, based on the novel of the same name by Edna Ferber. That year, the movie *Cimarron* won the Academy Award for Best Motion Picture. The opening credits of this movie included the following statement: "For certain descriptive passages in *Cimarron* Miss Ferber makes acknowledgement to *Hands Up*, by Fred Sutton and A.B. Macdonald."[20] So much for historical accuracy.

Respected literary critic and writer Burton Rascoe, a skeptic of Sutton's testimony, said of Sutton's *Hands Up!*:

> *This book is a treasure, a literary curiosity—the most comical lot of brummagem ever put together with scissors and paste, and doubly comical because Sutton has himself figuring personally in nearly every episode, either as an eye-witness or as one who got his information direct from the persons concerned. According to Sutton, he knew them all, from Wild Bill Hickok (his stuff about Wild Bill is taken from an article by Col. George W. Nichols in* Harper's *for February, 1867) to Henry Starr, to whom Sutton claims to have talked just before Starr was killed in 1921! Mr. Sutton was talking and Mr. MacDonald was writing this book in 1927. There are some comical pictures of Mr. Sutton, wearing chaps, cartridge belt with two guns, and holding a Winchester, and another of him holding "Belle Starr's famous Winchester."*[21]

Oxford Languages defines brummagem as "cheap, showy, or counterfeit," as in "a vile Brummagem substitute for the genuine article." Who knew?

In 1937, possibly in response to growing skepticism that he had ever met Wild Bill Hickok, Sutton doubled down on his fable and wrote an article, "My Personal Contact with James Butler Hickok." [22] It was his last Western fable; he died later that year at age seventy-seven. In the archives of the Kansas Historical Society are several Sutton items: a letter to archaeologist George Remsburg from Fred Sutton proclaiming his personal relationship with Billy the Kid, an autographed late-in-life photograph of Wyatt Earp inscribed *To my friend Fred E. Sutton, Wyatt Earp*, and lastly a ludicrous and somewhat disheartening cut-and-paste photo of "frontier sheriffs and Marshals" Wild Bill Hickok, Wyatt Earp, Bat Masterson, Bill Tilghman, and beaming, round-faced Fred Sutton, top hat and all, looking bemused but happy to be in such company, even if it is a falsehood designed by his own hand.

While Fred Sutton was perhaps a sorry impostor with attachment issues carrying out a childhood fantasy, Frank Tarbeaux was a swindler and con-man whose gambling specialty was three-card monte. Yet Tarbeaux made his own mark in the annals of impostors. He put himself at the same poker table with Captain Massie, Charley Rich, Carl Mann, and Wild Bill Hickok in *Deadwood* on August 2, 1876. He wrote in his autobiography:

> *Wild Bill Hickok was something else again. He was the greatest gunfighter in the West, Marshal of Abilene and Dodge City, killed twenty-five or thirty men, and was a hell roarer if there ever was one. He was also my pal.*
>
> *I was in the poker game in Mann and Manning's saloon in Deadwood, in '76, when "Wild Bill" was shot and killed. It happened that I had gone across the street to get a bite to eat when it happened, and got back only in time to see Bill dead. In that game were John Mann, Captain Massey, a Missouri River captain, and Charlie Rich, my partner. We used to spell each other, and that gave us an edge of being fresher than the others, I would play for awhile, and then Rich would take my place.*
>
> *This time I had left Rich playing our hand. The man who shot Bill through the back of the head was a half-witted hanger-on, half-crazed by booze. If I remember correctly, he was one of the McCoys, and was sent to do the job by Johnny Varnes, who had it in for Bill. Bill never saw McCoy in his life. The bullet went through Bill's head and hit Captain Massey in the arm. Right after "Wild Bill" was shot, I was*

in a stage station at Crazy Women's Fork, when a stage driver came in.
The waiter had been reading yellow-backed novels, I guess, and wore
his hair down his back.

Said the driver, "Did you hear the news about Bill's bein' killed?"
Said the waiter "What Bill?" "Wild Bill Hickok." "Wal," the waiter
said, "there's only a few of us left."[23]

Frank Tarbeaux was not at that poker table in the Number 10 Saloon in Deadwood on August 2, 1876, and he was not the founder of the Chisholm Trail. He was not a close friend of Frank and Jesse James, and he didn't shoot Bob Ford in Colorado. All these false claims and more can be read in his autobiography.

ENDNOTES

Introduction

1. John Malone, *North Topeka Times,* August 31, 1876.
2. Charles Gross to J. B. Edwards, April 26, 1922 ms letter excerpt, *William Elsey Connelley Papers,* WH905, Western History Collection, The Denver Public Library.
3. William F. Hooker, "The Camp-Fire," *Adventure Magazine* (August 3, 1920): 180.
4. John S. McClintock, *Pioneer Days in the Black Hills* (Norman, University of Oklahoma Press, 2000). 106.
5. *Manhattan Independent,* October 26, 1867.
6. Howard L. Hickok, letter to editor of *Newsweek* magazine, September 1, 1960. Cited online, cityofdeadwood.com, Wild Bill Hickok Collection.

1

1. Joseph Rosa, *They Called Him Wild Bill* (Norman, University of Oklahoma Press, *1987,* 2nd edition, 3rd printing). 10-14.
2. Howard L. Hickok, *The Hickok Legend,* manuscript excerpt, cited in Rosa, 14-15.
3. Mildred Fielder, *Wild Bill and Deadwood* (Seattle, Superior Publishing Company, 1965). 14-15.
4. Hickok, *Hickok Legend,* cited in Rosa, 14-15.
5. Edith Andrews Harmon, *Pioneer Settlers of Troy Grove, Illinois* (Decorah, Iowa, The Anundsen Publishing Company, 1973). 65-68.

2

1. Howard L. Hickok, *The Hickok Legend,* manuscript excerpt, cited in Rosa, 17.
2. "Steamboat Imperial," *Harpers Weekly,* August 8, 1863.
3. William E. Connelley, *Wild Bill and His Era* (New York, Cooper Square Publishers, *1972,* 2nd edition; 1st edition 1933). 18.
4. James Butler Hickok to Polly Hickok, September 28, 1856, ms letter, *Hickok Family Collection*, Kansas Historical Society, Topeka.
5. James Butler Hickok to Lydia Hickok, September 28, 1856, ms letter excerpt, *Hickok Family Collection*, KHS.
6. James Butler Hickok to Horace Hickok, November 24, 1856, ms letter excerpts, *Hickok Family Collection,* KHS.
7. Robert H. Williams, *With the Border Ruffians* (New York, Dutton, 1907).
8. Williams, *Border Ruffians,* 101-102.
9. S.T. Seaton to William Connelley, 09-27-1924, ts letter excerpts, *William Elsey Connelley Papers,* WH905, Western History Collection, The Denver Public Library.
10. Anonymous recollection, *Johnson County Kansas Atlas,* 1874.
11. James Butler Hickok to Celinda Hickok, April 22, 1858, ms letter excerpt, partially published in the auction catalog of Greg Martin Auctions dated June 16, 2003, *Letters, Photography, and Documents from the Estate of Celinda Hickok.*
12. James Butler Hickok to Horace Hickok, August 20, 1858, ms letter excerpt, *Hickok Family Collection,* KHS.

13. Don Russell, Editor, "Julia Cody Goodman's Memoirs of Buffalo Bill," *Kansas Historical Quarterly* (Winter, 1962): 44.

14. James Butler Hickok to Celinda Hickok, August, 1858, ms letter excerpt, *Hickok Family Collection*, KHS.

15. Williams, *Border Ruffians,* 106-108.

16. James Butler Hickok to Celinda Hickok, August, 1858, ms letter excerpt, *Hickok Family Collection*, KHS.

17. James Butler Hickok to Celinda Hickok, April 22nd, 1858, ms letter excerpt, partially published in the auction catalog of Greg Martin Auctions dated June 16, 2003, *Letters, Photography and Documents from the Estate of Celinda Hickok.*

18. Susan Andrews to William Connelley, May 1923, ms letter excerpts, cited in Joseph Rosa, *Wild Bill Hickok: The Man and His Myth (*Lawrence, University Press of Kansas, 1996). 211.

19. Greg Hermon, "Wild Bill's Sweetheart: The Life of Mary Jane Owen," *Real West Magazine* (February, 1987): 25.

20. James Butler Hickok to Horace Hickok, August 16, 1858, ms letter excerpt, *Hickok Family Collection*, KHS.

21. S. T. Seaton to William Connelley, September 27, 1924, ts letter excerpt. *William Elsey Connelley Papers*, WH905, Western History Collection, The Denver Public Library.

22. James Butler Hickok to Horace Hickok, Spring 1858, ms letter excerpts, *Hickok Family Collection*, KHS.

23. Greg Hermon, "Wild Bill Hickok's Johnson County Farm," *Kansas City Star* (12-6-1985).

24. Charles Gross to J. B. Edwards, ms letter excerpt, January 20, 1926, cited in Rosa, *They Called Him Wild Bill* (Norman, University of Oklahoma Press, *1987;* 2nd edition, 3rd printing): 30-31.

25. Polly Hickok to Horace Hickok, August 16, 1859, ms letter excerpt, *Hickok Family Collection*, KHS.

26. Horace Hickok to Lorenzo Hickok, August 21, 1859, ms letter excerpt, *Hickok Family Collection*, KHS.

27. Johnson County, Kansas Archives, Olathe, Kansas: July 7, 1859, Civil Case, Monetary Claim, Case #57, Accession 02-235.003, Location 00-04-02-02-10, Folder 0070.

28. William Connelley to J. B. Edwards, January 11, 1926, ms letter excerpt, *William Elsey Connelley Collection*, WH905, Western History Collection, The Denver Public Library.

3

1. Truman Blancett, "The Old Frontier," *Denver Post,* March 22, 1931.

2. Guy Butler to Horace Hickok, May 26, 1861, ms letter, *Hickok Family Collection,* Kansas Historical Society.

3. Jones & Cartwright to Horace Hickok, June 6, 1861, ms letter, *Hickok Family Collection*, KHS.

4. For further information on the myriad partnerships, sub-partnerships, and silent partnerships engendered by Russell, Majors and Waddell, see Raymond W. and Mary Lund Settle, War Drums and Wagon Wheels (University of Nebraska Press, Lincoln, 1966).

5. Celinda Hickok, ten-page circa 1900 manuscript statement relating some history of J. B. Hickok and the Hickok family, partially published in the auction catalog of Greg Martin Auctions dated June 16, 2003, *Letters, Photography, and Documents from the Estate of Celinda Hickok,* excerpts.
6. James Buel, *Heroes of the Plains* (St. Louis, Historical Publishing Company, 1881): 36-38.
7. Westport Border Star, 1859, cited in Joseph Rosa, *They Called Him Wild Bill* (Norman, University of Oklahoma Press, 1987, 2nd edition, 3rd printing):30-31.

4

1. Frank Wilstach, *Wild Bill Hickok* (Garden City, Doubleday, 1926): 59-68/Rosa, *They Called Him Wild Bill* (Norman, University of Oklahoma Press, 1987, 2nd edition, 3rd printing): 35-42/George Hansen, *Nebraska History Magazine,* Nebraska State Historical Society (April-June, 1927): 71-81.
2. Hansen, *Nebraska History Magazine,* April-June, 1927.
3. Frank Wilstach to William Connelley, October 30, 1926, ts letter excerpt, *William Elsey Connelley Papers,* WH905, Western History Collection, The Denver Public Library.
4. Frank Wilstach to William Connelley, December 16, 1926, ts letter excerpt, *William Elsey Connelley Papers,* WH905, Western History Collection, The Denver Public Library.
5. William Connelley to Frank Wilstach, December 23, 1926, ts letter excerpt, *William Elsey Connelley Papers,* WH905, Western History Collection, The Denver Public Library.
6. *Fairbury, Nebraska News* 1927, *Kansas City Journal* 1927, *Nebraska History Magazine,* April-June, 1927.
7. Hugh J. Dobbs, *Statement on Hickok trial,* Nebraska State Historical Society, Manuscripts Division, Lincoln.
8. Wilstach, *Wild Bill,* 69-70.
9. Mark Dugan, *Tales Never Told Around The Campfire* (Swallow Press, 1992): 51.

5

1. Horace Hickok, September 27, 1901 letter to the *Topeka Mail and Breeze,* excerpt, cited in Joseph Rosa, *They Called Him Wild Bill* (Norman, University of Oklahoma Press, 1974, 2nd edition, 3rd printing): 53.
2. National Archives, February 5, 1948 letter re. inquiry of Richard Corbyn concerning Hickok's records with the Department of the Army.
3. National Archives, February 5, 1948 letter re. inquiry of Richard Corbyn.
4. Records of the Quartermaster General, 1861-1865, National Archives, cited in Rosa, *They Called Him Wild Bill,* 53-54.
5. Records of the Quartermaster General, 1861-1865, National Archives, cited in Rosa, *They Called Him Wild Bill,* 53-54.
6. Records of the Quartermaster General, 1861-1865, National Archives , cited in Rosa *They Called Him Wild Bill,* 53-54.
7. George Hance, "The Truth About Wild Bill," *Topeka Mail and Breeze,* Dec. 20, 1901.
8. James Butler Hickok to William, June 24, 1862, ms letter, excerpt, published in the auction catalog of Greg Martin Auctions for June 16, 2003, *Letters, Photography, and Documents from the Estate of Celinda Hickok.*

9. James Butler Hickok to Lydia Hickok, July 8, 1862, cited in Joseph Rosa, *Wild Bill Hickok: The Man and His Myth* (Lawrence, University Press of Kansas, 1996): 32-33.

10. Rolla *Herald,* February 9, 1912.

11. Paul Campbell, "Dallas County Played Significant Role In Civil War, Kinzer Says," *Buffalo Reflex,* September 16, 2009.

12. R. I. Holcombe, *History of Greene County, Missouri,* Chapter 13, "Bloody Bones Kelso," 1883.

13. William E. Connelley, *John Kelso,* unpublished typescript chapter excerpt, *William Elsey Connelley Papers,* WH905, Western History Collection, The Denver Public Library.

14. Connelley, *John Kelso,* ts excerpt.

15. F. A. Carpenter, *History of the 17th Illinois Cavalry Volunteers* (no p., circa 1880s).

16. Rosa, *Wild Bill Hickok: The Man and His Myth,* 35.

17. William E. Connelley, *Wild Bill and His Era* (New York, Cooper Square Publishers, 1972, 2nd edition; 1st edition 1933): 66.

18. T. J. Estes, *Early Days and War Times In Northern Arkansas,* 1928, 15-16.

19. For an expansive review and intelligent treatise on the Price raid, see Howard N. Monett, *Action Before Westport 1864* (Kansas City, Missouri, Westport Historical Society, 1964).

20. John B. Sanborn, *The Campaign in Missouri in September and October, 1864.* (No publisher, no date): 32.

21. John Bradbury, ed. "The Civil War Letters of Lorenzo B. Hickok," *Newsletter of the Phelps County Historical Society,* October 1986, 4.

22. Lorenzo B. Hickok to Horace Hickok, July 16, 1863, ms letter, excerpt, *Hickok Family Collection,* Kansas Historical Society.

23. Lorenzo B. Hickok to Horace Hickok, March 4, 1864, ms letter, excerpt, *Hickok Family Collection,* KHS.

24. Lorenzo B. Hickok to Celinda Hickok, April 15, 1864, ms letter, excerpt, *Hickok Family Collection,* KHS.

25. Lorenzo B. Hickok to Celinda Hickok, July 26, 1864, ms letter, excerpt, published in the auction catalog of Greg Martin Auctions for June 16, 2003, *Letters, Photography, and Documents from the Estate of Celinda Hickok.*

26. Lorenzo B. Hickok to Horace Hickok, September 10, 1864, ms letter, excerpt, *Hickok Family Collection,* Kansas Historical Society.

27. Records of the Missouri Union Provost Marshal, 1861-1865.

28. Records of the Missouri Union Provost Marshal, 1861-1865, cited in Joseph Rosa, *They Called Him Wild Bill* (Norman, University of Oklahoma Press, 1987, 2nd edition, 3rd printing: 63-64.

29. Records of the Missouri Union Provost Marshal, 1861-1865, cited in Rosa, *They Called Him Wild Bill,* 64.

30. Records of the Missouri Union Provost Marshal, 1861-1865, cited in Rosa, *They Called Him Wild Bill,* 64.

31. Records of the Missouri Union Provost Marshal, 1861-1865.

32. Records of the Union Army, Southwest Missouri, 1861-1865, cited in Rosa, *They Called Him Wild Bill,* 64.

33. Records of the Union Army, Southwest Missouri, 1861-1865, cited in Rosa, *They Call Him Wild Bill,* 69.

34. Records of the Union Army, Southwest Missouri, 1861-1865, cited in Rosa, *They Called Him Wild Bill*, 69-70.

35. Records of the Missouri Union Provost Marshal, 1861-1865.

36. Records of the Missouri Union Provost Marshal, 1861-1865.

37. Records of the Missouri Union Provost Marshal, 1861-1865, cited in Rosa, *They Called Him Wild Bill*, 70.

⑥

1. Leo E. Huff, "Guerrillas, Jayhawkers and Bushwhackers in Northern Arkansas During the Civil War," *Arkansas Historical Quarterly*, Summer, 1965, 128-129, cited in Joseph Rosa, *Wild Bill Hickok: The Man and his Myth* (Lawrence, University Press of Kansas, 1996): 43.

2. George Ward Nichols, "Wild Bill," *Harpers New Monthly Magazine*, February 1867, excerpt.

3. State of Missouri vs. William Hickok—1865 Coroner's Report, Testimony of J. W. Orr, July 22nd, 1865, *Greene County Archives*, Springfield, Missouri.

4. State of Missouri vs. William Hickok—1865 Coroner's Report, Testimony of Eli Armstrong, *Greene County Archives*, Springfield, Missouri.

5. State of Missouri vs. William Hickok—1865 Coroner's Report, Testimony of Eli Armstrong, *Greene County Archives*, Springfield, Missouri.

6. State of Missouri vs. William Hickok—1865 Coroner's Report, Testimony of F. W. Scholten, *Greene County Archives*, Springfield, Missouri.

7. Robert Utley, *Life in Custer's Cavalry: Diaries and Letters of Albert and Jenny Barnitz 1867-1868*, New Haven, Yale Press, 1977): 37-38

8. Utley, *Life in Custer's Cavalry*, 37-38.

9. State of Missouri vs. William Hickok—1865 Trial Documents, Defense Attorney Phelps Proposed Instructions for the Jury, Greene County Archives, Springfield, Missouri. Judge Boyd rejected the proposed jury instructions written by defense attorney Phelps. Phelps' proposed instructions have been mistaken by some writers as being something different than what they actually are: the proposed jury instructions written by Phelps in the Hickok trial that were rejected by the judge in favor of the proposed jury instructions written by prosecuting lawyer Robert Fyan, because the judge believed Hickok was guilty. *The jury never saw these proposed instructions written by Phelps, nor would they. A*s it was then, it is still common today for the opposing lawyers in a jury trial to offer jury instructions to the judge that favor their own side. The judge may use one or the other instructions, but never would a judge use both. Several writers have completely mistaken Phelps' jury instructions for some sort of supplementary ruling from Judge Boyd that offered Hickok vindication. It was nothing of the kind, and it was certainly not written by Judge Boyd. See Joseph Rosa, *Wild Bill Hickok: The Man & His Myth*, 1996, 121-122. See also Rosa, *Wild Bill Hickok: Gunfighter*, University of Oklahoma Press, 2003, 94-95; and Steven Lubet (following Rosa), "Slap Leather! Legal Culture, Wild Bill Hickok, and the Gunslinger Myth," *UCLA Law Review*, Vol. 48, #6.

10. State of Missouri vs. William Hickok—1865 Coroner's Report, Testimony of Thomas D. Hudson, *Greene County Archives*, Springfield, Missouri.

11. State of Missouri vs. William Hickok—1865 Coroner's Report, Testimony of W. S. Riggs. *Greene Count Archives*, Springfield, Missouri.

12. State of Missouri vs. William Hickok—1865 Coroner's Report, Testimony of Lorenza F. Lee, *Greene County Archives,* Springfield, Missouri.

13. State of Missouri vs. William Hickok—1865 Coroner's Report, Testimony of Eli Armstrong, *Greene County Archives,* Springfield, Missouri.

14. State of Missouri vs. William Hickok—1865 Coroner's Report, Testimony of A. L. Budlong, *Greene County Archives,* Springfield, Missouri.

15. Utley, *Life in Custer's Cavalry,* 37-38.

16. State of Missouri vs. William Hickok—1865 Coroner's Report, Testimony of Dr. E. Ebert, *Greene County Archives,* Springfield, Missouri.

17. Dexter Fellows, *This Way To The Big Show: The Life Of Dexter Fellows* (New York, The Viking Press, 1936): 35-36.

18. William Connelley, 1925 interview transcript of J. T. Botkin, *William Elsey Connelley Collection,* WH905, Western History Collection, The Denver Public Library.

7

1. If the reader should think that Lachryma Christi is some kind of fine frontier liquor that no longer exists, as this writer did when first reading this, it is not that at all. The name Lachryma Christi means "the tears of Christ;" it is a fine Italian wine made from grapes grown on the slopes of Mt. Vesuvius overlooking Pompeii and the Bay of Naples. It is still sold today all over the world in both white and red varieties, and it is the only wine in the world that approximates very closely the same wine consumed by the ancient Romans.

2. *Junction City Weekly Union,* April 10, 1867, dateline Fort Harker, Kansas: *We make the following extracts from a letter written to the Boston Transcript, dated Fort Harker, Kansas April 5th....The great Indian expedition is at last on the war path...Wild Bill, whose incredible adventures you have all seen in* Harper's Magazine *for February, was with the party as a courier...In justice to Wild Bill we would state that he emphatically denies two of the Munchhausen tales related of him; the horse story and killing twelve men. He once killed three ranchmen who attacked his house, but he had the door between him and them [emphasis added]. Was this a confession six years after the fact? Or was this J. B. Hickok, tired of answering questions about the outrageous McCanles version put out by George Ward Nichols two months before, answering sarcastically and facetiously with a throw-away answer? Hickok obviously denied that he killed twelve men at Rock Creek. Further, it seems likely that the statement about killing the three ranchmen comes from the opinion of the reporter rather than Hickok.*

3. George Ward Nichols, "Wild Bill," *Harpers New Monthly Magazine,* February 1867.

4. Warrant for the arrest of William Hickok, January 13, 1866, charges unknown, *Greene County Archives,* Springfield, Missouri,

5. Eyewitness testimony of J. B. Hickok, in the matter of John Orr and Samuel Coleman, January 25, 1866, cited in R. I. Holcombe, *History of Greene County,* Missouri, 1883.

8

1. Within several years, and certainly by the time that J. B. Hickok moved to Kansas City in 1872, the Marble Hall Saloon in Kansas City would move into a bigger location in the 500 block of Main Street, which would become its permanent location.

2. Danny Bohen to William Connelley, December, 1925, ms letter excerpt, *William Elsey Connelley Collection*, WH905, Western History Collection, The Denver Public Library.

3. George Hance, "The Truth About Wild Bill," *Topeka Mail and Breeze*, December 20, 1901.

4. Charles Dawson, *Pioneer Tales of the Oregon Trail Through Jefferson County, Nebraska* (Topeka, Crane and Co., 1912):106-107.

5. James F. Meline, *Two Thousand Miles on Horseback: Santa Fe and Back: A Summer Tour Through Kansas, Nebraska, Colorado, and New Mexico, in the Year 1866* (New York, Hurd and Houghton, 1867, 1974, 1987, 2nd edition, 3rd printing).

6. Meline, *Two Thousand Miles*, 246-251.

7. William E. Connelley, *Wild Bill and His Era*, (New York, Cooper Square Publishers, 1972): 26-27.

8. *Meline*, Two Thousand Miles, 299.

9. "Julia Rockwell's Story," *Kansas City Star*, December 14, 1947, cited in Joseph Rosa, *They Called Him Wild Bill* (University of Oklahoma Press, Norman, 1974, 1987, 2nd edition, 3rd printing): 93.

10. William Connelley, *Wild Bill and His Era*, 93-94/Joseph Rosa, "Was Wild Bill Ever an Ump?" *Wild West Magazine*, June, 2011/"First Team a 'Knockout,'" *Kansas City Times*, April 27, 1927/Jeremy Drouin, "Did Wild Bill Hickok Ump a Baseball Game in Kansas City? KCQ Steps to the Plate," *Kansas City Public Library* and *Kansas City Star*, September 25, 2020.

11. Don Russell, *Lives and Legends of Buffalo Bill* (Norman, University of Oklahoma Press, 1960): 77-78.

12. Hickok lived with the Dunstons in Junction City for a period in 1866.

⑨

1. Case #482, John Tobin and William Wilson, larceny, District Court, District of Kansas, cited in Joseph Rosa, "J.B. Hickok, Deputy U.S. Marshal," *Kansas History, A Journal of the Central Plains*, Vol. 2, Number 4 (Winter 1979): 236.

2. James Drees, *Bloody Prairie, Volume 2* (The Hays Daily News, Hays, Kansas 1997): 27.

3. John Beach Edwards, *Early Days In Abilene* (Abilene, Kansas, *Abilene Daily Chronicle*, 1938).

4. Jeff Barnes, *The Great Plains Guide To Custer* (Mechanicsburg, PA, Stackpole Books, 2012): 18-20.

5. T. J. Stiles, *Custer's Trials* (New York, Alfred A. Knopf, 2015): 265-266.

6. Stiles, *Custer's Trials*, 293.

7. Elmo Scott Watson, ed. Theodore R. Davis, *Henry M. Stanley's Indian Campaign in 1867* (Westerners Brand Book, Bound Volume 2, 1945-46): 106-107.

8. Stiles, *Custer's Trials*, 266.

9. Stiles, *Custer's Trials*, 266.

10. Stiles, *Custer's Trials*, 268.

11. Stiles, *Custer's Trials*, 268.

12. Stiles, *Custer's Trials*, 268-269.

13. Stiles, *Custer's Trials*, 269.

14. Stiles, *Custer's Trials*, 273.

15. Stiles, *Custer's Trials*, 274.

16. Stiles, *Custer's Trials*, 274.

17. Stiles, *Custer's Trials*, 274.

18. Stiles, *Custer's Trials*, 275.

19. Stiles, *Custer's Trials*, 276.

20. Stiles, *Custer's Trials*, 276.

21. Danny Bohen to William Connelley, December 1925, ms letter excerpt, *William Elsey Connelley Collection*, WH905, Western History Collection, The Denver Public Library.

22. Blaine Burkey, *Custer, Come At Once! The Fort Hays Years of George and Elizabeth Custer* (Hays, Kansas, Society of Friends of Historic Fort Hays, 2nd Printing, 1991): 33.

23. Burkey, *Custer, Come At Once!*, 32.

24. Danny Bohen to William Connelley, December 1925, ms letter excerpt, *William Elsey Connelley Collection*, WH905. Western History Collection, The Denver Public Library.

25. Jim Gray, *Desperate Seed: Ellsworth, Kansas on the Violent Frontier* (Ellsworth, Kansas Cowboy Publications, 2009): 9, 11.

26. Burkey, *Custer, Come at Once!*, 33.

27. Gray, *Desperate Seed*, 9-10.

28. Charles Sternberg, *Life of a Fossil Hunter*, 1909, 11-13.

29. Colonel George Augustus Armes, *Ups and Downs of an Army Officer*, 1900, 232.

30. William Connelley, *Wild Bill and His Era* (New York, Cooper Square Publishers, 1972, 2nd edition, 1st edition 1933): 99.

31. Danny Bohen to William Connelley, December 1925, ms letter excerpt, *William Connelley Collection*, WH905, Western History Collection, The Denver Public Library.

32. Francis Cragin, *Early West Notebook*, Francis Cragin Collection, Colorado Historical Society, cited in Joseph Rosa, *The Man & His Myth* (Lawrence, University Press of Kansas, 1996): 90.

33. George Armstrong Custer, *My Life on the Plains* (New York, Sheldon and Co.,1874): 33-34.

34. Russell *Record*, December 5, 1938, cited in Drees, *Bloody Prairie Vol. 2*, 21.

35. Gray, *Desperate Seed*, 14.

36. Rosa, *J. B. Hickok*, Deputy U.S. Marshal, 237.

37) Manhattan *Independent*, October 26, 1867, cited in Joseph Rosa, *They Called Him Wild Bill* (Norman, Oklahoma University, 1974, 2nd edition, 3rd printing): 117.

38) Francis S. Wilson, *A History of Ellsworth County, Kansas* (Ellsworth County Historical Society, 1979).

39) Ellsworth *Tri-Weekly Advertiser*, December 25, 1867, cited in Gray, *Desperate Seed*, 18.

10

1. Danny Bohen to William Connelley, December 1925, ms letter excerpt, *William Elsey Connelley Collection*, WH905, Western History Collection, The Denver Public Library.

2. Nyle H. Miller and Joseph W. Snell, *Great Gunfighters of the Kansas Cowtowns, 1867—1886* (Lincoln, University of Nebraska, Bison Books, 1967): 117.

3. Joseph Rosa, "J. B. Hickok, Deputy U. S. Marshal," *Kansas History, A Journal of the Central Plains, Volume 2,* Number 4 (Winter 1979): 239-240.

4. Miguel Otero, *My Life on the Frontier* (New York, The Press of the Pioneers, 1935): 2-4, 10-17.

5. James Drees, *Bloody Prairie vol. 2* (Hays, Kansas, *The Hays Daily News,* 1997): 21.

6. Drees, *Bloody Prairie vol. 2,* 19.

7. Joseph Rosa, *They Called Him Wild Bill* (Norman, University of Oklahoma Press, 1974, 2nd edition, 3rd printing): *97-98.*

8. William Connelley interviews F. H. Chase, June 28, 1913, ts statement excerpt, *William Elsey Connelley Collection,* WH905, Western History Collection, The Denver Public Library.

9. John H. Putnam, "A Trip to the End of the Union Pacific in 1868," *Kansas Historical Quarterly,* vol. 13, no.3, 196-202.

10. Rosa, T*hey Called Him Wild Bill,* 121.

11. Colonel George Augustus Armes, *Ups and Downs of an Army Officer,* 1900, 271-272.

12. Armes, *Ups and Downs,* 273.

13. Danny Bohen to William Connelley, December 1924, ms. letter excerpt, *William Connelley Collection,* WH905, Western History Collection, The Denver Public Library.

14. T.J. Stiles, *Custer's Trials* (New York, Alfred A. Knopf, 2015): 316-319.

15. Armes, *Ups and Downs,* 278.

16. Armes, *Ups and Downs,* 279.

17. Armes, *Ups and Downs,* 283.

18. Armes, *Ups and Downs,* 283.

19. Armes, *Ups and Downs,* 285.

20. Armes, *Ups and Downs,* 285.

21. Armes, *Ups and Downs,* 285.

22. Armes, *Ups and Downs,* 285.

11

1. Letters Dispatched, 1869, Records of Fort Dodge, National Archives, cited in Joseph Rosa, *Wild Bill Hickok: The Man and His Myth* (Lawrence, University Press of Kansas, 1996): 91-92.

2. Hiram Robbins, "Wild Bill's Humor's," *Arkansaw Traveler (n.d.).*

3. Colonel George Augustus Armes, *Ups and Downs of an Army Officer,* 1900, 286.

4. Armes, *Ups and Downs,* 286.

5. Polly Hickok to Lorenzo Hickok, May 10, 1869, ms letter, published in the auction catalog of Greg Martin Auctions for June 16, 2003, *Letters, Photography, and Documents of the Estate of Celinda Hickok,* excerpt.

6. Howard Hickok, *The Hickok Legend,* cited in Joseph Rosa, *They Called Him Wild Bill* (Norman, University of Oklahoma Press, 1974, 2nd edition, 3rd printing): 131.

7. Howard Hickok, interview, cited in Rosa, *They Called Him Wild Bill,* 130.

8. James W. Buel, *Heroes of the Plains* (St. Louis, Historical Publishing Company, 1881): 106-110.

9. Ft. Wallace, Charles Woods to U. S. Marshal, May 8,1869, in Joseph Rosa, "J. B. Hickok: Deputy U. S. Marshal," *Kansas History, A Journal of the Central Plains,* Volume 2 Number 4 (Winter, 1979): 240.

10. Rosa, *J.B. Hickok,* 241.

11. Rosa, *J.B. Hickok,* 241-242.

12. Rosa, *J.B. Hickok,* 244.

13. Rosa, *J.B. Hickok,* 241-244.

14. Elizabeth Custer, *Following the Guidon* (NY, Harper and Bros., 1890): 160.

15 Elizabeth Custer, *Following the Guidon,* 161.

16. Matt Clarkson, "The Matthew Clarkson Manuscripts," ed. Rodney Staab, *Kansas History* (Winter, 1982): 259.

17. Records of Fort Hays, Letters Dispatched, 1867-1869, cited in Rosa, *They Called Him Wild Bill (*Norman, University of Oklahoma, 1974, 2nd edition, 3rd printing): 138-139.

18. James Drees, *Bloody Prairie, vol.2.* (Hays, Kansas, Hays Daily News, 1997): 22.

19. Annie Gilkeson to William Connelley, March 5, 1926, ts letter, *William Elsey Connelley Collection,* WH905, Western History Collection, The Denver Public Library.

20. Miguel Otero, *My Life on the Frontier* (New York, Press of the Pioneers, 1935):14.

21. Records of Fort Hays, Letters Dispatched, 1867-1869, cited in Rosa, *They Called Him Wild Bill,* 144-145.

22. Otero, *My Life on the Frontier,* 16-17.

23. Records of Fort Hays, Letters Received, 1867-1869, cited in Rosa, *They Called Him Wild Bill,* 145.

24. *Wichita Eagle,* September 14, 1876, citing statement of John Malone.

25. Blaine Burkey, *Wild Bill Hickok: The Law in Hays City* (Hays, Ellis County Historical Society, 1996): 8.

26. Harry Young, *Hard Knocks* (Portland, Wells and Company, 1915): 41-43.

27. Burkey, *Wild Bill Hickok,* 10.

28. Records of Fort Hays, Letters Sent, 1867—1869, cited in Rosa, *They Called Him Wild Bill,* 150.

29. Miller and Snell, *Great Gunfighters,* 123-124.

30. Rosa, *They Called Him Wild Bill,* 152.

31. Rosa, *They Called Him Wild Bill,* 149-153; "J. B. Hickok," 244-245.

32. Miller and Snell, *Great Gunfighters,* 126.

33. Adolph Roenigk, *Pioneer History of Kansas* (Denver, 1933): 182.

34. Rosa, *J.B. Hickok,* 246.

35. Rosa, *J.B. Hickok,* 247.

36. Rosa, *J.B. Hickok,* 246-248.

37. Rosa, *J.B. Hickok,* 248.

12

1. William E. Connelley, *Wild Bill and His Era* (New York, Cooper Square Publishers, 1972, 2nd edition, 1st edition 1933): 17.

2. J. C. Prine to William Connelley, February 28th, 1923, ms. letter, *William Elsey Connelley Collection,* WH905, Western History Collection, Denver Public Library.

3. *Newsletter,* Geary County Historical Society, September 28, 2020.

4. Joseph Rosa, *They Called Him Wild Bill* (Norman, University of Oklahoma Press, 1974, 2nd edition, 3rd printing): 171.

5. A. D. Gilkeson to H.L. Humphrey, *Dickinson County Biographical Sketches,* vol. 1, #3, files of the Kansas Historical Society.

6. Brian Pohanka, *A Summer on the Plains, 1870: The Diary of Annie Gibson Roberts* (Bryan, Texas, 1982): 43.
7. Rodney Staab ed., "Matthew Clarkson Manuscripts" *Kansas History* Winter,1982, 274-275.
8. Connelley, *Wild Bill and His Era*, 132-133.
9. Elizabeth Custer, *Following the Guidon* (New York, Harper, 1890): 164 -165.
10. 1909 journal of Sgt. John Ryan, cited in Sandy Barnard, *Ten Years With Custer* (Terre Haute, AST Press, 2001): 61, 107-108, 121-125.
11. William Webb, *Buffalo Land* (Cincinnati, E. Hannaford, 1872): 149.
12. Jeff Broome, "Wild Bill's Brawl With Two of Custer's Troopers," *Wild West* (December, 2012): 50-57.
13. Joseph Rosa, "J. B. Hickok, Deputy U. S. Marshal," *Kansas History, A Journal of the Central Plain*s, Volume 2, Number 4(Winter 1979): 249-250.
14. Percy Ebbutt, *Emigrant Life in Kansas* (Sonnenschein & Co. 1886): 12-13.

13

1. Theophilus Little, *Early Days In Abilene*, ms. loose leaf notebook, circa 1900, Abilene Historical Society.
2. Charles Gross to J. B. Edwards, April 13, 1922, ms letter, *John Beach Edwards Papers*, Kansas Historical Society.
3. Robert Dykstra, "*Wild Bill Hickok," Journal of the Central Mississippi Valley American Studies Association: Kansas Centennial Issue, 1961*, vol. 2, pages 20-48, 1871 *Abilene Minutes Book*, 32. Dykstra's outstanding essay on Hickok in Abilene is as fresh and informative today as it was when he wrote it for this academic journal sixty-three years ago. Dykstra utilized as the foundation of his essay two key municipal documents that had survived from 1871; the City of Abilene Minute Book and the City of Abilene Ordinance Book. He wanted to compare how the factual record represented in these municipal documents compared with the record of movies, books, even television. For this writer's purposes the information in the municipal documents, as cited by Dykstra, provide an opportunity to get even closer to what actually happened with Hickok in Abilene, inarguably his most famous and influential stint as a lawman.
4. Dykstra, 1871 Abilene Ordinance Book, *Wild Bill Hickok*, 32.
5. Charles Gross to J. B. Edwards, June 15, 1925, ms letter excerpt, *John Beach Edwards Papers*, Kansas Historical Society.
6. George Anderson, "Touring Kansas and Colorado in 1871: The Journal of George C. Anderson," *Kansas Historical Quarterly* (Autumn, 1956): 216.
7. Little, *Early Days In Abilene*.
8. Richard C. Mahron, *The Last Gunfighter: John Wesley Hardin* (College Station, Creative Publishing Company, 1995).
9. George Cushman, "Abilene, First of the Kansas Cow Towns," *Kansas Historical Quarterly*, August, 1940, 241-242.
10. Dykstra, 1871 Abilene Ordinance Book, *Wild Bill Hickok*, 33.
11. Dyastra, 1871 Abilene Ordinance Book, *Wild Bill Hickok*, 33.
12. Dykstra, 1871 Abilene Ordinance Book, *Wild Bill Hickok*, 34.
13. Dykstra, 1871 Abilene Minutes Book, *Wild Bill Hickok*, 34.
14. Dykstra 1871 Abilene Minutes Book, *Wild Bill Hickok*, 34.

15. Charles Gross to J. B. Edwards, June 15, 1925, ms letter excerpt, *John Beach Edwards Papers*, Kansas Historical Society.
16. Dexter Fellows, *This Way to the Big Show: The Life of Dexter Fellows* (New York, Viking Press, 1936): 35.
17. Gil Robinson, *Old Wagon Show Days* (Cincinnati, Brockwell Company, 1925): 129.
18. Robinson, *Old Wagon Show Days*, 130.
19. Charles Gross to J. B. Edwards, June 15, 1925, ms letter excerpt, *John Beach Edwards Papers,* Kansas Historical Society.
20. Dykstra, 1871 Abilene Minutes Book, *Wild Bill Hickok*, 34.
21. Dykstra, 1871 Abilene Minutes Book, *Wild Bill Hickok*, 34
22. Dykstra,1871 Abilene Minutes Book, *Wild Bill Hickok*, 34.
23. Little, *Early Days In Abilene.*
24. Charles Gross to J. B. Edwards, April 13, 1922, ms letter excerpt, *John Beach Edwards Papers*, Kansas State Historical Society.
25. Kansas City News, October 6, 1871, cited in Rosa, *Wild Bill Hickok: The Man and His Myth* (Lawrence, University Press of Kansas, 1996): 252.
26. Dykstra, 1871 Abilene Minutes Book, *Wild Bill Hickok*, 34.
27. Dykstra, 1871 Abilene Minutes Book, *Wild Bill Hickok*, 34.
28. Dykstra, 1871 Abilene Minutes Book, *Wild Bill Hickok*, 34-35.
29. Topeka Capital, August 30, 1908.
30. J. B. Edward statement, *John Beach Edwards Papers*, Kansas Historical Society.
31. James Drees, *Bloody Prairie vol.2,* (Hays, Kansas, Hays Daily News, 1997): 27.
32. Drees, *Bloody Prairie vol. 2,* 27.
33. Charles Gross to J. B. Edwards, June 15, 1925, ms letter excerpt, *John Beach Edwards Papers*, Kansas Historical Society.
34. Charles Lyon, Compendious History of Ellsworth County, Kansas, 1879.
35. Drees, *Bloody Prairie vol. 2,* 28.
36. Drees, *Bloody Prairie vol. 2,* 29.
37. William Connelley to Mrs. Ed Berry, January 21, 1926, ts letter, *William Elsey Connelley Collection*, WH905, Western History Collection, The Denver Public Library.
38. William Connelley to Ira Lloyd, January 26, 1926, ts letter excerpts, *William Elsey Connelley Collection*, WH905, Western History Collection. The Denver Public Library.
39. Mrs. Ed Berry to William Connelley, February 8, 1926, ms letter, *William Elsey Connelley Collection*, WH905, Western History Collection, The Denver Public Library.
40. William Connelley to Mrs. Ed Berry, February 13, 1926, ts letter excerpts, *William Elsey Connelley Collection*, WH905, Western History Collection, The Denver Public Library.

14
1. *National Cyclopaedia of American Biography, Vol.VI* (New York, James T. White and Co., 1896): 75-76/*Dictionary of American Authors*, nd., 68.
2. *History of Kansas City, Missouri,* ed. Theo S. Case (Syracuse, D. Mason & Co., 1888): 635-636.
3. *History of Kansas City, ed.* Theo S. Case, 636.
4. James W. Buel, *Heroes of the Plains* (St. Louis, Historical Publishing Co. 1881): 181, 213.
5. Jim Gray, *Desperate Seed: Ellsworth, Kansas on the Violent Frontier* (Kansas Cowboy Publications, Ellsworth, Kansas, 2009): 7, 14, 18.

6. Buel, *Heroes,* 50.
7. Buel, *Heroes*, 153-154.
8. Agnes Wright Spring, *Good Little Bad Man: The Life of Colorado Charley Utter* (Boulder, Pruett Publishing Co., 1987): 67.
9. Rosa, *They Called Him Wild Bill*, 166.
10. Rosa, *They Called Him Wild Bill*, 166.
11. Bob Kostoff, *The Niagara Falls Reporter,* "Wild Bill Hickock Rides the Range, Kills Lethargic Buffalo in Niagara Falls, Ont.," August 26, 2003.
12. Francis J. Petrie, *Niagara Falls Evening Reporter,* "Buffalo Hunt, Wild West Show Was Staged Here in 1872," September 17, 1966.
13. Joseph Rosa, "The Grand Buffalo Hunt at Niagara Falls," *Nebraska History Quarterly*, Vol. 86 (Winter, 2005): 11-13.
14. Buel, *Heroes*, 155-156.
15. Buel, *Heroes*, 213-215.

15

1. *The Springfield City Directory For 1873-74* (St. Louis, R. P. Studley Company, Printers, 1873): 64, 171.
2. *Springfield City Directory*, 1873-74, 74.
3. *Kansas City, Missouri City Directory*, 1873.
4. Joseph Rosa, "A Pistoleer Poet?", *True West Magazine*, September, 2001, 26.
5. Rosa, "A Pistoleer Poet?", 26.
6. *Springfield City Directory,* 1873-74, 1-180.
7. *Springfield City Directory,* 1873-74, 176.
8. Auction sales records of Swann Galleries, Heritage Auctions, and Cowan's Auctions.
9. Rosa, *They Called Him Wild Bill*, 242.
10. Hiram Robbins, "Wild Bill's Humors," *The Arkansaw Traveler*, undated.
11. *Jefferson City Peoples Tribune*, August 23, 1876.
12. William F. Cody, T*he Life of Hon. William F. Cody, Known as Buffalo Bill, the Famous Hunter, Scout and Guide: An Autobiography* (Hartford, Frank E. Bliss, 1879): 310.
13. Cody, *Autobiography*, 311.
14. Sandra A. Sagala, *Buffalo Bill on Stage* (Albuquerque, University of New Mexico Press, 2008): 21.
15. Sandra A. Sagala, *Buffalo Bill on Stage*, 23/Chicago Inter-Ocean, December 17, 1872.
16. Cody, *Autobiography*, 329.
17. Walter Noble Burns, *A Frontier Hero: Reminiscences of "Wild Bill" Hickok by his old Friend Buffalo Bill*, the Cowley (Wyoming) Progress, December 30, 1911.
18. Connelley, *Wild Bill and His Era*, 166.
19. Connelley, *Wild Bill and His Era*, 169.
20. *Pittsburgh Daily Leader*, 1973, nd.
21. Wilstach, *Wild Bill Hickok*, 218.
22. *Terre Haute Daily Express*, October 19, 1873.
23. Glenn Shirley, *Pawnee Bill: A Biography of Gordon Lillie*, 19.
24. Fellows, *This Way To The Big Show*, 33-34.
25. John Burke, *The Noblest Whiteskin*, (New York, Putnam, 1973): 107.

26. Robert Kane, *Outdoor Life Magazine,* June, 1906, cited in Rosa, *They Called Him Wild Bill,* 343-344.
27. Robert Kane, *Outdoor Recreation Magazine*, 1912.
28. Cody, *Autobiography*, 330-331.
29. *Williamsport Gazette & Bulletin*, November 26, 1873.
30. *Easton Daily Express*, December 15, 1873.

16

1. *Chicago Inter Ocean Magazine*, October 15, 1911.
2. Herschel Logan, *Buckskin and Satin* (Harrisburg, Stackpole, 1954): 90.
3. Sagala, *Buffalo Bill on Stage*, 52.
4. *Boston Herald,* October 2, 1927, "Buffalo Bill's Days in the Stage Recalled by Fellow Actor."
5. Cody, *Autobiography*, 333
6. Cody, *Autobiography*, 332-333.
7. Robbins, *Wild Bill's Humors.*
8. Frank Wilstach, *Wild Bill Hickok, The Prince of Pistoleers* (Garden City NY, Garden City Publishing, 1926): 225-226.
9. *Kansas City Times,* July 19, 1874.
10. Connelley, *Wild Bill and His Era*, 172-173.
11. Connelley, *Wild Bill and His Era*, 173.
12. Bill O'Neal, *Cheyenne: 1867 to 1903: A Biography of the Magic City of the Plains* (Eakin Press, 2006): 88, 110.
13. William F. Cody, *Life of Buffalo Bill*, 1879, Chapter 16.
14. James Buel, *Heroes of the Plains*, 1881.
15. Alfred Henry Lewis, "How Mr. Hickok Came to Cheyenne," *Saturday Evening Post.*
16. Joseph Rosa, *Wild Bill Hickok: The Man and His Myth* (University Press of Kansas, Lawrence, 1996): 57.
17. Joseph Rosa, *They Called Him Wild Bill* (University of Oklahoma Press, Norman, 1974, 2nd Edition): 266.
18. Agnes Wright Spring, *Good Little Bad Man: The Life of Colorado Charley Utter* (Boulder, Pruett Publishing, 1987): 125.
19. Spring, *Good Little Bad Man*, 125-126.
20. J. W. "Doc" Howard, *"Doc" Howard's Memoirs* (Denver, ca.1931): 18-19, cited in Rosa, "How Mr. Hickok Really Came to Cheyenne," in *Kansas and The West* (Topeka, Kansas State Historical Society 1976): 89.
21. J. W. "Doc" Howard, Memoirs, 19-20, cited in Rosa, "...Came to Cheyenne," in *Kansas and The West*, 91.

17

1. Danny Bohen to William Connelley, December 1925, ms letter excerpt, *William Elsey Connelley Collection*, WH905, Western History Collection, Denver Public Library.
2. J. W. "Doc" Howard, Memoirs, 19, cited in Rosa, "...Came to Cheyenne," in *Kansas and The West*, 94-95.
3. O'Neal, Cheyenne: 1867—1903, 88.
4. Annie D. Tallent, *The Black Hills, or The Last Hunting Ground of the Dakotahs*, 72-74.

5. South Dakota Hall of Fame, Chamberlin, South Dakota.
6. William F. Hooker, *The Prairie Schooner* (Chicago, Saul Brothers, 1918): 105.
7. William F. Hooker, "The Camp-Fire," *Adventure Magazine*, August 3, 1920, 180.
8. Buel, *Heroes of the Plains*, 181.
9. Buel, *Heroes of the Plains*, 181.
10. Buel, *Heroes of the Plains*, 181.
11. Mari Sandoz, *The Buffalo Hunters* (New York, Hastings House, 195): 259.
12. Rosa, *They Called Him Wild Bill*, 267-268.
13. Mari Sandoz to Joseph Rosa, November 3, 1956.
14. Joseph Rosa, *The Murder of Chief Whistler*, in Rosa, *They Called Him Wild Bill*, 207-221.
15. Rosa, *They Called Him Wild Bill*, 268.
16. Rosa, *They Called Him Wild Bill*, 268.

18

1. Charles Gross to J. B. Edwards, June 15, 1925, ms letter excerpt, *John Beach Edwards Papers*, Kansas Historical Society.
2. Linda A. Fisher and Carrie Bowers, *Agnes Lake Hickok: Queen of the Circus, Wife of a Legend* (Norman, University of Oklahoma Press, 2009): 229.
3. Fisher and Bowers, *Agnes Lake Hickok*, 229-230.
4. Wyoming State Archives.
5. Fisher and Bowers, *Agnes Lake Hickok*, 234.
6. William Secrest, "Bill Hickok's Girl on the Flying Trapeze," *Old West Magazine* (Winter, 1867): 68.
7. *Cincinnati Commercial Tribune*, January 29, 1928, cited in Jan Cerney, *Wild Bill Hickok and Agnes Lake* (United States, InstantPublisher.com, 2008): 135.
8. Agnes Hickok to Polly and Celinda Hickok, April 26, 1876, ms letter, *Hickok Family Collection*, Kansas Historical Society.
9. Buel, *Heroes*, 185.
10. James W. Buel to Lewis [Lorenzo] Hickok Esq., November 29, 1879, ms letter excerpt, published in the auction catalog of Greg Martin Auctions for June 16, 2003. *Letters, Photography, and Documents from the Estate of Celinda Hickok.*
11. James Butler Hickok to Agnes Hickok, June 2, 1876, ms letter, published in the auction catalog of Greg Martin Auctions for June 16, 2003. *Letters, Photography, and Documents from the Estate of Celinda Hickok.*
12. Buel, *Heroes*, 185-186.
13. Agnes Wright Spring, *Good Little Bad Man, The Life of Charley Utter* (Boulder, Pruett Publishing, 1987): 89.
14. Spring, *Good Little Bad Man*, 90—94.
15. William Secrest, *I Buried Hickok: The Memoirs of White Eye Anderson* (College Station, Creative Publishing Company, 1980): 92, 105.
16. Secrest ed., *I Buried Hickok*, 92.
17. Secrest ed., *I Buried Hickok*, 57.
18. Secrest ed., *I Buried Hickok*, 202.
19. Secrest ed., *I Buried Hickok*, 7-10.
20. Agnes Hickok to Polly Hickok, June 19, 1876, ms letter, *Hickok Family Collection*, Kansas Historical Society.

21. J. W. "Doc" Howard, Memoirs, cited in Spring, *Good Little Bad Man*, 95.

22. John Hunton, *The Diaries of John Hunton*, ed. Michael Griske, (Heritage Books, 2005): 86-87.

23. Agnes Hickok to Celinda Hickok, June 30, 1876, ms letter, *Hickok Family Collection*, Kansas Historical Society.

24. Secrest ed., *I Buried Hickok*, 92-93.

25. Doane Robinson, *History of South Dakota* (Chicago, 1930); volume three, 1767.

26. Secrest ed., *I Buried Hickok*, 93.

27. James McLaird, *Wild Bill Hickok & Calamity Jane: Deadwood Legends* (Pierre, South Dakota State Historical Society Press, 2008): 109-110.

28. Secrest ed. *I Buried Hickok*, 95-97, 99.

29. John S. McClintock, *Pioneer Days in the Black Hills* (Norman, University of Oklahoma Press, 2000): 65-75/Tallent, The Black Hills, 256-260.

30. Secrest ed., *I Buried Hickok*, 99-102/Annie D. Tallent, *The Black Hills, or the Last Hunting Ground of the Dakotahs* (St. Louis, Nixon Jones Printing Co., 1899): 256-260.

31. Leander P. Richardson, "A Trip to the Black Hills," *Scribner's Monthly Magazine*, February 1877.

32. Secrest ed., *I Buried Hickok*, note 31, p. 114.

33. Secrest ed., *I Buried Hickok*, 99 -102.

34. Richardson, "A Trip to the Black Hills."

35. Secrest ed. *I Buried Hickok*, 102-104.

36. Leander P. Richardson, letter to the *New York Sun*, 1893/ *True West*, November-December 1965, "Last Days of a Plainsman."

37. Secrest ed., *I Buried Hickok*, 116-117.

37B. Richardson, "A Trip to the Black Hills."

37C. Secrest ed., *I Buried Hickok,* 116-117.

38. Carl Mann, *Testimony in the Trial of Jack McCall*, excerpt, *Yankton Press* and *Dakotaian*, December 5, 1876.

39. Julia Rich Hogan, *Dead Man's Hand Dealt* By Charlie Rich, *The Rich Family Association Kinfolk Newsletter*, Fall/Winter 1980.

40. Peter LaFlemme, "I Heard the Shot That Killed Bill," *Rapid City Daily Journal*, November 6, 1949, cited in Fielder, *Wild Bill and Deadwood*, 86-87.

41. Secrest ed., *I Buried Hickok*, 120.

42. Wilstach, *Wild Bill Hickok*, 283-285.

43. Secrest ed., *I Buried Hickok*, 120-121.

44. Judge William L. Kuykendall, *Frontier Days: A True Narrative of Striking Events on the Western Frontier*, published 1917, Chapter XXIX.

45. Secrest ed., *I Buried Hickok*, 121.

46. Richardson, "A Trip to the Black Hills."

47. O. W. Coursey, "Wild Bill:" James Butler Hickok (Mitchell, South Dakota, Educator Supply Company, 1924): 60.

48. Agnes Hickok to Polly and Celinda Hickok, August 7, 1876, ms letter, *Hickok Family Collection*, Kansas Historical Society.

49. Lydia Barnes (Hickok) to Horace Hickok or Lorenzo Hickok, August 17, 1876, ms letter, *Hickok Family Collection*, Kansas Historical Society.

50. Lydia Barnes, Interview, *Chicago Daily Record*, December 26, 1896, cited in Rosa, *They Called Him Wild Bill*, 307.

51. Joseph Rosa, "Alias Jack McCall, A Pardon or Death," *The Trail Guide*, pub. quarterly by the Kansas City Posse, The Westerners. June 1967, vol. Two, 5, 9.

52. Rosa, *Alias Jack McCall*, 9.

53. Secrest ed., *I Buried Hickok*. 116.

54. Richardson, "A Trip to the Black Hills."

55. Secrest ed., *I Buried Hickok*, 121.

56. Seth Bullock, ms excerpt, cited in Thadd Turner, *Wild Bill Hickok: Deadwood City—End of Trail* (Universal Publishers, 2001): 159.

57. Watson Parker, *Deadwood: The Golden Years* (Lincoln, University of Nebraska Press, 1981): 77.

58. Harry Young, *Hard Knocks: A Life Story of the Vanishing West* (Pierre, South Dakota State Historical Society Press, 2005): 201.

59. Young, *Hard Knocks*, 201.

60. Young, *Hard Knocks*, 202-203.

61. Young, *Hard Knocks*, 203.

62. Young, *Hard Knocks*, 205.

63. Young, *Hard Knocks*, 213, 28.

64. John S. McClintock, *Pioneer Days in the Black Hills*, By One of the Early Day Pioneers (Norman, University of Oklahoma Press, 2000): 106.

65. Coursey, *Wild Bill*, 55-56.

66. Wilstach, *Wild Bill Hickok*, 295-296.

67. Connelley, *Wild Bill and His Era*, 203.

68. Agnes Hickok to Polly and Celinda Hickok, November 12, 1876, ms letter, *Hickok Family Collection*. Kansas Historical Society.

69. Wilstach, *Wild Bill Hickok*, 284.

70. Secrest ed., *I Buried Hickok*, 120.

71. Young, *Hard Knocks*, 220, 74.

72. Des Wilson, *Ghosts at the Table* (Philadelphia, DaCapo Press, 2008): 15.

73. Wilson, *Ghosts at the Table*, 15.

74. Wilson, *Ghosts at the Table*, 15-17.

75. Wilson, *Ghosts at the Table*, 18-19.

76. Wilson, *Ghosts at the Table*, 21.

77. Joseph Rosa, "Hickok's Last Gunfight," *Wild West Magazine* (December, 2008):

19

1. Department of Justice, Washington DC, letter excerpt of February 19, 1877, cited in Joseph Rosa, *They Called Him Wild Bill* (Norman, Oklahoma University Press, 1974, 1987 2nd edition, 3rd printing): 333.

2. Mary A. McCall, Louisville, Kentucky, letter to the Marshal of Yankton, cited in Rosa, *They Called Him Wild Bill*, 335.

3. O. W. Coursey, *Wild Bill* (Mitchell, S. D., Educator Supply Co., 1924): 65—67.

Appendix One

1. Alfred Henry Lewis, "Wild Bill Hickox," *Kansas City Evening Star*, August 3, 1895.

2. Alfred Henry Lewis, "How Mr. Hickok Came to Cheyenne," *Saturday Evening Post*, March 12, 1904.

3. Alfred Henry Lewis, *The Sunset Trail* (New York, A.L. Burt, 1905).

4. Bat Masterson, "A Few Scraps," *Denver Republican*, July 17, 1910.

5. Emerson Hough, *North of 36* (New York, McKinley, Stone and Mackenzie, 1923).

6. Stuart Lake, *Wyatt Earp, Frontier Marshal* (New York, Houghton Mifflin, 1931).

7. Stuart Lake, "Guns and Gunfighters," *Saturday Evening Post*, November 30, 1930.

8. Thomas Berger, *The Return of Little Big Man* (Boston, Little Brown and Co, 1999).

9. Joseph Rosa, *They Called Him Wild Bill* (Norman, University of Oklahoma Press, 1st edition, 1964): 248.

10. Joseph Rosa, *They Called Him Wild Bill* (Norman, University of Oklahoma Press, 1st edition, 1964): 248-249.

11. Joseph Rosa, *They Called Him Wild Bill* (Norman, University of Oklahoma Press, 2nd edition, 1974): 339.

12. Robert De Arment, *Bat Masterson* (Norman, University of Oklahoma Press, 1989): 8.

13. Theodore S. Case, *History of Kansas City, Missouri* (Syracuse, D. Mason & Co., 1888).

14. Frank Wornall, *Kansas City Star*.

Appendix Two

1. *Sioux Falls Daily Argus-Leader*, August 9, 1924.

2. *Deadwood Pioneer-Times*, August 22, 1925.

3. Leander Richardson, letter to the *New York Sun*, 1893.

4. Gil Robinson, *Old Wagon Show Days* (Cincinnati, Brockwell, 1925): 130-131.

5. Frank Wilstach, *Wild Bill Hickok, The Prince of Pistoleers* (Garden City, Garden City Publishing, 1925): 284.

6. John S. McClintock, *Pioneer Days in the Black Hills* (Norman, Oklahoma University Press, 2000): 114.

7. Richard B. Hughes, *Pioneer Years in the Black Hills* (Glendale, Cal. A.H. Clark Co., 1957): 162.

8. O. W. Coursey, *Wild Bill* (Mitchell, South Dakota, Educator Supply Company, 1924): 57.

9. Raymond Thorp, "Wild Bill's Famous Bullet," *Real West* magazine, May, 1961; 19, 58-59.

10. William Secrest, *I Buried Hickok: The Memoirs of White Eye Anderson* (College Station, Creative Publishing Company, 1980): 126.

11. Greg Martin Auctions, 18-page full color prospectus for upcoming auction dated Monday, June 16, 2003, titled *Letters, Photography, and Documents from the Estate of Celinda Hickok*/Prices realized, sheet for the Celinda Hickok auction of June 16, 2003.

12. *True West Magazine*, "Wyeth Sets Record with Hickok Oil," 09-01-2007.

13. *Field and Stream* magazine, "Is This the Gun Wild Bill Was Carrying When He Was Murdered in 1876?", 09-27-2013.

14. Ed McGivern, *Fast and Fancy Revolver Shooting*, 1932, 202-203.

15. Bonhams & Butterfield Auctions, One Page Color Promotion Sheet, An historic Smith & Wesson No. 2 Old Model Army revolver owned by Wild Bill Hickok, San Francisco, Auction Date 11-18-2013.

16. Reuters: "'Wild Bill' Hickok's Revolver Fails to Sell as Bids Stall at $220,000," 11-19-2013.

17. McClintock, *Pioneer Days*, 315.

18. reason.com blog, Jim Epstein, 7-22-2013, Broke City of Harrisburg Says Goodbye to Wild Bill Hickok's Knife, Doc Holliday's Dental Chair.

19. Secrest, *I Buried Hickok*, 121.

20. Coursey, *Wild Bill*, 58.

21. Wilstach, *Wild Bill Hickok*, 286.

22. McClintock, *Pioneer Days*, 112-114.

23. Jack Crawford, "Wild Bill's Grave," excerpt, *Virginia Evening Chronicle*, August 4, 1877. This excerpt from the poem was preceded by the line *Hear part of this letter— the last of this life.*

24. Wilstach, *Wild Bill Hickok*, 273-274.

25. Linda A. Fisher and Carrie Bowers, *Agnes Lake Hickok* (Norman, University of Oklahoma Press, 2009): 214-216.

26. Fisher and Bowers, *Agnes Lake Hickok*, 26.

27. Sarah Knott, *History in the Cards*, Cincinnati.com Visitors Guide, August 7, 2000.

28. Frank Wilstach to William Connelley, September 23, 1925, ts letter, *William Elsey Connelley Collection*, WH905, Western History Department, The Denver Public Library.

29. Frank Wilstach to William Connelley, October 5, 1925, ts letter, *William Elsey Connelley Collection*, WH905, Western History Department, The Denver Public Library.

30. Frank Wilstach to William Connelley, February 23, 1926, ts letter, *William Elsey Connelley Collection*, WH905, Western History Department, The Denver Public Library.

31. Frank Wilstach to William Connelley, December 16, 1926, ts letter, *William Elsey Connelley Collection*, WH905, Western History Department, The Denver Public Library.

32. Wilstach, *Wild Bill Hickok*, 273.

33. *Cincinnati Commercial Tribune*, January 29, 1928, cited in Cerney, "Wild Bill Hickok and Agnes Lake," 135.

34. *Big Piney Examiner*, August 29, 1929, cited in Cerney, *Wild Bill Hickok and Agnes Lake*, 149.

35. *Reliable Plant Magazine*, RP news wire, "United States Playing Card To Build Plant in Kentucky," 2009.

Appendix Three

1. Charley Utter to Dick & Brant Street, January 20, 1880, ms letter, *Hickok Family Collection*, Kansas Historical Society.

2. Lewis Schoenfield to Lorenzo Hickok, September 6, 1879, ms letter, *Hickok Family Collection*, Kansas Historical Society.

3. Lewis Schoenfield to Lorenzo Hickok, September 7, 1879, ms letter, *Hickok Family Collection*. Kansas Historical Society.

4. Lewis Schoenfield to Lorenzo Hickok, April 19, 1880, ms letter, *Hickok Family Collection*, Kansas Historical Society.

5. Lewis Schoenfield to Lorenzo Hickok, April 12, 1885, ms letter, *Hickok Family Collection*, Kansas Historical Society.

6. Lewis Schoenfield to Lorenzo Hickok, May 19, 1885, ms letter, *Hickok Family Collection*, Kansas Historical Society.

7. Henry Robinson to Horace D. Hickok, June 29, 1893, ms letter, *Hickok Family Collection*, Kansas Historical Society.

8. Cerney, *Wild Bill Hickok and Agnes Lake*, 184-185; Rosa, *They Called Him Wild Bill*, 230-233; McLaird, *Wild Bill Hickok & Calamity Jane*, 125-126.

9. Joseph B. Thoburn, *A Standard History of Oklahoma*, Volume IV, 1916, in Oklahoma County, Oklahoma Biographies 5. This is a who's who vanity publication apparently geared towards executives in investment, banking, and the oil business in that era.

10. *Saturday Evening Post*, April 10, 1926, "Fill Your Hand," Fred Sutton as told to A. B. MacDonald. This was the opening line of Sutton's fantasy.

11. *Saturday Evening Post*, April 10, 1926, "Fill Your Hand," Sutton to MacDonald.

12. *Saturday Evening Post*, April 10, 1926, "Fill Your Hand," Sutton to MacDonald.

13. *Saturday Evening Post*, April 10, 1926, "Fill Your Hand," Sutton to MacDonald.

14. *Saturday Evening Post*, April 26, 1926, "Hands Up!", Fred Sutton as told to A. B. McDonald.

15. Ramon Adams, *Six-Guns and Saddle Leather: A Bibliography of Books ands Pamphlets on Western Outlaws and Gunmen* (Norman, University of Oklahoma Press, 1969): 628.

16. Adams, *Six-Guns and Saddle Leather*, 202.

17. Adams, *Six-Guns and Saddle Leather*, 328.

18. Adams, *Six-Guns and Saddle Leather*, 675.

19. Carpe Librum, Rare Book and Manuscript Dealer, "Kansas City Mac": The Archives of A.B. McDonald, Archive introduction, 2020.

20. Screen credits for 1931 Academy Award-winning movie, *Cimarron*.

21. Burton Rascoe, *Belle Starr: The Bandit Queen* (Random House, New York, 1941): 314-315.

22. Fred E. Sutton, *My Personal Contact with James Butler Hickok* (Pony Express Courier, Placerville California, June 1937).

23. Donald Henderson Clarke, *The Autobiography of Frank Tarbeaux, as told to Donald Henderson Clarke* (New York, Vanguard Press, 1930): 57-58.

BIBLIOGRAPHY

Books and Pamphlets

Aarmes, Augustus, *Ups and Downs of an Army Officer,* 1900.
Adams, Oscar Fay, *Dictionary of American Biography,* 1901.
Adams, Ramon, *Six Guns and Saddle Leather: A Bibliography of Books and Pamphlets on Western Outlaws and Gunmen,* Norman, University of Oklahoma Press, 1969.
Barnard, Sandy, *Ten Years with Custer,* Terre Haute, AST Press, 2001.
Barnes, Jeff, *The Great Plains Guide to Custer,* Mechanicsburg, Stackpole Books, 2012.
Barnitz, Albert, *Life in Custer's Cavalry: Diaries and Letters of Albert and Jennie Barnitz, 1867-1868,* New Haven, Yale University Press, 1977.
Bennett, Estelline, *Old Deadwood Days,* Lincoln, University of Nebraska Press, 1982.
Berger, Thomas, *The Return of Little Big Man,* Boston, Little Brown and Co., 1999
Bliss, Frank E., *The Life of Hon. William F. Cody, Known as Buffalo Bill, the Famous Hunter, Scout and Guide: An Autobiography,* Hartford, 1879.
Buel, James W., *Heroes of the Plains,* St. Louis, Historical Publishing Company, 1881.
Buel, James W., *Life and Marvelous Adventures of Wild Bill, the Scout, Being a True and Exact History of all the Sanguinary Combats and Hairbreadth Escapes of the Most Famous Scout and Spy America Ever Produced,* Chicago, Belford, Clarke & Co., 1880.
Burke, John, *The Noblest Whiteskin,* New York, Putnam, 1973.
Burkey, Blaine, *Custer, Come At Once! The Fort Hays Years of George and Elizabeth Custer.* Hays, Society of Friends of Historic Fort Hays, 2nd Printing, 1991.
Wild Bill Hickok: The Law In Hays City, Hays, Ellis County Historical Society, 1996.
Carpenter, F.A., *History of the 17th Illinois Cavalry,* 1880's.
Case, Theodore S., ed., *History of Kansas City, Missouri,* Syracuse, D. Mason & Co., 1888.
Castel, Albert, *General Sterling Price and the Civil War in the West.* Baton Rouge, Louisiana State University Press, 1968.
Cerney, Jan, *Wild Bill Hickok and Agnes Lake,* USA, InstantPublisher.com, 2008.
Clarke, Donald Henderson, *The Autobiography of Frank Tarbeaux, as told to Donald Henderson Clarke,* New York, Vanguard Press, 1930.
Connelley, William F., *Wild Bill and His Era,* New York, Cooper Square Publishers, 1972, 2nd edition, 1st edition 1933.
Coursey, O.W., *Wild Bill: James Butler Hickok,* Mitchell, South Dakota, Educator Supply Company, 1924.
Custer, George Armstrong, *My Life on the Plains,* New York, Sheldon and Co., 1874.
Custer, Elizabeth, *Following the Guidon,* New York, Harper and Bros., 1890.
Dawson, Charles, *Pioneer Tales of the Oregon Trail Through Jefferson County, Nebraska,* Topeka, Crane and Co., 1912.
De Arment, Robert, *Bat Masterson: The Man and the Legend,* Norman, University of Oklahoma Press, 1989.
Devol, George H., *Forty Years a Gambler on the Mississippi,* Cincinnati, Devol & Haines, 1887.
Drees, James, *Bloody Prairie, Volume 2,* Hays, *The Hays Daily News,* 1997.
Dugan, Mark, *Tales Never Told Around the Campfire,* Athens, Ohio, Swallow Press, 1992.

Earl of Dunraven, *The Great Divide: Travels in the Upper Yellowstone in the Summer of 1874*, London, Chatto and Windus, 1876.

Edwards, John Beach, *Early Days in Abilene*, Abilene, Kansas, *Abilene Daily Chronicle*, 1938.

Estes, T.J., *Early Days and War Times in Northern Arkansas*, Yellville, Arkansas, 1928.

Fellows, Dexter, *This Way to the Big Show: The Life of Dexter Fellows*, New York, The Viking Press, 1936.

Fielder, Mildred, *Wild Bill and Deadwood*, Seattle, Superior Publishing Company, 1965.

Fisher, Linda A. and Carrie Bowers, *Agnes Lake Hickok: Queen of the Circus, Wife of a Legend*, Norman, University of Oklahoma Press, 2009.

Grasso, Christopher, ed., *Bloody Engagements: John R. Kelso's Civil War*, New Haven, Yale University Press, 2017.

Gray, Jim, *Desperate Seed: Ellsworth, Kansas on the Violent Frontier*, Ellsworth, Kansas Cowboy Publications, 2009.

Harmon, Edith Andrews, *Pioneer Settlers of Troy Grove, Illinois*, Decorah, Iowa, The Anundsen Publishing Company, 1973.

Heisler & Company, E.F., *Johnson County Kansas Atlas*, 1874.

Holcombe, R.I., *History of Greene County, Missouri*, St. Louis, Western Historical Company, 1883.

Hooker, William F., *The Prairie Schooner*, Chicago, Saul Brothers, 1918.

Horan, James D., *The Gunfighters*, New York, Gramercy Books, 2nd edition, 1994.

Hough, Emerson, *North of 36*, New York, McKinley, Stone and Mackenzie, 1923.

Howard, J. W. "Doc", *"Doc" Howard's Memoirs*, Denver, 1931.

Hughes, Richard B., *Pioneer Years in the Black Hills*, Glendale, Calif., Arthur Clark Company, 1957.

Hunton, John, *The Diaries of John Hunton*, ed. Michael Griske, Westminster, Maryland, Heritage Books, 2005.

Kansas City, Missouri City Directory, 1873.

Kuykendall, Judge William L., *Frontier Days: A True Narrative of Striking Events On the Frontier*, 1917.

Lake, Stuart, *Wyatt Earp, Frontier Marshal*, New York, Houghton Mifflin, 1931.

Logan, Herschel, *Buckskin and Satin*, Harrisburg, PA, Stackpole, 1954.

Londre', Felicia Hardison, *The Enchanted Years of the Stage: Kansas City at the Crossroads of American Theater, 1870-1930*, Columbia, Missouri, University of Missouri Press, 2007.

Mahron, Richard C., *The Last Gunfighter: JohnWesley Hardin*, College Station, Creative Publishing Company, 1995.

McClintock, John S., *Pioneer Days in the Black Hills*, Norman, University of Oklahoma Press, 2000.

McGivern, Ed, *Fast and Fancy Revolver Shooting*, 1932.

McIntyre, Stephen L., ed., *Springfield's Urban Histories: Essays on the Queen City of the Missouri Ozarks*, Springfield, Moon City Press, 2012.

McLaird, James, *Wild Bill Hickok and Calamity Jane*, Pierre, South Dakota, State Historical Society Press, 2008.

Meline, James F., *Two Thousand Miles on Horseback: Santa Fe and Back: A Summer Tour Through Kansas, Nebraska, Colorado, and New Mexico, in the Year 1866*. New York, Hurd and Houghton, 1867.

Miller, Nyle and Joseph W. Snell, *Great Gunfighters of the Kansas Cowtowns, 1867-1886,* Lincoln, University of Nebraska Press, Bison Books, 1967.

Monett, Howard N., *Action Before Westport,* Kansas City, Missouri, Westport Historical Society, 1964.

O'Neal, Bill, *Cheyenne: 1867 to 1903: A Biography of the Magic City of the Plains,* Fort Worth, Eakin Press, 2006.

Otero, Miguel, *My Life on the Frontier,* New York, The Press of the Pioneers, 1935.

Parker, Watson, *Deadwood: The Golden Years,* Lincoln, University of Nebraska Press, 1981.

Pohanka, Brian, *A Summer on the Plains, 1870: The Diary of Annie Gibson Roberts,* Bryan, Texas, 1982.

Rascoe, Burton, *Belle Starr: The Bandit Queen,* New York, Random House, 1941.

Rezatto, Helen, *Tales of the Black Hills,* Rapid City, S.D., Fenwyn Press, 1989.

Robinson, Doane, *History of South Dakota,* B.F. Bowen Publishers, 1904.

Robinson, Gil, *Old Wagon Show Days,* Cincinnati, Brockwell, 1925.

Roegnick, Adolph, *Pioneer History of Kansas,* Denver, 1930.

Rosa, Joseph, *They Called Him Wild Bill,* Norman, University of Oklahoma Press, 1987, 2nd edition, 3rd printing.
   Wild Bill Hickok: The Man and His Myth, Lawrence, University Press of Kansas, 1996.
   They Called Him Wild Bill, Norman, University of Oklahoma Press, 1964, 1st edition.

Russell, Don, *Lives and Legends of Buffalo Bill,* Norman, University of Oklahoma Press, 1960.

Sagala, Sandra S. *Buffalo Bill on Stage,* Albuquerque, University of New Mexico Press, 2008.

Sanborn, John B., *The Campaign in Missouri in September and October, 1864,* no publ., no date.

Sandoz, Mari, *The Buffalo Hunters,* New York, Hastings House, 1954.

Secrest, William, ed., *I Buried Hickok: The Memoirs of White Eye Anderson.* College Station, Creative Publishing Company, 1980.

Settle, Raymond W. and Mary Lund, *War Drums and Wagon Wheels,* Lincoln, University of Nebraska Press, 1966.

Shirley, Glenn, *Pawnee Bill: A Biography of Gordon Lillie,* Albuquerque, University of New Mexico Press, 1958.

Snell, Joseph W. and others, eds., *Kansas and The West,* Topeka, Kansas State Historical Society, 1976.

Spring, Agnes Wright, *Good Little Big Man: The Life of Colorado Charley Utter,* Boulder, Pruett Publishing Co., 1987.

Springfield, Missouri City Directory, 1873-74.

Sternberg, Charles, *Life of a Fossil Hunter,* Bloomington, Indiana University Press, 1990.

Stiles, T.J., *Custer's Trials,* New York, Alfred A. Knopf, 2015.

Tallent, Annie D., *The Black Hills, or The Last Hunting Grounds of the Dakotahs,* St. Louis, Nixon Jones Printing Company, 1899.

Thoburn, Joseph B., *A Standard History of Oklahoma,* Volume IV, 1916.

Turner, Thadd, *Wild Bill Hickok: Deadwood City – End of Trail,* USA, Universal Publishers, 2001.

Webb, William, *Buffalo Land,* Cincinnati, E. Hannaford & Co., 1872.

Wellman, Paul, *A Dynasty of Western Outlaws*, Lincoln, University of Nebraska Press, 1986.

White, James T. and Co., *National Cyclopedia of American Biography,* New York, 1896.

Williams, Robert, *With the Border Ruffians,* New York, Dutton, 1907.

Wilson, Des, *Ghosts at the Table,* Philadelphia, Da Capo Press, 2008.

Wilson, Francis S., *A History of Ellsworth County, Kansas,* Ellsworth, Ellsworth County Historical Society, 1979.

Wilstach, Frank, *Wild Bill Hickok,* Garden City, Doubleday, 1926.

Young, Harry, *Hard Knocks: A Life Story of the Vanishing West,* Pierre, South Dakota State Historical Society, 2005.

Magazines, Journals, Newsletters, Auction Records, and Digital Sources

Bradbury, John, ed., "The Civil War Letters of Lorenzo B. Hickok," *Newsletter of the Phelps County Historical Society,* October, 1986.

Bonhams & Butterfield Auctions, "An historic Smith & Wesson No.2 Old Model Army revolver owned by Wild Bill Hickok," One Page Color Auction Promotion Sheet, November 18, 2013.

Broome, Jeff, "Wild Bill's Brawl With Two of Custer's Troopers," *Wild West,* December, 2012.

Carpe Librum, Rare Book and Manuscript Dealer (digital) "Kansas City Mac: The Archives of A.B. McDonald, "Archive Introduction, 2020.

Chicago *Inter Ocean Magazine,* October 15, 1911.

Cowan's Auctions, *Sales Records for July 10, 2016.*

Dykstra, Robert, "Wild Bill in Abilene," *Journal of the Central Mississippi Valley American Studies Association: Kansas Centennial Issue,* 1961, Vol. 2.

Epstein, Jim, *reason.com blog,* "Broke City of Harrisburg Says Goodbye Says Goodbye To Wild Bill Hickok's Knife, Doc Holliday's Dental Chair." July 22, 2013.

Field and Stream, "Is This the Gun Wild Bill was Carrying When He Was Murdered in 1876?", September 27, 2013.

Greg Martin Auctions, Letters, Photography, and Documents from the Estate of Celinda Hickok, July 16, 2003.

Hansen, George W. "True Story of Wild Bill – McCanles Affray In Jefferson County, Nebraska, July 12, 1861" *Nebraska History Magazine,* April -June, 1927.

Heritage Auctions, *Sales Records for 2014.*

Hermon, Greg, "Wild Bill's Sweetheart: The Life of Mary Jane Owen, *Real West Magazine,* February, 1987.

Hooker, William F., "The Camp-Fire," *Adventure Magazine,* August 3, 1927.

Huff, Leo E., "Guerrillas, Jayhawkers and Bushwhackers in Northern Arkansas During the Civil War," *Arkansas Historical Quarterly,* Summer, 1965.

Kane, Robert A. "The D.A. vs. S.A. Controversary," *Outdoor Life,* June, 1906.

"I am prepared to believe any story of his skill or prowess that does not conflict with the laws of gravitation and physics" *Outdoor Recreation,* November, 1912.

Knott, Sarah, *Cincinnatti.com Visitors Guide,* "History in the Cards," August 7, 2000.

Lake, Stuart, "Guns and Gunfighters," *Saturday Evening Post,* November 30, 1930.

Lewis, Alfred Henry, "How Mr. Hickok Came to Cheyenne," *Saturday Evening Post*, March 12, 1904.

Masterson, Bat, "A Few Scraps," *The Denver Republican*, July 17, 1910.

Nichols, George Ward, "Wild Bill," *Harpers New Monthly Magazine*, February, 1867.

Putnam, John H., "A Trip to the End of the Union Pacific in 1868," *Kansas Historical Quarterly*, Vol. 13, no.3.

Reliable Plant Magazine (digital). RP news wire, "United States Playing Card To Build Plant in Kentucky, 2009.

Rich, Julia Hogan, "Dead Man's Hand Dealt By Charlie Rich," *The Rich Family Association Kinfolk Newsletter*, Fall/Winter, 1980.

Richardson, Leander P. "A Trip to the Black Hills," *Scribner's Monthly Magazine*, February, 1877.

"Last Days of a Plainsman," (letter to the New York Sun, 1893), *True West Magazine*, November-December, 1965.

Rosa, Joseph, "Alias Jack McCall: A Pardon or Death," *The Trail Guide*, June, 1967, Vol. 2.

"J.B. Hickok: Deputy U.S. Marshal," *Kansas History: A Journal of the Central Plains*, Vol. 2, Number 4, Winter 1979.

"A Pistoleer Poet?," *True West Magazine*, September, 2001.

"The Grand Buffalo Hunt at Niagara Falls," *Nebraska History Quarterly*, Vol. 86, Winter, 2005.

"Was Wild Bill Ever An Ump?, *Wild West Magazine*, June, 2011.

Russell, Don, ed., "Julia Cody Goodman's Memoirs of Buffalo Bill," *Kansas Historical Quarterly*, Winter, 1962.

Secrest, William, "Bill Hickok's Girl on the Flying Trapeze," *Old West Magazine*, Winter, 1967.

"Steamboat Imperial," *Harpers Weekly*, August 8, 1863.

Sutton, Fred, "Fill Your Hand! Fred Sutton as told to A.B. MacDonald," *Saturday Evening Post*, April 10, 1926.

"Hands Up!," Fred Sutton as told to A.B. MacDonald, *Saturday Evening Post*, April 26, 1926.

"My Personal Contact With James Butler Hickok," *Pony Express Courier*, Placerville, California, June, 1937.

Swann Galleries, New York City, *Sales Records for April 4, 1986*.

Thorp, Raymond, "Wild Bill's Famous Bullet," *Real West Magazine*, May, 1961.

True West Magazine, "Wyeth Sets Record With Hickok Oil," September, 2007.

Watson, Elmo Scott ed., "Theodore R. Davis: Henry M. Stanley's Indian Campaign in 1867" *Westerners Brand Book*, Vol. 2, 1945 – 1946.

Manuscript and Archival Sources

Abilene Historical Society, Theophilus Little, *Early Days In Abilene*, ms. looseleaf notebook, ca. 1900.

Denver Public Library, *William Elsey Connelley Collection*, WH905, Western History Collection.

Colorado Historical Society, *Francis Cragin Collection, Early West Notebook*.

Greene County Archives, Springfield, Missouri. *State of Missouri vs. William Hickok - Coroner's Report and Trial Documents*, 1865.

Hickok, Howard. L, *The Hickok Legend,* unpublished manuscript except for excerpts.
Johnson County, Kansas Archives, Olathe, Kansas, July 7, 1859, *Civil Case, Monetary Claim, Case #57, Accession 02-235.003, Location 00-04-02-02-10, Folder 0070.*
Kansas Historical Society, Topeka, Kansas, *John Beach Edwards Papers.*
Kansas Historical Society, Topeka, Kansas, *Hickok Family Collection,* Kansas Memory Collection,
Kansas Historical Society, Topeka, Kansas, *Records of Fort Hays, Letters Dispatched, 1867-1869.*
Kansas Historical Society, Topeka, Kansas, *Records of Fort Hays, Letters Received. 1867-1869.*
National Archives, *Records of Fort Dodge, Letters Dispatched, 1869.*
National Archives, *Inquiry Letter of Richard Corbyn, re. Hickok army records,* February 5, 1948.
National Archives, *Records of the Quartermaster General, 1861 – 1865.*
Nebraska State Historical Society, Manuscripts Division, *Hugh J. Dobbs, Statement on Hickok trial.*
Records of the Missouri Union Provost Marshal, 1861 – 1865.
Records of the Union Army, Southwest Missouri, 1861 – 1865.
Wyoming State Archives.

Newspapers

Abilene (Kansas) *Chronicle,* September 8, 1870
Abilene (Kansas) *Chronicle,* November 3, 1870
Abilene (Kansas) *Chronicle,* May 18, 1871
Abilene (Kansas) *Chronicle,* June 8, 1871
Abilene (Kansas) *Chronicle,* July 31, 1871
Abilene (Kansas) *Chronicle,* October 12, 1871
Abilene (Kansas) *Chronicle,* November 30, 1871
Arkansaw *Traveler,* n.d.
Atchison (Kansas) *Weekly Free Press,* March 2, 1867
Atchison (Kansas) *Free Press,* January 6, 1868
Austin (Texas) *Daily Democrat Statesman,* October 12, 1871
Black Hills (South Dakota) *Pioneer,* June 15, 1876
Black Hills (South Dakota) *Pioneer,* August 5, 1876
Black Hills (South Dakota) *Pioneer,* August 19, 1876
Black Hills (South Dakota) *Pioneer,* November 11, 1876
Black Hills (South Dakota) *Pioneer,* November 18, 1876
Black Hills (South Dakota) *Pioneer,* January 22, 1877
Black Hills (South Dakota) *Daily Times,* September 4, 1877
Black Hills (South Dakota) *Daily Times,* October 2, 1877
Big Piney (Wyoming) *Examiner,* August 29, 1929
Boston (Massachusetts) *Transcript,* April 4, 1867
Boston (Massachusetts) *Transcript,* April 6, 1867
Boston (Massachusetts) *Herald,* October 2, 1927
Brenham (Texas) *Banner,* October 16, 1871
Buffalo (Missouri) *Reflex,* September 16, 2009

Cheyenne (Wyoming) *Leader,* July 22, 1874
Cheyenne (Wyoming) *Leader,* July 31, 1874
Cheyenne (Wyoming) *Leader,* April 14, 1876
Cheyenne (Wyoming) *Leader,* May 3, 1876
Cheyenne (Wyoming) *Leader* June 8, 1876
Cheyenne (Wyoming) *Leader* August 12, 1876
Cheyenne (Wyoming) *Daily Leader,* March 7, 1876
Cheyenne (Wyoming) *Daily Leader,* September 1, 1876
Cheyenne (Wyoming) *Weekly Leader,* May 13, 1876
Cheyenne (Wyoming) *Weekly Leader,* August 17, 1876
Cheyenne (Wyoming) *Weekly Leader,* November 23, 1876
Cheyenne (Wyoming) *Weekly Leader,* November 30, 1876
Cheyenne (Wyoming) *Daily News,* October 7, 1874
Cheyenne (Wyoming) *Daily News,* December 3, 1874
Cheyenne (Wyoming) *Daily News,* March 26, 1875
Cheyenne (Wyoming) *Daily Sun,* March 8, 1876
Cheyenne (Wyoming) *Daily Sun,* April 30, 1876
Cheyenne (Wyoming) *Daily Sun,* September 14, 1877
Cheyenne (Wyoming) *Daily Sun,* September 28, 1877
Chicago (Illinois) *Inter-Ocean,* December 17, 1872
Chicago (Illinois) *Daily Record,* December 26, 1896
Chicago (Illinois) *Tribune,* August 25, 1876
Cincinnati (Ohio) *Commercial Tribune,* January 29, 1928
Clyde (Kansas) *Republican Valley Empire,* August 2,1870
Cowley (Wyoming) *Progress,* December 30, 1911.
Deadwood (South Dakota) *Pioneer Times,* August 22, 1925
Denver (Colorado) *Post,* March 22, 1931
Denver (Colorado) *Daily Times,* August 8, 1874
Denver (Colorado) *Rocky Mountain News,* July 31, 1874
Denver (Colorado) *Rocky Mountain News,* August 9, 1874
Denver (Colorado) *Republican,* July 17, 1910
Dickinson County (Colorado) *Chronicle,* February, 20, 1873
Easton (Illinois) *Daily Express,* December 15, 1873
Ellis County (Kansas) *Star,* August 17, 1876
Ellsworth (Kansas) *Democrat,* November 12, 1885
Ellsworth (Kansas) *Reporter,* September 26, 1878
Ellsworth (Kansas) *Reporter,* May 1, 1879
Ellsworth (Kansas) *Reporter,* November 12, 1885
Ellsworth (Kansas) *Tri-Weekly Advertiser,* December 25, 1867
Hays City (Kansas) *Railway Advance,* November 9, 1867
Hays City (Kansas) *Railway Advance,* June 1, 1868
Hays City (Kansas) *Railway Advance,* September 30, 1865
Hays City (Kansas) *Conservative,* December 14, 1867
Hays City (Kansas) *Sentinel,* September 28, 1869
Hays (Kansas) *Sentinel,* February 2, 1877
Hays (Kansas) *Sentinel,* January 18, 1878
Jefferson City (Missouri), *Peoples Tribune,* August 23, 1876

Johnson County (Kansas) *Democrat,* August 31, 1922
Junction City (Kansas) *Union,* July 23, 1870
Junction City (Kansas) *Union,* August 19,1871
Junction City (Kansas) *Union,* October 7, 1871
Junction City (Kansas) *Union,* August 19, 1876
Junction City (Kansas) *Weekly Union,* April 10, 1867
Junction City (Kansas) *Weekly Union,* May 11, 1867
Junction City (Kansas) *Weekly Union,* July 31, 1869
Kansas City, (Missouri) *News,* October 6, 1871
Kansas City (Missouri) *Times,* July 19, 1874
Kansas City (Missouri) *Times,* April 28, 1927
Kansas City (Missouri) *Star,* June 8, 1913
Kansas City (Missouri) *Star,* June 15, 1913
Kansas City (Missouri) *Star,* September 13, 1913
Kansas City (Missouri) *Star,* April 27, 1927
Kansas City (Missouri) *Star,* July 2, 1933
Kansas City (Missouri) *Star,* December 14, 1947
Kansas City (Missouri) *Star,* December 6, 1985
Kansas City (Missouri) *Star,* September 25, 2020
Kansas City (Missouri) *Evening Star,* August 3, 1895
Kansas (Topeka) *Daily Commonwealth,* November 18, 1869
Kansas (Topeka) *Daily Commonwealth,* March 1, 1873
Kansas (Topeka) *Daily Commonwealth,* March 14, 1873
(Kansas) Topeka *Daily Commonwealth,* July 21, 1874
Lawrence (Kansas) *Daily Tribune,* September 30, 1869
Leavenworth (Kansas) *Conservative,* February 1, 1867
Leavenworth (Kansas) *Daily Conservative,* February 1, 1867
Leavenworth (Kansas) *Daily Conservative,* February 19, 1867
Leavenworth (Kansas) *Daily Conservative,* August 12, 1867
Leavenworth (Kansas) *Daily Times,* August 13, 1867
Leavenworth (Kansas) *Daily Times,* October 21, 1877
Leavenworth (Kansas) *Daily Bulletin,* February 13, 1867
Leavenworth (Kansas) *Daily Commercial,* July 18, 1868
Leavenworth (Kansas) *Times and Conservative,* March 5, 1869
Leavenworth (Kansas) *Times and Conservative,* May 7, 1869
Leavenworth (Kansas) *Times and Conservative,* May 30, 1869
Leavenworth (Kansas) *Times and Conservative,* August 22, 1869
Leavenworth (Kansas) *Times and Conservative,* August 24, 1869
Leavenworth (Kansas) *Times and Conservative,* August 31, 1869
Leavenworth (Kansas) *Times and Conservative,* November 21, 1869
Manhattan (Kansas) *Independent,* October 26, 1867
Missouri (St. Louis) *Republican,* January 21, 1870
New York (New York) *Herald,* April 16, 1867
New York (New York) *Herald,* May 11, 1867
New York (New York) *Clipper,* April 12, 1873
New York (New York) *Clipper,* February 28, 1874
New York (New York) *Clipper,* March 7, 1874

Niagara Falls (New York) *Gazette,* August 28, 1872
Niagara Falls (New York) *Evening Reporter,* September 17, 1966
Niagara Falls (New York) *Reporter,* August 26, 2003
Olathe (Kansas) *Mirror,* June 6, 1901
Omaha (Nebraska) *Weekly Herald,* June 12, 1872
Omaha (Nebraska) *Daily Bee,* March 31, 1876
Omaha (Nebraska) *Daily Bee,* August 16, 1876
Pittsburgh (Pennsylvania), *Daily Leader,* n.d., 1973
Rapid City (South Dakota) *Daily Journal,* November 6, 1949
Reuters (New York) November 19, 2013
Rochester (New York) *Democrat and Chronicle,* March 13, 1874
Rolla (Missouri) *Herald,* February 9, 1912
Russell (Kansas) *Record,* December 5, 1938
St. Louis (Missouri) *Republican,* January 6, 1868
St. Louis (Missouri) *Republican,* March 15, 1873
St. Louis (Missouri) *Republican,* March 27, 1873
St. Louis (Missouri) *Republican,* March 23, 1876
St. Louis (Missouri) *Daily Democrat,* March 15, 1873
Saline County (Kansas) *Journal,* October 12, 1871
Saline County (Kansas) *Journal,* January 18, 1872
Sioux Falls (South Dakota) *Daily Argus Leader,* August 9, 1924
Springfield (Missouri) *Weekly Patriot,* August 10, 1865
Springfield (Missouri) *Patriot,* January 31, 1867
Terre Haute (Indiana) *Daily Express,* October 10. 1873
Terre Haute (Indiana) *Daily Express,* October 19, 1873
Topeka (Kansas) *Daily Commonwealth,* July 22, 1870
Topeka (Kansas) *Daily Commonwealth,* September 28, 1872
Topeka (Kansas) *Commonwealth,* December 9, 1869
Topeka (Kansas) *Commonwealth,* February 6, 1870
Topeka (Kansas) *Daily Record,* August 5, 1868
Topeka (Kansas) *State Record,* June 11, 1869
Topeka (Kansas) *State Record,* December 8, 1869
Topeka (Kansas) *State Record,* March 22, 1870
Topeka (Kansas) *Weekly Leader,* April 2, 1868
Topeka (Kansas) *Capitol,* August 30, 1908
Topeka (Kansas) *Mail and Breeze,* December 20, 1901
Toronto (Canada) *Globe,* August 28, 1872
Virginia *Evening Chronicle,* August 3, 1877
Warrensburg (Missouri) *Standard,* February 24, 1870
Warrensburg (Missouri) *Standard,* March 3, 1870
White Cloud (Kansas) *Chief,* December 9, 1869
Wichita (Kansas) *Eagle,* September 14, 1876
Williamsport (Pennsylvania) *Gazette and Bulletin,* November 26, 1873
Yankton (South Dakota) *Press and Dakotaian,* December 5, 1876

INDEX

Bunker Hill, Kansas, 153
Buntline, Ned, 68, 305, 310–324, 380, 429
Burke, Clinton, 477
Burke, Ed, 405
Burke, John, 316, 327, 330
Burns, N. H., 75
Burns, Walter Noble, 338–339
Burroughs, S. A., 246–248
Burroughs, William, 459
Bushwackers, 72, 74
Butler, Guy, 34, 39, 40–42, 44
Butler, Polly. *See* Hickok, Polly Butler
Butler, W. T., 199
Butterfield Overland Despatch, 272
Byram's Ford, Kansas City, Missouri, 70

C

Calamity Jane (Martha Jane Canary), 376–378, 380, 389, 402, 477–478
California, 190, 355, 371
  gold rush, 334, 344
  Pony Express to, 51, 123, 396
California Joe, 42, 389, 401, 409, 414
California Road, 24, 169, 219
Campbell, Bayless S., 18
Campbell, E. F., 162
Camp Carlin, Wyoming Territory, 345, 349, 351
Camp Supply, Indian Territory, 185, 207
Camp Walker, Indian Territory, 76
Canada, 122, 371
Canary, Martha Jane (Calamity Jane), 376–378, 380, 389, 402, 477–478
Carpenter, C. C., 367
Carpenter, F. A., 67, 424
Carr, General Eugene, 120, 178–179, 185, 186
Carr, Jeff, 345
Carson, George, 426–427
Carson, Josepha Jaramilla, 124

Carson, Kit, 42, 123–124, 253
Carson, Tom, 253, 263
Carter (prisoner at Fort Wallace), 192
Cartwright, Joseph, 40
Case, Theodore, 445, 446
Cassville, Missouri, 76, 78
Catterson, Robert, 34
cattle ranching/cattle trade, 4, 239–240, 265–266
Cayuga Indians, 293
CBS (television network), 432
CBS Evening News, 432
Cedar Bluffs, Dakota Territory, 380
Cedar Creek, Kansas, 23
Centennial Prairie, Dakota Territory, 415
Central Hotel, Junction City, Kansas, 223
Central Overland California & Pike's Peak Express Company, 48
Chambers, Annie, 280
Chapman, Herman, 75
Charleston, South Carolina, 285
Charlton Comics, 433
Chase, F. H., 174
Cherokee Indians, 138, 267
Cheyenne, Wyoming Territory, 5, 6, 55, 269, 335–341, 343–346, 348–351, 355–360, *360*, 362–375, 387, 409, 426–427
Cheyenne Indians, 44, 140, 146–148, 175, 178, 186–187, 431
Cheyenne River, Wyoming Territory, 301
Chicago, Illinois, 188–190, 233, 261, 284, 313, 355
Chicago Merchandise Mart, 456
Chilton, Mr., 291
Chivington, Colonel, 140, 148
Choctaw Indians, 275
Chouteau's Trading Post, Kansas, 26
Church, Bertha, 223
Church, Mr. and Mrs. E., 223
Cimarron (film), 482
Cimarron Crossing, 124

ACKNOWLEDGEMENTS

Any writer wishing to write about James Butler Hickok (aka Wild Bill Hickok) will of necessity walk through fields plowed and seeded by the late great Hickok scholar Joseph Rosa. With his magnum opus on Hickok in 1974, Rosa brought out James Butler Hickok as a real person, not just an amalgamation of the myths and legends by which most people considered his alter-ego. There is one piece of outstanding research by Joseph Rosa that is particularly important and illuminating of Hickok's life and era, undertaken by Rosa after historian Ramon Adams questioned if Hickok had ever actually been a deputy United States Marshal. Rosa's outstanding research produced extensive documented evidence of Hickok's five years as a deputy United States marshal. Rosa's work on this aspect of Hickok's life is the foundation of much of what is written in these pages on that subject. I and all writers on the life of James Butler Hickok are indebted to Joseph Rosa's literary contribution.

Yet the last fifty years have brought much new information about Wild Bill Hickok, sometimes from fugitive documents in obscure places. Hiding in the open for many years at the Denver Public Library has been the William Elsey Connelley Collection, a wide assortment of papers and documents that Connelley collected in preparation for his book that was published posthumously in 1933 as *Wild Bill and his Era.* (Connelley died in 1930.) The book was much smaller in volume than Connelley had envisioned, and much of the important material about Hickok that Connelley had collected remained unpublished. That material all ended up in the Denver Public Library's Western History Collection, where it still is today. Connelley did his research on Hickok in the 1920s, when many people who knew Hickok and the events in his life were still alive. Those interviews are much of what comprises the collection. My gratitude is immense to the Denver Public Library, who provided me twenty years ago with copies of many papers and letters from the collection, and then in 2022 gave me permission to quote from these papers in my book.

My thanks also to Des Wilson, English author of a brilliant history of poker, *Ghosts at the Table.* Des gave me permission to quote from his savvy takedown of the Aces and Eights legend that appeared in his book.

Thanks also to Dr. Ferrell Miller of the Geary County Historical Society, who gave me permission to publish from his wonderful anecdotal story, *Bertha Church Went to Town with Wild Bill Hickock.*

My thanks go to Dennis Garstang, member of the Kansas City chapter of Westerners, who let me review his insightful file on the town of Rolla, Missouri and Samuel Strawhun, who came west from that area.

I am indebted to Hickok family member Cynthia Rosinski, who gave me permission to publish passages from her mother Edith Harmon's family history of the Hickok family, *Pioneer Settlers of Troy Grove, Illinois.* Other than maudlin myths invented by early biographers, little was known about James Butler Hickok's childhood and teen years in Homer, Illinois, until Edith Harmon's family history was published in 1973. The opportunity to illuminate those youthful years of young James through the eyes of his own family is a valuable addition to this book.

Michael Wells of the Kansas City Public Library readily granted my request to publish an 1872 photograph of Kansas City's Main Street when this was the environ of James Butler Hickok.

Thanks also to Cynthia Edgerle of the Ellsworth County Historical Society for permission to publish a photograph of Anna Wilson (aka Indian Annie) and her daughter Birdie Daisy. This is the only known photograph of Indian Annie.

Thanks also to Tia Stenson-Cunningham and Rose Speirs of Deadwood History, Inc., for their help and cooperation in granting me permission to publish two early photographs of Deadwood.

Finally, special recognition must be given to the Kansas Historical Society, who have made accessible to the general public and researchers fifty-six letters of James Butler Hickok and his family in the KHS Hickok Family Collection.